Progressive Methods in Data Warehousing and Business Intelligence:
Concepts and Competitive Analytics

David Taniar
Monash University, Australia

INFORMATION SCIENCE REFERENCE

Hershey · New York

Director of Editorial Content:	Kristin Klinger
Director of Production:	Jennifer Neidig
Managing Editor:	Jamie Snavely
Assistant Managing Editor:	Carole Coulson
Typesetter:	Chris Hrobak
Cover Design:	Lisa Tosheff
Printed at:	Yurchak Printing Inc.

Published in the United States of America by
Information Science Reference (an imprint of IGI Global)
701 E. Chocolate Avenue, Suite 200
Hershey PA 17033
Tel: 717-533-8845
Fax: 717-533-8661
E-mail: cust@igi-global.com
Web site: http://www.igi-global.com

and in the United Kingdom by
Information Science Reference (an imprint of IGI Global)
3 Henrietta Street
Covent Garden
London WC2E 8LU
Tel: 44 20 7240 0856
Fax: 44 20 7379 0609
Web site: http://www.eurospanbookstore.com

Library of Congress Cataloging-in-Publication Data

Progressive methods in data warehousing and business intelligence : concepts and competitive analytics / David Taniar, editor.
       p. cm. -- (Advances in data warehousing and mining ; v. 3)
   Includes bibliographical references and index.
   Summary: "This book observes state-of-the-art developments and research, as well as current innovative activities in data warehousing and mining, focusing on the intersection of data warehousing and business intelligence"--Provided by publisher.
   ISBN 978-1-60566-232-9 (hardcover) -- ISBN 978-1-60566-233-6 (ebook)
   1. Business intelligence--Data processing. 2. Data warehousing. 3. Data mining. I. Taniar, David.
   HD38.7.P755 2009
   658.4'038--dc22
                                    2008024391

British Cataloguing in Publication Data
A Cataloguing in Publication record for this book is available from the British Library.

All work contributed to this book set is original material. The views expressed in this book are those of the authors, but not necessarily of the publisher.

Progressive Methods in Data Warehousing and Business Intelligence: Concepts and Competitive Analytics is part of the IGI Global series named *Advances in Data Warehousing and Mining* (ADWM) Series, ISBN: 1935-2646

Advances in Data Warehousing and Mining Series (ADWM)

ISBN: 1935-2646

Editor-in-Chief: David Taniar, Monash Univerisy, Australia

Progressive Methods in Data Warehousing and Business Intelligence: Concepts and Competitive Analytics

David Taniar, Monash University, Australia

Information Science Reference • copyright 2009 • 384pp • H/C (ISBN: 978-1-60566-232-9) • $195.00(our price)

Recent technological advancements in data warehousing have been contributing to the emergence of business intelligence useful for managerial decision making. Progressive Methods in Data Warehousing and Business Intelligence: Concepts and Competitive Analytics presents the latest trends, studies, and developments in business intelligence and data warehousing contributed by experts from around the globe. Consisting of four main sections, this book covers crucial topics within the field such as OLAP and patterns, spatio-temporal data warehousing, and benchmarking of the subject.

Data Mining and Knowledge Discovery Technologies

David Taniar, Monash University, Australia

IGI Publishing • copyright 2008 • 379pp • H/C (ISBN: 978-1-59904-960-1) • US $89.95(our price)

As information technology continues to advance in massive increments, the bank of information available from personal, financial, and business electronic transactions and all other electronic documentation and data storage is growing at an exponential rate. With this wealth of information comes the opportunity and necessity to utilize this information to maintain competitive advantage and process information effectively in real-world situations. Data Mining and Knowledge Discovery Technologies presents researchers and practitioners in fields such as knowledge management, information science, Web engineering, and medical informatics, with comprehensive, innovative research on data mining methods, structures, tools, and methods, the knowledge discovery process, and data marts, among many other cutting-edge topics.

Research and Trends in Data Mining Technologies and Applications

David Taniar, Monash University, Australia

IGI Publishing • copyright 2007 • 340 pp • H/C (ISBN: 1-59904-271-1) • US $85.46 (our price)

Activities in data warehousing and mining are constantly emerging. Data mining methods, algorithms, online analytical processes, data mart and practical issues consistently evolve, providing a challenge for professionals in the field. Research and Trends in Data Mining Technologies and Applications focuses on the integration between the fields of data warehousing and data mining, with emphasis on the applicability to real-world problems. This book provides an international perspective, highlighting solutions to some of researchers' toughest challenges. Developments in the knowledge discovery process, data models, structures, and design serve as answers and solutions to these emerging challenges.

The Advances in Data Warehousing and Mining (ADWM) Book Series aims to publish and disseminate knowledge on an international basis in the areas of data warehousing and data mining. The book series provides a highly regarded outlet for the most emerging research in the field and seeks to bridge underrepresented themes within the data warehousing and mining discipline. The Advances in Data Warehousing and Mining (ADWM) Book Series serves to provide a continuous forum for state-of-the-art developments and research, as well as current innovative activities in data warehousing and mining. In contrast to other book series, the ADWM focuses on the integration between the fields of data warehousing and data mining, with emphasize on the applicability to real world problems. ADWM is targeted at both academic researchers and practicing IT professionals.

Hershey • New York

Order online at www.igi-global.com or call 717-533-8845 x 100 –
Mon-Fri 8:30 am - 5:00 pm (est) or fax 24 hours a day 717-533-7115

Table of Contents

Section II
OLAP and Pattern

Section III
Spatio-Temporal Data Warehousing

Section IV
Benchmarking and Evaluation

Detailed Table of Contents

Section I
Conceptual Model and Development

There are many methods in the area of data warehousing to define requirements for the development of the most appropriate conceptual model of a data warehouse. There is no universal consensus about the best method, nor are there accepted standards for the conceptual modeling of data warehouses. Only few conceptual models have formally described methods how to get these models. Therefore, problems arise when in a particular data warehousing project, an appropriate development approach, and a corresponding method for the requirements elicitation, should be chosen and applied. Sometimes it is also necessary not only to use the existing methods, but also to provide new methods that are usable in particular development situations. It is necessary to represent these new methods formally, to ensure the appropriate usage of these methods in similar situations in the future. It is also necessary to define the contingency factors, which describe the situation where the method is usable. This chapter represents the usage of method engineering approach for the development of conceptual models of data warehouses. A set of contingency factors that determine the choice between the usage of an existing method and the necessity to develop a new one is defined. Three case studies are presented. Three new methods: user-driven, data-driven, and goal-driven are developed according to the situation in the particular projects and using the method engineering approach.

In the context of data warehouse design, a basic role is played by conceptual modeling, that provides a higher level of abstraction in describing the warehousing process and architecture in all its aspects, aimed at achieving independence of implementation issues. This chapter focuses on a conceptual model called the DFM that suits the variety of modeling situations that may be encountered in real projects of small to large complexity. The aim of the chapter is to propose a comprehensive set of solutions for conceptual modeling according to the DFM and to give the designer a practical guide for applying them in the context of a design methodology. Besides the basic concepts of multidimensional modeling, the other issues discussed are descriptive and cross-dimension attributes; convergences; shared, incomplete, recursive, and dynamic hierarchies; multiple and optional arcs; and additivity.

Chapter III

Entity resolution (also known as duplicate elimination) is an important part of the data cleaning process, especially in data integration and warehousing, where data are gathered from distributed and inconsistent sources. Learnable string similarity measures are an active area of research in the entity resolution problem. Our proposed framework builds upon our earlier work on entity resolution, in which fuzzy rules and membership functions are defined by the user. Here, we exploit neuro-fuzzy modeling for the first time to produce a unique adaptive framework for entity resolution, which automatically learns and adapts to the specific notion of similarity at a meta-level. This framework encompasses many of the previous work on trainable and domain-specific similarity measures. Employing fuzzy inference, it removes the repetitive task of hard-coding a program based on a schema, which is usually required in previous approaches. In addition, our extensible framework is very flexible for the end user. Hence, it can be utilized in the production of an intelligent tool to increase the quality and accuracy of data.

Chapter IV

Data Warehouses are increasingly used by commercial organizations to extract, from a huge amount of transactional data, concise information useful for supporting decision processes. However, the task of designing a data warehouse and evaluating its effectiveness is not trivial, especially in the case of large databases and in presence of redundant information. The meaning and the quality of selected attributes heavily influence the data warehouse's effectiveness and the quality of derived decisions. Our research is focused on interactive methodologies and techniques targeted at supporting the data warehouse design and evaluation by taking into account the quality of initial data. In this chapter we propose an approach for supporting the data warehouses development and refinement, providing practical examples and demonstrating the effectiveness of our solution. Our approach is mainly based on two phases: the first one is targeted at interactively guiding the attributes selection by providing quantitative information measuring different statistical and syntactical aspects of data, while the second phase, based on a set of 3D visualizations, gives the opportunity of run-time refining taken design choices according to data examination and analysis. For experimenting proposed solutions on real data, we have developed a tool, called ELDA (EvaLuation DAta warehouse quality), that has been used for supporting the data warehouse design and evaluation.

Chapter V

Dirk Draheim, University of Lunsbruck, Austria
Oscar Mangisengi, BWIN Interactive Entertainment, AG & SMS Data System, GmbH, Austria

Nowadays tracking data from activity checkpoints of unit transactions within an organization's business processes becomes an important data resource for business analysts and decision-makers to provide essential strategic and tactical business information. In the context of business process-oriented solutions, business-activity monitoring (BAM) architecture has been predicted as a major issue in the near future of the business-intelligence area. On the other hand, there is a huge potential for optimization of processes in today's industrial manufacturing. Important targets of improvement are production efficiency and product quality. Optimization is a complex task. A plethora of data that stems from numerical control and monitoring systems must be accessed, correlations in the information must be recognized, and rules that lead to improvement must be identified. In this chapter we envision the vertical integration of technical processes and control data with business processes and enterprise resource data. As concrete steps, we derive an activity warehouse model based on BAM requirements. We analyze different perspectives based on the requirements, such as business process management, key performance indication, process and state based-workflow management, and macro- and micro-level data. As a concrete outcome we define a meta-model for business processes with respect to monitoring. The implementation shows that data stored in an activity warehouse is able to efficiently monitor business processes in real-time and provides a better real-time visibility of business processes.

Section II
OLAP and Pattern

Chapter VI

Jorge Loureiro, Instituto Politécnico de Viseu, Portugal
Orlando Belo, Universidade do Minho, Portugal

OLAP queries are characterized by short answering times. Materialized cube views, a pre-aggregation and storage of group-by values, are one of the possible answers to that condition. However, if all possible views were computed and stored, the amount of necessary materializing time and storage space would be huge. Selecting the most beneficial set, based on the profile of the queries and observing some constraints as materializing space and maintenance time, a problem denoted as cube views selection problem, is the condition for an effective OLAP system, with a variety of solutions for centralized approaches. When a distributed OLAP architecture is considered, the problem gets bigger, as we must deal with another dimension—space. Besides the problem of the selection of multidimensional structures, there's now a node allocation one; both are a condition for performance. This chapter focuses on distributed OLAP systems, recently introduced, proposing evolutionary algorithms for the selection and allocation of the distributed OLAP Cube, using a distributed linear cost model. This model uses an extended aggregation lattice as framework to capture the distributed semantics, and introduces processing nodes' power and real communication costs parameters, allowing the estimation of query and maintenance costs in time units. Moreover, as we have an OLAP environment, whit several nodes, we will have parallel processing and then, the evaluation of the fitness of evolutionary solutions is based on cost estimation algorithms that simulate the execution of parallel tasks, using time units as cost metric.

Globalization and market deregulation has increased business competition, which imposed OLAP data and technologies as one of the great enterprise's assets. Its growing use and size stressed underlying servers and forced new solutions. The distribution of multidimensional data through a number of servers allows the increasing of storage and processing power without an exponential increase of financial costs. However, this solution adds another dimension to the problem: space. Even in centralized OLAP, cube selection efficiency is complex, but now, we must also know where to materialize subcubes. We have to select and also allocate the most beneficial subcubes, attending an expected (changing) user profile and constraints. We now have to deal with materializing space, processing power distribution, and communication costs. This chapter proposes new distributed cube selection algorithms based on discrete particle swarm optimizers; algorithms that solve the distributed OLAP selection problem considering a query profile under space constraints, using discrete particle swarm optimization in its normal(Di-PSO), cooperative (Di-CPSO), multi-phase (Di-MPSO), and applying hybrid genetic operators.

With the emergence of Semi-structured data format (such as XML), the storage of documents in centralised facilities appeared as a natural adaptation of data warehousing technology. Nowadays, OLAP (On-Line Analytical Processing) systems face growing non-numeric data. This chapter presents a framework for the multidimensional analysis of textual data in an OLAP sense. Document structure, metadata, and contents are converted into subjects of analysis (facts) and analysis axes (dimensions) within an adapted conceptual multidimensional schema. This schema represents the concepts that a decision maker will be able to manipulate in order to express his analyses. This allows greater multidimensional analysis possibilities as a user may gain insight within a collection of documents.

Despite their strategic importance, the wide-spread usage of decision support systems remains limited by both the complexity of their design and the lack of commercial design tools. This chapter addresses the design complexity of these systems. It proposes an approach for data mart design that is practical and that endorses the decision maker involvement in the design process. This approach adapts a development technique well established in the design of various complex systems for the design of data marts (DM): Pattern-based design. In the case of DM, a multidimensional pattern (MP) is a generic specification of analytical requirements within one domain. It is constructed and documented with standard, real-world entities (RWE) that describe information artifacts used or produced by the operational information systems (IS) of several enterprises. This documentation assists a decision maker in understanding the generic analytical solution; in addition, it guides the DM developer during the implementation phase. After over viewing our notion of MP and their construction method, this chapter details a reuse method composed of two adaptation levels: one logical and one physical. The logical level, which is independent of any data source model, allows a decision maker to adapt a given MP to their analytical requirements and to the RWE of their particular enterprise; this produces a DM schema. The physical specific level projects the RWE of the DM over the data source model. That is, the projection identifies the data source elements necessary to define the ETL procedures. We illustrate our approaches of construction and reuse of MP with examples in the medical domain.

Section III
Spatio-Temporal Data Warehousing

Chapter X

Concepción M. Gascueña, Polytechnic of Madrid University, Spain
Rafael Guadalupe, Polytechnic of Madrid University, Spain

The Multidimensional Databases (MDB) are used in the Decision Support Systems (DSS) and in Geographic Information Systems (GIS); the latter locates spatial data on the Earth's surface and studies its evolution through time. This work presents part of a methodology to design MDB, where it considers the Conceptual and Logical phases, and with related support for multiple spatio-temporal granularities. This will allow us to have multiple representations of the same spatial data, interacting with other, spatial and thematic data. In the Conceptual phase, the conceptual multidimensional model—FactEntity (FE)—is used. In the Logical phase, the rules of transformations are defined, from the FE model, to the Relational and Object Relational logical models, maintaining multidimensional semantics, and under the perspective of multiple spatial, temporal, and thematic granularities. The FE model shows constructors and hierarchical structures to deal with the multidimensional semantics on the one hand, carrying out a study on how to structure "a fact and its associated dimensions." Thus making up the Basic factEnty, and in addition, showing rules to generate all the possible Virtual factEntities. On the other hand, with the spatial semantics, highlighting the Semantic and Geometric spatial granularities.

One of the most complex issues of the integration and transformation interface is the case where there are multiple sources for a single data element in the enterprise Data Warehouse (DW). There are many facets due to the number of variables that are needed in the integration phase. This chapter presents our DW architecture for temporal integration on the basis of the temporal properties of the data and temporal characteristics of the data sources. If we use the data arrival properties of such underlying information sources, the Data Warehouse Administrator (DWA) can derive more appropriate rules and check the consistency of user requirements more accurately. The problem now facing the user is not the fact that the information being sought is unavailable, but rather that it is difficult to extract exactly what is needed from what is available. It would therefore be extremely useful to have an approach which determines whether it would be possible to integrate data from two data sources (with their respective data extraction methods associated). In order to make this decision, we use the temporal properties of the data, the temporal characteristics of the data sources, and their extraction methods. In this chapter, a solution to this problem is proposed.

Data warehousing is a popular technology, which aims at improving decision-making ability. As the result of an increasingly competitive environment, many companies are adopting a "bottom-up" approach to construct a data warehouse, since it is more likely to be on time and within budget. However, multiple independent data marts/cubes can easily cause problematic data inconsistency for anomalous update transactions, which leads to biased decision-making. This research focuses on solving the data inconsistency problem and proposing a temporal-based data consistency mechanism (TDCM) to maintain data consistency. From a relative time perspective, we use an active rule (standard ECA rule) to monitor the user query event and use a metadata approach to record related information. This both builds relationships between the different data cubes, and allows a user to define a VIT (valid interval temporal) threshold to identify the validity of interval that is a threshold to maintain data consistency. Moreover, we propose a consistency update method to update inconsistent data cubes, which can ensure all pieces of information are temporally consistent.

This chapter describes realization of distributed approach to continuous queries with kNN join processing in the spatial telemetric data warehouse. Due to dispersion of the developed system, new structural members were distinguished: the mobile object simulator, the kNN join processing service, and the query manager. Distributed tasks communicate using JAVA RMI methods. The kNN queries (k Nearest Neighbour) joins every point from one dataset with its k nearest neighbours in the other dataset. In our approach we use the Gorder method, which is a block nested loop join algorithm that exploits sorting, join scheduling, and distance computation filtering to reduce CPU and I/O usage

This chapter is concerned with multidimensional data models for spatial data warehouses. Over the last few years different approaches have been proposed in the literature for modelling multidimensional data with geometric extent. Nevertheless, the definition of a comprehensive and formal data model is still a major research issue. The main contributions of the chapter are twofold: First, it draws a picture of the research area; second it introduces a novel spatial multidimensional data model for spatial objects with geometry (MuSD – multigranular spatial data warehouse). MuSD complies with current standards for spatial data modelling, augmented by data warehousing concepts such as spatial fact, spatial dimension and spatial measure. The novelty of the model is the representation of spatial measures at multiple levels of geometric granularity. Besides the representation concepts, the model includes a set of OLAP operators supporting the navigation across dimension and measure levels.

Section IV
Benchmarking and Evaluation

Performance evaluation is a key issue for designers and users of Database Management Systems (DBMSs). Performance is generally assessed with software benchmarks that help, for example test architectural choices, compare different technologies, or tune a system. In the particular context of data warehousing and On-Line Analytical Processing (OLAP), although the Transaction Processing Performance Council (TPC) aims at issuing standard decision-support benchmarks, few benchmarks do actually exist. We present in this chapter the Data Warehouse Engineering Benchmark (DWEB), which allows generating various ad-hoc synthetic data warehouses and workloads. DWEB is fully parameterized to fulfill various data warehouse design needs. However, two levels of parameterization keep it relatively easy to tune. We also expand on our previous work on DWEB by presenting its new Extract, Transform, and Load (ETL) feature, as well as its new execution protocol. A Java implementation of DWEB is freely available online, which can be interfaced with most existing relational DMBSs. To the best of our knowledge, DWEB is the only easily available, up-to-date benchmark for data warehouses.

Chapter XVI

A *Star Schema Data Warehouse* looks like a star with a central, so-called *fact table*, in the middle, surrounded by so-called *dimension tables* with one-to-many relationships to the central fact table. Dimensions are defined as *dynamic* **or** *slowly changing* if the attributes or relationships of a dimension can be updated. Aggregations of fact data to the level of the related dynamic dimensions might be misleading if the fact data are aggregated without considering the changes of the dimensions. In this chapter, we will first prove that the problems of SCD (Slowly Changing Dimensions) in a datawarehouse may be viewed as a special case of the read skew anomaly that may occur when different transactions access and update records without concurrency control. That is, we prove that aggregating fact data to the levels of a dynamic dimension should not make sense. On the other hand, we will also illustrate, by examples, that in some situations it does make sense that fact data is aggregated to the levels of a dynamic dimension. That is, it is the semantics of the data that determine whether historical dimension data should be preserved or destroyed. Even worse, we also illustrate that for some applications, we need a history preserving response, while for other applications at the same time need a history destroying response. Kimball et al., (2002), have described three classic solutions/responses to handling the aggregation problems caused by slowly changing dimensions. In this chapter, we will describe and evaluate four more responses of which one are new. This is important because all the responses have very different properties, and it is not possible to select a best solution without knowing the semantics of the data.

Preface

This is the third volume of the *Advances in Data Warehousing and Mining* (ADWM) book series. ADWM publishes books in the areas of data warehousing and mining. The topic of this volume is data warehousing and OLAP. This volume consists of 16 chapters in 4 sections, contributed by researchers in data warehousing.

Section I on "*Conceptual Model and Development*" consists of five chapters covering various conceptual modeling, data cleaning, production process, and development.

Chapter I, "*Development of Data Warehouse Conceptual Models: Method Engineering Approach*" by Laila Niedrite, Maris Treimanis, Darja Solodovnikova, and Liga Grundmane, from University of Latvia, discusses the usage of method engineering approach for the development of conceptual models of data warehouses. They describe three methods, including (*a*) user-driven, (*b*) data-driven, and (*c*) goal-driven methods.

Chapter II, "*Conceptual Modeling Solutions for the Data Warehouse*" by Stefano Rizzi, University of Bologna, is a reprint from *Data Warehouses and OLAP: Concepts, Architectures and Solutions,* edited by R. Wrembel and C. Koncilia (2007). The chapter thoroughly discusses dimensional fact modeling. Several approaches to conceptual design, such as data-driven, requirement-driven, and mixed approaches, are described.

Chapter III, "*A Machine Learning Approach to Data Cleaning in Databases and Data Warehouses*" by Hamid Haidarian Shahri, University of Maryland, is also a reprint. It is initially published in *Handbook of Research on Fuzzy Information Processing in Databases*, edited by J. Galindo (2008). This chapter introduces entity resolution (or duplicate elimination) in data cleaning process. It also exploits neuto-fuzzy modeling in the context of entity resolution.

Chapter IV, "*Interactive Quality-Oriented Data Warehouse Development*" by Maurizio Pighin and Lucio Ieronutti, both from University of Udine, Italy, proposes quantitative and qualitative phases in data warehousing design and evaluation. They also present a tool that they have developed, called ELDA (EvalLuation DAta warehouse quality) to support data warehouse design and evaluation.

Chapter V, "*Integrated Business and Production Process Data Warehousing*" by Dirk Draheim, Software Competence Center Hagenberg, Austria, and Oscar Mangisengi, BWIN Interactive Entertainment and SMS Data System, Austria, is a chapter contributed by practitioners in industry. They focus on production process data based on business activity monitoring requirements.

Section II on "*OLAP and Pattern*" consists of 4 chapters covering multi-node OLAP systems, multi-dimensional patterns, and XML OLAP.

Chapter VI, "*Selecting and Allocating Cubes in Multi-Node OLAP Systems: An Evolutionary Approach*" by Jorge Loureiro, Instituto Politécnico de Viseu, Portugal, and Orlando Belo, Universidade do Minho, Portugal, focuses on multi-node distributed OLAP systems. They propose three algorithms: M-OLAP Greedy, M-OLAP Genetic, and M-OLAP Co-Evol-GA; the last two are based on genetic algorithm and evolutionary approach.

Chapter VII, "*Swarm Quant' Intelligence for Optimizing Multi-Node OLAP Systems*", also by Jorge Loureiro and Orlando Belo, also discusses multi-node OLAP systems. But in this chapter, they propose distributed cube selection algorithms based on discrete particle swarm optimizers to solve the distributed OLAP selection problem. They propose M-OLAP Discrete Particle Swarm Optimization (M-OLAP Di-PSO), M-OLAP Discrete Cooperative Particle Swarm Optimization (M-OLAP Di-CPSO), and M-OLAP Discrete Multi-Phase Particle Swarm Optimization (M-OLAP Di-MPSO).

Chapter VIII, "*Multidimensional Analysis of XML Document Contents with OLAP Dimensions*" by Franck Ravat, Olivier Teste, and Ronan Tournier, IRIT, Universite Toulouse, France, focuses on XML documents, where they present a framework for multidimensional OLAP analysis of textual data. They describe this using the conceptual and logical model.

Chapter IX, "*A Multidimensional Pattern Based Approach for the Design of Data Marts*" by Hanene Ben-Abdallah, Jamel Feki, and Mounira Ben Abdallah, from University of Sfax, Tunisia, concentrates on multi-dimensional patterns. In particular the authors describe multi-dimensional pattern from the logical and physical levels.

Section III on "*Spatio-Temporal Data Warehousing*" consists of 5 chapters covering various issues of spatial and spatio-temporal data warehousing.

Chapter X, "*A Multidimensional Methodology with Support for Spatio-Temporal Multigranularity in the Conceptual and Logical Phases*" by Concepción M. Gascueña, Carlos III de Madrid University, and Rafael Guadalupe, Politécnica de Madrid University, presents a methodology to design multi-dimensional database to support spatio-temporal granularities. This includes conceptual and logical phases which allow multiple representations of the same spatial data interacting with other spatial and thematic data.

Chapter XI, "*Methodology for Improving Data Warehouse Design using Data Sources Temporal Metadata*" by Francisco Araque, Alberto Salguero, and Cecilia Delgado, all from University of Granada, focuses on temporal data. They also discuss properties of temporal integration and data integration process.

Chapter XII, "*Using Active Rules to Maintain Data Consistency in Data Warehouse Systems*" by Shi-Ming Huang, National Chung Cheng University, Taiwan, John Tait, Sunderland University, UK, Chun-Hao Su, National Chung Cheng University, Taiwan, and Chih-Fong Tsai, National Chung Cheng University, Taiwan, focuses on data consistency, particularly from the temporal data aspects.

Chapter XIII, "*Distributed Approach to Continuous Queries with kNN Join Processing in Spatial Telemetric Data Warehouse*" by Marcin Gorawski and Wojciech Gębczyk, from Silesian Technical University, Poland, concentrates on continuous kNN join query processing, the context of spatial telemetric data warehouse, which is relevant to geospatial and mobile information systems. They also discuss spatial location and telemetric data warehouse and distributed systems.

Chapter XIV, "*Spatial Data Warehouse Modelling*" by Maria Luisa Damiani, Università di Milano, and Stefano Spaccapietra, Ecole Polytechnique Fédérale de Lausanne, is a reprint from *Processing and Managing Complex Data for Decision Support*, edited by Jérôme Darmont and Omar Boussaid (2006) The chapter presents multi-dimensional data models for spatial data warehouses. This includes a model for multi-granular spatial data warehouse and spatial OLAP.

The final section of this volume, Section IV on "*Benchmarking and Evaluation*", consists of two chapters, one on benchmarking data warehouses and the other on evaluation of slowly changing dimensions.

Chapter XV, "*Data Warehouse Benchmarking with DWEB*" by Jérôme Darmont, University of Lyon, focuses on the performance evaluation of data warehouses, in which it presents a data warehouse engineering benchmark, called DWEB. The benchmark also generates synthetic data and workloads.

Finally, Chapter XVI, *"Analyses and Evaluation of Responses to Slowly Changing Dimensions in Data Warehouses"* by Lars Frank and Christian Frank, from the Copenhagen Business School, focuses on dynamic data warehouses, where the dimensions are changing slowly. They particularly discuss different types of dynamicity, and responses to slowly changing dimensions.

Overall, this volume covers important foundations to researches and applications in data warehousing, covering modeling, OLAP and patterns, as well as new directions in benchmarking and evaluating data warehousing. Issues and applications, particularly in spatio-temporal, shows a full spectrum of the coverage of important and emerging topics in data warehousing.

David Taniar
Editor-in-Chief

Section I
Conceptual Model and Development

Chapter I
Development of Data Warehouse Conceptual Models:
Method Engineering Approach

Laila Niedrite
University of Latvia, Latvia

Maris Treimanis
University of Latvia, Latvia

Darja Solodovnikova
University of Latvia, Latvia

Liga Grundmane
University of Latvia, Latvia

ABSTRACT

There are many methods in the area of data warehousing to define requirements for the development of the most appropriate conceptual model of a data warehouse. There is no universal consensus about the best method, nor are there accepted standards for the conceptual modeling of data warehouses. Only few conceptual models have formally described methods how to get these models. Therefore, problems arise when in a particular data warehousing project, an appropriate development approach, and a corresponding method for the requirements elicitation, should be chosen and applied. Sometimes it is also necessary not only to use the existing methods, but also to provide new methods that are usable in particular development situations. It is necessary to represent these new methods formally, to ensure the appropriate usage of these methods in similar situations in the future. It is also necessary to define the contingency factors, which describe the situation where the method is usable. This chapter represents the usage of method engineering approach for the development of conceptual models of data warehouses. A set of contingency factors that determine the choice between the usage of an existing method and the necessity to develop a new one is defined. Three case studies are presented. Three new methods: user-driven, data-driven, and goal-driven are developed according to the situation in the particular projects and using the method engineering approach.

INTRODUCTION

Data warehouses are based on multidimensional models which contain the following elements: facts (the goal of the analysis), measures (quantitative data), dimensions (qualifying data), dimension attributes, classification hierarchies, levels of hierarchies (dimension attributes which form hierarchies), and attributes which describe levels of hierarchies of dimensions.

When it comes to the conceptual models of data warehouses, it is argued by many authors that the existing methods for conceptual modelling used for relational or object-oriented systems do not ensure sufficient support for the representation of multidimensional models in an intuitive way. Use of the aforementioned methods also ensures a waste of some of the semantics of multidimensional models. The necessary semantics must be added to the model informally, but that makes the model unsuitable for automatic transformation purposes. The conceptual models proposed by authors such as Sapia et al. (1998), Tryfona et al. (1999) and Lujan-Mora et al. (2002) are with various opportunities for expression, as can be seen in a comparison of the models in works such as (Blaschka et al., 1998), (Pedersen, 2000) and (Abello et al, 2001). This means that when a particular conceptual model is used for the modelling of data warehouses, some essential features

may be missing. Lujan-Mora et al. (2002) argue that problems also occur because of the inaccurate interpretation of elements and features in the multidimensional model. They say that this applies to nearly all conceptual models that have been developed for data warehousing. The variety of elements and features in the conceptual models reflect differences in opinion about the best model for data warehouses, and that means that there is no universal agreement about the relevant standard (Rizzi et al., 2006).

There are two possible approaches towards the development of a conceptual model. One can be developed from scratch, which means additional work in terms of the formal description of the model's elements. A model can also be developed by modifying an existing model so as to express the concepts of the multidimensional paradigm.

The conceptual models of data warehouses can be classified into several groups in accordance with how they are developed (Rizzi et al., 2006):

- Models based on the E/R model, e.g., ME/R (Sapia et al., 1998) or StarE/R (Tryfona et al., 1999);
- Models based on the UML., e.g., those using UML stereotypes (Lujan-Mora et al., 2002);
- Independent conceptual models proposed by different authors, e.g., Dimensional Fact Model (Golfarelli et al., 1998).

In the data warehousing field there exists the metamodel standard for data warehouses - the Common Warehouse Metamodel (CWM). It is actually a set of several metamodels, which describe various aspects of data warehousing. CWM is a platform independent specification of metamodels (Poole et al., 2003) developed so as to ensure the exchange of metadata between different tools and platforms. The features of a multidimensional model are basically described via an analysis-level OLAP package, however, CWM cannot fully reflect the semantics of all conceptual multidimensional models (Rizzi et al., 2006).

EXISTING METHODS FOR THE DEVELOPMENT OF CONCEPTUAL MODELS FOR DATA WAREHOUSES

There are several approaches to learn the requirements for a conceptual data warehouse model and to determine how the relevant model can be built. Classification of these approaches is presented in this section, along with an overview of methods, which exist in each approach. Weaknesses of the approaches are analysed to show the necessity to develop new methods. The positive aspects of existing approaches and the existence of many methods in each approach, however, suggests that several method components can be used in an appropriate situation.

We will use the method concept according to Brinkkemper (1996): "A method is an approach to perform a systems development project, based on a specific way of thinking, consisting of directions and rules, structured in a systematic way in development activities with corresponding development products."

There are several approaches how to determine the requirements for the development of a conceptual model for a data warehouse. The requirements for data warehouses are different than those which apply to other types of systems.

In the data warehousing field we can speak about information requirements (Winter & Strauch, 2003), (Goeken, 2005), as opposed to the functional requirements that are usually used.

The methods for developing of conceptual models for data warehouses can be split up into several groups (see Figure 1) on the basis of the approach that is taken:

- The data-driven approach (Artz, 2005), (List et al., 2002) is based on exploration of the models and data of data sources. The integration of models and data are essential in this approach. The conceptual model for a data warehouse comes from models of data sources via transformation. The analysis needs of an organisation are not identified at all, or are identified only partly.
- The requirements-driven approach (Winter & Strauch, 2003) is based on the elicitation of requirements in different ways. Some authors speak about more detailed subgroups that are based on various ways of requirements elicitation. For example, Artz (2005) speaks of a measurement-driven approach, List et al. (2002) refer to user-driven and goal-driven approaches, while Boehnlein and Ulbrich-vom-Ende (2000) speak of a process-driven approach.

All of the aforementioned approaches, including the data-driven approach, are ways of analysing the information requirements for data warehouses.

Data-driven methods have been proposed by many authors, including Golfarelli et al. (1998), Inmon (2002), and Phipps and Davis (2002). One of the best known is the semi-automatic method called the "Dimensional Fact Model" (Golfarelli et al., 1998), which creates a conceptual data warehouse model from existing ER model of a data source. Inmon (2002) proposes a rebuilt waterfall lifecycle for systems development, where the elicitation of the analysis needs of the

Figure 1. Approaches and methods for the development of conceptual models for data warehouses

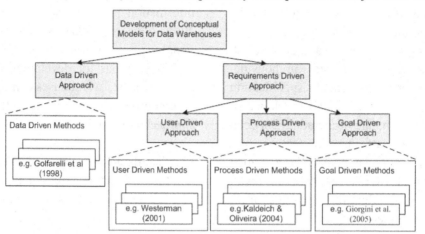

users occurs after the implementation of the data warehouse.

Most requirements-driven methods represent some aspects of the process-driven, goal-driven or user-driven methods. The exception is the "Information requirements-driven method" (Winter & Strauch, 2003). This is described by the authors as a four-step method for the engineering of requirements for data warehousing.

Process-driven methods are represented in (Boehnlein & Ulbrich-vom-Ende, 2000), and in methods developed for so called process data warehouse, e.g. (Kueng et al., 2001), (List et al., 2002). The "Metric driven approach" (Artz, 2005) can be seen as a version of the process-driven method. It begins with the identification of the most important business process that requires measurement and control. Kaldeich and Oliveira (2004) propose method, where a process model known as "As Is" and one called "To Be" are built, and they refer to the relevant analytical processes. A new ER model which includes the data that are necessary for data analysis is developed.

The goal-driven methods are, for example, the methods of Giorgini et al. (2005) and Bonifati et al. (2001). Giorgini et al. (2005) perform the requirements analysis from two perspectives - modelling of organisations and modelling of

decisions. Bonifati et al.(2001) present a method that consists of three steps - top-down analysis, bottom-up analysis, and integration. The authors use the Goal-Question-Metric approach for the top-down analysis. This makes it possible to identify the relevant organisation's goals.

The user-driven methods are described in (Westerman, 2001), (Goeken, 2005) and, in part, in (Kimball et al., 1998) to elicit user requirements. According to the "Kimball method" (Kimball et al., 1998), business users are interviewed to define the requirements. The goal of the interviews is to understand the work that users do and the way in which decisions are taken. IT experts are also interviewed so as to examine the available data sources. The existence and quality of data meant for analytical needs are estimated. The Wal-Mart method (Westerman, 2001) is designed for the implementation of business strategies. The author of the "Viewpoint" method (Goeken, 2005) states that the analysis of information needs is just one part of all requirements. The central object of the exploration should be the recipient of the information and his or her needs. To formalise these needs, Goeken (2005) proposes a method, which is based on the idea that many people with different needs are involved into the systems development process.

Often more than one approach is used in a particular method. When it comes to the combination of many sources, the Kimball method (Kimball et al., 1998), which involves four steps, can be mentioned. The other aforementioned methods also tend to be combinations of several approaches – two in most cases. The primary method is taken into account to determine the aforementioned classification. The goal-driven method of Bonifati et al. (2001), for instance, uses also the data-driven approach for certain specific purposes.

According to comparisons of all of the various approaches in the literature (List et al., 2002), (Winter & Strauch, 2003) and after an examination of the previous mentioned methods from various perspectives, certain strengths and weaknesses can be defined.

Strengths

- **For the user driven approach:** The elicitation of user requirements and the involvement of users, which is essential in data warehousing projects to ensure the successful use of the data warehouse that is created;
- **For the data driven approach:** This is the fastest way to define a data warehouse model;
- **For the process and goal driven approaches:** Essential business processes and indicators to measure these processes are identified. The model can be developed for an analysis of these indicators.

Weaknesses

- **For the user-driven approach:** Users do not have a clear understanding of data warehouses, about business strategies or organisational processes. It takes much more time to achieve consensus on requirements, and there are usually problems in prioritising the requirements;
- **For the data driven approach:** The models according to some methods are generated semi-automatically. Such models perhaps do not reflect all of the facts that are needed in analysing business goals. This is due to the nature of underlying models of data sources, which are built for operational purposes, not for data analysis.
- **For the process and goal driven approaches:** The model will reflect the opinion of senior management and a few experts, and it will correspond to a highly specialised issue. It is hard to predict the needs of all users. The model reflects business processes not processes of decision making.

To summarise, it can be said that more than one approach must usually be put to work to obtain a data model, which reflects the analytical needs of an organisation in a precise and appropriate way. The problem is choosing the method that is to be the primary method. There are several problems in this regard:

- There are no recommendations as to which approach is more suitable as the primary method in any given situation;
- There are no recommendations on which modelling technique to use, because none of the conceptual models satisfies all of the previously described criteria for expressiveness;
- There are no suggestions on how to describe the needs of users in terms of different levels of granularity in the information if different users have different requirements and different access rights;
- There are no accepted suggestions for particular business areas which approach and which modelling technique is more suitable.

THE METHOD ENGINEERING AND THE DEFINITION OF NEW METHODS

In this section we will propose three new methods, which have been developed in accordance with the ideas of method engineering. These are the user-driven, data-driven and goal-driven method. In each case the contingency factors are formulated and evaluated. The methods have been applied successfully in data warehousing projects at the University of Latvia.

Brinkkemper (1996) defines method engineering: "Method engineering is the engineering discipline to design, construct and adapt methods, techniques and tools for the development of information systems".

Method engineering involves one of three main strategies: development of a new method, method construction, and adaptation. A new method is developed, if no existing method is applicable. These methods are known as ad-hoc methods (Ralyte et al., 2003). Method construction means that a new method is built up from components or fragments of existing methods (Ralyte et al., 2003). This approach is called also an integration approach (Leppanen et al., 2007). Adaptation means that some components of an existing method are modified or may be passed over (Leppanen et al., 2007). We apply these strategies to components of methods presented in this chapter. Methods proposed here are new methods, which have been constructed from new, adapted or existing components of other methods.

A method can be considered to be a set of method components (Harmsen, 1997). Rolland (1997) uses the concept of context to describe the usage of method components. A context is defined as a pair <situation, decision>. The decision about the suitability of a method's fragment in a specific situation depends on 1) The purpose for which the fragment has been designed; 2) The technique for the achieving the goal, 3) The goal to be achieved (evaluation).

Rolland (1997) and Leppanen et al. (2007) stated that criteria for characterizing the situation of a method in the context of method engineering have been poorly defined. In the field of information systems development (ISD), many proposals have been made about contingency factors (Fitzgerald & Fitzgerald, 1999), (Mirbel& Ralyte, 2005), (Leppanen et al., 2007), e.g. contingency factors include the availability, stability and clarity of ISD goals, for instance, as well as the motivation of stakeholders. This can also be of assistance in methods construction in the method engineering field. .

Method representation is also important because method engineering should help to look at a variety of methods to find a useful one that exists or can be adapted, or it should help to construct a new one from useful components of other methods. The description of methods in this chapter is based on the Software Process Engineering Metamodel (OMG, 2005). The main elements of the metamodel are Activity, WorkProduct, and Role. Each activity can be divided up into the more detailed activities that are called steps.

We have based the description of each new method in this chapter on its process aspect. The sequence of activities and steps is described, and although the performers of activities are not analysed in detail, the related products are described. For activities or steps, the context and situation are analysed.

User Driven Method (UDM)

In this section we propose a user driven method (UDM) that we have developed according to method engineering principles. We will use examples from a case study to explain some method components. The method was successfully applied for the development of the data marts at the University of Latvia for the analysis of employees and students. The results about the experience of application of the user-driven method are published in detail in (Benefelds & Niedrite, 2004).

The situations in this project were used to identify the contingency factors that determine whether an existing method component can be used or adapted, or a new method component should be developed.

The process model of the UDM is characterized by the activities shown in Figure 2.

Activity 1. The definition of the problem area;

Activity 2. Interviewing. The employees to be interviewed are chosen and potential user groups are identified. Questions in the interviews are focused on the goals of the work, the quality criteria which exist, as well as the data that are needed for everyday data analysis.

Step 2.1. Making a list of employees to be interviewed – identification of user groups. We used existing method component, particularly, we performed this step according to Kimball's method (Kimball et al., 1998).

Step 2.2. Selection of questions for the interviews. To prepare to the interview we used existing method component, particularly, we performed this step according to Kimball's method (Kimball et al., 1998). Only the content of the interview template (Kimball et al., 1998) was adapted according to the project situation. A list of interview questions was produced and then adapted for each potential user group of the data warehouse. Answers that are given are registered into a table;

Step 2.3. Organising and conducting the interviews. We adapted existing method component, particularly, the groups of interviewed employees selected according to Kimball's method (Kimball et al., 1998) are merged also vertically in appropriate project situations.

Activity 3. Processing of the interview results. Interview results are processed with the help of two tables in the form of matrixes. The first, "Interest

Figure 2. The process model of the UDM

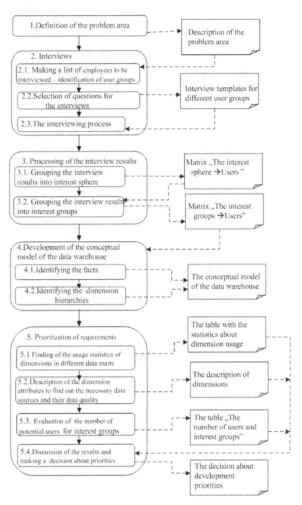

sphere ↔ Interviewees", is one in which each cell contains answers to the questions. The second one is "Interest groups ↔ Interviewees".

Step 3.1. Grouping the interview results into interest sphere. The interest sphere is defined as a grouping tool for similar requirements. The definition of these groups is made by the interviewer based on the answers to the interview questions; the interest sphere is the group of similar answers. The answers are summarized in the following matrix: one matrix dimension is „Interest sphere"; the second dimension is

Table 1. The fragment of the matrix "Interest sphere ↔ Interviewees"

	Students	Employees
Dean of Faculty of Pedagogy	The expected and real number of students by faculties. The number of graduates.	The number of professors, the list of employees by faculties, salaries
Chancellor	The number of students financed by the state and full-paying students	The salaries of the employees, the workload of the staff.

Table 2. The matrix "Interest groups"–"Interviewees"

	Students and PhDs	Employees	The finance resources
Chancellor	1	1	1.5
…			
The planning department manager	1	1	
…			
Dean of Faculty of Pedagogy	1	1	1.5
…			
	38	34	29.5

"Interviewees" (the interviewed user groups). The cells of the table contain answers, which characterize the needed analysis indicators. The Table 1 represents a fragment of the above mentioned matrix from the data warehouse project where the method was applied.

Step 3.2. Grouping the interview results into interest groups. This method component uses the table "Interest sphere ↔ Interviewees" and transforms it into the similar table "Interest group ↔ Interviewees". The similar interest spheres are merged into interest groups, which are larger groups used for prioritizing of the requirements.

This matrix served as a basis for analysing the number of potential users in each interest group. One dimension of the table is "Interest group". The second dimension is "Interviewees". The cells of the table contain the value k, where k=1, if the interviewed user group had a requirement from this interest group, k=1,5 - if the interviewee emphasized the particular issue as of the major priority for him or her. We have also applied extra coefficient p to emphasize the importance of the needs of a user or user group for the data analysis. For this category of users the value of the table cell is *k*p*.

The Table 2 represents a fragment of the above mentioned new matrix from the data warehouse project where the method was applied. We have used the following extra coefficients for the result analysis in our case study: p=1 - for faculties, p=2 - for top management and departments.

Activity 4. The development of the conceptual model of the data warehouse. This activity is based on the elicited analysis requirements. The ME/R notation is used to document the conceptual model.

Step 4.1. Identifying the facts. Fact attributes and dimensions are found out from the requirements. We adapted existing method component, particularly, the ME/R notation (Sapia et al., 1998) was used and an idea was added on how to analyse the documented statements of requirements.

Step 4.2. Identifying the dimension hierarchies. Data models of data sources are used to determine the hierarchies of dimension attributes. One of the data driven methods, e.g., DFM (Golfarelli et al., 1998) can be used. We adapted existing method component, particularly, DFM method was used. The adaptation means that a starting point is added to the DFM from the Step 4.1.

Activity 5. Prioritisation of requirements. The main goal of this step is to describe the dimension attributes so as to determine the necessary data sources and the quality of their data, the usage statistics of dimension in different data marts, and the number of potential users.

Step 5.1. Finding out the usage statistics of dimensions in different data marts. In this step the potential workload is estimated to develop the needed dimensions for different data marts. The existing method component, particularly, data warehouse "bus matrix" (Kimball et al., 1998) can be used.

Step 5.2. Description of the dimension attributes to find out the necessary data sources and their data quality. This step creates a table for the description of the dimensions and their attributes. The evaluation of the data quality and the description of necessary transformations are given. The goal of this step is to estimate the necessary resources for solving the data quality problems. Also it should be found out whether the data exist or not.

Step 5.3. Evaluation of the number of potential users for interest groups. This step groups the data marts into "Interest groups" identified in the previous steps; the number of potential users for each group is given. The information from the table "Interest groups"-"Interviewees" is used, the coefficients are not taken into account. The goal of this step is to estimate the number of potential users for data marts.

Step 5.4. Discussion of the results and making a decision about priorities. This step uses the following criteria for the prioritization and decision making:

- The potential number of users for each interest group, not only for the data mart;
- The potential number of users, when the coefficients are applied from the table "Interest groups"- "Interviewees". This number of users reflects to a greater extent the analysis needs, but not the needs to get the operational information;
- The existence and the quality of the necessary data from the data sources;
- The complexity of the data marts to be

developed, e.g. number of dimensions;
- The number of data sources.

The new UDM method uses four existing method components. Three existing method components have been adapted according to the situation. Five new method components have been built. The new method components are used mostly for the prioritisation of requirements. An overview of the method components is given in Table 3. The goal of the usage of the component is characterised. For each component a type is assigned - N for new components, A for adapted components or E for existing components. The origins of existing and adapted components are stated.

As far as the adapted components are concerned, two of the adaptation cases had user-driven method components as their origin. In one adaptation case, an existing data-driven method component (4.2.) was used. This choice was based on the fact that in most cases, only analysis dimensions are obtainable from interview results, while information about the hierarchical structure of attributes is rarely available.

The new user-driven method is characterized by the set of six contingency factors, which were identified during the evaluation of the method components (Table 3):

UDM_f1. One or several business processes, which should be measured are not distinguished;

UDM_f2. There are potentially many interviewees, which are performing data analysis;

UDM_f3. The broad spectrum of the requirements;

UDM_f4. The need to group the requirements according to their similarity to prioritize the requirements;

UDM_f5. The data analysis requirements, which are grouped, should be transformed into appropriate multidimensional conceptual model;

Table 3. An overview of the method components in the UDM

	ORIGIN	N/A/E	DESCRIPTION OF THE COMPONENT (GOAL; ADAPTATION, IF APPLICABLE)	CONT. FACTORS
1.1	IS	E	Definition of the problem area	UDM_f1
2.1	(Kimball et al, 1998)	E	Identifying of employees to be interviewed	UDM_f1; UDM_f2
2.2	(Kimball et al, 1998)	E	Preparing the interview. The content of the template is adapted according to the situation	UDM_f2
2.3	(Kimball et al, 1998)	A	Organising and conducting the interviews. The groups of interviewed employees are merged vertically in appropriate situations	UDM_f2
3.1	DW project situation	N	Structuring the results of interviews	UDM_f3; UDM_f4
3.2	DW project situation	N	1) Decreasing the number of the interest sphere from 3.1. step, if the prioritization is burdened; 2) Finding out the number of potential users for each interest sphere.	UDM_f3; UDM_f4
4.1	ME/R (Sapia et al, 1998)	A	Eliciting fact attributes and dimensions from the requirements; the ME/R notation is used and an idea is added on how to analyse the documented statements of requirements.	UDM_f5
4.2	DFM (Golfarelli et al., 1998)	A	Defining the dimension hierarchies. A starting point is added to the DFM from the step 4.1.	UDM_f5
5.1	(Kimball et al, 1998)	E	Estimating the potential workload to develop the needed dimensions for different data marts	UDM_f6
5.2	DW project situation	N	Estimating the data quality of data sources	UDM_f6
5.3	DW project situation	N	Estimating the number of potential users for different data marts	UDM_f6
5.4	DW project situation	N	Making the decision about development priorities	UDM_f6

UDM_f6. There are many requirements and it is necessary to prioritize them.

Data-Driven Method (DDM)

In this section we propose a data driven method (DDM) that we have developed according to method engineering principles. We will use examples from a case study to explain some method components. The method was successfully applied for the development of the data marts at the University of Latvia for the evaluation of the e-learning process using e-study environment WebCT. The results about the experience of ap-

plication of the data driven method are published in detail in (Solodovnikova & Niedrite, 2005). The situations in this project were used to identify the contingency factors that determine whether an existing method component can be used or adapted, or a new method component should be developed.

The process model of the DDM is given in the Figure 3 and consists of five activities.

Activity 1. The definition of the problem area. This activity is necessary because the underlying approach is data-driven. A global integrated data model of all data sources, if used, will contain

Figure 3. The process model of the DDM

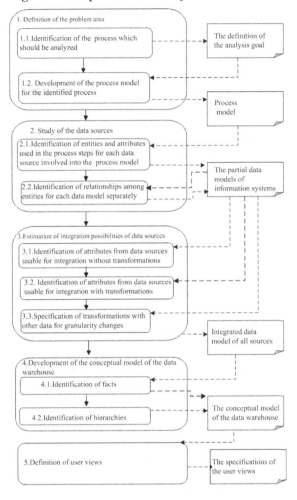

the information systems of the organization. The goal of the step is finding data sources, used by the process, which will be analysed. As a result, a limited process model is built, only processes that are related with the process from the step 1.1. are modelled. An existing process modelling technique can be adapted for this step.

In our case study for the analysis goal "E-learning analysis at the University of Latvia" we can consider the following process model (Figure 4).

Activity 2. The study of the data sources. The data models for each of the data sources used in the previous activity are developed. Only the data elements (entities and attributes), which are needed for the execution of the analysed process are included into the data model.

Step 2.1. Identification of entities and attributes used in the process steps for each data source involved into the process model. In this step limited data models are built, only the data used by processes of the 1.2. method component are included. For this step we can use a data modelling technique and adapt it according to the mentioned limitations.

Step 2.2. Identification of relationships among entities for each data model separately. For the definition of relationships among entities of each particular data model, the existing data models of data sources or data dictionaries of RDBMS are used. Existing methods e.g. data model analysis, metadata dictionary analysis are used.

a lot of unnecessary data not suitable for data analysis. To restrict this global data model and to build a subset of it we need to define the restriction principles.

Step 1.1. Identification of the process, which should be analyzed. The process, which should be analysed, is found out from the customer, but specific analysis needs and identifiers are not defined.

Step 1.2. Development of the process model for the identified process. A process model is made for the high level process from the Step 1.1. This model reflects the interaction between process steps and

In our case study as potential data sources involved into e-learning process, the following systems or files were discovered: 1) Student Information System (RDBMS); 2) WebCT web server log files that conform to the Common Log Format (CLF); 3) WebCT internal database, whose data were available through API and the result was obtained as an XML file. The data

Figure 4. The process model of e-learning process

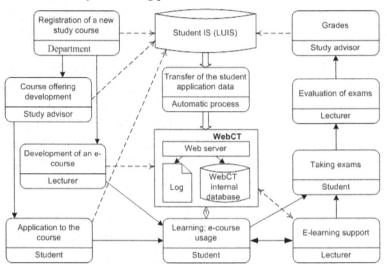

involved in e-learning processes are shown on the model, which reflects the data from all data sources (Figure 5).

Activity 3. Estimation of integration possibilities of data sources. Appropriate attributes from data sources are identified, whose values can be used for the integration of different data sources directly without or with transformations. The result of this activity is an integrated data model that corresponds to the analysed process.

Step 3.1. Identification of attributes from data sources usable for integration without transformations. Existing integration methods of data models can be used in this step. During this step attributes are discovered, which are common for many data models.

Step 3.2. Identification of attributes from data sources usable for integration with transformations. Existing integration methods of data models can be used. Integration problems are discovered and appropriate solutions to these problems are defined.

Step 3.3. Specification of transformations with other data for granularity changes. During this step the transformations for other data not only for the key attributes should be specified, if it is necessary. Existing integration methods of data models can be used. The result of this step is the specification of data aggregation for data integration purposes.

Activity 4. Development of the conceptual model of the data warehouse. The facts for the analysis are identified. The dimension hierarchies according to some known data-driven method are identified. For example, DFM is used. The previously identified fact attributes are used as the starting points for the building of the attribute trees. For each fact attribute its own attribute tree is built and further DFM steps also are applied.

Step 4.1. Identification of facts. Attributes are identified, which could be used as fact attributes. An existing data driven method can be adapted. We used DFM (Golfarelli et al., 1998), but we adapted it for the integrated data model. Searching for many-to-many relationships on each particular

Figure 5. Existing data of data sources

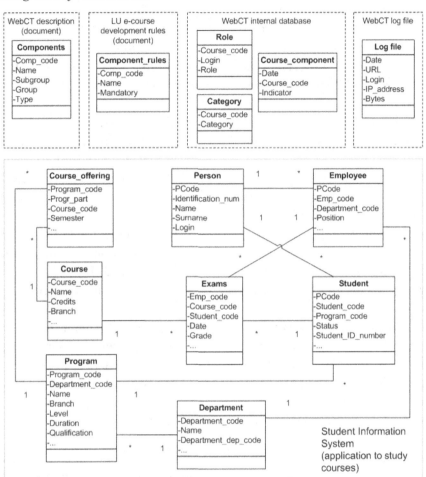

data model is used as a basis for drawing initial attribute trees according to the DFM method.

Step 4.2. Identification of hierarchies. In this step dimensions and hierarchies of dimension levels are identified. An existing data driven method can be adapted. We used DFM (Golfarelli et al., 1998), but we adapted it for the integrated data model. The global data model and the existing relationships between entities of data models of different data sources are used to extend the initially drawn attribute trees according to the DFM method.

Activity 5. Definition of the user views. According to the data driven approach user requirements are not discovered in detail before the development of a conceptual model of a data warehouse, therefore, two aspects exist concerning the users: 1) which data from the conceptual model are allowed or not for particular users; 2) which operations with the allowed data are applicable according to the data semantics.

The concept of users' views was introduced to formalize the analysis requirements and to provide a specification of access rights and reports for the developers. The users' views are defined based on the conceptual model of the data warehouse, the facts and possible data aggregation possibilities of this model, and the responsibilities of the particular user or user group. This approach is based on the assumption of Inmon (2002) that in a data warehouse the OLAP applications are developed iteratively.

The definitions of users' views are specified more accurately after discussing them with the customer.

The definition of each view is a set of m+2 elements $(R, G_m(L_{mj}), F)$, where $0 <= m <= n$; n– the number of dimensions and the other elements have the following meaning:

R - The identifier to be analysed: the name of the identifier, which is expressed in business terms and describes the fact, aggregation function, and the level of detail of dimension hierarchy;

$G_m(L_{mj})$– the restriction for the dimension D_m and for the hierarchy level L_{mj}, where $1 <= j <= k$; k – the number of levels of the dimension D_m; k $<= D_m$ number of attributes;

L_{m1} – hierarchy level used for the definition of the fact attribute, but L_{mk} – the top level of the hierarchy.

$G_m(L_{mj})$ could be labelled in three ways:

- Dimension_name$_m(L_{mj})$ // the restriction of analysis possibilities, where Dimension_name$_m$ is the name of the dimension D_m and the detail level for the analysis is provided until the hierarchy level L_{mj},

- Dimension_name$_m$ $(L_{mj} = $ „level_value") // the restriction of analysis possibilities. In this case only the instances of the dimension Dimension_name$_m$ with the value „level_value" of the hierarchy level L_{mj} are used.

- Dimension_name$_m$ $(L_{mj} = $ Value) // the restriction of data ownership; in this case the indicators are calculated for each individual user and the value of the dimension level L_{mj}; for each user a different allowed data set can be accessed depending on the *Value*

$F(f_x)$ - Function for the aggregation of facts, where f_x – fact attribute, $0 <= x <= z$, z – the number of fact attributes.

The definition of these constraints can be of two types - data analysis restriction or data ownership restriction:

- Data analysis restriction is a constraint, which is defined by the developer of the data warehouse based on the goal of the analysis; this restriction is provided for all users, which have this restriction defined within their user view. For example, the notation Course (Faculty) means that users can see the facts, which have the dimension Course, detailed until Faculty level.

- Data ownership restriction is a constraint, which means that allowed data are defined for a user depending on his or her position and department. For example, the notation Course (Faculty=Value) means that each user can see only the facts, which correspond to the courses of the faculty of a particular user.

Let us see an example from our case study - the management view definition. The management of the university is interested in evaluation of e-courses from the quantitative perspective of usage. The indicators, which characterize the e-course usage, are given in the management view in Table 4.

These indices can be compared with the financial figures of WebCT purchase and maintenance as well as finances, invested into the course development. The financial figures itself are not included into the data warehouse. The analysis comprises the whole university data; the granularity is up to the faculty level; the time dimension uses all reporting period or monthly data. The management is interested also in data about the activity of course designers or teaching assistants. The management view is characterized by the assessment at the end of the reporting period.

Table 4. Management view definition

Indices	Analysed dimensions and level of detail	Functions
Average activity (hits) of registered and active students	Course(faculty) Time(month) Role(role=student)	SUM(hits)/SUM(numb_of_active_st) SUM(hits)/SUM(numb_of_reg_st)
Average activity time of registered and active students	Course(faculty) Time(month) Role(role=student)	SUM(time)/SUM(numb_of_active_st) SUM(time)/SUM(numb_of_reg_st)
Number of sessions	Time(month); Session(category)	COUNT_DISTINCT (session_id)
Number of courses taught in the term	Course_offering (is_taught=yes)	COUNT_DISTINCT (course_id)
Number of active instructors	Role(role=designer or role= assistant)	COUNT_DISTINCT(person_id)

The method uses four existing components from other methods, adapts five existing components from other methods, and one new method component is built.

An overview about all method components is given in the Table 5. The designations used in this table are the same as in the case of the UDM and are described before Table 2. From adapted components for the DDM method it can be inferred that in three adaptation cases as a basic components are used method components which are not specific for the data warehousing field. Modelling and integration methods components from ISD field are used. Specific existing method components are used for discovering the elements of data warehouses: facts and hierarchies.

From the description of the method and its components also a set of contingency factors (seven factors), which characterize the data-driven method DDM, can be discovered:

DDM_f1. The process is new for the organization,

DDM_f2. Many data sources are involved, which should be integrated,

DDM_f3. One or several interrelated processes, which should be analysed, are identified,

DDM_f4. It is possible to get an integrated model of involved data sources,

DDM_f5. The indicators, which should be analysed, are not known,

DDM_f6. The analysis dimensions are not known also,

DDM_f7. There is only the analysis goal identified, but the analysis requirements are not known and there are no possibilities to find them out.

Goal-Driven Method (GDM)

In this section a goal driven method (GDM) for the development of a conceptual model of a data warehouse is proposed. The method was developed according to method engineering principles. The method was successfully applied for the development of the data marts at the University of Latvia for the process measurement of the student enrolment to study courses. The results about the experience of application of the data driven method are published in detail in (Niedrite et al., 2007). The situations in this project were used to identify the contingency factors that determine whether an existing method component can be used or adapted, or a new method component should be developed.

GDM is based on goal-question-(indicator)-metric (GQ(I)M) method (Park et al., 1996).

Table 5. An overview of method components of the DDM

	ORIGIN	N/A/ E	DESCRIPTION OF THE COMPONENT (GOAL; ADAPTATION, IF APPLICABLE)	CONT. FACTORS
1.1	IS	E	Finding the process to be analysed	DDM_f1
1.2	IS (process modelling)	A	Finding the data sources, used by the process, which will be analysed; a limited process model is built, only processes that are related with the given process are modelled.	DDM_f3
2.1	IS (data modelling)	A	Discovering the data used by each step of the process model, entities and attributes; limited data models are built, only the data used by processes of 1.2. component are included.	DDM_f2
2.2	IS (e.g. data model analysis)	E	Defining relationships between discovered entities in each particular data model	DDM_f2
3.1	IS, Integration of data models	E	Discovering attributes, which are common for many data models	DDM_f2
3.2	IS, Integration of data models	E	Discovering attributes, which are usable for integration with transformations	DDM_f2
3.3	Integration of data models	A	Discovering necessary activities for possible transformations of data sources of different data granularity; Specification of data aggregation for data integration purposes	DDM_f2
4.1	DFM	A	Discovering attributes, which could be used as facts; DFM is applied for the integrated data model	DDM_f4; DDM_f5
4.2	DFM	A	Identifying dimensions and hierarchies; DFM is applied for the integrated data model	DDM_f4; DDM_f6
5	project situation	N	Defining user views for different types of user groups according to the position, department and work functions	DDM_f7

A goal driven measurement process GQ(I)M proposed in (Park et al., 1996) is used as a basis for discovering indicators for the process measurement. The basic elements of the GQ(I)M method and their relationships are represented by the Indicator definition metamodel. An association between classes Indicator and Attribute is added to describe the necessary transformation function. This metamodel is described in detail in (Niedrite et al., 2007) and we will use it later in our method.

The process model of the GDM is given in the Figure 6 and consists of four activities.

Activity 1. Identification of indicators. Business goals, then measurement goals, and finally indicators are identified using the existing method

Figure 6. The process model of he GDM

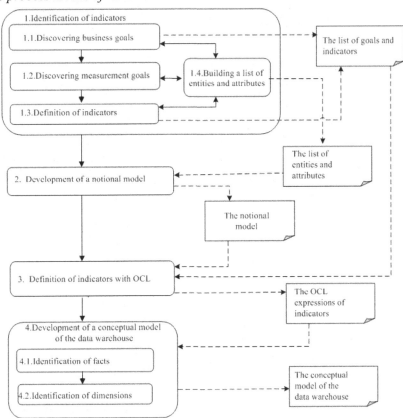

GQ(I)M (Park et al., 1996) and more detailed three steps can be considered according to GQ(I)M:

Step 1.1. Discovering business goals. Existing method component is used.

Step 1.2. Discovering measurement goals. Existing method component is used.

Step 1.3. Definition of indicators. Existing method component is used.

According to the GQ(I)M after the definition of measurement goals, questions that characterize achievement of the goals were formulated and indicators that answer these questions were identified. In our case study one of the identified measurement goals was "Improve the effectiveness of enrolment process from the students' viewpoint." We identified five questions, e.g.

"How many students could not enrol in courses through internet and why?" and also found out indicators that answer these questions. For our example question the corresponding indicators are I10 "Number of students with financial debt" and I11" Number of students with academic debt".

Activity 2. The development of notional model. Using GQ(I)M method together with identification of goals, questions, and indicators, also entities (process participants, objects, processes) and attributes are identified, which are involved into business processes. According to the GDM, a model named notional model is developed as a UML 2.0 Structure diagram. The notional model includes the identified entities and attributes and is an instance of the Indicator definition metamodel.

Figure 7. Notional Model of students' enrolment in courses

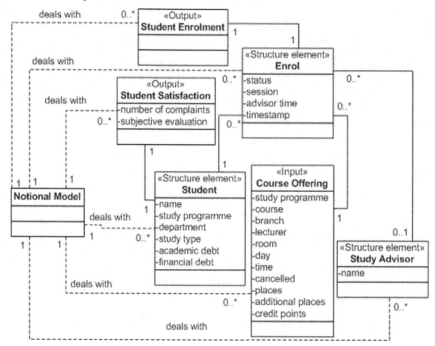

In our case study during the application of the GDM method in the development project of the data mart for the analysis of the enrolment process of students into the study courses, the notional model depicted in Figure 7 was developed.

Activity 3. The definition of indicators with OCL. The indicators, which were defined according to GQ(I)M, are afterwards defined with OCL expressions (OMG, 2006) based on the notional model. Transformation Functions from attributes to the indicators identified according to GQ(I)M method are formulated with OCL query operations that return a value or set of values using Entities, Attributes and associations from the Notional Model.

In our case study the indicators I10 and I11 that correspond to our example question are formulated with OCL in Table 6.

Activity 4. The development of the conceptual model of the data warehouse. The structure of all

OCL expressions is analysed to discover potential facts and dimensions.

Step 4.1. Identification of facts. OCL query operations (Table 6) that define Indicators are further analysed to design a data warehouse model. Firstly potential facts are identified. If a result of an operation is numerical, for example, sum(), size(), round(), multiplication, division, such values are considered as potential facts.

Step 4.2. Identification of dimensions. Potential dimensions and dimension attributes are determined. Initially classes, which appear in *context* clause of OCL query operations excluding the class Notional Model, are considered as

Table 6. Indicator formulation with OCL

I10	**context** Notional Model::I10():Integer **body:** Student → select(financial debt='Yes') → size()
I11	**context** Notional Model::I11():Integer **body:** Student → select(academic debt='Yes') → size()

potential dimensions. Their attributes correspond to dimension attributes. In addition other dimension attributes are derived from class attributes used in *select* clause of OCL query operations. These attributes are grouped into dimensions corresponding to classes that contain these attributes.

A data warehouse model (Figure 8) was produced for the case study indicators, including

also our two example indicators described in previous activities.

The GDM uses four existing method components. The result of these components is a set of identified indicators The method uses also four new method components. The method does not use adapted method components. An overview of the method components is given in Table 7. The designations used in this table are the same

Figure 8. The data warehouse model

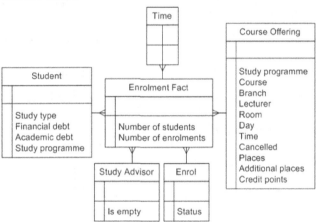

Table 7. An overview of method components of the GDM

	ORIGIN	N/A/E	DESCRIPTION OF THE COMPONENT (GOAL; ADAPTATION, IF APPLICABLE)	CONT. FACTORS
1.1	GQ(I)M	E(N)	Identification of business goals	GDM_f1; GDM_f2
1.2	GQ(I)M	E(N)	Identification of measurement goals	GDM_f1; GDM_f2
1.3	GQ(I)M	E(N)	Identification of indicators	GDM_f1; GDM_f2
1.4	GQ(I)M	E(N)	Development of the list of entities and attributes, which are involved in previous steps	GDM_f1; GDM_f2
2	project situation	N	Development of a data model from the entities and attributes according to the indicator definition metamodel	GDM_f3
3	project situation	N	Definition of indicators with OCL	GDM_f3
4.1.	project situation	N	Identification of facts	GDM_f3
4.2.	project situation	N	Identification of dimensions	GDM_f3

as in the case of the UDM and are described before Table 2.

For the goal-driven method GDM the following set of contingency factors was identified:

GDM_f1. One or several interrelated processes, which should be measured, are well-known;

GDM_f2. The indicators, which should be analysed, are not known;

GDM_f3. During the process of identification of the indicators it is possible to find out the set of entities and attributes that characterize the measured process.

CONCLUSION

Comparing the contingency factors discovered for each proposed new method, it is obvious that the situation during the construction of a new method should be analysed according to the following criteria (the values of given contingency factors are ignored):

- Is the process new for a particular organization;
- The number of processes to be measured;
- Is the process, which should be measured, identified (selected);
- The number of interviewees;
- The spectrum of analysis requirements,

Table 8. An overview and comparison of the contingency factors

	UDM	DDM	GDM
Is the process new	-	new DDM_f1	well-known GDM_f1
The number of processes	many UDM_f1	1 or some DDM_f3	1 or some GDM_f1
Is the process, which should be measured, identified	is not identified UDM_f1	are identified DDM_f3	are identified GDM_f1
The number of interviewees	many UDM_f2	-	-
The spectrum of analysis requirements	Broad UDM_f3 UDM_f6	-	-
Priorities of requirements	should be identified UDM_f4; UDM_f6	-	-
Number of data sources to be integrated	-	many DDM_f2	-
The models of data sources and the possibility to integrate them	-	well-known DDM_f4	Model is built GDM_f3
Indicators	are identified during interviews UDM_f5	are not known DDM_f5	are not known GDM_f2, are identified GDM_f3
Analysis dimensions	are identified during interviews UDM_f5	are not known DVM_f6	are not known GDM_f2, but are identified GDM_f3
The way of analysis	are identified during interviews UDM_f5	are not well-known DVM_f7	are not well-known GDM_f2, but are identified GDM_f3

- Are the priorities of requirements known;
- The number of data sources to be integrated,
- The models of data sources and the possibility to integrate them,
- Are the indicators identified,
- Are the analysis dimensions identified,
- The way of analysis.

Not for all proposed methods all these criteria are important. The values of these criteria for each method according to the contingency factors of methods derived from descriptions of methods and their components are given in the Table 8. If the criteria did not influence the decision during the development of the particular method, the cell in the table contains "-". The notation GDM_f1, for example, means that the first factor of GDM method is the source of the value in the cell.

To conclude, it can be said that eleven different contingency factors are identified, whose values have influenced the decisions about the approach that should be used. These contingency factors also determined method components that should be used, adapted, or built during the construction of a particular method.

ACKNOWLEDGMENT

This research was partially funded by the European Social Fund (ESF).

REFERENCES

Artz, J. (2005). Data driven vs. metric driven data warehouse design. In *Encyclopedia of Data Warehousing and Mining*, (pp. 223 – 227). Idea Group.

Abello, A., Samos, J., & Saltor, F. (2001). A framework for the classification and description of multidimensional data models. In *Proceedings of 12th Int. conf. on Database and Expert Systems Applications (DEXA)*, LNCS 2113, (pp. 668-677). Springer.

Benefelds, J., & Niedrite, L. (2004). Comparison of approaches in data warehouse development in financial services and higher education. In *Proceedings of the 6th Int. Conf. of Enterprise Information Systems (ICEIS 2004)*, *1*, 552-557. Porto.

Blaschka, M., Sapia, C., Hofling, G., & Dinter, B. (1998). Finding your way through multidimensional data models. In *Proceedings of 9th Int. Conf. on Database and Expert Systems Applications (DEXA)*, *LNCS 1460*, 198-203. Springer,

Boehnlein, M. & Ulbrich-vom-Ende, A. (2000). Business process-oriented development of data warehouse structures. In *Proceedings of Int. Conf. Data Warehousing 2000* (pp. 3-16). Physica Verlag.

Bonifati, A., Cattaneo, F., Ceri, S., Fuggetta, A., & Paraboschi, S. (2001). Designing data marts for data warehouses. In *ACM Transactions on Software Engineering and Methodology*, *10*(4), 452-483.

Brinkkemper, S. (1996). Method engineering: Engineering of information systems development methods and tools. In *Information and Software Technology*, *38*(4), 275- 280.

Fitzgerald, B. & Fitzgerald, G. (1999). Categories and contexts of information systems developing: Making sense of the mess. In *Proceedings of European Conf. on Information Systems*, (pp.194-211).

Giorgini, P., Rizzi, S., & Garzetti, M. (2005). Goal-oriented requirement analysis for data warehouse design. In *Proceedings of 8th ACM Int. Workshop DOLAP*, (pp. 47-56).

Goeken, M. (2005). Anforderungsmanagement bei der Entwicklung von data-warehouse-systemen. Ein sichtenspezifischer Ansatz. In *Procee-*

dings der DW 2004 - Data Warehousing und EAI, (pp. 167 – 186).

Golfarelli, M., Maio, D., & Rizzi, S. (1998). Conceptual design of data warehouses from E/R schemes. In *Proceedings of Hawaii Int. Conf. on System Sciences*, *7*, 334-343.

Harmsen, F. (1997). *Situational method engineering.* Dissertation Thesis, University of Twente, Moret Ernst & Young Management Consultants.

Inmon, W.H. (2002). *Building the data warehouse,* 3rd ed., Wiley Computer Publishing, p. 428.

Kaldeich, C., & Oliveira, J. (2004). Data warehouse methodology: A process driven approach. In *Proceedings of CAISE*, LNCS, *3084*, 536-549.

Kimball, R., Reeves, L., Ross, M., & Thornthwite, W. (1998). The data warehouse lifecycle toolkit: Expert methods for designing, developing and deploying data warehouses, (p. 771). John Wiley.

Kueng, P., Wettstein, T., & List, B. (2001). A holistic process performance analysis through a process data warehouse. In *Proceedings of the American Conf. on Information Systems*, (pp. 349-356).

Leppanen, M., Valtonen, K., & Pulkkinen, M. (2007). Towards a contingency framework for engineering an EAP method. In *Proceedings of the 30th Information Systems Research Seminar in Scandinavia IRIS2007.*

List, B., Bruckner, R. M., Machaczek, K., & Schiefer, J. (2002). A comparison of data warehouse development methodologies. Case study of the process warehouse. In *Proceedings of DEXA 2002, LNCS 2453*, (pp. 203-215). Springer.

Lujan-Mora, S., Trujillo, J., & Song, I. (2002). Extending the UML for multidimensional modeling. In *Proceedings of UML*, LNCS 2460, (pp. 290-304). Springer.

Mirbel, I., & Ralyte, J. (2005). Situational method engineering: Combining assembly-based and roadmap-driven approaches. In *Requirements Engineering*, *11*(1), 58-78.

Niedrite, L., Solodovnikova, D., Treimanis, M., & Niedritis, A. (2007). The development method for process-oriented data warehouse. In *WSEAS Transactions on Computer Research,,2*(2), 183 – 190.

Niedrite, L., Solodovnikova, D., Treimanis, M., & Niedritis, A. (2007). Goal-driven design of a data warehouse-based business process analysis system. In *Proceedings of WSEAS Int. Conf. on Artificial Intelligence, Knowledge Engineering And Data Bases AIKED '07.*

Object Management Group (2006). *Object constraint language (OCL) specification, v2.0.*

Object Management Group, (2005). *Software process engineering metamodel specification, v1.1.*

Park, R.E., Goethert, W.G., & Florac, W.A. (1996). Goal-driven software measurement – A guidebook. In *Technical Report, CMU/SEI-96-HB-002*, Software Engineering Institute, Carnegie Mellon University.

Pedersen, T. B. (2000). *Aspects of data modeling and query processing for complex multidimensional data*, PhD Thesis, Faculty of Engineering and Science, Aalborg University.

Phipps, C., & Davis, K.C. (2002). Automating data warehouse conceptual schema design and evaluation. In *Proceedings of the 4th Int. Workshop DMDW'2002*, CEUR-WS.org, *28*.

Poole, J., Chang, D., Tolbert, D., & Mellor, D. (2003). Common warehouse metamodel developers guide, (p. 704). Wiley Publishing.

Ralyte, J., Deneckere, R., & Rolland, C. (2003). Towards a generic model for situational method engineering. In *Proceedings. of CAiSE'03,* LNCS *2681,* 95-110. Springer-Verlag.

Rizzi, S., Abelló, A., Lechtenbörger, J., & Trujillo, J. (2006). Research in data warehouse modeling and design: Dead or alive? In *Proceedings of the 9th ACM Int. Workshop on Data Warehousing and OLAP (DOLAP '06)*, (pp. 3-10) ACM Press.

Rolland, C. (1997). A primer for method engineering. In *Proceedings of the INFormatique des ORganisations et Syst`emes d'Information et de D'ecision (INFORSID'97)*.

Sapia, C., Blaschka, M., Höfling, G., & Dinter, B. (1998). Extending the E/R model for the multidimensional paradigm. In *Proceedings of Advances in Database Technologies, ER '98 Workshops on Data Warehousing and Data Mining, Mobile Data Access, and Collaborative Work Support and Spatio-Temporal Data Management, LNCS 1552*, 105-116). Springer.

Solodovnikova, D., & Niedrite, L. (2005). Using data warehouse resources for assessment of E-Learning influence on university processes. In *Proceedings of the 9th East-European Conf. on Advances in Databases and Information Systems (ADBIS)*, (pp. 233-248).

Tryfona, N., Busborg, F., & Christiansen, J.G.B. (1999). StarER: A conceptual model for data warehouse design. In *Proceedings of ACM 2nd. Int. Workshop on Data warehousing and OLAP (DOLAP)*, USA, (pp. 3-8).

Westerman, P. (2001). *DatawWarehousing using the Wal-Mart model.* (p. 297). Morgan Kaufmann.

Winter, R., & Strauch, B. (2003). A method for demand-driven information requirements analysis in data warehousing projects. In *Proceedings of the 36th Hawaii Int. Conf. on System Sciences.*

Chapter II
Conceptual Modeling Solutions for the Data Warehouse

Stefano Rizzi
DEIS-University of Bologna, Italy

ABSTRACT

In the context of data warehouse design, a basic role is played by conceptual modeling, that provides a higher level of abstraction in describing the warehousing process and architecture in all its aspects, aimed at achieving independence of implementation issues. This chapter focuses on a conceptual model called the DFM that suits the variety of modeling situations that may be encountered in real projects of small to large complexity. The aim of the chapter is to propose a comprehensive set of solutions for conceptual modeling according to the DFM and to give the designer a practical guide for applying them in the context of a design methodology. Besides the basic concepts of multidimensional modeling, the other issues discussed are descriptive and cross-dimension attributes; convergences; shared, incomplete, recursive, and dynamic hierarchies; multiple and optional arcs; and additivity.

INTRODUCTION

Operational databases are focused on recording transactions, thus they are prevalently characterized by an OLTP (online transaction processing) workload. Conversely, data warehouses (DWs) allow complex analysis of data aimed at decision support; the workload they support has completely different characteristics, and is widely known as OLAP (online analytical processing). Traditionally, OLAP applications are based on *multidimensional modeling* that intuitively represents data under the metaphor of a cube whose cells correspond to events that occurred in the

Figure 1. The cube metaphor for multidimensional modeling

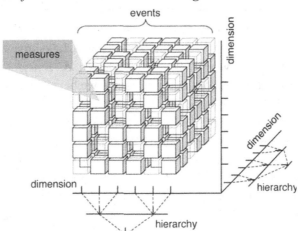

business domain (Figure 1). Each event is quantified by a set of measures; each edge of the cube corresponds to a relevant dimension for analysis, typically associated to a hierarchy of attributes that further describe it. The multidimensional model has a twofold benefit. On the one hand, it is close to the way of thinking of data analyzers, who are used to the spreadsheet metaphor; therefore it helps users understand data. On the other hand, it supports performance improvement as its simple structure allows designers to predict the user intentions.

Multidimensional modeling and OLAP workloads require specialized design techniques. In the context of design, a basic role is played by *conceptual modeling* that provides a higher level of abstraction in describing the warehousing process and architecture in all its aspects, aimed at achieving independence of implementation issues. Conceptual modeling is widely recognized to be the necessary foundation for building a database that is well-documented and fully satisfies the user requirements; usually, it relies on a graphical notation that facilitates writing, understanding, and managing conceptual schemata by both designers and users.

Unfortunately, in the field of data warehousing there still is no consensus about a formalism for conceptual modeling (Sen & Sinha, 2005). The entity/relationship (E/R) model is widespread in the enterprises as a conceptual formalism to provide standard documentation for relational information systems, and a great deal of effort has been made to use E/R schemata as the input for designing nonrelational databases as well (Fahrner & Vossen, 1995); nevertheless, as E/R is oriented to support queries that navigate associations between data rather than synthesize them, it is not well suited for data warehousing (Kimball, 1996). Actually, the E/R model has enough expressivity to represent most concepts necessary for modeling a DW; on the other hand, in its basic form, it is not able to properly emphasize the key aspects of the multidimensional model, so that its usage for DWs is expensive from the point of view of the graphical notation and not intuitive (Golfarelli, Maio, & Rizzi, 1998).

Some designers claim to use star schemata for conceptual modeling. A *star schema* is the standard implementation of the multidimensional model on relational platforms; it is just a (denormalized) relational schema, so it merely defines a set of relations and integrity constraints. Using the star schema for conceptual modeling is like starting to build a complex software by writing the code, without the support of and static, functional, or dynamic model, which typically leads to very poor results from the points of view of adherence to user requirements, of maintenance, and of reuse.

For all these reasons, in the last few years the research literature has proposed several original approaches for modeling a DW, some based on extensions of E/R, some on extensions of UML. This chapter focuses on an ad hoc conceptual model, the *dimensional fact model* (DFM), that was first proposed in Golfarelli et al. (1998) and continuously enriched and refined during the following years in order to optimally suit the variety of modeling situations that may be encountered in real projects of small to large complexity. The aim of the chapter is to propose a comprehensive set of solutions for conceptual modeling according to the DFM and to give a practical guide for applying them in the context of a design methodology. Besides the basic concepts of multidimensional modeling, namely facts, dimensions, measures, and hierarchies, the other issues discussed are descriptive and cross-dimension attributes; convergences; shared, incomplete, recursive, and dynamic hierarchies; multiple and optional arcs; and additivity.

After reviewing the related literature in the next section, in the third and fourth sections, we introduce the constructs of DFM for basic and advanced modeling, respectively. Then, in the fifth section we briefly discuss the different methodological approaches to conceptual design. Finally, in the sixth section we outline the open issues in conceptual modeling, and in the last section we draw the conclusions.

RELATED LITERATURE

In the context of data warehousing, the literature proposed several approaches to multidimensional modeling. Some of them have no graphical support and are aimed at establishing a formal foundation for representing cubes and hierarchies as well as

an algebra for querying them (Agrawal, Gupta, & Sarawagi, 1995; Cabibbo & Torlone, 1998; Datta & Thomas, 1997; Franconi & Kamble, 2004a; Gyssens & Lakshmanan, 1997; Li & Wang, 1996; Pedersen & Jensen, 1999; Vassiliadis, 1998); since we believe that a distinguishing feature of conceptual models is that of providing a graphical support to be easily understood by both designers and users when discussing and validating requirements, we will not discuss them.

The approaches to "strict" conceptual modeling for DWs devised so far are summarized in Table 1. For each model, the table shows if it is associated to some method for conceptual design and if it is based on E/R, is object-oriented, or is an ad hoc model.

The discussion about whether E/R-based, object-oriented, or ad hoc models are preferable is controversial. Some claim that E/R extensions should be adopted since (1) E/R has been tested for years; (2) designers are familiar with E/R; (3) E/R has proven flexible and powerful enough to adapt to a variety of application domains; and (4) several important research results were obtained for the E/R (Sapia, Blaschka, Hofling, & Dinter, 1998; Tryfona, Busborg, & Borch Christiansen, 1999). On the other hand, advocates of object-oriented models argue that (1) they are more expressive and better represent static and dynamic properties of information systems; (2) they provide powerful mechanisms for expressing requirements and constraints; (3) object-orientation is currently the dominant trend in data modeling; and (4) UML, in particular, is a standard and is naturally extensible (Abelló, Samos, & Saltor, 2002; Luján-Mora, Trujillo, & Song, 2002). Finally, we believe that ad hoc models compensate for the lack of familiarity from designers with the fact that (1) they achieve better notational economy; (2) they give proper emphasis to the peculiarities of the multidimensional model, thus (3) they are more intuitive and readable by nonexpert users. In particular, they can model some constraints related to functional dependencies (e.g., convergences

Table 1. Approaches to conceptual modeling

	E/R extension	object-oriented	ad hoc
no method	Franconi and Kamble (2004b); Sapia et al. (1998); Tryfona et al. (1999)	Abelló et al. (2002); Nguyen, Tjoa, and Wagner (2000)	Tsois et al. (2001)
method		Luján-Mora et al. (2002)	Golfarelli et al. (1998); Hüsemann et al. (2000)

and cross-dimensional attributes) in a simpler way than UML, that requires the use of formal expressions written, for instance, in OCL.

A comparison of the different models done by Tsois, Karayannidis, and Sellis (2001) pointed out that, abstracting from their graphical form, the core expressivity is similar. In confirmation of this, we show in Figure 2 how the same simple fact could be modeled through an E/R based, an object-oriented, and an ad hoc approach.

Figure 2. The SALE fact modeled through a starER (Sapia et al., 1998), a UML class diagram (Luján-Mora et al., 2002), and a fact schema (Hüsemann, Lechtenbörger, & Vossen, 2000)

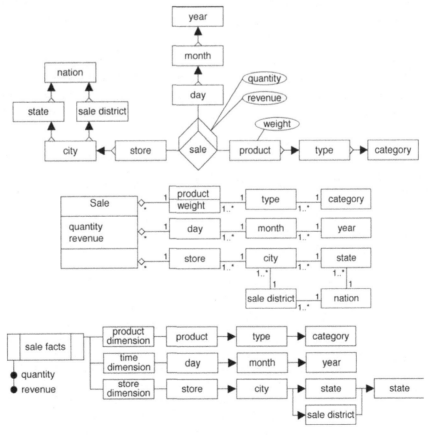

THE DIMENSIONAL FACT MODEL: BASIC MODELING

In this chapter we focus on an ad hoc model called the dimensional fact model. The DFM is a graphical conceptual model, specifically devised for multidimensional modeling, aimed at:

- Effectively supporting conceptual design
- Providing an environment on which user queries can be intuitively expressed
- Supporting the dialogue between the designer and the end users to refine the specification of requirements
- Creating a stable platform to ground logical design
- Providing an expressive and non-ambiguous design documentation

The representation of reality built using the DFM consists of a set of *fact schemata*. The basic concepts modeled are facts, measures, dimensions, and hierarchies. In the following we intuitively define these concepts, referring the reader to Figure 3 that depicts a simple fact schema for modeling invoices at line granularity; a formal definition of the same concepts can be found in Golfarelli et al. (1998).

Definition 1: A *fact* is a focus of interest for the decision-making process; typically, it models a set of events occurring in the enterprise world. A fact is graphically represented by a box with two sections, one for the fact name and one for the measures.

Examples of facts in the trade domain are sales, shipments, purchases, claims; in the financial domain: stock exchange transactions, contracts for insurance policies, granting of loans, bank statements, credit cards purchases. It is essential for a fact to have some *dynamic* aspects, that is, to evolve somehow across time.

Guideline 1: The concepts represented in the data source by frequently-updated archives are good candidates for facts; those represented by almost-static archives are not.

As a matter of fact, very few things are completely static; even the relationship between cities and regions might change, if some border were revised. Thus, the choice of facts should be based either on the average periodicity of changes, or on the specific interests of analysis. For instance, assigning a new sales manager to a sales department occurs less frequently than coupling a

Figure 3. A basic fact schema for the INVOICE LINE fact

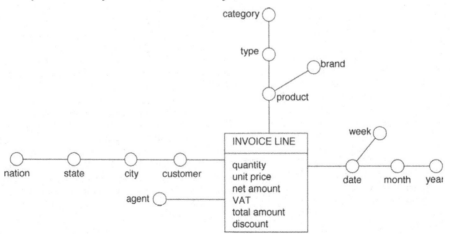

promotion to a product; thus, while the relationship between promotions and products is a good candidate to be modeled as a fact, that between sales managers and departments is not—except for the personnel manager, who is interested in analyzing the turnover!

Definition 2: A *measure* is a numerical property of a fact, and describes one of its quantitative aspects of interests for analysis. Measures are included in the bottom section of the fact.

For instance, each invoice line is measured by the number of units sold, the price per unit, the net amount, and so forth. The reason why measures should be numerical is that they are used for computations. A fact may also have no measures, if the only interesting thing to be recorded is the occurrence of events; in this case the fact scheme is said to be *empty* and is typically queried to count the events that occurred.

Definition 3: A *dimension* is a fact property with a finite domain and describes one of its analysis coordinates. The set of dimensions of a fact determines its finest representation granularity. Graphically, dimensions are represented as circles attached to the fact by straight lines.

Typical dimensions for the invoice fact are product, customer, agent, and date.

Guideline 2: At least one of the dimensions of the fact should represent time, at any granularity.

The relationship between measures and dimensions is expressed, at the instance level, by the concept of event.

Definition 4: A *primary event* is an occurrence of a fact, and is identified by a tuple of values, one for each dimension. Each primary event is described by one value for each measure.

Primary events are the elemental information which can be represented (in the cube metaphor, they correspond to the cube cells). In the invoice example they model the invoicing of one product to one customer made by one agent on one day; it is not possible to distinguish between invoices possibly made with different types (e.g., active, passive, returned, etc.) or in different hours of the day.

Guideline 3: If the granularity of primary events as determined by the set of dimensions is coarser than the granularity of tuples in the data source, measures should be defined as either aggregations of numerical attributes in the data source, or as counts of tuples.

Remarkably, some multidimensional models in the literature focus on treating dimensions and measures symmetrically (Agrawal et al., 1995; Gyssens & Lakshmanan, 1997). This is an important achievement from both the point of view of the uniformity of the logical model and that of the flexibility of OLAP operators. Nevertheless we claim that, at a conceptual level, distinguishing between measures and dimensions is important since it allows logical design to be more specifically aimed at the efficiency required by data warehousing applications.

Aggregation is the basic OLAP operation, since it allows significant information useful for decision support to be summarized from large amounts of data. From a conceptual point of view, aggregation is carried out on primary events thanks to the definition of dimension attributes and hierarchies.

Definition 5: A *dimension attribute* is a property, with a finite domain, of a dimension. Like dimensions, it is represented by a circle.

For instance, a product is described by its type, category, and brand; a customer, by its city and its nation. The relationships between dimension attributes are expressed by hierarchies.

Definition 6: A *hierarchy* is a directed tree, rooted in a dimension, whose nodes are all the dimension attributes that describe that dimension, and whose arcs model many-to-one associations between pairs of dimension attributes. Arcs are graphically represented by straight lines.

Guideline 4: Hierarchies should reproduce the pattern of interattribute functional dependencies expressed by the data source.

Hierarchies determine how primary events can be aggregated into secondary events and selected significantly for the decision-making process. The dimension in which a hierarchy is rooted defines its finest aggregation granularity, while the other dimension attributes define progressively coarser granularities. For instance, thanks to the existence of a many-to-one association between products and their categories, the invoicing events may be grouped according to the category of the products.

Definition 7: Given a set of dimension attributes, each tuple of their values identifies a *secondary event* that aggregates all the corresponding primary events. Each secondary event is described by a value for each measure that summarizes the values taken by the same measure in the corresponding primary events.

We close this section by surveying some alternative terminology used either in the literature or in the commercial tools. There is substantial agreement on using the term *dimensions* to designate the "entry points" to classify and identify events; while we refer in particular to the attribute determining the minimum fact granularity, sometimes the whole hierarchies are named as dimensions (for instance, the term "time dimension" often refers to the whole hi-

erarchy built on dimension *date*). Measures are sometimes called *variables* or *metrics*. Finally, in some data warehousing tools, the term *hierarchy* denotes each single branch of the tree rooted in a dimension.

THE DIMENSIONAL FACT MODEL: ADVANCED MODELING

The constructs we introduce in this section, with the support of Figure 4, are descriptive and cross-dimension attributes; convergences; shared, incomplete, recursive, and dynamic hierarchies; multiple and optional arcs; and additivity. Though some of them are not necessary in the simplest and most common modeling situations, they are quite useful in order to better express the multitude of conceptual shades that characterize real-world scenarios. In particular we will see how, following the introduction of some of this constructs, hierarchies will no longer be defined as trees to become, in the general case, directed graphs.

Descriptive Attributes

In several cases it is useful to represent additional information about a dimension attribute, though it is not interesting to use such information for aggregation. For instance, the user may ask for knowing the address of each store, but the user will hardly be interested in aggregating sales according to the address of the store.

Definition 8: A *descriptive attribute* specifies a property of a dimension attribute, to which is related by an *x*-to-one association. Descriptive attributes are not used for aggregation; they are always leaves of their hierarchy and are graphically represented by horizontal lines.

There are two main reasons why a descriptive attribute should not be used for aggregation:

Figure 4. The complete fact schema for the INVOICE LINE fact

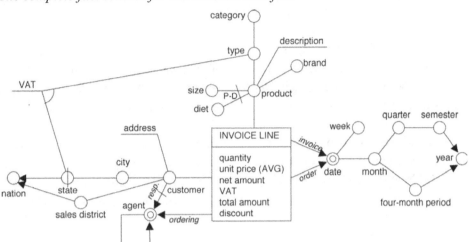

Guideline 5: A descriptive attribute either has a continuously-valued domain (for instance, the weight of a product), or is related to a dimension attribute by a one-to-one association (for instance, the address of a customer).

Cross-Dimension Attributes

Definition 9: A *cross-dimension attribute* is a (either dimension or descriptive) attribute whose value is determined by the combination of two or more dimension attributes, possibly belonging to different hierarchies. It is denoted by connecting through a curve line the arcs that determine it.

For instance, if the VAT on a product depends on both the product category and the state where the product is sold, it can be represented by a cross-dimension attribute as shown in Figure 4.

Convergence

Consider the geographic hierarchy on dimension *customer* (Figure 4): customers live in cities, which are grouped into states belonging to nations. Suppose that customers are grouped into sales districts as well, and that no inclusion relationships exist between districts and cities/states; on the

other hand, sales districts never cross the nation boundaries. In this case, each customer belongs to exactly one nation whichever of the two paths is followed (customer → city → state → nation or customer → sales district → nation).

Definition 10: A *convergence* takes place when two dimension attributes within a hierarchy are connected by two or more alternative paths of many-to-one associations. Convergences are represented by letting two or more arcs converge on the same dimension attribute.

The existence of apparently equal attributes does not always determine a convergence. If in the invoice fact we had a brand city attribute on the product hierarchy, representing the city where a brand is manufactured, there would be no convergence with attribute (customer) city, since a product manufactured in a city can obviously be sold to customers of other cities as well.

Optional Arcs

Definition 11: An *optional arc* models the fact that an association represented within the fact scheme is undefined for a subset of the events. An optional arc is graphically denoted by marking it with a dash.

For instance, attribute diet takes a value only for food products; for the other products, it is undefined.

In the presence of a set of optional arcs exiting from the same dimension attribute, their *coverage* can be denoted in order to pose a constraint on the optionalities involved. Like for IS-A hierarchies in the E/R model, the coverage of a set of optional arcs is characterized by two independent coordinates. Let a be a dimension attribute, and $b_1,..., b_m$ be its children attributes connected by optional arcs:

- The coverage is *total* if each value of a always corresponds to a value for at least one of its children; conversely, if some values of a exist for which all of its children are undefined, the coverage is said to be *partial*.
- The coverage is *disjoint* if each value of a corresponds to a value for, at most, one of its children; conversely, if some values of a exist that correspond to values for two or more children, the coverage is said to be *overlapped*.

Thus, overall, there are four possible coverages, denoted by T-D, T-O, P-D, and P-O. Figure 4 shows an example of optionality annotated with its coverage. We assume that products can have three types: food, clothing, and household, since expiration date and size are defined only for, respectively, food and clothing, the coverage is partial and disjoint.

Multiple Arcs

In most cases, as already said, hierarchies include attributes related by many-to-one associations. On the other hand, in some situations it is necessary to include also attributes that, for a single value taken by their father attribute, take several values.

Definition 12: A *multiple arc* is an arc, within a hierarchy, modeling a many-to-many association between the two dimension attributes it connects. Graphically, it is denoted by doubling the line that represents the arc.

Consider the fact schema modeling the sales of books in a library, represented in Figure 5, whose dimensions are date and book. Users will probably be interested in analyzing sales for each book author; on the other hand, since some books have two or more authors, the relationship between book and author must be modeled as a multiple arc.

Guideline 6: In presence of many-to-many associations, summarizability is no longer guaranteed, unless the multiple arc is properly *weighted*. Multiple arcs should be used sparingly since, in ROLAP logical design, they require complex solutions.

Summarizability is the property of correcting summarizing measures along hierarchies (Lenz & Shoshani, 1997). Weights restore summarizability,

Figure 5. The fact schema for the SALES fact

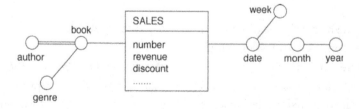

but their introduction is artificial in several cases; for instance, in the book sales fact, each author of a multiauthored book should be assigned a normalized weight expressing her "contribution" to the book.

Shared Hierarchies

Sometimes, large portions of hierarchies are replicated twice or more in the same fact schema. A typical example is the temporal hierarchy: a fact frequently has more than one dimension of type date, with different semantics, and it may be useful to define on each of them a temporal hierarchy month-week-year. Another example are geographic hierarchies, that may be defined starting from any location attribute in the fact schema. To avoid redundancy, the DFM provides a graphical shorthand for denoting hierarchy sharing. Figure 4 shows two examples of shared hierarchies. Fact INVOICE LINE has two date dimensions, with semantics invoice date and order date, respectively. This is denoted by doubling the circle that represents attribute date and specifying two *roles* invoice and order on the entering arcs. The second shared hierarchy is the one on agent, that may have two roles: the ordering agent, that is a dimension, and the agent who is responsible for a customer (optional).

Guideline 8: Explicitly representing shared hierarchies on the fact schema is important since, during ROLAP logical design, it enables ad hoc solutions aimed at avoiding replication of data in dimension tables.

Ragged Hierarchies

Let $a_1,..., a_n$ be a sequence of dimension attributes that define a path within a hierarchy (such as city, state, nation). Up to now we assumed that, for each value of a_1, exactly one value for every other attribute on the path exists. In the previous case, this is actually true for each city in the U.S., while it is false for most European countries where no decomposition in states is defined (see Figure 6).

Definition 13: A *ragged* (or *incomplete*) *hierarchy* is a hierarchy where, for some instances, the values of one or more attributes are missing (since undefined or unknown). A ragged hierarchy is graphically denoted by marking with a dash the attributes whose values may be missing.

As stated by Niemi (2001), within a ragged hierarchy each aggregation level has precise and consistent semantics, but the different hierarchy instances may have different length since one or more levels are missing, making the interlevel relationships not uniform (the father of "San Francisco" belongs to level state, the father of "Rome" to level nation).

There is a noticeable difference between a ragged hierarchy and an optional arc. In the first case we model the fact that, for some hierarchy instances, there is no value for one or more attributes *in any position of the hierarchy*. Conversely, through an optional arc we model the fact that there is no value for an attribute *and for all of its descendents*.

Figure 6. Ragged geographic hierarchies

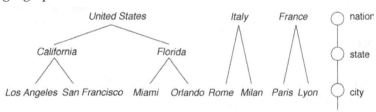

Guideline 9: Ragged hierarchies may lead to summarizability problems. A way for avoiding them is to fragment a fact into two or more facts, each including a subset of the hierarchies characterized by uniform interlevel relationships.

Thus, in the invoice example, fragmenting INVOICE LINE into U.S. INVOICE LINE and E.U. INVOICE LINE (the first with the state attribute, the second without state) restores the completeness of the geographic hierarchy.

Unbalanced Hierarchies

Definition 14: An *unbalanced* (or *recursive*) *hierarchy* is a hierarchy where, though interattribute relationships are consistent, the instances may have different length. Graphically, it is represented by introducing a cycle within the hierarchy.

A typical example of unbalanced hierarchy is the one that models the dependence interrelationships between working persons. Figure 4 includes an unbalanced hierarchy on sale agents: there are no fixed roles for the different agents, and the different "leaf" agents have a variable number of supervisor agents above them.

Guideline 10: Recursive hierarchies lead to complex solutions during ROLAP logical design and to poor querying performance. A way for avoiding them is to "unroll" them for a given number of times.

For instance, in the agent example, if the user states that two is the maximum number of interesting levels for the dependence relationship, the customer hierarchy could be transformed as in Figure 7.

Dynamic Hierarchies

Time is a key factor in data warehousing systems, since the decision process is often based on the evaluation of historical series and on the comparison between snapshots of the enterprise taken at different moments. The multidimensional models implicitly assume that the only dynamic components described in a cube are the events that instantiate it; hierarchies are traditionally considered to be static. Of course this is not correct: sales manager alternate, though slowly, on different departments; new products are added every week to those already being sold; the product categories change, and their relationship with products change; sales districts can be modified, and a customer may be moved from one district to another.[1]

The conceptual representation of hierarchy dynamicity is strictly related to its impact on user queries. In fact, in presence of a dynamic hierarchy we may picture three different temporal scenarios for analyzing events (SAP, 1998):

- **Today for yesterday:** All events are referred to the current configuration of hierarchies. Thus, assuming on January 1, 2005 the responsible agent for customer Smith has changed from Mr. Black to Mr. White, and that a new customer O'Hara has been acquired and assigned to Mr. Black, when computing the agent commissions all invoices for Smith are attributed to Mr. White, while only invoices for O'Hara are attributed to Mr. Black.
- **Yesterday for today:** All events are referred to some past configuration of hierarchies. In the previous example, all invoices for Smith are attributed to Mr. Black, while invoices for O'Hara are not considered.

Figure 7. Unrolling the agent hierarchy

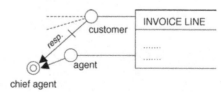

- **Today or yesterday (or historical truth):** Each event is referred to the configuration hierarchies had at the time the event occurred. Thus, the invoices for Smith up to 2004 and those for O'Hara are attributed to Mr. Black, while invoices for Smith from 2005 are attributed to Mr. White.

While in the agent example, dynamicity concerns an arc of a hierarchy, the one expressing the many-to-one association between customer and agent, in some cases it may as well concern a dimension attribute: for instance, the name of a product category may change. Even in this case, the different scenarios are defined in much the same way as before.

On the conceptual schema, it is useful to denote which scenarios the user is interested for each arc and attribute, since this heavily impacts on the specific solutions to be adopted during logical design. By default, we will assume that the only interesting scenario is today for yesterday—it is the most common one, and the one whose implementation on the star schema is simplest. If some attributes or arcs require different scenarios, the designer should specify them on a table like Table 2.

Additivity

Aggregation requires defining a proper operator to compose the measure values characterizing primary events into measure values characterizing each secondary event. From this point of view, we may distinguish three types of measures (Lenz & Shoshani, 1997):

- **Flow measures:** They refer to a time period, and are cumulatively evaluated at the end of that period. Examples are the number of products sold in a day, the monthly revenue, the number of those born in a year.
- **Stock measures:** They are evaluated at particular moments in time. Examples are the number of products in a warehouse, the number of inhabitants of a city, the temperature measured by a gauge.
- **Unit measures:** They are evaluated at particular moments in time, but they are expressed in relative terms. Examples are the unit price of a product, the discount percentage, the exchange rate of a currency.

The aggregation operators that can be used on the three types of measures are summarized in Table 3.

Table 2. Temporal scenarios for the INVOICE fact

arc/attribute	today for yesterday	yesterday for today	today or yesterday
customer-resp. agent	YES	YES	YES
customer-city	YES		YES
sale district			YES

Table 3. Valid aggregation operators for the three types of measures (Lenz, 1997)

	temporal hierarchies	nontemporal hierarchies
flow measures	SUM, AVG, MIN, MAX	SUM, AVG, MIN, MAX
stock measures	AVG, MIN, MAX	SUM, AVG, MIN, MAX
unit measures	AVG, MIN, MAX	AVG, MIN, MAX

Definition 15: A measure is said to be *additive* along a dimension if its values can be aggregated along the corresponding hierarchy by the sum operator, otherwise it is called *nonadditive*. A nonadditive measure is *nonaggregable* if no other aggregation operator can be used on it.

Table 3 shows that, in general, flow measures are additive along all dimensions, stock measures are nonadditive along temporal hierarchies, and unit measures are nonadditive along all dimensions.

On the invoice scheme, most measures are additive. For instance, quantity has flow type: the total quantity invoiced in a month is the sum of the quantities invoiced in the single days of that month. Measure unit price has unit type and is nonadditive along all dimensions. Though it cannot be summed up, it can still be aggregated by using operators such as average, maximum, and minimum.

Since additivity is the most frequent case, in order to simplify the graphic notation in the DFM, only the exceptions are represented explicitly. In particular, a measure is connected to the dimensions along which it is nonadditive by a dashed line labeled with the other aggregation operators (if any) which can be used instead. If a measure is aggregated through the same operator along all dimensions, that operator can be simply reported on its side (see for instance unit price in Figure 4).

APPROACHES TO CONCEPTUAL DESIGN

In this section we discuss how conceptual design can be framed within a methodology for DW design. The approaches to DW design are usually classified in two categories (Winter & Strauch, 2003):

- Data-driven (or supply-driven) approaches that design the DW starting from a detailed analysis of the data sources; user requirements impact on design by allowing the designer to select which chunks of data are relevant for decision making and by determining their structure according to the multidimensional model (Golfarelli et al., 1998; Hüsemann et al., 2000).

- Requirement-driven (or demand-driven) approaches start from determining the information requirements of end users, and how to map these requirements onto the available data sources is investigated only *a posteriori* (Prakash & Gosain, 2003; Schiefer, List & Bruckner, 2002).

While data-driven approaches somehow simplify the design of ETL (extraction, transformation, and loading), since each data in the DW is rooted in one or more attributes of the sources, they give user requirements a secondary role in determining the information contents for analysis, and give the designer little support in identifying facts, dimensions, and measures. Conversely, requirement-driven approaches bring user requirements to the foreground, but require a larger effort when designing ETL.

Data-Driven Approaches

Data-driven approaches are feasible when all of the following are true: (1) detailed knowledge of data sources is available *a priori* or easily achievable; (2) the source schemata exhibit a good degree of normalization; (3) the complexity of source schemata is not high. In practice, when the chosen architecture for the DW relies on a *reconciled level* (or *operational data store*) these requirements are largely satisfied: in fact, normalization and detailed knowledge are guaranteed by the source integration process. The same holds, thanks to a careful source recognition activity, in the frequent case when the source is a single relational database, well-designed and not very large.

In a data-driven approach, requirement analysis is typically carried out informally, based on simple requirement glossaries (Lechtenbörger, 2001) rather than on formal diagrams. Conceptual design is then heavily rooted on source schemata and can be largely automated. In particular, the designer is actively supported in identifying dimensions and measures, in building hierarchies, in detecting convergences and shared hierarchies. For instance, the approach proposed by Golfarelli et al. (1998) consists of five steps that, starting from the source schema expressed either by an E/R schema or a relational schema, create the conceptual schema for the DW:

1.   Choose facts of interest on the source schema
2.   For each fact, build an *attribute tree* that captures the functional dependencies expressed by the source schema
3.   Edit the attribute trees by adding/deleting attributes and functional dependencies
4.   Choose dimensions and measures
5.   Create the fact schemata

While step 2 is completely automated, some advanced constructs of the DFM are manually applied by the designer during step 5.

On-the-field experience shows that, when applicable, the data-driven approach is preferable since it reduces the overall time necessary for design. In fact, not only conceptual design can be partially automated, but even ETL design is made easier since the mapping between the data sources and the DW is derived at no additional cost during conceptual design.

Requirement-Driven Approaches

Conversely, within a requirement-driven framework, in the absence of knowledge of the source schema, the building of hierarchies cannot be automated; the main assurance of a satisfactory result is the skill and experience of the designer, and the designer's ability to interact with the domain experts. In this case it may be worth adopting formal techniques for specifying requirements in order to more accurately capture users' needs; for instance, the goal-oriented approach proposed by Giorgini, Rizzi, and Garzetti (2005) is based on an extension of the Tropos formalism and includes the following steps:

1.   Create, in the Tropos formalism, an *organizational model* that represents the stakeholders, their relationships, their goals as well as the relevant facts for the organization and the attributes that describe them.
2.   Create, in the Tropos formalism, a *decisional model* that expresses the analysis goals of decision makers and their information needs.
3.   Create preliminary fact schemata from the decisional model.
4.   Edit the fact schemata, for instance, by detecting functional dependencies between dimensions, recognizing optional dimensions, and unifying measures that only differ for the aggregation operator.

This approach is, in our view, more difficult to pursue than the previous one. Nevertheless, it is the only alternative when a detailed analysis of data sources cannot be made (for instance, when the DW is fed from an ERP system), or when the sources come from legacy systems whose complexity discourages recognition and normalization.

Mixed Approaches

Finally, also a few *mixed* approaches to design have been devised, aimed at joining the facilities of data-driven approaches with the guarantees of requirement-driven ones (Bonifati, Cattaneo, Ceri, Fuggetta, & Paraboschi, 2001; Giorgini et al., 2005). Here the user requirements, captured by means of a goal-oriented formalism, are matched with the schema of the source database to drive the algorithm that generates the conceptual schema for the DW. For instance, the approach proposed by Giorgini et al. (2005) encompasses three phases:

1. Create, in the Tropos formalism, an *organizational model* that represents the stakeholders, their relationships, their goals, as well as the relevant facts for the organization and the attributes that describe them.
2. Create, in the Tropos formalism, a *decisional model* that expresses the analysis goals of decision makers and their information needs.
3. Map facts, dimensions, and measures identified during requirement analysis onto entities in the source schema.
4. Generate a preliminary conceptual schema by navigating the functional dependencies expressed by the source schema.
5. Edit the fact schemata to fully meet the user expectations.

Note that, though step 4 may be based on the same algorithm employed in step 2 of the data-driven approach, here navigation is not "blind" but rather it is actively biased by the user requirements. Thus, the preliminary fact schemata generated here may be considerably simpler and smaller than those obtained in the data-driven approach. Besides, while in that approach the analyst is asked for identifying facts, dimensions, and measures directly on the source schema, here such identification is driven by the diagrams developed during requirement analysis.

Overall, the mixed framework is recommendable when source schemata are well-known but their size and complexity are substantial. In fact, the cost for a more careful and formal analysis of requirement is balanced by the quickening of conceptual design.

OPEN ISSUES

A lot of work has been done in the field of conceptual modeling for DWs; nevertheless some very important issues still remain open. We report some of them in this section, as they emerged during joint discussion at the *Perspective Seminar on "Data Warehousing at the Crossroads"* that took place at Dagstuhl, Germany on August 2004.

- **Lack of a standard:** Though several conceptual models have been proposed, none of them has been accepted as a standard so far, and all vendors propose their own proprietary design methods. We see two main reasons for this: (1) though the conceptual models devised are semantically rich, some of the modeled properties cannot be expressed in the target logical models, so the translation from conceptual to logical is incomplete; and (2) commercial CASE tools currently enable designers to directly draw logical schemata, thus no industrial push is given to any of the models. On the other hand, a unified conceptual model for DWs, implemented by sophisticated CASE tools, would be a valuable support for both the research and industrial communities.
- **Design patterns:** In software engineering, design patterns are a precious support for designers since they propose standard solutions to address common modeling problems. Recently, some preliminary attempts have been made to identify relevant patterns for multidimensional design, aimed at assisting DW designers during their modeling tasks by providing an approach for recognizing dimensions in a systematic and usable way (Jones & Song, 2005). Though we agree that DW design would undoubtedly benefit from adopting a pattern-based approach, and we also recognize the utility of patterns in increasing the effectiveness of teaching how

to design, we believe that further research is necessary in order to achieve a more comprehensive characterization of multidimensional patterns for both conceptual and logical design.

- **Modeling security:** Information security is a serious requirement that must be carefully considered in software engineering, not in isolation but as an issue underlying all stages of the development life cycle, from requirement analysis to implementation and maintenance. The problem of information security is even bigger in DWs, as these systems are used to discover crucial business information in strategic decision making. Some approaches to security in DWs, focused, for instance, on access control and multilevel security, can be found in the literature (see, for instance, Priebe & Pernul, 2000), but neither of them treats security as comprising all stages of the DW development cycle. Besides, the classical security model used in transactional databases, centered on tables, rows, and attributes, is unsuitable for DW and should be replaced by an ad hoc model centered on the main concepts of multidimensional modeling—such as facts, dimensions, and measures.

- **Modeling ETL:** ETL is a cornerstone of the data warehousing process, and its design and implementation may easily take 50% of the total time for setting up a DW. In the literature some approaches were devised for conceptual modeling of the ETL process from either the functional (Vassiliadis, Simitsis, & Skiadopoulos, 2002), the dynamic (Bouzeghoub, Fabret, & Matulovic, 1999), or the static (Calvanese, De Giacomo, Lenzerini, Nardi, & Rosati, 1998) points of view. Recently, also some interesting work on translating conceptual into logical ETL schemata has been done (Simitsis, 2005). Nevertheless, issues such as the optimization of ETL logical schemata are not very

well understood. Besides, there is a need for techniques that automatically propagate changes occurred in the source schemas to the ETL process.

CONCLUSION

In this chapter we have proposed a set of solutions for conceptual modeling of a DW according to the DFM. Since 1998, the DFM has been successfully adopted, in real DW projects mainly in the fields of retail, large distribution, telecommunications, health, justice, and instruction, where it has proved expressive enough to capture a wide variety of modeling situations. Remarkably, in most projects the DFM was also used to directly support dialogue with end users aimed at validating requirements, and to express the expected workload for the DW to be used for logical and physical design. This was made possible by the adoption of a CASE tool named WAND (warehouse integrated designer), entirely developed at the University of Bologna, that assists the designer in structuring a DW. WAND carries out data-driven conceptual design in a semiautomatic fashion starting from the logical scheme of the source database (see Figure 8), allows for a core workload to be defined on the conceptual scheme, and carries out workload-based logical design to

Figure 8. Editing a fact schema in WAND

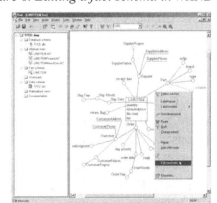

produce an optimized relational scheme for the DW (Golfarelli & Rizzi, 2001).

Overall, our on-the-field experience confirmed that adopting conceptual modeling within a DW project brings great advantages since:

- Conceptual schemata are the best support for discussing, verifying, and refining user specifications since they achieve the optimal trade-off between expressivity and clarity. Star schemata could hardly be used to this purpose.
- For the same reason, conceptual schemata are an irreplaceable component of the documentation for the DW project.
- They provide a solid and platform-independent foundation for logical and physical design.
- They are an effective support for maintaining and extending the DW.
- They make turn-over of designers and administrators on a DW project quicker and simpler.

REFERENCES

Abelló, A., Samos, J., & Saltor, F. (2002, July 17-19). YAM2 (Yet another multidimensional model): An extension of UML. In *Proceedings of the International Database Engineering & Applications Symposium* (pp. 172-181). Edmonton, Canada.

Agrawal, R., Gupta, A., & Sarawagi, S. (1995). *Modeling multidimensional databases* (IBM Research Report). IBM Almaden Research Center, San Jose, CA.

Bonifati, A., Cattaneo, F., Ceri, S., Fuggetta, A., & Paraboschi, S. (2001). Designing data marts for data warehouses. *ACM Transactions on Software Engineering and Methodology*, *10*(4), 452-483.

Bouzeghoub, M., Fabret, F., & Matulovic, M. (1999). Modeling data warehouse refreshment process as a workflow application. In *Proceedings of the International Workshop on Design and Management of Data Warehouses*, Heidelberg, Germany.

Cabibbo, L., & Torlone, R. (1998, March 23-27). A logical approach to multidimensional databases. In *Proceedings of the International Conference on Extending Database Technology* (pp. 183-197). Valencia, Spain.

Calvanese, D., De Giacomo, G., Lenzerini, M., Nardi, D., & Rosati, R. (1998, August 20-22). Information integration: Conceptual modeling and reasoning support. In *Proceedings of the International Conference on Cooperative Information Systems* (pp. 280-291). New York.

Datta, A., & Thomas, H. (1997). A conceptual model and algebra for on-line analytical processing in data warehouses. In *Proceedings of the Workshop for Information Technology and Systems* (pp. 91-100).

Fahrner, C., & Vossen, G. (1995). A survey of database transformations based on the entity-relationship model. *Data & Knowledge Engineering*, *15*(3), 213-250.

Franconi, E., & Kamble, A. (2004a, June 7-11). The GMD data model and algebra for multidimensional information. In *Proceedings of the Conference on Advanced Information Systems Engineering* (pp. 446-462). Riga, Latvia.

Franconi, E., & Kamble, A. (2004b). A data warehouse conceptual data model. In *Proceedings of the International Conference on Statistical and Scientific Database Management* (pp. 435-436).

Giorgini, P., Rizzi, S., & Garzetti, M. (2005, November 4-5). Goal-oriented requirement analysis for data warehouse design. In *Proceedings of the ACM International Workshop on Data Warehousing and OLAP* (pp. 47-56). Bremen, Germany.

Golfarelli, M., Maio, D., & Rizzi, S. (1998). The dimensional fact model: A conceptual model for data warehouses. *International Journal of Cooperative Information Systems, 7*(2-3), 215-247.

Golfarelli, M., & Rizzi, S. (2001, April 2-6). WAND: A CASE tool for data warehouse design. In *Demo Proceedings of the International Conference on Data Engineering* (pp. 7-9). Heidelberg, Germany.

Gyssens, M., & Lakshmanan, L. V. S. (1997). A foundation for multi-dimensional databases. In *Proceedings of the International Conference on Very Large Data Bases* (pp. 106-115), Athens, Greece.

Hüsemann, B., Lechtenbörger, J., & Vossen, G. (2000). Conceptual data warehouse design. In *Proceedings of the International Workshop on Design and Management of Data Warehouses*, Stockholm, Sweden.

Jones, M. E., & Song, I. Y. (2005). Dimensional modeling: Identifying, classifying & applying patterns. In *Proceedings of the ACM International Workshop on Data Warehousing and OLAP* (pp. 29-38). Bremen, Germany.

Kimball, R. (1996). *The data warehouse toolkit.* New York: John Wiley & Sons.

Lechtenbörger, J. (2001). *Data warehouse schema design* (Tech. Rep. No. 79). DISDBIS Akademische Verlagsgesellschaft Aka GmbH, Germany.

Lenz, H. J., & Shoshani, A. (1997). Summarizability in OLAP and statistical databases. In *Proceedings of the 9th International Conference on Statistical and Scientific Database Management* (pp. 132-143). Washington, DC.

Li, C., & Wang, X. S. (1996). A data model for supporting on-line analytical processing. In *Proceedings of the International Conference on Information and Knowledge Management* (pp. 81-88). Rockville, Maryland.

Luján-Mora, S., Trujillo, J., & Song, I. Y. (2002). Extending the UML for multidimensional modeling. In *Proceedings of the International Conference on the Unified Modeling Language* (pp. 290-304). Dresden, Germany.

Niemi, T., Nummenmaa, J., & Thanisch, P. (2001, June 4). Logical multidimensional database design for ragged and unbalanced aggregation. *Proceedings of the 3rd International Workshop on Design and Management of Data Warehouses,* Interlaken, Switzerland (p. 7).

Nguyen, T. B., Tjoa, A. M., & Wagner, R. (2000). An object-oriented multidimensional data model for OLAP. In *Proceedings of the International Conference on Web-Age Information Management* (pp. 69-82). Shanghai, China.

Pedersen, T. B., & Jensen, C. (1999). Multidimensional data modeling for complex data. In *Proceedings of the International Conference on Data Engineering* (pp. 336-345). Sydney, Austrialia.

Prakash, N., & Gosain, A. (2003). Requirements driven data warehouse development. In *Proceedings of the Conference on Advanced Information Systems Engineering—Short Papers,* Klagenfurt/Velden, Austria.

Priebe, T., & Pernul, G. (2000). Towards OLAP security design: Survey and research issues. In *Proceedings of the ACM International Workshop on Data Warehousing and OLAP* (pp. 33-40). Washington, DC.

SAP. (1998). *Data modeling with BW.* SAP America Inc. and SAP AG, Rockville, MD.

Sapia, C., Blaschka, M., Hofling, G., & Dinter, B. (1998). Extending the E/R model for the multidimensional paradigm. In *Proceedings of the International Conference on Conceptual Modeling*, Singapore.

Schiefer, J., List, B., & Bruckner, R. (2002). A holistic approach for managing requirements of data warehouse systems. In *Proceedings of the Americas Conference on Information Systems*.

Sen, A., & Sinha, A. P. (2005). A comparison of data warehousing methodologies. *Communications of the ACM, 48*(3), 79-84.

Simitsis, A. (2005). Mapping conceptual to logical models for ETL processes. In *Proceedings of the ACM International Workshop on Data Warehousing and OLAP* (pp. 67-76). Bremen, Germany.

Tryfona, N., Busborg, F., & Borch Christiansen, J. G. (1999). starER: A conceptual model for data warehouse design. In *Proceedings of the ACM International Workshop on Data Warehousing and OLAP*, Kansas City, Kansas (pp. 3-8).

Tsois, A., Karayannidis, N., & Sellis, T. (2001). MAC: Conceptual data modeling for OLAP. In *Proceedings of the International Workshop on Design and Management of Data Warehouses* (pp. 5.1-5.11). Interlaken, Switzerland.

Vassiliadis, P. (1998). Modeling multidimensional databases, cubes and cube operations. In *Proceedings of the 10th International Conference on Statistical and Scientific Database Management*, Capri, Italy.

Vassiliadis, P., Simitsis, A., & Skiadopoulos, S. (2002, November 8). Conceptual modeling for ETL processes. In *Proceedings of the ACM International Workshop on Data Warehousing and OLAP* (pp. 14-21). McLean, VA.

Winter, R., & Strauch, B. (2003). A method for demand-driven information requirements analysis in data warehousing projects. In *Proceedings of the Hawaii International Conference on System Sciences*, Kona (pp. 1359-1365).

ENDNOTE

[1] In this chapter we will only consider dynamicity at the instance level. Dynamicity at the schema level is related to the problem of evolution of DWs and is outside the scope of this chapter.

Chapter III
A Machine Learning Approach to Data Cleaning in Databases and Data Warehouses

Hamid Haidarian Shahri
University of Maryland, USA

ABSTRACT

Entity resolution (also known as duplicate elimination) is an important part of the data cleaning process, especially in data integration and warehousing, where data are gathered from distributed and inconsistent sources. Learnable string similarity measures are an active area of research in the entity resolution problem. Our proposed framework builds upon our earlier work on entity resolution, in which fuzzy rules and membership functions are defined by the user. Here, we exploit neuro-fuzzy modeling for the first time to produce a unique adaptive framework for entity resolution, which automatically learns and adapts to the specific notion of similarity at a meta-level. This framework encompasses many of the previous work on trainable and domain-specific similarity measures. Employing fuzzy inference, it removes the repetitive task of hard-coding a program based on a schema, which is usually required in previous approaches. In addition, our extensible framework is very flexible for the end user. Hence, it can be utilized in the production of an intelligent tool to increase the quality and accuracy of data.

INTRODUCTION

The problems of data quality and data cleaning are inevitable in data integration from distributed operational databases and online transaction processing (OLTP) systems (Rahm & Do, 2000). This is due to the lack of a unified set of standards spanning over all the distributed sources. One of the most challenging and resource-intensive phases of data cleaning is the removal of fuzzy duplicate records. Considering the possibility of a large number of records to be examined, the removal requires many comparisons and the comparisons demand a complex matching process.

The term *fuzzy duplicates* is used for tuples that are somehow different, but describe the same real-world entity, that is, different syntaxes but the same semantic. Duplicate elimination (also known as entity resolution) is applicable in any database, but critical in data integration and analytical processing domains, where accurate reports and statistics are required. The data cleaning task by itself can be considered as a variant of data mining. Moreover, in data mining and knowledge discovery applications, cleaning is required before any useful knowledge can be extracted from data. Other application domains of entity resolution include data warehouses, especially for dimension tables, online analytical processing (OLAP) applications, decision support systems, on-demand (lazy) Web-based information integration systems, Web search engines, and numerous others. Therefore, an adaptive and flexible approach to detect the duplicates can be utilized as a tool in many database applications.

When data are gathered form distributed sources, differences between tuples are generally caused by four categories of problems in data, namely, the data are incomplete, incorrect, incomprehensible, or inconsistent. Some examples of the discrepancies are spelling errors; abbreviations; missing fields; inconsistent formats; invalid, wrong, or unknown codes; word transposition; and so forth as demonstrated using sample tuples in Table 1.

Very interestingly, the causes of discrepancies are quite similar to what has to be fixed in data cleaning and preprocessing in databases (Rahm & Do, 2000). For example, in the extraction, transformation, and load (ETL) process of a data warehouse, it is essential to detect and fix these problems in dirty data. That is exactly why the elimination of fuzzy duplicates should be performed as one of the last stages of the data cleaning process. In fact, for effective execution of the duplicate elimination phase, it is vital to perform a cleaning stage beforehand. In data integration, many stages of the cleaning can be implemented on the fly (for example, in a data warehouse as the data is being transferred in the ETL process). However, duplicate elimination must be performed after all those stages. That is

Table 1. Examples of various discrepancies in database tuples

Discrepancy Problem	Name	Address	Phone Number	ID Number	Gender
	John Dow	Lucent Laboratories	615 5544	553066	Male
Spelling Errors	John Doe	Lucent Laboratories	615 5544	553066	Male
Abbreviations	J. Dow	Lucent Lab.	615 5544	553066	Male
Missing Fields	John Dow	-	615 5544	-	Male
Inconsistent Formats	John Dow	Lucent Laboratories	(021)6155544	553066	1
Word Transposition	Dow John	Lucent Laboratories	615 5544	553066	Male

what makes duplicate elimination distinctive from the rest of the data cleaning process (for example, change of formats, units, and so forth).

In order to detect the duplicates, the tuples have to be compared to determine their similarity. Uncertainty and ambiguity are inherent in the process of determining fuzzy duplicates due to the fact that there is a range of problems in the tuples, for example, missing information, different formats, and abbreviations. Our earlier work (Haidarian-Shahri & Barforush, 2004) explored how fuzzy inference can be suitably employed to handle the uncertainty of the problem. Haidarian-Shahri and Barforush described several advantages of the fuzzy expert system over the previously proposed solutions for duplicate elimination. One important advantage is getting rid of the repetitive task of hand-coding rules using a programming language that is very time consuming and difficult to manipulate. This chapter introduces the utilization of neuro-fuzzy modeling on top of the Sugeno method of inference (Takagi & Sugeno, 1985) for the first time to produce an adaptive and flexible fuzzy duplicate elimination framework. Here, we elaborate on how our architecture is capable of learning the specific notion of record similarity in any domain from training examples. This way, the rules become dynamic, unlike hand-coded rules of all the previous methods (Galhardas et al., 2001; Hernandez & Stolfo, 1998; Low, Lee, & Ling, 2001; Monge & Elkan, 1997), which in turn assists in achieving better results according to the experiments. Enhancing this novel framework with machine learning and automatic adaptation capabilities paves the way for the development of an intelligent and extendible tool to increase the quality and accuracy of data.

Another chapter of this book by Feil and Abonyi includes an introduction to fuzzy data mining methods. One data cleaning operation may be to fill in missing fields with plausible values to produce a complete data set, and this topic is studied in the chapter by Peláez, Doña, and La Red.

The rest of this chapter is organized as follows. First, we give an account of the related work in the field of duplicate elimination. Then, we describe the design of our architecture. The section after that explains the adaptability and some other characteristics of the framework. Then, we evaluate the performance of the framework and its adaptation capabilities. Finally, we summarize with a conclusion and future directions.

RELATED WORK

Generally, data cleaning is a practical and important process in the database industry and different approaches have been suggested for this task. Some of the advantages of our framework over the previous work done on fuzzy (approximate) duplicate elimination are mentioned here. These points will become clearer later as the system is explained in detail in the next sections.

First, the previously suggested fixed and predefined conditions and declarative rules used for comparing the tuples were particularly difficult and time consuming to program (using a programming language), and the coding had to be repeated for different table schemas (Galhardas et al., 2001; Hernandez & Stolfo, 1998; Low et al., 2001; Monge & Elkan, 1997). Our framework uses natural-language fuzzy rules, which are easily defined with the aid of a GUI (graphical user interface). Second, the program (i.e., thresholds, certainty factors [Low et al., 2001] and other parameters) had to be verified again to allow any minor change in the similarity functions. Hence, the hand-coded rules were inflexible and hard to manipulate. Unlike any of the earlier methods, the design of our framework allows the user to make changes flexibly in the rules and similarity functions without any coding.

Third, in previous methods, the rules were static and no learning mechanism could be used in the system. Exploiting neuro-fuzzy modeling equips the framework with learning capabilities.

This adaptation feature is a decisive advantage of the system, and the learning not only minimizes user intervention, it also achieves better results than the user-defined rules, according to the experiments. Therefore, the task of fine-tuning the rules becomes automatic and effortless. Fourth, the design of our system enables the user to easily manipulate different parts of the process and implement many of the previously developed methods using this extendible framework. None of the previous methods take such a comprehensive approach.

Most previous approaches similarly use some form of rules to detect the duplicates. As mentioned above, the design of our framework and deployment of fuzzy logic provides some unique characteristics in our system. The utilization of fuzzy logic not only helps in handling of uncertainty in a natural way, it also makes the framework adaptive using machine learning techniques. Particularly, the learning mechanism in the framework improves performance and was not existent in any of the previous approaches.

SNM (sorted neighborhood method) from Hernandez and Stolfo (1998) is integrated into our framework as well. Hernandez and Stolfo propose a set of rules encoded using a programming language to compare the pairs of tuples. The knowledge-based approach introduced by Low et al. (2001) is similar to our work in the sense of exploiting coded rules to represent knowledge. However, Low et al. do not employ fuzzy inference and use a certainty factor for the coded rules and for the computation of the transitive closures, which is not required here. In our approach, the knowledge base is replaced with fuzzy rules provided by the user. AJAX (Galhardas et al., 2001) presents an execution model, algorithms, and a declarative language similar to SQL (structured query language) commands to express data cleaning specifications and perform the cleaning efficiently. In contrast to our system, these rules are static and hard to manipulate. Nevertheless, the use of a declarative language such as SQL

instead of a procedural programming language is very advantageous. Raman and Hellerstein (2001) describe an interactive data cleaning system that allows users to see the changes in the data with the aid of a spreadsheet-like interface. It uses the gradual construction of transformations through examples, using a GUI, but is somewhat rigid; that is, it may be hard to reverse the unwanted changes during the interactive execution. The detection of anomalies through visual inspection by human users is also limiting.

Elmagarmid, Ipeirotis, and Verykios (2007) provide a good and recent survey of various duplicate elimination approaches. Chaudhuri, Ganti, and Motwani (2005) and Ananthakrishna, Chaudhuri, and Ganti (2002) also look at the problem of fuzzy duplicate elimination. Note that the use of the word *fuzzy* is only a synonym for approximate, and they do not use fuzzy logic in any way. Ananthakrishna et al. use the relations that exist in the star schema structure in a data warehouse to find the duplicates. Sarawagi and Bhamidipaty (2002) use active learning to train a duplicate elimination system; that is, examples are provided by the user in an interactive fashion to help the system learn.

FLEXIBLE ENTITY RESOLUTION ARCHITECTURE

Detecting fuzzy duplicates by hand using a human requires assigning an expert who is familiar with the table schema and semantic interpretation of attributes in a tuple; he or she must compare the tuples using expertise and conclude whether two tuples refer to the same entity or not. So, for comparing tuples and determining their similarity, internal knowledge about the nature of the tuples seems essential. Developing a code for this task as proposed by previous methods is very time consuming. Even then, the user (expert) has to deal with parameter tuning of the code by trial and error for the system to work properly.

For finding fuzzy duplicates, Hernandez and Stolfo suggest SNM, in which a key is created for each tuple such that the duplicates will have similar keys. The key is usually created by combining some of the attributes, and the tuples are sorted using that key. The sort operation clusters the duplicates and brings them closer to each other. Finally, a window of size w slides over the sorted data, and the tuple, entering the window, is compared with all the w-1 tuples in the window. Hence, performing $n(w$-1) comparisons for a total of n tuples.

A detailed workflow of the duplicate elimination framework is demonstrated in Figure 1. The principal procedure is as follows: to feed a pair of tuples (selected from all possible pairs) into a decision making system and determine if they are fuzzy duplicates or not. First, the data should be cleaned before starting the duplicate elimination phase. That is essential for achieving good results. In a dumb approach, each record is selected and compared with all the rest of the tuples, one by one (i.e., a total of $n(n$-1) comparisons for n records).

To make the process more efficient, the cleaned tuples are clustered by some algorithm in hope of collecting the tuples that are most likely to be duplicates in one group. Then, all possible pairs from each cluster are selected, and the comparisons are only performed for records within each cluster. The user should select the attributes that are important in comparing two records because some attributes do not have much effect in distinguishing a record uniquely. A neuro-fuzzy inference engine, which uses attribute similarities for comparing a pair of records, is employed to detect the duplicates.

This novel framework considerably simplifies duplicate elimination and allows the user to flexibly change different parts of the process. The framework was designed with the aim of producing a user-friendly and application-oriented tool in mind that facilitates flexible user manipulation. In Figure 1, by following the points where the user (expert) can intervene, it is observed that the forthcoming items can be easily selected from a list or supplied by the user (from left to right).

Figure 1. A detailed workflow of the framework

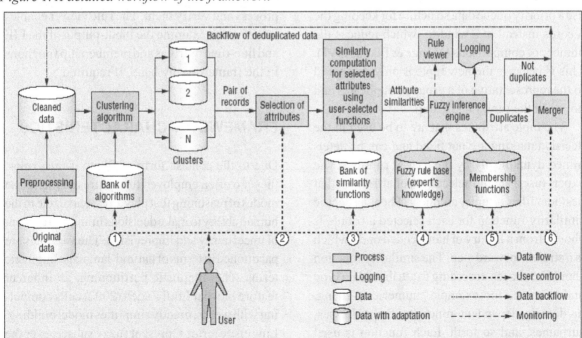

1. Clustering algorithm
2. Attributes to be used in the comparison of a pair of tuples
3. Corresponding similarity functions for measuring attribute similarity
4. Fuzzy rules to be used in the inference engine
5. Membership functions (MFs)
6. Merging strategy

Most of the above items are explained in this section. Fuzzy rules and membership functions will be explained further in the next sections. Steps 4 and 5 involving the fuzzy rules and membership functions are where the machine learning occurs by using ANFIS (adaptive network-based fuzzy inference system). In this framework, the creation of a key, sorting based on that key, and a sliding window phase of the SNM method is a clustering algorithm. The moving window is a structure that is used for holding the clustered tuples and actually acts like a cluster. The comparisons are performed for the tuples within the window. Any other existing clustering algorithm can be employed, and a new hand-coded one even can be added to the bank of algorithms. For example, another option is to use a priority queue data structure for keeping the records instead of a window, which reduces the number of comparisons (Monge & Elkan, 1997). This is because the new tuple is only compared to the representative of a group of duplicates and not to all the tuples in a group.

The tuple attributes that are to be used in the decision making are not fixed and can be determined dynamically by the user at runtime. The expert (user) should select a set of attributes that best identifies a tuple, uniquely. Then, a specific similarity function for each selected attribute is chosen from a library of hand-coded ones, which is a straightforward step. The similarity function should be chosen according to attribute data type and domain, for example, numerical, string, or domain-dependent functions for addresses, surnames, and so forth. Each function is used

for measuring the similarity of two corresponding attributes in a pair of tuples. In this way, any original or appropriate similarity function can be easily integrated into the fuzzy duplicate elimination framework. The fuzzy inference engine combines the attribute similarities and decides whether the tuples are duplicates or not using the fuzzy rules and membership functions as explained in Haidarian-Shahri and Barforush (2004) and Haidarian-Shahri and Shahri (2006). The details are related to how we use the Mamdani method of inference.

At the end, the framework has to eliminate the detected duplicates by merging them. Different merging strategies can be utilized as suggested in the literature (Hernandez & Stolfo, 1998), that is, deciding on which tuple to use as the prime representative of the duplicates. Some alternatives are using the tuple that has the least number of empty attributes, using the newest tuple, prompting the user to make a decision, and so on. All the merged tuples and their prime representatives are recorded in a log. The input-output of the fuzzy inference engine (FIE) for the detected duplicates is also saved. This information helps the user to review the changes in the duplicate elimination process and verify them. The rule viewer enables the expert to examine the input-output of the FIE and fine-tune the rules and membership functions in the framework by hand, if required.

FRAMEWORK CHARACTERISTICS

Due to the concise form of fuzzy if-then rules, they are often employed to capture the imprecise modes of reasoning that play an essential role in the human ability to make decisions in an environment of uncertainty and imprecision. The variables are partitioned in terms of natural-language linguistic terms. This linguistic partitioning, an inherent feature of what Lotfi Zadeh (2002) calls computing with words, greatly simplifies model building. Linguistic terms represent fuzzy subsets over the corresponding variable's domain. These terms are what we actually use in our everyday linguistic reasoning as we speak. Consequently, the rules can be easily defined by the expert.

It has been shown that the decision-making process is intrinsically difficult, taking into account the ambiguity and uncertainty involved in the inference. It is also time consuming and quite impossible to assign a human to this task, especially when dealing with large amounts of data. The system has a robust design for fuzzy duplicate elimination, and has several interesting features, as explained here.

Adaptation and Learning Capabilities

The fuzzy reasoning approach provides a fast and intuitive way of defining the rules by the expert in natural language with the aid of a simple GUI. This eliminates the repetitive process of hard-coding and reduces the development time. An example of a rule in this framework is as follows: IF (Last-NameSimilarity is *high*) ∧ (FirstNameSimilarity is *high*) ∧ (CodeSimilarity is *high*) ∧ (Address-Similarity is *low*) THEN (Probability = 0.9). In this rule, LastNameSimilarity is a linguistic variable and high is a linguistic term that is characterized by an MF. The definition of linguistic variable can be found in Zadeh (1975a, 1975b, 1975c) and in another chapter of this book, written by Xexeo. Generally, the antecedent part of each rule can include a subset (or all) of the attributes that the user has selected previously. The consequence or output of the rule represents the probability of two tuples being duplicates.

In the rules for the Mamdani method of inference (Mamdani, 1976), the output variable is fuzzy. The Mamdani method is utilized when the rules and hand-drawn MFs are defined by the user without any learning and adaptation. This method is more intuitive and suitable for human input. Humans find it easier to state the rules that have fuzzy output variables, such as Probability

= high. On the other hand, in the rules for the Sugeno method of inference (Takagi & Sugeno, 1985), the output variable is defined by a linear equation or a constant, for example Probability = 0.85. This is computationally more efficient and works better with adaptive techniques. Hence, learning can be applied on top of a Sugeno fuzzy inference system (FIS). In grid partitioning or subtractive clustering (as explained in this section), the user only determines the number of membership functions for each input variable to form the initial structure of the FIS. This way, there is no need to define any rules or MFs by hand. The adaptation mechanism will handle the rest, as we will explain.

Fuzzy rules specify the criteria for the detection of duplicates and the rules effectively capture the expert's knowledge that is required in the decision-making process. In our system, the only tricky part for the expert is to determine the fuzzy rules and membership functions for the inference engine. By taking advantage of neuro-fuzzy techniques (Jang & Sun, 1995) on top of the Sugeno method of inference, the framework can be trained using the available numerical data, which mitigates the need for human intervention. The numerical data used for training are vectors. Each vector consists of the attribute similarities of a pair of tuples (inputs of the fuzzy inference engine) and a tag of zero or one (output of the FIE) that determines whether the pair is a duplicate or not. Note that the results of employing the Mamdani method of inference, which merely employs the rules provided by the user in natural language without any learning, is quite acceptable as presented in Haidarian-Shahri and Barforush (2004). Adding adaptation and learning capabilities to the framework enhances the results, as shown in the experiments. Later, we will explain more about the training process and the number of training examples that are required. The details of the adaptation process are provided in Jang and Sun.

The process of constructing a fuzzy inference system is called fuzzy modeling, which has the following features.

- Human expertise about the decision-making process is integrated into the structure determination of the system. This usage of domain knowledge is not provided by most other modeling methods. Structure determination includes determining the relevant inputs, the number of MFs for each input, the number of rules, and the type of fuzzy model (e.g., Mamdani, Sugeno).

- When numerical input-output data for the system to be modeled are available, other conventional system identification methods can be employed. The term *neuro-fuzzy modeling* refers to applying learning techniques developed in the neural networks literature to parameter identification of FISs. Parameter identification deals with recognizing the shape of MFs and the output of rules, to generate best performance.

By employing ANFIS, the membership functions are molded into shape and the consequence of the rules are tuned to model the training data set more closely (Jang, 1993; Jang & Sun, 1995). The ANFIS architecture consists of a five-layered adaptive network, which is functionally equivalent to a first-order Sugeno fuzzy model. This network (i.e., fuzzy model) can be trained when numerical data are available. The adaptation of the fuzzy inference system using machine learning facilitates better performance. When numerical input-output data are not available, the system merely employs the rules provided by the user in natural language as explained in Haidarian-Shahri and Barforush (2004).

In essence, the spirit of a fuzzy inference system is "divide and conquer"; that is, the antecedents of fuzzy rules partition the input space into a number of local fuzzy regions, while the consequents describe the behavior within a given region. In our experiments, grid partitioning (Bezdek, 1981) and subtractive clustering (Chiu, 1994) are used to divide (partition) the problem space and determine the initial structure of the fuzzy system. Then ANFIS is applied for learning and fine-tuning of the parameters. Grid partitioning uses similar and symmetric MFs for all the input variables to generate equal partitions without clustering. The subtractive clustering method partitions the data into groups called clusters and generates an FIS with the minimum number of rules required to distinguish the fuzzy qualities associated with each of the clusters.

Two methods are employed for updating the membership function parameters in ANFIS learning: (a) back-propagation (BP) for all parameters (a steepest descent method), and (b) a hybrid method consisting of back-propagation for the parameters associated with the input membership functions, and least-squares estimation for the parameters associated with the output membership functions. As a result, the training error decreases in each fuzzy region, at least locally, throughout the learning process. Therefore, the more the initial membership functions resemble the optimal ones, the easier it will be for the parameter training to converge.

The most critical advantage of the framework is its machine learning capabilities. In previous methods used for duplicate elimination, the expert had to define the rules using a programming language (Hernandez & Stolfo, 1998; Low et al., 2001). The task of determining the thresholds for the rules and other parameters, like the certainty factor, was purely done by trial and error (Low et al.). In this system, not only is the hard-coding, but the system also adapts to the specific meaning of similarity based on the problem domain using the provided training examples. Even in cases when numerical data for training is unavailable, the framework can be utilized using the membership functions and simple commonsense rules provided by the expert to achieve acceptable performance. It is very valuable to consider that, although there might be other learning mechanisms that are feasible to be utilized for this task, none are likely to be so accommodative and user friendly to allow the framework (tool) to operate with and without training data. Haidarian-Shahri and Barforush (2004) report on the use of the system and handling of uncertainty without any training.

Note that, here, the learning is done at a meta-level to capture the specific notion of record similarity, which is the quantity that needs to be measured for the detection of fuzzy duplicate records. This is more than developing trainable similarity functions for specific types of fields or domain-independent similarity functions. In fact, this framework allows the user to employ any previously developed and complex learnable string similarity measure (Bilenko & Mooney, 2003; Monge & Elkan, 1997) in the duplicate elimination process, as shown in Step 3 of Figure 1.

Other Features

Other features of the framework are briefly described here. More details can be found in Haidarian-Shahri and Barforush (2004) and Haidarian-Shahri and Shahri (2006). When the expert is entering the rules, he or she is in fact just adding the natural and instinctive form of reasoning as if performing the task by hand. Here, the need for the time-consuming task of hard-coding a program and its parameter tuning is eliminated. Additionally, by using fuzzy logic, uncertainty is handled inherently in the fuzzy inference process, and there is no need for a certainty factor for the rules.

The user can change different parts of the framework, as previously illustrated in Figure 1. Consequently, duplicate elimination is performed very flexibly. Since, the expert determines the clustering algorithm, tuple attributes, and corresponding similarity functions for measuring their similarity, many of the previously developed methods for duplicate elimination can be integrated into the framework. Hence, the framework

is quite extendible and serves as a platform for implementing various approaches.

Obviously, domain knowledge helps the duplicate elimination process. After all, what are considered duplicates or data anomalies in one case might not be in another. Such domain-dependent knowledge is derived naturally from the business domain. The business analyst with subject-matter expertise is able to fully understand the business logic governing the situation and can provide the appropriate knowledge to make a decision. Here, domain knowledge is represented in the form of fuzzy rules, which resemble humans' way of reasoning under vagueness and uncertainty. These fuzzy if-then rules are simple, structured, and manipulative.

The framework also provides a rule viewer and a logging mechanism that enables the expert to see the exact effect of the fired rules for each input vector, as illustrated in Haidarian-Shahri and Barforush (2004) and Haidarian-Shahri and Shahri (2006). This, in turn, allows the manipulation and fine-tuning of problematic rules by hand, if required. The rule viewer also provides the reasoning and explanation behind the changes in the tuples and helps the expert to gain a better understanding of the process.

PERFORMANCE AND ADAPTATION EVALUATION

For implementing the fuzzy duplicate elimination framework, the Borland C++ Builder Enterprise Suite and Microsoft SQL Server 2000 are used. The data reside in relational database tables and are fetched through ActiveX Data Object (ADO) components. The Data Transformation Service (DTS) of MS SQL Server is employed to load the data into the OLE DB Provider. The hardware setup in these experiments is a Pentium 4 (1.5 GHz) with 256 MB of RAM and the Windows XP operating system.

The data set used in our experiments is made up of segmented census records originally gathered by Winkler (1999) and also employed in some of the previous string matching projects (Cohen, Ravikumar, & Fienberg, 2003). The data are the result of the integration of two different sources, and each source has duplicates as well as other inconsistencies. The table consists of 580 records, of which 332 are unique and 248 are duplicates. The records are very similar to the ones shown in Table 1. For the purpose of these experiments and investigating the effectiveness of the approach, a simple similarity function is used in our implementation, which only matches the characters in the two fields and correspondingly returns a value between zero and one. That is, the more characters two strings have in common, the more their similarity would be. This is basically using the Jaccard string similarity measure. For two strings s and t, the similarity measure would return the ratio of intersection of s and t to the union of s and t. However, by adding smarter and more sophisticated attribute similarity functions that are domain dependant (handling abbreviations, address checking, etc.), the final results can only improve. The fuzzy inference process is not explained here and the reader can refer to Mamdani (1976), Takagi and Sugeno (1985), and Haidarian-Shahri and Shahri (2006) for more details.

Four attributes, namely, last name, first name, code, and address, are selected by the expert and employed in the inference process. The basic SNM is used for the clustering of records. Two linguistic terms (high and low) are used for the bell-shaped hand-drawn membership functions of the input variables, as shown in Figure 2 (left), which allows for the definition of a total of 2^4 rules. The output variable consists of three linguistic terms (low, medium, high), as demonstrated in Figure 2 (right). Humans find it easier to state the rules that have fuzzy output variables, as in the Mamdani method. The expert adds 11 simple rules, similar to the following, in natural language, with the aid of a GUI.

- IF (LastNameSimilarity is *low*) ∧ (FirstNameSimilarity is *high*) ∧ (CodeSimilarity is *high*) ∧ (AddressSimilarity is *high*) THEN (Probability is *medium*).
- IF (LastNameSimilarity is *low*) ∧ (FirstNameSimilarity is *low*) THEN (Probability is *low*).

To evaluate the performance of the approach and adaptation effectiveness, recall and precision are measured. Recall is the ratio of the number of retrieved duplicates to the total number of duplicates. False-positive error (FP_e) is the ratio of the number of wrongly identified duplicates to the total number of identified duplicates. Precision is equal to $1 - FP_e$. Obviously, the performance of the system is better if the precision is higher at a given recall rate. The precision-recall curves

Figure 2. Linguistic terms (low, high) and their corresponding membership functions for the four input variables (on the left), and the linguistic terms (low, medium, high) for the output variable (on the right)

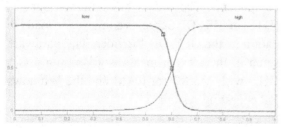 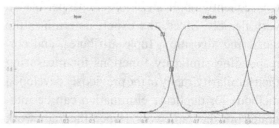

for hand-drawn membership functions and the FISs resulting from applying ANFIS are shown in Figure 3. For all the cases in this figure, two linguistic terms (membership functions) are used for each input variable.

Several hand-drawn bell-shaped MFs are tested using different crossing points for the *low* and *high* terms. The best results are achieved with the crossing point at 0.6 as shown in Figure 2, and the curve labeled "Best Hand-Drawn" and plotted in Figure 3 is for that shape. When using adaptation, the initial structure of the FIS is formed using grid partitioning, and the user does not specify any rules or MFs. Different combinations of hybrid and back-propagation learning on bell and Guassian shapes are experimented with and it is observed that the trained FISs perform better than the FIS using hand-drawn MFs and user-defined rules. Hybrid learning on Gaussian MFs shows the best performance and achieves a 10 to 20% better precision at a given recall rate.

In Figure 3, note that by using a very simple hand-drawn shape and primitive rules defined by the expert, the system is able to detect 70% of the duplicates with 90% precision without any programming. The resultant data are more accurate and quite acceptable (Haidarian-Shahri & Barforush, 2004). By employing learning, the framework even achieves better results, successfully detecting 85% of the duplicates with 90% precision. The data set used for the training consists of the comparisons performed for a window size of 10. A total of 5,220 comparisons are recorded and the duplicates are marked. Each vector in the training data set consists of the four attribute similarities and a tag of zero (not duplicate) or one (duplicate). This data set is broken into three equal parts for training, testing, and validation. In the ANFIS training process, the FIS is trained using the training data set, the error rate for the validation data set is monitored, and parameters, which perform best on the validation data set (not the training data set), are chosen for the inference system. Then the FIS is tested on the testing data set. This way, model overfitting on the training data set, which degrades the overall performance,

Figure 3. Comparison of user-generated and grid-partitioned FISs using different combinations of learning and MF shapes

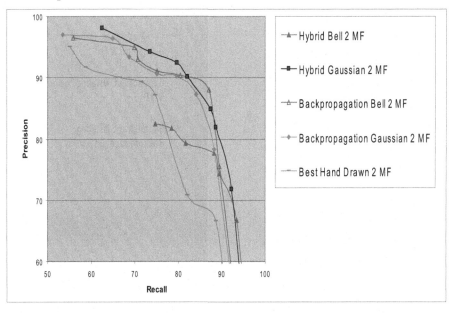

is avoided. Cross-validation ensures that the system learns to perform well in the general case, that is, for the unseen data.

As our initial conjecture (Haidarian-Shahri & Barforush, 2004), the experiments showed that using more than two linguistic terms (high and low) for input variables does not improve the results because when the similarity of attributes (as measured by the user-selected function) is not high, the actual similarity value and the difference between the attributes are of no significance. Hence, there is no need for more than two terms. Having two linguistic terms also limits the total number of possible rules.

Figure 4 show the effect of ANFIS learning on the consequence part of the rules (decision surface) at epochs 0, 10, and 26. The training was performed for 30 epochs, and these epoch

Figure 4. The effect of ANFIS learning on the consequence (z-value) part of the rules; the learning algorithm gradually produces a decision surface that matches the training data.

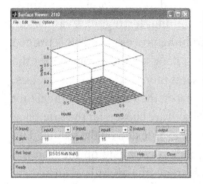 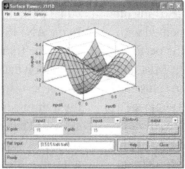 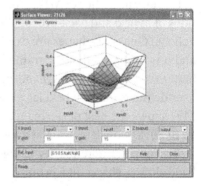

Figure 5. Comparison of grid partitioning and subtractive clustering for the initial structure of an FIS and using different learning methods

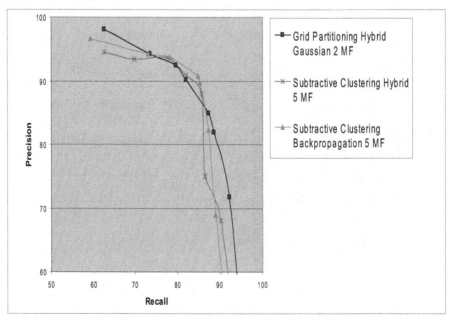

numbers are chosen to demonstrate the gradual change of the decision surface during the training procedure. It illustrates the underlying effect of training on the dynamic fuzzy rules. Note that the ANFIS is capable of adapting to produce a highly nonlinear mapping between input and output in the n-dimensional problem space. Here, two dimensions are shown: the hybrid learning algorithm, and grid partitioning to perform the initial division of the problem input space. The consequence (z-value) of a rule determines the probability of a pair of tuples being duplicates. As demonstrated in Figure 4, rule consequences are all set to zero at the start, and the learning algorithm gradually produces a decision surface that matches the training data as much as possible, reducing the error rate. Figure 4 is showing the change of the first-name and last-name input variables, marked as input3 and input4, respectively. The tuples have four attributes, namely, code, address, first name, and last name.

Figure 5 demonstrates the precision-recall curve for the best trained FIS resulting from grid partitioning and the FISs generated using subtractive clustering with hybrid and back-propagation learning. Here, subtractive clustering uses five MFs per input variable. The performance is similar for the three cases in the figure. Therefore, subtractive clustering is also quite effective for partitioning.

By employing a set of simple rules, easily worded in natural language by the user who is familiar with the records, acceptable results are achieved. In this approach, very little time is spent on phrasing the rules, and the burden of writing hard-code with complex conditions is mitigated. This is not a surprise because intuitiveness and suitability for human comprehension is the inherent feature of fuzzy logic. To top that off, when training data are available, our design exploits neuro-fuzzy modeling to allow users to de-duplicate their integrated data adaptively and effortlessly. This even alleviates the need for specifying obvious rules and regular membership functions.

CONCLUSION

In this chapter, we introduce a novel and adaptive framework for de-duplication. Essentially, it would not be possible to produce such a flexible inference mechanism without the exploitation of fuzzy logic, which has the added benefit of removing time-consuming and repetitive programming. Utilizing this reasoning approach paves the way for an easy-to-use, accommodative, and intelligent duplicate elimination framework that can operate with or without training data. Therefore, with this framework, the development time for setting up a de-duplication system is reduced considerably. The results show that the system is capable of eliminating 85% of the duplicates at a precision level of 90%.

The advantages of utilizing fuzzy logic in the framework for fuzzy duplicate elimination include the ability to specify the rules in natural language easily and intuitively (domain knowledge acquisition), the ability to remove the hard-coding process, framework extendibility, fast development time, flexibility of rule manipulation, inherent handling of uncertainty of the problem without using different parameters, and most importantly, adaptability. If training data are not available, duplicate elimination is done using the natural-language rules and membership functions provided by the user. Furthermore, if training data are available, the use of ANFIS and machine learning capabilities virtually automates the production of the fuzzy rule base and specification of the membership functions.

All together, these features make the framework very suitable and promising to be utilized in the development of an application-oriented commercial tool for fuzzy duplicate elimination, which is our main future goal. Perhaps another interesting future line of work is to implement this approach using standard fuzzy data types and the clustering technique defined in (Galindo, Urrutia, & Piattini, 2006), which defines some fuzzy data types and many fuzzy operations on these values using FSQL (fuzzy SQL) with 18 fuzzy comparators, like FEQ (fuzzy equal), NFEQ (necessarily FEQ), FGT (fuzzy greater than), NFGT (necessarily FGT), MGT (much greater than), NMGT (necessarily MGT), inclusion, and fuzzy inclusion.

ACKNOWLEDGMENT

The authors would like thank helpful comments and suggestions by Dr. Galindo and anonymous reviewers, which increased the quality of this chapter.

REFERENCES

Ananthakrishna, R., Chaudhuri, S., & Ganti, V. (2002). Eliminating fuzzy duplicates in data warehouses. In *Proceedings of 28ᵗʰ International Conference on Very Large Databases (VLDB '02)*.

Bezdek, J. C. (1981). *Pattern recognition with fuzzy objective function algorithms*. New York: Plenum Press.

Bilenko, M., & Mooney, R. J. (2003, August). Adaptive duplicate detection using learnable string similarity measures. *Proceedings of the Ninth ACM SIGKDD International Conference on Knowledge Discovery and Data Mining (KDD'03)*, Washington, DC (pp. 39-48).

Chaudhuri, S., Ganti, V., & Motwani, R. (2005). Robust identification of fuzzy duplicates. In *Proceedings of the 21ˢᵗ international Conference on Data Engineering (ICDE'05)*, Washington, DC (pp. 865-876).

Chiu, S. (1994). Fuzzy model identification based on cluster estimation. *Journal of Intelligent & Fuzzy Systems, 2*(3).

Cohen, W., Ravikumar, P., & Fienberg, S. (2003). A comparison of string distance metrics for name-matching tasks. In *Proceedings of the Eighth International Joint Conference on Artificial Intelligence: Workshop on Information Integration on the Web (IIWeb-03)*.

Elmagarmid, A. K., Ipeirotis, P. G., & Verykios, V. S. (2007). Duplicate record detection: A survey. *IEEE Transactions on Knowledge and Data Engineering, 19*(1), 1-16.

Galhardas, H., Florescu, D., et al. (2001). Declarative data cleaning: Language, model and algorithms. In *Proceedings of the 27ᵗʰ International Conference on Very Large Databases (VLDB'01)*, Rome (pp. 371-380).

Galindo, J., Urrutia, A., & Piattini, M. (2006). *Fuzzy databases: Modeling, design and implementation*. Hershey, PA: Idea Group Publishing.

Haidarian Shahri, H., & Barforush, A. A. (2004). A flexible fuzzy expert system for fuzzy duplicate elimination in data cleaning. *Proceedings of the 15ᵗʰ International Conference on Database and Expert Systems Applications (DEXA'04)* (LNCS 3180, pp. 161-170). Springer Verlag.

Haidarian Shahri, H., & Shahri, S. H. (2006). Eliminating duplicates in information integration: An adaptive, extensible framework. *IEEE Intelligent Systems, 21*(5), 63-71.

Hernandez, M. A., & Stolfo, S. J. (1998). Real-world data is dirty: Data cleansing and the merge/purge problem. *Data Mining and Knowledge Discovery, 2*(1), 9-37.

Jang, J. S. R. (1993). ANFIS: Adaptive network-based fuzzy inference systems. *IEEE Transactions on Systems, Man, and Cybernetics, 23*(3), 665-685.

Jang, J. S. R., & Sun, C. T. (1995). Neuro-fuzzy modeling and control. *Proceedings of the IEEE*, 378-406.

Low, W. L., Lee, M. L., & Ling, T. W. (2001). A knowledge-based approach for duplicate elimination in data cleaning. *Information Systems, 26*, 585-606.

Mamdani, E. H. (1976). Advances in linguistic synthesis of fuzzy controllers. *International Journal on Man Machine Studies, 8*, 669-678.

Monge, A. E., & Elkan, P. C. (1997, May). An efficient domain-independent algorithm for detecting approximately duplicate database records. *Proceedings of the SIGMOD 1997 Workshop on Data Mining and Knowledge Discovery* (pp. 23-29).

Rahm, E., & Do, H. H. (2000). Data cleaning: Problems and current approaches. *Bulletin of the IEEE Computer Society Technical Committee on Data Engineering, 23*(4), 3-13.

Raman, V., & Hellerstein, J. M. (2001). Potter's Wheel: An interactive data cleaning system. In *Proceedings of the 27th International Conference on Very Large Databases (VLDB'01)*, Rome (pp. 381-390).

Sarawagi, S., & Bhamidipaty, A. (2002). Interactive deduplication using active learning. *Proceedings of Eighth ACM SIGKDD International Conference on Knowledge Discovery and Data Mining (KDD '02)* (pp. 269-278).

Takagi, T., & Sugeno, M. (1985). Fuzzy identification of systems and its applications to modeling and control. *IEEE Transactions on Systems, Man, and Cybernetics, 15*, 116-132.

Winkler, W. E. (1999). *The state of record linkage and current research problems* (Publication No. R99/04). Internal Revenue Service, Statistics of Income Division.

Zadeh, L. A. (1975a). The concept of linguistic variable and its application to approximate reasoning: Part I. *Information Sciences, 8*, 199-251.

Zadeh, L. A. (1975b). The concept of linguistic variable and its application to approximate reasoning: Part II. *Information Sciences, 8*, 301-357.

Zadeh, L. A. (1975c). The concept of linguistic variable and its application to approximate reasoning: Part III. *Information Sciences, 9*, 43-80.

Zadeh, L. A. (2002). From computing with numbers to computing with words: From manipulation of measurements to manipulation of perceptions. *International Journal on Applied Mathematics and Computer Science, 12*(3), 307-324.

KEY TERMS

Data Cleaning: Data cleaning is the process of improving the quality of the data by modifying their form or content, for example, removing or correcting erroneous data values, filling in missing values, and so forth.

Data Warehouse: A data warehouse is a database designed for the business intelligence requirements and managerial decision making of an organization. The data warehouse integrates data from the various operational systems and is typically loaded from these systems at regular intervals. It contains historical information that enables the analysis of business performance over time. The data are subject oriented, integrated, time variant, and nonvolatile.

Machine Learning: Machine learning is an area of artificial intelligence concerned with the development of techniques that allow computers to learn. Learning is the ability of the machine to improve its performance based on previous results.

Mamdani Method of Inference: Mamdani's fuzzy inference method is the most commonly seen fuzzy methodology. It was proposed in 1975 by Ebrahim Mamdani as an attempt to control a steam engine and boiler combination. *Mamdani-type inference* expects the output membership functions to be fuzzy sets. After the aggregation process, there is a fuzzy set for each output variable that needs defuzzification. It is possible, and in many cases much more efficient, to use a single spike as the output membership function rather than a distributed fuzzy set. This type of output is sometimes known as a *singleton* output membership function, and it can be thought of as a "predefuzzified" fuzzy set. It enhances the efficiency of the defuzzification process because it greatly simplifies the computation required by the more general Mamdani method, which finds the centroid of a two-dimensional function. Rather than integrating across the two-dimensional function to find the centroid, you use the weighted average of a few data points. Sugeno-type systems support this type of model.

OLAP (Online Analytical Processing): OLAP involves systems for the retrieval and analysis of data to reveal business trends and statistics not directly visible in the data directly retrieved from a database. It provides multidimensional, summarized views of business data and is used for reporting, analysis, modeling and planning for optimizing the business.

OLTP (Online Transaction Processing): OLTP involves operational systems for collecting and managing the base data in an organization specified by transactions, such as sales order processing, inventory, accounts payable, and so forth. It usually offers little or no analytical capabilities.

Sugeno Method of Inference: Introduced in 1985, it is similar to the Mamdani method in many respects. The first two parts of the fuzzy inference process, fuzzifying the inputs and applying the fuzzy operator, are exactly the same. The main difference between Mamdani and Sugeno is that the Sugeno output membership functions are either linear or constant.

Chapter IV
Interactive Quality–Oriented Data Warehouse Development

Maurizio Pighin
IS&SE-Lab, University of Udine, Italy

Lucio Ieronutti
IS&SE-Lab, University of Udine, Italy

ABSTRACT

Data Warehouses are increasingly used by commercial organizations to extract, from a huge amount of transactional data, concise information useful for supporting decision processes. However, the task of designing a data warehouse and evaluating its effectiveness is not trivial, especially in the case of large databases and in presence of redundant information. The meaning and the quality of selected attributes heavily influence the data warehouse's effectiveness and the quality of derived decisions. Our research is focused on interactive methodologies and techniques targeted at supporting the data warehouse design and evaluation by taking into account the quality of initial data. In this chapter we propose an approach for supporting the data warehouses development and refinement, providing practical examples and demonstrating the effectiveness of our solution. Our approach is mainly based on two phases: the first one is targeted at interactively guiding the attributes selection by providing quantitative information measuring different statistical and syntactical aspects of data, while the second phase, based on a set of 3D visualizations, gives the opportunity of run-time refining taken design choices according to data examination and analysis. For experimenting proposed solutions on real data, we have developed a tool, called ELDA (EvaLuation DAta warehouse quality), that has been used for supporting the data warehouse design and evaluation.

INTRODUCTION

Data Warehouses are widely used by commercial organizations to extract from a huge amount of transactional data concise information useful for supporting decision processes. For example, organization managers greatly benefit from the availability of tools and techniques targeted at deriving information on sale trends and discovering unusual accounting movements. With respect to the entire amount of data stored into the initial database (or databases, hereinafter DBs), such analysis is centered on a limited subset of attributes (i.e., datawarehouse measures and dimensions). As a result, the datawarehouse (hereinafter DW) effectiveness and the quality of related decisions is strongly influenced by the semantics of selected attributes and the quality of initial data. For example, information on customers and suppliers as well as products ordered and sold are very meaningful from data analysis point of view due to their semantics. However, the availability of information measuring and representing different aspects of data can make easier the task of selecting DW attributes, especially in presence of multiple choices (i.e., redundant information) and in the case of DBs characterized by an high number of attributes, tables and relations. Quantitative measurements allow DW engineers to better focus their attention towards the attributes characterized by the most desirable features, while qualitative data representations enable one to interactively and intuitively examine the considered data subset, allowing one to reduce the time required for the DW design and evaluation.

Our research is focused on interactive methodologies and techniques aimed at supporting the DW design and evaluation by taking into account the quality of initial data. In this chapter we propose an approach supporting the DW development and refinement, providing practical examples demonstrating the effectiveness of our solution. Proposed methodology can be effectively used (i) during the DW construction phase for driving and interactively refining the attributes selection, and (ii) at the end of the design process, to evaluate the quality of taken DW design choices.

While most solutions that have been proposed in the literature for assessing data quality are related with semantics, our goal is to propose an interactive approach focused on statistical aspects of data. The approach is mainly composed by two phases: an analytical phase based on a set of metrics measuring different data features (quantitative information), and an exploration phase based on an innovative graphical representation of DW ipercubes that allows one to navigate intuitively through the information space to better examine the quality and distribution of data (qualitative information). The interaction is one of the most important feature of our approach: the designer can incrementally define the DW measures and dimensions and both quality measurements and data representations change according to such modifications. This solution allows one to evaluate rapidly and intuitively the effects of alternative design choices. For example, the designer can immediately discover that the inclusion of an attribute negatively influences the global DW quality. If the quantitative evaluation does not convince the designer, he can explore the DW ipercubes to better understand relations among data, data distributions and behaviors.

In a real world scenario, DW engineers greatly benefit from the possibility of obtaining concise and easy-to-understand information describing the data actually stored into the DB, since they typically have a partial knowledge and vision of a specific operational DB (e.g., how an organization really uses the commercial system). Indeed, different organizations can use the same system, but each DB instantiation stores data that can be different from the point of view of distribution, correctness and reliability (e.g., an organization never fills a particular field of the form). As a result, the same DW design choices can produce different informative effects depending on the data actually stored into the DB. Then, although the attributes selection is primarily based on data semantics, the availability of both quantitative and qualitative information on data could greatly support the DW design phase. For example, in the presence of alternative choices (valid from semantic point of view), the designer can select the attribute characterized by the most desirable syntactical and statistical features. On the other hand, the designer can decide to change his design choice if he discovers that the selected attribute is characterized by undesirable features (for instance, an high percentage of null values).

This chapter is structured as follows. First, we survey related work. Then we present the methodology we propose for supporting the DW design process, and ELDA (EvaLuation DAta-warehouse quality), a tool implementing such methodology. In last section we describe the experimental evaluation we have carried out for demonstrating the effectiveness of our solution. Finally, we conclude the chpater by discussing ongoing and future works.

RELATED WORKS

In the literature, different researchers have been focused on data quality in operational systems and a number of different definitions and methodologies have been proposed, each one characterized by different quality metrics. Although Wang [1996a] and Redman [1996] proposed a wide number of metrics that have become the reference models for data quality in operational systems, in the literature most works refer only to a limited subset (e.g., *accuracy*, *completeness*, *consistency* and *timeliness*). Moreover, literature reviews e.g., [Wang et al. 1995] highlighted that there is not a general agreement on these metrics, being the concept of quality strongly context dependent. For example, *timeliness* has been defined by some researchers in terms of whether the data are out of date [Ballou and Pazer 1985], while other researchers use the same term for identi-

fying the availability of output on time [Kriebel 1978][Scannapieco et al. 2004][Karr et al. 2006]. Moreover, some of the proposed metrics, called *subjective metrics* [Wang and Strong 1996a] e.g., *interpretability* and *easy of understanding*, require an evaluation made by questionnaires and/or interviews [Lee et al. 2001] and then result more suitable for qualitative evaluations rather than quantitative ones. Jeusfeld and colleagues [1998] adopt a meta modeling approach for linking quality measurements to different abstraction levels and user requirements, and propose a notation to formulate quality goals, queries and measurements. An interesting idea is based on detecting discrepancies among objective and subjective quality measurements [Pipino et al. 2002][De Amicis and Batini 2004].

Some researchers have been focused on methods for conceptual schema development and evaluation [Jarke et al. 1999]. Some of these approaches e.g., [Phipps and Davis 2002] include the possibility of using the user input to refine the obtained result. However, these solutions typically require to translate user requirements into a formal and complete description of a logical schema.

An alternative category of approaches employs objective measurements for assessing data quality. In this context, an interesting work has been presented in [Karr et al. 2006], where quality indicators are derived by analyzing statistical data distributions. Another interesting work based on objective measurements has been proposed in [Calero et al. 2001], where a set of metrics measuring different features of multidimensional models have been presented. However, although based on metrics that have same similarity with our proposal (number of attributes, number of keys, etc.), this solution evaluates the DW quality considering the DW schema but not the quality of initial data.

A different category of techniques for assessing data quality concerns Cooperative Information Systems (CISs). In this context, the DaQuinCIS project proposed a methodology [Scannapieco et al. 2004][Missier and Batini 2003] for quality measurement and improvement. The proposed solution is primarily based on the premise that CISs are characterized by high data replication, i.e. different copies of the same data are stored by different organizations. From data quality prospective, this feature offers the opportunity of evaluating and improving data quality on the basis of comparisons among different copies. Data redundancy has been effectively used not only for identifying mistakes, but also for reconciling available copies or selecting the most appropriate ones.

From data visualization point of view, some researchers have been focused on proposing innovative solutions for DW representations. For example, Shekhar and colleagues [2001] proposed *map cube*, a visualization tool for spatial DWs; taken a base map, associated data tables and cartographic preferences, the proposed solution is able to automatically derive an album of maps displaying the data. The derived visualizations can be browsed using traditional DW operators, such as drill-down and roll up. However, as the need to understand and analyze information increases, the need to explore data advances beyond simple two dimensional representations; such visualizations require analysts to view several charts or spreadsheets sequentially to identify complex and multidimensional data relationships.

Advanced three dimensional representations enable analysts to explore complex, multidimensional data in one screen. In this context, several visualization and interaction techniques have been proposed, each one characterized by different functionalities, goals and purposes. The Xerox PARC User Interface Research Group has conducted an extensive research in this field, focusing on hierarchical information and proposing a set of general visualization techniques, such as *perspective walls*, *cone trees*, *hyperbolic* and *disk trees* [Robertson et al., 1993]. Different tools based on such visualization techniques have been developed; for example, in [Noser and Stucki,

2000] has been presented a web-based solution that is able to visualize and query large data hierarchies in an efficient and versatile manner starting from data stored into relational DBs. A different category of visualization techniques and tools adopt solutions that are specific to the considered application domain. A specific data visualization application is *NYSE 3-D Trading Floor* [Delaney, 1999], a virtual environment designed for monitoring and displaying business activities. The proposed application integrates continuous data streams from trading systems, highlights unusual business and system activities, and enables the staff to pinpoint where complex events are taking place. In the context of urban planning, an explorative work has been presented in [Coors and Jung, 1998]; the proposed tool, called *GOOVI-3D*, provides access and interaction with a spatial DB storing information for example on buildings. An important feature supported by the tool is the possibility to query data and observe its effects directly on data representation (e.g., the user is interested in finding buildings characterized by less than five floors). Three dimensional visualizations have been successfully employed also for representing temporal data in the medical domain, where they are used for displaying and analyzing the huge amount of data collected during medical treatments and therapies. An interesting visualization and interaction technique has been proposed in [Chittaro, Combi and Trapasso, 2003], where the specific domain of hemodialysis is considered.

For the specific context of DWs, there are not three dimensional solutions targeted at effectively supporting the DW design. More specifically, we are interested in proposing visualization and interaction techniques that are specifically devoted to highlight relations and data proprieties from data distributions point of view. Although traditional three dimensional representations can be adopted for such purposes (e.g., 3D bar charts), they do not provide the DW designer with the control needed for data examination and exploration.

PROPOSED METHODOLOGY

In this chapter we propose an interactive methodology supporting the DW design and evaluating the quality of taken design choices. Our solution is mainly based on two phases (see Figure 1): the first one is targeted at guiding the attributes selection by providing quantitative information evaluating different data features, while the second phase gives the opportunity of refining taken design choices according to qualitative information derived from the examination and exploration of data representations.

More specifically, for the first phase we define a set of metrics measuring different syntactical and statistical aspects of data (e.g., percentage of null values) and evaluating information directly derived from initial DBs (e.g., attributes types) and the current version of the DW schema (e.g., active relations). By combining obtained indexes, we derive a set of quantitative measurements highlighting the set of attributes that are more suitable to be included into the DW as dimensions and measures. According to derived information and considering data semantics, the expert can start to define a preliminary version of the DW schema (specifying the initial set of DW measures and dimensions). Given such information, for the second phase we propose interactive three-dimensional representations of DW ipercubes that allow one to visually evaluate the effects of the preliminary design choices. This solution allows

one to navigate through the data intuitively, making easier the task of studying data distributions in the case of multiple dimensions, discovering undesirable data features, or to confirm selected DW measures and dimensions. If the expert catches some unexpected and undesirable data feature, he can go back to the previous phase for refining his design choice, e.g., excluding some attributes and including new dimensions and/or measures. It is important to note that each modification of the DW schema causes the indexes re-computation on the fly and the possibility of exploring different DW ipercubes. These two phases can be executed till the expert find the good compromise between his needs and the quantitative and qualitative results provided by our methodology. In the following, we describe in detail the quantitative and qualitative phases we propose for supporting the DW design process.

Quantitative Phase

Quantitative phase is based on the global indicators $M_m(t_j, a_i)$ and $M_d(t_j, a_i)$ estimating how much the attribute a_i belonging to the table t_j is suitable to be used respectively as DW measure and dimension. Information on the final DW design quality $M(DW)$ is then derived by considering the indicators of selected attributes. The global indicators $M_m(t_j, a_i)$ and $M_d(t_j, a_i)$ are derived by combining the indexes computed by a set of metrics, each one designed with the aim of

Figure 1. General schema of the proposed methodology

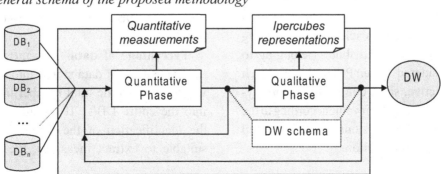

capturing a different (syntactical or statistical) aspect of data. More specifically, we differently weight each measured feature using a set of coefficients: negative coefficients are used when the measurement involves an undesirable feature for a specific point of view of the analysis (dimension or measure), while positive coefficients are used in the case of desirable features. It is important to note that in our experiments we simply use unitary values for the coefficients (i.e. −1 and 1), postponing to further evaluations the accurate tuning of these values.

The metrics we propose refer to three different DB elements:

- **Tables of a DB:** These metrics are able to measure general features of a given table, such as the percentage of numerical attributes of the table. The two indicators $MT_m(t_j)$ and $MT_d(t_j)$ measuring how much the table t_j is suitable to extract respectively measures and dimensions are derived by combining the indexes computed by these metrics.

- **Attributes of a table:** At a level of a single table, these metrics measure salient characteristics of data, such as the percentage of null values of an attribute. The two indicators $MA_m(a_i)$ and $MA_d(a_i)$ evaluating if the attribute a_i provides value added respectively as dimension and measure are derived by combining the indexes computed by these metrics.

- **Relations of a DB:** These metrics estimate the quality of DB relations. The quality indicator $MR(t_j)$ measuring the quality of the relations involving the table t_j is used during the attributes selection for refining the indexes of the attributes belonging to the considered table. Proposed approach is interactive, since quality indicators dynamically change their value according to the measures and dimensions actually selected for the DW construction.

In this chapter, we give an informal and intuitive description of the proposed metrics; a deeper mathematical and formal description for some metrics can be found in [Pighin and Ieronutti, 2007].

Table Metrics

In this Section, we describe the set of metrics $mt_{e=1..k}$ (being k the total number of table metrics, in this chapter $k = 5$) and corresponding indexes we propose for DB tables. With these metrics, we aim at taking into account that different tables could play different roles and then result more/less suitable for extracting measures and dimensions. The indicators $MT_m(t_j)$ and $MT_d(t_j)$ measuring how much the table t_j is suitable to extract measures and dimensions are derived by linearly combining the indexes computed by the metrics $mt_{e=1..k}$ using respectively the set of coefficients $ct_{m,e}$ and $ct_{d,e}$. The indicators $MT_m(t_j)$ and $MT_d(t_j)$ are used: (i) to support the selection of the tables for the DW definition, (ii) to differently weight the indexes computed on the attributes belonging to different tables. In particular, the two indicators are derived as follows:

$$MT_p(t_j) = \frac{\sum_{e=1}^{k}\left(ct_{p,e} * mt_e(t_j)\right)}{k}$$

where $p = d$ (dimension) or m (measure), $e = 1,...,k$ identifies the metric, j identifies the table, and $ct_{p,e}$ is the coefficient of the table-metric e. In the following, we briefly describe the metrics $mt_{e=1..5}$ we propose for DB tables and corresponding coefficients.

Percentage of data. This metric measures the percentage of data stored into a given table with respect to the total number of data stored into the entire DB(s). If the analysis concerns the identification of the tables that are more suitable to extract measures, the corresponding coefficient is positive ($ct_{m,1} > 0$) since tables storing transactional information are generally characterized by a higher number of data with respect to the other types of tables. On the other hand, the coefficient for dimensions is negative ($ct_{d,1} < 0$) since tables concerning business objects definitions (e.g., products or clients) are typically characterized by a lower number of data than transactional archives.

Rate attributes/records. This metric computes the rate between the number of attributes and the number of records in the considered table. If the analysis concerns the identification of tables that are more suitable to extract dimensions, the corresponding coefficient is positive ($ct_{d,2} > 0$) since tables concerning business objects definitions are characterized by a number of attributes that is (typically lower but) comparable with the number of records stored into the table. On the other hand, the coefficient for measures is negative ($ct_{m,2} < 0$) since generally in transactional archives the number of records and the number of attributes have a different order of magnitude.

In/our relations. This metric measures the rate between incoming and outgoing relations. Given a *one-to-many* relation connecting the tables t_{j1} and t_{j2}, in this chapter we consider the relation as incoming from the point of view of the table t_{j2}, while outgoing from the point of view of t_{j1}. If the analysis concerns the identification of tables that are more suitable to extract measures, the corresponding coefficient is positive ($ct_{m,3} > 0$) since these tables are generally characterized by an higher number of incoming relations than outgoing ones. For example, the table storing information on the bill is linked by a number of other tables storing for example information on sold products, sales agent and on the customer. For the opposite reason, the coefficient for dimensions is negative ($ct_{d,3} < 0$).

Number of relations. This metric considers the total number of relations involving the considered table. The computed index estimates the relevance of the table, since tables characterized

by many relations typically play an important role into the DB. Since an high number of relations is a desirable feature for both measures and dimensions point of view, both coefficients are positive ($ct_{m,4}$ and $ct_{d,4} > 0$).

Percentage of numerical attributes. This metric derives the percentage of numerical attributes into the considered table. Integers, decimal numbers and date are considered by this metric as numerical data. Since tables storing information related with transactional activities are generally characterized by an high number of numerical attributes, the coefficient for measures is positive ($ct_{m,5} > 0$). Indeed, these tables typically contain many numerical attributes, such as ones storing information on the amount of products sold, the date of the sale, the price of different products and the total bill. On the other hand, tables storing information on products, customers and sellers are characterized by an higher number of alphanumerical attributes (e.g., specifying the customer/seller address). For this reason, if the analysis concerns the identification of the tables that are more suitable to extract dimensions, the corresponding coefficient is negative ($ct_{d,5} < 0$).

Attribute Metrics

In this Section, we describe the set of metrics $ma_{h=1..r}$ (being r the total number of attribute metrics, in this chapter $r = 6$) and corresponding indexes we propose for DB attributes. The global indicators $MA_m(a_i)$ and $MA_d(a_i)$ measuring how much the attribute a_i is suitable to be used respectively as measure and dimension are derived by differently combining the indexes derived by the metrics $ma_{h=1..r}$ using respectively the set of coefficients $ca_{m,h}$ and $ca_{d,h}$. In particular, the two indicators are derived as follows:

$$MA_p(a_i) = \frac{\sum_{h=1}^{r}\left(ca_{p,h} * ma_h(a_i)\right)}{r}$$

where $p = d$ (dimension) or m (measure), $h = 1,...,r$ identifies the metric, i identifies the attribute, and $ca_{p,h}$ is the coefficient of the attribute-metric h considering the role p of the attribute. In the case of a DW attribute derived as a combination of more than one DB attributes, the corresponding index is derived as the mean of the indexes related to the DB attributes. In the following, we briefly describe the metrics $ma_{h=1..6}$ we propose for DB attributes and corresponding coefficients.

Percentage of null values. This metric measures the percentage of attribute data having null values. Although simple, such measurement provides an important indicator concerning the relevance of an attribute since, independently from its role, attributes characterized by an high percentage of null values are not suitable to effectively support decision processes. For example, an attribute having a percentage of null values greater than 90% is characterized by a scarce informative content from the analysis point of view. For this reason, both coefficients for this metric are negative ($ca_{m,1}$ and $ca_{d,1} < 0$), highlighting that the presence of an high number of null values is an undesirable feature for both dimensions and measures.

Number of values. The index computed by this metric concerns the extent in which the attribute assumes different values on the domain. More specifically, the metric behaves like a cosine function: if an attribute assumes a small number of different values (e.g., in the case of units of measurement where only a limited number of different values is admitted), the metric derives a value that is close to 1. A similar value is derived in the case of attributes characterized by a number of values that equals the total number of table records (e.g., when the attribute is the primary key of a table). Intermediate values are computed for the other cases according to the cosine behavior.

If the analysis concerns the evaluation of how much an attribute is suitable to be used as dimension, the corresponding coefficient is positive ($ca_{d,2} > 0$), since both attributes assuming a limited number of different values and ones characterized by a large number of different values can be effectively used for exploring the data. For example, an attribute storing information on the payment type (e.g., cash money or credit card) is suitable to be used as dimension and typically it is characterized by limited number of different values. On the other extreme, an attributes storing information on product or customer codes is also suitable to be used as dimension and typically it is characterized by an high number of different values. With respect to the measures choice, the coefficient is negative ($ca_{m,2} < 0$) because attributes characterized by (i) few values are generally not suitable to be used as measures, since they do not contain discriminatory and predictive information, and (ii) a large number of different values can correspond to keys and then result unsuitable to be used as measures. On the other hand, attributes storing information related to transactional activities (then, suitable to be used as measures) are characterized by a number of values (e.g., purchase money or number of elements sold) that is lower with respect to the total number of records.

Degree of clusterization. This metric measures the extent in which the attribute values are clustered on the domain. If the analysis concerns the evaluation of how much an attribute is suitable to be used as dimension, the corresponding coefficient is positive ($ca_{d,3} > 0$), since attributes that are suitable to be used as dimensions (e.g., numerical codes and names of products, customers and supplier) typically are clusterizable. On the other hand, the coefficient for measures is negative ($ca_{m,3} < 0$), since attributes suitable to be used as measures generally are characterized by values that tend to spread over the domain. It is important to highlight that this metric does not consider the data distribution into clusters, but only the total number of clusters into the attribute domain.

Uniformity of distribution. This metric measures how much the values of an attribute are equally distributed on the domain. The possibility of highlighting uniform distributions enables our methodology to identify attributes that are suitable to be used as measures, since typically they are not characterized by uniform distributions (e.g., normal distribution). For example, it is more probable that the distribution of values of an attribute storing information on the customer is more similar to an uniform distribution with respect to the distribution of an attribute storing information on the bill (typically characterized by a Gaussian distribution).

For this reason, if the analysis concerns the evaluation of how much an attribute is suitable to be used as a measure, the corresponding coefficient is negative ($ca_{m,4} < 0$). On the other hand, if the analysis concerns dimensions, the corresponding coefficient is positive ($ca_{d,4} > 0$); indeed, the more values are uniformly distributed on the domain (or in the considered subset), the more effectively the analyst can explore the data.

Keys. This metric derives a value both taking into account if the considered attribute belong or not to primary and/or duplicable keys. The coefficient for dimensions is positive ($ca_{d,5} > 0$) since attributes belonging to the primary or secondary keys often identify look-up tables and then they are the best candidates for the DW dimensions. On the other hand, the coefficient for measures is negative ($ca_{m,5} < 0$) since attributes belonging to primary or secondary keys typically are not suitable to be used as measures.

Type of attribute. This metric returns a float value according to the type of the attribute (alphanumerical strings = 0, whole numbers or temporal data = 0.5, real numbers = 0). Typically numerical attributes are more suitable to be used as measures rather than being used as dimensions; for this reason, the coefficient for measures is positive ($ca_{m,6} > 0$). On the other hand, in the case of dimensions, the corresponding coefficient is negative ($ca_{d,6} < 0$) since business objects defini-

tions are often coded by alphanumerical attributes. Moreover, alphanumerical attributes are rarely use in a DW as measures due to the limited number of applicable mathematical functions (e.g., *count* function).

Relation Metrics

In this Section, we describe the set of metrics $MR_{s=1..f}$ (being f the total number of relation metrics, in this chapter $f = 2$) and corresponding indexes we propose for DB relations. These metrics have been designed with the aim of measuring the quality of relations by considering (i) data actually stored into the DB and (ii) relations actually used into the DW. Information on relations quality is used during the DW construction to dynamically refine the indexes referring to DB attributes and tables. As a result, unlike table and attribute indexes that are computed only once on the initial DB, these indexes are updated whenever the DW schema changes (e.g., new measures are included into the DW). This solution allows the methodology to consider the quality of the relations that are actually used for exploring the data into the DW, enabling to (i) better support the user during the selection of measures and dimensions, and (ii) estimate more precisely the final DW design quality.

For the evaluation, we define $MR(a_{i1}, a_{i2})$ as a quality indicator for the relation directly connecting the attributes a_{i1} and a_{i2}.

In particular, such indicator is derived by combining the indexes computed by the metrics $MR_{s=1..f}$ as follows:

$$MR(a_{i1}, a_{i2}) = \frac{\sum_{s=1}^{f} MR_s(a_{i1}, a_{i2})}{f}$$

where $s = 1, ..., f$ identifies the metric, while a_{i1} and a_{i2} the DB attributes connected by a direct relation. Once these indicators are computed, our methodology derives for each table t_j the indicator

$MR_d(t_j)$ and $MR_m(t_j)$ evaluating the quality of the relations involving the considered table respectively from dimensions and measures point of view. For such evaluation, we consider not only direct relations (i.e., relations explicitly defined in the initial DB schema), but also indirect ones (i.e., relations defined as a sequence of direct relations). In the following, we first describe the procedure used for deriving $MR_m(t_j)$ (the indicator $MR_d(t_j)$ is computed using a similar procedure), and in the following subsections we briefly present the two metrics we propose for direct relations.

Let T_d be the set of tables containing at least one DW dimension, the indicator $MR_m(t_j)$ is computed by deriving the whole set of indirect relations connecting the tables belonging to T_d to the considered table t_j. Then, the procedure computes for each indirect relation the corresponding index by multiplying the quality indicators of direct relations constituting the considered indirect relation. Finally, if there are one or more relations involving the considered table, $MR_m(t_j)$ corresponds to the index characterizing the best indirect relation.

Percentage of domain values. Given a relation directly connecting the attributes a_{i1} and a_{i2}, this metric computes the percentage of values belonging to the *relation domain* (i.e. the domain of the attribute a_{i1}) that are actually instantiated into the *relation codomain* (i.e. the domain of the attribute a_{i2}). Such percentage provides information on the quality of relation; in particular, the more greater is such percentage, the more higher the relation quality is.

Uniformity of distribution. This metric evaluates if the domain values are uniformly distributed on the relation codomain. The measured feature positively influences the quality of the relation, since uniform distributions allow one to better explore the data with respect to situations in which values are clustered.

Data Warehouse Quality Metric

Our methodology derives for each attribute a_i belonging to the table t_j the two global indicators $M_d(t_j, a_i)$ and $M_m(t_j, a_i)$ indicating how much the attribute is suitable to be used in the DW respectively as dimension and measure. These indicators are computed by combining the attribute, table and relation indexes described in previous sections. More specifically, these indicators are derived as follows:

$$M_p(t_j, a_i) = MT_p(t_j)*MA_p(a_i)*MR_p(t_j) \qquad a_i \in t_j$$

where $p = d$ (dimensions) or m (measure), i and j identify respectively the considered attribute and table, MT_p, MA_p and MR_p are respectively the table, attribute and relation indexes.

Once all indicators are computed, our methodology derives two ordered lists of DB attributes: the first list contains the attributes ordered according to M_d, while the second one according to M_m. The two functions $rank_d(a_i)$ and $rank_m(a_i)$ derive the relative position of the attribute a_i respectively into the first and second (ordered) list. It is important to note that while M_m and M_d are used for deriving information concerning the absolute quality of an attribute, $rank_d(a_i)$ and $rank_m(a_i)$ can be used for evaluating the quality of an attribute with respect to the quality of the other DB attributes.

Finally, let D_{dw} be the set of n_d attributes chosen as DW dimensions and M_{dw} the set of n_m attributes selected as measures, the final DW design quality $M(DW)$ is estimated as follows:

$$M(DW) = \frac{\sum_{\substack{a_i \in M_{dw} \\ a_i \in t_j}} M_m(t_j, a_i) + \sum_{\substack{a_i \in D_{dw} \\ a_i \in t_j}} M_d(t_j, a_i)}{n_m + n_d}$$

Qualitative Phase

The qualitative phase is based on an interactive three dimensional representation of DW ipercubes that allows one to better evaluate data distributions and relations among attributes selected in the previous phase. In particular, each DW ipercube (characterized by an arbitrary number of different dimensions and measures) can be analyzed by exploring and studying different sub-cubes, each one characterized by three dimensions and one measure. Each dimension of the representation corresponds to a descriptive attribute (i.e., dimension), while each point into the three dimensional space corresponds to a numeric field (i.e., measure). At any time the user can change the considered measure and dimensions and the ipercube representation changes according to such selection.

Since representing each fact as a point into the ipercube space can be visually confusing (e.g., millions of records are represented as millions of points overlapping each other), we propose to simplify the representation by discretizing the three dimensional space and using different functions for grouping facts falling into the same discretized volume, represented by a small cube.

The user can interactively change the granularity of the representation by modifying the level of discretization (consequently, the cubes resolution) according to his needs. Small cubes are more suitable for accurate and precise analysis, while a lower level of discretization is more suitable whenever it is not required an high level of detail (e.g., for providing an overview of data distribution).

In general, the user could select both a particular grouping function and the granularity of the representation according to the purposes and goals of the analysis. The main grouping functions are count, sum, average, standard deviation, minimum and maximum value. For example, the user could select the count function for studying the distribution of products sold to different clients during the last year. In particular, both representations depicted in Figure 2 refer to such kind of data, but they differ from the point of view of representation granularity.

Additionally, we propose a set of interaction techniques for allowing the user to intuitively explore the DW ipercubes. More specifically, we suggest the use of the color coding, slice and dice, cutting plane, detail-on-demand and dynamic queries techniques for enabling the user to analyze

Figure 2. Representing the same data using (a) 8 and (b) 24 discretizations

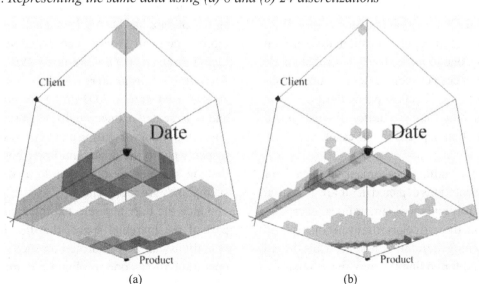

(a)   (b)

the ipercubes, visual representations that can also be examined using multiple point of view. We separately present and discuss in more detail the above techniques in the following subsections.

It is important to note that the real-time interaction is achieved into the visualization since most proposed interaction techniques work on aggregated data (i.e., a discretized version of the initial ipercube); such solution allows one to reduce considerably the time for performing the required computations.

Color Coding

In the proposed representation, a *color coding* mechanism is used for mapping numerical data to visual representations. This solution allows one to intuitively evaluate data distributions and easily identify the outliers, avoiding to examine and interpret numerical values [Schulze-Wollgast et al., 2005]. The proposed mapping allows the user to:

- Choose between using two or more control points (each one associating a value with a color) and select appropriate control points,
- Fine-tune color coding, by controlling the transitions between colors. In particular, the user can set the parameter used for exponential interpolation between colors. With respect to linear interpolation, this solution allows one to more clearly highlight subtle differences between values [Schulze-Wollgast et al., 2005] and is particularly effective when values are not uniformly distributed (as it often happens in our case).

The color coding mechanism employed for both representations depicted in Figure 2 is based on two control points and a simple linear interpolation between the two colors: the cyan color is used for representing the minimum value, while the red color is used for coding the maximum value.

It is important to note that the user can interactively modify the exponent of the interpolation and the visualization changes in real-time according to such modification. This functionality provides the user with the possibility of intuitively and interactively exploring numeric data from a qualitative point of view. In this chapter, most figures refer to representations based on a color coding mechanism characterized by two control points (cyan and red respectively for the minimum and maximum value).

Slice and Dice

In the context of DWs, *slice* and *dice* are the operations that allow one to break down the information space into smaller parts to better focus the data examination and analysis on specific dimensions ranges. In the proposed interaction technique, the selection of data subset is performed through rangesliders (i.e., graphical widget that allows one to select an interval of values), each one associated to a different ipercube dimension. By interacting with the rangesliders, the user has the possibility to select proper ranges of domain values and the visualization changes in real-time according to such selection. For example, Figure 3 (a) depicts the initial ipercube where all facts are considered and represented into the corresponding visualization. In Figure 3 (b) only a subset of data has been selected and visualized; more specifically, only records satisfying the logic formula *(CARTE <* **product** *< INDURITORI)* AND *(CROAZIA<***broker***<GRECIA)* AND *(2002-10-21 <* **sold date** *< 2003-01-24)* are considered and represented. Conceptually, each rangeslider controls a couple of cutting planes corresponding respectively to the upper and lower bounds of a domain subinterval; only data located between such planes are represented.

Once the user has selected the appropriated part of the ipercube space, the dice (or slice) operations can be performed on such data; this operation allows one to obtain a more detailed

Figure 3. Using rangesliders for selecting a specific subset of ipercube data: (a) the whole set of records is considered, (b) different ranges of domain values are considered and (c) a dice operation is performed on the specified data subset

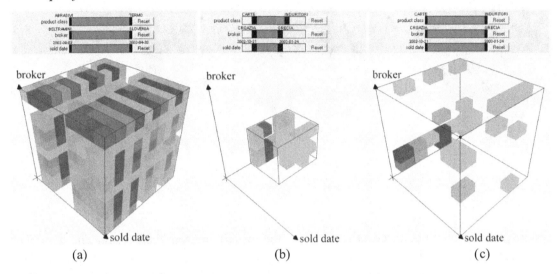

(a)　　　　　　　　　　　(b)　　　　　　　　　　　(c)

visualization concerning the selected ipercube space, as depicted in Figure 3 (c). It is important to note that such operation can be performed time after time to incrementally increase the level of detail of the visualization, giving at each step the opportunity of identifying the most interesting part of the information space.

Cutting Plane

In computer graphics, the term *occlusion* is used to describe the situation in which an object closer to the viewpoint masks a geometry further away from the viewpoint. This problem can considerably affect the effectiveness of three dimensional visualizations, especially in the case of representations characterized by a high number of different objects and geometries. There are mainly two solutions for overcoming the occlusion problem. The first one is based on the usage of semitransparent (i.e., partially transparent) objects. For example, it has been demonstrated that such solution has positive effects on navigation performance (Chittaro and Scagnetto, 2001). Unfortunately, this solution can not be effectively

applied together with color coding mechanisms, since modifications to the degree of transparency of an object heavily influence the colors perception for both close (semitransparent) and distant (solid) geometries.

Another solution is based on the usage of *cutting planes*, virtual planes that are used for partitioning the three dimensional space in two parts; only objects belonging to one partition are displayed into the visualization, while the other ones are hidden (they become completely transparent).

In the proposed methodology, a cutting plane can be used for exploring the ipercube in the case of dense data. The user can interactively modify the vertical position and the orientation of the cutting plane, allowing one to examine internal parts of the ipercube. Figure 4 demonstrates the benefits of such solution. In particular, Figure 4 (a) depicts an ipercube characterized by dense data; from such representation, the user cannot derive any information concerning the internal data, since only data belonging to the ipercube surfaces is visible. By modifying the rotation and position of the cutting plane the user can

Figure 4. Exploring the ipercube representation using the cutting plane technique

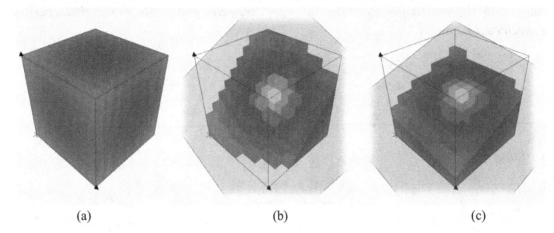

(a)	(b)	(c)

easily explore the entire ipercube, discovering for example that the minimum value is positioned at the centre of the ipercube, as depicted in Figure 4 (b) and (c), where two different rotations are used for exploring the data.

Detail-On-Demand

In the proposed representation, we suggest also the use of the *detail-on-demand* method: starting from a data overview, the user has the possibility of obtaining detailed information referring to a particular part of data without loosing sight of the ipercube overview. Then, instead of incrementally refining the analysis using slice and dice operations, the detail-on-demand technique allows the user to go deep into data, enabling to access information at the lowest level of detail. In particular, as soon as the user selects a specific part of the ipercube representation, both textual and numerical information on records corresponding to the selection is retrieved and visualized.

Dynamic Queries

Dynamic queries [Shneiderman, 1994] are a data analysis technique that is typically used for exploring a large dataset, providing users with a fast and easy-to-use method to specify queries

and visually present their result. The basic idea of dynamic queries is to combine input widget, called *query devices*, with graphical representation of the result. By directly manipulating query devices, user can specify the desired values for the attributes of elements in the dataset and can thus easily explore different subset of data. Results are rapidly updated, enabling users to quickly learn interesting proprieties of data. Such solution has been successfully employed in different application domains, such as real estate [Williamson and Shneiderman, 1992] and tourism [Burigat et al., 2005].

We adopt the dynamic queries technique for making easier the task of identifying the subset of data satisfying particular measure proprieties through a set of rangesliders, the same graphical widget use for performing slice and dice operations (see Section "Slice and Dice"). Instead of acting on dimensions ranges, in this case the rangesliders are used for querying the values concerning different grouping functions. More specifically, by interacting with such graphical widget, the user can modify the range of values for a specific grouping function and the visualization is updated in real-time; as a result, only data satisfying all conditions are displayed into the representation. Supported conditions refer to available grouping functions, i.e. count, average, sum, maximum, minimum and standard deviation. This solution allows one to easily highlight data (if exist) characterized by particular proprieties (e.g., outliers). For example, in Figure 5 we consider the ipercube characterized by "broker", "sold date" and "product class" as dimensions and "product quantity" as measure. By interacting with two rangesliders (one for each constraint), the user has the possibility to easily identify the information spaces characterized by more than a certain number of records (see Figure 5 (a) and (b)) and where the total number of products sold is less than a given threshold (see Figure 5 (c)). It is important to note that all representations depicted in Figure 5 refer to the counting function (highlighted in green). As a result, the color of each cube codes the number of records falling in the corresponding discretized volume; any time the user can decide to change such choice by simply selecting a different grouping function (e.g., sum function) and the color mapping of the representation changes according to such selection.

Viewpoint Control

In traditional tabular data representations, the *pivot* allows one to turn the data (e.g., swapping rows and columns) for viewing it from different perspectives. However, in the case of two dimensional representations the available possibilities are very limited. One of the most important feature of three dimensional data representations is the possibility of observing the content from different points of view (called *viewpoints*). This way, users can gain a deeper understanding of the subject and create more complete and correct mental models to represent it [Chittaro and Ranon, 2007]. For example, different viewpoints can be designed with the purpose of focusing the user attention towards different data aspects or with the aim of highlighting particular relations among data. Indeed, the benefits provided by the availability of alternative viewpoints have been successfully exploited by several authors (e.g., [Li et al., 2000][Campbell et al., 2002]) for proposing three dimensional representations characterized by effective inspection possibilities.

The ipercube representation can be explored by using three different viewpoint categories: *free*, *fixed* and *constrained*. The first category allows the user to completely control the orientation of the viewpoint; with such control, the user has the possibility of freely positioning and orienting the point of view to better observe a particular

Figure 5. Querying and visualizing data ipercube

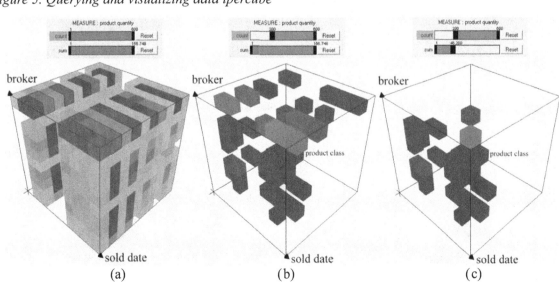

(a)   (b)   (c)

aspect of the representation. However, such freedom can introduce exploration difficulties, especially in the case of users that are not expert in navigating through three dimensional spaces. In this situation, the effort spent in controlling the viewpoint overcomes the benefits offered by such navigation freedom.

In the second category the viewpoint position and orientation is pre-determined; the user can explore the representation from different points of view by simply changing the currently selected viewpoint. For such purpose, we suggest eight viewpoints (one for each ipercube vertex) that provide the users with meaningful axonometric views of the ipercube representation (see Figure 6).

The last category of viewpoints is the more interesting from data exploration and analysis point of view. Each viewpoint is constrained to a different three dimensional surface, meaning that it is positioned to a fixed distance with respect to the surface and oriented perpendicularly with respect to the surface. If the surface changes its position and/or orientation, the corresponding viewpoint position and orientation are updated according to the constraints.

We proposed seven constrained viewpoints, one constrained to the cutting plane (see Section "Cutting Plane") and the remaining viewpoints constrained to the six dice planes (see Section "Scle and Dice"). As a result, each constrained viewpoint is able to focus the user attention toward parts of the representation involved in the current interaction, simplifying at the same time the complexity of the visualization and reducing the effort required for controlling the viewpoint.

ELDA TOOL

ELDA (EvaLuation DAtawarehouse quality) is a tool designed for experimenting proposed methodology on real data. It has been developed by carefully taking into account human-computer interaction issues and focusing on computation performance. The task of evaluating a DW using ELDA is mainly composed by two phases, separately described in the following sections.

Quantitative Phase

In ELDA the quantitative phase is composed by two sequential steps. In the first step ELDA (i)

Figure 6. The same ipercube observed by using different fixed viewpoints

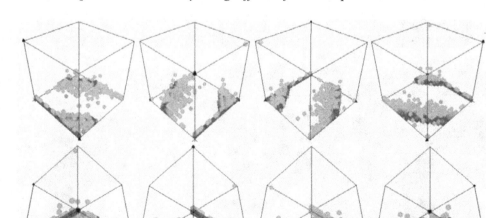

Figure 7. Graphical User Interface of ELDA supporting the selection of DW attributes

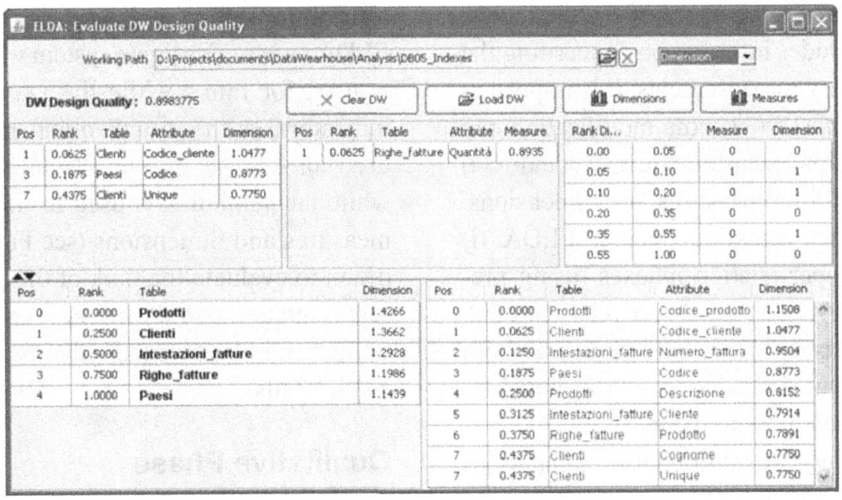

computes table and attribute indexes (see Sections "Table metrics" and "Attribute metrics"), and (ii) measures the main features of direct relations (see Section "Relation metrics"). The time required for such measurements strictly depends on the number of records stored into the DB(s). For example, in our experiments (involving tens of tables, hundreds of attributes and millions of records) the computation takes about ten minutes on a Pentium 4 2GHz processor with 1Gb ram.

Once all indexes are computed, in the second step ELDA combines them with the corresponding coefficients to derive (i) for each DB table t_j the global indicators $MT_d(t_j)$ and $MT_m(t_j)$, and (ii) for each DB attribute a_i belonging to the table t_j the global indicators $M_d(t_j, a_i)$ and $M_m(t_j, a_i)$. More specifically, according to the current role of the analysis (i.e. dimension or measure), the tool ranks and visualizes into two ordered lists the corresponding indicators, as depicted in the lower part of Figure 7. As a result, tables and attributes that are more suitable for the selected role are positioned in the first rows of the lists. In addition to quality measurements specified in the last column of lists depicted in Figure 7, ELDA also provides information both on the absolute (first column) and relative (second column) po-

sition of the considered DB element (table and attribute) into the corresponding ranked list. As soon as the user changes the point of view of the analysis (e.g., from dimension to measure), the tool updates the ranked lists according to the current user choice.

An important functionality offered by ELDA is the possibility of filtering the list of DB attributes. In particular, the tool visualizes only the attributes belonging to the tables that have been selected into the tables list. This functionality is particularly effective in the case of DBs characterized by an high number of tables and attributes; in such situations, the user can start the analysis only by considering the attributes belonging to high-ranked tables, and then extend the analysis to the other attributes.

Ranked and filtered attributes list can be effectively used for supporting the selection of DW measures and dimensions, since is a concise but effective way for providing users with statistical and syntactical information. According to semantic considerations and guided by computed quality indicators, the user can start to include dimensions and measures by directly clicking on the corresponding rows of the list. As a result, selected attributes are added to the list of DW measures or dimensions depending on the current role of the analysis; beside the name of the attributes, ELDA also includes information concerning the computed quality measurements. It is important to note that each DW schema modification can cause the inclusion/exclusion of (direct or indirect) relations connecting measures and dimensions. Every time such situation occurs, ELDA (i) recomputes proper relation indexes (using pre-computed information on direct relations) and (ii) consequently refines at selection-time both tables and attributes indicators, ranking both lists according to new measurements.

The following two additional functionalities have been designed with the aim of making easier and more intuitive the task of evaluating taken DW design choices. The first functionality consists in counting the number of selected DW measures and dimensions falling into different rank intervals. For such evaluation, ELDA subdivides the rank values into six intervals; the more the number of attributes fall into the first intervals, the more taken choices are evaluated by the tool as appropriated. In the example depicted in Figure 7, the selected measure falls into the second interval, while dimensions fall respectively into the second, third and fifth intervals.

The second functionality offered by the tool

is the possibility to visually represent the quality of taken DW design choices. For such purpose, ELDA uses a coordinate system where the x-axis is used for ranks while the y-axis for quality indicators. In the visualization small points are used for representing unselected DB attributes, while the symbol X is used for identifying DW measures and dimensions (see Figure 8). In addition to evaluate the rank of the attributes, this representation also allows one to analyze the trend of quality indicators (e.g., the user can discover sudden falls).

Qualitative Phase

The second phase concerns the qualitative evaluation of taken design choices. At any time the user can require to visualize a particular DW ipercube by selecting the corresponding attributes choosing among the dimensions and measures included into the current version of the DW schema. This way, the user has the possibility to constantly verify the correctness of his choices, without requiring to concretely build the entire DW for discovering unexpected and undesirable data features.

For such qualitative analysis, ELDA provides the user with several controls and functionalities that allow one to interactively explore and examine data representations. More specifically, at the beginning the user has to specify the set of dimensions, the measure and the related grouping function to be used for the analysis. Moreover, the user has also the possibility of selecting the proper granularity of the representation taking into account two factors. First, the choice is influenced by the required resolution of the representation. For example, while high-resolution representations are more suitable for accurate and precise analysis, lower resolutions are more suitable for providing the user with a data distribution overview. Second, since the granularity influences the time required for the computation, the choice also depends on the available processing power. For example, in our experiments (involving tens

Figure 8. Visually representing the quality of taken design choices for dimensions

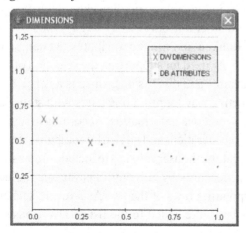

of tables, hundreds of attributes and millions of records, performed on a Pentium 4 2GHz processor with 1Gb ram) the ipercube computation takes about 2 and 20 seconds using respectively 10 and 30 discretizations. However, once the representation is computed and visualized, the interaction and exploration techniques discussed in previous sections (es., cutting plane, dynamic queries and viewpoint control) can be executed in real-time since performed on aggregated data.

According to user selections, ELDA computes and visualizes the corresponding three dimensional ipercube representation on the right part of the graphical user interface (see right part of Figure 9). Then, the user has the possibility of exploring and navigating through the data by interacting with several controls (see left part of Figure 9) and the visualization changes in real-time according to such interactions. In the example depicted in Figure 9, a specific subpart of the dimensions space is considered and visualized (specifying the range of values for the attributes *sold date* and *broker*, see the top-left part of the figure) and a particular fixed viewpoint is selected for observing the representation.

The user has the possibility to gradually focus the analysis on a specific part of the ipercube using slice and dice operations, or directly obtain detailed information concerning a particular part of the ipercube by simply selecting the corresponding cube into the representation. More specifically, as soon as the mouse pointer is over a specific part of the visualization, information on dimensions concerning the (implicitly) selected space appears on the screen, as depicted in Figure 10 (a). If the user is interested in studying in more detail data falling into such space, he has simply to click the corresponding volume; a detailed report including information on all records falling into the selected volume is then displayed. Such report is displayed into a separate windows that also includes information on the grouping functions referred to the selected subset of data, as depicted in Figure 10 (b).

At any time of the evaluation, the user can change the color coding mechanism for highlighting subtle differences between data values. For such purpose, the user can choose a proper number of control points, the color associated to each control point, and the exponent used for the interpolation. For example, in the representations depicted in Figure 11, three different coding are employed for representing the same ipercube. While the representations depicted in Figure 11

Figure 9. Graphical User Interface of ELDA supporting the qualitative phase

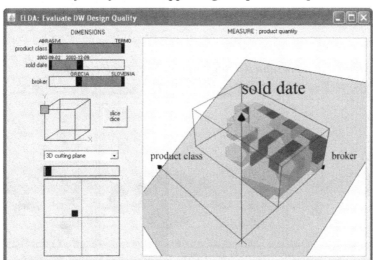

Figure 10. Obtaining detailed information concerning a particular subset of data

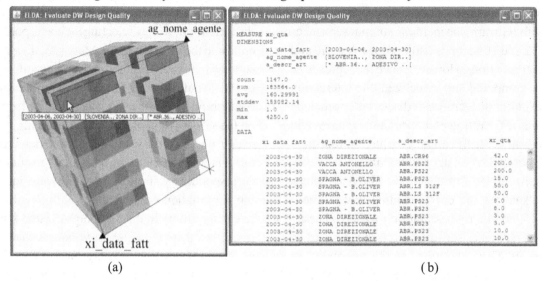

(a)   (b)

(a) and (b) differ in both the number of control points and the color associated to each control point, Figure 11 (b) and (c) differ only in the exponent used for the interpolation.

More specifically, the color coding employed for the ipercube represented in Figure 11(a) is characterized by three control points: the yellow color is employed for the minimum value, cyan color for the value located at the middle of values range, while purple color is used for the maximum value. A linear interpolation is used for mapping intermediate colors. On the other hand, two control points characterize the coding of both representations depicted in Figure 11 (b) and (c); the two coding differ only from the point of view of color interpolation. In Figure 11(a) a linear interpolation is used for the mapping, while the representation depicted in Figure 11(b) employs an exponential interpolation (in this case, the exponent equals 4) for deriving intermediate colors. In the considered examples, the latter representation is able to highlight more clearly subtle differences into the values.

If during the data exploration the user discover some unexpected and undesirable data features, he can go back to the previous phase to refine

Figure 11. The same ipercube represented using three different color coding

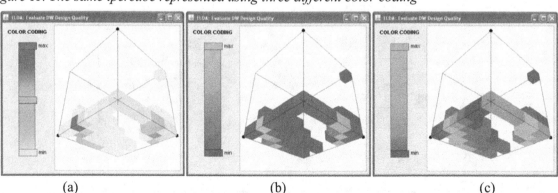

(a)   (b)   (c)

her design choices, e.g., excluding some DW dimensions and measures. It is interesting to note that although designed mainly for supporting the evaluation of data distributions, the visualization and interaction techniques proposed for the qualitative analysis allow one also to perform some preliminary data analysis, e.g., intuitive identification of the most sold products, interesting customers and productive brokers.

EXPERIMENTAL EVALUATION

We have experimented proposed methodology on three DBs subsets of two real world ERP (Enterprise Resource Planning) systems. Considered DBs, called respectively *DB01*, *DB02* and *DB03*, are characterized by tens of tables, hundreds of attributes and millions of records. In particular, while DB01 and DB02 correspond to different instantiations of the same DB schema (it is the same business system used by two different commercial organizations), DB03 has a different DB schema (it is based on a different ERP system).

For the experimental evaluation, we asked to an expert to build an unique (and relatively simple) schema for a selling DW by selecting the attributes that are the most suitable to support decision processes. The DW build by the expert is characterized by a star schema where six attributes are used as measures ($n_m = 6$) and nine as dimensions ($n_d = 9$). Starting from this schema, we build three DWs, filling them with the three different DB sources. As a result, the attributes chosen to build the first two DWs are physically the same (since they belong to the same DB schema), while a different set of attributes (characterized by the same semantics with respect to ones selected for previous DWs) are chosen for the DW03 construction.

Then, we have experimented our methodology for testing its effectiveness by considering the above three case studies. The analysis is mainly targeted at evaluating if the proposed metrics effectively support quantitative analysis by taking into account (i) the structure of the initial DB (in this experiment, two different DB schemas are considered), (ii) data actually stored into the initial DB (in this experiment, three different data sources are considered), and (iii) the DW schema (in this experiment, an unique DW schema is considered). We have then evaluated both if during the DW construction the proposed methodology effectively drives design choices and, at the end of the quantitative phase, if it can be used for deriving information on the final DW design quality.

Quantitative Phase

In the first phase of our experiment, we have considered the metrics we propose for the DB tables and evaluated their effectiveness in highlighting tables that are suitable to be used for extracting measures and dimensions. The global indexes MT_d and MT_m for the three DBs are summarized respectively in Table 1 (a) and (b). Derived quality measurements for the DB tables are consistent with our expectations; for example, for both DB01 and DB02, the procedure highlights that *xsr* and *intf* are tables suitable for extracting measures since these tables store selling and pricing information. It is interesting to note that although based on the same DB schema, different indexes are computed for DB01 and DB02 due to different data distributions. A similar good result is obtained for DB03, where the tables *bolla_riga* and *bolla_riga_add* store the same kind of information stored into *xsr*, while *mag_costo* stores pricing information on products. With respect to dimensions choice, our procedure highlights both in DB01 and DB02 the tables *gum* and *zon*; indeed, the first table stores information on customers categories, while the second one stores geographical information on customers. A similar result is obtained for DB03, since the tables *anagrafico_conti* and *gruppo_imprend*, storing information respectively on customer accounts and product categories.

Table 1. List of DB01, DB02 and DB03 tables ranked according to (a) MT_d and (b) MT_m

(a) Dimensions

Tables of DB01	MT_d
zon	0.8814
gum	0.8645
smag	0.8514
...	...

Tables of DB02	MT_d
gum	0.7481
zon	0.7463
...	...

Tables of DB03	MT_d
ord_tipo	0.8716
anagrafico_conti	0.8689
gruppo_imprend	0.8660
...	...

(b) Measures

Tables of DB01	MT_m
xsr	0.8521
org	0.8420
intf	0.8340
...	...

Tables of DB02	MT_m
xsr	0.8316
intf	0.8276
...	...

Tables of DB03	MT_m
bolla_riga	0.8468
bolla_riga_add	0.8462
mag_costo	0.8333
...	...

In the second phase of the experiment, we have considered the metrics we propose for the attributes. We summarize in Table 2 (a) and (b) the quality indicators respectively from dimensions and measures point of view. The computed indexes are consistent with our expectations; for example, in both DB01 and DB02 the attributes *zn_sigla* and *mp_sigla* result suitable to be used as dimensions; indeed, the first attribute stores geographical information on customers and sellers, while the second one collects information on payment types. Additionally, our procedure identifies *lio_prezzo* and *xr_valore* as the attributes that are more suitable to be used as measures in DB01. This is consistent with the semantics of data, since the first attribute stores pricing information on special offers, while the

second one refers to invoices amounts. Also in the case of DB02 the procedure highlights attributes storing money-related information; for example, the attribute *mv_imp_val* stores information on accounts movements. A good result is also obtained for DB03; in this case, the procedure correctly identifies *tipo_ord* and *cod_moneta* as attributes suitable to be used as dimensions and less effective as measures. Indeed, these attributes store information respectively on types of orders and moneys. On the other hand, the attribute *qta_ordinata* storing information on the number of products ordered by the customer, it results suitable to be used as measure.

In the third phase of our experiment, we have considered the DW built by the expert and analyzed the rank of selected attributes in order to evaluate the effectiveness of our methodology in correctly measuring the quality of the attributes according to their role into the DW. In Table 3 and Table 4 we report respectively the measures and dimensions chosen for building the three DWs and related ranks.

To better evaluate the results, we illustrate in Figure 12 the whole set of DB attributes ranked according to M_m and M_d, highlighting the measures and dimensions chosen by the expert to built the DW. It is interesting to note that most selected attributes (in the figure, represented by red X) are located in the upper-left part of the figures, meaning that the derived quality indicators are consistent with the expert design choices.

The final step of the quantitative phase concerns the evaluation of the derived global indicators measuring the quality of the considered DWs. From computed measurements, DW01 results the better DW, while DW02 result the worst one, due to both the low quality of data stored into the selected DB attributes and the initial DB schema. In particular, the following global indicators are computed: M(DW01)=0.8826, M(DW02)=0.6292 and M(DW03) = 0.8504.

Table 2. Attributes of DB01, DB02 and DB03 ranked according to (a) MA_d and (b) MA_m

(a) Dimensions   (b) Measures

Attributes of DB01	MA_d	$rank_d$
mp_sigla	0.7268	0.0000
zn_sigla	0.6843	0.0024
...	...	...

Attributes of DB01	MA_m	$rank_m$
lio_prezzo	0.7467	0.0000
xr_valore	0.7443	0.0024
...	...	...

Attributes of DB02	MA_d	$rank_d$
zn_sigla	0.6828	0.0000
ps_sigla_paese	0.6694	0.0015
mp_sigla	0.6692	0.0030
...	...	...

Attributes of DB02	MA_m	$rank_m$
mv_imp_val	0.7512	0.0000
ra_importo_val	0.7486	0.0015
ra_pag_val	0.7423	0.0030
...	...	...

Attributes of DB03	MA_d	$rank_d$
tipo_ord	0.7078	0.0000
cod_moneta	0.6830	0.0020
...	...	...

Attributes of DB03	MA_m	$rank_m$
nro_ordine	0.6767	0.0000
qta_ordinata	0.6502	0.0020
...	...	...

Table 3. Ranking of DW01, DW02 and DW03 measures

DW	SOURCE		M_m			$rank_m$		
	DB01 and DB02	DB03	DW01	DW02	DW03	DW01	DW02	DW03
product quantity	*xr_qta*	*qta_spedita*	1.0369	0.9291	0.9616	0.0123	0.0193	0.0081
product price	*xr_valore*	*riga_prezzo*	1.2145	1.1629	0.7925	0.0000	0.0044	0.1071
broker commission	*xr_prov_age*	*provv_ag1*	0.9999	0.0000	0.8164	0.0197	1.0000	0.0727
customer discount	*xr_val_sco*	*sc_riga*	0.9608	0.0000	0.8914	0.0468	1.0000	0.0222
product last cost	*a_ult_prz_pag*	*costo_f1*	1.0477	0.8452	0.9255	0.0074	0.0400	0.0121
product std. cost	*a_prz_pag_stand*	*costo_f2*	0.0339	0.8758	0.9255	0.9634	0.0267	0.0121

Table 4. Ranking of DW01, DW02 and DW03 dimensions

DW	SOURCE		M_d			$Rank_d$		
	DB01 and DB02	DB03	DW01	DW02	DW03	DW01	DW02	DW03
product	a_sigla_art	cod_articolo	1.0648	1.0712	1.0128	0.0000	0.0000	0.0060
product class	smg_tipo_codice	cod_ricl_ind_ricl_f1	0.7906	0.7803	0.7092	0.0343	0.0133	0.0986
warehouse class	a_cl_inv	cod_ricl_ind_ricl_f2	0.6098	0.0000	0.7092	0.1397	1.0000	0.0986
customer	sc_cod_s_conto	conti_clienti_m_p	0.8094	0.7497	0.7977	0.0294	0.0192	0.0523
customer class	gu_codice	cod_gruppo	0.6789	0.7479	0.9381	0.0833	0.0222	0.0141
province	xi_prov	cod_provincia	0.5576	0.7009	0.9482	0.1961	0.0385	0.0101
country	ps_sigla_paese	elenco_stati_cod_iso	0.7770	0.8403	0.8044	0.0368	0.0074	0.0483
broker	ag_cod_agente	conti_fornitori_m_p	0.9302	0.0000	0.6179	0.0025	1.0000	0.0986
commercial zone	zn_sigla	cod_zona_comm	0.7977	0.7348	0.9070	0.0368	0.0266	0.0201

Figure 12. Quality measurements for DB01, DB02 and DB03 attributes from dimensions (left figures) and measures (right figures) point of view

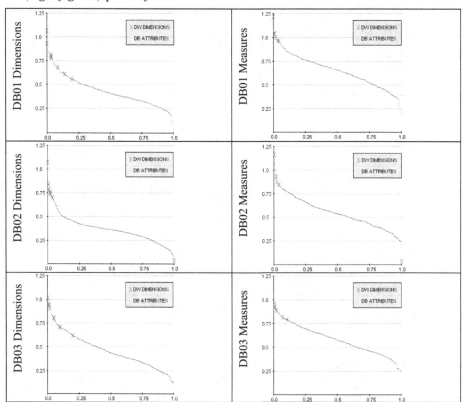

Qualitative Phase

At the end of the quantitative phase, we have used the ELDA tool to visually analyze taken design choices for better evaluating if data distributions are coherent with the designer expectations or are characterized by some unexpected and undesirable behavior. For such purpose, we have considered, visualized and analyzed different ipercubes using possible combinations of selected DW dimensions and measures. With respect to the quantitative phase that allows one to derive concise information concerning the general data features, the qualitative evaluation better highlights relations among data, giving to the user also the possibility of focusing the attention on specific data subset.

Although in the real experiment we have examined several DW ipercubes, some at different levels of detail also performing slice and dice operations, in the following we provide only an example demonstrating the effectiveness of our technique in highlighting particular data features.

In particular, we compare three ipercubes that are equivalent from a semantic point of view, but characterized by different data distributions since referring to data stored into a different DW (i.e., DW01, DW02 and DW03, see Figure 13). The considered ipercubes are characterized by the attributes *Product*, *Sold Date* and *Customer* as dimensions, and *Product Sold* as measure. Moreover, the counting function is used for aggregating the data. As a result, in the resulting visualizations the cyan color is used for identifying parts of the ipercube characterized by a limited number of records where the attribute *Product Sold* does not assume a null value. On the other hand, red cubes identifying parts of the information space characterized by an higher number of records. If all records falling into a specific part of the ipercube are characterized by null values for the selected measure, the corresponding volume in the three dimensional visualization is completely transparent.

Starting from these considerations, different data behaviors outcrops from the visualizations derived by ELDA (in Figure 13 the three columns refer to visualizations concerning different DWs, while the rows display the same representation observed by two different points of view).

In particular, by observing Figure 13(a) one can easily note that DW01 stores data that are not equally distributed into the time domain (Y axis of the representation), since there is a period where any data has been recorded by the information system. From data distribution point of view in the time domain, the other two DWs do not exhibit such behavior.

On the other hand, the representation of the DW02 ipercube highlights a different data distribution feature: from such visualization one can identify an undesirable data behavior (i.e., an evident data clusterization) for the attribute *Product*. By examining the visualization in more detail (i.e., using the detail-on-demand technique), we discovered that most records are characterized by the same attribute value corresponding to the default value that is assigned to the attribute when the user using the information system does not fill the corresponding field. We discovered a similar but less evident behavior in the DW01 ipercube, since also in this case ELDA highlighted an interval (corresponding to the default attribute value) into the *Product* domain where most data are recorded. However, data stored into the remaining part of the domain is more dense with respect to the previous case.

We have also employed constraints viewpoints for better examining data distributions consid-

Figure 13. Visualizing semantically equivalent ipercubes of (a) DW01, (b) DW02 and (c) DW03

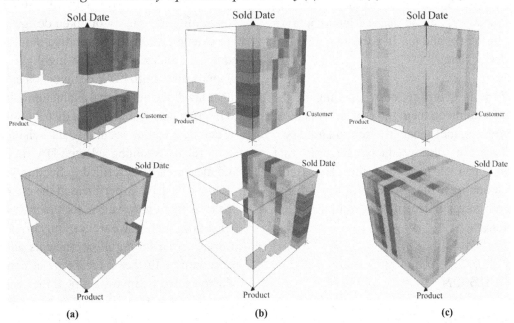

(a) (b) (c)

Figure 14. Using a constrained viewpoint for analyzing the trend of data through the time domain

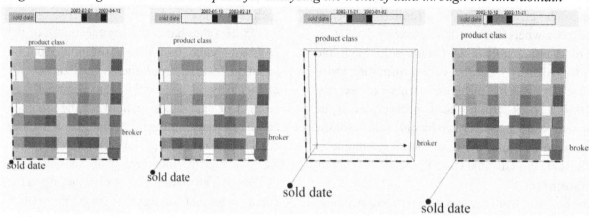

ering different values of one dimension. In the following, we consider only the DW01 ipercube characterized by the attributes *Product Class*, *Sold Date* and *Broker* as dimensions, and *Product Sold* as measure. By observing the ipercube representation using a viewpoint constrained to the upper bound of the attribute *Sold Date* and changing such value, the user can interactively examine data distribution in different time of year, as depicted in Figure 14 (where the color indicates the average number of products sold). Additionally, some preliminary information concerning the data analysis can be derived by comparing Figure 14 (a), (b) and (c). In particular, one can easily derive that:

- There is a broker (corresponding to the last column on the right) that has sold most products, independently from their class;
- There are some products categories that have been sold more than other classes (corresponding to the second, fifth, seventh and ninth rows), independently from a specific broker.

CONCLUSION

In this chapter, we have proposed an interactive methodology supporting the DW design and evalu-

ating from both quantitative and qualitative point of view the quality of taken design choices. For the quantitative evaluation we propose a set of metrics measuring different syntactical and statistical data features, while for the qualitative evaluation we propose visualization and interaction techniques effectively supporting data exploration and examination during the DW design phase. Our solution has been successfully experimented on three real DWs, the experimental evaluation demonstrated the effectiveness of our proposal in providing both quantitative and qualitative information concerning the quality of taken design choices. For example, from a quantitative point of view, computed indexes correctly highlighted some inappropriate initial DW design choices. On the other hand, the qualitative evaluation allowed us to interactively examine data distributions more in detail, discover peculiar data behaviors and study relations among selected DW dimensions and measures, as described in Section "".

Since we have experimented the quantitative phase using unitary values for the metrics coefficients (i.e., 1 or -1), we are currently investigating if an accurate tuning of coefficients allows the procedure to further increase its effectiveness. Moreover, we are investigating if the conditional entropy and mutual information can be used for automatically discovering correlations among attributes in order to enable our methodology to suggest alternative design choices during the DW creation. For example, an attribute could represent a valid alternative to another attribute if (i) it is strongly correlated with the second attribute and (ii) its quality is higher with respect to the one measured for the second attribute.

We have recently started at testing our metrics on completely different contexts for evaluating if its effectiveness is independent from the specific application domain; we then shift from ERP systems to applications collecting information on undergraduates, university employers and professors and to DB of motorways crashes. This evaluation is also targeted at highlighting possible limitations of the proposed methodology and can elicit new requirements.

Although designed for providing the user with qualitative information concerning data distributions, we have recently started at evaluating the effectiveness of adopting the proposed three dimensional representation and related interaction techniques not only for the design, but also for data analysis. More specifically, we intend to identify main limitations of our proposal and novel functionalities to be included into ELDA for improving its effectiveness from data analysis point of view.

REFERENCES

Ballou, D.P, Wang, R.Y., Pazer H.L., & Tayi, G.K. (1998). Modelling information manufacturing systems to determine information product quality., *Management Science, 44*(4), 462–484.

Ballou, D.P., & Pazer, H.L. (1985). Modeling data and process quality in multi-input, multi-output information systems. *Management Science, 31*(2), 150–162.

Burigat, S., Chittaro, L., & De Marco, L. (2005) Bringing dynamic queries to mobile devices: A visual preference-based search tool for tourist decision support. *Proceedings of INTERACT 2005: 10th IFIP International Conference on Human-Computer Interaction* (pp. 213-226). Berlin: Springer Verlag.

Calero, C., Piattini, M., Pascual, C., & Serrano, M.A. (2001). Towards data warehouse quality metrics. *Proceedings of International Workshop on Design and Management of Data Warehouses*, (pp. 2/1-10).

Campbell, B., Collins, P., Hadaway, H., Hedley, N., & Stoermer, M. (2002). Web3D in ocean science learning environments: Virtual big beef creek. *Proceedings of the 7th International Conference on 3D Web Technology*, (pp. 85-91). New-York: ACM Press.

Chengalur-Smith, I.N., Ballou, D.P., & Pazer, H.L. (1999). The impact of data quality information on decision making: An exploratory analysis. *IEEE Transactions on Knowledge and Data Engineering, 11*(6), 853-864.

Chittaro, L., & Scagnetto, I. (2001). Is semitransparency useful for navigating virtual environments? *Proceedings of VRST-2001: 8th ACM Symposium on Virtual Reality Software & Technology*, (pp. 159-166). New York: ACM Press.

Chittaro, L., Combi, C., & Trapasso, G. (2003, December). Data mining on temporal data: A visual approach and its clinical application to hemodialysis. *Journal of Visual Languages and Computing, 14*(6), 591-620.

Chittaro, L., & Ranon, R. (2007). Web3D technologies in learning, education and training: Motivations, issues, opportunities. *Computers & Education Journal, 49*(1), 3-18.

Coors, V., & Jung, V. (1998). Using VRML as an interface to the 3D data warehouse. *Proceedings of the third Symposium on Virtual Reality Modeling Language*. New York: ACM Press.

De Amicis, F., & Batini, C. (2004). A methodology for data quality assessment on financial data. *Studies in Communication Sciences, 4*,(2), 115-136.

Delaney, B. (1999). The NYSE's 3D trading floor. *IEEE Computer Graphics and Applications 19*(6), 12-15.

English, L.P. (1999). Improving data warehouse & business information quality: Methods for reducing costs and increasing profits. Wiley and Sons.

Jarke, M., Jeusfeld, M.A., Quix, C., & Vassiliadis, P. (1999). Architecture and quality in data warehouses: An extended repository approach. *Information Systems, 24*(3), 229-253.

Jeusfeld, M.A., Quix, C., & Jarke, M. (1998). Design and analysis of quality information for data warehouses. *Proceedings of the International Conference on Conceptual Modeling*, (pp. 349-362).

Karr, A.F., Sanil, A.P., & Banks, D.L. (2006). Data quality: A statistical perspective. *Statistical Methodology, 3*(2), 137-173.

Kriebel, C.H. (1978). Evaluating the quality of information systems. *Proceedings of the BIFOA Symposium*, (pp. 18-20).

Lee, Y.W., Strong, D.M., Kahn, B.K., & Wang, R.Y. (2001). AIMQ: A methodology for information quality assessment. *Information and Management, 40*(2), 133-146.

Li, Y., Brodlie, K., & Philips, N. (2001). Web-based VR training simulator for percutaneous rhizotomy. *Proceedings of Medicine Meets Virtual Reality*, (pp. 175-181).

Missier, P., & Batini, C. (2003). An information quality management framework for cooperative information Systems. *Proceedings of Information Systems and Engineering*, (pp.25–40).

Noser, H., & Stucki, P. (2003). Dynamic 3D visualization of database-defined tree structures on the World Wide Web by using rewriting systems.

Proceedings of the International Workshop on Advance Issues of E-Commerce and Web-Based Information Systems, (pp. 247-254). IEEE Computer Society Press.

Phipps, C., & Davis, K. (2002). Automating data warehouse conceptual schema design and evaluation. *Proceeding of DMDW*, (pp. 23-32).

Pighin, M., & Ieronutti, L. (2007). From database to datawarehouse: A design quality evaluation. *Proceedings of the International Conference on Enterprise Information Systems, INSTICC Eds.*, Lisbon, POR, (pp. 178-185).

Pipino, L., Lee, Y., & Wang, R. (2002. Data quality assessment. *Communications of the ACM, 45*(4), 211-218.

Redman, T.C. (1996). *Data quality for the information age.* Artech House.

Redman, T.C. (1998). The impact of poor data quality on the typical enterprise. *Communications of the ACM, 41*(2), 79-82.

Robertson, G.G., Card, S.K., & Mackinlay, J.D. (1993). Information visualization using 3D interactive animation. *Communications of the ACM 36*(4), 57-71.

Scannapieco, M., Virgillito, A., Marchetti, C., Mecella, M., & Baldoni, R. (2004). The DaQuinCIS architecture: A platform for exchanging and improving data quality in cooperative information systems. *Information Systems, 29*(7), 551-582.

Schulze-Wollgast, P., Tominski, C., & Schumann, H. (2005). Enhancing visual exploration by appropriate color coding. *Proceedings of International Conference in Central Europe on Computer Graphics, Visualization and Computer Vision*, (pp. 203-210).

Shekhar, S., Lu, C., Tan, X., Chawla, S., & Vatsavai, R. (2001). Map cube: A visualization tool for spatial data warehouses. As *Chapter of Geographic Data Mining and Knowledge Discovery*,

Harvey J. Miller and Jiawei Han (eds.), Taylor and Francis.

Shneiderman, B. (1994). Dynamic queries for visual information seeking.*seeking. IEEE Software, 11(6), 70-77.*

Wang, R.Y., Strong, D.M. (1996a). Beyond accuracy: What data quality means to data consumers. *Journal of Management Information Systems, 12*(4), 5-33.

Wang, R.Y., & Strong, D.M. (1996b). *Data quality systems evaluation and implementation.*London: Cambridge Market Intelligence Ltd.

Wang, R.Y., Storey, V.C., & Firth, C.P. (1995). A framework for analysis of data quality research. *IEEE Transactions on Knowledge and Data Engineering, 7*(4), 623-640.

Williamson, C., Shneiderman, B. (1992). The dynamic HomeFinder: Evaluating dynamic queries in a real-estate information exploration System. *Proceedings of the Conference on Research and Development in Information Retrieval (SIGIR 92),* (pp. 338–346). New-York: ACM Press.

Chapter V
Integrated Business and Production Process Data Warehousing

Dirk Draheim
University of Lunsbruck, Austria

Oscar Mangisengi
BWIN Interactive Entertainment, AG & SMS Data System, GmbH, Austria

ABSTRACT

Nowadays tracking data from activity checkpoints of unit transactions within an organization's business processes becomes an important data resource for business analysts and decision-makers to provide essential strategic and tactical business information. In the context of business process-oriented solutions, business-activity monitoring (BAM) architecture has been predicted as a major issue in the near future of the business-intelligence area. On the other hand, there is a huge potential for optimization of processes in today's industrial manufacturing. Important targets of improvement are production efficiency and product quality. Optimization is a complex task. A plethora of data that stems from numerical control and monitoring systems must be accessed, correlations in the information must be recognized, and rules that lead to improvement must be identified. In this chapter we envision the vertical integration of technical processes and control data with business processes and enterprise resource data. As concrete steps, we derive an activity warehouse model based on BAM requirements. We analyze different perspectives based on the requirements, such as business process management, key performance indication, process and state based-workflow management, and macro- and micro-level data. As a concrete outcome we define a meta-model for business processes with respect to monitoring. The implementation shows that data stored in an activity warehouse is able to efficiently monitor business processes in real-time and provides a better real-time visibility of business processes.

INTRODUCTION

In the continuously changing business environment nowadays manufacturing organizations can benefit from one unified business environment that brings production process data and business data together in real-time. We believe in a balanced view on all activities in the modern enterprise. A focus on the mere administration side of businesses is to narrow. The production process must be incorporated into information management from the outset, because excellence in production is a fundament of today's businesses (Hayes & Wheelright, 1984). In fact, manufacturers generate incredible amounts of raw data in production processes, however, they are often not used efficiently yet. The rationales of turning production process data into information in industrial manufacturing are to improve production processes, competitiveness, and product qualities; enabling management to understand where inefficiencies exist and to optimize production processes, and to prepare smart business decisions for high-level management, such as to provide an accurate picture of occurrences on the production process. As a result, the need for highly integrated control and information systems as data resources for Business Intelligence (BI) applications is essential to addressing the emerging challenges.

Data Warehousing currently is almost identical to BI tools for supporting decision-making. A data warehouse (DW) stores historical data, which are integrated from different data sources, and it is organized into multidimensional data (Kimball, Ross & Merz, 2002; Inmon, 2002). Data in a DW is dynamically processed by an On-Line Analytical Processing (OLAP) tool (Codd, Codd & Salley, 1993) for high-level management to make decisions. Although DWs have been developed over a decade, they are still inadequate for answering the needs of BI applications. DW does not provide data based on events and lacks process-context. DW stores end measures, i.e., aggregated reference data, rather than process checkpoints (Creese, 2005). However, those processes, events, or activities always occur in business processes as well as production processes.

Workflow management (WfM) systems (Hollingworth, 1995) have been developed in the last decade to help automating business processes of organizations. Today's workflow technology products known as business process management suites (Miers, Harmon & Hall, 2006) enable the tracking of data in business processes. Furthermore, Business Activity Monitoring (BAM) - a current business intelligence trend (Dresner, 2002; Mangisengi, Pichler, Auer, Draheim & Rumetshofer, 2007) – enables monitoring business process activities of an organization.

Based on our experience in successfully implementing an activity warehouse for monitoring business activities for integrating enterprise applications (Mangisengi et al., 2007), we argue that the workflow technology supported by Service-Oriented Architecture (SOA) and BAM technology are potential technologies for industrial manufacturing to optimize and improve production processes and business processes as well as product quality measures.

In this paper we envision the vertical integration of technical processes and control data with business processes and enterprise resource data. This paper presents a meta-model of an activity warehouse for integrating business and production process data in industrial manufacturing. We approach BAM requirements for deriving the meta-model of the activity warehouse.

This work is structured as follows. The next section gives related work. Then, research background and motivation are presented. Afterwards, we present production process data based on BAM requirements. Furthermore, we present a meta-model of integrated business and production process data. Finally, a conclusion and future research are given in the last section.

RELATED WORK

Recently there exists research work in the literature for the architecture of Business Activity Monitoring, workflow management systems, and real-time data warehousing. We summarize research works as follows. The architecture of BAM is initialized and introduced in (Dresner, 2002; Nesamoney, 2004; Hellinger & Fingerhut, 2002; White, 2003; McCoy, 2001). The concept of process warehouse has been introduced for different purposes, such as in (Nishiyama, 1999) a process warehouse focuses on a general information source for software process improvement. Then, (Tjoa, List, Schiefer & Quirchmayr, 2003) introduces a data warehouse approach for business process management, called a process warehouse, and in (Pankratius & Stucky, 2005) they introduce a process warehouse repository. Furthermore, in relation to data warehousing, (Schiefer, List & Bruckner, 2003) propose an architecture that allows for transforming and integrating workflow events with minimal latency providing the data context against which the event data is used or analyzed. An extraction, transformation, and loading (ETL) tool is used for storing a workflow events stream in a Process Data Store (PDS).

In reference to our previous work in (Mangisengi et al., 2007), we have successfully implemented Business-Activity Monitoring for integrating enterprise applications and introduced an activity warehouse model for managing data for monitoring business activity.

There is a huge potential for optimization of processes in today's industrial manufacturing. Optimization is a complex task. A plethora of data that stems from numerical control and monitoring systems must be accessed, correlations in the information must be recognized, and rules that lead to improvement must be identified. Despite concrete standardization efforts, existing approaches to this problem often remain low-level and proprietary in today's manufacturing projects. The several manufacturing applications that

make up an overall solution are isolated spots of information rather than well-planned integrated data sources (Browne, Harhen & Shivnan, 1996) and this situation has not yet been overcome in practice. Current efforts in manufacturing execution systems address this. For example, STEP (Standard of Product Model Data) (ISO 2004) standardizes the description of both physical and functional aspects of products. ISO 15531 (MANDATE) (ISO 2005; Cutting-Decelle & Michel, 2003) provides a conceptual data model for manufacturing resources, manufacturing engineering data, and manufacturing control data. Both STEP and ISO 15531 are examples of standards that already pursue a data-oriented viewpoint on the manufacturing scenario.

Research Background and Motivation

Because of the huge potential for optimization of processes in today's industrial manufacturing to improve production efficiency and product quality, we endeavor to bring data warehousing to the area of industrial manufacturing. Product qualities, product processes, business processes, or process optimizations can be improved by capturing production process and business process data in detail. They must be tracked and stored in a repository, and then they are monitored and analyzed using a tool. Problems that occurred in business processes as well as in production processes must be solved and improvements must be identified.

An integrated business and production process landscape in industrial manufacturing is given in Figure 1. The figure shows that the integrated business and production processes are divided into four layers, i.e., Enterprise Resource Planning (ERP), Production Planning and Control (PPC), Manufacturing Execution System (MES), and Numerical Control (NC). Two layers (i.e., ERP and PPC) consist of business processes and its workflows, whereas the rest of the layers consist of production processes and its workflows.

In this paper we discuss in more detail production processes in industrial manufacturing and briefly present it. A production system consists of three systems, namely input, execution, and output systems. The input system receives raw materials that will be processed in an execution system, an execution system processes the raw material from inputs and contains a production process, and the output system manages finished products from the execution system.

Figure 1 shows that a production process can be divided into a set of processes (i.e., *PP Process 1, ..., PP Process 3*) that is controlled and executed by the MES Process 1 and provides a sequential production system. Furthermore, the MES Process 2 executes and controls other processes (i.e., *PP Process 4, ..., PP Process* 6) after it receives a signal from the PP Process 3. A process within the production process may consist of a set of production process activities. A production process is rich in machine activities and works at regular intervals; in addition, it is a long-running production transaction from input to output system. Within the interval, a checkpoint of activities occurs in the production process.

In industrial manufacturing, production process and business process data are generated by activities and events and they are rich in process-context. We face the issue that DWs used for business intelligence applications for analytical processing are inadequate data resource to address those purposes. On the other hand, the process-context data cannot be stored in DW. Therefore, we need a repository that can be used for storing the necessary items. We argue that an integration of process-oriented data and data that stem from applications in industrial manufacturing could provide powerful information for making decisions.

PRODUCTION PROCESS DATA BASED ON BUSINESS ACTIVITY MONITORING REQUIREMENTS

In this section we present our approach for managing production processes and business processes

Figure 1. An integrated business and production process landscape in industrial manufacturing

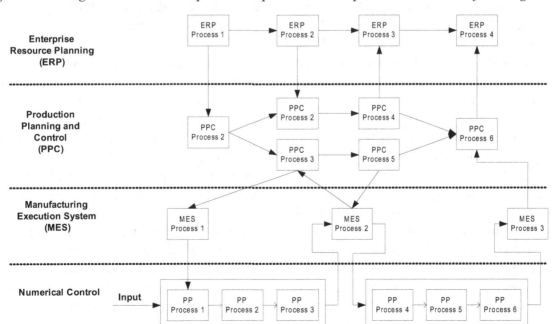

Figure 2. A conceptual hierarchical model of a production process

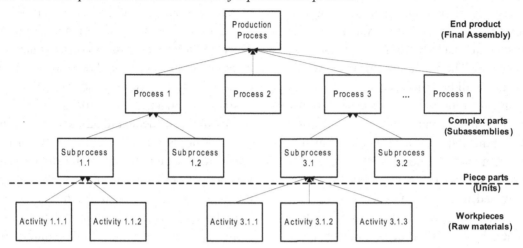

in industrial manufacturing based on business activity monitoring requirements. We use a top-down approach to derive a meta-model.

A Conceptual Hierarchical Structure of a Production Process

In order to monitor events, checkpoints and activities of a production process, a model of a production process is necessary. In reference to our previous work, a conceptual hierarchical structure of a business process in general has been introduced (Mangisengi et al., 2007). There exist similarities between a business process and a production process in general. The similarities can be listed as follows:

- A unit transaction in a production process or a business process is assumed as a long-running transaction and is valid at intervals.
- A production process as well as a business process can be organized into a hierarchical structure that represents different levels of importance from the highest level process to the lowest level process, or vice-versa.
- A production process as well as business process may be decomposed into a set of processes.

- An activity is the lowest level process that represents a particular process of a production process.

Based on the similarities between a business process and production process, a model of the production process hierarchical structure is given in Figure 2.

Relationship between Business Activity Monitoring and Business Process Management

A BAM architecture consists of components such as Business Process Optimization (BPO) and Key Performance Indicators (KPI) for supporting business optimization by providing business metric information. It must be able to support event-driven decision making by rules-based monitoring and reporting, real-time integration of event and context, and comprehensive exception-alert capabilities (Nesamoney, 2004). Furthermore, Business Process Management (BPM) technology aims at enhancing the business efficiency and responsiveness and optimizing the business process of an organization in order to improve business services (Chang, 2004; McDaniel, 2001).

BPM has closed relationship to the BAM system in general and the business strategy of an organization in particular. Thus, the BAM and BPM systems support data as follows:

- **Strategic data:** The strategic data provides the result of an organization that can be achieved and its hypotheses. Also, it can be supported by the scorecards
- **Tactical data:** The tactical data controls and monitors the business process activities and its progress in detail and supports a contextual data.
- **Business metrics data:** The business metrics data supports the strategic improvements for the higher level goals. It supports departments and teams to define what activities must be performed

A Production Process Workflow in Industrial Manufacturing

In this section we present a workflow technology for industrial manufacturing. Manufacturing organizations integrate production processes and business processes.

Common Workflow

The common characteristics of all workflow applications are that they are concerned with the registration of information and with tracking that information in a simulated environment; it is possible to determine the status of information while it is in the environment and which stakeholders are responsible for performing activities pertaining to that information. For the common workflow requirement, the following data in the activity warehouse are as follows:

- **Tracking activity:** The tracking activity data deal with the checkpoints of production process activities of a unit transaction in industrial manufacturing. It provides the

history of activities of a unit transaction.

- **Status activity:** The status activity data provide the status of a unit transaction after the execution of a production process activity. The current status also is used by an actor to decide for executing the next activity of the production process and in addition to arrange the executions of workflow in order.

Tree-Dimensional Workflow

An activity is the lowest level process of a production process and can be represented as a three-dimensional workflow. The three dimensions of an activity of a checkpoint in the production process are as follows:

The tree-dimensional workflow, e.g., process and actor, is represented by the dimension *process* and the dimension *actor* respectively, whereas an action is given by a method for the particular process and actor.

Timing Data

Timing data aims at recording when activities are executed. An activity warehouse has to deal with the entry date of an activity. In our approach for modeling the activity warehouse, we separate between the execution time and the measurement data for an activity.

In order to optimize the performance of a production process and its efficiency, the activity warehouse must be able to capture the execution time of an activity up to seconds, milliseconds, or even microseconds. Therefore, the activity warehouse uses the following attributes for the time efficiencies given in the time efficiency section.

Measurement Data

To optimize production processes and its business performances, an activity warehouse supports a set of attributes for metric data (e.g., the cost efficiency) and a set of time efficiency attributes.

The measurement data and the time efficiencies must be tracked in very detail for the checkpoints of business process activities of transactions. Furthermore, like OLAP tools, measurement data can be aggregated against the dimension tables. In the context of BAM, data stored in the activity warehouse must be able to provide an event-driven decision-making that means the lowest data level or an activity can be used to make decision for the business process efficiency. For example, the lowest business process data can be used for finding unexpected problems in the business process. To support the measurement data for the activity warehouse, we classify measurement data into groups as follows:

Macro Level Data

Macro level data represent end measurements of a unit transaction that are stored in operational data management. They will be extracted, transformed, and loaded from the operational storage and, furthermore, they are stored in the data warehouse.

Micro Level Data

Micro level data is the lowest activity data in a production process. The micro level data is defined as a checkpoint data of a production process activity of a unit transaction. The micro level data is distinguished into time efficiency data and measurement data. Micro level data includes data as follow:

Time Efficiency

In a production process there are many data acquisition applications, and their acquisition time must be captured and measured. Furthermore, the existence of the time efficiency requirements is very important in activity warehousing. The time efficiency is to measure time in data acquisition application in production processes as well as

business processes. The activity warehouse provides the time efficiency attributes to measure the performance and efficiency of business process. Attributes for the time efficiency are dependent on the business optimization performance requirements. A set of time efficiency attributes could be as follows:

- **Cycle time:** The cycle time is the total elapsed time, measured from the moment when a request enters the systems to when it leaves it. This is the time measure that is most obvious to the customer.
- **Work time:** The worked time is that the activities that execute the request are worked on. Practically, activities are sometimes idle or waiting for other activities to finish and for this reason cycle time and work time are not the same.
- **Time worked:** It concerned with the actual time of work expanded on the request. Sometimes more than one person is working on a request at one time. Thus, time worked is not the same as work time.
- **Idle time:** The idle time refers to when an activity or process is not doing anything.
- Transit time. The time spent in transit between activities or steps.
- **Queue time:** The time that a request is waiting on a critical resource; the request is ready for processing, however it waiting for resources from another activity to reach it.
- **Setup time:** The time required for a resource to switch from one type of task to another.

Cost Efficiency

The cost efficiency attributes depend on the value of the attributes time efficiencies and the value of activity per hour. They provide cost efficiency data to optimize the business processes and to calculate the cost of production processes as well as business processes.

The macro and micro level data enable the business process management tools to monitor and drill down data from the macro level data to the micro level data as well as horizontal and vertical rolling-down to each individual transaction or production and business processes. Using these functionalities, an organization can improve the visibility of the overall performance of the organization at both the macro and micro level data.

BUSINESS AND PRODUCTION PROCESS DATA META MODEL

A meta-model of the activity warehouse consists of a set of dimension tables, namely the dimension *State*, the dimension *Process*, and the dimension *Actor*, the attribute of a unit transaction, a set of cost efficiency attributes, and a set of time efficiency attributes. The activity warehouse is directly coupled with a unit transaction of business or production processes. Attributes of the activity warehouse table are given as follows:

AW (UnitTransID, StateID, ActivityID, ActorID, CostOfProductionProcess, CostOfBusinessProcess, CycleTime, WorkTime, Timeworked, IdleTime, TransitTime, QueueTime, SetupTime)

In this activity warehouse, we show two costs as examples for calculating production processes and business processes. Other costs can be extended dependent on the cost requirements. Other attributes (i.e., CycleTime, WorkTime, Timeworked, IdleTime, TransitTime, QueueTime, and SetupTime) provide at least recorded times. Meanwhile, attributes of dimension tables of the activity warehouse are given as follows:

State (StateID, Description, Category)
Process (ActivityID, Description, Subprocess, Process)
Actor (ActorID, Description, FirstName, LastName, Role)

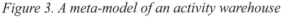

Figure 3. A meta-model of an activity warehouse

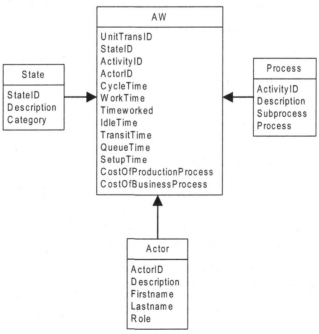

The activity warehouse of integrated business process and production process activities data are presented in Figure 3. The dimension Process shows the categorization of business processes and production processes.

CONCLUSION

In this paper we have presented a meta-model of an integrated business and production process data warehousing. The advantage of the model enables detecting failures of business processes as well as production processes in real-time using a business-activity monitoring tool. Furthermore, costs of production and business processes can be directly summarized and aggregated according to activities, sub-processes, or processes. In addition, performances of business and production processes can be reported and informed in real-time.

REFERENCES

Browne, J., Harhen, J., & Shivnan, J. (1996). *Production management systems*. Addison-Wesley.

Chang, J. (2004). The current state of BPM technology. *Journal of Business Integration*.

Codd, E.F., Codd, S.B., & Salley, C.T. (1993). Providing OLAP (On-Line Analytical Processing) to user analysts: An IT mandate. *White Paper*, E.F. Codd & Associates.

Creese, G. (2005). Volume analytics: Get ready for the process warehouse. *DMReview*. http://www.dmreview.com.

Cutting-Decelle, A.F., & Michel, J.J. (2003). ISO 15531 MANDATE: A standardized data model for manufacturing management. *International Journal of Computer Applications in Technology*, *18*(1-4).

Dresner, H. (2002). Business activity monitoring: New age BI?. *Gartner Research LE-15-8377*.

Hayes, R., & Wheelright, S. (1984). *Restoring our competitive edge*: *Competing through manufacturing*. John Wiley & Sons.

Hellinger, M., & Fingerhut, S. (2002). Business activity monitoring: EAI meets data warehousing. *Journal of Enterprise Application Integration (EAI)*.

Hollingworth, D. (1995). *The workflow reference model*. Technical Report TC00-1003, Workflow Management Coalition, Lighthouse Point, Florida, USA.

Inmon, W. (2002). *Building the data warehouse*. John Wiley & Sons.

ISO (2004). ISO Technical Committee TC 184/ SC 4. ISO 10303-1:1994. *Industrial automation systems and integration - Product data representation and exchange - Part 1: Overview and fundamental principles*. International Organization for Standardization.

ISO (2005). ISO Technical Committee 184/SC 4. ISO 15531-32 (2005). *Industrial automation systems and integration - Industrial manufacturing management data: Resources usage management - Part 32: Conceptual model for resources usage management data*. International Organization for Standardization.

Kimball, R., Ross, M., & Merz, R. (2002). *The data warehouse toolkit*: *The complete guide to dimensional modeling*. John Wiley & Sons.

Mangisengi, O., Pichler, M., Auer, D., Draheim, D., & Rumetshofer, H. (2007). Activity warehouse: Data management for business activity monitoring. *Proceeding from the Ninth International Conference of Enterprise Information Systems (ICEIS)*, Madeira, Portugal.

McCoy, D. (2001). *Business activity monitoring: The promise and the reality*. Gartner Group.

McDaniel, T. (2001). Ten pillars of business process management. *Journal of Enterprise Application Integration (EAI)*.

Miers, D., Harmon, P., & Hall, C. (2006). The 2006 BPM suites report. *Business Process Trends*.

Nesamoney, D. (2004). BAM: Event-driven business intelligence for the real-time enterprise. *DM Review, 14*(3).

Nishiyama, T. (1999). Using a process warehouse concept a practical method for successful technology transfer. *Proceeding from the Second International Symposium on Object-Oriented Real Time Distributed Computing, IEEE Computer Society*, Saint Malo.

Pankratius, V., & Stucky, W. (2005). A formal foundation for workflow composition, workflow view definition, and workflow normalization based on Petri Nets. *Proceeding from the Second Asia-Pacific Conference on Conceptual Modeling (APCCM 2005)*.

Schiefer, J., List, B., & Bruckner, R.M. (2003). Process data store: A real-time data store for monitoring business processes. *Lecture Notes in Computer Science, Database and Expert Systems Applications (DEXA)*, Springer-Verlag.

Tjoa, A.M., List, B., Schiefer, J., & Quirchmayr, G. (2003). The process warehouse – A data warehouse approach for business process management. *Intelligent Management in the Knowledge Economy*, (p. 112-126). Edward Elgar Publishing.

White, C. (2003). Building the real-time enterprise. *The Data Warehousing Institute, TDWI Report Series*, A101 Communications Publication.

Section II
OLAP and Pattern

Chapter VI
Selecting and Allocating Cubes in Multi–Node OLAP Systems:
An Evolutionary Approach

Jorge Loureiro
Instituto Politécnico de Viseu, Portugal

Orlando Belo
Universidade do Minho, Portugal

ABSTRACT

OLAP queries are characterized by short answering times. Materialized cube views, a pre-aggregation and storage of group-by values, are one of the possible answers to that condition. However, if all possible views were computed and stored, the amount of necessary materializing time and storage space would be huge. Selecting the most beneficial set, based on the profile of the queries and observing some constraints as materializing space and maintenance time, a problem denoted as cube views selection problem, is the condition for an effective OLAP system, with a variety of solutions for centralized approaches. When a distributed OLAP architecture is considered, the problem gets bigger, as we must deal with another dimension—space. Besides the problem of the selection of multidimensional structures, there's now a node allocation one; both are a condition for performance. This chapter focuses on distributed OLAP systems, recently introduced, proposing evolutionary algorithms for the selection and allocation of the distributed OLAP Cube, using a distributed linear cost model. This model uses an extended aggregation lattice as framework to capture the distributed semantics, and introduces processing nodes' power and real communication costs parameters, allowing the estimation of query and maintenance costs in time units. Moreover, as we have an OLAP environment, whit several nodes, we will have parallel processing and then, the evaluation of the fitness of evolutionary solutions is based on cost estimation algorithms that simulate the execution of parallel tasks, using time units as cost metric.

INTRODUCTION

The revolution operated at business environment and technology level motivated Data Warehousing (DWing). Globalization has generated highly competitive business environments, where proper and timely decision making is critical for the success or even the survival of organizations. Decision makers see their business on a multidimensional perspective and, mainly, need information of aggregated nature. These concomitant factors impose a new class of applications coined as On-Line Analytical Processing (OLAP).

The success of the DWing and OLAP concept brings to them an increasing number of new users and more and more business information areas. Its enlargement is a natural consequence: the stored data becomes huge, as well as the number of users. This reality imposes a high stress on the hardware platform, as OLAP query answers might be given in seconds. Some solutions were proposed and implemented, being two of them the most relevant: the pre-aggregation and materializing of queries and the distribution of data structures.

The former is an extension of the DWing concept, as an eagger approach (Widom, 1995): why waiting for a query to scan and compute the answer? The aggregation of possible huge detailed data to answer to an aggregated query may take a long time (possibly some hours or days) and then, the pre-computing and materializing of aggregated queries' answers, denoted as materialized views, cuboids or subcubes (Deshpande et al, 1997) (mainly used from now on), jointly named as materialized OLAP cubes or OLAP structures, are, certainly, a *sine qua non* performance condition in OLAP systems.

The second solution is, naturally, another view of the old maxim *"divide ut imperes"*: as OLAP users increase and structures get huge, we may distribute them by several hardware platforms, trying to gain the known advantages of database distribution: a sustained growth of processing capacity (easy scalability) without an exponential increase of costs and an increased availability of the system, as it eliminates the dependence from a single source. And this distribution may be achieved in different ways. 1) Creating different cubes, each one inhabiting in a different hardware platform: that's the solution coined as data mart approach; 2) distributing the OLAP cube by several nodes, inhabiting in close or remote sites, interconnected by communication links: that's a multi-node OLAP approach (M-OLAP); 3) using, as base distribution element, not the subcube, but only a part of it, a component called subcube fragment. Those solutions may be conjunctly applied, building, on its largest creation, the Enterprise Data Warehouse or the Federated Data Marts. But those creations, a materialization of the referred advantages, don't come for free. Many problems have to be solved, being the most relevant the so called "cube view selection problem", an optimizing issue derived from the former referred solution: materialization of subcubes.

As the number of these structures (and especially size and refresh cost) is huge, we have to select only the most beneficial ones, based on the maxim that "an unused subcube is almost useless". Periodically, or almost in real-time, we may decide which of the subcubes are the most beneficial and provide for its materialization and update (possibly adding or discarding some of them). Also, when the distributed OLAP approach gets on the stage, other disadvantages may be pointed: the increased complexity of DW administration and a huge dependency on the proper selection and allocation (into the several nodes) of the data cube, a question which is partially answered by the proposals of this paper: a new algorithm for the selection and allocation of distributed OLAP cubes, based on evolutionary approaches, which uses a linear cost model that introduces explicit communication costs and node processing power, allowing the use of time as the reference cost unit.

OPTIMIZING SOLUTIONS ISSUES AND RELATED WORK

The proper allocation of data cubes was heavily investigated for the centralized approach, where many algorithms were proposed, using mainly two kinds of techniques: greedy heuristics and genetic algorithms. The distributed approaches only recently came to stage.

All solutions have in common: 1) a cost model that allows the estimation of query (and maintenance) costs; 2) an algorithm that tries to minimize the costs: query costs or query and maintenance costs; and 3) constraints that may be applied to the optimizing process: a) maximal materializing space, and b) maximal maintenance window size that corresponds to an imposed limit of maintenance costs.

Linear Cost Model and Lattice Framework

The multidimensional model, the base characteristic of any OLAP system, may be seen as a data cube, concept introduced in (Gray, Chaudury, and Bosworth, 1997) as a generalization of the SQL group-by operator to meet the users' online investigation of data from various viewpoints. It is a multidimensional redundant projection of a relation, built upon the values of the cube dimensions. In this greed, each cell contains one or more measures ("living" cells values), all characterized by the same coordinates combination (dimension/level instance).

(Harinarayan, Harinarayan, Rajaraman, and Ullman, 1996) introduced the cube *lattice*, a direct acyclic graph (Figure 1), whose inspection allows to extract the constituent elements: subcubes or cuboids (Albrecht et al., 1999) (in any vertex), named by the dimensions/hierarchies grouped there, e.g. subcube $(p--)$ is a group by product, and the dependency relations between each subcube pair (edges).

*Figure 1. OLAP cube **lattice** with three dimensions: product, supplier and time, generating $2^3=8$ possible subcubes*

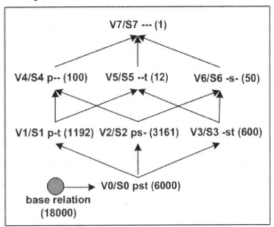

Using ~ as the dependence relation (derived-from, be-computed-from), we say that c_i depends on c_j, denoted as $c_i \sim c_j$ if any query answered by c_i can also be answered by c_j. However, the reverse is not true. In Figure 1, $(p - t) \sim (pst)$ or $(p--) \sim (ps-)$ but $(p-t) \not\sim (p--)$. With this dependence relation we may define the ancestors and descendents of a subcube c_i in a subset M of all possible subcubes, as follows:

$$Anc(c_i, M) = \{c_j \mid c_j \in M \text{ and } c_i \sim c_j\},$$

$$Des(c_i, M) = \{c_j \mid c_j \in M \text{ and } c_j \sim c_i\}.$$

Any ancestor of a subcube may be used to calculate it. The reverse is valid for the subcube's descendent. In Figure 1, subcube $(p--)$ may be computed from $(ps-)$, $(p - t)$ or even (pst). Aggregation costs will vary according to the size (in brackets in Figure 1) of the used subcube, lower for $(p - t)$, higher for (pst). The subcubes' size and dependence relations allow to define straightforwardly the least ancestor as: $Lanc(c_i, M) = \min_{c_j \in Anc(c_i)} |c_j|$. In the previous example, $Lanc((p--), M) = (p - t)$.

Cube Selection and Allocation Problems

The number of subcubes of a real OLAP system is usually huge. In Figure 1 we have only 8 possibilities, but even a simple cube, with 4 dimensions and 4 hierarchy levels by dimension, will have $4 \times 4 \times 4 \times 4 = 256$ subcubes. A real OLAP system has normally 4-12 dimensions (Kimball, 1996). Another example may be, for instance: if we have 5 dimensions, three of them with a four level hierarchy and the remaining two, with 5 levels, we will have $4 \times 4 \times 4 \times 5 \times 5 = 1600$ possible subcubes. Its total size and time to refresh would be intolerable. One has to decide the set of subcubes to be materialized, knowing the queries' profile: a subcube that's never been used has, probably, no interest. But, given the subcubes' dependence relations (represented as edges in Figure 1), a subcube may be used to answer a query (directly) or answer to other queries by further aggregating (indirect answer). In the maintenance process, this is valid: a subcube may be used to generate others or to compute deltas to refresh other subcubes.

Summing up, a subcube may be used to answer (or to refresh) a lot of other queries (subcubes), or, reversely, a query (or subcube) may be answered (or generated) by a number of others: its ancestors. This number, as a general rule, grows with the level of the subcube in the *lattice* structure (considering that the most aggregated subcube has the higher level), and it surely grows with the number of dimensions and hierarchies. Then, in real OLAP systems, the number of subcubes is high, as well as the possible ancestors of a given subcube. The number of alternatives to update a subcube or to answer a query is enormous. The selection of the most efficient subset of the possible subcubes (known as cube or views selection problem) able to answer to a set of queries, given a set of constraints (space or time to refresh) is a problem characteristically NP-hard (Harinarayan, Harinarayan, Rajaraman, and Ullman, 1996) and its solution is restricted to approximated ones.

Distributed Dependent Lattice

In this work, the cube view selection problem is extended to the space dimension. We deal with the minimizing of query and maintenance costs of a subcube distribution in a node set interconnected by an arbitrary communication network (Figure 2). Each node contains a dependent *lattice*, representative of the possible subcubes located there and its relationships, connected to other nodes by dashed lines that represent the communication channels, due to the distributed scenario. Each *lattice* vertex is linked to other not only with edges that show the dependences of intra-node aggregations, but also with other edges, that denote the communication channels, generating inter-node dependencies (as a subcube in one node may be computed using subcubes in other nodes). These edges connect subcubes in the same granularity level in different nodes of the M-OLAP architecture. In practice, they allow representing the additional communication costs that occur due to subcube or delta data transfer between nodes.

In Figure 2, the dashed line shows the dependence between subcubes *(-st)* inhabiting in all nodes. In the same figure, there is a graph that models the same dependence, supposing a fully connected network. Each link represents the communication costs C_{ij} that incur with the transport of one subcube between nodes i and j.

As communication is bidirectional, each subcubes is spilt in two (itself and its reciprocal), and the links that use third nodes are eliminated (avoiding cycles). Each link models the connection of minimal cost between two nodes. This graph will repeat itself for each of the subcubes in the *lattice*. In each node, one virtual vertex is included to model the virtual root (base relation – detailed DW table or data sources in a virtual DW), supposed to be located in node zero. This relation will be used as a primary source of data, for two different situations: when there isn't any competent subcube in any node that may be used

Figure 2. Distributed Lattice, adapted from (Bauer & Lehner, 2003). The dashed line shows the inter-node dependencies at the same level of granularity relating to the communication interconnections

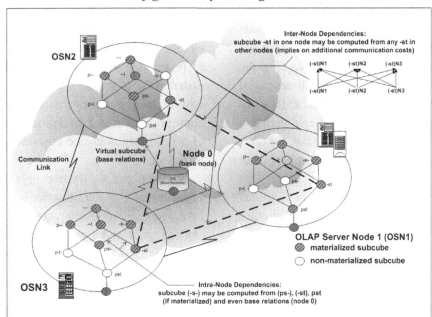

to answer a query (or its cost proved to be higher than the cost of using the base relation), and also, as the data source for the maintenance process. The processing cost of using base relations is, usually, many times higher, than the greatest processing cost of any *lattice*'s subcubes.

Related Work

The cube or views selection problem is very important in OLAP systems, and it has deserved a particular interest by the scientific community. Although there is a diversity of proposals, they

Figure 3. Two dimensional characterization of the OLAP cube selection problem, conjointly with used selecting logic and heuristics and proposals' references

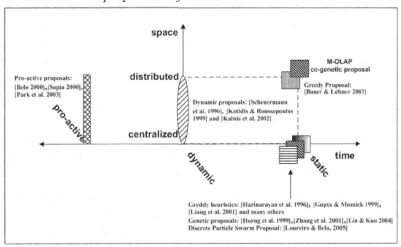

may be characterized, based on its essence, as a two dimensional perspective (**Figure 3**): 1) time, which dictates the elapsed interval between recalibration of OLAP structures as the real needs change (being then static, dynamic and pro-active, respectively); and 2) space, governing the distribution of the materialized multidimensional structures (centralized, and distributed). Concerning to static proposals, another dimension would make sense: selecting logic; but, for now, we prefer to restrict the characterization, and put the additional dimension as a label.

In Figure 3, the squares represent solutions in two great families of algorithms, and another recent proposal: greedy heuristics (Harinarayan, Harinarayan, Rajaraman, and Ullman, 1996; Gupta & Mumick, 1999; Liang, Wang, and Orlowska, 2004), genetic algorithms (Horng, Chang, Liu, and Kao, 1999; Lin & Kuo, 2004; Zhang, Yao, and Yang, 2001) and discrete particle swarm algorithm (Loureiro & Belo, 2006c) act upon centralized structures of great dimensions (the DW's materialized views or Data Marts), as they don't allow a reconfiguration in short periods, being then relatively static (thence the name).

The ellipse presented in the figure represents dynamic approaches (Scheuermann, Shim, and Vingralek, 1996); Kotidis, & Roussopoulos, 1999; Kalnis, Mamoulis, and Papadias, 2002). They act at cache level, of low size, and its materialization doesn't imply extra costs overhead. In the same figure, the rectangle shows the proactive proposals: they introduce the speculative perspective, trying to predict the users' needs, and, with that knowledge, prepare in advance the suitable OLAP structures. Prefetching caches or cube restructuring (by dynamic recomputing of future useful subcubes) are possible solutions in this class of proposals (Belo, 2000; Park, Kim, and Lee, 2003; Sapia, 2000) and employ a cache whose admission and substitution of subcubes (or fragments) politics uses a prediction of its future usefulness.

Quitting the time axis, we enter in the distributed approaches. The first proposal has emerged only recently. The traditional solutions have now new issues: nodes' processing power and nodes' storage space, communication costs and parallel processing. In (Bauer & Lehner, 2003) cube distribution is solved with a greedy approach, with materialized space constraint, considering communication costs and processing power only as a ratio. Maintenance costs are explicitly not included.

In this paper, we try to evolve the cost model towards real world entities: we have a number of heterogeneous nodes characterized by a maximal storage space and a processing power, interconnected with a heterogeneous communication network, characterized by real network and communication parameters. We also consider maintenance costs as an additive to query cost and we're going to use genetic and co-evolutionary genetic algorithms, trying to surpass the known disadvantages of greedy approaches: as a non-look-back construction heuristic, its proposed solutions may be clearly non-optimal.

COSTS IN THE M-OLAP ENVIRONMENT

We're going to consider that the spatial range of the distribution is short: a few meters or some near buildings, meaning this that a local area network, possibly with a high bandwidth, links the OLAP architecture's nodes. But this distributed scenario may be extended even more: the nodes may inhabit at remote sites, far from each other, and a wide area network (WAN) may be considered, what would change the considered communication parameters. Thus, this latter architecture is a generalization of the former one. Now, as query users may be geographically widespread (which is common, given the globalization and consequent dispersion of decision competences), there may be place for additional query savings (as the data sources may be sited at near places, lowering communication costs). But this scenario, given nowadays user's needs and the available technology, is, as generally accepted, no more than an academic model entity.

A new study and research may be performed, trying to find the border conditions that would justify such architectural paradigm. If maintenance costs are not considered (as is the case of dynamic proposals), that architecture makes all sense, as, supposing the geographic distribution of queries, transporting OLAP data to their utilization, which is possible with a correct allocation of the subcubes to nodes, will imply lower communication costs and faster answering times. Also, a possible priority level of users (imagine CEO needs that might be satisfied in a hurry) may justify the remote OLAP sites. But, when maintenance costs are taken in account, the local use of OLAP data implies an extra cost (the move of data needed to update the OLAP structures).

The core question that has to be answered, given a widespread OLAP architecture and a geographic and priority query profile, is to know when the query savings surpass the maintenance costs. Simply, we may say that, if maintenance costs are low and there is a concentration of high priority queries in any distant site, remote OLAP nodes may be beneficial. Having a cost model (that is an easy extension of the one that we are about to describe), we may intend to conduct an analytical analysis towards the solution of that function. But, this discussion is clearly beyond the purpose of the present work and then, in this paper, our M-OLAP architecture is restricted to a limited area, considering only local OLAP nodes.

The purpose of any OLAP system is the minimization of query costs (and possibly the maintenance ones), having a space constraint by node that has to obey to the maintenance time constraint previously defined (we consider that the DW has a twofold division: query time period and maintenance period). The distributed nature of M-OLAP architecture results in two distinct kinds of costs: 1) intrinsic costs due to scan/aggregation or integration, known from now on as processing costs, and 2) communication costs. Both are responsible for the query and maintenance costs. To compute the processing cost it is assumed that the linear cost model (Harinarayan, Harinarayan, Rajaraman, and Ullman, 1996) is used, in which the cost of evaluating a query equals the number of non-null cells in the aggregated cube used to answer the query. Communication costs are function of a set of parameters that characterizes the way data travels by inter-node connections and the communication technology.

As said, in this paper, instead of using records as the unit of costs, we are going to use time, as it matches the purpose of the undertaken optimization – minimizing the answering time to the user's queries – and, on the other hand, time also comes to sight concerning to the other cost: maintenance time.

Intrinsic Processing Costs

Previously, we presented the *lattice* and dependence relations that allow the computation of a subcube using any ancestor. No matter if we have to calculate a subcube to perform its maintenance (incremental or integral), or to answer a query named by this subcube, the processing costs are the same, essentially due to three main reasons: 1) a subcube query has a subcube as target, so, it can be nominated by the target subcube on its own; 2) a subcube whose cells have the aggregations related to all attributes that appear in any query's selection condition , may be used to answer to the query; 3) besides, if the target subcube isn't materialized, the lattice structure may be inspected to ancestors' searching. If only a part of the subcube is processed, as when a delta maintenance method is used, or if a selection condition exists in the query (and suitable indexes), that may be accounted by a factor, here denoted as extent, u_e (update extent) and q_e (query extent) respectively.

Then the intrinsic processing costs, of a subcube s_i, assuming the linear cost model is $C_p(S_i) = |Anc(S_i)|$, and query costs $Cq(Qi, M) = Cp(Qi, M).fq_i.q_{e_i}$,

where fq_i is the frequency of the query i. Expressing this cost in terms of the cube notion, where there is a mapping from the query set Q to the subcube set S: $Cq(Qi, M) = |Anc(Si, M)|.fq_i.q_{e_{q_i}}$.

Its minimization

$$Cq(Qi, M) = Min(|Anc(Si, M)|).fq_i.q_{e_{q_i}} \qquad (1)$$

where $Min(|Anc(Si, M)|)$ is the minimum live ancestor (MLA) (Shim, Scheuermann, and Vingralek, 1999) the ancestor of S_i of minimal size that is materialized in M.

A similar expression may be deduced concerning to maintenance costs, only having to add an additional term, corresponding to the integration costs, proportional to the size of the generated subcube or delta.

Communication Costs

The following parameters will be used to define, in the context of this work, a communication link: Binary Debit (BD), a measure of the number of bits (liquid or total) that traverse a communication channel by unit of time (in bps) and Latency (La), a measure of the time elapsed between the communication request (or need) and its effective beginning. Many other parameters may be considered as Transit Delay (TD), Size Packet (Sp), Time to Make a Connection (TMC), used in connectionless links; it may also include time spending to virtual channel establishing. But, given the space range of the communication links considered in this study, the communication cost of transmitting data between nodes i and j can be assumed to be linear and restricted to, as follows:

$$CC_{ij} = Np * Sp / BD + La \qquad (2)$$

where Np is the number of data packets to transfer.

We may also consider the cost of query redirecting, which corresponds to the transmission of the message between the accepting node and answering node. In this case, it is supposed that this message has a constant size of 100 bytes.

M-OLAP Environment Total Costs

Summing up, the model we intend to design might be a generic one, able to be applied on multi node OLAP architectures. Contributing to query costs, it's important to consider the costs of data scan (and aggregate) of the ancestor's cube on its own (*Csa*) and the costs incurred in its transmission and query redirecting (*Ccom*). Then, the total costs of answering a query Qi, at a node j, are the sum of the intrinsic processing costs (eq. 1) with communication costs (eq. 2), if the living ancestor is located in any node except for j. If we have a set of queries Q,

$$Cq(Q, M) = \sum_{q_i \in Q} min(|Anc(S_i, M)| + Ccom|S_i|).fq_{q_i}.q_{e_{q_i}} \qquad (3)$$

Similarly, to maintenance cost, we have to sum the costs of data scan (and aggregate) of the ancestor subcube on its own, the costs incurred in its transmission and the costs of its integration into the destination node. Then, the maintenance costs of a distribution M of subcubes is:

$$Cm(M) = \sum_{S_i \in M} min(|Anc(S_i, M)| + Ccom(S_i) + |S_i|).f_u.u_e \qquad (4)$$

Adopting time as the cost referential, the processing power of an OLAP node where Anc_s or Anc_{q_i} inhabits may be used to convert records in time, what comes to introduce a new model parameter, Pp_{Node}, the processing power of Node n, in $records.s^{-1}$.

Finally, using equation 2, equations 3 and 4 may be rewritten as (see Equation 5. and Equation 6.) where $|S_i|.8.8$, is the size (in bits) of subcube

Equation 5.

$$Cq(Q, M) = \sum_{q_i \in Q} \min(|Anc(S_i, M)| / Pp_n + (|S_i|.8 + 100).8) / BD + 2.La).fq_{q_i}.qe_{q_i} \tag{5}$$

Equation 6.

$$Cm(M) = \sum_{S_i \in M} \min(|Anc(S_i, M)| / Pp_n + |S_i|.8.8 / BD + La + |S_i|).f_u.u_e \tag{6}$$

S_i (supposing that each cell has 8 bytes – size of a double type number in many representations), that may have to be corrected to an integer number of packets, if the communication link has a minimal packet size.

PRACTICAL EXAMPLE

We shall consider the distributed *lattice* of Figure 1 and a M-OLAP architecture with 3 OLAP server nodes. The architecture is presented in Figure 4, where all communication and node parameters are also shown.

To simplify, let's suppose that each OSN supports the OLAP database and also serves a users' community, accepting its queries, analyzing then in order to decide the node where it may be answered, providing its possible redirection. That is saying that in this simplified architecture, we don't have dedicated middleware server(s), but that function is executed on a peer-to-peer basis by all OSNs. In this example, we also consider that the communication costs between the user

Figure 4. A user poses a query Q (ps-) using a LAN to a M-OLAP architecture with three OLAP server nodes, interconnected with a high speed network with BD=1Gbps and La=50ms. The query answering costs are shown in brackets, whose minimal value must be selected

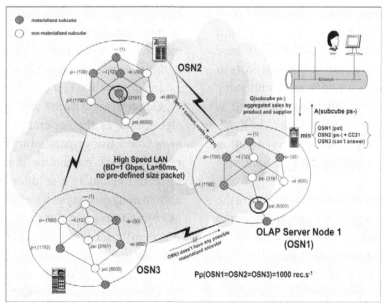

and any of the OSN are equal, and, then, they may be despised.

The user connects to OSN1 and poses a query Q *(ps-)*, pretending to know the aggregated sales by product and supplier. In Figure 4, the subcubes marked with a circle are the ancestors of subcube *(ps-)*, possible sources of query answer. If OSN1 supplies the answer, only processing costs has to be considered; OSN3 cannot be used, as none of its materializing subcubes is able to answer the query; subcube *(ps-)* of OSN2 may be used, having also communication costs (shown in the same figure).

Applying eq. 5,

Cq(Q*(ps-)*,M)=6000/1000 = 6 s, if *(pst)* of OSN1 was used;
Cq(Q*(ps-)*,M)=3164/1000+(3164*8*8+100*8)/ 1E9+2*0.05 = 3.26 s, if *(ps-)* of OSN2 was used.

This way, OSN2 is elected to answer to this query.

PROPOSED ALGORITHMS

In order to demonstrate our approach we present three distinct algorithms: the first one is of a greedy type (M-OLAP Greedy), derived from the proposal in (Bauer & Lehner, 2003), where we add the maintenance costs to the total costs to minimize; the second is based on an evolutionary approach (M-OLAP Genetic); and the third is based on a co-evolutionary approach (M-OLAP Co-Evol-GA). The purpose of this triple solution is related with the affording of a comparative valuation.

The choice of the co-evolutionary variant of the genetic algorithm was settled by its indication to problems of high complexity (Potter & Jong, 1994), which will be certainly the case of a real DW. The original co-evolutionary genetic algorithm was modified in such a way that its performance in cube

selection and allocation problem was improved, as we shall see. The normal genetic approach was also developed to compare and appraise the effective advantages of the co-evolutionary genetic algorithm, justifying its use.

We also designed and developed parallel query and maintenance cost estimation algorithms (to be used as fitness function in genetic algorithms and to allow the computation of the gain in the Greedy algorithm). In this paper, we discuss informally and present formally the query cost algorithm, whose design is based on some approaches referred in (Loureiro & Belo, 2006b), where a parallel design is described, and also a formal presentation of three maintenance cost estimation algorithms.

M-OLAP Greedy Algorithm

The M-OLAP Greedy algorithm is a multi-node extended version using greedy heuristics. It may use two benefit metrics: gain and density of gain. Its formal description is shown in Algorithm 1.

Basically, the algorithm takes a distributed aggregation *lattice* and storage limit per OLAP node as input. As long as storage capacity is left into each node, the algorithm selects the peer node/subcube with the highest benefit to materialize. Moreover, to solve ties when there are two or more identical benefits values, a strategy to pick the one at the network node which has the highest storage space left is applied.

Introduction to Genetic Algorithms

Genetic algorithms are population based algorithms, as they operate on a *population* of *individuals*, using a parallel approach to the search process. Every population is called *generation*. Each individual is a solution for the problem, known as a *phenotype*. Solutions are represented as *chromosomes*, in this case, on a binary form. A general description of a genetic algorithm (GA) may be found in (Goldberg, 1989). In its very core, a genetic algorithm tries to capitalize, in complex solutions for problems, the biological

Algorithm 1. M-OLAP greedy algorithm

```
Input:   L // Lattice with all granularity's combinations
    E=(E₁... Eₙ.) ; Q=(Q₁... Qₙ) // Maximal storage nodes' space and Query set and its nodes' distribution
    P=(P₁... Pₙ.); X=(X₁... Xₙ.) // Nodes' processing power and Connections and their parameters
Output: M // Materialized subcubes selected and allocated

Begin
// initialize with all empty nodes; in node 0 inhabits the base virtual relation,
// whose size is supposed to be 3x the subcube of lower granularity
    M← { c₀ }

    While ( ∃ Eₙ > 0 AND ∃ c : B(M ⋃ {c}) > B(M)  Do:  // while there is available storage space in any node and a possible benefit

        c_opt ←  ∅ ; B ( { c_opt },M) : ←  0; // searching of a subcube c in any node with maximal benefit
        ForEach node n:

            ForEach (c ∈ {L – M} ) // not yet materialized subcubes in the node; compute the query gain to each of descendent subcubes

                ForEach ( i ∈ { descendent (c) } )
                    B ({c},M,P,X) ← B({c}, M,P,X) + (C (i, M,P,X) – C (i, M ⋃ {c},P,X))

                End ForEach
                B ({c},M,P,X) ← B({c}, M,P,X) – CM(c, M,P,X) // subtract maintenance costs
            End ForEach
            If (B{c}, M,P,X) > B({c_opt}, M,P,X) // tests c as the subcube that provides the maximal gain
                c_opt ← c
            End If
        End ForEach
        If ( Eₙ – Size( {c_opt} ) > 0) // if there is available storage space, adds the optimal subcube to M

            M ← M ⋃ {c_opt} ; P ← Update (P, M);  // adds the newly select subcube to M and update processing power

            X[i...n] ← Update (X[i...n], M);  Eₙ ← Eₙ – size( {c_opt} ) // update BD available in each connection and storage space in node n
        Else
            Eₙ ← 0
        End If
    EndWhile
    Return (M)
End
```

evolution process, a known successful and robust fitness method.

Genetic algorithms (Holland, 1992) may search hypothesis spaces, having complex inter-acting parts, where the impact of each one in the generic fitness hypothesis may be difficult to model. Basically, a genetic algorithm begins with a random population (groups of *chromosomes*) and, in each *generation*, some parents are selected and an *offspring* is generated, using operations that try to mimic biological processes, usually, *crossover* and *mutation*. Adopting the *survival of the fittest principle*, all chromosomes are evaluated using a *fitness function* to determine their fitness values (the quality of each solution), which are then used to decide whether the individuals are kept to propagate or discarded (through the selection process). Individuals with higher fitness have a corresponding higher probability of being kept and thus generating offspring, contributing to the genetic fund of the new population. The new generated population replaces the old one and

the whole process is repeated until a specific termination criterion is satisfied, usually, a given number of generations. The chromosome with the highest fitness value in the last population gives the solution to the problem.

Given the scope of this paper, we only give some details about the genetic operators and selection mechanism. As said early, GA use mainly two kinds of genetic operators: Crossover and Mutation. The crossover operation is used to generate offspring by exchanging bits in a pair of individuals (parents), although multi-parents may be also possible. There are diverse forms of crossovers, but here we adopted the simplest, the one point crossover. A randomly generated point is used to split the genome and the portions of the two individuals divided by this point are changed to form the offspring. The mutation operator is a means of the occasional random alteration of the value of a genome, changing some elements in selected individuals. It introduces new features that may not be present in any member of the

Figure 5. Co-evolutionary approach where the normal genetic population is divided into subpopulations, known as species

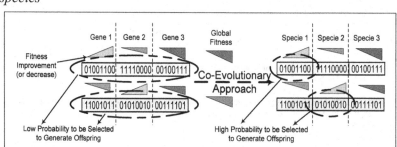

population, leading to additional genetic diversity, which helps the searching process to escape from local optimal traps.

M-Olap Co-Evolutionary Genetic Algorithm with Semi-Random Genome Completion

With complexity problem rising, a genetic algorithm shows an increasing difficulty to attain good solutions. As the fitness evaluation is global, an improvement in a gene of the chromosome may be submerged by degradations in other(s), being lost the good gene, as the individual will have a low global fitness value and its survival probability will be low too.

As we can see in Figure 5 (at left), a positive evolution was observed in the first and second genes of individual one and two, respectively, but, as fitness evaluation is made globally, those improvements are submerged by the degradation of one or more of the other genes of the individual, resulting in a low global fitness. Both individuals have then a low probability of being selected to generate offspring, and the gene improvement will be, probably, lost. But this weakness might be surpassed, if each gene was the genome of one individual: any improvement may generate offspring, as the fitness is now evaluated gene by gene (where each gene is now a population's member). We have to pay an additional cost corresponding to a higher number of fitness evaluations (s many times as the species' number), but the final balance may be profitable. This is the proposal described in (Potter & Jong, 1994), where the cooperative

evolutionary approach is described. The solution's hind arose with the perception that to the evolution of increasing complex structures, explicit notions of modularity have to be introduced, in order to provide a reasonable evolution opportunity for complex solutions, as interacting co-adapted components. Figure 5 (at right) shows the solution, where each gene population forms a specie (a different population).

In practice: 1) the population is composed of several subpopulations (denoted as species), each one representing a component of the potential solution; 2) the complete solution is obtained by the congregation of the representative members of each of the present species; 3) the credit granting to each specie is defined in terms of the fitness of the complete solutions where specie's members participate; 4) the evolution of each specie is like the one of a standard genetic algorithm – in Algorithm 2 it is shown the formal description of the M-OLAP Co-Evolutionary Genetic algorithm (M-OLAP Co-Evol-GA).

The fitness evaluation referred previously in 3) may be done in two different ways: at the initial generating population phase (generation 0), the genome completion is made by randomly selecting individuals of each of the other species; in all other generations (evolutionary phase), the best individual of the other species is chosen. That is precisely here that the co-genetic approach may reveal some limitations: if there are specific interdependences, as it is the case, given the subcubes'

Algorithm 2. M-OLAP co-evolutionary genetic algorithm with semi-random complete genome completion

```
Input:   L // Lattice with all granularity's combinations
         E=(E₁... Eₙ.) ; Q=(Q₁... Qₙ) // Maximal storage nodes' space and query set and its distribution
         P=(P₁... Pₙ.); X=(X₁... Xₙ.) // Nodes' processing power and connections and their parameters
Output: M // Materialized subcubes selected and allocated

Begin
// initialize with all empty nodes; in node 0 inhabits the base virtual relation, whose size is supposed to be 3x the subcube of lower
granularity
     M← { c₀ }
     ForEach node n // generate the initial population: each specie represents the subcubes to materialize in each node
        Popn(gen) ← randomly generating each specie's population
        While                        do: // randomly discard subcubes to meet the spatial constraint
             ∑     | Sᵤ |> Eₙ
           sᵤ∈M
           a ← random number [1...max.subcubes]; Mₙ ← Mₙ \ {Suₐ} // Mₙ = Su1...n,n, represents the subcubes in node n
        End While
     Next n
     ForEach node n // evaluate the fitness of each individual in Popn(gen)
        ForEach individual i in Mn
           // global_genome is generated with the gen. of indiv./specie in evaluation + the gen. of random indiv. of each of the other
species
           global_genome ← Popₙ(gen)
           ForEach node \{n} nn
              global_genome ? global_genome ∪ random(Popₙₙ(gen))
           Next nn
           fitness ( i ) ← fₐ (global_genome, M,I,P,X) // fitness of individual I, where fₐ is the fitness function
        Next i
     Next n
     While termination criterion = false do // loop: evolution of the population
        gen ← gen + 1
        ForEach node n
           Clear the new population Popₙ(gen)
           While | Popₙ(gen)| < population_size do
              select two parents form Popₙ(gen - 1) with a selection mechanism and apply genetic operators
              perform crossover
              perform mutation
              Mₙ ← Map(Popₙ(gen)ₙ) // Mₙ is the mapping of genome to corresponding materialized subcubes
              Mₙ ← R(Mₙ) // invokes the repair method method if the genoma corresponds to an invalid M
                         // repairing may be random, by minimal fitness density loss or minimal fitness loss
              Popₙ(gen) ← UnMap(Mₙ)// unmaps Mₙ and places the offspring into Popₙ(gen)
           EndWhile
           ForEach individual i in Mn // fitness evaluation of each individual in Popₙ(gen)
              global_genome ← genome(i) // puts in global_genome the genome of individual i
              For each node \ {n} nn // generates global_genome with the best or a random individual of the remaining species
                 global_genome ← global_genome ∪ indiv_max_adapt(Popₙₙ(gen)) OR random (Popₙₙ(gen))
              Next nn
              fitness ( i ) ← fₐ (global_genome, M,I,P,X) // evaluation of the fitness of individual i
           Next i
        Next n
     End While
     Return (M) // returns genomes of best individual of each specie that altogether show the best fitness
End
```

inter and intra-nodes relationships, a better solution may be invalidated if in another node the best individual implies in higher maintenance costs due to the solution's "improvement", without surpassing improvements in query costs. As the evolution operates specie by specie, the algorithm falls in a dead lock loop: an improvement in the best individual of specie S1 is invalidated by the better individual in specie S2 and reversely. Then, it is impossible for the algorithm to visit some of the areas, and the search of new promising solutions is progressively restricted, taking place a premature convergence phenomenon. The algorithm falls in sub-optimal solutions from where it's impossible to get out (not even a casual chirurgic mutation will cause the surpassing of this local minimum, as mutations operate also at specie's level).

To solve this problem, we have to allow that the selection of individuals of other species to generate a "complete solution genome" isn't so deterministic. Instead of selecting only the best genome in each of the other species, other individuals, for each specie, are randomly selected too. The situation is apparently solved, but a complete random selection of the individuals (as in generation 0) caused non-convergence phenomenon. Then, an intermediate solution was adopted: with probability p the best individual of each specie is selected; otherwise, a random individual of the same specie is chosen. Using a threshold, this "completion genome selection mechanism" may be more or less close to the (Potter & Jong, 1994), proposal. We also made another change in the original co-evolutionary genetic algorithm: we introduced an inter-specie crossing, with probabilistic hybrid production, tending to make possible a greater genetic diversity, whose final effects are similar to a large scale mutation.

M-OLAP Cube Selection Problem Genetic Coding

In order to apply a genetic algorithm to any problem, we have to solve two main issues: 1) how to code the problem into the genome and

2) how to evaluate each solution (defining the fitness function).

The former question is straightforward (shown in Figure 6). As we deal with a combinatorial problem, each subcube may be (1) or may not be (0) materialized in each node, and any combination of materialized / non-materialized subcube may be admissible, having then to observe the applied constraints. In terms of the genome of each element of the population in the genetic algorithm, this may be coded as a binary string: each bit has the information about the materialization of each subcube. E.g. the materialized cube views M of the 3 node's lattice in Figure 6 is coded as (11001011010100100011101), as shown on the corresponding genetic mapping.

When co-evolutionary genetic mapping is on concern, it's almost the same, but, as we have seen in the last section, we have three species (as many as the number of OLAP nodes); so, each genome has the information of M concerning to each node. Only the juxtaposition of the genome of individuals of all three species builds a solution.

Figure 6. Genetic coding of the distributed cube selection and allocation problem into the genome of a normal and co-evolutionary genetic algorithms

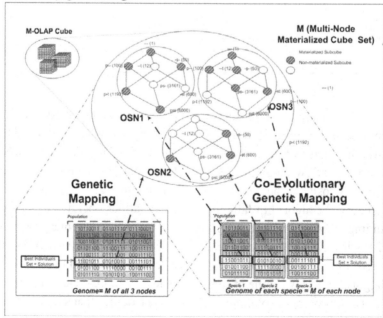

Fitness Function: Cost Estimation Algorithms

Let's discuss the second question left in the last section: how to evaluate each proposed solution.

As we discussed, we deal with two kinds of costs, whose minimizing is the objective function of the algorithms. Then, to develop the fitness func-

tion, we must apply eq. 5 and 6, but with parallel tasks execution. This way, we used maintenance cost estimation algorithms described in (Loureiro & Belo, 2006b), which may be looked for further details, especially concerning to parallel execution tasks simulation. We also design and developed a query costs estimation algorithm, M-OLAP PQ-CEA, which is the acronym of Multi-Node OLAP

Algorithm 3. M-OLAP PQCEA, a multi-node OLAP parallel query cost estimation algorithm

```
Input:   L // Lattice with all granularity's combinations
         Ei=(Ei_{1,1...n},...,Ei_{n,...n}) // Extension of query use of each node/subcube
         Fi=(Fi_{1...n,1},...., Fi_{1...n,n},Si)// Query's nodes distribution and frequency
         M=(Su_{1...n,1},...., Su_{1...n,n}) // Subcubes' allocation to nodes
         P=(P_1... P_n.) // Processing power in each node
         X=(X_1... X_n.) // // Communication connections and their parameters

Output:  C(Q,(I,M,Fi,Ei,P,X))// answering cost to queries given M, Fi, Ei, P and X

  1. Initialization: C(Q)← 0, nWindow; // query cost=0
     1.1. Batch loading: loads batch with all queries to process
  2. Query processing:
     2.1. For Each Query Q in Batch
        2.1.1. Finds materialized node/subcube n_s:
               // looks for an ancestor that is the ancestor of lower cost or the one with the next lower cost
               // (when is looking for alternate ancestors), ancestor is a peer node/subcube
               n_s ← next minimal ancestor(Q)
               costProc← costScan/Aggr(n_s) // cost of producing s(Q) from s into node n, where s(Q) is subcube Q
               costComm← costComm(s(Q),n→n(Q)) // cost of transporting s(Q) from n to n(Q), the node where was received Q
        2.1.2. If there isn't any ancestor, uses the base relation:
               n← 0; // 0 is the base node
               costProc← baseCost // processing cost is the defined base processing cost
               costComm← costComm(s(q),0→n(Q)) // cost of transporting s(Q) from base node to n(Q)
     2.2. Alocates query processing of Q to node n OR try to find an alternate ancestor OR Closes current window
          if there isn't any idle node able to process Q from any minimal ancestor within an admissible cost:
        2.2.1. If found an ancestor but busyNode[n]=true
               // an ancestor is found but is located at a busy node: try to find another alternate ancestor
               look for alternate ancestor = true
               repeat 2.1.1. thru 2.1.2.
        2.2.1. If there are no materialized ancestors AND is not looking for alternate ancestor AND base node is idle
               // allocates processing of Q to base node and adds costs to current window costs
               busyNode[0] ←true, valUsoProc[0] ← costProc, valUsoCom[0,n(Q)] ← valUsoCom[0,n(Q)]+costComm
               Process Next Query
        2.2.2. Else If there is no materialized ancestor AND is not looking for alternate ancestor AND base node busy
               // current query only may be answered by base relation but base node is already busy:
               // nothing more could be done to surpass the conflict; we have to close this window and reprocess this query
               currWinProcCost← max(costProc[any node] // computes the maximal proc. cost of any node
               currWinCommCost← max(costComm[any node→any node] // computes maximal comm. cost of any comm. link
               busyNode[any node] ← false; // all nodes are set to idle
               nWindow++; // increments window number
               // query cost updating
               C(Q) ← C(Q) + currWinProcCost+currWinCommCost* F(Q)*E(Q) // F(Q) and E(Q)are query frequency and extension
               Reprocess Current Query
        2.2.3. Else If is looking for an alternate ancestor AND none is found
               // nothing more can be done, close this window and reprocess current query
               Execute processing alike 2.2.1.
        2.2.4. Else If is looking for alternate ancestor AND found one AND query cost admissible
               // found alternate node at an admissible cost: process this query
               busyNode[n] ←true, valUsoProc[n] ← costProc, valUsoCom[n,n(Q)] ← valUsoCom[n,n(Q)]+costComm
               Process Next Query
        2.2.5. Else If is looking for alternate ancestor AND found one AND query cost not admissible
               // an alternate ancestor is found but its costs is higher than the admissible; close this window and reprocess current query
               Execute processing alike 2.2.2.
        2.2.6. Else If is not looking for alternate ancestor and an ancestor is found
               // process current query and allocate answering node
               Execute processing alike 2.2.4.
     2.3. // all queries processed: accumulates cost of last window
          currWinProcCost← max(costProc[any node] // computes the maximal proc. cost of any node
          currWinCommCost← max(costComm[any node→any node] // computes maximal comm. cost of any comm. link
          C(Q) ← C(Q) + currWinProcCost + currWinCommCost*F(Q)*E(Q) // F(Q) and E(Q)query frequency and extension
  3. Return Query cost:
     Return C(Q) // returns estimated query cost
```

Parallel Query Cost Estimation Algorithm, whose formal description is made in Algorithm 3.

This algorithm supposes a batch with all queries and then tries to allocate queries to OSNs on a parallel fashion, trying to use the inherent parallelism of M-OLAP architecture. To compute the costs, the algorithm uses the window concept adopted and described in (Loureiro & Belo, 2006b), a simpler version of pipeline processing of tasks, no more than a way to divide the time into succeeding discrete intervals, where tasks run in a parallel fashion, and which time value (the maximal cost of any set of conjoint tasks that forms a transaction) are latter used to compute the total cost of query answering.

As run-time speed is at premium, we select heuristics that aren't so complicated. It won't execute any query look-ahead function in order to make any try to perform query reordering, when the next query has to be processed by an already busy node. When such a situation occurs, it only tries to find an alternate ancestor which may be processed by a free node. If this strategy was no longer successful, it simply conforms to the situation, and one or more nodes have no tasks to perform in this window (something like a stall when talking about pipeline processing). Possibly, that heuristic leads to a pessimistic approach, but certainly more optimistic and near to reality than the simpler sequential query execution, where only one node would be used in each time interval.

Summarizing, this means that, in each window, if a query is allocated to node *x* and that same node would be usually elected to process next query, the algorithm doesn't look for another (future) unanswered query to allocate to other free node, but it tries to find an alternate ancestor, that may be processed into a free node, although at a higher cost. But this cost must be within a defined threshold (a defined parameter, a factor applied to current window size), meaning this that it only accepts the other ancestor, if its cost was not much higher than the total processing costs of the current window. Then, the use of alternate

subcube, implies almost no extra cost, as it uses time already spent to process other query(ies) on allocated node(s), putting a lazy node to work.

EXPERIMENTAL EVALUATION

We used an object oriented approach in the design of the algorithms. Subsequently, in the implementation phase, we made some adjusts in order to optimize the performance.

Classes

Figure 7 shows the simplified class diagram of the developed system. In this diagram, classes corresponding to the general and specific base parameters and also the I/O services are shown as subsystems. This diagram wasn't implemented in a "pure" form. We opted by arrays to store the intensive data processing structures, as its performance is considered the fastest and the algorithms' performance is at premium.

A brief analysis to the algorithms allows retaining the main architectural components and corresponding classes related to the:

1. Data cube, with subcubes' information, dimensional hierarchies (including parallel hierarchies support) and frequency and extension of updates (classes Cube, SubCube, DimParallel, DimHierarq, SCubesDependencies);
2. Queries, identifying the queries, receiving node, its frequency and utilization extension (class QueryNode);
3. M-OLAP architecture, as OLAP server nodes, available materialization storage space, processing power, connection links and its functional parameters and some additional information: installed hardware, localization, etc., (class Nodes and CommLinks);

Figure 7. Simplified class diagram, corresponding to the system's data classes, developed to an experimental evaluation of the algorithms

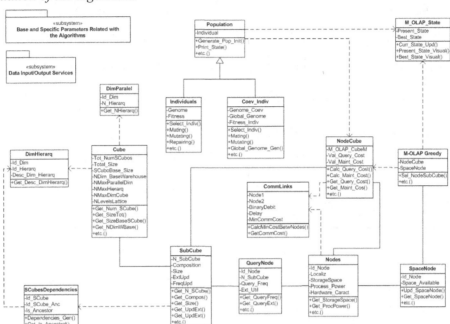

4. Global and specific parameters set, that allows the system to know how to set up the data structures of the algorithms and manage the algorithm's run-time (subsystem Base and Specific Parameters Related with the Algorithms);

5. Data structures that support the state managed by the algorithms, as: distribution of subcubes by the different nodes (M_OLAP_State class); to the *greedy* algorithm, the available space in each node (Space_Node class), and, for the *genetic* algorithm, genomes' population (Population, Individuals and Coev_Indiv classes);

6. M-OLAP greedy algorithm (M-OLAP Greedy class)

7. Query and maintenance cost estimation of any cube distribution (Node_Cube class);

8. Present state and best solution achieved by the algorithms, and visualization of these states(class M_OLAP_State);

9. Input/output data services (Data Input/Output Services subsystem), generating the data

persistence concerning to internal states or statistical information used in experimental tests.

Algorithms Application

For test data, we have used the test set of Benchmark's (TPC-R 2002), selecting the smallest database (1 GB), from which we selected 3 dimensions (customer, product and supplier). To broaden the variety of subcubes, we added additional attributes to each dimension (as shown in Figure 8), generating hierarchies, as follows: customer (*c-n-r-all*); product (*p-t-all*) and (*p-s-all*); supplier (*s-n-r-all*). It's important to emphasize that the product dimension shows parallel hierarchies. This way, the algorithm's implementation should bear this characteristic. As we have 3 dimensions, each one with 4 hierarchies, that makes a total of 4x4x4=64 possible subcubes, presented in Table 1, jointly with their sizes (in tuples). We also supposed that the cost of using base relations is three times the cost of subcube cps. Greedy2PRS Algorithm

Table 1. Generated subcubes with dimensions described in [TPC-R 2002] and described additional hierarchies' attributes

Subcube	Size	Subcube	Size	Subcube	Size	Subcube	Size
0 cps	6,000,000	16 nps	5,000,000	32 rps	4,000,000	48 -ps	800,000
1 cpn	6,000,000	17 npn	5,000,000	33 rpn	4,000,000	49 -pn	800,000
2 cpr	6,000.000	18 npr	5,000,000	34 rpr	4,000,000	50 -pr	800,000
3 cp-	6,000.000	19 np-	5,000,000	35 rp-	1,000,000	51 -p-	200,000
4 css	5,000,000	20 nss	500,000	36 rss	2,500,000	52 -ss	500,000
5 csn	5,000,000	21 nsn	30,000	37 rsn	6,250	53 -sn	1,250
6 csr	5,000,000	22 nsr	6,250	38 rsr	1,250	54 -sr	250
7 cs-	5,000,000	23 ns-	1,250	39 rs-	25	55 -s-	5
8 cts	5,390,000	24 nts	800,000	40 rts	3,000,000	56 -ts	1,500,000
9 ctn	5,390,000	25 ntn	30,000	41 rtn	18,750	57 -tn	3,750
10 ctr	5,390,000	26 ntr	18,750	42 rtr	3,750	58 -tr	750
11 ct-	5,390,000	27 nt-	3,750	43 rt-	750	59 -t-	150
12 c-s	6,000,000	28 n-s	250,000	44 r-s	50,000	60 --s	100,000
13 c-n	2,500,000	29 n-n	625	45 r-n	125	61 --n	25
14 c-r	500,000	30 n-r	125	46 r-r	25	62 --r	25
15 c--	150	31 n--	25	47 r--	5	63 ---	1

Figure 8. Dimensional hierarchies on customer, product and supplier dimensions of a TPC-R Benchmark database subset (using ME/R notation (Sapia, Blaschka, Höfling, and Dinter, 1998))

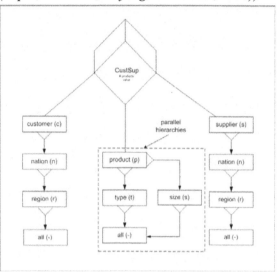

(Loureiro & Belo, 2006b) was used to compute the maintenance cost, supposing u_e=0.1 to all OSNs. Concerning to query cost estimation, q_e=1.

Figure 9 shows the simulation architecture: three OSN plus the base relation (considered as node 0) and a network. OLAP distributed middleware is in charge of receive user queries and provide for its OSN allocation, and correspond-

ing redirecting. As in the example of Figure 4, it is supposed that middleware services run into each OSN, on a peer-to-peer approach, although one or many dedicated servers may also exist.

Figure 9. M-OLAP architecture with distributed OLAP middleware

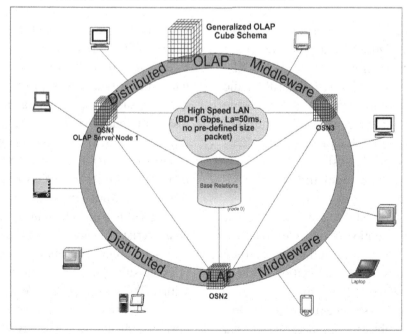

To simplify the computations, it is supposed that communication costs between OSNs and any user are equal (using a LAN), and then, may be neglected. Although remote user access may also be considered (through a WAN / Intranet), case where we would have to consider extra communication costs (and, perhaps, remote OSNs, possibly inhabiting clients or OLAP proxy servers), but this discussion and evaluation is left to a future work. We generated random query profiles (normalized in order to have a total number equal to the number of subcubes) that were supposed to induce the optimized M (materialized set of selected and allocated subcubes).

Performed Tests and Obtained Results

In the initial test we wanted to gain some insights about the tuning of some parameters of genetic algorithms, and then beginning the test set. We observed the easy convergence of both algorithms, even with small populations (e.g. 50). Moreover, we have seen immediately the superior performance of the co-Evolutionary variant, confirming

the choice made. Also both genetic algorithms have a superior performance than the Greedy algorithm. Then, we performed the initial test, where we evaluated comparatively the performance of all algorithms and the impact of the number of individuals of the population on the quality of the solutions achieved. We generated three different random query distributions, where all queries are present, only its frequency is different, but the total of queries is normalized to a number equal to the number of subcubes, what is saying that for any query distribution $\sum_{i=1}^{n} f_i = n$, where n is the number of subcubes and f_i, the frequency of query i. As genetic algorithms are inherently stochastic, each result of the test is the average of several runs of the algorithms (a number between three and seven). For the initial test, we used a population of 100 individuals and a maximal materializing space by node of 10% of the total materializing space needed to store all subcubes. The used genetic parameters appeared in Table 2.

The obtained results are shown in Figure 10. As we can see, M-OLAP Co-Evolutionary Genetic Algorithm with semi-random genoma completion

Table 2. Genetic parameters used in the most of the performed tests

Number of Generations	500
Selection type	Binary tournament (or competition) selection. Pick two randomly selected members and with 85% probability the fittest individual is selected. This probability intends to preserve the genetic diversity.
% Crossing	90%
Cross-Over	One point
Cross-Over Point	Randomly generated for each generation
% Mutation	5
Mutation probability	1 in each 8 bits
Way of dealing with invalid solutions	Randomly pick one bit set to 1 (corresponding to a materialized subcube) and setting it to 0 (the corresponding subcube becomes non-materialized). The process is repeated until the total materializing space is below the maximal materializing space, for generation, crossing and mutation operations.
Random Co-Evolutionary Genetic Genome Completion	With probability P=80%, the best individual of the other species is selected; with 1-P, a random individual is selected.
Inter Species Crossing Probability	10%

has a superior performance in all three query sets, with an average superiority of 33% in face to Normal GA and of 44% when compared to the Greedy algorithm. Another interesting feature of the algorithms that we are interested in analyzing is the speed in achieving the solution. For the same test, Figure 11 shows the evolution of the quality of the proposed solutions of both genetic algorithms. An initial fast evolution followed by an evolution with slower rate is clear. Around generation 100, there's an almost null variation,

signifying that the convergence has happened. This is an example, and other test conditions might behave differently, but these three clear stages may be identified. Also, this plot shows the superiority of co-Evolutionary algorithm version.

Concerning to the impact of the number of individuals in the population, we performed this same test with populations of 20, 50, 100 (of initial test), 200 and 500. Figure 12 shows the test's results. We observed that when the population was 20, the M-CoEvol-GA algorithm

Figure 10. Comparative performance of greedy and genetic algorithms (normal and co-evolutionary) for a population of 100 elements and a materializing space of 10%

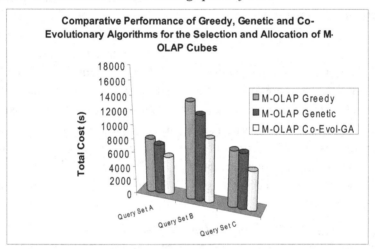

Figure 11. Evolution of the quality of the proposed solutions of both genetic algorithms

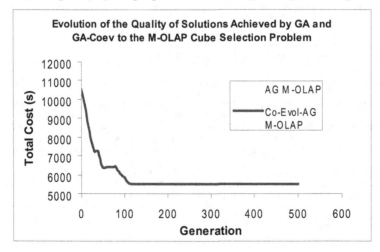

Figure 12. Impact of the population's individual's number on the quality of the achieved solutions of both genetic algorithms

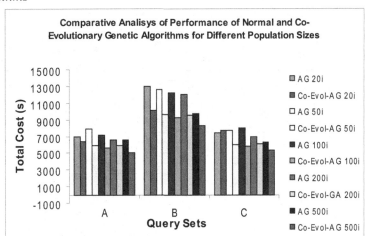

had difficulties to converge (it hadn't converged after 500 generations in several runs, especially when applied to query set C, what explains the bad obtained results for that case). Globally, we have observed that the number of the population's individuals has a positive impact on the quality of the solution. A 20 to 500 increase implies an increase of about 22% for normal GA and 30% for co-Evolutionary GA. This behavior is in pace with the information referred in (Lin & Kuo, 2004) although the GA is then applied to centralized OLAP approach.

A second test set tries to evaluate the behavior of the algorithms concerning to the complexity of the OLAP cube. For this purpose we used two different cube *lattices*: The original 64 cube with subcubes (that we will refer as cube A) and another one, more extensive, with 256 subcubes (referred

as cube B), generated from the former, adding another dimension: time, with hierarchy day(d)-month(m)-year(y)-all. The size of the new OLAP cube supposes one year of data and probabilities of generating a cell that is shown in Table 3.

With these assumptions, we generated the *lattice* shown on Table 4. Also, we generated other queries distribution (also normalized), which we have used to test all algorithms when applied to the cube B.

The results of total costs achieved when the algorithms were applied to cube B confirmed the results obtained with cube A: M-OLAP Co-Evol-GA is the best performer of them all. An example of the obtained results is shown in Table 5, for 100 individuals' population.

This test may also answer to another important evaluation feature of the algorithms: their scalability. We have to analyze the run-time of all three algorithms and measure the impact of the number of subcubes in the execution speed. This may also be used to evaluate the complexity of the algorithms, and, then, Table 5 also shows the run time needed to achieve the final solution. Its inspection shows that Greedy algorithm is the fastest when cube A is used. But that's not true for cube B: it shows an exponential increase of

Table 3. Probabilities of generating cells concerning the time dimension, using the existent 3 dimensions lattice.

New dim.	Existent lattice cube views			
Hierarchie	low-level	1 dim. colapsed	2 dim. colapsed	all colapsed
d(day)	20%	40%	60%	100%
m(month)	60%	80%	90%	100%
y(year)	90%	95%	100%	100%
- (all)	100%	100%	100%	100%

Table 4. Generated subcubes for the 256 cube lattice adding a time dimension with hierarchy day-month-year-all to the former customer-product-supplier dimensions

SubCube		Size	SubCube		Size	SubCube		Size	SubCube		Size
0	cpsd	438.000.000	64	cpsm	43.200.000	128	cpsy	5.400.000	192	cps-	6.000.000
1	cpnd	438.000.000	65	cpnm	43.200.000	129	cpny	5.400.000	193	cpn-	6.000.000
2	cssd	365.000.000	66	cssm	36.000.000	130	cssy	4.500.000	194	css-	5.000.000
3	ctsd	437.270.000	67	ctsm	43.128.000	131	ctsy	5.391.000	195	cts-	5.990.000
4	npsd	365.000.000	68	npsm	36.000.000	132	npsy	4.500.000	196	nps-	5.000.000
5	cprd	438.000.000	69	cprm	43.200.000	133	cpry	5.400.000	197	cpr-	6.000.000
6	csnd	365.000.000	70	csnm	36.000.000	134	csny	4.500.000	198	csn-	5.000.000
7	ctnd	437.270.000	71	ctnm	43.128.000	135	ctny	5.391.000	199	ctn-	5.990.000
8	c-sd	876.000.000	72	c-sm	57.600.000	136	c-sy	5.700.000	200	c-s-	6.000.000
9	npnd	365.000.000	73	npnm	36.000.000	137	npny	4.500.000	201	npn-	5.000.000
10	nssd	36.500.000	74	nssm	3.600.000	138	nssy	450.000	202	nss-	500.000
11	ntsd	58.400.000	75	ntsm	5.760.000	139	ntsy	720.000	203	nts-	800.000
12	rpsd	292.000.000	76	rpsm	28.800.000	140	rpsy	3.600.000	204	rps-	4.000.000
13	cp-d	876.000.000	77	cp-m	57.600.000	141	cp-y	5.700.000	205	cp--	6.000.000
14	csrd	365.000.000	78	csrm	36.000.000	142	csry	4.500.000	206	csr-	5.000.000
15	ctrd	437.270.000	79	ctrm	43.128.000	143	ctry	5.391.000	207	ctr-	5.990.000
16	c-nd	365.000.000	80	c-nm	24.000.000	144	c-ny	2.375.000	208	c-n-	2.500.000
17	nprd	365.000.000	81	nprm	36.000.000	145	npry	4.500.000	209	npr-	5.000.000
18	nsnd	2.190.000	82	nsnm	216.000	146	nsny	27.000	210	nsn-	30.000
19	ntnd	6.570.000	83	ntnm	648.000	147	ntny	81.000	211	ntn-	90.000
20	n-sd	36.500.000	84	n-sm	2.400.000	148	n-sy	237.500	212	n-s-	250.000
21	rpnd	292.000.000	85	rpnm	28.800.000	149	rpny	3.600.000	213	rpn-	4.000.000
22	rssd	182.500.000	86	rssm	18.000.000	150	rssy	2.250.000	214	rss-	2.500.000
23	rtsd	219.000.000	87	rtsm	21.600.000	151	rtsy	2.700.000	215	rts-	3.000.000
24	-psd	116.800.000	88	-psm	7.680.000	152	-psy	760.000	216	-ps-	800.000
25	cs-d	730.000.000	89	cs-m	48.000.000	153	cs-y	4.750.000	217	cs--	5.000.000
26	ct-d	874.540.000	90	ct-m	57.504.000	154	ct-y	5.690.500	218	ct--	5.990.000
27	c-rd	73.000.000	91	c-rm	4.800.000	155	c-ry	475.000	219	c-r-	500.000
28	np-d	730.000.000	92	np-m	48.000.000	156	np-y	4.750.000	220	np--	5.000.000
29	nsrd	456.250	93	nsrm	45.000	157	nsry	5.625	221	nsr-	6.250
30	ntrd	1.368.750	94	ntrm	135.000	158	ntry	16.875	222	ntr-	18.750
31	n-nd	91.250	95	n-nm	6.000	159	n-ny	593	223	n-n-	625
32	rprd	292.000.000	96	rprm	28.800.000	160	rpry	3.600.000	224	rpr-	4.000.000
33	rsnd	456.250	97	rsnm	45.000	161	rsny	5.625	225	rsn-	6.250
34	rtnd	1.368.750	98	rtnm	135.000	162	rtny	16.875	226	rtn-	18.750
35	r-sd	7.300.000	99	r-sm	480.000	163	r-sy	47.500	227	r-s-	50.000
36	-pnd	116.800.000	100	-pnm	7.680.000	164	-pny	760.000	228	-pn-	800.000
37	-ssd	73.000.000	101	-ssm	4.800.000	165	-ssy	475.000	229	-ss-	500.000
38	-tsd	219.000.000	102	-tsm	14.400.000	166	-tsy	1.425.000	230	-ts-	1.500.000
39	c--d	32.850.000	103	c--m	1.620.000	167	c--y	150.000	231	c---	150.000
40	ns-d	182.500	104	ns-m	12.000	168	ns-y	1.187	232	ns--	1.250
41	nt-d	547.500	105	nt-m	36.000	169	nt-y	3.562	233	nt--	3.750
42	n-rd	18.250	106	n-rm	1.200	170	n-ry	118	234	n-r-	125
43	rp-d	146.000.000	107	rp-m	9.600.000	171	rp-y	950.000	235	rp--	1.000.000
44	rsrd	91.250	108	rsrm	9.000	172	rsry	1.125	236	rsr-	1.250
45	rtrd	273.750	109	rtrm	27.000	173	rtry	3.375	237	rtr-	3.750
46	r-nd	18.250	110	r-nm	1.200	174	r-ny	118	238	r-n-	125
47	-prd	116.800.000	111	-prm	7.680.000	175	-pry	760.000	239	-pr-	800.000
48	-snd	182.500	112	-snm	12.000	176	-sny	1.187	240	-sn-	1.250
49	-tnd	547.500	113	-tnm	36.000	177	-tny	3.562	241	-tn-	3.750
50	--sd	21.900.000	114	--sm	1.080.000	178	--sy	100.000	242	--s-	100.000
51	n--d	5.475	115	n--m	270	179	n--y	25	243	n---	25
52	rs-d	3.650	116	rs-m	240	180	rs-y	23	244	rs--	25
53	rt-d	109.500	117	rt-m	7.200	181	rt-y	712	245	rt--	750
54	r-rd	3.650	118	r-rm	240	182	r-ry	23	246	r-r-	25
55	-p-d	43.800.000	119	-p-m	2.160.000	183	-p-y	200.000	247	-p--	200.000
56	-srd	36.500	120	-srm	2.400	184	-sry	237	248	-sr-	250
57	-trd	109.500	121	-trm	7.200	185	-try	712	249	-tr-	750
58	--nd	5.475	122	--nm	270	186	--ny	25	250	--n-	25
59	r--d	1.095	123	r--m	54	187	r--y	5	251	r---	5
60	-s-d	1.095	124	-s-m	54	188	-s-y	5	252	-s--	5
61	-t-d	32.850	125	-t-m	1.620	189	-t-y	150	253	-t--	150
62	--rd	5.475	126	--rm	270	190	--ry	25	254	--r-	25
63	---d	365	127	---m	12	191	---y	1	255	----	1

run-time with the number of subcubes (3,103,992 / 72,965 = 42.53) for a four times increase of the subcubes' number. This is in pace with the referred complexity of the original *greedy* algorithm's complexity ($O(kn^2)$ (Kalnis, Mamoulis, and Papadias, 2002)), is also squared in n, but it's dependent of k (number of the selected subcubes). In the M-OLAP Greedy, as we have N nodes, the former complexity values might be multiplied by N.

The same kind of analysis may be performed on GA. According to (Lin & Kuo, 2004), the original genetic algorithm with greedy repair has reported a value of $O(grn^2\log n)$, where g is the number of generations, r the size of the population and n the number of subcubes. Here we don't have greedy repair, but a N nodes number. Then, the complexity is only linear for Normal GA (771,319 / 237,739 = 3.2) and co-Evolutionary GA (2,802,646 / 323,906 = 8.6).

But the last analysis is somewhat fallacious: we compare final solutions run time, not the run time needed to achieve a given solution quality, in this case, the run time of Greedy algorithm. These new objectives produced the results that are shown in Table 6. The superiority of GA is perfectly visible; in this case normal GA seems to have the best relation speed / solution quality. The reason may be related with the inter-specie crossing that favoring the genetic diversity, hurts the speed of convergence. It's the price to pay for the observed high superiority concerning to the final solution quality.

Another important measure of the scalability of the algorithms is related with its performance behavior when the number of architecture's nodes was changed. Then, we performed another test using a 10 OSN + base node architecture, also

Table 5. Total costs, generations and run-time returned by greedy, normal and co-evolutionary genetic algorithms when applied to the 64 and 256 subcubes cube of an M-OLAP architecture, with 3 OSN + base node

3 OSN+1 nodes		64 SubCubes Cube	256 SubCubes Cube
Greedy	Final Solution Quality	7,790	801,174
Algorithm	Run Time	72,965	3,103,592
Genetic	Final Solution Quality	7,152	628,134
M-OLAP	Generations Needed	353	299
Algorithm	Run Time	237,739	771,319
Co-Evolutionary	Final Solution Quality	5,501	505,285
Genetic	Generations Needed	187	295
M-OLAP	Run Time	323,906	2,802,646

Table 6. Comparative analysis of costs, generations and run-time returned by greedy, normal and co-evolutionary genetic algorithms when applied to the 64 and 256 subcubes cube of an M-OLAP architecture, with 3 OSN + base node

3 OSN+1 nodes		64 SubCubes Cube	256 SubCubes Cube
M-OLAP	Final Solution Quality	7,790	801,174
Greedy	Run Time	72,965	3,103,592
M-OLAP	Comparable Sol. Quality	7,622	743,556
Genetic	Generations Needed	160	70
Algorithm	Run Time	116,077	197,534
M-OLAP	Comparable Sol. Quality	6,975	766,542
Co-Evolutionary	Generations Needed	27	80
Genetic Alg.	Run Time	55,833	582,969

for 10% materializing space by node, and using Cube A (64 subcubes).

This time, maintaining the former genetic parameters, normal GA reveals itself as the best performer. We observed that M-OLAP Co-Evol-GA has a difficult convergence. Looking for possible causes we thought immediately of inter-specie crossing as the disturbance cause. As the number of nodes is high, the 10% probability of inter-specie crossing works as a high mutation operator that hurts the evolution process. Then, we changed it to 2% and we also changed mutation tax to 2%, trying to limit the disturbance factors. The results are shown in Table 7. A better scalability of GA is clear, better for normal version. But this conclusion is somewhat changed if we compare the run time needed to co-Evolutionary version to achieve a solution comparable to normal GA when applied to 10 OSN+1: we observed that after 170 generations, co-Evolutionary GA version achieved a cost of 8,241, with a run time of 1,952.147, clearly less than the run time needed to achieve the final solution (about four times less).

We repeated the test for a population of 200 individuals: the results confirmed the conclusions, but now the quality of the genetic solutions was even better. We obtained a cost of 7,124 for normal GA, with a run time of 518,616 and 4,234, with a run time of 16,409,446 for co-Evolutionary version. And the quality was even improved when more generations (and run time) was allowed: 6,524/2,240,411 and 3,971/20,294,572, for the same values/algorithms respectively.

Run time values of 20,000 seconds are clearly excessive, but remember that we have used a laptop with an AMD Athlon XP-M 2500 processor. If a more powerful computer was used the execution times will be substantially lower and then inside real time limits. Also, a *peer-to-peer* parallel version may be intended, as it is of easy design and implementation, because of the remarkable parallel characteristics of co-Evolutionary GA. Both solutions will avoid the referred long run-time restriction and the performance gains will justify completely the extra power consumed.

This same test may also be used to gain some insights on the scale-up of the M-OLAP architecture. The estimated total cost was almost the same when a 3 OSN+1 or 10 OSN+1architecture were tested. This means that the M-OLAP architecture has an easy scale-up: an increase of query load accompanied by a proportional increase of power (processing and storage) almost maintains the total costs (the same query answering speed and size of maintenance window).

Still concerning to run time tests, it's also important to extend the preliminary analysis of the complexity already made when we discussed the results of Table 5. We now evaluate the impact of the number of individuals of the GA population and the execution run time costs. We used again all test parameters and conditions that generate the values shown in Figure 12. Then, we performed a tests' sequence with populations of 20, 50, 100, 200 and 500 individuals. The results are reported on the plot of Figure 13.

Table 7. Total costs, generations and run-time returned by greedy, normal and co-evolutionary genetic algorithms when applied to the 3 and 10 OSN + base node M-OLAP architecture

64 SubCubes		3 OSN+1 Nodes	10 OSN+1 Nodes
M-OLAP Greedy Algorithm	Final Solution Quality	7,790	12,461
	Run Time	72,965	517,243
M-OLAP Genetic Algorithm	Final Solution Quality	7,152	8,430
	Generations Needed	353	270
	Run Time	237,739	377,853
M-OLAP Co-Evolutionary Genetic Alg.	Final Solution Quality	5,501	6,811
	Generations Needed	187	670
	Run Time	323,906	8,036,837

Figure 13. Impact of the population individuals' number on the run-time of normal and co-evolutionary genetic algorithms, when applied to 64 subcubes cube and for 10% materializing space per node

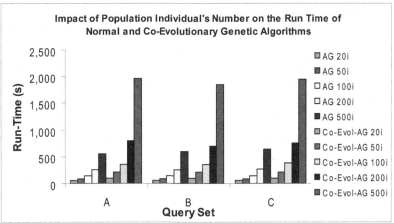

It's obvious the independence of run time with relation to the query set and it's also clear that it has a direct relation with the number of individuals of the population, confirming the analysis of (Lin & Kuo, 2004). What is more, it's clear that the co-Evolutionary version is substantially slower than the normal version. The reason for this behavior is simple: all genetic operations and fitness evaluation are directly proportional to the individuals' number; also, when co-Evolutionary version is

on concern, the number of fitness evaluations is higher, proportional to the number of nodes (equal to the number of species).

The next test tries to evaluate the impact of the materializing space limit by node on the quality of the solutions proposed by all three algorithms. This test may be highly valuable, as it gives some insights on the "best profit" materializing space. This way, we ran the algorithms for materializing spaces of 1, 2, 3, 5, 10, 20 and 30% of total mate-

Figure 14. Impact of the materializing space limit (by node) on the quality of solutions returned by greedy, normal and co-evolutionary genetic algorithms, when applied to 64 subcubes cube and a 3+1 nodes M-OLAP architecture

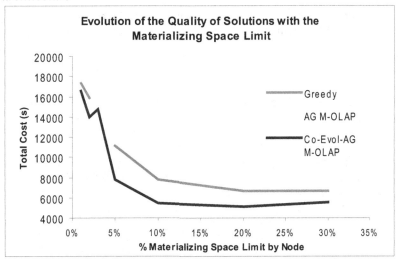

rializing space needed to store all subcubes. We used again the 3+1 M-OLAP architecture, OLAP cube A (64 subcubes) and genetic parameters of the last test. The results returned by the algorithms execution are shown in Figure 14.

Once again the GA co-Evolutionary version shows its high performance, being consistently better than all the others. It's also clear that materializing space brings profits, with an initial high return that progressively slows. If, initially, query cost savings x maintenance cost balance bends clearly to the first plate (as any materializing subcube may be very useful to query answering), the situation is progressively changing (with maintenance cost increase), and somewhere between 20% and 30%, the equilibrium point is reached. Beyond this value, any new materialized subcube has a maintenance cost that isn't justified by query cost savings, probably because constitute redundant or quasi-redundant subcubes. This behavior justifies the 10% materializing space limit that was used on almost all performed tests.

This experimental evaluation tests' set wouldn't be finished if we didn't have evaluated the impact of variations on some of the selected genetic parameters on the global performance of GA. Among all the parameters and possible combinations, we selected to research: 1) the behavior of GA when varying the mutation tax; 2) the impact of the way of dealing with invalid genomas (when any produced solution has a total materializing space that surpasses the node's space limit); 3) the selection type; and 4) for competition selection type, analyzing the impact of the best individual selection probability value.

For the test of research 1) we used a 3+1 M-OLAP architecture, a population of 100 individuals and probability of inter-specie crossing of 2%. The results shown in Figure 15 confirmed, once again, that the co-Evolutionary version of GA is the best performer for every mutation tax used, until non-convergence phenomenon had happened.

Also, an opposite behavior of both algorithms is apparent. GA seems to improve its performance with increases on the mutation tax, while co-Evolutionary version has losses, although not severe. Remember that inter-specie crossing works as a large scale mutation, which explains the observed behavior. The selected value of 5% for almost all

Figure 15. Plot of the variation of solution's quality varying the mutation tax for normal and co-evolutionary genetic algorithms when applied to the 3+1 M-OLAP nodes cube selection and allocation problem

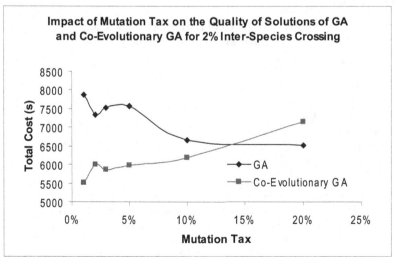

experiments is reasonable, even though the 10% value seems to be more adjusted here, but, as we have used a 5% inter-specie crossing, not a 2% (as in this experiment), a 10% mutation tax would probably imply a non-convergence phenomenon. Also, the 5% value seems to be the one that is the most equilibrate, not favoring one algorithm in detriment of the other.

For the second test of this set we used the same population and M-OLAP architecture. We set the mutation tax to 2 % and inter-specie crossing also at 2%. We implemented two other ways of dealing with invalid genomas (the ones whose corresponding M surpasses the maximal materializing space by node), besides the random method (denoted as R), used in all test experiments performed till now:

1. A greedy algorithm described in (Lin & Kuo, 2004), that tries to eliminate the subcubes that imply a lower density loss of fitness (cost increase caused by removing subcube i / size of removed subcube i), denoted as genome repair type D (from **D**ensity); we used this type only for the generation step of the genetic algorithms. The reason for this restricted use is simple: this repair type, as being very time consuming, can't be used in the evolution phase, because it would have to be used as many times as the number of generations, or even twice (as in each generation it might be used after crossing and after mutation), and, then, its run-time would be enormous.

2. Acting on the evolution process in order to deny invalid genomes, only allowing the generation of genomes whose corresponding cube size is below the materializing space limit, denoted as repair type V (only **V**alid genomas); we use this solution only for mutation genetic operator.

All genetic algorithms have two distinct running phases: population's generation and evolution. The evolution phase may be divided into crossing and mutation (genetic operator's phases), although other operations (using other genetic operators, e.g. inversion) may be also introduced. In each of these phases, it may be necessary to fix the genome of any individual. This way, the dealing with invalid genomes may be performed in three different phases: 1) in the generation of the genetic population, 2) during or after the crossing operation and 3) in the mutation phase. For each of these repairs, one of the methods may be used, and, then, the genomes fixing is denoted with three letters, corresponding to the ways of dealing with invalid genomes in each of the three phases. E.g. RRR means that a random way is used in all three phases: generation, crossing and mutation. Given the referred restrictions of genome fixing usage, we will have RRR, DRR and RRV invalid genome dealing. Table 8 shows the results of the running of both genetic algorithms using query set A and each of the three genome fix/repair combined methods. All values are the average of four to six running of the algorithms.

A table sight shows immediately that none of the new repair methods is a remarkable panacea, as they don't evidence a high gain in the solutions' quality. A detailed analysis of the values shows that inverse repair greedy method (used in the

Table 8. Comparative table of quality and run-time execution of normal and co-evolutionary genetic algorithms using three distinct combinations of genome fix/repair methods

	Genetic Algorithm		Co-Evolutionary GA	
	Total Cost	Run-Time	Total Cost	Run-Time
Invalid M dealing: RRR	7.182	155.036	6.037	406.037
Invalid M dealing: DRR	7.439	1.236.431	5.967	1.400.108
Invalid M dealing: RRV	6.967	173.969	5.569	287.854

generation phase, being part of DRR combination) isn't profitable (relating to RRR), as it simply doesn't improve the cost (or it does, but only a little bit), and implies a great run-time increase. Otherwise, repair type V applied to the mutation operation is valuable, especially in the co-Evolutionary genetic algorithm version. Those results raise the future research interest for other repair methods of this type, which may be included into the crossing operator.

For test three of this set we implemented another selection mechanism: proportional method as the one originally proposed by Holland (Holland, 1992) among other available standard selection schemes (Blickle & Thiele, 1996) (e.g. truncation and linear or exponential ranking). Here we implemented it as a scheme denoted as roulette wheel method (Goldberg, 1989). The name roulette is paradigmatic of the selection mechanism: a roulette is built, where the slots of the roulette wheel are determined based on the probabilities of individuals surviving into the next generation. These probabilities are calculated by dividing the fitness values of the individuals by the sum of the fitness values of the current pool of individuals. Adding the probability of the current individual to the probability of the previous creates the slot. For example, if probability of individual 1 and 2 were 0.24 and 0.12, respectively, then slot 1 will range from 0-0.24 while slot 2 will range from 0.25-0.36. The last slot will have an upper value of 1. In summary, each individual in the population will occupy a slot size that is proportional to its fitness value. When the ball rounds the roulette, as a fittest individual has a corresponding large slot, its selection probability will be correspondingly higher. In the algorithm, a random number

is generated that determines the slot where the ball stops on the roulette.

The results of this test are shown in Table 9. In the allowed 300 generations, the normal GA sometimes didn't converge and co-Evolutionary version never did. The problem may be explained by the lower selection pressure due to the undesirable property that arises from the fact that proportional selection not to be translation invariant (Maza & Tidor, 1993), and some scaling methods (Grefenstette & Baker, 1989) or "over selection" (Koza, 1992) must be used. In spite of this, especially normal GA showed better results, may be due only to random search and luck, or simply because a number substantially higher of generations to be needed, due to the selection intensity being to low, even in early stages of the evolution. The authors in (Blickle & Thiele, 1996) conclude that proportional selection is a very unsuited selection scheme. All those results and discussion confirms our choice of the binary tournament selection method.

Due to the panoply of selection methods (and variants) proposed in the literature, may be it would be interesting to research its impact onto the performance onto these genetic algorithms when applied to this particular problem. Especially rank selection methods and fitness uniform selection strategy described in (Hutter, 2002) seems to deserve further research.

Finally, for test four we used the same genetic parameters as in test two of this set, with invalid M dealing type RRR (random discard of subcubes after the population's generation and all genetic operators). We want to evaluate the impact of the probability of selecting the fittest individual when using the binary tournament selection. To this

Table 9. Comparative performance when using two different selection methods: the former competition and proportional methods

Selection Method	Genetic Algorithm	Co-Evolutionary GA
Competition	7,380	5,880
Roullete	6,650	6,160

Figure 16. Impact of the probability of selecting the fittest individual when used the competition selection method for the normal and co-evolutionary genetic algorithms.

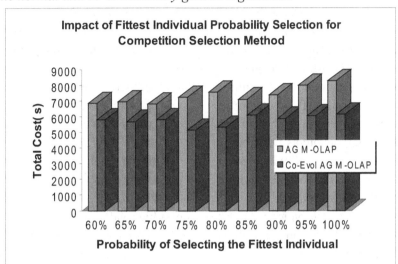

purpose, we varied the probability of selecting the fittest individual from 60 to 100%, in 5% increases when performing the test using query set A. The results of this test are shown in Figure 16.

A brief analysis allows concluding that this probability doesn't have a great impact on the quality of the achieved solutions, but more pronounced on the normal GA algorithm. Values of 85-90% will be a good choice as they don't favor any of the algorithms, as was the example of values of 75-80%, which would be great for GA-Coev, at cost of GA-Normal performance. Values of 60-70% would be also good, but it was observed that the algorithms didn't converge. These observations do justify the choice of the value of 85 and 90% used in the most of performed tests.

CONCLUSION AND FUTURE WORK

The algorithms that were proposed allow, in a simplified way, to manage a distributed OLAP system, capitalizing the advantages of computing and data distribution, with light administration costs. As it was noted, having the cube schema

as base, the frequency of subcube usage and its node access, the M-OLAP architecture and its network connections, Greedy and Genetic algorithms proposed an OLAP structure distribution that minimized query and maintenance costs. This work improves existent proposals in four different ways: 1) it deals with real world parameter values, concerning to nodes, communication networks and the measure value – time, clearly near the way of measure users' satisfaction and maintenance window size; 2) it introduces maintenance cost into the cost equation to minimize; 3) it introduces also genetic proposals onto the distributed OLAP cube selection problem, proposing both a normal and co-Evolutionary version; and 4) it uses as fitness function (for GA) and for compute the gain (for Greedy algorithms) query and maintenance cost estimation algorithms that simulates the parallel execution of tasks (using the inherent parallelism of the M-OLAP architecture).

The experimental results of the simulation seem to show the superiority of genetic algorithms, when applied to the M-OLAP cube selection and allocation problem. In fact, concerning to the quality of the solutions achieved by the algorithms, while the M-OLAP GA is better than the M-OLAP Greedy, the co-Evolutionary version is the best.

The run-time execution results show an easy scalability of GA in both directions: cube's complexity and nodes number. Moreover, another interesting conclusion of the simulation's results is the easy scale-up of the M-OLAP architecture.

These algorithms may compose the core of a subsystem that we may denote as Distributed Data Cube Proposal Generator, to which other algorithms that we will refer soon (as part of future work proposals) may be added.

The design of a *workbench* which includes Greedy, Genetic and Particle Swarm Algorithms and other supporting classes and data structures, with special relevance for the query and maintenance estimation algorithms, would allow the execution of simulations and comparative evaluation of performance of different OLAP architectures. Yet better, the system may be provided with heuristics, or other learning mechanisms, that allow the selection of the suitable algorithm to the specific case, the switching between algorithms or even cooperation among them (Krink & Løvbjerg, 2002), in the solution of the same case. This subsystem may be included in a broad system constituting the Distributed Middleware of Figure 9, implemented as a multi-agent system that will allow the full automation of the use and maintenance of distributed OLAP structures under the control of and supplying system's state information to the DW administrator. This distributed system would be charged of:

1. Queries accepting, acting to provide their answering (knowing where the best subcube able to provide the answer is located);
2. The process of storing the history of posed queries as well as several statistics;
3. The extraction of information related to the utility of subcubes with a possible speculative approach, trying to guess its future usage;

4. The generation of the new M-OLAP cube distribution proposal;
5. The process of maintenance of OLAP structures: subcubes or deltas generation and its transmission to the proper nodes;
6. The broadcasting of information about the global subcubes' distribution, to allow component 1 to compute the best way to answer to a posed query.

Further improvements may be intended, especially the research of type V mechanisms for applying to the crossing operator, which may be of a high value, and also evaluate the impact of multi-point and multi parent crossing and the inclusion of an inversion operator. Also, the use of genetic local search, a hybrid heuristic that combines the advantages of population-based search and local optimization, deserves further research in the near future.

Recent developments in other life inspired algorithms, known as particle swarm optimization (Kennedy & Eberhart, 1995), motivated us for the opening of another research direction. We have already designed, developed and tested a discrete particle swarm algorithm, having applied it to the centralized cube selection problem (Loureiro & Belo, 2006c) with promising results (Loureiro & Belo, 2006a). We intend, in near future, to extend the spatial application environment to a distributed OLAP architecture, developing and testing an M-OLAP version of Discrete Particle Swarm Algorithm. Also, we plan to introduce a new distributed non-linear cost model, with corresponding query and maintenance cost estimation algorithms design and development. These must also include parallel tasks execution simulation, implemented as a pipeline fashion. All these works are already in progress and show interesting results. Moreover, the inclusion of the dual constraint on the optimizing process (materializing space and time) will be tried in all described M-OLAP cube selection and allocation algorithms.

REFERENCES

Albrecht, J., Bauer, A., Deyerling, O., Gunzel, H., Hummer, W., Lehner, W., & Schlesinger, L. (1999). Management of multidimensional aggregates for efficient online analytical processing. *Proceedings: International Database Engineering and Applications Symposium*, Montreal, Canada, (pp. 156-164).

Bauer, A., & Lehner, W. (2003). On solving the view selection problem in distributed data warehouse architectures. *Proceedings: 15th International Conference on Scientific and Statistical Database Management (SSDBM'03), IEEE*, (pp. 43-51).

Belo, O. (2000). Putting intelligent personal assistants working on dynamic hypercube views updating. *Proceedings: 2nd International Symposium on Robotics and Automation (ISRA'2000)*, Monterrey, México.

Blickle, T., & Thiele, L. (1996). A comparison of selection schemes used in evolutionary algorithms. *Evolutionary Computation 4*(4), 361-394.

Maza, M., & Tidor, B. (1993). An analysis of selection procedures with particular attention paid to proportional and Bolzmann selection. In Stefanic Forrest (ed.) *Proceedings of the Fifth International Conference on Genetic Algorithms*, San Mateo, CA. (pp. 124-131) Morgan Kaufmann Publishers.

Deshpande, P. M., Naughton, J. K., Ramasamy, K., Shukla, A., Tufte, K., & Zhao, Y. (1997). Cubing algorithms, storage estimation, and Storage and processing alternatives for OLAP. *Data Engineering Bulletin, 20*(1), 3-11.

Goldberg, D.E. (1989). *Genetic algorithms in search, optimization, and machine learning.* Reading, MA: Addison-Wesley.

Gray, J., Chaudury, S., & Bosworth, A. (1997). Data cube: A relational aggregation operator generalizing group-by, cross-tabs and subtotals. *Data Mining and Knowledge Discovery 1*(1), 29-53.

Grefenstette, J..J., & Baker, J.E. (1989). How genetic algorithms work: A critical look at implicit parallelism. In J. David Schaffer, (ed.) *Proceedings: the Third International Conference on Genetic Algorithms*, San Mateo, CA, (pp. 20-27). Morgan Kaufmann Publishers

Gupta, H., & Mumick, I.S. (1999). Selection of views to materialize under a maintenance-time constraint. *Proceedings of the International Conference on Database* Theory.

Harinarayan, V., Rajaraman, A., & Ullman, J. (1996, June). Implementing data cubes efficiently. *Proceedings ACM SIGMOD*, Montreal, Canada, (pp. 205-216).

Holland, J.H. (1992). *Adaptation in natural and artificial systems.* Cambridge, MA, (2nd edition): MIT Press.

Horng, J.T., Chang, Y.J., Liu, B.J., & Kao, C.Y. (1999). Materialized view selection using genetic algorithms in a data warehouse. In *Proceedings of World Congress on Evolutionary Computation*, Washington D.C.

Hutter, M. (2002, May). Fitness uniform selection to preserve genetic diversity. *Proceedings in the 2002 Congress on Evolutionary Computation (CEC-2002)*, Washington D.C, USA, *IEEE* (pp. 783-788).

Kalnis, *P., Mamoulis, N., & D., Papadias (2002). View selection using randomized search. Data Knowledge Engineering, 42*(1), 89-111.

Kennedy, J., & Eberhart, R. C. (1995). Particle swarm optimization. In *Proceedings of the International Conference on Neural Networks*, IV. Piscataway, NJ: IEEE Service Center, (pp. 1942-1948).

Kimball, R. (1996). Data warehouse toolkit: Practical techniques for building dimensional data warehouses. John Wiley & Sons.

Kotidis, Y., & Roussopoulos, N. (1999, June). Dynamat. A dynamic view management system for data warehouses. In *Proceedings of the ACM SIGMOD International Conference on Management of Data*, Philadelphia, Pennsylvania, (pp. 371-382).

Koza, J.R. (1992). Genetic programming: On the programming of computers by means of natural selection. Cambridge, Massachusetts: MIT Press.

Krink, T., & Løvbjerg, M. (2002, September 7-11). The life cycle model: Combining particle swarm optimization, genetic algorithms and hillclimbers. In *Proceedings of the 7th International Conference on Parallel Problem Solving from Nature (PPSN VII)*, Granada, Spain. *Lecture Notes in Computer Science, 2439*, 621-630. Springer.

Liang, W., Wang, H., & Orlowska, M.E. (2004). Materialized view selection under the maintenance cost constraint. *Data and Knowledge Engineering, 37*(2), 203-216.

Lin, W.-Y., & Kuo, I-C. (2004). A genetic selection algorithm for OLAP data cubes. *Knowledge and Information Systems, 6*(1), 83-102. Springer-Verlag London Ltd.

Loureiro, J., & Belo, O. (2006ᵃ, January). Life inspired algorithms for the selection of OLAP data cubes. In *WSEAS Transactions on Computers, 1*(5), 8-14.

Loureiro, J., & Belo, O. (2006b, October 2-6). Evaluating maintenance cost computing algorithms for multi-node OLAP systems. In *Proceedings of the XI Conference on Software Engineering and Databases (JISBD2006)*, Sitges, Barcelona, (pp. 241-250).

Loureiro, J., & Belo, O. (2006c, May 23-27). A discrete particle swarm algorithm for OLAP data cube selection. In *Proceedings of 8th International Conference on Enterprise Information Systems (ICEIS 2006)*, Paphos, Cyprus, (pp. 46-53).

Park, C.S., Kim, M.H., & Lee, Y.J. (2003, November). Usability-based caching of query results in OLAP systems. *Journal of Systems and Software, 68*(2), 103-119.

Potter, M.A., & Jong, K.A. (1994). A cooperative coevolutionary approach to function optimization. In *The Third Parallel Problem Solving From Nature*. Berlin, Germany: Springer-Verlag, (pp. 249-257).

Sapia, C., Blaschka, M, Höfling, & Dinter, B. (1998). Extending the E/R model for the multi-dimensional paradigm. In Advances in Database Technologies (ER'98 Workshop Proceedings), Springer-Verlag, 105-116.

Sapia, C. (2000, September). PROMISE – Modeling and predicting user query behavior in online analytical processing environments. In *Proceedings of the 2nd International Conference on Data Warehousing and Knowledge Discovery (DAWAK'00)*, London, UK, Springer.

Scheuermann, P., Shim, J., & Vingralek, R. (1996, September 3-6). WATCHMAN: A data warehouse intelligent cache manager. In *Proceedings of the 22th International Conference on Very Large Data Bases VLDB'96*, Bombay, (pp. 51-62).

Shim, J., Scheuermann, P., & Vingralek, R. (1999, July). Dynamic caching of query results for decision support systems. In *Proceedings of the 11th International Conference on Scientific and Statistical Database Management*, Cleveland, Ohio.

Transaction Processing Performance Council (TPC) TPC Benchmark R (decision support) Standard Specification Revision 2.1.0. tpcr_2.1.0.pdf, available in http://www.tpc.org.

Widom, J. (1995, November). Research problems in data warehousing. In *Proceedings of the Fourth International Conference on Information and Knowledge Management (CIKM '95)*, Baltimore, Maryland, (pp. 25-30), Invited paper.

Zhang, C., Yao, X., & Yang, J. (2001, September). An evolutionary approach to materialized views selection in a data warehouse environment. *IEEE Trans. on Systems, Man and Cybernetics, Part C, 31*(3).

Chapter VII
Swarm Quant' Intelligence for Optimizing Multi–Node OLAP Systems

Jorge Loureiro
Instituto Politécnico de Viseu, Portugal

Orlando Belo
Universidade do Minho, Portugal

ABSTRACT

Globalization and market deregulation has increased business competition, which imposed OLAP data and technologies as one of the great enterprise's assets. Its growing use and size stressed underlying servers and forced new solutions. The distribution of multidimensional data through a number of servers allows the increasing of storage and processing power without an exponential increase of financial costs. However, this solution adds another dimension to the problem: space. Even in centralized OLAP, cube selection efficiency is complex, but now, we must also know where to materialize subcubes. We have to select and also allocate the most beneficial subcubes, attending an expected (changing) user profile and constraints. We now have to deal with materializing space, processing power distribution, and communication costs. This chapter proposes new distributed cube selection algorithms based on discrete particle swarm optimizers; algorithms that solve the distributed OLAP selection problem considering a query profile under space constraints, using discrete particle swarm optimization in its normal(Di-PSO), cooperative (Di-CPSO), multi-phase (Di-MPSO), and applying hybrid genetic operators.

INTRODUCTION

Nowadays, economy, with globalization (market opening and unrulement) shows a growing dynamic and volatile environment. Decision makers submerged into uncertainty are eager for something to guide them, in order to make timely, coherent and adjusted decisions. Within this context a new Grail was born: information as condition for competition. Data Warehouses (DW) emerged, naturally, as a core component in the constitution of organization's informational infrastructure. Their unified, subject oriented, non-volatile and temporal variability preserving vision, allowed them to become the main source of information concerning business activities.

The growing interest on DW's information by knowledge workers has motivated a fast enlargement of the business enclosed areas. Also the adoption of Data Warehousing (DWing) by most of Fortune 400's enterprises has helped to make the huge size of today's DW (hundreds of GB or even tenths of TB). A query addressed to such a database has necessarily a long run-time, but they must be desirably short, given the on-line appanage characteristic of OLAP systems. This emphasis on speed is dictated by two orders of reasons: 1) OLAP users' need to take business decisions in a few minutes, in order to accompany the fast change of markets, operated in short time intervals; 2) the strong dependence of the productivity of CEO's, managers and all knowledge workers and decision makers of enterprises in general, on the quickness of the answers to their business questions.

However, this constant need for speed seems to be blocked by the huge amount of DW data: a query like "show me the sales by product family and month of this year related to last year" may force a scanning and aggregation of a significant portion of the fact table in the DW. This is something that could last for hours or days, even disposing, hypothetically, of powerful hardware and suitable indexes.

The adoption of a DWing "eagger" (Widom, 1995) approach allowed to solve this problem through the generation and timely updating of the so called materialized views, summary tables or subcubes (mainly used from now on). In essence, they are *Group By* previously calculated and stored by any kind of dimensions/hierarchies' combinations. These subcubes need space and especially time, enlarging the size of the DW even more, perhaps one hundred times bigger, since the number of subcubes may be very large, causing the well-known "data explosion". So, it is crucial to restrict the number of subcubes and select those that prove to be the most useful, due to their ratio utilization/occupied space. This is, in the essence, the views selection problem: selecting the right set of subcubes to materialize, in order to minimize query costs, characteristically NP-hard (Harinarayan, Rajaraman, and Ullman, 1996).

Two constraints may be applied to the optimization process: the space that is available to cube materializing and the time disposable to the refreshing process. But multidimensional data continues growing and the number of OLAP users too. These concomitant factors impose a great stress over OLAP underlying platform: a new powerful server was needed or simply empower the architecture with the aggregated power of several small (general purpose) servers, distributing multidimensional structures and OLAP queries through the available nodes. That's what we called Multi-Node OLAP architecture, shown in Figure 1.

A number of OLAP Server Nodes (OSN) with predefined storage and processing power, connected through a network, using real characteristics of communication inter-node links, which may freely share data or issue aggregation queries to other nodes participating in a distributed scenario, constitutes the M-OLAP component, where inhabit the multidimensional structures. This system serves a distributed knowledge worker community, which puts a set of queries on their daily routine. This brings to

Figure 1. Multi-Node OLAP (M-OLAP) Architecture and corresponding framing (data sources, DW, ETLs processes, and administration and restructuring engine)

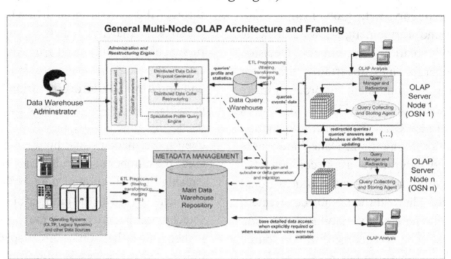

OLAP the known advantages of data distribution and processing proficiently, like increased availability, communication costs reduction, simpler and cheaper hardware and loading and processing distribution.

However, there is a price to pay: increased management complexity, mainly related to the selection and distribution of the OLAP data structures. Nevertheless, this disadvantage would vanish, as shown in Figure 1, where the administrator and restructuring engine that is in charge of this management, under the control of the DW administrator and in a simple and automatic way. Into this component we focus on the distributed data cube proposal generator, that, using a query profile induced from the query data warehouse and maybe with some speculative addict (provided by the speculative profile query engine), might generate the new data cube proposal which the distributed data cube restructuring will bring into action. But this component has now to deal with a new dimension: space. The proficiency of the OLAP system is bounded not only by the proper subcube selection, as in the classical centralized OLAP architecture, but also by their spatial al-

location (the assignment of subcubes to the node (or nodes) where they will be materialized). For that purpose, we propose the application of a new optimization paradigm: particle swarm optimization (PSO) that has been widely and successfully used in optimization problems in several domains.

This paper is organized as follows: in the beginning we have a summary of some proposals of solutions to cube selection problem in centralized and distributed DW environments, focusing on the several used algorithm's families. Afterwards, we discuss the factors that are responsible for query and maintenance costs in distributed environments, being shown, at the end, the proposed cost model. Then, we introduce the generic PSO algorithm in its discrete form, two variations (cooperative and multi-phase versions) and several possible hybrids; this section ends with the formal presentation of three proposed algorithms: Discrete Particle Swarm Optimization Original (Di-PSO), Discrete Cooperative Particle Swarm Optimization (Di-CPSO) and Discrete Multi-Phase Particle Swarm Optimization (Di-MPSO). Next we report the experimental performance study, using a database architecture somewhat complex (with four OLAP-server nodes) and an OLAP cube derived of TPC-R database, with 3 dimensions and 4 hierarchies per dimension (including one with parallel hierarchies). The paper ends with the conclusions and some future work.

RELATED WORK

OLAP optimization consists in a balancing between performance and redundancy. The classical cube selection problem was first studied in (Harinarayan, Rajaraman, and Ullman, 1996), being, since then, the object of a great research effort by the scientific community.

In spite of the great diversity of proposals, they may be characterized, in their essence, by a three-dimensional perspective, as shown in Figure 2: 1) time, which dictates the elapsed interval between re-calibration of OLAP structures as the real needs change (a pro-active approach will have a negative time, as the maintenance's interval is made attending to the future needs, the recalibration is made in advance); 2) space, governing the distribution of the materialized multidimensional structures and 3) selecting logic, according to the methods or heuristics used to build the solution.

Time splits naturally the first dimension into 3 parts and generates an according number of solutions' classes: static (long), dynamic (immediate and actual) and pro-active (future). The second dimension classifies the solutions as centralized and distributed. Finally, an analysis to the third dimension shows that most of the solutions are in the greedy algorithms domain (shown as a square). Some others are based in genetic algorithms (triangles), random selection with iterative search, simulated annealing or a combination of both and, recently, using Discrete Particle Swarm Optimization, but for the centralized architecture, showed as a star.

It's important to report some considerations, though short, about each of the categories defined before. Due to imposed space constraints, we'll make here only a brief analysis of the proposals in each of these categories.

Let us look at the first dimension: elapsed time between re-calibration of OLAP structures. The well known static proposals are based in several greedy heuristics (Harinarayan, Rajaraman, and Ullman, 1996; Shukla, Deshpande, and Naughton, 1998; Gupta & Mumick, 1999; Liang,, Wang, and Orlowska, 2001) or in genetic algorithms (Horng, Chang, Liu, and Kao, 1999; Zhang, Yao, and Yang, 2001; Lin & Kuo, 2004), and they usually act at great size structures. They don't allow a complete reconfiguration in short intervals, as the costs of that operation may be prohibitively high, thence its name "static", once it is relatively stable through time. The dynamic approach (Scheuermann, Shim, and Vingralek, 1996; Kotidis & Roussopoulos, 1999) intends to act at cache level, of short size. Besides, they don't usually imply additional costs to their materialization. Finally, pro-active proposals, with cache prefetching or restructuring (with dynamic recalculation of future needed subcubes) are two possible ways for finding solutions in this proposals class (Belo, 2000; Sapia, 2000). Moreover, the subsumption of future appraisal of subcubes (or fragments) in the admission and substitution cache politics is proposed in (Park, Kim, and Lee, 2003), being classified as pro-active proposals too. To completely characterize them we need an extra dimension that shows whose method is used to gain insight into the future.

The second dimension is related to OLAP cube distribution. The majority of solutions is focused in a centralized approach, because it is the most applied, and also, until a few time ago, the only one that was being implemented. The distributed solution has come to stage very recently (Bauer & Lehner, 2003), mainly devoted to organizations that operate at global scale, based on a greedy heu-

Figure 2. Three dimensional proposals' solutions characterization to cube selection problem

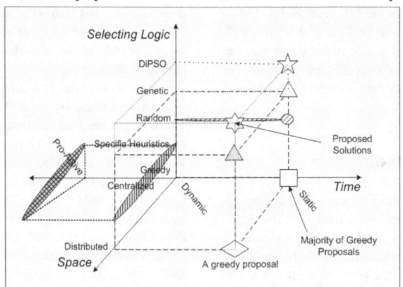

ristic. A genetic and co-evolutionary approach has been recently proposed (Loureiro & Belo, 2006b) (in the figure showed as a shaded triangle).

Finally, the third dimension cuts the solution set in several families: "greedy heuristics" family is one possible name for the first. By far, that's the solution which has the greatest number of proposals. It was introduced in (Harinarayan, Rajaraman, and Ullman, 1996), in the shape of an algorithm GSC (greedy under space constraint), which was the base of the heuristics of all family: it proposes the benefit concept and a starting point with an empty set of views, which is incrementally added with the view that had the maximum benefit per unit of space, in terms of the decreasing of query costs.

Many other proposals might be pointed, that have been adding several heuristics to the basic one, enlarging the domain of applicability and introducing new constraints, as it is the important case of maintenance time constraint included in (Gupta & Mumick, 1999; Liang,, Wang, and Orlowska, 2001). A detailed description and comparative analysis may be found in (Yu, Choi, Gou, and Lu, 2004).

The second family brings up the cube selection genetic algorithms (Holland, 1992) (the triangle in the figure). Genetic algorithms achieve better or at least equal solutions, compared to greedy algorithms (Horng, Chang, Liu, and Kao, 1999; Zhang, Yao, and Yang, 2001; Lin & Kuo, 2004). In (Loureiro & Belo, 2006c), it is proposed a genetic algorithm, M-OLAP genetic, and M-OLAP co-genetic (a co-evolutionary version) (Potter & Jong, 1994) of the classical genetic algorithm, where there isn't only one population of individuals (solutions) but one set of subpopulations, known as species. Besides, to introduce the co-evolutionary variant, it also includes an evolution on the process of how to build the global genome (known as context vector). These algorithms extend the application domain of genetic algorithms to distributed OLAP architectures. The co-evolutionary variant showed a better performance than the classical genetic one, achieving analogous solutions (in terms of total costs), in a number of generations and processing time spent somewhat shorter. It's also important to refer to the random search proposals. They try to give an answer to the problem of greedy algorithms, which are too slow and therefore unsuitable in high dimensionality DW's.

Finally, let's talk about random search proposals. They try to give an answer to the problem of greedy algorithms, which are too slow and therefore unsuitable in high dimensionality DW's. In (Kalnis, Mamoulis, and Papadias, 2002), it is proposed one heuristic that used a pool (with size matching the space constraint) to which are added views (previously ordered) until the time constraint is broken. Selection and removing of views may be done using three search heuristics: iterative improvement (II), simulated annealing (SA) and two-phase optimization (2PO), which combines the former ones, allowing the creation of three algorithms. These are employed to the views selection problem under space constraint, showing 2PO algorithm to achieve solutions of equally good quality related to GSC algorithm in running times three orders of magnitude less (for a 15-dimensional DW).

QUERY ANSWERING AND MAINTENANCE COSTS

The distributed nature of the M-OLAP architecture results in two distinct kinds of costs: 1) intrinsic costs due to scan / aggregation or integration, from now on known as processing costs and 2) communication costs. Both are responsible for the query and maintenance costs. The purpose of the system is the minimization of query costs (and possibly the maintenance ones), having a space constraint by node that has to obey to the maintenance time constraint previously defined (we consider that the M-OLAP has a twofold division: query time period and maintenance period). To compute the processing cost it is assumed that the linear cost model is used (Harinarayan, Rajaraman, and Ullman, 1996), in which the cost of evaluating a query equals the number of non-null cells in the aggregated cube used to answer the query. Instead of using records, in this paper

we're going to use time for the unit of costs, as it matches the purpose of the undertaken optimization – minimizing the answering time to the user's queries – and, on the other hand, time also comes to sight in the maintenance time constraint.

Distributed Dependent Lattice

Figure 3 shows a distributed dependent *lattice* (Harinarayan, Rajaraman, and Ullman, 1996), of dimensions product, supplier and time, when immersed in a three-nodes architecture. Each node contains the possible subcubes located there, connected to all other nodes by arrows that represent the communication channels, due to the distributed scenario. In each lattice vertex there aren't only the edges that show the dependences of intra-node aggregations, but also other edges that denote the communication channels. These edges connect subcubes at the same granularity level in different nodes of the M-OLAP. In practice, they allow to represent the additional communication costs that occur because of the computation of each subcube using another one inhabiting in a different node. In Figure 3, the dashed line shows the dependence between subcubes (ps-) inhabiting in all nodes. In the center of the same figure, there is a graph that models the same dependence. Each arrow represents the communication costs C_{ij} that incur with the transport of one subcube between nodes *i* and *j*. As communication is bidireccional, each of the subcubes is spilt in two (itself and its reciprocal), and the links that use third nodes are eliminated (avoiding the cycles). Each link will model the connection of minimal cost between two nodes. This graph will repeat itself for each of the subcubes in the architecture.

It will be included one virtual vertex, in each lattice, that models the virtual root (which stands for the base relation – detailed DW table or data sources in a virtual DW), supposed to be located in node 0. This relation will be used as the primary source of data, being used in two different situations: when there isn't any competent subcube in

Figure 3. Distributed Lattice. The dashed line shows the inter-node dependence in the same level of granularity relating to the communication interconnections. The graph in top right shows the dependences among the nodes related to subcube (ps-)

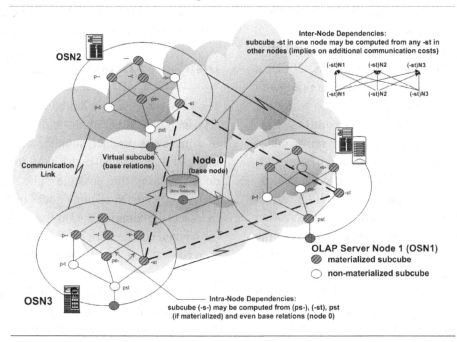

any node that may be used to answer a query and also as a data source for the maintenance process. Obviously, the processing cost of using this base relation is bigger than the highest processing cost of any lattice's subcube.

Communication Costs

Nowadays, communication services are mainly hired to telecommunication's operators. This ensures to the contractor that there are connections between each of its nodes and a QoS (Quality of Service) (Walrand & Varaiya, 2000) defined in terms of a number of parameters. Anyway, we may also use any other communication network lines to connect nodes, e.g. simple switched telephone lines or leased lines. For this discussion, the following parameters will be used to define a communication link:

- Binary Debit (BD), a measure of the number of bits (liquid or total) that traverse a communication channel by unit of time (in bps). When there is a contract of communication services this is called CIR - Committed Information Rate.

- Transit Delay (TD), mandatory to isochronous applications (e.g. video on demand). In transactional applications it can be relaxed, given its ability to adapt to the link's conditions. This way, these applications are also known as best-effort.

- Size packet (Sp) is the size of the packet that may be transported in the communication link, if it is applicable. Any costs of initiating a data packet may also be added (Cini) (Huang & Chen, 2001).

- Time to Make a Connection (TMC), used in connectionless links. It may include the time spent to a virtual channel establishing.

Thus, the communication cost of transmitting data between nodes i and j can be assumed to be a linear function as follows:

$$CC_{ij} = N_p \cdot (C_{ini} + S_p / BD) + TD + TMC \quad (3.1),$$

where N_p is the number of data packets to transfer.

Query and Maintenance Total Costs

The processes involved in subcube computing (see section 3.1) may be transposed to query answering. In fact, 1) an OLAP query is addressed to a particular subcube, then, it can be nominated by the subcube itself; 2) a subcube whose cells contain aggregations of all attributes that appear in a query select condition may be used to answer it; 3) besides, even if the exact subcube isn't materialized, the distributed dependent **lattice** structure may be explored to find another subcube that may be used as an aggregation source. A subcube like this is named ancestor (Anc), and may be defined as $Anc(s_i, M) = \{s_j | s_j \in M$ and $s_i \sim s_j\}$ where M is the set of materialized subcubes and $\sim$ is the dependence relation (derived-from, be-computed-from).

Recall that in a distributed **lattice**, the subcube cost is computed as the sum of processing costs (Cp) and communication costs (Cc). Then $C(s_i) = Cp(Anc(s_i)) + Ccom(s_i)$, being the general purpose its minimization. In short, we have to find a subcube whose sum of scan and aggregation cost of one of its ancestors with the communication cost is minimal.

Given a subcube distribution M in the several nodes and a query set Q,

$$Cq(Q, M) = \sum_{q \in Q} \min((Cp(Anc(q_i, M) + Ccom(q_i)) * fq_{i_i} * eq_{i_i}$$
$$(3.2)$$

is the query cost answering and

$$Cm(M) = fu \sum \min((Cp(Anc(s_i, M).eu_{s_i} \quad (3.3)$$

the maintenance cost of M.

Assuming a linear cost model, $Cb(s_i) = |s_i|$, and then

$$Cq(Q, M) = \sum_{q \in Q} \min(|Anc(q_i, M)| + Ccom|q_i|) * fq_{q_i} * eq_{q_i}$$
$$(3.4)$$

and

$$Cm(M) = \sum_{S_i \in M} \min(|Anc(S_i, M)| + Ccom|S_i|) . fu_{s_i} . eu_{s_i}$$
$$(3.5)$$

Adopting time as the cost referential, the processing power of the **OLAP** node where Anc_{s_i} or Anc_{q_i} inhabits may be used to convert records in time, what comes to introduce a new model parameter, Cp_{Node}, the processing power of Node n, in records.s^{-1}.

Finally, using eq. 3.1, eqs. 3.4 and 3.5 may be rewritten as (see equation 3.6) where $Np = int(|S_i| * 8 * 8 / Sp) + 1$, and $|S_i| * 8 * 8$ is the size (in bits) of subcube $_{Si}$, (supposing each cell has 8 bytes – amount of memory space used by a double identifier). The same considerations apply to Np related to q_i.

Equation 3.6

$$Cq(Q, M) = \sum_{q_i \in Q} \min(|Anc(q_i, M)| / Cp(No_{Ancqi}) + (Np.(Cini + Sp / BD) + TD + TMC)) * fq_{q_i} * eq_{q_i}$$

$$Cm(M) = \sum_{S_i \in M} \min(|Anc(S_i, M)| / Cp(No_{AncSi}) + (Np.(Cini + Sp / BD + TD + TMC)) * fu_{s_i} * eu_{s_i} \quad (3.6)$$

PARTICLE SWARM OPTIMIZATION AND PROPOSED ALGORITHMS

Several search algorithms have a biological motivation, trying to mimic a characteristic aspect of what can be called "life". There's a simple reason: life (as its biological basic aspect, or, at a higher level, as the social and cognitive behavior), is a perpetual process of adaptation to the environmental conditions, requiring a continuous demand of solutions in face of succeeding new problems. The best known algorithms in this huge domain, are 1) evolutionary algorithms, where the most representatives and most used are probably genetic algorithms, 2) swarm algorithms that may take the form of particle swarm algorithms and ant colony optimization, and finally, 3) artificial immune systems. As said in section 2, algorithms of class 1) and 2) has been already applied to cube selection in a centralized DW, and class 2) also to he distributed approach. Now we are proposing the use of swarm algorithms to the same problem too.

Particle Swarm Optimization

The origin of the particle swarm concept lies in the simulation of a simplified social system. In the beginning, the Particle Swarm Optimization (PSO) authors were looking for a graphic simulation of the gracious but unpredictable choreography of a bird flock, modeling a social and cognitive behavior. After many modifications, the authors realized that the conceptual model was, in fact, an optimizer, that was proposed in (Kennedy & Eberhart, 1995; Eberhart & Kennedy, 1995). This approach assumes a population of individuals represented as binary strings or real-valued vectors – fairly-primitive agents, called particles, which can fly on an n-dimensional space, whose position in a n-dimensional space will bring its instant fitness. This position may be altered by the application of an interactive procedure that uses a velocity vector, allowing a progressively best adaptation to its environment. It also assumes that individuals are social by nature, and thus capable of interacting with others within a given neighborhood. For each individual, there are two main types of information available: the first one is his own past experiences (known as individual knowledge), the *pbest* (particle best) position, and the other one is related to the knowledge about its neighbor's performance (referred as cultural transmission), *gbest* (global best) position.

There are two main versions of the PSO algorithm: the initial version, a continuous one, where the particles move in a continuous space, and the discrete or binary version, known as discrete particle swarm optimization (Di-PSO), shown in a simple form in Algorithm 1, proposed in (Kennedy & Eberhart, 1997), where the space is discretized. Although similar, the spatial evolution of particles in the former is addictive and continuous, meaning that its next location is computed adding the velocity to the position where the particle is at the moment. The discrete space doesn't allow the addictive continuous relation space-velocity. It is substituted by the introduction of the probabilistic space: the particle's position will be given by a probability dependent of its velocity, using the rule

$$if\ rnd() < sig(v_i^{k+1})\ then\ s_i^{k+1} = 1;\ else\ si^{k+1} = 0$$
$$(4.1)$$

where $sig(v_i^k) = \dfrac{1}{1 + \exp(-v_i^k)}$, being v_i^k the velocity of the particle i at the kth iteration.

The location of the particle is now a state (then the epithet *"quantic"*). The direct and deterministic relation between space and velocity is discarded. A casualistic vector is introduced; even if the particle maintains the same velocity, its state may change.

The formula that rules the particle's dynamic concerning to velocity is:

$$v_i^{k+1} = wv_i^k + c1.rnd().(pbest - s_i^k) + c2.rnd().(gbest - s_i^k)$$

$$(4.2)$$

meaning that changes in the particle's velocity are affected by its past velocity and by a vector that tends to push it to its best past location, related to its own past success knowledge – *pbest*, and another vector, that pushes it to the best position already reached by any particle, corresponding to the global knowledge - *gbest*. *W*, called inertia, corresponds to the probability level of changing state even without changing velocity – then, it is a mutation probability; *c1* and *c2* are two constants which control the degree to which the particle favors exploitation or exploration.

To prevent the system from running away, when the particles' oscillation becomes too high, the velocity of the particle is limited by a v_{max} parameter and the following rule:

$$if \, vi > v_{max}, \, then \, v_i = v_{max}; \, if \, v_i < -v_{max}, \, then \, v_i = -v_{max};$$

$$(4.3)$$

This rule conceptually means that a limit is imposed to the maximal probability of a bit to achieve the 0 or the 1 value. Since the sigmoid function is used, the exploration of new solutions

will be encouraged if v_{max} is short, in opposition to the expected behavior in continuous PSO.

Variants and Hybrids to the Discrete Particle Swarm Optimization

Many variations have been proposed to the PSO base version, mainly including 1) cooperation (Van den Bergh & Engelbrecht, 2004) and 2) multi-phase swarms with hill-climbing (Al-Kazemi & Mohan, 2002). Some nuances and hybrids has been also proposed as 3) genetic hybridization (Løvbjerg, Rasmussen, and Krink, 2001; Angeline, 1998); and 4) mass extinction (Xie, Zhang, and Yang, 2002).

The cooperative version mainly differs from the original version in the number of swarms: several for the first and only one in the second. It is named in (Van den Bergh & Engelbrecht, 2004, to the PSO continuous version, cooperative swarms, due to the cooperation among the swarms. Here, it is migrated to the discrete version. Instead of each particle be allow to fly over all dimensions, it is restricted to the dimensions of only a part of the problem (in this case, the node boundary). But the fitness can only be computed with a global position of a particle. Then, we need a scheme to build a general position, where the particle is included. This is achieved with the denoted context

Algorithm 1. Standard discrete (quantic) PSO algorithm

1.	*Initialization*: randomly initialize a population of particles (position and velocity) in the n-dimensional space.
2.	*Population loop*: **For each** particle, **Do**:
	2.1. Own goodness evaluation and pbest update: evaluate the 'goodness' of the particle. **If** its goodness > its best goodness so far, **Then** update pbest.
	2.2. *Global goodness evaluation and gbest update*: **If** the goodness of this particle > the goodness that any particle has ever achieved, **Then** update gbest.
	2.3. *Evaluate*: apply equation (4.2) and rule (4.3).
	2.4. *Particle position update*: apply rule (4.1).
3.	*Cycle*: **Repeat** Step 2 **Until** a given convergence criterion is met, usually a pre-defined number of iterations.

vector: a virtual global positioning of particles, where each particle's position will be included (into the corresponding dimensions of the node). Some details the way of creating this context vector will be given later, in next section.

Multi-phase version is a variant where is proposed the division of the swarm into several groups, each one being in one of possible phases, switching from phase to phase by the use of an adaptive method: phase change occurs if no global best fitness improvement is observed in S recent iterations. In practice, in one phase, one group moves towards gbest, while the other moves in opposite direction. It uses also hill-climbing. The genetic hybridization comes with the possibility of particles having offspring (Løvbjerg, Rasmussen, and Krink, 2001), whose equations are shown also in next section, and the selection of particles (Angeline, 1998). Selection is simply performed by the substitution, in each loop, of a specified number of particles *S*, by an equal number of others with greater fitness that has been previously cloned. Mass extinction (Xie, Zhang, and Yang, 2002) is the artificial simulation of mass extinctions which have played a key role in shaping the story of life on Earth. It is performed simply by reinitializing the velocities of all particles at a predefined extinction interval (Ie), a number of iterations.

Proposed Algorithms

The proposed algorithms are hybrid variations of the three discrete PSO shown previously, including hybridization and mass extinction.

Problem coding in Di-PSO is a simple mapping of each possible subcube in one dimension of the discrete space. As we have n nodes, this implies a n*subcubes_per_lattice number of dimensions of Di-PSO space. If the particle is at position=1 (state 1) in a given dimension, that means the corresponding subcube/node is materialized; in its turn, position=0 of the particle implies that the subcube is not materialized.

Table 1. Space mapping paradigm observed in Di-PSO problem coding

Dimension or Shape	Corresponding Subcube
X	0
Y	1
Z	2
Triangle	3
Square	4
Pentagon	5
Hexagon	6
Heptagon	7

Mapping process for the 3 nodes M-OLAP *lattice* may be seen in Figure 4.

As we need 8 dimensions per node and we are restricted by the orthogonal x,y,z dimensions, we opted by the representation of the particle's position by 5 geometric shapes that represent the remaining 5 dimensions: a triangle for subcube 3, a square for subcube 4, a pentagon for subcube 5, a hexagon for subcube 6 and a heptagon for subcube 7. The space mapping paradigm is shown in Table 1.

Each geometric shape may be black (a one) or white (a zero) reflecting the particle's position in the corresponding dimension. The position of particle is, in this case, P1(10101001 00011101 00101001). If the cooperative version is on concern, each particle flies into a 8 dimensions' space and in this case we may have a particle P1 (of swarm 1, mapped to node 1, with dimensions 0 to 7) and a context vector, represented here by virtual particles' position, which corresponds to dimensions 8 to 15 (swam 2) and 16 to 23 (swarm 3), e.g. the gbest position of swarms 2 and 3.

As we apply a per node space constraint, the particles' move may produce invalid solutions. In this work, instead of applying a fitness penalty that will only avoid the fault particle to become pbest or gbest, we employ a repair method, which randomly un-materialize subcubes generating

Figure 4. Cube selection and allocation problem mapping in M-OLAP environment in discrete PSO n-dimensional space

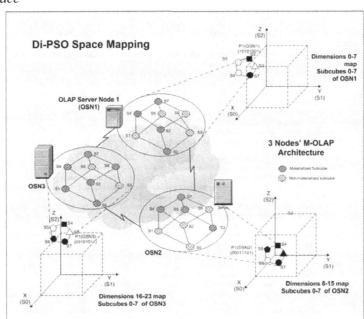

velocities accordingly, until the particle's proposal is valid. A more complex repair method was tried (that eliminated materialized subcubes which implied the least fitness loss, employing an inverse greedy method), but the performance gain didn't justify the processing cost.

M-OLAP Discrete Particle Swarm Optimization (M-OLAP Di-PSO)

In **Algorithm 2** we formally present the M-**OLAP** Di-PSO algorithm, based in the PSO discrete standard version. It was given genetic skills, using mating and selection operators.

Selection is implemented by the simple substitution of particles. In each loop a specified number of particles S will be substituted by an equal number of others with greater goodness that has been previously cloned. The substitution process may be done in several ways, with an elitism (Mitchell, 1996) level increasingly descending: 1) by taking randomly two particles in S, substituting

the one with lower goodness by *gbest* particle; 2) by replacing any randomly taken particle in S by *gbest,* and, for the rest of them, taking randomly pairs of particles and replacing the one of the pair with lower goodness by any other third particle; 3) by taking randomly pairs of particles in S and replacing the one with lower goodness by its peer. In all the described substitution methods, the particle's original *pbest* is retained, becoming the initial particle's position.

In the mating process, position and velocity are always crossed among dimensions corresponding to the same node and applying the following equations:

$$sun_1(x_i) = p_i * parent_1(x_i) + (1.0 - p_i) * parent_2(x_i)$$

and

$$sun_2(x_i) = p_i * parent_2(x_i) + (1.0 - p_i) * parent_1(x_i)$$

(4.4)

Algorithm 2. Distributed cube selection and allocation algorithm using discrete particle swarm optimization with breeding and selection in a M-OLAP environment (M-OLAP Di-PSO algorithm)

---

1. Initialization - randomly initialize a population of particles (position and velocity) in the n-dimensional space:

    1.1. *Randomly generate* the *velocity* of each particle being its position a) also randomly generated or b) according to the formulas that rule the particle's dynamics.

    1.2. *Repairing* those particles that don't satisfy space constraint, changing its position.

    1.3. *Maintenance cost computing* of the cube distribution proposed by each particle, being repeated 1.1. and 1.2. to the particles that don't obey to the defined constraint.

    1.4. *Initial goodness computing*, updating *pbest* and *gbest*.

    1.5. *Showing the distribution of solutions* of this initial swarm and also of the *pbest* solution.

2. Population Loop - **For each** particle, **Do**:

    2.1. *Using the formulas* that rule the particle's dynamics.

        2.1.1. v_i^{k+1} *computing*: to apply equation (4.1) and rule (4.3).

        2.1.2. *position updating*: to apply equation (4.2).

    2.2. *Repairing* those particles that don't satisfy space constraint, changing its position and velocity.

    2.3. *Maintenance cost computing* of the cube distribution proposed by each particle, being repeated 2.1.1. and 2.1.2. to the particles that don't obey to the defined constraint, what means that only the particle's moving that generates valid solutions is allowed.

    2.4. *Cross operator applying* using formulas (4.4) e (4.5), repairing those particles that don't obey to space constraints, just allowing crossings that generate particles that obey to the maintenance time constraints.

    2.5. *Own goodness evaluation and pbest update*: evaluate the 'goodness' of the particle. **If** its goodness > its best goodness so far, **Then** update *pbest*.

    2.6. *Global goodness evaluation and gbest update*: **If** the goodness of this particle > the goodness that any particle has ever achieved, **Then** update *gbest*.

    2.7. *Selection and cloning* with substitution operator applying.

    2.8. *Showing the distribution of solutions* of the actual swarm and also of the *pbest* solution.

3. Cycle: **Repeat** Step 2 **Until** a given convergence criterion is met, usually a pre-defined number of iterations.

---

where p_i is a uniformly distributed random value between 0 and 1.

$$sun_1(v) = (patent_1(v) + parent_2(v) / (|\, parent_1(v) + parent_2(v)|\,) * |parent_1(v)|$$

and

$$sun_2(v) = (parent_1(v) + parent_2(v) / (|\, parent_1(v) + parent_2(v)|\,) * |parent_2(v)|$$

$$(4.5)$$

It iterates the whole swarm and, with *bp* (*breeding probability*), one particle is marked to mate. From the marked breeding set group (*bg*), a pair of them is randomly taken, and then the formulas are applied (4.4 and 4.5) to generate the offspring particles, an operation to be repeated until *bg* is empty. The offspring particles replace their parents, keeping the population constant.

M-OLAP Discrete Cooperative Particle Swarm Optimization (M-OLAP Di-CPSO)

This algorithm is a multi-swarm cooperative version of the former and is presented in **Algorithm 3**. Its main difference is that it deals with many swarms whose particles' moves are restricted to subspace regions (in this case, the corresponding node dimensions).

Although the basic idea of cooperative swarms was already proposed in (Løvbjerg, Rasmussen, and Krink, 2001), nevertheless in terms of a sub-populations' hybrid model, in (Van den Bergh & Engelbrecht, 2004), it is formally presented, and in a more complete way.

In M-**OLAP** Di-CPSO all hybrid characteristics of M-OLAP Di-PSO are kept, now applied to each swarm, governed by rules that govern the particles' dynamic in the discrete multidimensional space. In practice, there's a swarm for each node of the M-OLAP architecture. In this case, the position of each particle in each swarm will determine whether the subcubes are materialized or not in the corresponding node. To evaluate the goodness of a particle, a "context vector" (Van den Bergh & Engelbrecht, 2004) is used, which is no more than a vector built by the position of gbest in each swarm. Mapping the PSO space to the cube selection and allocation problem, this vector corresponds to the best cube distribution until that moment.

To compute the goodness of one particle of a swarm (node), its own vector will substitute the homologous (*gbest* of the same swarm) in the context vector, thus following the goodness computing. In the proposed algorithm, some variations were introduced to this scheme: not only the aforementioned manner of vector context generating, but also the use of a probabilistic selection as follows: to each swarm, and with a *p* probability, the *gbest* vector is selected, and with *(1-p)* probability a particle is randomly selected in the same swarm. This scheme was successfully used with genetic co-evolutionary algorithms, in the same problem (Loureiro & Belo, 2006b), allowing the algorithm's escape from local minimums; here we expect it is also useful, although it may be

eventually less relevant, given the probabilistic nature of the particle's position.

M-OLAP Discrete Multi-Phase Particle Swarm Optimization (M-OLAP Di-MPSO)

We opted by using the smallest number of groups and phases: two for each. In this case, equation 4.2 is changed to

$$v^{k+1} = c_v.wv_i^k + c_x.c2.rnd\ 9().s_i^k + c_g.c2.rnd().gbest)$$

$$(4.6)$$

where the signs of coefficients (c_v, c_x and c_g) determine the direction of the particle movement. At any given time, each particle is in one of the possible phases, determined by its preceding phase and the number of iterations executed so

Algorithm 3. Distributed cube selection and allocation algorithm addressing a M-OLAP architecture using a discrete cooperative particle swarm optimization with breeding and selection

> *1. Initialization* - randomly initialize n swarms (one for each architecture's node) of particles (position and velocity):
>   1.1. Randomly generate the *velocity* of each particle being its position a) also randomly generated or b) according to the formulas that rule the particle's dynamics.
>   1.2. *Repairing* those particles that don't satisfy space constraint, changing its position.
>   1.3. *Generating initial context vector*, taking randomly one particle of each swarm;
>   1.4. *Initial repairing of the temporary context vector*: computing the maintenance cost of each temporary context vector component (related to one node), rebuilding it if it offends the maintenance constraint, updating the initial context vector with the corrected components.
>   1.5. *Maintenance cost computing* of the cube distribution proposed by each particle, being repeated 1.1. and 1.2. to the particles that don't obey to the defined constraint, using the initial context vector generated and constrained in 1.3. and 1.4.
>   1.6. *Initial goodness computing*, updating *pbest* and *gbest*.
>   1.7. *Generate the context vector* of the initial population.
>   1.8. *Showing the distribution of solutions* of this initial swarm and also of the *pbest* solution.
> *2. Populations Loop* - **For Each** swarm and **For Each** particle, **Do**:
>   2.1. *Using the formulas* that rules the particle's dynamics:
>   2.1.1. v_i^{k+1} *computing*: to apply equation (4.1) and rule (4.3).
>   2.1.2. *position updating*: to apply equation (4.2).
>   2.2. *Repairing* those particles that don't satisfy space constraint, changing its position.
>   2.3. *Maintenance cost computing* of the cube distribution proposed by each particle, being repeated 2.1.1. and 2.1.2. to the particles that don't obey to the defined constraint, what means that only the particle's moving that generates valid solutions is allowed.
>   2.4. *Cross operator applying* using formulas (4.4) e (4.5), repairing those particles that don't obey to space constraints, just allowing crossings that generate particles that obey to the maintenance of time constraints.
>   2.5. *Own goodness evaluation and pbest update*: evaluate the 'goodness' of the particle. **If** its goodness > its best goodness so far, **Then** update *pbest*.
>   2.6. *Global goodness evaluation and gbest update*: **If** the goodness of this particle > the goodness that any particle has ever achieved, **Then** update *gbest*.
>   2.7. *Selection and cloning* with substitution operator applying.
>   2.8. *Showing the distribution of solutions* of the actual swarm and also of the *pbest* solution.
> *3. Cycle*: **Repeat** Step 2 **Until** a given convergence criterion is met, usually a pre-defined number of iterations.

far. Within each phase, particles fall into different groups with different coefficient values for each group. In our experiments we used for phase 1, (1, -1, 1) for group 1 and (1, 1, -1) for group 2. In phase 2 the coefficients are switched.

This swarm optimizer version also uses hill climbing which only permits particle position to change if such a change improves fitness. This way, each particle's current position is better that its previous position, hence eq. 4.6 doesn't contain a separate term corresponding to *pbest*. Hill climbing would require a fitness test whenever a dimension was updated. This would require an enormous amount of fitness evaluations, which would imply a very long running time. This way, it performs a fitness evaluation only after transitory updating a randomly chosen fraction (*s*) of consecutive velocity vector components. Only if changes improve fitness the updates will be committed. The interval from where *s* is randomly chosen is allowed to decrease with the running of the algorithm. Another variation of the algorithm was also tried, where, if no improvement of fitness if achieved, the interval was extended and a re-evolution of the particle in *s* dimensions is tried. But this modified version has a worst performance that the former and then it was disregarded.

EXPERIMENTAL PERFORMANCE STUDY

In the experimental study of the two algorithms, we have used the test set of Benchmark's (TPC-R 2002), selecting the smallest database (1 GB), from which we selected 3 dimensions (customer, product and supplier). To broaden the variety of subcubes, we added additional attributes to each dimension, forming the hierarchies shown in **Figure 5**.

Equations (3.6) will be used to compute the following costs: 1) the query answer costs of a multi-node M distribution of subcubes (the proposed solution of each particle or of a particle in a

Figure 5. Dimensional hierarchies on customer, product and supplier dimensions of a TPC-R Benchmark database subset

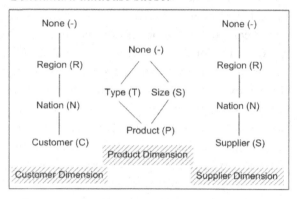

context vector), whose minimization is the global purpose of the algorithms, supposing $e_q=1$; and 2) the maintenance costs, that might be obeyed as constraints, supposing e_u and $f_u=1$.

Concerning to the cost estimation algorithms, we opted by the use of the architecture's parallelism when estimating costs, allowing that multiple queries or subcubes/deltas can be processed using different OSNs and communication links. This implied the control of conflicts and resource allocation with the use of succeeding windows to discretize time and separate each parallel processing where multiple tasks may occur. With these general rules in mind, we will use the Greedy2PRS Algorithm proposed in (Loureiro & Belo, 2006c), which may be looked for further details, specially concerning to parallel execution tasks simulation. We also used a query costs estimation algorithm, M-OLAP PQCEA, which is the acronym of Multi-Node OLAP Parallel Query Cost Estimation Algorithm, also used in (Loureiro & Belo, 2006b).

The system components were implemented in Java, appealing to the following classes:

- ParamAlgPSwarm, that loads and supplies the working parameters which rule the PSO algorithms, an extension of the base parameters;

- ParticleSwarm, that allows the creation of swarm objects, keeping the state and supplying a set of services to the main classes;
- PSONormal, that implements M-OLAP Di-PSO algorithm;
- PSOCoop, the M-OLAP Di-CPSO algorithm; and
- M-DiPSO, the M-OLAP multi-phase discrete algorithm.

The system, as a whole, uses the services of four other classes:

- **NodeCube:** Responsible for the computing of query and maintenance costs, attending to the model and the cost formulas stated in section 3.4, whose query and maintenance algorithms are already described;
- **QualifQuerySCube:** Able to compute and to dispose the dependence relations between subcubes, using nothing more than the dimension and hierarchies definitions and the naming of each subcube by a string (e.g. cps, for the subcube 1 in Table 2);
- **StateDistrib:** Makes available the necessary services to the visualization of the instant state of the particles' spatial distribution and also the best distribution attained so far;
- **OutBook:** Used to output the results, through a set of services of data output.

It's also used another set of classes that loads and makes available data related to the M-OLAP architecture and environment:

- Base architectural parameters;
- The cube (subcubes, sizes, dimensions, parallel hierarchies);
- The network's connections (characteristics as: BD, delay, size of packet, etc.);
- The queries and their spatial distribution;
- Nodes, their storage capacity and processing power.

As we have 3 dimensions, each one with 4 hierarchies, that makes a total of 4x4x4=64 possible subcubes, that are presented in Table 2, jointly with their sizes (in tuples). Let's also suppose that the cost of using base relation is 18 M tuples (3 times the cost of subcube cps).

In this simulation we supposed a three OSNs (with materializing space=10% of total cube space and a processing power of 15E3 records.s-1) plus the base relations (e.g. a DW - considered as node 0 with processing power of 3E4 records.s-1) and a network with BD=1Gbps and delay=[15,50]ms. An OLAP distributed middleware is in charge of receive user queries and provide for its OSN allocation, and corresponding redirecting. It is supposed that middleware services run into each OSN, on a peer-to-peer approach, although one or many dedicated servers may also exist. To simplify the computations, it is supposed that communication costs between OSNs and any user are equal (using a LAN), and then may be neglected. We generated a random query profile (normalized in order to have a total number equal to the number of subcubes) that was supposed to induce the optimized M (materialized set of selected and allocated subcubes).

Initially we have performed some tests to gain insights about the tuning of some parameters of Di-PSO algorithms, e.g. Vmax, w, c1 and c2. We also used some information about the values used in other research works. Then, we selected Vmax=10, w=[0.99,1.00], varying linearly with the number of iterations and c1=c2=1.74. We generated the initial velocity vector randomly and the initial position with (eq. 4.1). As said in section 4, each invalid solution was randomly repaired. As we have three base Di-PSO variants, often we will perform a comparative evaluation, applying each one in turn to the same test. Given the stochastic nature of the algorithms, all presented values are the average of 10 runs.

It's important to refer, globally, that in all the tests the convergence of all algorithms is verified, showing their ability to find a solution to the cube

Table 2. Generated subcubes with dimensions and hierarchies shown in Fig. 5 as described in (TPC-R 2002)

Subcube		Size	Subcube		Size	Subcube		Size	Subcube		Size
0	cps	6,000,000	16	nps	5,000,000	32	rps	4,000,000	48	-ps	800,000
1	cpn	6,000,000	17	npn	5,000,000	33	rpn	4,000,000	49	-pn	800,000
2	cpr	6,000,000	18	npr	5,000,000	34	rpr	4,000,000	50	-pr	800,000
3	cp-	6,000,000	19	np-	5,000,000	35	rp-	1,000,000	51	-p-	200,000
4	css	5,000,000	20	nss	500,000	36	rss	2,500,000	52	-ss	500,000
5	csn	5,000,000	21	nsn	30,000	37	rsn	6,250	53	-sn	1,250
6	csr	5,000,000	22	nsr	6,250	38	rsr	1,250	54	-sr	250
7	cs-	5,000,000	23	ns-	1,250	39	rs-	25	55	-s-	5
8	cts	5,990,000	24	nts	800,000	40	rts	3,000,000	56	-ts	1,500,000
9	ctn	5,990,000	25	ntn	90,000	41	rtn	18,750	57	-tn	3,750
10	ctr	5,990,000	26	ntr	18,750	42	rtr	3,750	58	-tr	750
11	ct-	5,990,000	27	nt-	3,750	43	rt-	750	59	-t-	150
12	c-s	6,000,000	28	n-s	250,000	44	r-s	50,000	60	--s	100,000
13	c-n	2,500,000	29	n-n	625	45	r-n	125	61	--n	25
14	c-r	500,000	30	n-r	125	46	r-r	25	62	--r	25
15	c--	150	31	n--	25	47	r--	5	63	---	1

selection and allocation problem. Tests' results were shown in graphical form; some of them aren't sufficiently clear but yet capable of showing the global insights. Other results are shown as tables, allowing the exhibition of some details.

First test was designed to allow the evaluation of the impact of the particles' number on the quality of the solution, using in this case only the Di-PSO. The results are shown in **Figure 6**.

As we can see, a swarm with a higher number of particles achieved good solutions after a reduced number of iterations; but if a number of generations were allowed, the difference between the quality of the solutions of a great and a small swarm vanished.

Table 3 allows performing a trade-off analysis of quality vs. run-time. Referring to the table, we may observe that, e.g., the 200 particles' swarm achieved a solution with a cost of 5,914 after 200 iterations spending 402 seconds. A swarm of 10 particles achieves an identical solution after 700 iterations on 71 seconds and a 20 particles' swarm after 500 iterations spending 101 seconds. For 40 and 100 particles the results are poorer: Di-PSO needs 600 and 450 iterations spending 237 and 443 seconds, respectively. After these results, we selected a swarm population of 20 particles for all subsequent tests, as a good trade-off between quality of final solution and run-time execution.

Figure 6. Impact of particle's swarm number on the goodness of the solutions for Di-PSO algorithm

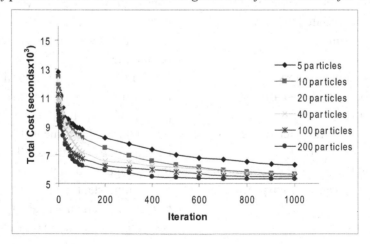

Table 3. Quality and run-time execution of M-OLAP Di-PSO algorithm for different particles swarm's number

Particles	At 200 iterations		At 400 iterations		At 500 iterations		At 600 iterations		At 700 iterations		At 800 iterations		At 1000 iterations	
	Cost	Run-Time	Cost	Run-Time	Cost	Run-Time	Cost	Run-Time	Cost	Run-Time	Cost	Run-Time	Cost	Run-Time
10	7475	22	6558	41	6312	50.5	6152	60.5	5924	71	5800	82.5	5655	103.5
20	7080	44	6137	80.5	5922	101	5834	126.5	5743	136	5659	158	5573	200.5
40	6555	84.5	6263	167.5	6118	199.5	6025	237.5	5840	277.5	5707	252.5	5537	393.5
100	6264	196	5958	394.5	5810	500	5698	595	5566	721.5	5506	803	5469	1008.5
200	5914	402.5	5467	812	5406	1008.5	5365	1110.5	5349	1422	5311	1621.5	5304	2022

Figure 7 shows the run-time of the M-OLAP Di-PSO algorithm for different number of swarm particles, all for 1000 iterations. As we can see, the run-time linearly increases with the number of swarm particles, with a value of ten seconds. particle^{-1}. This shows that if we can use a low number of particles without hurting the quality of solutions the run-time will be kept into controlled values.

Next test evaluates comparatively the performance (in terms of quality and how fast it as achieved) of M-OLAP Di-PSO, Di-CPSo and

Figure 7. Run-time execution of M-OLAP Di-PSO algorithm varying the number of swarm's particles

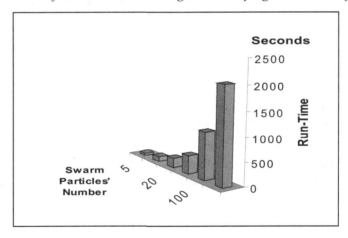

Figure 8. Quality achieved by M-OLAP Di-PSO, M-OLAP Di-CPSO and M-OLAP Di-MPSO algorithms

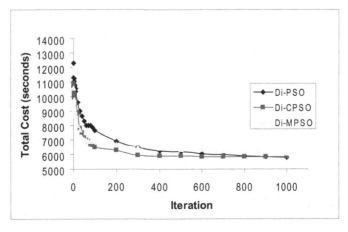

Di-MPSO algorithms. The results are shown in Figure 8.

As we can verify, cooperative and multi-phase versions achieve a good solution in a lower number of iterations. As the interval between evaluations is short, any improvement has a high probability of being captured. But, if a high number of iterations was allowed, normal and cooperative versions achieve almost the same quality and the multi-phase behaves poorer. A trade-off analysis of quality vs. run-time shows that, even for a low number of iterations (e.g. 100), where Di-CPSO and Di-MPSO performs better, we observed that Di-CPSO spends 89 seconds to achieve a 6507 solution. For a similar solution, Di-PSO uses 63 seconds to achieve a 6479 solution. For Di-MPSO x Di-PSO the plate bends higher to the second: 8,875 in 175 sec. vs. 6,893 in 43 sec.

Next test tries to evaluate if mass extinction will be also beneficial when PSO is applied to this kind of problem. Then we executed M-OLAP Di-PSO algorithm varying Ie. We used Ie from the set [10, 20, 50, 100, 500] and also the no mass extinction option. **Figure 9** shows the obtained results. As we can see, for low values of *Ie*, the algorithm has a poorer performance compared to the algorithm with no mass extinction. The best

value seems to happen with *Ie*=100, where ME option surpasses the no mass extinction use.

To complete the tests, we have to study the behavior of M-OLAP Di-PSO and M-OLAP Di-CPSO algorithms in their genetic hybrid versions. It was observed that the genetic operator has a weak impact. Concerning to genetic crossing, **Figure 10** shows the results of the test.

Although the number of series is high, we can observe that only for M-OLSP Di-PSO and for 20% crossing, this operator seems to be beneficial. All other values (10, 40 and 60%) hurt the

Figure 10. Impact of genetic crossing for M-OLAP Di-PSO and Di-CPSO algorithms onto the quality of proposed solutions

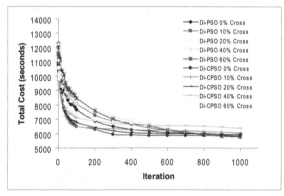

Figure 9. Impact of mass extinction onto the quality of solutions proposed by M-OLAP Di-PSO algorithm

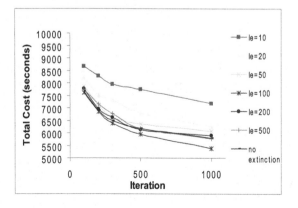

Figure 11. Impact of genetic crossing for M-OLAP Di-PSO and Di-CPSO algorithms onto the quality of proposed solutions (detail only for 0 and 20% crossing)

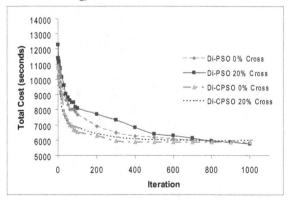

quality. **Figure 11** allows confirming this first observation. As we can see, 20% crossing from Di-PSO seems to be beneficial. The same isn't true for Di-CPSO. As crossing is, in this case, performed as an intra-node operation, it seems that no further information is gained. The opposite happens to Di-PSO: the inter-node crossing seems to be interesting. Even for this version, higher crossing values disturb the swarm and damage the quality of the achieved solutions.

The last test evaluates the scalability of algorithms, concerning to the number of M-OLAP nodes. We used M-OLAP Di-PSO algorithm. The two others, as similar in terms of complexity (cost estimation algorithms and loop design) must have the same behavior. We used the same 3 nodes M-OLAP architecture and another with 10 nodes. We generate another query profile, also normalized to a total frequency of 64 queries by node. The plot of **Figure 12** shows the observed run-time and corresponding ratio.

As we can see, an increase of 10/3=3.3 for the number of nodes implies a run-time increase of 3.8, showing a quasi-linearity and the easy support by the algorithms of M-OLAP architectures with many nodes. This is an interesting characteristic, as M-OLAP architecture evidenced a good scale-up by the simulations described in (Loureiro & Belo, 2006c).

Figure 12. Run-time of M-OLAP Di-PSO algorithm for 3 and 10 nodes' architecture and corresponding ratio.

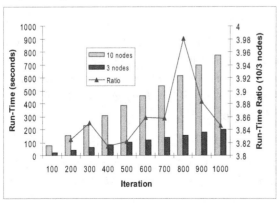

CONCLUSION AND FUTURE RESEARCH ISSUES

This paper focus on the use of discrete particle swarm optimization to solve the cube selection and allocation problem for distributed and multidimensional structures typical of M-OLAP environments, where we have several nodes interconnected with communication links. These communication facilities extend the subcubes' dependencies beyond the node borders, generating intra-node dependencies.

The aim of this study is to evaluate the comparative performance of some variants of the discrete particle swarm optimization algorithm. The experimental simulated tests that we performed shown that this kind of optimization allows the design and building of algorithms that stand as good candidates to this problem. Given the nature of the M-OLAP architecture:

- We used a cost model that extends the existing proposals by the explicit inclusion of parameters as communication costs and processing power of OLAP nodes;
- The query and maintenance cost estimation algorithms simulate the parallelization of tasks (using the inherent parallelisms of the M-OLAP architecture), keeping the calculated values closer to real values.

These features of the cost model and computing algorithms are particularly interesting, especially for the maintenance cost estimation, if maintenance cost constraints were applied.

We tested not only the original PSO discrete version, but also a cooperative and a multi-phase approach. A set of proposed variations in the PSO continuous version was also included in the developed algorithms.

Globally, the tests allow us to conclude that all algorithms achieve good solutions, but the multi-phase version seems to perform poorer in this kind of problem (it is neither faster nor it achieves a better final solution). The observed performance of this algorithm constituted a real disappointment. In fact, it would be expectable that the algorithm performed better, according to the referred results (Al-Kazemi & Mohan, 2002). Maybe it's not suitable to this kind of problem or some detail of design and implementation might have been missed.

Concerning to the cooperative version, it achieves good solutions in a fewer iterations than the normal one, but, in terms of execution time, this is not really true, as the first needs an *n* times number of fitness evaluations. The quality of the final solution is almost the same for both.

Mass extinction seems to be interesting, concerning that the extinction interval is carefully selected. In this case, the experimental results show that a value of 1/10 of the number of iterations improves the quality of achieved solutions.

Concerning to genetic swarm operators, our results seem to advise only crossing operator for Di-PSO with a low crossing percent (this case 20%).

The discussed algorithms may support the development of a system capable of automating the OLAP cube distribution (being a part of the distributed data cube proposal generator of the system shown in Figure 1), making management tasks easier, thus allowing the gain of the inherent advantages of data and processing distribution without the incurrence in management overhead and other normally associated costs.

Given the M-OLAP scope of the proposed algorithms, the scalability is at premium. The performed tests ensure it, not only by showing the relative independence of the quality of the solution in face to the swarm particles' number, but also by the only slight growth of the run-time with the number of the M-OLAP architecture's nodes.

For future research issues, it will be interesting to perform the comparative valuation of these algorithms against the greedy and genetic ones, but using another cost model (Loureiro & Belo, 2006a), introducing non-linearities. This may

result in further conclusions that may conceive a number of rules of thumb about the adjustment of any of the algorithms to the specificity of the real problem. As all algorithms were already designed and implemented having a global system in mind where each one is a component, it may be conceived and developed something like a *workbench* addressing the cube selection problem.

Moreover, the inclusion of another parameter in the cost model, related to the differentiation between rebuilt subcubes and incremental ones, concerning to the maintenance process, may allow the coexistence in the same M-OLAP system of delta's incremental maintenance (typical for the maintenance of great static structures) and by subcube rebuilding (for dynamic or even pro-active cubes selection and allocation). This will be of high interest, because it enlarges the range of application of all algorithms in new real situations.

REFERENCES

Al-Kazemi, B. & Mohan, C.K. (2002). Multi-phase discrete particle swarm optimization. *Proceedings from the International Workshop on Frontiers in Evolutionary Algorithms*, (pp. 622-625).

Angeline, P. (1998, May 4-9). Using selection to improve particle swarm optimization. Proceedings from *The IEEE International Conference on Evolutionary Computation (ICEC'98)*, Anchorage, Alaska, USA.

Bauer, A., &Lehner, W. (2003). On solving the view selection problem in distributed data warehouse architectures. *Proceedings from the 15th International Conference on Scientific and Statistical Database Management (SSDBM'03), IEEE*, (pp. 43-51).

Belo, O. (2000, November). Putting intelligent personal assistants working on dynamic hypercube views updating. *Proceedings of 2nd Inter-*

national Symposium on Robotics and Automation (ISRA'2000), Monterrey, México.

Van den Bergh, F., & Engelbrecht, A.P. (2004, June). A cooperative approach to particle swarm optimization. *IEEE Transactions on Evolutionary Computation, 8*(3), 225-239.

Eberhart, R.C., & Kennedy, J. (1995). A new optimizer using particle swarm theory. *Proceedings from the Sixth International Symposium on Micro Machine and Human Science*, Nagoya, Japan, IEEE Service Center, Piscataway, NJ, (pp. 39-43).

Eberhart, R. C., & Shi, Y. (2001). Particle swarm optimization: Developments, applications and resources. *Proceedings from the 2001 Congress on Evolutionary Computation,.1*, 81-86.

Gupta, H., & Mumick, I.S. (1999). Selection of views to materialize under a maintenance-time constraint. *Proceedings from the International Conference on Database Theory.*

Harinarayan, V., Rajaraman, A., & Ullman, J. (1996, June). Implementing data cubes efficiently. In *Proceedings of ACM SIGMOD*, Montreal, Canada, (pp. 205-216).

Holland, J.H. (1992). Adaptation in natural and artificial systems. Cambridge, MA, (2nd edition): MIT Press

Horng, J.T., Chang, Y.J., Liu, B.J., & Kao, C.Y. (1999, July). Materialized view selection using genetic algorithms in a data warehouse. *Proceedings from the World Congress on Evolutionary Computation*, Washington D.C.

Huang, Y.-F., & Chen, J.-H. (2001). Fragment allocation in distributed database design. In *Journal of Information Science and Engineering 17*(2001), 491-506.

Kalnis, P., Mamoulis, N., & Papadias, D. (2002). View selection using randomized search. In *Data Knowledge Engineering, 42*(1), 89-111.

Kennedy, J., & Eberhart, R.C. (1995). Particle swarm optimization. *Proceedings from the IEEE Intl. Conference on Neural Networks* (Perth, Australia), *4*,1942-1948, IEEE Service Center, Piscataway, NJ..

Kennedy, J., & Eberhart, R.C. (1997). A discrete binary version of the particle swarm optimization algorithm. *Proceedings from the 1997 Conference on Systems, Man and Cybernetics (SMC'97)*, (pp. 4104-4109).

Kotidis, Y., & Roussopoulos, N. (1999, June). Dynamat: A dynamic view management system for data warehouses. *Proceedings from the ACM SIGMOD International Conference on Management of Data*, Philadelphia, Pennsylvania, (pp. 371-382).

Liang, W., Wang, H., & Orlowska, M.E. (2001). Materialized view selection under the maintenance cost constraint. In *Data and Knowledge Engineering, 37*(2), 203-216.

Lin, W.-Y., & Kuo, I-C. (2004). A genetic selection algorithm for OLAP data cubes. *Knowledge and Information Systems, 6*(1), 83-102. Springer-Verlag London Ltd.

Loureiro, J., & Belo, O. (2006[a], June 5-9). A non-linear cost model for multi-node OLAP cubes. *Proceedings from the CAiSE'06 Forum*, Luxembourg, (pp. 68-71).

Loureiro, J. &Belo, O. (2006b, December 11-14). An evolutionary approach to the selection and allocation of distributed cubes. *Proceedings from 2006 International Database Engineering & Applications Symposium (IDEAS2006)*, Delhi, India, (pp. 243-248).

Loureiro, J., & Belo, O. (2006c, October 3-6). Evaluating maintenance cost computing algorithms for multi-node OLAP systems. *Proceedings from the XI Conference on Software Engineering and Databases (JISBD2006)*, Sitges, Barcelona, (pp. 241-250_.

Løvbjerg, M., Rasmussen, T., & Krink, T. (2001). Hybrid particle swarm optimization with breeding and subpopulations. *Proceedings from the 3rd Genetic and Evolutionary Computation Conference (GECCO-2001).*

Mitchell, M. (1996). *An introduction to genetic algorithms.* Cambridge, MA: MIT Press.

Park, C.S., Kim, M.H., & Lee, Y.J. (2003, November). Usability-based caching of query results in OLAP systems. *Journal of Systems and Software, 68*(2), 103-119.

Potter, M.A., & Jong, K.A. (1994). A cooperative coevolutionary approach to function optimization. *The Third Parallel Problem Solving From Nature.* Berlin, Germany: Springer-Verlag, (pp. 249-257).

Sapia, C. (2000, September). PROMISE – Modeling and predicting user query behavior in online analytical processing environments. *Proceedings from the 2nd International Conference on Data Warehousing and Knowledge Discovery (DAWAK'00),* London, UK: Springer LNCS.

Scheuermann, P., Shim, J., & Vingralek, R. (1996, September 3-6). WATCHMAN: A data warehouse intelligent cache manager. *Proceedings from the 22th International Conference on Very Large Data Bases VLDB'96,* Bombay, (pp. 51-62).

Shi, Y., & Eberhart, R.C. (1999). Empirical study of particle swarm optimization. *Proceedings from the 1999 Congress of Evolutionary Cmputation, 3,* 1945-1950. IEEE Press.

Shukla, A., Deshpande, P.M., & Naughton, J.F. (1998). Materialized view selection for multidimensional datasets. *Proceedings of VLDB.*

Transaction Processing Performance Council (TPC): TPC Benchmark R (decision support) Standard Specification Revision 2.1.0. tpcr_2.1.0.pdf, available at http://www.tpc.org

Walrand, J., & Varaiya, P. (2000). *High-performance communication networks.* The Morgan Kaufmann Series in Networking.

Widom, J. (1995, November). Research problems in data warehousing. *Proceedings from the Fourth International Conference on Information and Knowledge Management (CIKM '95),* invited paper , Baltimore, Maryland, (pp. 25-30).

Xie, X.-F., Zhang, W.-J., & Yang, Z.-L. (2002). Hybrid particle swarm optimizer with mass extinction. *Proceedings from the Int. Conf. on Communication, Circuits and Systems (ACCCAS),* Chengdhu, China.

Yu, J.X., Choi, C-H, Gou, G., & Lu, H. (2004, May). Selecting views with maintenance cost constraints: Issues, heuristics and performance. *Journal of Research and Practice in Information Technology, 36*(2.

Zhang, C., Yao, X., & Yang, J. (2001, September). An evolutionary approach to materialized views selection in a data warehouse environment. *IEEE Trans. on Systems, Man and Cybernetics, Part C, 31*(3).

Chapter VIII
Multidimensional Anlaysis of XML Document Contents with OLAP Dimensions

Franck Ravat
IRIT, Universite Toulouse, France

Olivier Teste
IRIT, Universite Toulouse, France

Ronan Tournier
IRIT, Universite Toulouse, France

ABSTRACT

With the emergence of Semi-structured data format (such as XML), the storage of documents in centralised facilities appeared as a natural adaptation of data warehousing technology. Nowadays, OLAP (On-Line Analytical Processing) systems face growing non-numeric data. This chapter presents a framework for the multidimensional analysis of textual data in an OLAP sense. Document structure, metadata, and contents are converted into subjects of analysis (facts) and analysis axes (dimensions) within an adapted conceptual multidimensional schema. This schema represents the concepts that a decision maker will be able to manipulate in order to express his analyses. This allows greater multidimensional analysis possibilities as a user may gain insight within a collection of documents.

INTRODUCTION

The rapid expansion of information technologies has considerably increased the quantity of available data through electronic documents. The volume of all this information is so large that comprehension of this information is a difficult problem to tackle.

Context: Data Warehousing and Document Warehousing

OLAP (On-Line Analytical Processing) systems (Codd et al., 1993), with the use of multidimensional databases, enable decision makers to gains insight into enterprise performance through fast and interactive access to different views of data organised in a multidimensional way (Colliat, 1996). Multidimensional databases, also called data marts (Kimball, 1996), organise data warehouse data within multidimensional structures in order to facilitate their analysis (see Figure 1).

Multidimensional modelling (Kimball, 1996) represents data as points within a multidimensional space with the "cube" or "hypercube" metaphor. This user-oriented approach incorporates structures as well as data in the cube representation. For example, in Figure 2, the *number of keywords* used in a scientific publication is analysed according to three analysis axes: the *authors*, the *dates* and the *keywords* of these publications. A "slice" of the cube has been extracted and is represented as a table on the right hand side of Figure 2.

In order to design multidimensional databases, multidimensional structures were created to represent the concepts of analysis subjects, namely *facts*, and analysis axes, namely *dimensions* (Kimball, 1996). Facts are groupings of analysis indicators called *measures*. Dimensions are composed of *parameters* hierarchically organised that model the different levels of detail of an analysis axis. A parameter may be associated to complementary information represented by *weak attributes* (e.g. the name of the month associated to its number in a dimension modelling time). The Figure 3 illustrates through a star schema (Kimball, 1996) the multidimensional structures of the cube representation displayed in Figure 2. Graphic notations come from (Ravat et al., 2008)

Figure 1. Architecture of a decisional system

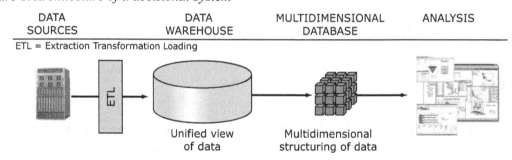

Figure 2. Cube representation of a multidimensional database and extracted "slice"

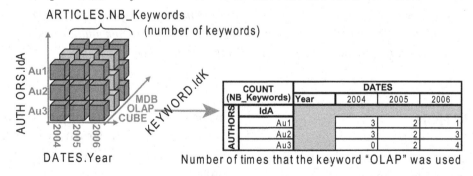

COUNT (NB_Keywords)	DATES			
IdA	Year	2004	2005	2006
Au1			3	2	1
Au2			3	2	3
Au3			0	2	4

Number of times that the keyword "OLAP" was used

Figure 3. Star schema of a multidimensional database

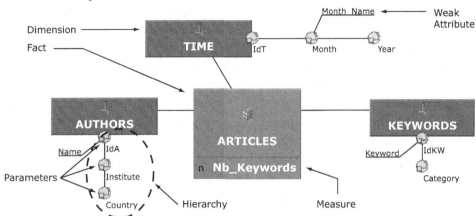

and are inspired by (Golfarelli et al., 1998). Fact and dimension concepts will be presented in more details hereinafter.

According to a recent survey (Tseng et al., 2006), decision support systems have only excavated the surface layers of the task. Multidimensional analysis based multidimensional analysis of numerical data is nowadays a well mastered technique (Sullivan, 2001). These multidimensional databases are built on transactional data extracted from corporate operational information systems. But only 20% of information system data is transactional and may be easily processed (Tseng et al., 2006). The remaining 80%, i.e. documents, remain out of reach of OLAP systems due to the lack of adapted tools for processing non numeric data such as textual data.

OLAP systems provide powerful tools, but within a rigid framework inherited from databases. Textual data, less structured than transactional data is harder to handle. Recently XML[1] technology has provided a vast framework for sharing and spreading documents throughout corporate information systems or over the Web. The XML language allows data storage in an auto-descriptive format with the use of a grammar to specify its structure: DTD (Document Type Definition) or XSchema[2]. Slowly, semi-structured documents started to be integrated within data warehouses

and the term document warehousing emerged (Sullivan, 2001), with tools such as Xyleme[3]. Consequently, structured or semi-structured documents are becoming a conceivable data source for OLAP systems.

Nowadays, the OLAP environment rests on a quantitative analysis of factual data, for example, the number of products sold or the number of times a keyword is used in a document (see Mothe et al., 2003 for a detailed example). We whish to go further by providing a more complete environment. Systems should not be limited to quantitative analysis but should also include qualitative analyses. However, quantitative data must be correctly handled within OLAP systems. These systems aggregate analysis data with the use of aggregation functions. For example, the total number of times a keyword was used in a document during each year is obtained by summing each individual number of times that the keyword was used by each author. The aggregation is done through a Sum aggregation function. The problem is that quantitative data is generally non additive and non numeric, thus standard aggregation functions (e.g. Sum or Average) cannot operate. In (Park et al., 2005), the authors suggest the use of adapted aggregation functions and in (Ravat et al., 2007) we defined such a function. In the rest of this paper, throughout our examples, we shall use a simple textual based aggregation function: Top _ KEYWORDS (Park et al., 2005).

In order to provide more detailed analysis capacities decision support systems should be able to provide the usage of nearly all 100% of corporate information system data. Documents or Web data could be directly integrated within analysis processes. Not taking into account these data sources would inevitably lead to the omission of relevant information during an important decision-making process or the inclusion of irrelevant information and thus producing inaccurate analyses (Tseng et al., 2006). Going beyond Fankhauser et al., 2003 writings, we believe that XML technology allows considering the integration of documents within an OLAP system. As a consequence, the key problem rests on the multidimensional analysis of documents. The actual OLAP environment does not deal with the analysis of textual data. Besides, textual data have a structure and a content that could be handled with adapted analysis means. The analysis of textual documents allows a user to gain a global vision of a document collection. Looking for information that does not exist within a document collection would represent a loss of time for the user. The opposite could be crucial in terms of decision making.

Related Works

We consider two types of XML documents (Fuhr & Großjohann, 2001):

- *Data-centric XML documents* are raw data documents, mainly used by applications to exchange data (as in e-business application strategies). In this category, one may find lists and logs such as: invoices, orders, spreadsheets, or even "dumps" of databases. These documents are very structured and are similar to database content.

- *Document-centric XML documents* also known as text-rich documents are the traditional paper documents, e.g. scientific

articles, e-books, website pages. These documents are mainly composed of textual data and do not have an obvious structure.

We divide related works into three categories:

- Integrating XML data within data warehouses;
- Warehousing XML data directly;
- Integrating documents within OLAP analysis.

The first category presents the integration of XML data within a data warehouse. (Golfarelli et al., 2001 and Pokorný, 2001) propose to integrate XML data from the description of their structure with a DTD. (Vrdoljak et al., 2003 and Vrdoljak et al., 2006) suggest creating a multidimensional schema from the XSchema structure definition of the XML documents. (Niemi et al., 2002) assembles XML data cubes on the fly from user queries. (Zhang et al., 2003) proposes a method for creating a data warehouse on XML data. An alternative to integrating XML data within a warehouse consists in using federations. This is the case when warehousing the XML data within the data warehouse may not be taken into consideration, i.e. in case of legal constraints (such as rights on data) or physical constraints (when data change too rapidly for an efficient warehouse refreshing process). In this federation context, the authors of (Jensen et al., 2001; Pedersen et al., 2002 and Yin et al., 2004) describe an application that first splits queries between two warehousing systems (one for the traditional data, one for the XML data) and second federates the results of processed queries.

The second category represents warehousing of complex data in XML format. Due to the complexity of this data type the solution is to physically integrate them within a native XML warehouse. Two research fields have been developed.

The first is centred on adapting the XML query language (XQuery[4]) for analytics, i.e. easing the expression of multidimensional queries with this language. Notably with: the addition of a grouping operator (Beyer et al., 2005 and Bordawerkar et al., 2005); the adaptation of the Cube operator (Gray et al., 1996) to XML data (Wiwatwattana et al., 2007); and the aggregation of XML data with the use of its structure (Wang et al., 2005).

The second field is centred on creating XML warehouses. In (Nassis et al., 2004), the authors propose a special xFACT structure that allows the definition of a document warehouse (Sullivan, 2001) using XML format with complex factual data. In (Boussaid et al., 2006), the authors describe a design process as well as a framework for an XML warehouse. They offer the multidimensional analysis of complex data but only within a numerical context (i.e. all indicators or measures are numeric). In (Khrouf et al., 2004), the authors describe a document warehouse, where documents are regrouped by structure similarity. A user may run multidimensional analyses on document structures but still with numerical indicators (e.g. a number of structures).

The third category concerns the addition of documents within the OLAP framework and is divided into three subcategories:

Firstly, by associating numerical analysis to information retrieval techniques, the authors of (Pérez et al., 2005 and Peréz et al., 2007) propose to enrich a multidimensional analysis. They offer to return to the user documents which are relevant to the context of the ongoing analysis. As a consequence, the decision maker has available complementary information concerning the current analysis. However, there is no analysis of the documents, the user must read all the relevant documents in order to take advantage of them.

Secondly, four works suggested the use of the OLAP environment for the analysis of document collections. In (McCabe et al., 2000) and (Mothe et al., 2003), the authors suggest the use of multidimensional analyses to gain a global vision of document collections with the analysis of the use of keywords within the documents. With

this, the user may specify information retrieval queries more precisely by an optimised use of the keywords. In (Keith et al., 2005) and (Tseng et al., 2006), the authors suggest the use of the OLAP environment for building cooccurence matrices. With these four propositions, document contents are analysed according to a keyword dimension (results are similar to the table presented in Figure 2). Textual data (the content of documents) are modelled through analysis axes but not subjects of analysis. Analysis indicators (or measures) are always numeric (the number of times a keyword is used...). Thus, only quantitative analyses and not qualitative analyses are expressed.

Thirdly, with the direct analysis of the documents. In (Khrouf et al., 2004), the authors allow the multidimensional analysis of document structures. Finally, in (Park et al., 2005), the authors use the xFACT structure (Nassis et al., 2004) and introduce the concept of multidimensional analysis of XML documents with the use of text mining techniques. In a complementary manner, we introduced an aggregation function for keywords through the use of a "pseudo-average" function (Ravat et al., 2007). This function aggregates a set of keywords into a smaller and more general set, thus reducing the final number of keywords.

These advanced propositions are limited: 1) apart from the two last propositions, textual data is not analysed and systems use mainly numeric measures to go round the problem; 2) the rare textual analyses rests on keywords whereas contents and structure are ignored; 3) document structures are almost systematically ignored; and 4) there exists no framework for the specification of non numeric indicators.

Objectives and Contributions

The major objective of this work is to go beyond the analysis capacities of numeric indicators and to provide an enriched OLAP framework that associates the actual quantitative analysis capabilities to new qualitative analysis possibilities. However, the analysis of textual data is not as reliable as the analysis of numerical data.

By *multidimensional analysis of documents*, we mean the multidimensional analysis of textual data sources (i.e. documents) in an OLAP environment. In order to be compatible with the rigid environment inherited from data warehouses, we consider structured or semi-structured documents. For example, XML documents that represent the proceedings of scientific conferences, the diagnoses of patient files from a hospital information system, quality control reports...

We propose an extension of a constellation model described in (Ravat et al., 2008), allowing the specification of textual measures. Contrarily to (Park et al., 2005), we whish to specify a formal framework for textual measures in order to facilitate multidimensional analysis specification. We also revise the previously proposed dimension categories (Tseng et al., 2006), in order to take into account the dimension that characterises document structures. Modelling document structures allows a greater flexibility for analysis specifications on textual data.

This chapter is structured as follows: the second section defines our multidimensional model, where we introduce the concept of textual measure as well as the concept of a structure dimension. The third section presents the logical level of our proposition while the fourth section describes the analysis of textual data within the framework.

CONCEPTUAL MULTIDIMENSIONAL MODEL

Current multidimensional models are limited for the analysis of textual data. Nevertheless, actual star or constellation schemas (Kimball, 1996) are widely used. As a consequence, we propose to extend a constellation model specified in (Ravat et al., 2008) in order to allow the conceptual modelling of analyses of document collections.

By *document collection* we mean a set of documents homogeneous in structure corresponding to an analysis requirement. These collections are supposed to be accessible through a document warehouse (Sullivan, 2001). We invite the reader to consult recent surveys (Torlone, 2003; Abello et al., 2006 and Ravat et al., 2008) for an overview of multidimensional modelling.

Due to the rigid environment inherited from data warehouses, we consider the document collections to be composed of structured or semi-structured documents, e.g. scientific articles stored in XML format. Moreover, the specification of dimensions over the structure of documents requires a collection that is homogeneous in structure.

Formal Definition

A textual constellation schema is used for modelling an analysis of document contents where this content is modelled as a subject of analysis.

Definition. A *textual constellation schema CT* is defined by $CT = (F^{CT}, D^{CT}, Star^{CT})$, where:

- $F^{CT} = \{F_1,...,F_m\}$ is a set of *facts*;
- $D^{CT} = \{D_1,...,D_n\}$ is a set of *dimensions*;
- $Star^{CT} = F^{CT} \rightarrow 2^{D^{CT}}$ is a function that associates each fact to its linked dimensions.

Note that a textual star schema is a constellation where F^{CT} is a singleton ($F^{CT} = \{F_1\}$). The notation 2^D represents the power set of the set D.

Definition. A *fact F* is defined by $F = (M^F, I^F, IStar^F)$ where:

- $M^F = \{M_1,...,M_n\}$ is a set of *measures*;
- $I^F = \{i^F_1,...,i^F_q\}$ is a set of fact instances;
- $IStar^F : I^F \rightarrow I^{D1} \times ... \times I^{Dn}$ is a function that associates the instances of the fact F to the instances of the associated dimensions D_i.

Definition. A *measure M* is defined by $M = (m, F_{AGG})$ where:

- m is the measure;
- $F_{AGG} = \{f_1,...,f_x\}$ is a set of aggregation functions compatible with the additvity of the measure, $f_i \in (\text{SUM}, \text{AVG}, \text{MAX}...)$.

Measures may be additive, semi-additive or even non-additive (Kimball, 1996), (Horner et al., 2004).

Definition. A *dimension D* is defined by $D = (A^D, H^D, I^D)$ where:

- $A^D = \{a^D_1,...,a^D_u\}$ is a set of *attributes* (parameters and weak attributes);
- $H^D = \{H^D_1,...,H^D_x\}$ is a set of *hierarchies* that represent the organisation of the attributes, A^D of the dimension;
- $I^D = \{i^D_1,...,i^D_p\}$ is a set of *instances* of the dimension.

Definition. A *hierarchy H* is defined by $H = (Param^H, Weak^H)$ where:

- $Param^H = <p^H_1, p^H_2,..., p^H_{np}, All>$ is an ordered set of attributes, called *parameters* (with $\forall k \in [1..np]$, $p^H_k \in A^D$);
- $Weak^H : Param^H \rightarrow 2^{A^D - Param^H}$ is an application that specifies the association of some attributes (called *weak attributes*) to parameters.

All hierarchies of a dimension start by the same parameter: a common root $p^H_1 = a^D_1$, $\forall H \in H^D$ and end with the generic parameter of highest granularity (*All*). Note that the parameter *All* is never displayed in graphical representations as it tends to confuse users (Malinowski et al., 2006).

Different Types of Measures

To answer to the specificities of document collections, we define an extension of the classical concept of measure. In this way, we distinguish two types of measures: numerical measures and textual measures.

A *numerical measure* is a measure exclusively composed of numerical data. It is either:

- **Additive:** All traditional aggregation functions may be used (SUM, AVERAGE, MINIMUM, MAXIMUM);
- **Semi-additive:** Thus representing instant measures (stock levels, temperature values...) where only limited aggregation functions may be used (the SUM aggregation function is not compatible).

For a measure $M = (m, F_{AGG})$, F_{AGG} allows the specification of a list of compatible aggregation function. Note that a non-additive measure is never considered numerical in our framework.

A *textual measure* is a measure where data is both non numeric and non additive. The content of a textual measure may be a word, a set of words, a structured text such as paragraph or even a whole document. We distinguish two types of textual measures:

- A *raw textual measure*: is a measure whose content corresponds to the complete content of a document or a fragment of a document (e.g. the full textual content of an XML article bereft of all XML tags that structure it);
- An *elaborated textual measure* is a measure whose content comes from a raw textual measure and passed through a certain amount of pre-processing. For example, a textual measure composed of keywords is an elaborated textual measure. This type of measure could be obtained from a raw textual measure where stop words would have been removed and only the most significant keywords relative to the context of the document would have been preserved with algorithms such as those presented in (Baeza-Yates & Ribeiro-Neto, 1999).

With a non additive measure, only generic aggregation functions may be used (e.g. COUNT and LIST). However, in (Park et al., 2005), the authors suggest the use of aggregation functions inspired from text mining techniques, such as TOP _ KEYWORDS that returns the n major keywords of a text and SUMMARY that generates the summary of a textual fragment. More recently, we have proposed a new function, AVG _ KW (Ravat et al., 2007) that exclusively operates on textual measures composed of keywords and that combines several keywords into a more general keyword according to a "pseudo-average" function.

Note that other types of measures could be considered, such as geographic measures (Han et al., 1998), but they are out of the scope of this paper.

Special Data Requires Special Dimensions

When designing OLAP analyses from document data, the authors of (Tseng et al., 2006) distinguish three types of dimensions:

1. **Ordinary dimensions:** These dimensions are composed of extracted data from the contents of analysed documents. Data is extracted and then organised in a hierarchical manner. A dimension with the major keywords of the documents organised according to categories is an ordinary dimension, e.g. (Keith et al., 2005 and Mothe et al., 2003).

2. *Meta-data dimension:* Data from this dimension are composed of the meta-data extracted from the documents, e.g. the authors, the editor or the publication date of a scientific article. Dublin Core[5] meta-data represents some of these meta-data.

3. **Category dimension:** These dimensions represent dimensions composed with keywords extracted from a categorisation hierarchy (or ontology) such as Wordnet[6]. Each

document is linked to the related elements of the hierarchy (manually or automatically).

To these three types of dimension, we define two other:

4. **Structure dimension:** This dimension models the common structure of the documents that compose the analysed collection. A textual constellation may hold a set of structure dimensions, but a fact may only be linked to a unique structure dimension: let $D^{STR} = \{D_{S1}, \ldots, D_{Sn}\}$ be a set of structure dimensions; $D^{STR} \subset D^{CT}$, these dimensions are part of the textual constellation CT and: $\|D^{STR}\| \le \|F^{CT}\|$ and $\forall F \in F^{CT}$, $\nexists (D_{Si} \in D_{STR} \wedge D_{Sj} \in D^{STR}) | (D_{Si} \in Star^{CT}(F) \wedge D_{Sj} \in Star^{CT}(F))$

5. **Complementary dimensions:** These dimensions are composed from complementary data sources. For example, complementary information concerning article authors.

Note that although category dimensions may be seen as complementary dimensions their roles are not the same. Category dimensions partition documents according to an existing categorisation hierarchy or ontology based on the document content. Complementary dimensions are more "complementary meta-data" dimensions. They do not partition documents according to content but rather to auxiliary meta-data.

However, notice also that ordinary dimensions (Tseng et al., 2006) are scarcely used in our model because the document content is modelled through our textual measures. Moreover, these dimensions are not well suited, as in (Mothe et al., 2003), this type of dimension is very delicate to implement, as it requires a large amount of pre-processing as well as being "*non-strict*" dimensions (Malinowski et al., 2006). This is due to the fact that considering document contents as a measure has never been addressed before.

Structure dimensions are constructed from extracted document structures (i.e. the common

DTD or XSchema of the analysed document collection). Each parameter of this dimension models the different levels of granularity of a same document. That is, the set of text that will be used by the specific textual aggregation functions. Structure dimensions model both the generic structure (i.e. *section, subsection, paragraph...*) and the specific structure with the use of attributes such as *Section_Type, Paragraph_Type...* For example, *introduction* and *conclusion* are section types whereas *definition* and *theorem* (...) are paragraph types. The specific structure is extracted from the XML tags that determine the different elements within the XML document.

Complementary dimensions represent all classic dimensions that one may come across within a standard OLAP framework (e.g. customer or product dimensions).

Application

In order to analyse the activities of a research unit, a decision maker analyses the content of a document collection that are composed of scientific articles. These articles have a header with a common structure and have a certain amount of meta-data. Amongst these meta-data, one may find: the name of the authors, their affiliations (institute, country...), the date of publication of the article, a list of keywords...

The articles are also characterised by an organisation of their content according to the hierarchical structure of the XML data:

- A *generic structure*. The articles are composed of paragraphs grouped into subsections, themselves grouped into sections. Regarding sections, they are regrouped into articles.
- A *specific structure*. This structure may be seen as a description of the generic elements of the generic structure. Thus, types of sections: introduction, conclusion... and types of paragraphs: definition, example, theorem...

The elements that compose the generic and the specific structure are extracted from the documents by an analysis of the XML tags that divide document contents. This is done in a semi-automatic way in order to solve possible conflicts.

The textual star schema corresponding to this analysis of scientific publications is presented in Figure 4. This schema has the advantage of completing the one presented in the introduction of this document (see Figure 3). The new schema

Figure 4. Example of a textual star schema for the multidimensional analysis of documents

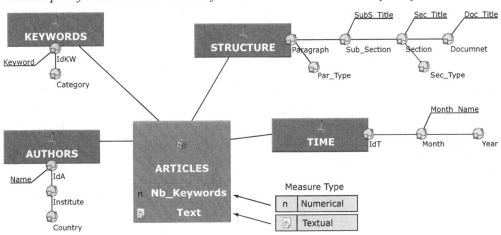

provides the possibility of analysing the meta-data and the keywords of the documents as in the four previous propositions (McCabe et al., 2000, Mothe et al., 2003, Keith et al., 2005 and Tseng et al., 2006). Moreover, this schema allows the analysis of the contents of the documents with the use of the document structure. Compared to the example presented in introduction, a raw textual measure has been added to the fact *ARTICLES* as well as a new dimension *STRUCTURE*. Note that, in this example, the three other dimensions are meta-data dimensions.

The dimension *STRUCTURE* is composed of parameters that model the generic and specific structure of the document collection. Each param-eter represents a specific granularity of the mea-sure *Text* (paragraphs, subsections, sections).

LOGICAL MODEL: MULTIDIMENSIONAL LOGICAL MODEL

Underneath the conceptual framework based on textual constellations previously presented, the logical level of the environment is based on an extension of R-OLAP (Relational OLAP) technol-ogy (Kimball, 1996). The architecture is presented in Figure 5. It is composed of two storage spaces: a multidimensional database (1) and a XML data storage space (2). In the multidimensional database, each dimension is represented by a relational table and fact table(s) acts as a central pivot hosting foreign keys pointing towards the different dimension tables (Kimball, 1996). XML documents are stored separately in a document warehouse (large XML objects in a relational database which we consider to be accessed as XML files). These documents are linked to the factual data with an XPath expression. In our example, there is an XPath expression for each paragraph.

Tables are built from either document data (or-dinary, meta-data dimensions and measure data) or complementary data (category and complemen-tary dimensions). The structure dimension is built from the internal structure of the articles. This structure is extracted by scanning the DTD of the XML documents. Each text fragment is associated to its source document with an XPath expression that designates the position of the element within the document. The system uses XQuery expres-sions to select and return document fragments. For example `"article/section[@Id=1]/paragraph"`

Figure 5. Logical representation of a textual star schema

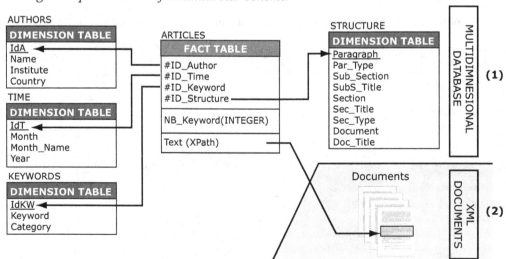

designates all the paragraphs of the first sections (sections whose id is equal to 1) of all articles.

Note that if the *Id* attribute does not exist, it is possible to replace it with the number of the element (here a section). This is possible due to the fact that, at a same level, XML elements are sequentially ordered.

In case of storage space problems it is possible not to duplicate the document textual contents within the fact table. In this case, only an XPath expression is stored to access to the textual data within the XML storage space. Nevertheless, this approach has the drawback of increasing the system disk I/O load. A solution is the use of adapted materialised views but with a control over their size, as we are in a case where storage space is a problem. This solution would at least reduce the system processing time of the aggregation process.

In order to implement "non-covering" hierarchies (Malinowski et al., 2006), we use virtual values at the logical level. Thus, an article without any subsection would have a unique "dummy"

subsection within every section. This is an interesting solution to handle section introduction paragraphs that are usually before the first subsection of a section.

DATA EXAMPLE

The Figure 6 presents a small dataset of a star textual schema (note that not all multidimensional data are represented).

Multidimensional Analysis of Textual Data

Multidimensional OLAP analyses present analysed subject data according to different detail levels (also called granularity levels). The process aggregates data according to the select level with the use of aggregation functions such as SUM, MIN, MAX, AVERAGE... In Table 1, a decision maker wishes to analyse the number of theorems by month and by author (1). In order to obtain a more global vision, the decision maker aggregates monthly

Figure 6 Data example

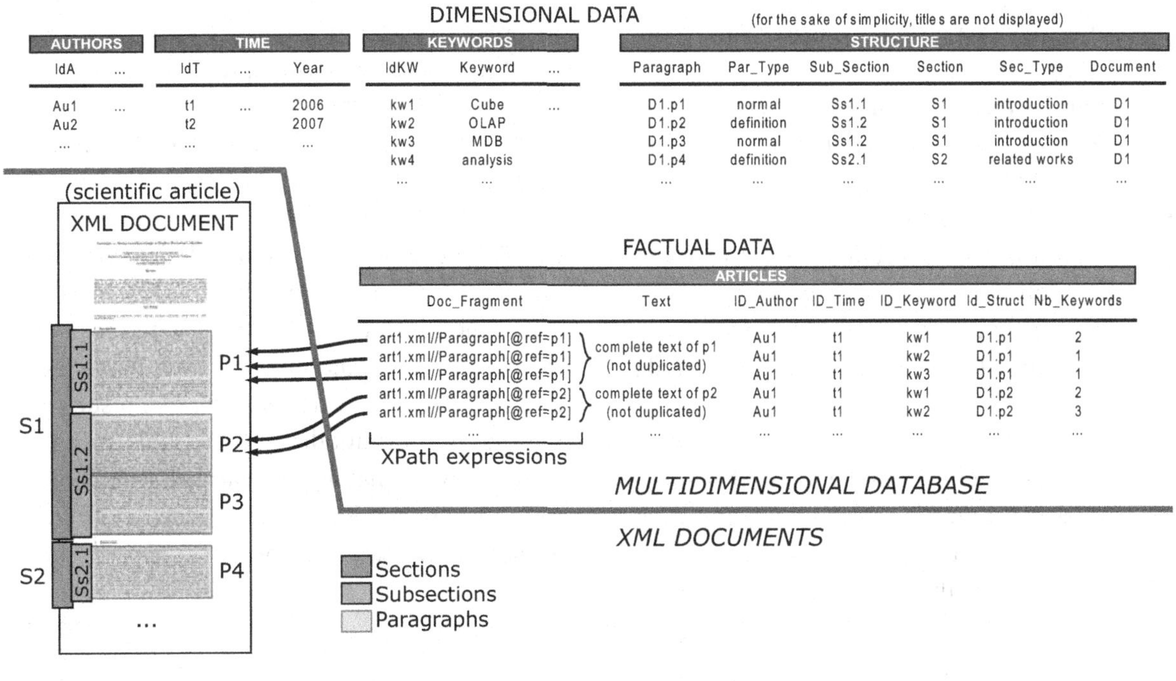

Table 1. (1) Number of theorems per author and per month; (2) total by year.

(1)

COUNT (Text)		TIME				
	Year	2006			2007	
	Month	Sept.	Nov.	Dec.	Jan.	Feb.
AUTHORS	IdA					
	Au1	3	4	2	2	2
	Au2	2	2	3	6	7
STRUCTURE.Par_Type = 'Theorem'						

(2)

COUNT (Text)		TIME	
	Year	2006	2007
AUTHORS	IdA		
	Au1	9	4
	Au2	7	13
STRUCTURE.Par_Type = 'Theorem'			

data into yearly data (2). He thus projects an aggregated value of theorems (the total number) for each pair (author, year).

Aggregating Textual Data

The analysis of textual measures requires specific aggregation means. Current aggregation functions do not have the capacity to take as input textual data. Within the standard OLAP environment, only generic aggregation functions Count and Identity (also called List) may be employed on data that are non numeric and non additive.

Along with the two generic aggregation functions (Count and List), we suggest the use of the following aggregation functions:

- **Summary:** A function that generates the summary of a textual measure (Park et al., 2005).
- **Top_Keyword:** A function that returns the n major keywords of a textual measure (Park et al., 2005).
- **Avg_Kw:** A function that tries to aggregate keywords into an "average" keyword. More precisely, this function aggregates sets of keywords into more general keywords with a controlled loss of semantic (Ravat et al., 2007).

Within the examples, in the rest of this document, we shall use the Top _ Keyword aggregation function. This function takes as input a fragment of text and returns the n major keywords of the fragment (stopwords excluded). In our examples, we shall limit ourselves to the two major keywords (n = 2).

Contrarily to numeric measure analysis, the analysis of textual measures may cruelly lack precision. Indeed, aggregation functions that operate on text are not as robust as basic functions such as sum or average. To compensate this problem, the *STRUCTURE* dimension provides flexibility during multidimensional analyses. With this dimension, the user may easily change the level of detail used by the aggregation function, thus overcoming the lack of precision that may occur when analysing textual data with a greater flexibility in the specification of analyses.

Analysis Example

In order to ease comprehensiveness, we shall use throughout this example a pseudo query language for the specification of analyses. The language allows the specification of an *analysis subject*; the elements to be placed within the *column* and *line* headers; the level of granularity (with the use of the structure dimension); and possibly a restriction on the content with the use of the specific structure (e.g. with the use of *Paragraph_Type* and *Section_Type* parameters of the *STRUCTURE* dimension). The results are viewed within a multidimensional table (mTable), adapted for displaying textual data (see Table 1 for an example with numerical data and Figure 7 for a textual data example).

Example. In the following example, the decision maker analyses a collection of scientific articles. The analysis deals with the publications of two authors *Au1* and *Au2* during *2005* and *2006*, where the major keywords of each set of documents are displayed. These keywords are aggregated at the *section* granularity level and the analysis is limited to the contents of the introductions of each document. Thus the aggregation function selects the major keywords of the *introductions* of all articles. The Figure 7 presents the results of this analysis which is specified with the following expression:

```
Subject: TOP _ KEYWORDS(ARTICLES.Text)
Lines: AUTHORS.IdA='Au1' OR AUTHORS.
IdA='Au2'
Columns: TIME.Year=2005 OR TIME.
Year=2006
Granularity Level: STRUCTURE.Section
Restriction: STRUCTURE.Type _
Sec='introduction'
```

The restitution interface is a multidimensional table (mTable) (Gyssens et al., 1997 and Ravat et al., 2008). In this table, during the analysis of textual measures, each cell that has a result is in fact a hypertext link to a Web page that has the detailed list of the aggregated elements. Contrarily to the system presented in (Tseng et al., 2006), where the interface returns the complete text, the displayed list of elements use XPath expression to access only the fragments corresponding to the designated granularity (a *section* in our case and not the whole article).

Definition. A *multidimensional table T* (*mTable* for short) is a matrix of *lines×columns* cells, with each cell defined as $c_{ij} = (R, Lk)$ where:

- *R* is an aggregated result;
- *Lk* is a hypertext link.

The link *Lk* leads to a Web page that contains the aggregated result of the linked cell as well as a list of elements that were used to generate the aggregation. Each source element is listed as an XPath expression that links the element to the corresponding fragment of text of the document.

Example. In *2006*, *Au1* has published at least two articles (see Figure 7): *ARTICLE12* and *ARTICLE23*. The major keywords of both introductions of these articles are *OLAP* and *Query*: $c_{Au1,2006}=(R=\{OLAP, Query\}, Lk_{Au1,2006})$. Note that the XPath expressions are specified at the granularity level selected within the STRUCTURE dimension. For instance, in our example, the introduction of the document corresponds to all the paragraphs that compose the section whose type is introduction.

Another example is the list of all theorems written by an author during a year. This analysis is expressed by the following expression:

```
Subject: LIST(ARTICLES.Text)
Lines: AUTHORS.IdA='Au1' OR AUTHORS.
IdA='Au2'
Columns: TIME.Year=2005 OR TIME.
Year=2006
Granularity Level: STRUCTURE.Document
Restriction: STRUCTURE.Type _
Par='Theorem'
```

The selection of all the theorems of an article is done by applying a restriction on the type of paragraph (*Type_Par*). The granularity level is the complete document; this is specified by the *Document* parameter of the STRUCTURE dimension. As a consequence, the aggregation function shall regroup the elements to be aggregated for each article. Had the user selected the COUNT aggregation function, he would have obtained, for each cell of the multidimensional table, a number corresponding to the number of theorems per article (see Table 1 (2)).

CONCLUSION

In this document we have proposed to extend previous works on the multidimensional analysis

Figure 7. Restitution interface with an analysis example

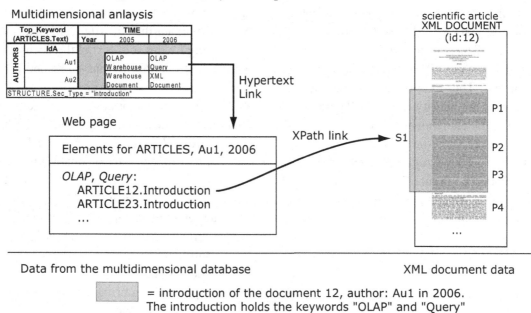

Multidimensional anlaysis

scientific article
XML DOCUMENT
(id:12)

Hypertext
Link

XPath link

Web page

Elements for ARTICLES, Au1, 2006

OLAP, Query:
  ARTICLE12.Introduction
  ARTICLE23.Introduction
  ...

Data from the multidimensional database

XML document data

= introduction of the document 12, author: Au1 in 2006.
The introduction holds the keywords "OLAP" and "Query"

of documents in order to obtain extended analysis capacities in the OLAP environment.

We have adapted a constellation model (Ravat et al., 2008); by the addition of textual measures as well as a specific dimension that represents the structure of documents. This dimension provides more flexibility to the user in order to have a better reliability during the aggregation of textual data. The dimension also allows the specification of complex analyses that rest on specific elements of a document collection. Besides, the model supports multiple analyses with a constellation schema. In order to return to the user understandable results, we have adapted a multidimensional table. This table allows the display of fragments of the documents corresponding to the data sources from which originate the aggregations that are displayed within the table.

This aim of this proposition is to provide extended analysis capabilities to a decision maker. Textual data that pass through information systems are under-exploited due to the lack of management from actual systems. We think an adapted OLAP environment will provide new analysis perspectives for the decision making process.

We are currently finishing the extension of a prototype (GraphicOLAPSQL) based on the RDBMS Oracle 10g2 and a client Java interface. Documents are stored in large XML objects within an XML database. Queries are expressed with a graphic manipulation of the conceptual elements presented within a textual star or constellation schema (see Ravat et al., 2008 for more details on the graphic query language and the associated prototype GraphicOLAPSQL).

Several future works are considered. Firstly, throughout our examples we have used a multidimensional table as a restitution interface for textual data analysis. This tabular structure is well adapted to the restitution of numerical analysis data, but when it comes to non numerical data such as text, the display may easily be overloaded. Thus, we wish to investigate on the use of more adapted restitution interfaces for textual data. Secondly, as documents do not only contain text, but also graphs, figures or even references, we wish to adapt the environment for all types of contents not reducing the system to only multidimensional numerical or textual analysis.

REFERENCES

Abelló, A., Samos J., & Saltor, F. (2006). YAM²: A multidimensional conceptual model extending UML. *Journal of Information Systems (IS)*, *31*(6), 541-567.

Baeza-Yates, R.A., & Ribeiro-Neto, B.A. (1999). *Modern information retrieval*. ACM Press/Addison-Wesley.

Beyer, K.S., Chamberlin, D.D., Colby, L.S., Ozcan, F., Pirahesh, H., & Xu Y. (2005). Extending XQuery for analytics, *ACM SIGMOD Int. Conf. on Management of Data (SIGMOD)* (pp. 503–514). ACM Press.

Bordawekar, R., & Lang, C. A. (2005). Analytical processing of XML documents: Opportunities and challenges. *SIGMOD Record, 34*(2), 27-32.

Boussaid, O., Messaoud, R.B., Choquet, R., & Anthoard, S. (2006). X-Warehousing: An XML-based approach for warehousing complex data. In *10th East European Conf. on Advances in Databases and Information Systems (ADBIS 2006)* (pp. 39–54). Springer.

Codd, E.F., Codd, S.B., & Salley, C.T. (1993). *Providing OLAP (On Line Analytical Processing) to user analyst: An IT mandate*, technical report, E.F. Codd and associates, (white paper de Hyperion Solutions Corporation).

Colliat, G. (1996). OLAP, relational, and multidimensional database systems. *SIGMOD Record, 25*(3), 64-69.

Fankhauser, P., & Klement, T. (2003). XML for data warehousing chances and challenges (Extended Abstract). In *5th Int. Conf. on Data Warehousing and Knowledge Discovery (DaWaK 2003)* (pp. 1-3). Springer.

Fuhr, N., & Großjohann, K. (2001). XIRQL: A query language for information retrieval in XML documents. In *Proceedings of the 24th Intl. Conf. on Research and Development in Information Retrieval (SIGIR 2001)* (pp. 172–180). ACM Press.

Golfarelli, M., Maio, D., & Rizzi, S. (1998). The dimensional fact model: A conceptual model for data warehouses, invited paper. *Intl. Journal of Cooperative Information Systems (IJCIS)*, *7*(2-3), 215-247.

Golfarelli, M., Rizzi, S., & Vrdoljak, B. (2001). Data warehouse design from XML sources. In *4th ACM Int. Workshop on Data Warehousing and OLAP (DOLAP 2001)* (pp. 40-47). ACM Press.

Gray, J., Bosworth, A., Layman, A., & Pirahesh, H. (1996). Data cube: A relational aggregation operator generalizing group-by, cross-tab, and sub-total. In *12th Int. Conf. on Data Engineering (ICDE)* (pp. 152-159), IEEE Computer Society.

Gyssens, M., & Lakshmanan, L.V.S. (1997). A foundation for multi-dimensional databases, *23rd Int. Conf. on Very Large Data Bases (VLDB)* (pp. 106-115), Morgan Kaufmann.

Han, J., Stefanovic, N., & Koperski, K. (1998). Selective materialization: An efficient method for spatial data cube construction. In *Research and Development in Knowledge Discovery and Data Mining (PAKDD'98)* (pp. 144-158). Springer.

Horner, J., Song, I-Y., & Chen, P.P. (2004). An analysis of additivity in OLAP systems. In *7th ACM Int. Workshop on Data Warehousing and OLAP (DOLAP 2004)* (pp. 83-91). ACM Press.

Jensen, M.R., Møller, T.H., & Pedersen, T.B. (2001). Specifying OLAP cubes on XML data, *13th Int. Conf. on Scientific and Statistical Database Management (SSDBM)* (pp. 101-112). IEEE Computer Society.

Keith, S., Kaser, O., & Lemire, D. (2005). Analyzing large collections of electronic text using

OLAP. In *APICS 29th Conf. in Mathematics, Statistics and Computer Science* (pp. 17-26). Acadia University.

Khrouf, K., & Soulé-Dupuy, C. (2004). A textual warehouse approach: A Web data repository. In Masoud Mohammadian (Eds.), *Intelligent Agents for Data Mining and Information Retrieval* (pp. 101-124), Idea Publishing Group (IGP).

Kimball, R. (1996). *The data warehouse toolkit.* Ed. John Wiley and Sons, 1996, 2nd ed. 2003.

Malinowski, E., & Zimányi, E. (2006). Hierarchies in a multidimensional model: From conceptual modeling to logical representation. *Journal of Data & Knowledge Engineering (DKE), 59*(2), 348-377.

McCabe, C., Lee, J., Chowdhury, A., Grossman, D. A., & Frieder, O. (2000). On the design and evaluation of a multi-dimensional approach to information retrieval. In *23rd Int. ACM Conf. on Research and Development in Information Retrieval (SIGIR)* (pp. 363-365). ACM Press.

Mothe, J., Chrisment, C., Dousset, B., & Alau, J. (2003). DocCube: Multi-dimensional visualisation and exploration of large document sets. *Journal of the American Society for Information Science and Technology (JASIST), 54*(7), 650-659.

Nassis, V., Rajugan R., Dillon T.S., & Rahayu, J.W. (2004). Conceptual Design of XML Document Warehouses, *6th Int. Conf. on Data Warehousing and Knowledge Discovery (DaWaK 2004)* (pp. 1-14). Springer.

Niemi, T., Niinimäki, M., Nummenmaa, J., & Thanisch, P. (2002). Constructing an OLAP cube from distributed XML data. In *5th ACM Int. Workshop on Data Warehousing and OLAP (DOLAP)* (pp.22-27). ACM Press.

Park, B-K., Han, H., & Song, I-Y. (2005). XML-OLAP: A multidimensional analysis framework for XML warehouses. In *6th Int. Conf. on Data*

Warehousing and Knowledge Discovery (DaWaK) (pp.32-42). Springer.

Pedersen, D., Riis, K., & Pedersen, T.B. (2002). XML-extended OLAP querying. *14th Int. Conf. on Scientific and Statistical Database Management (SSDBM)* (pp.195-206), IEEE Computer Society.

Pérez, J.M., Berlanga, Llavori, R., Aramburu, M.J., & Pedersen, T.B. (2005). A relevance-extended multi-dimensional model for a data warehouse contextualized with documents. In *8th Intl. Workshop on Data Warehousing and OLAP (DOLAP)* (pp.19-28), ACM Press.

Pérez-Martinez, J.M., Berlanga-Llavori, R.B., Aramburu-Cabo, M.J., & Pedersen, T.B. (2007). Contextualizing data warehouses with documents. *Decision Support Systems (DSS)*, available online doi:10.1016/j.dss.2006.12.005.

Pokorný, J. (2001). Modelling stars using XML. In *4th ACM Int. Workshop on Data Warehousing and OLAP (DOLAP)* (pp.24-31). ACM Press.

Ravat, F., Teste, O., & Tournier, R. (2007). OLAP aggregation function for textual data warehouse. In *9th International Conference on Enterprise Information Systems (ICEIS 2007)*, vol. DISI (pp. 151-156). INSTICC Press.

Ravat, F., Teste, O., Tournier, R., & Zurfluh, G. (2008). Algebraic and graphic languages for OLAP manipulations. *Int. j. of Data Warehousing and Mining (DWM), 4*(1), 17-46.

Sullivan, D. (2001). *Document warehousing and text mining*, Wiley John & Sons Inc.

Torlone, R. (2003). Conceptual multidimensional models. In M. Rafanelli (ed.), *Multidimensional Databases: Problems and Solutions* (pp. 69-90). Idea Publishing Group.

Tseng, F.S.C., & Chou, A.Y.H (2006). The concept of document warehousing for multi-dimensional modeling of textual-based business intelligence.

Decision Support Systems (*DSS*), *42*(2), 727-744.

Vrdoljak, B., Banek, M., & Rizzi S. (2003). Designing Web warehouses from XML schemas. In *5th Int. Conf. on Data Warehousing and Knowledge Discovery* (*DaWaK*) (pp. 89-98). Springer.

Vrdoljak, B., Banek, M., & Skocir, Z. (2006). Integrating XML sources into a data warehouse. In *2nd Int. Workshop on Data Engineering Issues in E-Commerce and Services* (*DEECS 2006*) (pp. 133-142). Springer.

Wang, H., Li, J., He, Z., & Gao, H. (2005). OLAP for XML data. In *5th Int. Conf. on Computer and Information Technology* (*CIT*) (pp. 233-237), IEEE Computer Society.

Wiwatwattana, N., Jagadish, H.V., Lakshmanan, L.V.S., & Srivastava, D. (2007). X³: A cube operator for XML OLAP. In *23rd Int. Conf. on Data Engineering* (*ICDE*) (pp. 916-925). IEEE Computer Society.

Yin, X., & Pedersen, T.B. (2004). Evaluating XML-extended OLAP queries based on a physical algebra. In *7th ACM Int. Workshop on Data Warehousing and OLAP* (*DOLAP*) (pp.73-82). ACM Press.

Zhang, J., Ling, T.W., Bruckner, R.M., & Tjoa, A.M. (2003). Building XML data warehouse based on frequent patterns in user queries. In *5th Int. Conf. on Data Warehousing and Knowledge Discovery* (*DaWaK*) (pp. 99-108). Springer.

ENDNOTES

[1] Extensible Markup Language (XML), from http://www.w3.org/XML/

[2] XML Schema (XSchema), from http://www.w3.org/XML/Schema

[3] Xyleme Server, from http://www.xyleme.com/xml_server

[4] XML Query Language (XQuery), from http://www.w3.org/XML/Query

[5] Dublin Core Metadata initiative (DCMI) de http://dublincore.org/

[6] Wordnet, a lexical database for the English language, from http://wordnet.princeton.edu/

Chapter IX
A Multidimensional Pattern Based Approach for the Design of Data Marts

Hanene Ben-Abdallah
University of Sfax, Tunisia

Jamel Feki
University of Sfax, Tunisia

Mounira Ben Abdallah
University of Sfax, Tunisia

ABSTRACT

Despite their strategic importance, the wide-spread usage of decision support systems remains limited by both the complexity of their design and the lack of commercial design tools. This chapter addresses the design complexity of these systems. It proposes an approach for data mart design that is practical and that endorses the decision maker involvement in the design process. This approach adapts a development technique well established in the design of various complex systems for the design of data marts (DM): Pattern-based design. In the case of DM, a multidimensional pattern (MP) is a generic specification of analytical requirements within one domain. It is constructed and documented with standard, real-world entities (RWE) that describe information artifacts used or produced by the operational information systems (IS) of several enterprises. This documentation assists a decision maker in understanding the generic analytical solution; in addition, it guides the DM developer during the implementation phase. After over viewing our notion of MP and their construction method, this chapter details a reuse method composed of two adaptation levels: one logical and one physical. The logical level, which is independent of any data source model, allows a decision maker to adapt a given MP to their analytical requirements and to the RWE of their particular enterprise; this produces a DM schema. The physical specific level projects the RWE of the DM over the data source model. That is, the projection identifies the data source elements necessary to define the ETL procedures. We illustrate our approaches of construction and reuse of MP with examples in the medical domain.

INTRODUCTION

Judicious decision making within an enterprise heavily relies nowadays on the ability to analyze large data volumes generated by the enterprise daily activities. To apprehend the difficulties and often impossibility of manual analyses of huge data volumes, decision makers have manifested a growing interest in installing decision support systems (DSS) on top of their computerized information systems (IS) (Kimball R. 1996). This interest triggered the proposition of several methods dealing with various phases of the DSS life cycle. However, two main difficulties impede the wide spread adoption of so far proposed methods. One difficulty stems from the fact that some methods presume that decision makers have a good expertise in IS modeling; this is the case of bottom-up DSS design methods (Golfarelli M., Maio D. & Rizzi S. 1998a), (Golfarelli M., Lechtenbörger J., Rizzi S. & Vossen G. 1998b), (Hüsemann, B., Lechtenbörger, J. & Vossen G. 2000), (Chen Y., Dehne F., Eavis T., & Rau-Chaplin A. 2006), (Cabibbo L. & Torlone R. 2000) and (Moody L. D. & Kortink M. A. R. 2000). The second difficulty is due to the fact that other methods rely on the ability of decision makers to define their analytical needs in a rigorous way that guarantees their loadability from the data in the operational IS; this is the case of top-down DSS design methods (Kimball 2002), (Tsois A., Karayannidis N. & Sellis T. 2001).

Independently of any design method and software tool used during its development, a DSS is typically organized into a data warehouse (DW) gathering all decisional information of the enterprise. In addition, to facilitate the manipulation of a DW, this latter is reorganized into data marts (DM) each of which representing a subject-oriented extract of the DW. Furthermore, a DM uses a *multidimensional* model that structures information into facts (interesting observations of a business process) and dimensions (the recording and analysis axes of observations). This model enables decision makers to write *ad hoc* queries and to manipulate/analyze easily the results of their queries (Chrisment C., Pujolle G., Ravat F., Teste O. & Zurfluh G. 2006).

Despite the advantages of this dedicated multidimensional model, the design of the DM schema remains a difficult task. Actually, it is a complex, technical process that requires a high expertise in data warehousing yet, it conditions the success and efficiency of the obtained DM.

The originality of the work presented in this chapter resides in proposing a DM design approach that relies on the reuse of generic OLAP requirement solutions we call *multidimensional patterns* (MP). In fact, reuse-based development is not a novel technique in itself; it has been applied for several application domains and through various techniques, *e.g.*, design patterns (Gamma E., Helm R., Johnson J. & Vlissides J. 1999), components (Cheesman J. & Daniels J. 2000), and more recently the OMG model driven architecture (MDA) (OMG 2003). However, the application of reuse techniques in the design of DSS has not been well explored.

More specifically, this chapter presents a pattern-based method for the construction of DM schemes. By analogy to a design pattern, which represents a generic solution to a reoccurring problem in a given application domain, we consider a *multidimensional pattern* as a typical standard, conceptual solution defined as a generic star-schema in one activity domain of the enterprise (Feki J. & Ben-Abdallah H. 2007). This concept of MP can be used in a top-down design approach either to prototype, or to build a DSS directly on top of the enterprise's operational system. Such a DSS can be either light (a set of independent DMs), or complete (a DW-dependant set of DMs). In the first case, decision makers define their OLAP requirements by adapting/reusing several MPs to derive DM schemes. This MP reuse context is well suited for small enterprises that are generally unable to bear the relatively high cost of a system containing both a DW and several DMs; instead, they often adopt a simplified architecture limited to a set of DM answering particular analytical requirements. On the other hand, if an enterprise can afford the construction of a complete DSS, the DM schemes derived from a set of MPs can be transformed and merged to derive the DW model (Feki J., Nabli A., Ben-Abdallah. H & Gargouri F. 2008). Note that this derivation method of a DW model from the DM schemes adheres to the MDA approach.

Given this role of MP in the design of (complete/light) DSS, the main objective of this chapter is to present a DM schema design approach based on MP reuse. This reuse is conducted at two consecutive levels:

1. A *logical* level that is independent of the data model of the target IS and where the decision maker specifies their analytical requirements via the MP. At this level, the MP documentation assists the decision maker both in understanding the MP and in relating it to their particular IS; and
2. A *physical* level that enables the decisional designer to obtain a DM schema documented with the computerized "objects" (tables, columns, ...) in the target IS. This second level prepares for the ETL process.

To illustrate the feasibility of our DM schema design method, this chapter shows its application on two MP in the *medical domain*. The choice of the medical domain is due to the great interest that arises from the synergistic application of computational, informational, cognitive, organizational, and other sciences whose primary focus is the acquisition, storage, and use of information in this domain (Zheng K. 2006). In fact, as health care costs continue to spiral upward, health care institutions are under enormous pressure to create a cost-effective system by controlling operating costs while maintaining the quality of care and services (Zheng K. 2006). To create such systems, they first have to analyze the performance of current systems/procedures.

The remainder of this chapter is organized as follows: First, we position the presented work within current DSS design methods. Secondly, we briefly overview our MP construction method and introduces sample MP to illustrate our reuse method. Then, we present the logical and physical reuse levels. Finally, we summarize our contributions and outline our future works.

RELATED WORK

In this section, we first overview current DSS design approaches in general. Secondly, we present DSS used within the medical domain in order to outline some OLAP requirements in this domain; in the third section, we show how a decision maker can specify these requirements by reusing our multidimensional patterns.

Decision Support Systems (DSS)

In the context of DSS development, the majority of research efforts focused on proposing theoretical grounds for DW design methods. They provided for three types of DM schema construction approaches: 1) a bottom-up approach (Golfarelli M., Maio D. & Rizzi S. 1998), (Moody L. D. & Kortink M. A. R. 2000), (Hüsemann, B., Lechtenbörger, J. & Vossen G. 2000), (Cabibbo L. & Torlone R. 2000), (Moody L. D. & Kortink M. A. R. 2000) and (Chen Y., Dehne F., Eavis T., & Rau-Chaplin A. 2006); 2) a top-down approach (Kimball 2002), (Tsois A., Karayannidis N. & Sellis T. 2001); or 3) a mixed approach (Böhnlein M. & Ulbrich-vom Ende A. 1999), (Bonifati A., Cattaneo F., Ceri S., Fuggetta A. & Paraboschi S. (2001), (Phipps C. & Davis, K. (2002)). In addition, to facilitate the application of these approaches, several researchers laid the theoretical ground for CASE tools. For instance, (Abello A., Samos J. & Saltor F. 2003) implemented a set of operations for the semantic navigation in star schemes; these operations assist a decision maker in understanding the various levels of measure aggregations and in refining their OLAP requirements. A second example is the work of (Ravat F., Teste O. & Zurfluh G. 2006) which proposed a graphical query language for an OLAP algebra.

In a complementary effort, other researchers tried to define well-formedness constraints for DM schemes to guarantee both the consistency of the loaded data, and the correctness of the query results. In this context, (Carpani F. & Ruggia R. 2001) proposed an integrity constraint language to enhance a multidimensional data model; (Hurtado C.A. & Mendelzon A.O. 2002) presented several constraints for OLAP dimensions; (Lechtenbörger J. & Vossen G. 2003) defined multidimensional normal forms for the design of DW; and (Ghozzi F. 2004) formalized several syntactic and semantic (*i.e.,* data-based) constraints for multidimensional data. The proposed constraints are a vital assistance means both for the design of a DM, and for a DW design tool in general. However, they do not spare the decision maker from the theoretical complexity behind a DM design.

On the other hand, the complexity of system design was addressed for several decades in other application domains like information systems. Reuse was put forward as a design approach that accelerates the development time and improves the quality of the developed systems. Among the various reuse techniques, design patterns have been the most widely used (Gamma E., Helm R., Johnson J. & Vlissides J. 1999) and are integrated in latest reuse techniques based on models (OMG 2003). The concept of patterns has also been adopted for processes to describe an established approach or a series of actions in software development (OMG 2006). In general, a pattern is described by a name, a motivation, a type, a structure, and possibly a context of reuse and typical reuse examples.

In the domain of information systems, several efforts were invested to introduce patterns for the development of this type of systems (Saidane M. & Giraudin J.P. 2002). However, in the domain of DSS, to our knowledge, only the research group

SIG of IRIT[1] has investigated the application of patterns. The researchers in this group proposed a DSS development method, called BIPAD (Business Intelligence Patterns for Analysis and Design) (Annoni E. 2007). The proposed method represents business processes as patterns that are used to guide the development of a DSS. In other words, it specifies the development process of a DSS. Hence, it differs from our approach that deals with OLAP design patterns, *i.e.,* it offers product patterns.

Decision Support Systems in the Medical Domain

Independently of their application domain, we can divide DSS into two categories depending on the impact of their usage: long-term or short-term. The first category of DSS is often used for strategic planning and it relies on data covering a long time period. In the medical domain, this category of DSS can be used for strategic decision making for a population, for instance, face to climatic and/or social criteria, to measure the performance of doctors, and/or the efficiency of treatments prescribed for a disease… Within this category of DSS, (Bernier E., Badard T., Bédard Y., Gosselin P. & Pouliot J. 2007) developed an interactive spatio-temporal web application for exchanging, integrating, summarizing and analyzing social, health and environmental geospatial data. This system has two objectives: better understanding the interactions between public health and climate changes, and facilitating future decision making by public health agencies and municipalities. It provides answers for analytical requirements *pre-defined* from a collection of geo-referenced indicators; these latter were identified by specialists and end-users as relevant for the surveillance of the impacts of climate changes on public health. For instance, this system can answer the following analytical requirements: the number of people with respiratory diseases split by sex and in a specific geographic area; the number of people with a given disease living in apartment buildings in a particular geographic area; the number of people with cardiovascular, respiratory and psychological diseases, whose age is between 5 and 65 years and who live in a heat wave area. Because the analytical requirements are pre-defined within this system, a decision maker cannot modify them easily to specify their particular OLAP requirements. In addition, since the system is developed through a top-down approach, a decision maker has no guarantee on the satisfiability of any new requirements they may add.

On the other hand, the second category of DSS provides for tactical decisions and requires fresh, and at times, near-real time data. Within this category, we find several DSS in the medical domain known as Clinical Decision Support Systems (CDSS). These systems form an increasingly significant part of clinical knowledge management technologies, through their capacity to support clinical processes and to use best-known medical knowledge. In fact, CDSS are "active knowledge systems which use two or more items of patient data to generate case specific advice" (Zheng K. 2006). Such advice takes the form of alerts and reminders, diagnostic assistance, therapy critiquing and planning, prescribing decision support, information retrieval, and image recognition and interpretation (Zheng K. 2006) (Payne T. H. 2000).

Among the developed CDSS, we find *Clinical Reminder System* (CRS) (Zheng. K. 2006), *Antimicrobial System* (Payne T. H. 2000) and *Computerized Patient Record System* (CPRS) (Payne T. H. 2000). These systems aim at improving care quality by providing clinicians with just-in-time alerts and recommended actions. They were developed based on a set of patient scenarios and protocols for preventive care and chronic strategies of disease treatments. However, to build these CDSS, clinicians can clearly benefit from a DSS that allows them to analyze, for instance, treatments prescribed for a certain

disease as a function of patients (their age, sex ...), test results of patients with a particular disease, and during a certain period... In deed, *UnitedHealth Group*, a large health maintenance organization, analyzed the billing information to design patient reminder treatment strategies for diabetic patients, heart-attack survivors, and women at risk of breast cancer (Zheng. K. 2006). Such DSS used to develop a CDSS can be built using our pattern-based approach.

MULTIDIMENSIONAL PATTERNS

In this section, we first present our concept of multidimensional pattern. Secondly, we overview our practical MP construction method.

Multidimensional Patterns

A *multidimensional pattern* is a conceptual solution for a set of decisional requirements; it is *subject oriented, domain specific, generic, documented,* modeled as a *star schema*, and designed for the *OLAP requirements specification* for the DM/DW design.

In the above definition, *subject oriented* means that the pattern gathers elements that allow the analyses of a particular analytical need (fact). In addition, the MP *genericity* ensures that the pattern covers most potential analyses of the modeled fact, independently of a particular enterprise. The MP *documentation* explains the limits and the conditions of its reuse. In addition, the pattern is *specific to one activity domain* of the enterprises where the fact is relevant. Finally, an MP is modeled as *a star schema* built on a single fact (*e.g.,* hospitalization, prescription, billing) since this model is the keystone in multidimensional modeling; it can be used to derive other multidimensional schemes, *e.g.,* Snowflake and Constellation.

MP Construction

Figure 1 illustrates the tree steps of our MP construction approach. Except for the classification step, which is manually done, the other two steps are automatically conducted.

As illustrated in Figure 1, our MP construction approach is based on RWE representing the artifacts of information circulating in *multiple* enterprises, *e.g.,* a patient fiche, a hospitalization file, a billing form, a delivery order, an application interface, etc (Ben-Abdallah M., Feki J. & Ben-Abdallah H. 2006b). These RWE are used to build and to document the PM at the same time. In fact, the MP documentation facilitates the reuse of the pattern; in particular, it facilitates the correspondence between the RWE used in the pattern and those RWE in the target IS. In addition, this association prepares for the generation of the loading procedures.

In order to guarantee the construction of generic MP, *i.e.,* independent of a particular enterprise, our construction approach starts with the standardization of RWE gathered from various enterprises. This standardization relies on an empirical study that collects the data items present in the different RWE, their presence rates, as well as their common names and formats (Ben-Abdallah M., Feki J. & Ben-Abdallah H. 2006a). The presence rates of the RWE data items serve as indicators on their importance in the domain and, consequently, as indices of their analytical potential. In addition, the standardization of the RWE element names resolves any naming conflicts and prepares a "dictionary" for the domain, which can be useful during the MP reuse.

Once standardized, the RWE are classified into *fact entities* (FE) *and basic entities* (BE) (Feki J. & Ben-Abdallah H. 2007). A FE materializes a daily activity/transaction in the enterprise; con-

Figure 1. Multidimensional pattern construction approach.

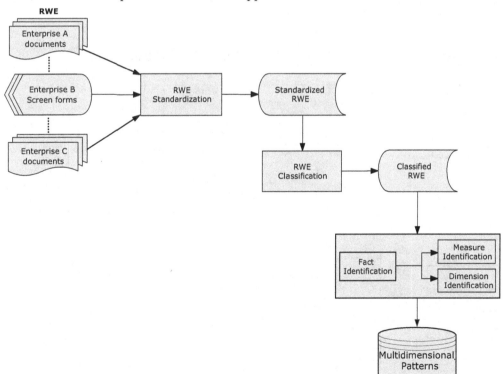

sequently, it produces a potential fact with a set of measures. On the other hand, a BE supplies data for a FE and defines the interpretation context of a transaction; thus, a BE is useful in finding dimensions and dimensional attributes. In (Feki J. Ben Abdallah M., & Ben-Abdallah H. 2006a), we defined a set of classification rules based on the structure of the RWE.

As fixed in EDI standards, any fact entity contains three parts: header, body and summary (UNECE 2002). The header contains identifying and descriptive information in addition to the transaction date. The body contains transactional data pertinent to basic entities and/or refers to other fact entities. Finally, the summary generally contains aggregate totals and/or data with exhaustive values. Figure 2 illustrates a sample set of classified RWE, where the FE "*Hospitalization File*" is surrounded by three BE. These BE are referred to by the FE and complement it with information answering *who, where,* and *when* questions.

Once the RWE are classified, our MP construction approach extracts from them multidi-

mensional elements (*i.e.*, measures, dimensions, attributes and hierarchies): Measures are directly extracted from the FE (*e.g., Hospitalization File*), whereas dimensional attributes (*e.g., Patient sex, age...*) are extracted from the BE linked to the FE. During the extraction of multidimensional elements, we keep track of the source entities of each retained multidimensional element; this information documents the pattern and later helps in its reuse.

Furthermore, we defined a set of extraction rules that rely on typing and occurrence information of the elements (Ben Abdallah M., Feki J. & Ben-Abdallah H. 2006a). For instance, measures can only come from numeric and reoccurring data items in a FE, whereas dimensional attributes come from character data items in a BE.

One limit of our measure identification rules is that they identify only elementary measures, *i.e.*, measures that are not derived like the number of hospitalization days, the quantity of doses taken during a certain period, the duration of chirurgical act... However, the MP developer and/or the decision maker can exploit the RWE documenting

Figure 2. An example of a fact entity (FE) surrounded by three basic entities (BE)

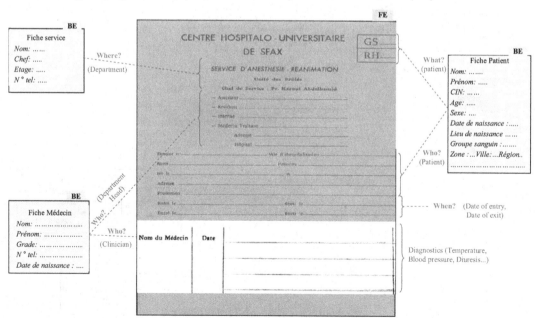

the MP to add any interesting, derivable (computed) measure. The added measures would be computed based on data present in the RWE, and thus are guaranteed to be loadable.

On the other hand, the extraction step may identify too many multidimensional elements, which may produce a complex pattern. In order to limit the complexity of the constructed patterns, we use the statistical results of the standardization (step 1, Figure 1) to eliminate infrequent multidimensional elements (*i.e.,* those with a presence rate under a predefined threshold). Furthermore, naturally, not all retained elements have the same importance/genericity in the domain of the pattern. To distinguish between elements with different genericities, we propose to classify them into three genericity levels: *important, recommended* and

optional. We have limited the number of levels to three after our empirical studies in three domains; these studies revealed strong concentrations of the presence rates around three dominant values forming three groups. However, the MP designer can choose more genericity levels.

With our distinction of the genericity levels, important elements (dimensions, measures and attributes) constitute the *core* almost invariant of the pattern; that is, they are omni present in all analyses in the pattern domain. On the other hand, the recommended and optional elements are relatively less significant and form the *variable part* of the pattern; that is, they are most likely adapted in the reuse phase depending on the decision maker requirements.

Figure 3. P1: MP analyzing the fact "Hospitalization".

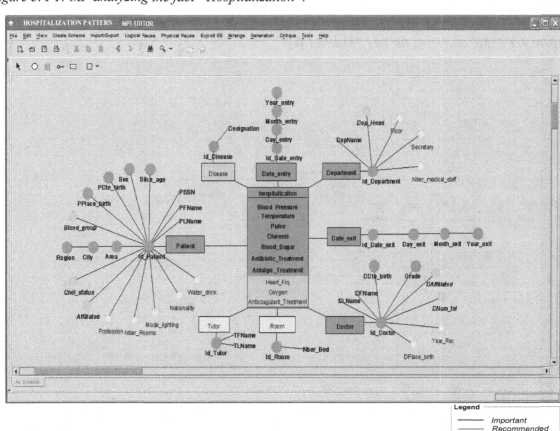

MP Examples

Based on our construction approach, we built four MP in the medical domain covering the analysis subjects *Hospitalization, Prescription, Medical Test* and *Appointment*. We constructed these patterns from two hundred documents collected from one public university hospital, two public and regional hospitals, three private hospitals and ten medical laboratories. We constructed these patterns with our MP construction tool, called MP-Builder (Ben Abdallah M., Ben said N., Feki J. & Ben-Abdallah H. 2007) and we edited them with our reuse tool MP-Editor (Ben Abdallah M., Feki J. & Ben-Abdallah H., 2006b).

Figure 3 shows the *Hospitalization* pattern that allows the analysis of this fact according to eight dimensions (*Disease, Patient, Department, Doctor, Date_entry, Date_exit, Tutor and Room*). These dimensions are organized in hierarchies

(*e.g., Address* of *Patient*) of parameters (*e.g., City, Area*... of the dimension *Patient, Specialty* of a *Doctor*). For this pattern, the fact was constructed on the FE *Hospitalization File* (Figure 2) and, for example, the dimension *Patient* was identified from the BE *"Patient File"*. Note that, the pattern designer and/or the decision maker can modify this automatically constructed pattern: for example, they may add the measure *Days_Hos* (the number of hospitalization days) derived from the two dimensions *Date_entry* and *Date_exit*. In addition, this pattern can be used by managers to analyze, for example instance, patient stays within a department during a specific period, doctor loads in a department, etc. On the other hand, clinicians can use this same pattern to analyze, for instance: blood pressure of patients older than a certain age and living in a particular (heat) area; diuresis of hospitalized patients drinking a certain type of water and having a kidney disease; oxygen

Figure 4. P2: MP analyzing the fact "Medical Test"

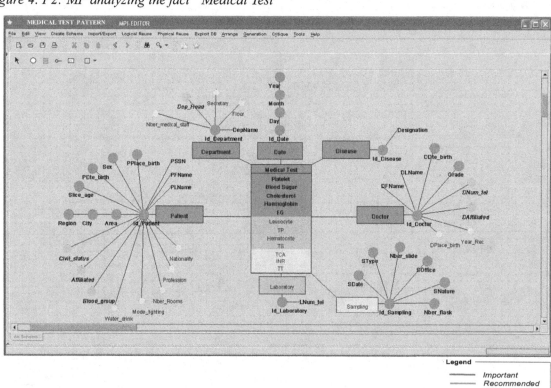

of patients living in less than a certain number of rooms and having a contagious disease, etc. These medical OLAP requirements can be the basis of both a DSS for strategic planning like the spatio-temporal system (Bernier E., Badard T., Bédard Y., Gosselin P. & Pouliot J. 2007), and a DSS used to build a CDSS such as *CRS* (Zheng. K. 2005), *cf.*, the related section.

Figure 4 illustrates a second pattern that analyzes the fact *Medical Test* according to seven dimensions (*Disease, Patient, Department, Doctor, Date, Laboratory* and *Sampling*). This fact records several results of medical tests (*Platelet, Blood Sugar, Cholesterol* ...). This pattern can be used to supply data that interest more the medical staff (diagnostics taken for a specific disease, results of medical tests for a patient during a year ...). The supplied data can be also used to build a CDSS and/or to guide clinicians in indicating diagnostics for a patient, defining strategies for a population according to their age, etc.

For the above two patterns (P_1 and P_2), we considered the analytical elements with presence rates higher than 75 % as important (*e.g.*, the dimensions *Patient, Doctor, Department...*), those with presence rates between 50 % and 75 % as recommended (*e.g.*, the dimensions *Disease, Laboratory*), whereas those with presence rates between 50 % and 10 % as optional (*e.g.*, the dimensions *Room, Sampling*). On the other hand, we rejected the elements whose presence rates are less than 10 %. In our MP diagrams, the three genericity levels are graphically distinguished in order to assist the decision maker while reusing these MP.

The reuse of one of these patterns for a target IS builds a DM star schema and projects it over the computerized data model of that target IS. As depicted in Figure 5, we manage the reuse at two levels: i) a *logical* level conducted by the decision maker and that is independent of the data model of the target IS; and ii) a technical *physical* level

Figure 5. Logical and physical levels of an MP reuse

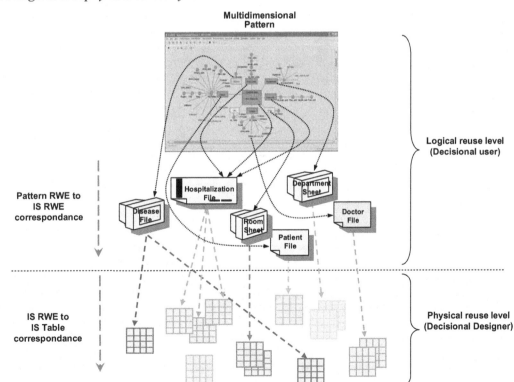

conducted by decisional designers and that treats the projection steps.

The division of the reuse phase into two levels has a twofold motivation. First, it helps separating the OLAP requirements specification from the DM design; this alleviates the complexity of the DM development process. Secondly, the division aims at delaying the introduction of technical, implementation aspects during the DM design; this better motivates the decision maker to participate more intensively in the OLAP requirements specification.

MP REUSE: THE LOGICAL LEVEL

The logical reuse level is performed in two steps: *pre-instantiation* of the pattern, followed by *instantiation* of its entities by the RWE of the target, operational system.

Pattern Pre-Instantiation

By definition, a pattern, built around and documented by RWE, is a generic schema that decision makers can modify and adapt according to their particular analytical needs. For example, they can remove measures, dimensions, hierarchies and/or parameters. The addition of a multidimensional element is allowed provided that the added element can be traced to RWE of the target IS; this restriction ensures the loadability of the added elements. However, we believe that the addition operation is imperceptibly necessary, since an MP is generic and, therefore, it covers all possible multidimensional elements of its domain. It can be, however, used to add for instance aggregate/derived measures; as we noted in the previous section, this type of measures cannot be identified by our MP construction method.

Figure 6. P$_{manager}$: a pre-instantiation example of the Hospitalization pattern.

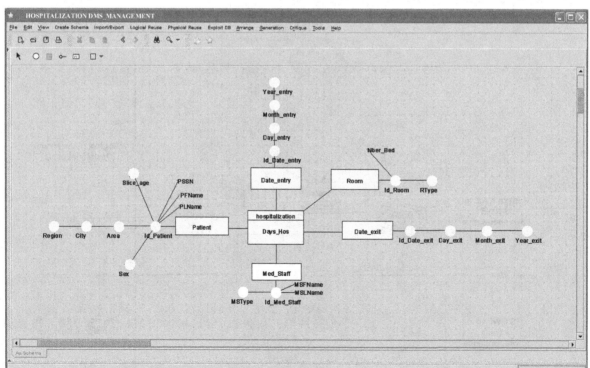

On the other hand, the deletion operations can be carried out mainly on the variable part of the pattern, *i.e.,* on the elements marked as recommended or optional. Thus, a decision maker should not invest much effort on the core of the pattern, considered as the stable part.

Figure 6 and 7 show two pre-instantiations ($P_{manager}$ and $P_{clinician}$) of the *Hospitalization* pattern (Figure 3). $P_{manager}$ and $P_{clinician}$ were pre-instantiated by, respectively, a manager and a member of a medical staff. The manager was interested in analyzing the loads of the medical staff (Doctors, nurses, anesthetists...) according to their type/category during a certain period. To express these requirements, the manager started from the *Hospitalization* pattern, removed the dimensions *Disease*, *Tutor* and *Department*, all the measures, several hierarchies (*H_Civil_Status* from the *Patient* dimension...) and parameters (*Blood_group* from the dimension *Patient*...),

renamed the dimension *Doctor* into *Med_Staff* and added the parameter *MSType* from the documenting RWE *Medical Staff File*. Furthermore, the manager also wanted to know room utilization per type (reanimation, operation...) during a certain period; thus, they added the parameter *RType* to the dimension *Room*. In addition, to analyze the number of hospitalization days, the manager added the measure *Days_Hos* derived from the dimensions *Date_entry* and *Date_exit*; they chose to keep these dimensions in order to know, for example, patients hospitalized during a specific period.

On the other hand, a clinician can use the same pattern to derive $P_{clinician}$ and analyze, for example, diagnostics (Pressure Blood, Temperature, Heart_Frq...) carried by doctors according to their specialty, for a specific disease. In this case, the clinician added to the dimension *Doctor* the parameter *Specialty*. In addition, he/she can

Figure 7. $P_{clinician}$: a pre-instantiation example of the pattern P_1

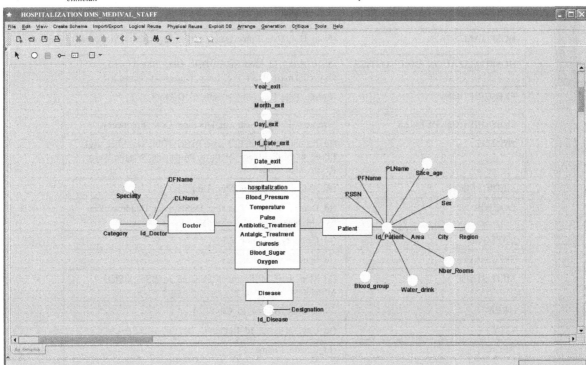

also analyze treatments (Antibiotic_Treatment, Antalgic_Treatment...) taken by patients suffering from a specific disease during a certain period.

To manage the logical reuse step, we have defined a set of algebraic operators that a decision maker can use to derive a star schema from a pattern. These algebraic operators are formalized in (Feki J. & Ben-Abdallah H. 2007) to guarantee the well-formedness of the derived DM schema (Ghozzi F. 2004) (Hurtado C.A, & Mendelzon A.O. 2002).

Note that once a pattern is pre-instantiated, the genericity levels are no longer significant. That is, all the decisional elements have the same importance and representation (*cf.*, Figure 6 and 7).

Instantiation of the RWE

Recall that an MP is documented with the standardized RWE used to build it. Being standard, these RWE are independent of any particular

Table 1. RWE instantiation for the star-schema $P_{manager}$.

PATTERN RWE	IS RWE
Hospitalization File	Hospitalization File
Patient File	Patient File
Doctor File	Medical Staff File
Room Sheet	Room File

IS. However, in order to derive a particular DM schema, these RWE must be associated with those of the target IS (Table 2). This is the objective of the instantiation step.

For a pattern P, the set of all its entities, noted as *Rwe(P)*, is the union of the RWE defining its fact, measures, dimensions and their attributes. The instantiation of the RWE of a pattern P associates each element of *Rwe(P)* with RWE of the target IS. Any element without a correspondent RWE in the target IS should be eliminated (or carefully

Table 2. Part of a relational schema of a private polyclinic X.

HOSPITALIZATION	(Num_Hos, Date_Entry, Date_Exit,..., Id_Patient#, Id_Room#)
HOSPITALIZATION_DIAGNOSTICS	(Num_Hos #, Id_Med_Staff#, Date_Diag, Blood_press, Oxygen, Drain, Heart_Frq, Temp, Diuresis, Glucose,...)
PRESCRIPTION	(Presno, Pres_Date, Id_Patient#, Id_Doctor#, ...)
PRESCRIPTION_DETAILS	(Presno #, Ref_Medicament, Duration, Dose, Frequency ...)
PATIENT	(Id_Patient, PFName, PLName, PSSN, PTel, Sex, Slice_Age, PDate_of_birth, PPlace_of_birth, Profession, Weight, Waist, PType, Area_Code#...)
MEDICAMENT	(Ref_Medicament, Des_Med, Unit,...)
DOCTOR	(Id_Doctor, DFname, DLname, DSSN, Dtel, Daddress, Year_Rec, Id_Specialty#, Id_Category#...)
CATEGORY	(Id_Category, Catname, ...)
SPECIALTY	(Id_Specialty, Spename, ...)
MED_STAFF	(Id_Med_Staff, MSFname, MSLname, MSSSN, MStel, MSaddress, MSType...)
AREA	(Area_Code, Aname, Id_City#, ...)
CITY	(Id_City, CTname , Id_Region#, ...)
REGION	(Id_Region, Rname, ...)
ROOM	(Id_Room, RType, ...)

examined by the DM designer); this ensures that the DM is "well derived" for the target IS and that all its elements are loadable.

Table 1 illustrates a sample correspondence between the RWE of the *Hospitalization* pattern and those of the pre-instantiated pattern $P_{manager}$.

The result of the logical instantiation is a DM schema documented with RWE that are specific to one target operational system. However, this DM schema is still independent of the IS computerized data model and any specific implementation platform. The complete instantiation requires the correspondence of its RWE with the computer "objects" (tables, columns...). This correspondence is called *physical reuse*.

MP REUSE: THE PHYSICAL LEVEL

The physical reuse level is a technical process where the decisional designer is the principal actor. They can be assisted by the operational IS designer. In the case of a relational data model[2], the assistance mainly aims at identifying the database tables implementing each RWE (used in the derived DM schema). In this task, the decisional designer exploits the inter-table links materialized through referential integrity constraints.

RWE-Tables Association

This step aims at projecting the data source over the RWE used in the logically instantiated pattern (*i.e.*, DM schema). To accomplish this step, we define one rule to determine the tables that implement each basic entity, and another to determine the tables materializing each basic entity.

To illustrate the RWE-Table association rules, we will use the relational data source of a private polyclinic *X* described in Table 2; the primary keys in this database are underlined and the foreign keys are followed by the sharp sign (#).

Identification of Tables of a Fact Entity

In general, each measure within a fact has several instances referring to the same fact, *e.g.*, blood pressure, temperature or heart frequency taken by doctors for a hospitalized patient. Therefore, a FE models a *master-detail* relationship where the master table represents the *fact* table and the detail table is that of the measures.

Table 3. A sample RWE-Tables correspondance

RWE of Pmanager / IS Tables	HOSPITALIZATION	HOSPITALIZATION_DIAGNOSTICS	PATIENT	AREA	CITY	REGION	ROOM	MED_STAFF	DOCTOR	MEDICAMENT	CATEGORY	SPECIALTY	PRESCRIPTION	PRESCRIPTION_DETAILS
(FE) Hospitalization File	R1	R1												
(BE) Patient File			R2	R2	R2	R2			Unused Tables of the source DB					
(BE) Medical Staff File								R2						
(BE) Room File							R2							

We identify the tables of a fact entity in an IS (denoted as FE^{IS}) by the following rule:

R1: *The table T containing the identifier of the fact entity FE^{IS} and each table directly referring to T (by a foreign key) and containing a measure in FE^{IS}.*

Identification of tables of a basic entity

Because of the normalization process of the relations, a basic entity in the target IS (noted BE^{IS}) is generally modeled by:

R2: *The table T containing the identifier of the basic entity BE^{IS}, and each table T' belonging to the transitive closure of T such as T' is not a table implementing a RWE.*

Recall that the transitive closure of a table T is the set of all tables T' directly or indirectly referenced by T through the functional dependency of the foreign key of T on the primary key of T'.

Table 3 illustrates the matrix of correspondence between the data source tables (*cf.*, Tab1) and the RWE of the DM (Figure 6). For example, for the FE *Hospitalization File* (generating the fact *Hospitalization* of the DM $P_{manager}$ in Figure 6), rule *R1* identifies the tables HOSPITALIZATION and HOSPITALIZATION_DIAGNOSTICS. These tables contain all data of the FE *Hospitalization File*.

Note that the tables identified by the rule *R1* completely define the recording context of the measures. That is, they represent each measure's dependence on the date and on the entities to which it is related by its identifier.

In addition, for the BE *Patient File* (which builds the *Patient* dimension in $P_{manager}$ of Figure 6), the rule *R2* identifies first the table PATIENT and then the three tables AREA, CITY and REGION. Joining these three tables through their primary/ foreign key columns builds the implementation of the BE *Patient File* and gathers the data of the *Patient* dimension.

RWE Data-Items Association with Table Columns

Recall that the DM is actually reduced to the multidimensional elements present in both the RWE and the computerized IS. In addition, according to our MP construction approach, each multidimensional element comes from one single data item in the RWE. Consequently, the association between a table column and a DM element is a one-to-one function.

The objective of this section is to show the existence of a minimal subset of the database tables that implements a RWE when the database is normalized (*i.e.*, in CODD's Third Normal Form). This guaranties a finite and minimal number of joins. For this, we adapt the concept of *Schema Graph* (Golfarelli M., Lechtenbörger J., Rizzi S. & Vossen G. 2004) used to model data dependencies among the elements of a DM schema. Our adapted graph, called *RWE-Graph,* represents the dependencies among the tables of a RWE implementation. We use this graph to show the existence of a minimal implementation, which is deduced from the properties of dependency graphs.

Properties of dependency graphs

In the presentation of the properties of a functional dependency graph, we adopt the standard notations in relational databases, where capital letters from the beginning of the alphabet (A, B …) denote single attributes and from the end of the alphabet (X, Y, Z) denote sets of attributes. We restrict our attention to simple functional dependencies, noted as $A \rightarrow B$.

Recall that, in the literature of the database field (Maier, 1983) (Lechtenbörger, J. 2004), a set F of functional dependencies (FD) is *canonical* if it verifies the three following properties:

a. $(X \rightarrow Y \in F) \Rightarrow |Y| = 1$ (*i.e.*, Y is a single attribute),

b. $(X \rightarrow A \in F) \wedge (Y \subset X) \Rightarrow (Y \nrightarrow A)$ (*i.e.*, A is fully dependent on X), and

c. $(F' \subsetneq F) \Rightarrow (F' \not\equiv F)$; (*i.e., F is minimal*).

Moreover, for every set *F* of FD, there is at least one *canonical cover*; that is, a canonical set of FD that is equivalent to *F* (Maier 1983); (Golfarelli M., Lechtenbörger J., Rizzi S. & Vossen G. 2004). In addition, as proven in (Golfarelli M., Lechtenbörger J., Rizzi S. & Vossen G. 2004), if all functional dependencies in *F* are simple and form an acyclic graph, then *F* admits a *unique* minimal, canonical cover. The functional dependency $X \rightarrow Y$ is said to be simple iff $|X| \cong |Y| = 1$.

RWE-Graph Construction

In order to define our concept of *RWE-Graph*, we will use the following notation:

- *P* : a multidimensional pattern, logically instantiated;
- Rwe^{IS} : the set of RWE from the computerized IS used in *P*; and
- T^{IS} : a set of database tables from the target IS used for the physical instantiation; these tables are determined from Rwe^{IS} by applying the rules of the previous section.

Definition. A *RWE-Graph* of a RWE *r* is a directed graph $G = (\{E\} \cup U, F)$ with nodes $\{E\} \cup U$ and arcs *F*, where:

- *E* is the *first* table identified either by rule *R1* (if *r* is a fact entity), or by rule *R2* (if *r* is a basic entity);
- *U* is the set of *remaining* tables identified either by rule *R1* (if *r* is a fact entity), or by rule *R2* (if *r* is a basic entity); and
- *F* is a *canonical set* of simple FD defined on $(\{E\} \cup U)$ such that:

$$T_1 \rightarrow T_2 \in F \text{ iff } \exists X \subseteq \text{ForeignKey}(T_1) : X = \text{PrimaryKey}(T_2) \wedge X \neq \varphi$$

where the function *ForeignKey* (respectively, *PrimaryKey*) returns the set of foreign keys (the primary key[3]) of a table.

Note that the node *E* has no incoming edges. In addition, there is a path from *E* to every node in *U*. Recall that for each RWE *r* in an instantiated pattern *P*, its corresponding tables reference one another through foreign-primary keys; hence, the RWE-graph of a RWE *r* is a connected graph that starts from the root table *E*.

Figure 8. A basic entity Patient of a private polyclinic X (a) and its RWE-Graph (b)

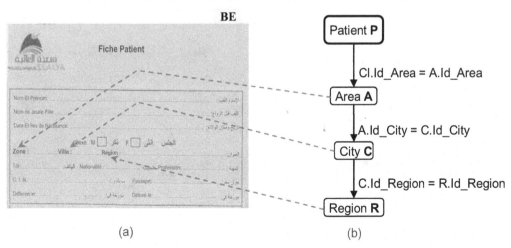

(a)   (b)

Furthermore, the set of arcs F in the RWE-graph of a RWE r is a *canonical set*:

a. the arcs in F represent simple dependencies: every foreign key (considered as a monolithic attribute) functionally determines its corresponding primary key;

b. since the functional dependencies we consider are limited to key attributes, each foreign key completely determines its corresponding primary key;

c. F is a minimal set: since we assumed the data source to be in the new third normal form (*i.e.*, BCNF for Boyce-Codd Normal Form), then F contains *no redundant* dependencies; and finally,

d. the fact that G is *acyclic* can be proven by induction and because if a mutual dependency exists between the keys of two tables, then this logically implies the existence of a single table; otherwise, the data source contains redundant data. In fact, mutual

dependencies should exist only among attributes belonging to the same table.

Using the above four properties of the RWE-Graph G, we can infer that G admits a *unique, minimal canonical cover* (Golfarelli M., Lechtenbörger J., Rizzi S. & Vossen G. 2004). The minimality of G is an important property, since it ensures the construction of non-redundant objects with a minimum number of joins.

Example

Figure 8 shows an example of a RWE *Patient* and its corresponding RWE-Graph. Each arc in the RWE-Graph is labeled with the predicate of an equi-join between the tables of its source and destination nodes.

The RWE-Graph can be used to construct trivially a relational view: This corresponds to a query to gather the columns from all tables of the RWE-Graph, where the join predicate of the query

Figure 9. Correspondence between RWE elements and table columns in MPI-Editor.

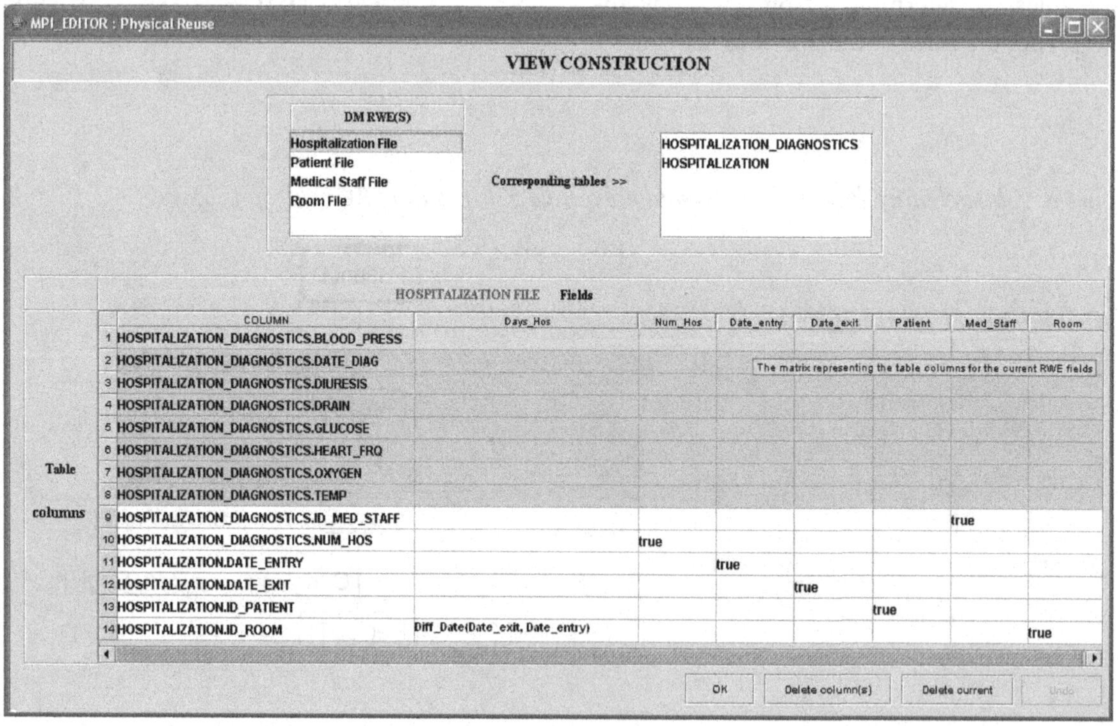

is the conjunction of the predicates representing the arcs of the graph.

For the RWE *Patient* example of Figure 8, and according to its *RWE-graph*, this entity is simulated by the view resulting from a query comprising three equi-joins over the four tables PATIENT, AREA, CITY and REGION.

The correspondence between elements of a RWE and columns of their identified tables requires its validation from the DM designer. Indeed, our correspondence is principally linguistic, *i.e.,* an element of a RWE has either the same name of its associated table column or a synonym. In order to facilitate the validation, our tool of MP reuse presents the designer with an automatically constructed correspondence matrix.

Figure 9 shows the correspondence matrix for elements of the RWE *"Hospitalization File"* and the two pertinent tables HOSPITALIZATION and HOSPITALIZATION_DIAGNOSTICS. For example, the element *Med_Staff* in this file is associated to the column *Id_Med_Staff* of the table HOSPITALIZATION_DIAGNOSTICS. In addition, for computed elements, *e.g., Days_Hos,* the correspondence matrix shows the computing function, *e.g.,* the function *Diff_Date(Date_exit, Date_entry)* which calculates the difference between the two dates *Date_exit* and *Date_entry.*

Once the decision-maker validates the correspondences between the RWE elements and table columns, they can be passed on to the loading phase. They present the DM developer specific data tables they can use to define the necessary ETL procedures.

CONCLUSION

This work introduced the concept of multidimensional pattern (MP), both as an assistance means for the expression of analytical requirements by decision makers, and as a tool for data mart (DM) schema design. An MP is a typical solution specifying a set of analytical requirements for a given domain of activity and independently of any data model of a particular IS. In addition, an MP is constructed based on standard real world entities (RWE) which are easier to understand and to adapt by decision makers for their OLTP system.

An MP can be reused either to prototype and/or to construct data marts for a particular IS, or to construct a complete DSS (*i.e.,* the data marts first and then the data warehouse). In this chapter, we presented a two-level reuse method for the first case: At the *logical level,* the decision maker first adapts an MP to their specific analytical requirements, then (s)he establishes the correspondences between the RWE of the pattern and those of the target IS; consequently, the resulting DM schema is closely related to the enterprise. At the *physical level,* the DSS designer retrieves, from the target computerized IS, the tables necessary for the loading process of the derived DM schema. To identify the tables implementing a RWE in the target IS, we have defined two rules that assist the designer in this task. The identified tables are vital assistance to the definition of ETL procedures.

To evaluate our DM design approach, we have already applied it in three domains: commercial (Ben Abdallah M., Feki J., Ben-Abdallah H. 2006a), medical, and financial. In this chapter, we showed patterns from the medical domain analyzing the subjects *Hospitalization* and *Medical Test.* We showed how these patterns can be used by both medical staff and organization managers to specify their OLAP requirements. Then, we applied the steps of our reuse approach on the *Hospitalization* pattern.

We are currently working on two research axes. In the first, we are conducting further experimental evaluations with the help of managers of local enterprises and clinicians and managers in other polyclinics. These evaluations will allow us to judge better the genericity of the so far constructed patterns, as well as the soundness of our rules at the physical reuse level.

In the second research axis, we are integrating our pattern-based design approach within the OMG model-driven architecture. With this development approach, we would cover the conceptual, logical and physical levels of a DM/DW modeling. In addition, we would provide for the automatic passages between the models at the three levels. At the conceptual level, we consider the patterns as computation independent models (CIM) that capitalize domain expertise. A CIM can be transformed through our logical reuse approach to derive a platform independent model (PIM) that represents specific OLAP requirements. On the other hand, the logically instantiated pattern (PIM) can be transformed to a platform specific model (PSM) adapted to a particular DBMS. For this third modeling level, we are currently pursuing the definition of the transformation rules for relational OLAP (*ROLAP*). To do so, we need to formalize the platform description model (PDM) of a relational DBMS from the query language description and user manual of the DBMS. Then, we need to define the merging rules of the PIM and PDM.

REFERENCES

Abello, A., Samos, J., & Saltor F. (2003). Implementing operations to navigate semantic star schemas. *Proceedings of the Sixth International Workshop on Data Warehousing and OLAP (DOLAP 2003)* (pp. 56–62). New York: ACM Press.

Annoni, E. (2007, November). Eléments méthodologique pour le développement de systèmes décisionnels dans' un contexte de réutilisation. Thesis in computer sciences, University Paul Sabatier, Toulouse, France.

Ben-Abdallah, M., Feki, J., & Ben-Abdallah, H. (2006, 9-11 Mai). Designing Multidimensional patterns from standardized real world entities. *International Conference on Computer and Communication Engineering ICCCE'06*, Kuala Lumpur, Malaysia.

Ben-Abdallah, M., Feki, J., & Ben-Abdallah, H. (2006, 7-9 December). MPI-EDITOR : Un outil de spécification de besoins OLAP par réutilisation logique de patrons multidimensionnels. *Maghrebian Conference on Software Engineering and Artificial Intelligence MCSEAI'06*, Agadir, Morocco.

Ben-Abdallah, M., Ben, Saïd N., Feki, J., & Ben-Abdallah, H. (2007, November). MP-Builder : A tool for multidimensional pattern construction , *Arab International Conference on Information Technology (ACIT 2007)*, Lattakia, Syria.

Bernier, E., Badard, T., Bédard, Y., Gosselin, P., & Pouliot, J. (2007). Complex spatio-temporal data warehousing and OLAP technologies to better understand climate-related health vulnerabilities. *Special number of International Journal of Biomedical Engineering and Technology on "Warehousing and Mining Complex Data: Applications to Biology, Medicine, Behavior, Health and Environment".*

Böhnlein, M., & Ulbrich-vom, Ende, A. (1999). Deriving initial data warehouse structures from the conceptual data models of the underlying operational information systems.

Bonifati, A., Cattaneo, F., Ceri, S., Fuggetta, A., & Paraboschi, S. (2001, October). Designing data marts for data warehouse. *ACM Transaction on Software Engineering and Methodology, ACM, 10*, 452-483.

Cabibbo, L., & Torlone, R. (2000). The design and development of a logical OLAP system. *2nd International Conference of Data Warehousing and Knowledge Discovery (DaWaK'00)*, London, UK: Springer, LNCS 1874, (pp. 1-10).

Carpani, F., & Ruggia, R. (2001). An integrity constraints language for a conceptual multidimensional data model. *13th International Conference on Software Engineering & Knowledge Engineering (SEKE'01)*, Argentina.

Codd, E.F. (1970, June). A relational model of data for large shared data banks. *Communication of the ACM, 13*(6), 3776-387.

Cheesman, J., & Daniels, J. (2000). UML Components: A simple process for specifying component-based software. Addison Wesley.

Chen, Y., Dehne, F., Eavis, T., & Rau-Chaplin, A. (2006). Improved data partitioning for building large ROLAP data cubes in parallel. *Journal of Data Warehousing and Mining, 2(*1), 1-26.

Chrisment, C., Pujolle, G., Ravat, F., Teste, O., & Zurfluh, G. (2006). *Bases de données décisionnelles.* Encyclopédie de l'informatique et des systèmes d'information. Jacky Akoka, Isabelle Comyn-Wattiau (Edition.), Vuibert, I/5, pp. 533-546.

Feki, J., & Ben-Abdallah, H. (2006, 22-24 Mai). Star patterns for data mart design: Definition and logical reuse operators. *International Conference on Control, Modeling and Diagnosis ICCMD'06*, Annaba Algeria.

Feki, J., Ben-Abadallah, H., & Ben Abdallah, M. (2006). Réutilisation des patrons en étoile. *XXIVème Congrès INFORSID'06*, (pp. 687-701), Hammamet, Tunisie.

Feki, J., & Ben-Abdallah, H. (2007, March). Multidimensional pattern construction and logical reuse for the design of data marts. *International Review on Computers and Software (IRECOS)*, 2(2), 124-134, ISSN 1882-6003.

Feki, J., Majdoubi, J., & Gargouri, F. (2005, July). A two-phase approach for multidimensional schemes integration. *17th International Conference on Software Engineering and Knowledge Engineering (SEKE'05)*, (pp. 498-503), Taipei, Taiwan, Republic of China. ISBN I-891706-16-0.

Feki, J., Nabli, A., Ben-Abdallah, H., & Gargouri, F. (2008, August). An automatic data warehouse conceptual design approach. encyclopedia of data warehousing and mining, John Wang Edition (To appear August).

Gamma, E., Helm, R., Johnson, J. & Vlissides, J. (1999). *Design patterns: Elements of reusable object-oriented software.* Addisson-Wesley.

Ghozzi, F. (2004). Conception et manipulation de bases de données dimensionnelles à contraintes. *Thesis in computer sciences,* University Paul Sabatier, Toulouse, France.

Golfarelli, M., Maio, D., & Rizzi, S. (1998). Conceptual design of data warehouses from E/R schemes. *31st Hawaii International Conference on System Sciences.*

Golfarelli, M., Rizzi, S., & Saltarelli, E. (2002). WAND: A case tool for workload-based design of a data mart. SEBD, (pp. 422-426).

Golfarelli, M., Lechtenbörger, J., Rizzi, S., & Vossen, G. (2004). Schema versioning in data warehouses. *S. Wang et al. (Eds.): ER Workshops 2004, LNCS 3289, (*pp. 415-428). *Berlin, Heidelburg:* Springer-Verlag.

Hurtado, C.A., & Mendelzon, A.O. (2002, June). OLAP dimension constraints. *21st ACM SIGACT-SIGMOD-SIGART Symposium on Principles of Database Systems (PODS'02),* Madison, USA, (pp. 169-179).

Hüsemann, B., Lechtenbörger, J., & Vossen, G. (2000). Conceptual data warehouse design. *Proc. of the Int'l Workshop on Design and Management of Data Warehouses*, Stockholm, Sweden, (pp. 6.1-6.11).

Kimball, R. (2002). *The data warehouse toolkit.* New York, Second Edition: Wiley

Lechtenbörger, J., Hüsemann, B. J., & Vossen. (2000). Conceptual data warehouse design. *International Workshop on Design and Management of Data Warehouses*, Stockholm, Sweden, (pp. 6.1-6.11).

Lechtenbörger, J., & Vossen, G. (2003, July). Multidimensional normal forms for data warehouse design. *Information Systems Review, 28*(5), 415-434.

Lechtenbörger, J. (2004). Computing unique canonical covers for simple FDs via transitive reduction. *Technical report, Angewandte Mathematik und Informatik,* University of Muenster, Germany: Information Processing Letters.

Maier, D. (1983). The theory of relational databases. *Computer Science Press.*

Moody, L. D., & Kortink, M. A. R. (2000). From enterprise models to dimensional models: A methodology for data warehouses and data mart design. *International Workshop on Design and Management of Data Warehouses,* Stockholm, Sweden, (pp. 5.1-5.12).

OMG (2003). Object Management Group (OMG), MDA Guide 1.0.1., omg/2003-06-01.

OMG (2006). Object Management Group (OMG), Business Process Modeling Notation Specification.http://www.bpmn.org/Documents/OMG%20Final%20Adopted%20BPMN%201-0%20Spec%2006-02-01.pdf.

Payne, T.H. (2000). Computer decision support systems. *Chest: Official Journal of the American College of Chest Physicians, 118,* 47-52.

Phipps, C., & Davis, K. (2002). Automating data warehouse conceptual schema design and evaluation. *DMDW'02*, Canada.

Ravat, F., Teste, O., Zurfluh, G. (2006, June). Algèbre OLAP et langage graphique. *XIVème congrès INFormatique des ORganisations et Systèmes d'Information et de Décision (INFORSID'06)*, Tunisia, (pp. 1039-1054)

Saidane, M., & Giraudin, J.P. (2002). Ingénierie de la coopération des systèmes d'information. *Revue Ingénierie des Systèmes d'Information (ISI), 7*(4), Hermès.

Tsois, A., Karayannidis, N., & Sellis, T. (2001). MAC: Conceptual data modeling for OLAP. *International Workshop on Design and Management of Data Warehouses (DMDW'2001)*, Interlaken, Switzerland.

UNECE (2002). UN/CEFACT - ebXML Core Components Technical Specification, Part 1 V1.8. http//www.unece.org/cefact/ebxml/ebXML_CCTS_Part1_V1-8.

Zheng, K. (2006, September 2006). Design, implementation, user acceptance, and evaluation of a clinical decision support system for evidence-based medicine practice. *Thesis in information systems and health informatics*, Carnegie Mellon University, H. John Heinz III School of Public Policy and Management, Pittsburgh, Pennsylvania.

ENDNOTES

[1] Institut de Recherche en Informatique de Toulouse-France

[2] We choose the relational model since it has been the most commonly used model during the three last decades.

[3] When the primary key of a table is a list of attributes, we can regard it as a monolithic attribute.

Section III
Spatio-Temporal Data Warehousing

Chapter X
A Multidimensional Methodology with Support for Spatio–Temporal Multigranularity in the Conceptual and Logical Phases

Concepción M. Gascueña
Polytechnic of Madrid University, Spain

Rafael Guadalupe
Polytechnic of Madrid University, Spain

ABSTRACT

*The Multidimensional Databases (MDB) are used in the Decision Support Systems (DSS) and in Geographic Information Systems (GIS); the latter locates spatial data on the Earth's surface and studies its evolution through time. This work presents part of a methodology to design MDB, where it considers the Conceptual and Logical phases, and with related support for multiple spatio-temporal granularities. This will allow us to have multiple representations of the same spatial data, interacting with other, spatial and thematic data. In the Conceptual phase, the conceptual multidimensional model—FactEntity (FE)—is used. In the Logical phase, the rules of transformations are defined, from the FE model, to the Relational and Object Relational logical models, maintaining multidimensional semantics, and under the perspective of multiple spatial, temporal, and thematic granularities. The FE model shows constructors and hierarchical structures to deal with the multidimensional semantics on the one hand, carrying out a study on how to structure "a fact and its associated dimensions." Thus making up the Basic factEnty, and in addition, showing rules to generate all the possible Virtual factEntities. On the other hand, with the spatial semantics, highlighting the **Semantic** and **Geometric spatial granularities**.*

INTRODUCTION

The traditional databases methodologies propose to design these in three phases: Conceptual, Logical and Physical.

In the Conceptual phase, the focus is on the data types of the application, their relationships and constraints. The Logical phase is related to the implementation of the conceptual data model in a commercial Databases Manager System (*DBMS*), using a model more near to implementation, as for example the Relational, *R* model. In the Physical phase, the model of the physical design is totally dependent on the commercial *DBMS* chosen for the implementation.

In the design of Multidimensional databases (*MDB*), from a Conceptual focus, most of the models proposed use extensions to operational models such as Entity Relation (*ER)* or Unified Modeling Language (*UML*). But these models do not reflect the multidimensional or spatial semantics, because they were created for other purposes. From a Logical focus, the models gather less semantics that conceptual models. The *MDB*, as commented (Piattini, Marcos, Calero & Vela, 2006), have an immature technology, which suggests that there is no model accepted by the Scientific Community to model these databases.

The *MDB* allow us to store the data in an appropriate way for its analysis. How to structure data in the analysis and design stage, gives guidelines for physical storage. The data should be ready for the analysis to be easy and fast.

On the other hand the new technologies of databases, allow us the management of terabytes of data in less time than ever. It is now possible, to store space in databases, not as photos or images but as thousands of points and to store the evolution of space over time. But the spatial data cannot be treated as the rest of the data, as they have special features. The same spatial data can be observed and handled with different shapes and sizes. The models must enable us to represent this feature. It is of interest to get multiple interconnected representations of the same spatial object, interacting with other spatial and thematic data.

This proposal seeks to resolve these shortcomings, providing a conceptual model multidimensional, with support for multiple spatial, temporal and thematic related granularities, and rules for converting it into logical models without losing this semantics.

We propose to deal the spatial data in *MDB* as a dimension, and its different representations with different granularities. But we ask:

- How to divide the spatial area of interest?
- How to represent this area in a database?
- In what way?
- How big?

We answer, with the adequate space granularities. We study the spatial data and we distinguish two spatial granularity types, *Semantic* and *Geometric*. Next we define briefly these concepts, for more details read (Gascueña & Guadalupe, 2008), (Gascueña & Guadalupe, 2008c).

In the *Semantic spatial* granularity the area of interest is classified by means of semantic qualities such as: administrative boundaries, political, etc. A set of *Semantic granularities* consider the space divided into units that are part of a total, *"parts-of"*. These parts only change over time. And each *Semantic granularity* is considered a different spatial element.

A *Geometric spatial* granularity is defined as the unit of measurement in a Spatial Reference System, (*SRS)* according to which the properties of space are represented, along with geometry of representation associated with that unit. The geometry of representation can be points, lines and surfaces, or combinations of these. A spatial data can be stored and represented with different granularities. In Figure 1 we see a spatial zone divided into Plot and represented with surface and point geometric types.

Figure 1. Represented zones in surface and points geometries

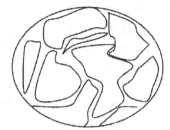 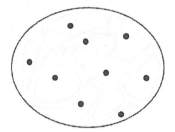

The *Temporal granularity* is the unit of measure chosen on the time domain to represent the variation of an element, for example the granularities with respect to day, month and year have the granules 7/7/1953, 7/1953, 1953 respectly.

Our object is to develop a methodology of design for *MDB*, considering the Conceptual and Logical phases. Where in the *Conceptual* phase, the model called *FactEntity* (*FE*) presented in (Gascueña & Guadalupe, 2008), (Gascueña & Guadalupe, 2008b) is used. And in *Logical* phase some rules to transform the *FE* model in the Relational (*R*) and Object Relational (*OR*) logical models are defined, without loss of multidimensional semantics and low prospects of multiple spatial, temporal and thematic granularities.

This work is structured as follows: in Section 2, we will see the Conceptual Phase of the methodology proposed. Section 3, include the Logical Phase. In section 4, we show an example of application. The section 5 we will expose related works, and in section 6, some conclusions and future work are shown.

CONCEPTUAL PHASE

We define the *FactEntity (FE)* conceptual multidimensional model that supports, on the one hand multidimensional semantics and generation of data derived automatically, and on the other hand, the spatial semantics emphasizing the spatio-temporal multigranularities, which allows us to have multiple representations of the same spatial

element, depending on the need of the application and of the thematic data that accompanies the spatial data. In addition *FE* model has graphic representation. Next, we briefly define the functionality of the *FE* model, for more details see (Gascueña & Guadalupe, 2008).

Multidimensional Semantics in the FactEntity Model

The *FE* model is based on the Snowflake logical model, (Kimball, 1996), but from a conceptual approach adding cardinality and exclusivity, and new concepts, builders and hierarchical structures, which allow us to represent in a diagram, *what* data will be stored, *where* to find it, and *how* to derive it. This model has two main elements: *dimension* and *factEntity*, and distinguishes between: *basic* and *derived* data. The *factEntities* are classified in *Basic* and *Virtual*. It's about of analyze a *fact* object of study, from different perspectives or *dimensions*, and with varying degrees of detail or *granularities*. Thus, we distinguish between *basic fact* and *derived fact*. A *fact* contains one or more *measures*.

A *dimension* can have different granularities, these are represented with different levels (one for each granularity), and several levels form one hierarchy where the lowest level is called *leaf level*. A dimension can have more one hierarchy, but only one *leaf level*.

A *Basic factEntity* is composed of only one "*Basic fact*" object of study and the *leaf levels* of its dimensions associated, and this is repre-

Figure 2. Metamodel made up with the ER model, which gathers the Basic factEntity semantics, this is highlighted in bold

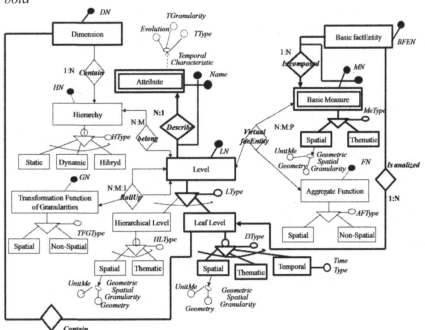

sented explicitly in the scheme. A *Basic fact* is composed of one of several *"Basic measures"*. We highlight the semantics of the *Basic factEntities* in a metamodel of the *FE* model (Gascueña & Guadalupe, 2008b), made up with the extend *ER* model. We see the entities and relationship that participate, highlighted in bold into Figure 2.

In order to navigate between hierarchies, some multidimensional operators are necessary; we can see some in the Table 1.

The *Virtual factEntities* are formed by *derived data*, which are made up of the "evolution" of *basic data*, when the Rollup is realized on one or more dimensions.

The *Virtual factEntities* are composed of *"Derived measures"* of a processed *Basic measure*, and the Cartesian product of the subgroups composed for its associated dimensions, where at least one dimension is involved with a level greater than the *leaf level*. This is not represented explicitly in the *FE* scheme.

We highlight the semantics of the *Virtual factEntities* on a metamodel of the *FE* model, made up with the extended *ER* model. We see the entities and relationship that participate, highlighted in bold into Figure 3.

The *FE* model allows us to represent on the *FE* scheme two types of functions, ones the func-

Table 1. Some multidimensional operators.

Navigating through the levels of hierarchy
Roll-up: Navigating from lower level to higher level
Drill-Dow: Navigating from higher level to lower level
Selecting elements
Slice, Dice: Selection and projection of elements

*Figure 3. Metamodel made up with the ER model, which gathers the **Virtual factEntity** semantics, this is highlighted in bold*

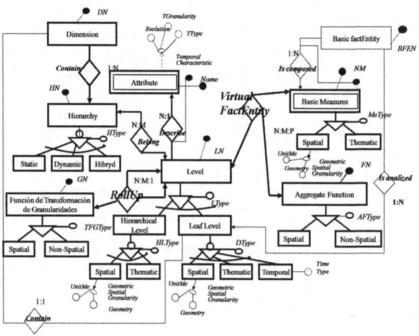

tions that are used to change the granularities, when necessary. This is interesting above all, in changes of, *Semantic* and *Geometric* spatial granularities. And other of ones to represent, the functions used on the "*Basic fact measures,*" when the granularity of each dimension changes. So, we can generate the *Virtual factEntities* in an automatic way.

The *FE* model introduces all the necessary information for the *Virtual factEntities* to be created, at the Logical and Physical phases of modelling. It is in these phases where it is decided:

- Which *Virtual factEntities* will be made?
- How these will be stored, such as:
  - *Aggregates*, the derived data will be calculated and stored.
  - *Pre-aggregates*, the derived data will be requiring new calculation, based on other previously aggregates data.
  - The definitions of generation rules only will are saved.
- *What* form, on tables, views, materialized views, dimensional arrays, etc?

Spatial Semantics in the FactEntity Model

Spatial data type is defined as an abstract type which contains: an identifier, a unit of measure within a spatial reference system (*SRS*), a geometry of representation associated with this unit, and a dimension associated with this geometry. We consider the Open Geographic Information System (*OGIS*) specifications for spatial data, and their topological relationships, to represent the spatial data in a geometric way, see some in Table 2.

In this study is of interest, the spatial data when they are present in a *factEntity* as representation of measures or dimensions.

Table 2. Spatial data and topological relations

Spatial data type		Topological relationshipa	
Surface	ᗡ	Cross surface and line	𝒷
Line	~	Cross line and line	⚡
Point	●	Cros point and line	⌐

Hierarchy Types

The *FE* model to collect the spatio-temporal multigranularity, considers three hierarchy types: *Dynamic*, *Static* and *Hybrid*, (Gascueña & Guadalupe, 2008a), (Gascueña & Guadalupe, 2008b).

In *Dynamic hierarchy* the navigation through the different granularities, imply changes in the *basic measures*; it is appropriated for modelling thematic dimensions or *Semantic* granularity of spatial dimensions. In *Static hierarchy* the changes of granularity on this hierarchy does not imply changes in the *basic measures*, it just changes the spatial representation; it is appropriated for modeling the different *Geometric* spatial granularities of spatial dimensions. The *Hybrid hierarchy* is a mixture of the two previous one; it is appropriated to represent the related *Semantic* and *Geometric* spatial granularities.

Temporal Semantics in the FactEntity Model

Temporal Characteristic

The *FE* model considers the temporal characteristics: *Type of Time*, *Evolution*, and *Granularity*, (Gascueña & Guadalupe, 2008), (Gascueña & Guadalupe, 2008b).

The *Type of Time* represents the "*moments of time*" in which the qualities of an object are valid, for the domain of application. The *FE* model considers: *Valid* and *Transaction* time. The *Transaction time* is the time in which the changes of an element are introduced in a database; this

is represented in the *FE* model as *TT*. The *Valid time* is the real time when an element changes, this is represented in the *FE* model as *VT*. Also the combination of both *Transaction* and *Valid time* is represented for *TVT*.

The *Evolution* of an element can be: *Specific* and *Historical*. The *Specific evolution* only gathers the last time in which a change has happened together with the new value of element. The *Historical evolution* keeps all the values and times when the changes have happened.

The granularity is a partition of the time domain chosen to represent an event; this represents the update frequency of an object/element.

The Time in the Structures of the FE Model

The *FE* model, allows representing temporal characteristics on different structures such as *factEntity*, *attribute* and *hierarchical level*. The *Temporal factEntity* registers the "temporal evolution" of *fact measures* and it is supported by the Time Dimension. The *Temporal Attribute*, any attribute can have its own temporal characteristics, and these are independent of the characteristic of rest of the attributes associated to it. The *Temporal Level* is supported by introducing the temporal characteristics on the primary attribute of this level.

Spatio-Temporal Multigranularity

The *spatio-temporal multigranularity* has two orthogonal notions, spatial and temporal granularities, which are considered as a discrete partition of space and time respectively.

The *spatial multigranularity* is a feature that allows us to represent a space of interest with different *Semantic* spatial granularities and where each *Semantic* spatial granularity, may have one or more different *Geometric* spatial granularities. Different spatial granularities (*Semantic* and *Geometric*) can be interlinked and associated with a space object.

The *temporal multigranularity* is a feature that allows us to represent the changes of an element or group, with different temporal granularities.

The *spatio-temporal multigranularity* is a spatial feature that allows us to represent a space

of interest with *spatial* and *temporal multigranularity* interrelated.

Graphical Representation of the FactEntity Model

We observe in Figure 4 and Table 3, the constructors used for the *FE* model.

In Figure 5 we can see an example of a *Location* spatial dimension that has different types of spatial granularities. The a) option has three *Semantic* granularities, and one representation spatial (surface, m), and is modeled with a *Dynamic hierarchy*. The b) option has a single *Semantic* granularity with three *Geometric* granularities:

Figure 4. Notations for the FactEntity Model

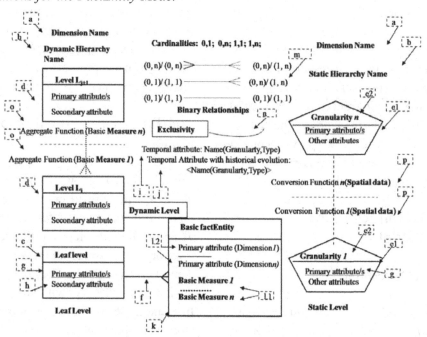

Table 3. Explanation of the constructors of the FactEntity Model

a) Dimension name	b) Hierarchy name
c) Leaf level	d) Level of Dynamic Hierarchy
e) e.1) Level of Static Hierarchy different from leaf level e.2) Geometric spatial granularity	f) Parent-child relation
g) Primary attribute	h) Secondary attribute
i) Temporal attribute	j) Attribute with historical evolution
k) Basic FactEntity	l) l.1) Basic Measures l.2) Primary attribute of each dimension
m) Cardinalities: minimum and maximum number of members related between two consecutive levels	n) Exclusivity
o) Functions applied on the measures when Rollup is done	p) Functions to reach a coarser granularity between levels

Figure 5. Different types of spatial granularities handled with different types of hierarchies

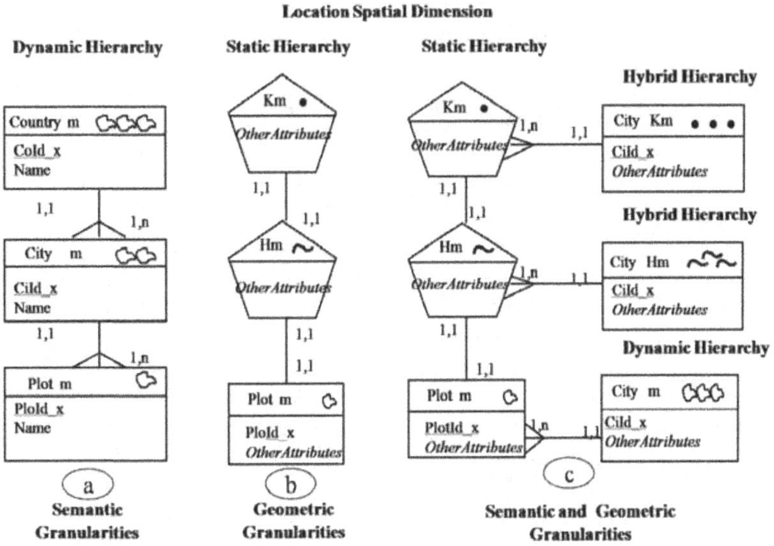

(surface, m), (line, Hm), and (point, km), and are modeled with a *Static hierarchy*. And the c) option has two *Semantic* granularities with three inter-related *Geometric* granularities; these are modeled with one *Static*, one *Dynamic* and two *Hybrid hierarchies*.

The *FE* model allows us to represent on the scheme, the functions that are used to change the *Semantic* and *Geometric* spatial granularities. See Table 4 and 5. We present some functions in Table 4, these can be equivalent to those presented in (Berloto, 1998), which conserve the topological consistency.

In Figure 6 we have add on the schema of Figure 5, the functions of transformation applied to change a granularity to a greater one.

The *FE* model also allows us to represent the functions used on the *fact measures*, on the scheme when the granularities of dimension change; see some in Tables 5 and 6.

Table 4. Functions used to change geometric granularity

Conversion Spatial Functions	
lineConvert	It converts an open line to a point
SurfConvert	It converts a surface and its bounding lines to a line
SurConvertPoint	It converts a simple surface and its bounding to a point
Generalization	It does not change the way, but reduces the details

Table 5. Spatial functions used to change semantic granularity

Distributive	Convex hull, geometric union, geometric intersection
Algebraic	Center of n geometric points, center of gravity
Holistic	Equi-partition, nearest-neighbor index
User Defined	

Figure 6. Functions of transformation applied to change a granularity to a greater one, on spatial hierarchies

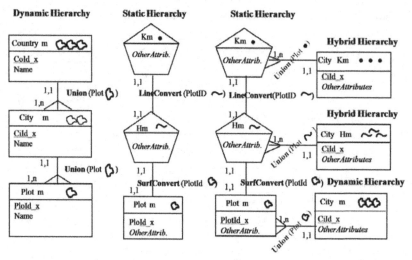

Location Spatial Dimension

Table 6. Thematic aggregation functions

Distributive	Sum, Min, Max,... Refuse aggregates of a lower level of a hierarchy in order to calculate the aggregates for higher level
Algebraic	Average, Variance, Standard deviation,.... Need an additional treatment for reusing the values
Holistic	Median, most frequent, rank.. Required new calculations using the data of the leaf level
User Defined	

Example 1

Next we analyze an example of application with a *Basic factEntity* and dimensions with multiple granularities.

We want to know the amount of products collected every semester in the plots of certain cities. Also we want to store the number of inhabitants of each city, which is updated each month.

In the first step we choose the constructors. In Figure 7 we see the scheme made up with the *FE* model. We are modelling with:

- A Basic factEntity.
- A fact = KProd fact measure.
- A Time dimension with three granularities.

- A Products dimension without any hierarchy.
- A spatial dimension with two semantic and three geometric granularities.
- A temporal attribute (Inhabitants), with Valid Time type, Month temporal granularity and Historical evolution.

In the second step we include semantics in the schema. We introduce the functions applied on the *fact measures* and those applied to change the *spatial granularities*. So, we can observe how it is possible to generate the *Virtual factEntities* in an automatic way. See Figure 8.

Figure 7. FE scheme with multiple granularities.

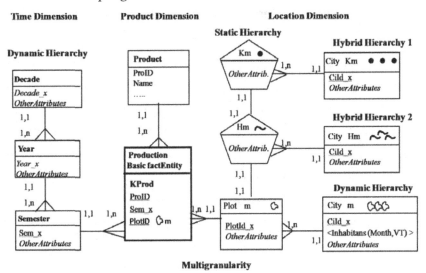

Example 2

We want to study the evolution of riverbeds and plots within a geographic area. See Figure 9.

In Figure 9 we see a schema with an example with two spatial dimensions present in the *Basic factEntity* and any *fact measure*. Here we only want the evolution of spatial elements.

Note that Location dimension has not spatial representation, so it is treated as a thematic dimension. In addition we observe that though there are not, fact measures, the intersection of spatial data evolves through of Location dimension. Also it is possible to gather this evolution, if we so wish.

Figure 8. The specifications between levels provide semantics in the model

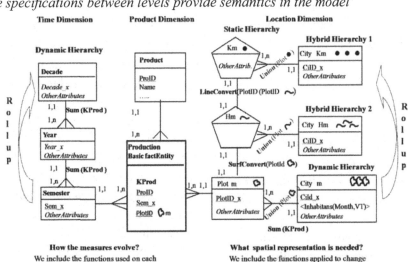

Figure 9. Example with two spatial dimensions present in a Basic factEntity and any measure

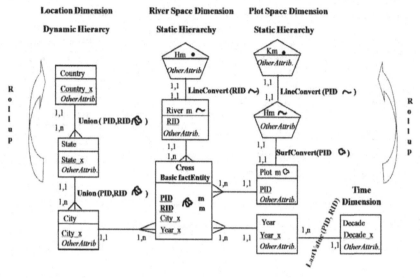

Spatial functions applied when the geometric granularities are changed allow us to generate easily the *Virtual factEntities* desired

In conclusion, the new multidimensional characteristics included in our *FE* model, are:

- The incorporation of new hierarchy types called: *Static*, *Dynamic* and *Hybrid* to gather related different granularities.
- The definition of the new concepts of *Basic* and *Virtual factEntities*. In addition a clear distinction is made between *basic* and *derived* data.
- It lets us deal with multiple spatio-temporal granularities, which are related and interacting with the rest of the elements.

LOGICAL PHASE

We show rules to transform the constructors of the *FE* model, to the *R* and *OR* logic models, taking into account the multidimensional semantics and stressing:

- The transformation of the different hierarchy types under the prospects for the multigranularities.

- And the rules to transform temporal characteristics of the elements.

Relational Logical Model

The *Relational* model introduced by Cood in 1970, is one of the logical data models most used by the commercial *DBMS*. The most important elements of *R* model are relations (tables) and attributes (columns).

In this logical phase, we will indistinct use the words: relation or table, and attribute or column. A relational *scheme* is composed, by the table name and the column name together with its data type. One relational *instance* is identified of unique way in a row or tuple into the associated table. The order of rows and columns in a table is not important. A *relation* is defined as a set of tuples not ordered.

The main constraints of the *R* model are the *primary key*, the *referential integrity* and the *entity integrity*, for more details to see (Elmasri & Navathe, 2007). Where, the *primary key* is a subset of attributes in each relationship that identifies each tuple in unique way. And the *foreign key* is a set of attributes in a relationship, which is the same as a *primary key* in another relationship. The *referential integrity* and the *entity integrity* are with regarding the *primary key* and the *foreign key*.

In the traditional *DB* the data types of the attributes are called domains and are limited to basic domains such as: Integer, Real, Alphanumeric, date, etc; the user defined types are not allowed. This complicates quite a bit the treatment of spatial data in the *R* model.

Extensions of the Relational Model

The *Object Relational* model emerges as an extension to the *R* model, which allows the use of user defined types. The *OGIS* provides standard specifications, to include new types of data in the *OR* model. This permits us, to collect spatial characteristics in new domains and abstract data types (*ADT*) under the relational paradigm.

The SQL3/SQL99 is the standard proposed for Object-Oriented *DBMS*. This accepts user defined data types within a relational database.

The *OGIS* standard, recommends a set of types and spatial functions, for the processing of spatial data and *GIS*. The recommendations of *OGIS* standards are reflected in SQL3. The spatial data is seen as an *ADT*.

Transforming Elements

Next, we show some valid rules for transforming the constructors of *FE* model into the *R* and *OR* models.

This work follows the *OGIS* specifications and it uses abstract data types to define the spatial domain in the *OR* model.

Transforming Attributes

Each attribute becomes a column of the table associated, and each primary attribute becomes the *primary key* of its associated table.

Parent-Child Between Dimensional Levels

This proposal does not consider N:M interrelationships among dimensional hierarchical levels. An ideal conceptual model where a "*child*" (member of a lower level) has only a "*parent*" (member of a higher level) is considered here. See Table 7.

Note, that *Parent* means members of the superior level, and *child/children,* mean members of the inferior level.

In a binary relationship the primary key of the upper level table is propagated to the lower level table as a column (*Foreign Key*).

Table 7. Possible cardinalities implied between members of consecutive levels

Superior Level	Inferior Level	Meaning
1,1	1,n	Each parent has a child or more. Each child a single parent
1,1	0,n	It is possible to have parent s with zero or various children . Each child has a single parent
1,0	1,n	Each parent has one or various children. Each child has zero or one parent.
1,0	0,n	Parents with zero or several children. Children with zero or one parent.
1,0	1,1	Parents with only a child. Children with zero or one parent.
1,0	0,1	Parents with zero or one child. Children with zero or one parent.

Transforming Dimensions

To transform dimensions we take into account, whether this dimension has hierarchies or whether it only includes a *leaf level*.

In all the cases, each *leaf level* converts into a table/relationship "*leaf table*"; the attributes are transformed into columns, and the primary attribute becomes the primary key of this table.

Since a dimension can have several hierarchies, we must also to take into account:

- *Whether there is only one hierarchy*, each hierarchical level can be transformed into separate tables or be included in the "*table leaf*" according to the criteria of normalization and number of secondary attributes contained in the higher levels.
- *Whether there are more than one hierarchy*, we think that they should be treated independently from each other, but this will depend on the semantics of the application.

Next we consider dimensions that have only one hierarchy.

Transformation of All Levels into a Singular Leaf Table

We choose this option when:

- Never mind that the tables are not normalized (i.e. with data redundancy).
- There is little or no secondary attribute at higher levels of the *leaf level*.

This option includes all the *primary attributes* of all the levels (granularities), within the "*leaf table*", and also the secondary attributes associated with each level. We are not considering this option adequate, if there is more of a hierarchy in one dimension.

It may not be necessary to include the primary attributes of all levels, as part of the primary key of this "*leaf table*" but the choice of the primary key is totally dependent on the semantics of modelled discourse universe.

Example 3

We choose a Location dimension, without spatial representation, with a hierarchy: Country / City / Plot, see the *FE* diagram in Figure 10. The dimensional hierarchy is converted into a singular table, the "*leaf table*", which contains primary and secondary attributes of the three different granularities, see leaf table in figure 10. This is an example where it is not necessary to include all the identifier attributes from the highest levels to make up the primary key of the "*leaf table*".

Note, the columns that form the primary key are underlined and bold, as in this example, City and Plot. The examples are represented with tables in a tabular way and containing data, to make them easier to understand.

Transformation into One Table for Each Level

We opt for the normalization, i.e. one table for each level of each hierarchy in the following cases:

- There is more than one hierarchy.
- There is only one hierarchy with many secondary attributes at each level.

In this case we don't want to have data redundancy. We are taking this election to transform the hierarchical schema of previous example 3. The Figure 11 shows the Location dimension converted in three tables, one for each level.

We observe that each transformed table has its own attributes and primary keys. Note that the *foreign keys* are in italics.

Transforming factEntities

A *Basic factEntity* is converted in a *fact table*. The *Virtual factEntities* are generated processing the

Figure 10. Transformation of a Location dimension into a singular leaf table not normalized.

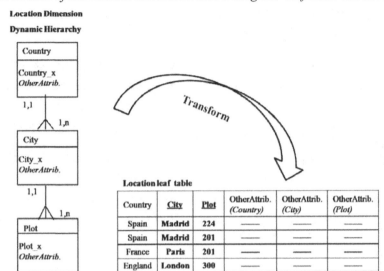

Figure 11. Transformation of a Location dimension in normalized tables that represent the third level, the second level and the leaf level.

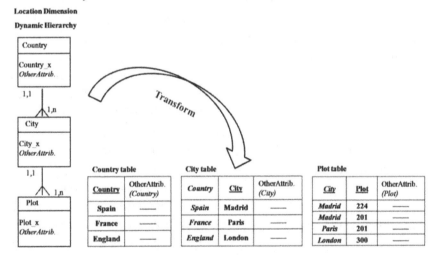

Basic factEntity. The *FE* model provides everything necessary to explain how these are created, but not all the possibilities will be necessary for the analysis, and not all that will be needed will be stored in permanent tables. Next, we see some possibilities.

Basic factEntity

Each *Basic factEntity* becomes a *fact table*, which contains all the *foreign keys*, propagated from all *leaf levels* of its associated dimensions, and all *basic measures*. The *primary key* of this table is formed with a set of these *foreign keys*.

Sometimes, in some domains of application, surrogacy keys are chosen, which are distinct to the inherited keys, thus avoiding excessively long keys.

Virtual factEntities

The *Virtual factEntities* are created when the dimensions are "deployed" forming hierarchies and are composed of derived data:

- *Derived basic measures* formed applying Aggregation functions.
- *Derived leaf levels* which are formed with the Cartesian product of all possible subgroups that can be formed with the *m* dimensions associated with each *fact*.

Thus, for a set of *m* dimensions SD = $[D_1,...,D_m]$, it is possible to form groups of *one* dimension, *two* dimensions, *m-1* dimensions and *m* dimensions. The *Virtual factEntities* can be created with the subsets of the Cartesian product of the previous subgroups. We clarify this in the next examples.

Example 4

We see the potential *factEntities* that can be generated with a set of four dimensions, and a *fact* composed of *Basic measures*.

SD = $[D_1, D_2, D_3, D_4]$; fact = $[m_1...m_k]$.

First

We find the different aggregate subgroups that we can form, in respect to one, two, three and four dimensions.

We apply the following formula:

$[D_i x...xD_p]$ / $\forall i \in [1,...,m] \land \forall p \in [1,...,m] \land (p > i$ or $p = \emptyset)$ where $\emptyset$ is the empty set *(Formula 1)*

In this example m = 4.

For i = 1 Λ p = Ø,2,3,4 ⇨

- Subgroups with one dimension: $\{D_1\}$.
- Subgroups with two dimensions: $\{D_1,D_2\}$; $\{D_1,D_3\}$; $\{D_1,D_4\}$.
- Subgroups with three dimensions: $\{D_1,D_2,D_3\}$;$\{D_1,D_2,D_4\}$; $\{D_1,D_3,D_4\}$.
- Subgroups with four dimensions: $\{D_1,D_2,D_3,D_4\}$.

For i = 2 Λ p = Ø,3,4 ⇨

- Subgroups with one dimension: $\{D_2\}$.
- Subgroups with two dimensions: $\{D_2,D_3\}$; $\{D_2,D_4\}$.
- Subgroups with three dimensions: $\{D_2,D_3,D_4\}$.
- Subgroups with four dimensions: Ø.

For i = 3 Λ p = Ø,4 ⇨

- Subgroups with one dimension: $\{D_3\}$.
- Subgroups with two dimensions: $\{D_3,D_4\}$.
- Subgroups with three dimensions: Ø.
- Subgroups with four dimensions: Ø.

For i = 4 Λ p = Ø ⇨

- Subgroups with one dimension: $\{D_4\}$.
- Subgroups with two dimensions: Ø.
- Subgroups with three dimensions: Ø.
- Subgroups with four dimensions: Ø.

Now, we group these subgroups by number dimensions

- Subgroups with one dimension: $\{D_1\}$; $\{D_2\}$; $\{D_3\}$; $\{D_4\}$.
- Subgroups with two dimensions: $\{D_1,D_2\}$; $\{D_1,D_3\}$; $\{D_1,D_4\}$; $\{D_2,D_3\}$; $\{D_2,D_4\}$; $\{D_3,D_4\}$.

- Subgroups with three dimensions: $\{D_1, D_2, D_3\}$; $\{D_1, D_2, D_4\}$; $\{D_1, D_3, D_4\}$; $\{D_2, D_3, D_4\}$.
- Subgroups with four dimensions: $\{D_1, D_2, D_3, D_4\}$.

Second

The *Cartesian product* is applied on each of the previous subgroups, taking into account that in some domains of application, the order in which we choose the elements to make up the subgroup will be significant. For example, sometimes it will be different the result of applying the *Cartesian product* on the subset (D_1, D_2, D_3), that applying the *Cartesian product* on the subsets: (D_2, D_1, D_3) or (D_3, D_1, D_2), which have changed the order of some of the elements.

Thirdly

We note below, the generic structure that the *Virtual factEntities* have grouping elements according to *Cartesian subgroups* obtained in the previous step.

Virtual FactEntity = ([D_ix...xD_p], {$G_j(me_j)$}).

Where:

$(D_i x \ldots x D_p)$ *represent the Cartesian Product*, $\forall i \in [1,\ldots,4] \wedge \forall p \in [1,\ldots,4] \wedge (p > i)$.

And

($Gj(mej)$ is the set of Gj compatible functions with the basic measure (me_j)$\forall j \in [1,\ldots,k]$).

Example 5

We specify the example 4 above, in a three-dimensional model with different granularities and a generic *fact* composed of *Basic measures*:

- *Time Dimension*: Day, Month.
- *Product Dimension*: Article.
- *Location Dimension*: Village, City, Country.
- *Fact*: set Basic Measures.

First

We apply the formula 1, to obtain the following subgroups:

- Subgroups of one dimension: {Time}, {Product}; {Location}.
- Subgroups with two dimensions: {Time, Product}; {Time, Location}; {Product, Location}.
- Subgroups with three dimensions: {Time, Product, Location}.

Second

Now, we apply the *Cartesian* product on the previous Subgroups:

Subgroups of three dimensions: {Time x Product x Location}:

- Subgroup to *Basic FactEntity*: {Day, Article, Village}
- Subgroups to *Virtual FactEntities*: {Day, Article, City}; {Day, Article, Country}; {Month, Article, Village}; {Month, Article, City}; {Month, Article, Country}.

Subgroups of two dimensions: {Time x Product}; {Time x Location}; {Product x Location}:

- Subgroups to *Virtual FactEntities*:
  {Time x Product}: {Day, Article}; {Month, Article}.
  {Time x Location}: {Day, Village}; {Day, City}; {Day, Country}; {Month, Village}; {Month, City}; {Month, Country}.

{Product x Location}: {Article, Village}; {Article, City}; {Article, Country}.

Subgroups of one dimension: {Time}, {Product}, {Location}:

- Subgrupos for *Virtual FactEntities*:
  {Time}: {Day}, {Month}.
  {Product}: {Article}.
  {Location}: {Village}, {City}, {Country}.

Depending on whether we select ones, or other combinations, the *basic measures* suffer various transformation processes. The *FE* model explains how this process should be realize, and represents the functions to be applied on these measures, according to the change of granularities of the dimensions, which allow us to generate Virtual *factEntities* automatically.

Thirdly

Next, we see the *structure* of some *factEntities*, built with subgroups generated in the previous step:

- *Basic FactEntity* = (Day, Article, Village, *Basic Measures*).
- A *Virtual FactEntity* = (Month, Article, Country, {G (*Basic Measures*)}).
- B *Virtual FactEntity* = (Article, {G (*Basic Measures*)}).
- C *Virtual FactEntity* = (Month, Country, {G (*Basic Measures*)}).

Where, {G (*Basic Measures*)} is the set of *Derived Measures* and G is the set of compatible functions with these *Basic Measures*.

Selection of Virtual factEntities

Not all possible combinations or Cartesian subgroups are necessary for the analysis of the *fact measures*. We will have to ask:

- What are the needs of the application?
- What are the more frequent queries?
- What is the physical space available to store the data, etc.. ?

In line with the criteria chosen, and depending on the application, the structure will contain each *Virtual FactEntity* selected is determined. So opting for:

- Permanent tables.
- Views.
- Materialized views.
- Under demand.

Next we explain briefly these concepts.

Permanent Tables

We will store the more consulted *Virtual factEntities* in *permanent tables*, or the more complicated, or those that can serve as the basis for more elaborated further queries.

Views

A view is a table that does not contain data, only contain the structure. The data contained in other permanent tables, are processed and loaded into the view when this is invoked.

The *Virtual factEntity views* are created with processed data from *dimensions* and *basic measures*.

Materialized Views

A *materialized view* is a special view that store data in a permanent way. These data are obtained and processed from other base tables. Each certain time the views are "refreshed" with the updates made in such *base tables*.

Under Demand

Some times it is not necessary to store the data of the *Virtual FactEntities* and these data are generated under demand, i.e., the data are derived and processed at the moment of use. Thus, only the rules and formulas of generation are keeping. This is used in queries that are seldom required, or easy queries which need little manipulation.

Conclusions

Not all possible combinations or Cartesian subgroups are necessary for the analysis of the *fact measures*. We will have to ask:

- What are the needs of the application?
- What are the more frequent queries?
- What is the physical space available to store the data?
- Etc.

The *Virtual factEntities* are significant because they are the base on the study of the *facts*, and are also the support for the process of decision-making. They provide a way to examine the data, from different perspectives and with varying degrees of detail. Thus, it is important, to define perfectly, and to choose appropriately: *what Virtual factEntities* will be necessary and *which* will be stored.

It is here where the *FE* model, provides a framework for creating the necessary structures, allowing choosing the most relevant for each domain of application.

Transformation of Spatial Granularities

To transform spatial data we can use the *R* or *OR* models. In the *R* model, each spatial domain is represented in a new relation/table. In the *OR* model, each spatial domain is represented as an abstract type of data, which is included as a column in a relational table.

The examples presented in this section suppose spatial data modeled as: geometry of surface type with four points, where the last is just like the first, it is enough to store three points; geometry of line type with two points; and geometry of point type, and also each point has two coordinates.

Next, we see examples using the two options *R* or *OR* models. We distinguish between *Semantic* and *Geometric* granularities.

Semantic Spatial Granularity

To transform a spatial dimension with one hierarchy and several semantic spatial granularities, we have two options: to convert the whole hierarchy into one *"leaf table"*, or to convert each level of the hierarchy (each granularity) into a table, see example 6.

Figure 12. FE scheme of a Location Dimension with a hierarchy, which has various Semantic spatial Granularities and only one Geometric spatial Granularity

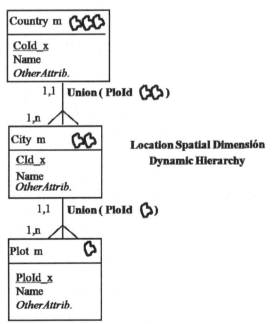

Example 6

We consider the previous example 3 with spatial data. We expand the scheme of Figure 10 with the spatial representation. In figure 12, we can see a Location Dimension with three *Semantic* granularities and only one *Geometric* granularity, expressed in surface geometry and meter as the associated measurement unit.

We do the transformation to the *R* model and the spatial data are converted into relational tables.

In the Following the two options of transformation are considered.

Option 1: Transformation into one Table with all Levels of the Semantic Spatial Granularities

The transformation of the hierarchy dimensional of Figure 12 is performed in a single "*leaf table*" which contains the three *Semantic* spatial granularities, see Table 8 a). The secondary attributes of each level are all kept on the same table.

Two tables are used to transform spatial data to *R* model. One table (Plot Table) contains the identified and the three points that define each plot. The other table (Point Table), gathers the coordinates of each point. See Tables 8 b) and 8 c) respectively.

Table 8 a. Leaf table of Location Dimension is non- normalized

Location leaf table

Surface Plot, m (PloId)	City U(Plot, Surf) (CId)	City Name	Country U(Plot, Surf) (CoId)	Country Name	OtherAttrib. (Co,Ci.,Plot)
id211	id21	Madrid	id2	Spain	———
id212	id21	Madrid	id2	Spain	———
id221	id22	Guadalajara	id2	Spain	———
id311	id31	Paris	id3	France	———
id411	id41	London	id4	England	———

Tables 8 b. and 8 c. Here we see spatial data in relational tables

b)

Plot Table (Surface, m)

PloId	Point 1	Point 2	Point 3
id211	p1211	p2211	p3211
id212	p1212	p2212	p3212
id221	p1221	p2221	p3221
id311	p1311	p2311	p3311
id411	p1411	p2411	p3411

c)

Point Table (Point, m)

Point	X	Y
p1211	x_{1211}	y_{1211}
p2211	x_{2211}	y_{2211}
p3211	x_{3211}	y_{3211}
p1212	x_{1212}	y_{1212}
p2212	x_{2212}	y_{2212}
——	——	——

Tables 9. a) Transformed table from level third. b) Transformed table of second level.

a)

Country table

CoId Union(Plot,Surface)	Country	OtherAttrib.
id2	Spain	——
id3	France	——
id4	England	——

b)

City table

(CoId)	(CId) Union(Plot,Surface)	City Name	OtherAttrib
id2	id21	Madrid	——
id2	id22	Guadalajara	——
id3	id31	Paris	——
id4	id41	London	——

Table 10. a) Table transformed, of leaf level. b) and c) relational tables for spatial data

a) Plot table (leaf)

(CId)	Plot, m (PloId)	OtherAttrib
id21	id211	———
id21	id212	———
id22	id221	———
id31	id311	———
id41	id411	———

b) Point Plot table

PloId	Point 1	Point 2	Point 3
id211	p1211	p2211	p3211
id212	p1212	p2212	p3212
id221	p1221	p2221	p3221
id311	p1311	p2311	p3311
id411	p1411	p2411	p3411

c) Point table

Point	X	Y
p1211	x_{1211}	y_{1211}
p2211	x_{2211}	y_{2211}
p3211	x_{3211}	y_{3211}
p1212	x_{1212}	y_{1212}
p2212	x_{2212}	y_{2212}
———	———	———

Option 2: Transformation at a Table for Each Level of Semantic Spatial Granularity

In this case the hierarchy of figure 12, is transformed into one table for each S*emantic* granularity, see Tables: 9 a), 9 b) and 10 a). To Keep the spatial component of spatial data, we are using relational tables, see Table: 10 b) and 10 c).

Geometric Spatial Granularity

To transform several *Geometric* granularities into *R* or *OR* models, we can opt to transform the whole hierarchy of geometry of representation into a single table, or store each geometry in a different table, see example 7.

Example 7

A *Location* dimension with spatial data and a single semantic level called Plot is considered, but with different *Geometric* granularities such as: (surface, m), (line, Hm) and (point, Km). We use the *FE* model to obtain the design scheme, see Figure 13. The functions used to change to another larger *Geometric* granularity are explicitly represented in the scheme.

The scheme allows the representation of the different secondary attributes on each *Geometric* spatial granularity. They are included here as "*OtherAttrib*".

Figure 13. Scheme FE of Location dimension, which has various Geometric spatial granularities

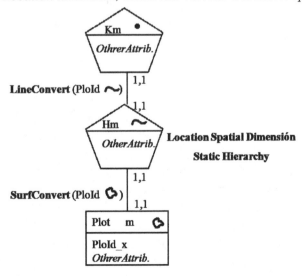

Option 1: Transformation in only one Non- Normalized Table for All the Geometric Spatial Granularity Levels

The Static hierarchy of Figure 13 is transformed into a single "*leaf table*" that contains the three spatial levels. To reach the coarse granularities the transformation functions explicitly represented in the scheme are used. See Table 11. Each spatial level contains the spatial data and the secondary attributes (*OtherAttrib.*). Each secondary attribute and the spatial identifier are transformed into a col-

umn of this *leaf table*. For the spatial component, one table for each, geometry of representation is created. All geometries are represented by points, see Tables: 12, 13, and 14.

Note that the relational tables that contain spatial data are normalized. Table 12 contains plots represented as surface with three points, Table 13, contains plot represented as lines with two points, and Table 14, contains the plots represented as a point, and in addition the points of all the previous tables. Each point has two coordinates and one associate unit of measure.

Table 11. Three geometric spatial granularities for the same spatial data type in the leaf table

Plot leaf table with multirepresentation

Plot Surface (PloId, m)	(Plot Line, Hm) SurfConvert (PloId,m) = (PloId, Hm)	(PlotPoint, Km) LineConvert (PloId,Hm) = (PloId, Km)	OtherAttrib.
id211	id211L	id211P	——
id212	id212L	id212P	——
id221	id221L	id221P	——
id311	id311L	id311P	——
id411	id411L	id411P	——

Tables 12. and 13. Relational tables with spatial data of (surface, m) and (lines,Hm) types, respectively

SurfacePlot Table (three points, m)

PloId, m	Point 1	Point 2	Point 3
id211	p1211	p2211	p3211
id212	p1212	p2212	p3212
id221	p1221	p2221	p3221
id311	p1311	p2311	p3311
id411	p1411	p2411	p3411

LinePlot Table (two points, Hm)

PloId, Hm	Point 1	Point 2
id211L	p1211L	p2211L
id212L	p1212L	p2212L
id221L	p1221L	p2221L
id311L	p1311L	p2311L
id411L	p1411L	p2411L

Table 14. We have a relational table with spatial points

Points Table (points with two coordinates and units of measure)

Point	X	Y	Measure Unit
id211P	x_{1211p}	y_{1211p}	Km
id212P	x_{2121p}	y_{2121p}	Km
id221P	x_{2211p}	y_{2211p}	Km
——	——	——	——
p1211 L	x_{1211L}	y_{1211L}	Hm
p2211L	x_{2211L}	y_{2211L}	Hm
——	——	——	——
p1211	x_{1211}	y_{1211}	m
p2211	x_{2211}	y_{2211}	m
——	——	——	——

Option 2: Transformation into Normalized Tables, one Table for each Geometric Spatial Granularity Level

Now, we perform the transformation of the Static hierarchy of Figure 13, into normalized tables, i.e. one relational table for each *Geometric* granularity, which also includes its secondary attributes transformed into columns, see Tables: 15, 16, 17.

In summary to choose the most appropriate option such as, a table or more, we can consider the rules and criteria of transformation shown for the dimensions in general.

What will be more efficient?

- It depends on the domain of application.
- The amount of data.
- The consultations carried out.
- From space available, and so on.

Semantic and Geometric Spatial Granularities

We consider several options to transform a spatial dimension with different *Semantic* and *Geomet-*

Table 15. Geometric granularity of surface type with its secondary attributes in a relational table

SurfacePlot table (three points, m)

PloId, m	Point 1	Point 2	Point 3	OtherAttrib.
id211	p1211	p2211	p3211	——
id212	p1212	p2212	p3212	——
id221	p1221	p2221	p3221	——
id311	p1311	p2311	p3311	——
id411	p1411	p2411	p3411	——

Table 16. Geometric granularity of line type with its secondary attributes in a relational table

LinePlot table (two point, m)

PloId	(PlotLine, Hm) SurfConvert (PloId, m) = (PloId, Hm)	Point 1	Point 2	OtherAttrib.
id211	id211L	p1211L	p2211L	——
id212	id212L	p1212L	p2212L	——
id221	id221L	p1221L	p2221L	——
id311	id311L	p1311L	p2311L	——
id411	id411L	p1411L	p2411L	——

Table 17. Geometric granularity of point type with its secondary attributes in a relational table

PointPlot table (two coordinates, Km)

PloId	(Plot, Point, Km) LineConvert (PloId, Hm) = (PloId, Km)	X	Y	OtherAttib.
id211	id211P	x_{1211p}	y_{1211p}	——
id212	id212P	x_{2121p}	y_{2121p}	——
id221	id221P	x_{2221p}	y_{2221p}	——
id311	id311P	x_{3112p}	y_{3112p}	——
id411	id411P	x_{4112p}	y_{4112p}	——

ric granularities in the *R* and *OR* logical models. These are analyzed as follows:

a. A single table with all the different granularities, *Semantic* and *Geometric*.

b. A table with the all *Semantic* granularities and other table for all the *Geometric* granularities.

c. A table for each *Semantic* granularity with its associated *Geometric* granularities.

d. A table for each hierarchical dimensional level, i.e. each *Semantic* and *Geometric* granularities.

e. Each hierarchy is handled independently and with different options. This depends completely on each application to be modelled.

When we say table we refer equally to a relational table or an object relational table, depending on the model chosen for the transformation. In the first case, the spatial data are transformed into relational tables, as seen in the previous examples. In the latter case, each spatial datum is converted into a column as an object or *ADT*. In all the options we suppose that secondary attributes are propagated together with its associated granularities.

In the example 8, we analyze different ways of transforming interrelated *Semantic* and *Geometric* spatial granularities using the *OR* model with *ADT*.

Example 8

A Location dimension with spatial data and spatial granularities is considered, as is detailed below:

- *Semantic* granularities: City, Plot.
- *Geometric* granularities of Plot leaf level: (Surface, m), (Line, Hm), (Point, Km).
- *Geometric* granularities of City level, (these are dependent and derived from the Plot Geometric granularities): Union (Surface, m), Union (Line, Hm), Union (Point, Km).

Figure 14. FE scheme of a Location dimension with interrelated semantic and geometric granularities

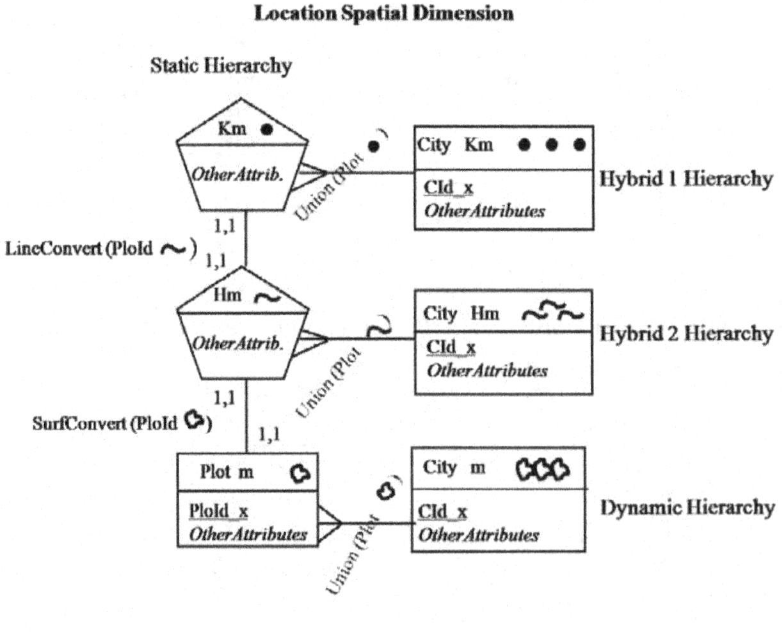

In Figure 14, we see the scheme made up with the *FE* model, which gathers this semantics.

Transformation into Object Relational Model

We previously define some *ADT* necessary to make up the transformation.

We define an *ADT* for the *Point* geometry figure:

Point type is an Object (

- X: Number type;
- Y: Number type;
- Unit: String type;
- Transformation Function (LineConvert(P1 *Point* Type, P2 *Point* Type) RETURN *Point* Type)).

We define an *ADT* for the *Line* geometry figure:

Line type is an Object (

- P1: Point Type;
- P2: Point Type;
- Transformation Function (SurfConvert(Sx *Surface* Type) RETURN *Line* Type));

We define an *ADT* for the *Surface* geometry figure:

Surface type is an Object (

- P1: Point Type;
- P2: Point Type;
- P3: Point Type;
- Transformation Function (Generalization (Sx *Surface* Type) RETURN *Surface* Type)).

We define an *ADT* for each set of previous types:

- *SetSurface* type is a S*et* of object of *Surface* type.
- *SetLine* type is a *Set* of object of *Line* type.
- *SetPoint* type is a *Set* of object of *Poin*t type.

The *Point ADT* has two attributes of Number type (coordinates), an alphanumeric attribute (unit), and a transformation function that lets us to change one Line geometric type into a Point geometric type.

The *Line ADT* is composed for two attributes of *Point* type and has a transformation function that changes, one Surface geometric type into a Line geometric type.

The *Surface ADT* has three attributes of *Point* type and a transformation function of generalization, which changes the granularity without changing the form.

We choose these *ADT* simple to present our examples. However the *ADT* can be defined as complicated as needed. For example, you can define a line with more than two points, a surface with more than four points, and so on. In addition, each type of data can use a variety of functions, many of which are specified in the standard *OGIS*.

In Figure 14 we have a *Static* hierarchy, a *Dynamic* hierarchy and two *Hybrid* hierarchies. We use the options: a), b) c), and d), shown above, to transform these hierarchies into *OR* model.

In the definitions of the tables following, the column highlighted will be the primary keys, and the column in italics will be the foreign keys. We define the Sdom as the set of basic domains such as: Number, String, Alphanumeric, date, etc.

Option a) All the Semantic and Geometric Granularities are Transformed into one Singular Table

It performs the transformation of all hierarchies into a single table with an *ADT* for each spatial granularity.

TotalLocation Table (

- PloId: Number,
- SurfacePlot: Surface,
- LinePlot = SurfConvert (SurfacePlot): Line,
- PointPlot = LineConvert (LinePlot): Point,
- Other Plot Attributes: Sdom,
- CId: Alphanumeric,
- SurfaceCity = Union (SurfacePlot): SetSurface,
- LineCity = Union (LinePlot): SetLine,
- PointCity = Union (PointPlot): SetPoint,
- Other City Attributes: Sdom).

Option b) The Semantic Granularities are Transformed into one Table and Geometric Granularities Are Transformed Into another Table

The following table contains *leaf level*, and the secondary level of *Dynamic* hierarchy.

SemanticLocation Table (

- PloId: Number,
- CId: Alphanumeric,
- SurfacePlot: Surface,
- Other Plot Attributes: Sdom,
- SurfaceCity = Union (SurfacePlot): SetSurface,
- Other City Attributes: Sdom).

The following table contains the second and third level of the *Static* hierarchy, the third level of the *Hybrid 2* hierarchy, and the fourth level of the *Hybrid 1* hierarchy.

GeometricLocation Table (

- *PloId*: Number, (Foreign Key of *SemanticLocation*),

- *CId*: Alphanumeric, (Foreign Key of *SemanticLocation*)
- LinePlot: SurfConvert (*SemanticLocation. SurfacePlot*): Line,
- PointPlot: LineConvert (LinePlot): Point,
- LineCity = Union(LinePlot): SetLine,
- PointCity = Union (PointPlot): SetPoint,
- Other Plot Attributes: Sdom,
- Other City Attributes: Sdom).

Option c) Each Semantic Granularity Together with its Geometric Granularities Associates, are Transformed into a Table

The following table contains the *leaf level*, and the second and third levels of *Static* hierarchy.

Plot Table (

- PloId: Number,
- *CId*: Alphanumeric, (Foreign Key of *City* table)
- SurfacePlot: Surface,
- LinePlot: SurfConvert (SurfacePlot): Line,
- PointPlot: LineConvert (LinePlot): Point,
- Other Plot Attributes: Sdom).

The following table contains the second level of *Dynamic* hierarchy, the third level of *Hybrid 2* hierarchy, and the fourth level of *Hybrid 1* hierarchy.

City Table (

- CId: Alphanumeric,
- SurfaceCity = Union (*Plot*.SurfacePlot): SetSurface,
- LineCity = Unión (*Plot*.LinePlot): SetLine,
- PointCity = Union (*Plot*.PointPlot): SetPoint,
- Other City Attributes: Sdom).

Option d) Each Semantic and GeoMetric Granularity is Transformed into a Table

The following table contains the *leaf level (Semantic and Geometric granularity)*.

SemanticPlot Table (

- PloId: Number,
- *CId*: Alphanumeric (Foreign Key of *SemanticCity*),
- SurfacePlot: Surface,
- Other Plot Attributes: Sdom).

The following table contains the second level of the *Static* hierarchy (*the Geometric granularity is changed*)

LinePlot Table (

- *PloId*: Number, (Foreign Key of *SemanticPlot*)
- *CId*: Alphanumeric (Foreign Key of *LineCity*)
- LinePlot = SurfConvert (*SemanticPlot.SurfacePlot*): Line
- Other Plot Attributes: Sdom).

The following table contains the third level of the *Static* hierarchy (*the Geometric granularity is changed*)

PointPlot Table (

- *PloId*: Number, (Foreign Key of *LinePlot*)
- *CId*: Alphanumeric (Foreign Key of *PointCity*),
- PointPlot = LineConvert (*LinePlot*.LinePlot): Point,
- Other Plot Attributes: Sdom).

The following table contains the second level of the *Dynamic* hierarchy (*the Semantic and Geometric granularities are changed*).

SemanticCity Table (

- *CId*: Alphanumeric,
- SurfaceCity = Union (*SemanticPlot.* SurfacePlot): SetSurface,
- Other City Attributes: Sdom).

The following table contains the third level of *Hybrid 2* hierarchy (*the Semantic and Geometric granularities are changed).*

LineCity Table (

- *CId*: Alphanumeric, (Foreign Key of *SemanticCity*),
- LineCity = Union (*LinePlot.***LinePlot***): SetLine,
- Other City Attributes: Sdom).

The following table contains the fourth level of *Hybrid 1* hierarchy (*the Semantic and Geometric granularities are changed).*

PointCity Table (

- *CId*: Alphanumeric, (Foreign Key of *LineCity)*,
- PointCity = Union (*PointPlot.***PointPlot***): SetPoint,
- Other City Attributes: Sdom).

Transformation of Temporal Elements

In the following, the transformation rules for the constructors of *FE* model with temporal characteristics are given.

Temporal attributes; Time type and Granularity

The temporal attributes are handled as *ADT*; these collect the temporal characteristics, type of time and granularity.

Here we see an example of three possible definitions of *ADT*, to collect the three types of time considered: *VT*, *TT*, and *TVT*.

We define a temporal *ADT* for a generic attribute "A", with *VT* and we call this A_*VT-Temporal*.

A_*VTTemporal* type is an Object (

- *ValidTime*: Date type, (*with the format of the granularity*),
- *Value*: type of A attribute,
- Transformation Function of Granularity (T A_*VTTemporal type*) RETURN A TV Tempo-ral type).

We define a temporal *ADT* for a generic attribute "A", with *TT* that we call A_*TTTemporal*.

A_*TTTemporal* type is an Object (

- *TransactionTime*: Date Type, (*with the format of the granularity*),
- *Value*: type of A attribute,
- Transformation Function of Granularity (T A_*TTTemporal type*) RETURN A_*TTTemporal type*).

We define a temporal *ADT* for a generic attribute "A", with *TVT* that we call A_*TVTTemporal*.

A_*TVTTemporal* type is an Object (

- *ValidTime*: Date type, (*with the format of the granularity*),
- *TransactionTime*: Date type, (*with the format of the granularity*),
- *Value*: type of A attribute,

- Transformation Function of Granularity (T A_*TVTTemporal type*) RETURN A_*TVT-Temporal type*).

Where:

The *Value attribute* represents the values of the "A temporal attribute" and must be defined in its associated domain.

The attributes of Date type gather the type of time *VT* and *TT*, and the temporal granularity is defined with the format of these attributes.

The transformation function added allows changing granularities.

Evolution

To transform the *evolution* characteristic the following is taken into account:

The *Specific evolution* is covered defining the attribute as a temporal *ADT*, as seen in the preceding paragraph.

The *Historical evolution* of an attribute is represented by a list of values of defined *ADT*. For example you can use the *OR* constructor, "list", as shown below:

- A attribute: list < A_*VTTemporal* Type > type.
- A attribute : list < A_*TTTemporal* Type > type.
- A attribute : list < A_*TVTTemporal* Type > type.

Temporal Levels

The levels with temporal characteristics are transformed into temporal tables, as explained below.

Time Type and Granularity

The SQL2 proposes an extension that allows the definition of the temporal characteristics of a table, broadening the CREATE TABLE statement with the following structure:

CREATE TABLE AS Time Type <granularity>

Evolution

The *Historic evolution* is handled using the *Version of Tuples* method, this is typical of *R* databases, where every tuple represents a version of the information.

Attributes of Date type are added to each tuple, according to the types of time used, as shown below:

Transaction Time: two attributes (Initial Transaction, End Transaction) of Date type are added.

Valid Time: two attributes (Initial Valid Time, End Valid Time) of Date type, are added.

Transaction and Valid Time: four attributes (Initial Transaction, End Transaction, Initial Valid Time and End Valid Time) of Date type are added.

In *Specific evolution* only the last value and the date of the updated of temporal level are considered, therefore sometimes it is not necessary to include the attributes that make the final times of Transaction and Valid, although this depends on the needs of the application.

Temporal factEntities

The temporal characteristics of the *factEntities* are spread into the associated *fact table*. The granularity is marked by the Time dimension. The type of time generally is the Valid time. The *fact table* is a historical table. Usually it doesn't have modifications or deletions. Although there are massive loads of data, with new values of the *fact measures* and *dimensional leaf levels*.

EXAMPLES OF TRANSFORMATION

Next, we will apply the transformation rules defined in the previous section, to transform the *FE* scheme obtained in Figure 7 (which corresponds at the example 1), into *OR* model. Let's opt for a normalized form.

Product Dimension

The Product dimension only has the *leaf level*. This is transformed into a table.

Products Table (

- ProID: Number,
- Name: Alfanumeric,
- Other Product Attributes: Sdom).

Time Dimension

Each level of the Dynamics hierarchy of Time Dimension becomes a relational table. The *parent-child* relationship makes the primary key of Decades table be spread to Years table, and that the primary key of Years table it be spread to Semesters table.

Decades Table(

- Decade_x: Date,
- Other Decade attributes: Sdom).

Years Table (
- Year_x: Date,
- *Decade_x*: Date, (Foreign key of Decades),
- Other Year attributes: Sdom).

Semesters Table (

- Sem_x: Date,
- *Year_x*: Date, (Foreign key of Years),
- Other Semester attributes: Sdom).

Location Dimension

The Location dimension has different *Geometric* and *Semantics* spatial granularities. To transform these into the *OR* model, we are going to follow the rules of section shown above, option d). It transforms each *Semantic* granularity and each *Geometric* granularity into a different table.

We are using the defined *ADT* in the previous section.

SurfacePlots Table (

- PlotID_x: Number,
- *CiID_x*: Alfanumeric, (Foreign key of SurfaceCitys)
- SurfacePl: Surface ADT,
- Other SurfacePlot attributes: Sdom).

LinePlots Table (

- *PlotID_x*: Number, (Foreign key of SurfacePlots)
- *CiID_x*: Alfanumeric, (Foreign key of LineCitys)
- LinePl = SurfConvert (SurfacePlots.SurfacePl): Line ADT,
- Other LinePlot attributes: Sdom).

PointPlots Table (

- *PlotID_x*: Number, (Foreign key of LinePlots)
- *CiID_x*: Alfanumeric, (Foreign key of PointCitys)
- PointPl = LineConvert (LinePlots.LinePl): Point ADT,
- Other PointPlot attributes: Sdom).

SurfaceCitys Table (

- CiID_x: Alfanumeric,
- SurfaceCi = Union (SurfacePlots.SurfacePl): SetSurface ADT,

- Inhabitantes: list < Inhabitantes VTTempal ADT>,
- Other SurfaceCity attributes: Sdom).

LineCitys Table (

- CiID_x: Alfanumeric, (Foreign key of LinePlots),
- LineCi = Union (LinePlots.LinePl): SetLine ADT,
- Other LineCity attributes: Sdom).

PointCitys Table (

- CiID_x: Alfanumeric, (Foreign key of LineCitys),
- PointCi = Union (PointPlots.PointPl): SetPoint ADT,
- Other PointCity attributes: Sdom).

Production Basic factEntity

The *Production Basic factEntity* converts into one *fact table*, which contains a column for the *Kprod Basic measure*, and one column for each *primary key* from the "*leaf tables*" of its associated dimensions, which are propagated as *foreign keys*.

We choose the set of all inherited keys to make up the primary key of the *Production fact table*.

Basic facEntity ⇨

Productions Table (

- *PlotID_x*: Number, (Foreign key of SurfacePlots),
- *ProID*: Number, (Foreign key of Products)
- *Sem_x*: Date, (Foreign key of Semesters),
- *Year_x*: Date, (Foreign key of Semesters),
- KProd: Number (basic measure)).

In this example we do not include spatial representation in the *fact table*.

Virtual factEntities

Now, we can to make up the **Virtual factEntities** wanted. We apply the rules shown in example 4.

Virtual FactEntity = $([D_i x \ldots x D_p], \{G_j(me_j)\})./$ $i \in [1,\ldots,m] \wedge \forall p \in [1,\ldots,m] \wedge (p > i)$. *In this example* $m = 3$.

First

We form all the possible groups with the dimension, we apply the formula 1:

$[D_i x \ldots x D_p] / \forall i \in [1,\ldots,3] \wedge \forall p \in [1,\ldots,3] \wedge (p > i)$.

For i = 1 Λ p = Ø,2,3 ⇨

- Subgroups with one dimension: $\{D_1\}$.
- Subgroups with two dimensions: $\{D_1, D_2\}$; $\{D_1, D_3\}$.
- Subgroups with three dimensions: $\{D_1, D_2, D_3\}$.

For i = 2 Λ p = Ø,3 ⇨

- Subgroups with one dimension: $\{D_2\}$.
- Subgroups with two dimensions: $\{D_2, D_3\}$.
- Subgroups with three dimensions: Ø.

Now we group the previous subgroups by number of dimensions

Where D_1 = Product; D_2 = Location; D_3 = Time

- Subgroups with one dimension:
  - o {Product}.
  - o {Location}.
  - o {Time}.
- Subgroups with two dimensions:
  - o {Product, Location}.
  - o {Product, Time}.
  - o {Location, Time}.
- Subgroups with three dimensions:
  - o {Product, Location, Time}.

Second

We apply the *Cartesian* product on the previous subgroups.

- {Product}:
  1. {Product}.
- {Location}:
  2. {Plot}.
  3. {City}.
- {Time}:
  4. {Semester}.
  5. {Year}.
  6. {Decade}.
- {Product x Location}:
  7. {Product, Plot}.
  8. {Product, City}.
- {Product x Time}:
  9. {Product, Semester}.
  10. {Product, Year}.
  11. {Product, Year}.
- {Location x Time}:
  12. {Plot, Semester}.
  13. {City, Semester}.
  14. {Plot, Year}.
  15. {City, Year}.
  16. {Plot, Decade}.
  17. {City, Decade}.
- {Product x Location x Time}:
  18. {Product, Plot, Semester}.
  19. {Product, City, Semester}.
  20. {Product, Plot, Year}.
  21. {Product, City, Year}.
  22. {Product, Plot, Decade}.
  23. {Product, City, Decade}.

The previous possibilities that have the elements of Location Dimension can be generated with different representations.

Thirdly

The *Virtual factEntities* are generated using some of the Cartesian products of the previous step. We analyze an illustrative example:

Example 9

We want to know the number of products collected for every City and Year and with spatial representation.

Definition of Virtual factEntities

The associated *Virtual factEntity* corresponds to the number 15, of the previous step. We call it *VFE_ProductCityYear* and it is made up as follows:

Structure

(Location/City, Time/Year, *KProdD*).

Derived Data

((CiID_x, CitySpatial = UNION(*PlotGeometric*)), Year, SUM(KProd)).

Where:

- The *Location* dimension is represented with the *City Semantic* spatial granularity. The *Geometric* spatial granularities are dependent on the *Geometric spatial granularity* of Plot, and are represented, as:
  - o The identifier of City.
  - o UNION(PlotGeometry)). Where PlotGeometry can be any of the available representations for Plot.
- The *Time dimension* is expressed with year granularity.
- The *KProdD measure* is derived from *KProd basic measure*, and is expressed as SUM(*KProdD*).

In summary, as has been noted, the scheme offers all possibilities for creating *Virtual factEntities* with derived data, and which allows us to analyze data with multiple spatial and temporal representations.

Transformation of Virtual factEntities

Next, we represent connected the structure and the definition of data derived of *VFE_ProductCityYear*. Thus, we define as a relation/table:

VFE_ProductCityYear Relation (

- *CiID_x*: Alfanumeric,
- CitySpatial = UNION(PlotGeometry. PlotID_x): SGeometry
- *Year* = Date, (Format, YYYY),
- QuantityProd = SUM(KProd)): Number).

Where:

- *PlotGeometry* can be: Surface, Line, or Point.
- *SGeometry* represents any *ADT* such as: SSurface, SLine, SPoint.

This relation can be transformed into a physical table, a materialized view, etc. We choose to store only the rules to obtain the structures and the derived data.

Next, we see how can to obtain the data of this *VFE_ProductCityYear* Relation.

Ways of to Obtain Derive Data

To obtain data derived: First we define an intermediate view without spatial representation.

CREATE VIEW V_*ProductCityYear* (
AS

- SELECT SurfacePlot.CiID_x "City", Production.Year "Year", Sum(KProd) "Quantity"

- FROM Production, SurfacePlot
- WHERE Production.PlotID_x = Surface-Plot. PlotID_x
- GROUP BY (SurfacePlot.CiID_x, Production.Year).

We need another step to obtain the spatial representation. According to the desired representation we have three different views:

With representations of Surfaces

CREATE VIEW V_*ProductCityYear*_Surface(AS

- SELECT V.City, Union(SP.SurfacePI) "Surfaces", V.Year, V.Quantity
- FROM SurfacePlots SP, V_*ProductCityYear* V
- WHERE V.PlotID_x = SP.PlotID_x).

With Representations of Lines

CREATE VIEW V_*ProductCityYear*_Line(AS

- SELECT V.City, Union(LP.LinePI) "Lines", V.Year, V.Quantity
- FROM LinePlots LP, V_*ProductCityYear* V
- WHERE V.PlotID_x = LP.PlotID_x).

With Representations of Point

CREATE VIEW V_*ProductCityYear*_Point(AS

- SELECT V.City, Union(PP.PointPI), V.Year, V.Quantity
- FROM PointPlots PP, V_*ProductCityYear* V
- WHERE V.PlotID_x = PP.PlotID_x).

Thus, a scheme resulted of transforming *VFE_ProductCityYear Virtual factEntity* into *OR* model could have the following elements:

- *VFE_ProductCityYear* Relation.
- V_*ProductCityYear*.
- V_*ProductCityYear*_Surface.
- V_*ProductCityYear*_Line.
- V_*ProductCityYear*_Point.

Furthermore, whether the *VFE_ProductCityYear* relationship, is considered as permanent tables or materialized views, they can use the same structure and derived data that previous views provide.

Conclusion

We have found in these examples how *Virtual factEntities* can be elected and generated automatically, since the scheme provides information on: *where* the data are, *how* to reach them, and *what* functions should be applied for these to be derived. This facilitates for the end user the choice: of *what Virtual factEntities* are needed, *which* will be stored, and at *what* level of detail.

RELATED WORK

Most of the models proposed to design MDB from a conceptual approach are basing on concepts modelled from traditional databases and present extensions to the *ER* model such as in (Sapia, Blaschka, Höfling & Dinter, 1999). Other models, (Malinowski & Zimanyi, 2004) and (Golfarelli, Mario & Rizzi, 1998), adopt the starting point of an *ER* model providing guidelines for its transformation into a multidimensional model. In the StarER model (Tryfona, Busborg & Borch, 1999), there is a proposal to use the Star multidimensional model together with an extension of the *ER* model. Other authors present extensions to the *UML* model, such as (Luján-Mora, Trujillo & Song, 2006), and (Abelló, Samos, Saltor, 2006). Although researchers such as (Torlone, 2003) and (Kimball, 1996) consider, as we do, that the traditional data models are not adapted to represent the special semantics of multidimensional databases. Some classifications of the most important characteristics that must be gathered in a conceptual multidimensional model are shown in (Torlone, 2003), (Abello, Samos & Saltor, 2006), (Malinowski & Zimanyi, 2004) and (Luján-Mora, Trujillo & Song, 2006). In (Abello, Samos & Saltor, 2006) propose to design the conceptual phase in three levels of detail increasing in complexity. With this design approach, a model is presented in (Abello, Samos & Saltor, 2002) and (Abelló, Samos & Saltor, 2006), which uses an extension of *UML* model. The model in (Torlone, 2003) is presenting from a conceptual point of view and it specifies the basic and advanced characteristics that an ideal multidimensional conceptual model would have. A classification of the different hierarchies (with regard to the cardinality between the different hierarchical levels) that must support a model is showing in (Malinowski & Zimanyi, 2004). This work is completing in (Malinowski & Zimanyi, 2005), where it is defining as transforming these hierarchies into the logical model under the relational paradigm. In (Gascueña & Guadalupe, 2008), (Gascueña & Guadalupe, 2008b) a specific conceptual multidimensional model called FactEntity is shown; this model is not considered for its authors how a extension of any model; in addition various types of hierarchies (with regard to the implication that have the navigation between hierarchical levels on the basic measures), are presented. In (Gascueña & Guadalupe, 2008c) is realized a study comparative between several multidimensional models, and are added the new characteristic that a multidimensional conceptual model would have to support multiples spatio-temporal granularities.

Introducing Space and Time in Multidimensional Models

Three types of space dimensions (depending on the fact that the space elements are included in all, some or none of the levels of the dimensional hierarchies) and two types of measures (space or numerical measures) are distinguishing in (Stefanovic, Han & Koperski, 2000). In (Malinowski & Zimanyi, 2004) the inclusion of the spatial data at a hierarchical level or as measures is proposing, though they do not include the spatial granularity. In (Malinowski & Zimanyi, 2005), the same authors present a classification of the space hierarchies following the criteria set in (Malinowski & Zimanyi, 2004) (with regard to the cardinality). A study is presenting on the temporality of the data at column and row level in (Malinowski & Zimanyi, 2006) and (Malinowski & Zimanyi, 2006b) . In (Gascueña , Cuadra & Martínez, 2006) is studied the multigranularity of the spatial data from a logical approach. In (Gascueña, Moreno & Cuadra, 2006) is detail a comparative view of how to deal with the spatio-temporal multigranularity with two different logical models: *OO* and Multidimensional. In (Gascueña & Guadalupe, 2008),(Gascueña & Guadalupe, 2008b) we define spatial granularity concepts highlighting two types of *Semantic* and *Geometric* spatial granularities, in addition we use different types of hierarchies to support the treatment of multiples spatio-temporal granularities and how these are related.

Introducing Space and Time in Object Oriented Models

In general, the treatment of multigranularity in *OO* models exists, as in the work of (Camossi, Bertolotto, Bertino & Guerrini, 2003) and (Camossi, Bertolotto, Bertino & Guerrini, 2003b) that extends Object Data Management Group *ODMG*, for the inclusion of this concept in its model called Spatio Temporal ODMG *ST_ODMG*. The *ST_ODMG* model supports the handling of entities with a spatial extension that changes their position on temporary maps. It provides a frame for mapping the movement of a moving spatial entity through a geographic area, where the spatial objects can be expressing at different levels of detail. In (Khatri, Ram & Snodgrass, 2006) a study on the spatio-temporal granularities by means of ontology is carrying out. They propose to model it in two phases: first, by using a conventional conceptual *ER* model, without considering spatial or temporal aspects, it would model "what". In the second phase, it completes with notations or labels that gather the associated semantics of time and space, "when and where", as well as the movement of the spatial objects, although they only handle one granularity for each spatial data. In (Parent, Spaccapietra & Zimanyi, 1999) it shows the MADS model as an extension of the *ER* model, although it uses *OO* elements and some authors present it as a hybrid between *OO* and *ER*. It uses complex structures and abstract types of data to support the definition of domains associated with space and time over object and relations. But none of the models proposed above distinguish, between *Semantic* and *Geometric* spatial granularities, as our proposal has done.

Supporting Multi-Representation

In reference (Parent, Spaccapietra & Zimanyi, 2006) an extension to the *MAD* model is added to handle multiple resolutions in the geographic databases. It presents four orthogonal dimensions in order to model: data structures, space, time and representation. It distinguishes two approaches to support multiple spatial resolutions. The *multi-resolution* approach only stores the data of the upper level of resolution, delegating the simplification and space generalization to the databases system. The *multi-representational* approach stores the data at different levels of resolution and allows the objects to have multiple geometries. In (Bedard, 1999) and (Bedard, 1999b) objects with different interpretations and scales are defined. In (Timpf, 1999) series of maps are used and handle with hierarchies. In (Jones, Kidner, Luo, Bundy & Ware, 1996) objects with different representations (multi-scale) are associated. In (Stell, Worboys & 1998) the objects at different

levels of detail are organized, such as stratified maps. In (Bedard & Bernier, 2002) the concept of "VUEL" (View Element) and new definitions of multi-representation are introduced with four dimensions: semantics, graphic, geometry and associated scale. It proposes to model the space using the expressivity of the multidimensional models, where the spatial data is dealt with in the table of facts and the dimensions are marking the different semantics of multi-representation, although it is not a multidimensional model. The Geo_Frame_T model (Vargas da Rocha, Edelweiss & Iochpe, 2001) uses the *OO* paradigm and an extension of *UML* model, and introduces a set of temporal and space stereotypes to describe the elements and the class diagram. The Temporal Spatial *STER* model is presented in (Tryfona, Price & Jensen, 2003) as an extension of the *ER* model maintaining the concepts used in *ER* and including sets of spatial entities.

None of these models support multidimensional concepts, neither do they distinguish between *Semantic* and *Geometric* spatial granularities, the reason why they are not adapted to model the multidimensional semantic. In (Gascueña & Guadalupe, 2008), (Gascueña & Guadalupe, 2008b) the *FE* model gathers, on the one hand the multidimensional semantics, and on the other hand the spatial semantics; in addition a study on the way of divide a space of interest, to introduce this in a *MDB*, is made up; and concepts as *Semantic* and *Geometric* spatial granularities are presented. This allows showing in the conceptual phase of modelled the multiples representations wished for each spatial data.

This section has carried out the study of data models from the focus of *MDB* and from the focus of traditional databases. We observe that the most of the proposed models are handled from Conceptual or Logical perspectives, but that none of them intends a continued methodology and whit support to the spatio- temporal multigranularity, as we do. We presented a way to model *MDB*, separating clearly the two phases, since in this scope these sometimes are confused, in addition we suggesting rules to transform the conceptual model into logical model, but without losing sight both the multidimensional and the spatial semantics, and among latest the interrelated spatio-temporal multigranularities.

CONCLUSION AND FUTURE LINES OF RESEARCH

In this work we have studied and developed how handled the different types of spatial granularities. We have proposed part of a methodology for designing multidimensional databases in the Conceptual and Logical phases. We have used the definition of the new concepts, constructors and structures that the FactEntity conceptual model proposes. This model is presented in (Gascueña & Guadalupe, 2008), (Gascueña & Guadalupe, 2008b) and collects: multidimensional, spatial and temporal semantics. We explain the semantics of the *Basic* factEntity and *Virtual* factEntity with a metamodel made up with the *ER* model. Furthermore we define rules, to convert the elements of FactEntity model, into the *R* and *OR* logical models, discussing various possibilities, and under the perspectives of multiples spatial and temporal granularities, and without loss of the multidimensional semantics. In addition we have included examples and illustrations to clarify our exposure. Finally we present a case of use complete using the proposal methodology.

We also believe that the FactEntity model can be used in those applications where it is of interest to study spatial elements with different granularities, although they are not geographically located.

We futures lines of research are oriented towards the formal definition of the FactEntity model with logical formulas and BNF grammars. The realization of a Case tool that allows us to automate the FactEntity model and the transformation rules for *DBMS*. We will define rules to preserve the consistency of the temporal elements in a *MDB*. Furthermore we want apply the FactEntity model in techniques of Data Mining and we want to study and analyse the impact that various factors, such as scale, resolution, perception, etc.., have on the choice of adequate spatial granularity. Also we will try to search for applications of the FactEntity model in various research areas such as Medicine, Biology, Banking, etc. We also are interested in the application of the model to study the evolution of phenomena such as earthquakes, hurricanes, floods etc.., and their implications on the landscape.

REFERENCES

Abello, A., Samos, J., & Saltor, F. (2006). *A data warehouse multidimensional models classification*. Technical Report LSI-2000-6. Universidad de Granada.

Abelló, A., Samos, J., & Saltor, F. (2002). *YAM2 (Yet Another Multidimensional Model): An extension of UML*. In *Proceedings of the Int. DB Engineering and Application Symposium*, (pp. 172-181).

Abelló, A., Samos, J., & Saltor, F. (2006). *YAM2, A multidimensional conceptual model extending UML. Information Systems, 31*(6),541-567.

Bedard, Y. (1999). *Visual modeling of spatial databases: towards spatial PVL and UML. Geomantic 53*(2), 169-186.

Bedard, Y., & Bernier, E. (2002). *Supporting multiple representations with spatial databases views management and the concept of VUEL. Proceedings of the Joint Workshop on Multi-Scale Representations of Spatial Data, ISPRS*.

Berloto, M. (1998). *Geometric modeling of spatial entities at multiple levels of resolution*. PhD Thesis, Uni. degli Studi di Genova.

Bettini, C., Jajodia, S., & Wang, S. (2000). *Time granularities in databases, data mining and temporal reasoning*, Secaucus, NJ, USA. Ed. New York: Springer-Verlag Inc. Secaucus, NJ, USA.

Borges, K. A. V., Davis Jr., C.A.., & Laender, A. H. F. (2001). *OMT-G: An object-oriented data model for geographic applications Geo Informatics 5*(3), 221-260.

Camossi, E., Bertolotto, M., Bertino, E., & Guerrini, G. (2003). *ST_ODMG: A multigranular spatiotemporal extension of ODMG Model.* Technical Report DISI-TR-03-09, Università degli Studi di Genova.

Camossi, E., Bertolotto, M., Bertino, E., & Guerrini, G. (2003b). *A multigranular spactiotemporal data model. Proceedings of the 11th ACM international symposium.* Advances in GIS, (pp. 94-101). New Orleans, USA.

Elmasri, R, & Navathe, S.(2007). *Fundamental of database systems*, Pearson International/Addison Wesley Editorial, 5ª edition.

Gascueña, C. M., Moreno, L., & Cuadra, D. (2006). *Dos Perspectivas para la Representación de la Multi-Granularidad en Bases de Datos Espacio-Temporales.* IADIS 2005 conferences.

Gascueña, C. M., Cuadra, D., & Martínez, P. (2006). *A multidimensional approach to the representation of the spatiotemporal multi-granularity. Proceedings of the 8th International Conference on Enterprise Information Systems,* Cyprus. ICEIS 2006.

Gascueña, C. M., & Guadalupe, R. (2008). *Some types of spatio-temporal granularities in a conceptual multidimensional model. Proceedings from the 7th International Conference, Bratislava, Slovak APLIMAT 2008.*

Gascueña, C. M., & Guadalupe, R.. (2008). *Some types of spatio-temporal granularities in a conceptual multidimensional model. Aplimat-Journal of Applied Mathematics, 1*(2), 215-216.

Gascueña, C. M., & Guadalupe, R. (2008). *A study of the spatial representation in multidimensional models. Proceedings of the 10th International Conference on Enterprise Information Systems,* Spain, ICEIS 2008.

Gascueña, C. (2008). *Proposual of a conceptual model for the Representation of spatio temporal multigranularity in multidimensional databases.* PhD Thesis. University Politecnica of Madrid, Spain.

Golfarelli, M., Mario, D., & Rizzi, S. (1998). *The dimensional fact model: A conceptual model for data warehouses.* (IJCIS) *7*(2–3), 215-247.

Jones, C.B., Kidner, D.B., Luo, L.Q., Bundy, G.L., & Ware, J.M. (1996). Databases design for a multi-scale spatial information system. *Int. J., GIS 10*(8), 901-920.

Khatri, V., Ram, S., & Snodgrass, R. T. (2006). *On augmenting database design-support environments to capture the geo-spatio-temporal data semantic,* 2004, Publisher Elsevier Science Ltd, *31*(2), 98-133.

Kimball, R. (1996). *The data warehouse toolkit.* John Wiley & Sons Ed.,

Luján-Mora, S., Trujillo, J., & Song, Il- Yeol. (2006). A UML profile for multidimensional modeling in data warehouses. *DKE, 59*(3), 725-769.

Malinowski, E., & Zimanyi, E. (2004). *Representing spatiality in a conceptual multidimensional model.* Proceedings of the 12th annual ACM international workshop on GIS. Washington, DC, USA.

Malinowski, E., & Zimanyi, E. (2004). OLAP hierarchies: A conceptual perspective. In *Proceedings of the 16th Int. Conf. on Advanced Information Systems Engineering,* (pp. 477-491).

Malinowski, E., & Zimanyi, E. (2005). Spatial hierarchies and topological relationships in the spatial multiDimER model. *Lecture Notes in Computer Science, 3567,* p. 17.

Malinowski, E., & Zimanyi, E. (2006). *Inclusion of time-varying measures in temporal data warehouses dimensions. Proceedings of the 8th International Conference on Enterprise Information Systems*, Paphos, Cyprus.

Malinowski, E., & Zimanyi, E. (2006b). *A conceptual solution for representing time in data warehouse dimensions.* Proceedings of the 3rd Asia-Pacific (APCCM2006), Hobart, Australia.

Parent, C., Spaccapietra, S., & Zimanyi, E. (1999). *Spatio-temporal conceptual models: Data structures+space+time. Proceedings of the 7th ACM Symposium on Advances in Geographic Information Systems*, Kansas City, USA.

Parent, C., Spaccapietra, S., & Zimanyi, E. (2006). *The MurMur project: Modeling and querying multi-representation spatio-temporal databases. Information Systems, 31*(8), 733-769.

Piattini, Mario G., Esperanza, Marcos, Coral, Calero, & Belén, Vela. (2006). *Tecnología y diseño de bases de datos*, Editorial: Ra-Ma.

Sapia, C., Blaschka, M., Höfling, G., & Dintel, B. (1999). Extending the E/R model for the multidimensional paradigm. *Advances in DB Technologies. LNCS1552*, Springer-Verlag.

Stefanovic, N., Han, J., & Koperski, K. (2000). Object-based selective materialization for efficient implementation of spatial data cubes. *IEEE Trans. on Knowledge and Data Engineering, 12*(6), 938-958.

Stell, J., & Worboys, M. (1998). Stratified map spaces: A formal basic for multi-resolution spatial databases. *Proceedings of the 8th International Symposium on Spatial Data Handling, SDH'98* (pp. 180-189).

Timpf, S. (1999). Abstraction, level of detail, and hierarchies in map series. *International Conference on Spatial Information Theory, COSIT'99*, LNCS 1661, (pp. 125-140).

Torlone R. (2003). *Conceptual Multidimensional Models. In Multidimensional databases: problems and solutions*, pages 69-90, Idea Group Publishing, Hershey, PA, USA.

Tryfona, N., Busborg, F., & Borch, J. (1999). *StarER a conceptual model for data warehouse design. In Proceedings of the 2nd ACM Int. Workshop on DW and OLAP*, (pp. 3-8).

Tryfona, N., Price, R., & Jensen, C. S.(2003). *Conceptual Models for Spatio-temporal Applications.* In M. Koubarakis et al. (Eds.), Spatio-Temporal DB: The CHOROCHRONOS Approach (pp. 79-116). Berlin, Heidelberg: Verlag.

Vargas, da Rocha, L., Edelweiss, L. V., & Iochpe, C. (2001). GeoFrame-T: A temporal conceptual framework for data modelin. *Proceedings of the ninth ACM international symposium on Advances in GIS*, Atlanta, GA, USA.

Chapter XI
Methodology for Improving Data Warehouse Design using Data Sources Temporal Metadata

Francisco Araque
University of Granada, Spain

Alberto Salguero
University of Granada, Spain

Cecilia Delgado
University of Granada, Spain

ABSTRACT

One of the most complex issues of the integration and transformation interface is the case where there are multiple sources for a single data element in the enterprise Data Warehouse (DW). There are many facets due to the number of variables that are needed in the integration phase. This chapter presents our DW architecture for temporal integration on the basis of the temporal properties of the data and temporal characteristics of the data sources. If we use the data arrival properties of such underlying information sources, the Data Warehouse Administrator (DWA) can derive more appropriate rules and check the consistency of user requirements more accurately. The problem now facing the user is not the fact that the information being sought is unavailable, but rather that it is difficult to extract exactly what is needed from what is available. It would therefore be extremely useful to have an approach which determines whether it would be possible to integrate data from two data sources (with their respective data extraction methods associated). In order to make this decision, we use the temporal properties of the data, the temporal characteristics of the data sources, and their extraction methods. In this chapter, a solution to this problem is proposed.

INTRODUCTION

The ability to integrate data from a wide range of data sources is an important field of research in data engineering. Data integration is a prominent theme in many areas and enables widely distributed, heterogeneous, dynamic collections of information sources to be accessed and handled.

Many information sources have their own information delivery schedules, whereby the data arrival time is either predetermined or predictable. If we use the data arrival properties of such underlying information sources, the Data Warehouse Administrator (DWA) can derive more appropriate rules and check the consistency of user requirements more accurately. The problem now facing the user is not the fact that the information being sought is unavailable, but rather that it is difficult to extract exactly what is needed from what is available.

It would therefore be extremely useful to have an approach which determines whether it would be possible to integrate data from two data sources (with their respective data extraction methods associated). In order to make this decision, we use the temporal properties of the data, the temporal characteristics of the data sources and their extraction methods. Notice that we are not suggesting a methodology, but an architecture. Defining a methodology is absolutely out of the scope of this paper, and the architecture does not impose it.

It should be pointed out that we are not interested in how semantically equivalent data from different data sources will be integrated. Our interest lies in knowing whether the data from different sources (specified by the DWA) can be integrated on the basis of the temporal characteristics (not in how this integration is carried out).

The use of DW and Data Integration has been proposed previously in many fields. In (Haller, Proll, Retschitzgger, Tjoa, & Wagner, 2000) the Integrating Heterogeneous Tourism Information data sources is addressed using three-tier architecture. In (Moura, Pantoquillo, & Viana, 2004) a Real-Time Decision Support System for space missions control is put forward using Data Warehousing technology. In (Oliva & Saltor, A Negotiation Process Approach for Building Federated Databases, 1996) a multi-level security policies integration methodology to endow tightly coupled federated database systems with a multi-level security system is presented. In (Vassiliadis, Quix, Vassiliou, & Jarke, 2001) a framework for quality-oriented DW management is exposed, where special attention is paid to the treatment of metadata. The problem of the little support for automatized tasks in DW is considered in (Thalhamer, Schrefl, & Mohania, 2001), where the DW is used in combination with event/condition/action (ECA) rules to get an active DW. Finally, in (March & Hevner, 2005) an integrated decision support system from the perspective of a DW is exposed. Their authors state that the essence of the data warehousing concept is the integration of data from disparate sources into one coherent repository of information. Nevertheless, none of the previous works encompass the aspects of the integration of the temporal parameters of data.

In this chapter a solution to this problem is proposed. Its main contributions are: a DW architecture for temporal integration on the basis of the temporal properties of the data and temporal characteristics of the sources, a Temporal Integration Processor and a Refreshment Metadata Generator, that will be both used to integrate temporal properties of data and to generate the necessary data for the later DW refreshment.

Firstly, the concept of DW and the temporal concepts used in this work and our previous related works are revised; following our architecture is presented; following section presents whether data from two data sources with their data extraction methods can be integrated. Then we describe the proposed methodology with its corresponding algorithms. Finally, we illustrate the proposed methodology with a working example.

FEDERATED DATABASES AND DATA WAREHOUSES

Inmon (Inmon, 2002) defined a Data Warehouse as "a subject-oriented, integrated, time-variant, non-volatile collection of data in support of management's decision-making process." A DW is a database that stores a copy of operational data with an optimized structure for query and analysis. The scope is one of the issues which defines the DW: it is the entire enterprise. In terms of a more limited scope, a new concept is defined: a Data Mart (DM) is a highly focused DW covering a single department or subject area. The DW and data marts are usually implemented using relational databases, (Harinarayan, Rajaraman, & Ullman, 1996) which define multidimensional structures. A *federated database system* (FDBS) is formed by different *component database systems*; it provides integrated access to them: they co-operate (inter-operate) with each other to produce consolidated answers to the queries defined over the FDBS. Generally, the FDBS has no data of its own, queries are answered by accessing the component database systems.

We have extended the Sheth & Larson five-level architecture (Sheth & Larson, 1990), (Samos, Saltor, Sistac, & Bardés, 1998), which is very general and encompasses most of the previously existing architectures. In this architecture three types of data models are used: first, each component database can have its own native model; second, a *canonical data model* (CDM) which is adopted in the FDBS; and third, external schema can be defined in different *user models*.

One of the fundamental characteristics of a DW is its temporal dimension, so the scheme of the warehouse has to be able to reflect the temporal properties of the data. The extracting mechanisms of this kind of data from operational system will be also important. In order to carry out the integration process, it will be necessary to transfer the data of the data sources, probably specified in different data models, to a common

data model, that will be the used as the model to design the scheme of the warehouse. In our case, we have decided to use an OO model as canonical data model, in particular, the object model proposed in the standard ODMG 3.0.

ODMG has been extended with temporal elements. We call this new ODMG extension as ODMGT. This is also our proposal: to use for the definition of the data ware-house and data mart schema an object-oriented model as CDM, enhanced with temporal features to define loading of the data warehouse and data marts.

ARCHITECTURE EXTENSION WITH TEMPORAL ELEMENTS

Taking paper (Samos, Saltor, Sistac, & Bardés, 1998) as point of departure, we propose the following reference architecture (see Figure 1):

Native Schema. Initially we have the different data source schemes expressed in its native schemes. Each data source will have, a scheme, the data inherent to the source and the metadata of its scheme. In the metadata we will have huge temporal information about the source: temporal data on the scheme, metadata on availability of the source, availability of the log file or delta if it had them, etc.

Some of the temporal parameters that we consider of interest for the integration process are (Araque, Salguero, & Delgado, Information System Architecture for Data Warehousing):

- **Availability Window (AW):** Period of time in which the data source can be accessed by the monitoring programs responsible for data source extraction.
- **Extraction Time (ET):** Period of time taken by the monitoring program to extract significant data from the source.

- **Granularity (Gr):** It is the extent to which a system contains discrete components of ever-smaller size. In our case, because we are dealing with time, it is common to work with granules like minute, day, month…
- **Transaction time (TT):** Time instant when the data element is recorded in the data source computer system. This would be the data source TT.
- **Storage time (ST):** Maximum time interval for the delta file, log file, or a source image to be stored.

Preintegration. In the *Preintegration* phase, the semantic enrichment of the data source native schemes is made by the conversion processor. In addition, the data source temporal metadata are used to enrich the data source scheme with temporal properties. We obtain the component scheme (CST) expressed in the CDM, in our case, ODMGT (ODMG enriched with temporal elements).

Component and Export Schemas. Apart from the five-scheme levels mentioned (Sheth & Larson, 1990), three more different levels should be considered:

- **Component Scheme T (CST):** the conversion of a Native Scheme to our CDM, enriched so that temporal concepts could be expressed.
- **Exportation Scheme T (EST):** it represents the part of a component scheme which is available for the DW designer. It is expressed in the same CDM as the Component Scheme.
- **Data Warehouse Scheme:** it corresponds to the integration of multiple Exportation Schemes T according to the design needs expressed in an enriched CDM so that temporal concepts could be expressed.

From the CST expressed in ODMGT, the negotiation processor generates the export schemes (EST) expressed in ODMGT. These EST are the part of the CST that is considered necessary for its integration in the DW.

Integration. From many data sources EST schemas, the DW scheme is constructed (expressed in ODMGT). This process is made by the Integration Processor that suggests how to integrate the Export Schemes helping to solve semantic heterogeneities (out of the scope of this paper). In the definition of the DW scheme, the DW Processor participates in order to contemplate the characteristics of structuring and storage of the data in the DW.

Two modules have been added to the reference architecture in order to carry out the integration of the temporal properties of data, considering the extraction method used: the *Temporal Integration Processor* and the *Metadata Refreshment Generator*.

The *Temporal Integration Processor* uses the set of semantic relations and the conformed schemes obtained during the detection phase of similarities (Oliva & Saltor, A Negotiation Process Approach for Building Federated Databases, 1996). This phase is part of the integration methodology of data schemes. As a result, we obtain data in form of rules about the integration possibilities existing between the originating data from the data sources (minimum granularity, if the period of refreshment must be annotated between some concrete values). This information is kept in the Temporal Metadata Warehouse. In addition, as a result of the Temporal Integration process, a set of mapping functions is obtained. It identifies the attributes of the schemes of the data sources that are self-integrated to obtain an attribute of the DW scheme.

The *Metadata Refreshment Generator* determines the most suitable parameters to carry

Figure 1. Functional architecture

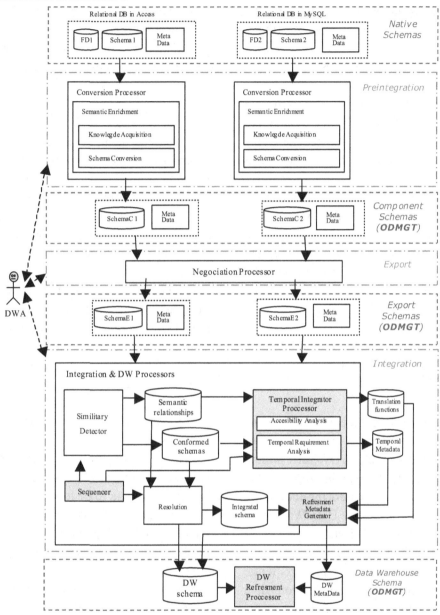

out the refreshment of data in the DW scheme (Araque & Samos, Data warehouse refreshment maintaining temporal consistency, 2003). The DW scheme is generated in the resolution phase of the methodology of integration of schemes of data. It is in this second phase where, from the minimum requirements generated by the temporal integration and stored in the Temporal Metadata

warehouse, the DW designer fixes the refreshment parameters. As result, the DW scheme is obtained along with the Refreshment Metadata necessary to update the former according to the data extraction method and other temporal properties of a concrete data source.

Obtaining of the DW scheme and the Export schemes is not a linear process. We need the Integration and Negotiation Processors collaborate in an iterative process where the participation of the local and DW administrators is necessary (Oliva & Saltor, A Negotiation Process Approach for Building Federated Databases, 1996).

Data Warehouse Refreshment. After temporal integration and once the DW scheme is obtained, its maintenance and update will be necessary. This function is carried out by the DW Refreshment Processor. Taking both the minimum requirements that are due to fulfill the requirements to carry out integration between two data of different data sources (obtained by means of the Temporal Integration module) and the integrated scheme (obtained by the resolution module) the refreshment parameters of the data stored in the DW will be adjusted.

TEMPORAL PROPERTIES INTEGRATION

After the initial loading, warehouse data must be regularly refreshed, and modifications of operational data since the last DW refreshment must be propagated into the warehouse so that the warehouse data reflects the state of the underlying operational systems (Araque, Data Warehousing with regard to temporal characteristics of the data source, 2002), (Araque, Real-time Data Warehousing with Temporal Requirements, 2003), (Araque, Integrating heterogeneous data sources with temporal constraints using wrappers, 2003).

Data Sources

Data sources can be operational databases, historical data (usually archived on tapes), external data (for example, from market research companies or from the Internet), or information from the already existing data warehouse environment. They can also be relational databases from the line of business applications. In addition, they can reside on many different platforms and can contain structured information (such as tables or spreadsheets) or unstructured information (such as plain text files or pictures and other multimedia information).

Extraction, transformation and loading (ETL) (Araque, Salguero, & Delgado, Monitoring web data sources using temporal properties as an external resources of a Data Warehouse, 2007) are data warehousing processes which involve extracting data from external sources, adapting it to business needs, and ultimately loading it into the data warehouse. ETL is important as this is the way data actually gets loaded into the warehouse.

The first part of an ETL process is to extract the data from the source systems. Most data warehousing projects consolidate data from different source systems. Each separate system may also use a different data organization/format. Common data source formats are relational databases and flat files, but there are other source formats. Extraction converts the data into records and columns.

The transformation phase applies a series of rules or functions to the extracted data in order to derive the data to be loaded.

During the load phase, data is loaded into the data warehouse. Depending on the organization's requirements, this process can vary greatly: some data warehouses merely overwrite old information with new data; more complex systems can maintain a history and audit trail of all the changes to the data.

Data Capture

DWs describe the evolving history of an organization, and timestamps allow temporal data to be maintained. When considering temporal data for DWs, we need to understand how time is reflected in a data source, how this relates to the structure of the data, and how a state change affects existing data. A number of approaches have been explored (Bruckner & Tjoa, 2002):

- **Transient data:** Alterations and deletions of existing records physically destroy the previous data content.
- **Semi-periodic data:** Typically found in the real-time data of operational systems where previous states are important. However, almost all operational systems only retain a small history of the data changes due to performance and/or storage constraints.
- **Periodic data:** Once a record has been added to a database, it is never physically deleted, nor is its content ever modified. Instead, new records are always added to reflect updates or even deletions. Periodic data thus contain a complete record of any data changes.
- **Snapshot data:** A stable view of data as it exists at some point in time.

Capture is a component of data replication that interacts with source data in order to obtain a copy of some or all of the data contained therein or a record of any changes (Castellanos, 1993). In general, not all the data contained in the source is required. Although all the data could be captured and unwanted data then discarded, it is more efficient to capture only the required subset. The capture of such a subset, with no reference to any time dependency of the source, is called static capture. In addition, where data sources change with time, we may need to capture the history of these changes. In some cases, performing a static capture on a repeated basis is sufficient. However, in many cases we must capture the actual changes that have occurred in the source. Both performance considerations and the need to transform transient or semi-periodic data into periodic data are the driving force behind this requirement. This type is called incremental capture.

Static capture essentially takes a snapshot of the source data at a point in time. This snapshot may contain all the data found in the source, but it usually only contains a subset of the data. Static capture occurs from the first time a set of data from a particular operational system is to be added to the data warehouse, where the operational system maintains a complete history of the data and the volume of data is small.

Incremental capture is the method of capturing a record of changes occurring in a source data set. Incremental capture recognizes that most data has a time dependency, and thus requires an approach to efficiently handle this. As the volume of changes in a set of data is almost always smaller than the total volume, an incremental capture of the changes in the data rather than a static capture of the full resulting data set is more efficient.

Delayed capture occurs at predefined times, rather than when each change occurs. In periodic data, this behaviour produces a complete record of the changes in the source. In transient and semi-periodic data, however, the result in certain circumstances may be an incomplete record of changes that have occurred. These problems arise in the case of deletions and multiple updates in transient and semi-periodic data.

There are several data capture techniques, and static capture is the simplest of these. Incremental capture, however, is not a single topic. It can be divided into five different techniques, each of which has its own strengths and weaknesses. The first three types are immediate capture, whereby changes in the source data are captured immediately after the event causing the change to occur. Immediate capture guarantees the capture of all changes made to the operational system irrespective of whether the operational data is transient, semi-periodic, or periodic. The first three types are:

- Application-assisted capture, which depends on the application changing the operational data so that the changed data may be stored in a more permanent way
- Triggered capture, which depends on the database manager to store the changed data in a more permanent way

- Log/journal capture, which depends on the database manager's log/journal to store the changed data

Because of their ability to capture a complete record of the changes in the source data, these three techniques are usually used with incremental data capture. In some environments, however, technical limitations prevent their use, and in such cases, either of the following two delayed capture strategies can be used if business requirements allow:

— Timestamp-based capture, which selects changed data based on timestamps provided by the application that maintains the data.

— File comparison, which compares versions of the data in order to detect changes.

Temporal Concepts

In order to represent the data discussed previously, we use a time model consisting of an infinite set of instants Ti (time points on an underlying time axis). This is a completely ordered set of time points with the ordering relation '≤' (Bruckner & Tjoa, 2002). Other temporal concepts may also be necessary:

- An *instant* is a time point on an underlying time axis.
- A *timestamp* is a time value associated with some object, e.g. an attribute value or a tuple.
- An *event* is an instantaneous fact, i.e. something occurring at an instant.
- The *lifespan* of an object is the time over which it is defined. The valid-time lifespan of an object refers to the time when the corresponding object exists in the modelled reality. Analogously, the transaction-time lifespan refers to the time when the database object is current in the database.

- A *temporal element* is a finite union of n-dimensional time intervals. These are finite unions of valid time intervals, transaction-time intervals, and bitemporal intervals, respectively.
- A *time interval* is the time between two instants.
- The *transaction time* (TT) of a database fact is the time when the fact is current in the database and may be retrieved.
- The *valid time* (VT) of a fact is the time when the fact is true in the modelled reality. A fact may have any number of associated instants and intervals, with single instants and intervals being important in special cases. Valid times are usually supplied by the user.

We can represent the temporal characteristics of the data source with the temporal concepts presented previously. It is therefore possible to determine *when* the data source can offer the data and *how* this data changes over time (temporal characteristics). This can be represented in the temporal component schema and used by the DW administrator to decide how to schedule the refreshment activity. It depends on the temporal properties of the data source.

Temporal Properties of Data

The DW must be updated periodically in order to reflect source data updates. The operational source systems collect data from real-world events captured by computer systems. The observation of these real-world events is characterized by a delay. This so-called propagation delay is the time interval it takes for a monitoring (operational) system to realize an occurred state change. The update patterns (daily, weekly, etc.) for DWs and the data integration process (ETL) result in increased propagation delays.

Having the necessary information available on time means that we can tolerate some delay (be it seconds, minutes, or even hours) between the time of the origin transaction (or event) and the time when the changes are reflected in the warehouse environment. This delay (or latency) is the overall time between the initial creation of the data and its population into the DW, and is the sum of the latencies for the individual steps in the process flow:

- Time to capture the changes after their initial creation.
- Time to transport (or propagate) the changes from the source system to the DW system.
- Time to have everything ready for further ETL processing, e.g. waiting for dependent source changes to arrive.
- Time to transform and apply the detail changes.
- Time to maintain additional structures, e.g. refreshing materialized views.

It is necessary to indicate that we take the following conditions as a starting point:

- We consider that we are at the E of the ETL component (Extraction, Transformation and Loading). This means we are treating times in the data source and in the data extraction component. This is necessary before the data is transformed in order to determine whether it is possible (in terms of temporal questions) to integrate data from one or more data sources.
- Transforming the data (with formatting changes, etc.) and loading them into the

DW will entail other times which are not considered in the previous "temporal characteristic integration" of the different data sources.
- We suppose that we are going to integrate data which has previously passed through the semantic integration phase.

We consider the following temporal parameters to be of interest on the basis of the characteristics of the data extraction methods and the data sources (Figure 2):

- VTstart: time instant when the data element changes in the real world (event). At this moment, its Valid Time begins. The end of the VT can be approximated in different ways which will depend on the source type and the data extraction method. The time interval from VTstart to VTend is the lifespan.
- TT: time instant when the data element is recorded in the data source computer system. This would be the transaction time.
- W: time instant when the data is available to be consulted. We suppose that a time interval can elapse between the instant when the data element is really stored in the data source computer system and the instant when the data element is available to be queried. There are two possibilities:
  o that W <VDstart (in this case, the data element would only be available on the local source level or for certain users)
  o that VDstart <= W <VDend (in this case, the data element would be avail-

Figure 2. Temporal properties of data

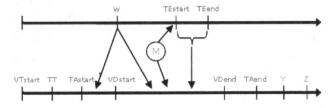

able for monitoring by the extraction programs responsible for data source queries)

- VD: Availability Window(Time interval). Period of time in which the data source can be accessed by the monitoring programs responsible for data source extraction. There may be more than one daily availability window. Then:
  - o VDstart, time instant when the availability window is initiated
  - o VDend, time instant when the availability window ends
- TE: Extraction Time(Time interval). Period of time taken by the monitoring program to extract significant data from the source. Then:
  - o TEstart, time instant when the data extraction is initiated.
  - o TEend, time instant when the data extraction ends.
  - o We suppose that the TE is within the VD in case it were necessary to consult the source to extract some data. In other words, VDstart< TEstart < TEend < VDend.
- M: time instant when the data source monitoring process is initiated. Depending on the extraction methods, M may coincide with TEstart.
- TA: maximum time interval storing the delta file, log file, or a source image. We suppose that during the VD, these files are available. This means that the TA interval can have any beginning and any end, but we suppose that it at least coincides with the source availability window. Therefore, TAstart <= VDstart and VDend <= TAend.
- Y: time instant from when the data is recorded in the DW.
- Z: time instant from when certain data from the DW are summarized, passed from one type of storage to another because they are considered unnecessary.

From VTstart to Z represents the real life of a data element from when it changes in the real world until this data element moves into secondary storage. Y and Z parameters it is not considered to be of immediate usefulness in this research.

By considering the previous temporal parameters and two data sources with their specific extraction methods (this can be the same method for both), we can determine whether it will be possible to integrate data from two sources (according to DWA requirements).

DATA INTEGRATION PROCESS

Prior to integration, it is necessary to determine under what parameters it is possible and suitable to access the sources in search of changes, according to their availability and granularity, obtained automatically by the tool of the previous section. This process is carried out by the pre-integration algorithm. It is only possible to determine these parameters previously if there is some pattern related to the source availability. The parameters obtained as a result shall be used in the specific integration algorithms whenever the data sources are refreshed (M).

One of the most complex issues of the integration and transformation interface is the case where there are multiple sources for a single element of data in the DW. For example, in the DW there is a data element that has as its source data element a1 from legacy application A and a data element b1 from legacy application B. If it is possible to temporally integrate the data from both sources (on the basis of their temporal properties), semantic integration is undertaken and the result is stored in the DW.

The integration methodology, shown in Figure 2, consists of a set of processes that define the rules for capturing a parameter from a single source as well as integrate a set of values semantically equivalent coming from different data sources. It has two phases, shown in Figure 3: *Temporal integration* (A) and *Generation of Refresh metadata* (B). The elements of the architecture that are of interest in this paper have been shadowed in Figure 3.

The temporary process of integration can also be divided into two different tasks: the analysis of the accessibility of both sources and the analysis of temporal requirements. The first of the previous tasks, which this article is focused on, verifies that certain temporary parameters common to any type of extraction method are satisfied, so the integration can be carried out, whereas the second one, which would be carried out only in the case of surpassing the first task, is focused on determining whether the integration of specific sources of data is possible. We obtain as a result data in form of rules about the integration possibilities existing between the data of the sources (the minimum granularity that can be obtained, the intervals in which refreshment should be performed, etc). The second task will be explained in temporal requirements algorithm section.

In the second phase the most suitable parameters are selected to carry out the refreshment process of the data. It is in this second phase where, from the minimum requirements selected by the temporary first stage of integration, the DW designer sets the refreshment parameters.

These parameters can be set automatically by the system taking care of different criteria (like the maximum level of detail, the no-saturation of the communication resources, etc). As a result, the necessary metadata are obtained so that the DW can be refreshed coherently depending on the type of extraction method and other temporary characteristics of the data sources.

This process does not guarantee that the integration of all of the changes detected in the sources can be carried out satisfactorily. Instead, what it guarantees is that the process of integration of a change can be carried out only and exclusively the times that are necessary to obtain the objectives proposed by the DW designer, attending to aspects related to the refreshment and the availability of the data.

Accessibility Algorithm

Given two data sources, the first task to do is to determine the smallest sequence in the intersection of the set of the availability window values of both data sources that is repeated periodically. We will denominate this concept *"common pattern of availability"*. For example, if the availability window of a data source is repeated every thirty six hours and the window of another is repeated

Figure. 3. System architecture

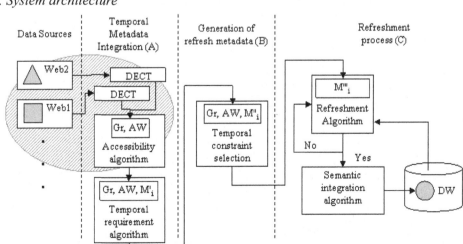

Figure 4. "Common pattern of availability"

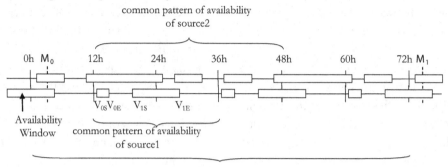

every twenty four hour, the "common pattern of availability" will be an interval of duration equal to seventy two hours (see Figure 4).

The algorithm, shown in Figure 5, first determines the maximum level of detail which both data sources can provide. For example, if a source provides data with a level of detail of a day, whereas another one provides them at an hour level, it is not possible to integrate them to obtain a level of detail better than a day (hours, minutes, seconds …).

It can occur that the unit (the granule) of the level of detail that can be obtained after the integration of both data sources has a length greater than the *"common pattern of availability"*. For example, that a granularity at day level can be obtained and the length of the common pattern is of several hours. In this case, querying the data sources once a day would be enough (it does not make sense to check a data source more often than it is going to be stored). Therefore, the maximum interval width of refreshment in the algorithm is adjusted to the length of the unit of the level of detail, obtained by means of the function "interval" in the algorithm. The value of the period of sampling could be, in the case of the previous example, multiple of a day (two days, three days, one week …). Within the com-

Figure 5. Accessibility algorithm

```
In:
    source[] : list of sources that contains the semantically equivalent parameter to
                integrate
    commonAW : common Availability Window pattern.
Out:
  M[] : list of instants to query the sources

If commonAW is periodical then
    GrMax = MinDetail(Granularity(source[1]), Granularity(source[2]), …)
    // Example: day = MinDetail(hour, day)
    If interval(GrMax) >= interval(commonAW) then
        LongestAW = LongestAWInterval(commonAW)
        M[0] = LongestAW.Start
        RefresmentInterval = interval(GrMax)
    Else
        i = 0, j = 0
        While interval(GrMax)*j < Interval(commonAW).end
            If all sources are accessible at interval(GrMax)*j
                M[i] = interval(GrMax)*j
                    i++
            j++
Else
    "It is not possible to determine the integration process previously"
```

mon pattern the moment in which the interval of maximum length begins is chosen to make the refreshment in which both sources are available, so that there is more probability to satisfy the restrictions imposed in the second phase, the *Analysis of Temporal Requirements* (out of scope of this paper). This interval is determined by the "*LongestAWInterval*" function.

In case that the unit (the *granule*) of the level of detail that can be obtained after the integration of both data sources has a length smaller than the common pattern of availability, it is necessary to determine in what moments within the common pattern both data sources are going to be available to refresh their data. Since it does not make sense to refresh a data more often than is going to be stored, only values that distant the length of the integrated granularity unit are chosen.

For example, if the granularity with which the data are going to be integrated correspond to "seconds", the instants will be temporarily distanced one second. Then it is verified that, for all those instants of the common pattern, both data sources are accessible. If it is successful it will be added to the set of instants (M) in which the refreshment can be made.

Some of the instants included in the M set will be discarded in the following phase because they do not fulfil some of the specific requirements that depend on the precise kind of sources. In this case, due to the fact that we are integrating web data sources which usually are simply HTML flat files, we will use a *File Comparison*-based method to do the integration process. This method consists on compare versions of the data in order to detect changes (Araque, Salguero, Delgado, & Samos, Algorithms for integrating temporal properties of data in Data Warehousing , 2006).

Every extracting method has its own requirements. If we are using a *File Comparison*-based method we need to ensure that the following sentence is valid:

$$(ET(DS1) \; U \; ET(DS2)) \subset (AW(DS1) \cap AW(DS2))$$

where ET(X) is the time needed to extract a change from the source X (*Extraction Time*), AW(X) is the *Availability Window* of the source X and DS1 and DS2 are both data sources. In other words, we cannot carry out the integration process of both data sources more often than the time we need to extract the changes. Obviously, if we need thirty seconds to extract the changes from a source and forty seconds to extract them from another source, it is not possible to integrate them every minute because we are not able to get the changes from both data sources so quickly.

Temporal Requirements Algorithms

In the following paragraphs, we shall explain how verification would be performed in order to determine whether data from data sources can be integrated. It is necessary to indicate that if we rely on 5 different extraction methods, and the combination of these two at a time, we would have 15 possible combinations. In this article, we shall focus on only two cases: firstly, the combination of two sources, one with the File Comparison method (FC) and the other with the Log method (LOG); secondly, the combination of two sources both with the same log method (LOG).

We suppose that the data recorded in the delta and log files have a timestamp which indicates the moment when the change in the source occurred (source TT). The following paragraphs describe the crosses between extraction methods on an abstract level, without going into low level details which shall be examined in subsequent sections.

LOG – FC. In this case, the LOG method extracts the data from the data source and provides us with all the changes of interest produced in the source, since these are recorded in the LOG file. The

FC method, on the other hand, only provides us with some of the changes produced in the source (depending on how the source is monitored). We will therefore be able to temporally integrate only some of the changes produced in both sources. Integration of the TT parameter would not be possible as the FC method does not have this parameter. On an abstract level, we can say that temporal integration may be carried out during all of the previously mentioned temporal parameters or characteristics except TT.

The granularity is a parameter that is inherent to the data source, while the refreshment period depends on the DW designer. This is true in all

cases except for the case of data sources with File Comparison extracting method, in which the level of detail of the changes is determined by the time elapsed between two consecutives images of the data source.

Let suppose the data sources in Figure 6. The maximum level of detail we can obtain for the parameter *level* once integrated (and the rest of attributes) is a day, i.e. the highest level of detail available in both data sources. In the temporal warehouse metadata repository is generated a rule that states this fact. This rule implies, in addition, a restriction in the process of refreshment. It does not make sense to query the data sources more

Figure 6. LOG and FC integration process example

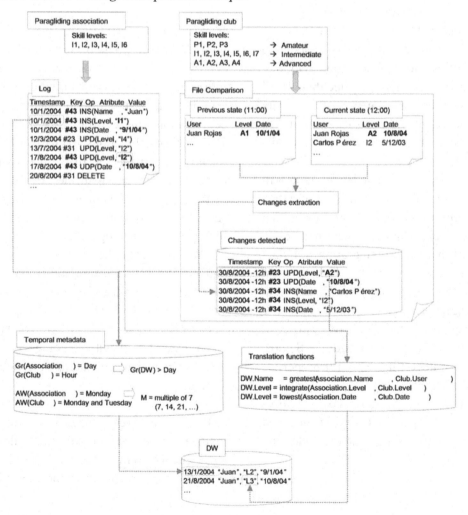

frequently than the level of detail used to store the parameter in the warehouse. Thus, in this case, there is reason to query the data sources more than once a day. Moreover, since these sources can be accessed simultaneously only on Mondays, the period of refreshment should be multiple of seven days (once a week, once every two weeks, once every three weeks, once a month, …), and should be twenty-three hours and fifty-nine minutes length.

LOG – LOG. In this case, we carry out the temporal integration of data (from the same or different sources) extracted with the same method. From the source where the data are extracted with the LOG method, all the produced changes are available. We will therefore be able to temporally integrate all the changes produced in both sources. On an abstract level, we can say that temporal integration may be carried out during all of the previously mentioned temporal properties.

Prior to integration, it is necessary to determine under what parameters it is possible and suitable to access the sources in search of changes, according to their availability and granularity (Gr) This process is carried out by the pre-integration algorithm. It is only possible to determine these parameters previously if there is some pattern related to the source availability (Figure 7). The parameters obtained as a result shall be used in the specific integration algorithms whenever the data sources are refreshed (M). If it is possible to temporally integrate the data from both sources (on the basis of their temporal properties), semantic integration is undertaken and the result is stored in the DW.

Data sources. By way of example to show the usefulness of these algorithms, an application is used which has been developed to maximize the flight experience of soaring pilots. These pilots depend to a large extent on meteorological conditions to carry out their activity and an important

Figure 7. Integration Process

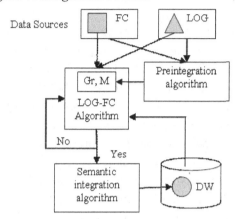

part of the system is responsible for handling this information. Two data sources are used to obtain this type of information:

• The US National Weather Service Web site. We can access weather measurements (temperature, pressure, humidity, general conditions and wind speed and direction) every hour in every airport in the world. It is a FC data source.

• In order to obtain a more detailed analysis and to select the best zone to fly, pilots use another tool: the SkewT diagram. The SkewT, or sounding chart, is a vertical snapshot of temperature, dew point and winds above a point on the earth. These soundings are carried out in some airports every twelve hours by launching a balloon sounding. It is a LOG data source.

The information provided by both data sources is semantically equivalent in certain cases. Given an airport where soundings are carried out, the lower layer meteorological information obtained in the sounding and that obtained from a normal meteorological station must be identical if relating to the same instant. In order to integrate these data, it is necessary to use the algorithms described in the following section.

Algorithm for FC – LOG

Every time the data source with the FC method is accessed, the value of the parameter to be integrated is extracted and this is compared with its last known value. If there has been a change, it is necessary to search for the associated change in the LOG source in order for integration to be performed. Since the LOG source might have collected more than one change in the period which has elapsed since the last refreshment, only the last change occurring in this period is taken into account. This is verified by consulting the TT value of the change in question.

If integration was possible, the value of the variable which stores the previous value of the FC-type source is updated. If integration was not possible, the value of this variable is not updated, so that if the change is detected in the LOG source in subsequent refreshments, integration can be carried out even if there has been no further change in the value of the parameter in the FC source.

Figure 8 represents the evolution of the meteorological data sources from the example which we are following (one source with a LOG extraction method and another with an FC method). If the designer wants to obtain this information with a daily level of detail, the integration process of the change "A" detected in the temperature would be carried out in the following way: every twenty-four hours, both sources are consulted; if the temperature value on the airport website has changed in relation to our last stored one, the two changes of the same parameter which

have occurred in the source corresponding to the soundings in the last twenty-four hours are recovered (as they are carried out every twelve hours and all the changes are recorded). The value from the website is then semantically integrated with the latest one of these. The algorithm for FC – LOG is as follows:

```
available = true
If any source is not periodical
  available = CheckAvailabilityW(Log)
  available = CheckAvailabilityW & avail-
able
If availabile = true
  newValue^Fc = readValue(FC)
  If newValue^Fc <> oldValue^Fc
    newValue^Log = last log value
    If TT(newValue^Log) < M_{i-1}
      ;Imposible to integrate the change
      ;because it still has not been
      ;detected in the Log source.
    If-not
      result=Integrate(newValue^Fc,newValue^Log)
    oldValue^Fc = newValue^Fc
```

Algorithm for LOG – LOG

This algorithm maintains a record of the changes which still remain to be detected in both sources. Every so often, the algorithm is executed and the two data sources from this temporal record are consulted and the pairs of changes are integrated. The first change is obtained in the source 1 of the parameter to be integrated. This change must take place after the record which indicated the first change which could not be integrated.

If either of these two changes has occurred since the last refreshment, this means that this

Figure 8. LOG – FC

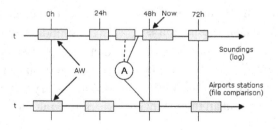

is the first time that a change in some source has been recorded and so integration may be carried out. Since this is a log, all the changes repeated in both sources must appear and must also be ordered temporally.

Figure 9 shows an integration example of two log-type data sources. The third time that the data sources are consulted (instant M3), it is not possible to integrate change "A" because it is still unavailable in one of the sources. The instant corresponding to the change detected is saved and no action is taken until the following refreshment. The fourth time that the sources are consulted, the temporal record is read first. In this case, change "A" is recorded in the second data source, and we therefore know that this change has not been integrated previously. It is then integrated semantically and the main loop of the algorithm is reiterated. When change "B" is detected in both sources, integration may be carried out directly. The algorithm is as follows:

```
available = true
allChanges = true
If any source is not periodical
 available = CheckAvailabilityW(Log)
 available = CheckAvailabilityW & available
If Now - LastTimeRefreshed < ST
 allChanges = false
If availabile = true & allChanges = true
 Repeat
  v1 = firstChangeAfter(updatedTo, Log1)
  v2 = firstChangeAfter(updatedTo, Log2)
  If TT(v1) > M_{i-1} || TT(v2) > M_{i-1}
   result = integrate(v1, v2)
   updatedTo = min(TT(v1), TT(v2))
while v1 <> null && v2 <> null
```

EXAMPLE

A Decision Support System (DSS) being based on a DW (March & Hevner, 2005) is presented as an example. This can be offered by Small and Medium-Sized Enterprises (SMEs) as a plus for adventure tourism. Here, a DSS (Figure 10) is used to assist novel and expert pilots in the decision-making process for a soaring trip (Araque, Salguero, & Abad, Application of data warehouse and Decision Support System in Soaring site recommendation, 2006).

These pilots depend to a large extent on meteorological conditions to carry out their activity and an important part of the system is responsible for handling this information. Two web data sources are mainly used to obtain this kind of information:

- The US National Weather Service Website. We can access weather measurements (temperature, pressure, humidity, etc) in every airport in the world.
- In order to obtain a more detailed analysis and to select the best zone to fly, pilots use another tool: the SkewT diagram. The SkewT, or sounding chart, is a vertical snapshot of temperature, dew point and winds above a point on the earth.

The information provided by both data sources is semantically equivalent in certain cases. In order to efficiently integrate these data, it is necessary to use the algorithm described in the previous

Figure 9. LOG – LOG

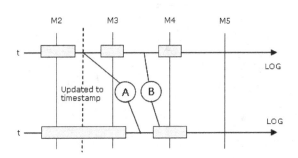

section. It is needed to use an efficient approach because these kinds of services are offered by SMEs which often have limited resources. The continuous integration of Web data sources may result in a collapse of the resources they use to communicate with their clients, which are not designed to support the laborious task of maintaining a DW up to date.

In our approach, the DW Administrator (DWA) introduces the data sources temporal properties in *DECT* tool (Araque, Real-time Data Warehousing with Temporal Requirements, 2003), (Araque, Integrating heterogeneous data sources with temporal constraints using wrappers, 2003) and selects the parameters to integrate, for example the temperature. This tool is able to determine the maximum level of detail (granularity) provided by each data source after a period of time. It uses an algorithm to determine the frequency of the changes produced at the data source. We approximate the granularity of the source by selecting the smallest interval that take place between two consecutive changes.

In the first source, the information about the temperature can be precise with a detail of "minute" (for example, that at 14 hours and 27 minutes there were a temperature of 15°C), whereas in the second case it talks about the temperature with a detail of "hour" (for example, that at 14 hours there were 15°C). The reason is that in the first source has been detected more than one change within an hour at least once, whereas in the second

source all the changes has been detected at least one hour distanced.

It can also determine the time intervals in which this information is available to be queried. Let us suppose that the first data source is always available, but the second one is only accessible from 23:10 to 00:10 and from 12:00 to 15:59 (availability window). Common pattern of availability would include, therefore, a whole day. Applying the accessibility algorithm we would obtain all possible instants of querying in which both sources are accessible and are distanced an interval equal to the maximum integrated granularity unit each other (hourly in the example we are using). Using the values of this example we would obtain {00:00, 12:00, 13:00, 14:00, 15:00}.

For each one of the previous set of instants is necessary to verify that the extraction and integration of the data sources would be possible. For this purpose we use the second algorithm mentioned in the previous section (out of the scope of this paper).

To help DWA in this process we have developed a tool that is able of performing both algorithm described in this paper: *Accessibility Algorithm* and *Analysis of Temporal Requirements*. A capture of this tool can be seen in Figure 11.

Using the data extracted from Web data sources a DSS for adventure practice recommendation can be offered as a post-consumption value-added service by travel agencies to their customers. Therefore, once a customer makes an on-line

Figure 10. Motivation example applied to tourism area

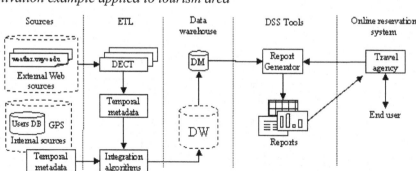

reservation, the travel agency can offer advice about adventure practices available in the area that customer may be interested in. Due to the high risk factor accompanying most adventure sports, a regular information system is far from being accurate. A more sophisticated ICT system is required in order to extract and process quality information from different sources. In this way, the customer can be provided with true helpful assistance to be aided in the decision-making process.

While logging reservation systems do not need supplementary information as weather forecast, other products in the tourist industry, such as eco-tourism can take a tremendous advantage of last-minute DW. The system allows to query a last-minute DW and use the output report to filter the on line availability of outdoor activities offered by the on line reservation system.

ACKNOWLEDGMENT

This work has been supported by the Andalucía Research Program under project GR2007/07-2 and by the Spanish Research Program under projects EA-2007-0228 and TIN2005-09098-C05-03.

Figure 11. DWA tool for analyzing the refreshment process.

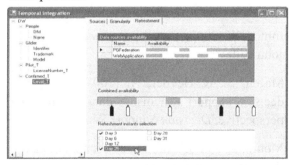

CONCLUSION AND FUTURE WORK

We have presented our work related to Data Warehouse design using data sources temporal metadata. The main contributions are: DW architecture for temporal integration on the basis of the temporal properties of the data and temporal characteristics of the sources, a Temporal Integration Processor and a Refreshment Metadata Generator, that will be both used to integrate temporal properties of data and to generate the necessary data for the later DW refreshment. In addition, we proposed a methodology with its corresponding algorithms.

Actually we are working about using a parallel fuzzy algorithm for integration process in order to obtain more precise data in the DW. The result is more precise because several refreshments of data sources are semantically integrated in a unique DW fact (Carrasco, Araque, Salguero, & Vila, 2008), (Salguero A. , Araque, Carrasco, Vila, & Martínez, 2007), (Araque, Carrasco, Salguero, Delgado, & Vila, 2007).

On the other hand, our work is now centred on use of a canonical data model based on ontologies to deal with the data sources schemes integration. Although it is not the first time the ontology model has been proposed for this purpose, in this case the work has been focused on the integration of spatio-temporal data. Moreover, to our knowledge this is the first time the metadata storage capabilities of some ontology definition languages has been used in order to improve the DW data refreshment process design (Salguero, Araque, & Delgado, Using ontology metadata for data warehousing, 2008), (Salguero, Araque, & Delgado, Data integration algorithm for data warehousing based on ontologies metadata, 2008), (Salguero & Araque, Ontology based data warehousing for improving touristic Web Sites, 2008).

REFERENCES

Araque, F. (2002). Data warehousing with regard to temporal characteristics of the data source. *IADIS WWW/Internet Conference*. Lisbon, Portugal.

Araque, F. (2003). Integrating heterogeneous data sources with temporal constraints using wrappers. *The 15th Conference On Advanced Information Systems Engineering. Caise Forum*. Klagenfurt, Austria.

Araque, F. (2003). Real-time data warehousing with temporal requirements. *Decision Systems Engineering, DSE'03 (in conjunction with the CAISE'03 conference)*. Austria: Klagen-furt/Velden.

Araque, F., & Samos, J. (2003). Data warehouse refreshment maintaining temporal consistency. *The 5th Intern. Conference on Enterprise Information Systems, ICEIS*. Angers, France.

Araque, F., Carrasco, R., Salguero, A., Delgado, C., & Vila, M. (2007). Fuzzy integration of a Web data sources for data warehousing. *Lecture Notes in Computer Science, 4739. ISSN: 0302-9743. Springer-Verlag*.

Araque, F., Salguero, A., & Abad, M. (2006). Application of data warehouse and decision support system in soaring site recommendation. *Information and Communication Technologies in Tourism, ENTER 2006*. Lausanne, Switzerland: Springer Verlag.

Araque, F., Salguero, A., & Delgado, C. Information system architecture for data warehousing. *Lecture Notes in Computer Science*. ISSN: 0302-9743. Springer-Verlag.

Araque, F., Salguero, A., & Delgado, C. (2007). Monitoring Web data sources using temporal properties as an external resources of a data warehouse. *The 9th International Conference on Enterprise Information Systems*, (pp.. 28-35). Funchal, Madeira.

Araque, F., Salguero, A., Delgado, C., & Samos, J. (2006). Algorithms for integrating temporal properties of data in data warehousing. *The 8th Int. Conf. on Enterprise Information Systems (ICEIS)*. Paphos, Cyprus.

Bruckner, R., & Tjoa, A. (2002). Capturing delays and valid times in data warehouses: Towards timely consistent analyses. *Journal of Intelligent Information Systems (JIIS), 19*(2,)169-190. *Kluwer Academic Publishers*.

Carrasco, R., Araque, F., Salguero, A., & Vila, A. (2008). Applying fuzzy data mining to tourism area. En J. Galindo, *Handbook of Research on Fuzzy Information Processing in Databases*. Hershey, PA, USA: Information Science Reference.

Castellanos, M. (1993). *Semiautomatic semantic enrichment for the integrated access in interoperable databases. PhD thesis,* . Barcelona, Spain: Dept. Lenguajes y Sistemas Informáticos, Universidad Politécnica de Cataluña, Barcelona.

Haller, M., Proll, B., Retschitzgger, W., Tjoa, A., & Wagner, R. (2000). Integrating heterogeneous tourism information in TIScover - The MIRO-Web approach. *Proceedings Information and Communication Technologies in Tourism, ENTER*. Barcelona , Spain

Harinarayan, V., Rajaraman, A., & Ullman, J. (1996). Implementing data cubes efficiently. *Proceedings of ACM SIGMOD Conference*. Montreal: ACM.

Inmon, W. (2002). *Building the Data Warehouse*. John Wiley.

March, S., & Hevner, A. (2005). Integrated decision support systems: A data warehousing perspective. *Decision Support Systems* .

Moura, J., Pantoquillo, M., & Viana, N. (2004). Real-time decision support system for space missions control. *International Conference on*

Information and Knowledge Engineering. Las Vegas.

Oliva, M., & Saltor, F. (1996). A negotiation process approach for building federated databases. *The 10th ERCIM Database Research Group Workshop on Heterogeneous Information Management,* (pp. 43-49). Prague.

Oliva, M., & Saltor, F. (2001). Integrating multilevel security policies in multilevel federated database systems. In B. Thuraisingham, R. van de Riet, K.R. Dittrich, and Z. Tari, editors. Boston: Kluwer Academic Publishers.

Salguero, A., & Araque, F. (2008). Ontology based data warehousing for improving touristic Web Sites. *International Conference. International Conference e-Commerce 2008.* Amsterdam, The Netherlands.

Salguero, A., Araque, A., Carrasco, R., Vila, M., & Martínez, L. (2007). Applying fuzzy data mining for soaring area selection. *Computational and ambient intelligence - Lecture Notes in Computer Science, 450,* 597-604, *ISSN: 0302-9743.*

Salguero, A., Araque, F., & Delgado, C. (2008). Data integration algorithm for data warehousing based on ontologies metadata. *The 8th International FLINS Conference on Computational Intelligence in Decision and Control (FLINS).* Madrid, Spain.

Salguero, A., Araque, F., & Delgado, C. (2008). Using ontology metadata for data warehousing. *The 10th Int. Conf. on Enterprise Information Systems (ICEIS).* Barcelona, Spain.

Samos, J., Saltor, F., Sistac, J., & Bardés, A. (1998). Database architecture for data ware-housing: An evolutionary approach. *Proceedings Int'l Conf. on Database and Expert Systems Applications* (pp.. 746-756). Vienna: In G. Quirchmayr et al. (Eds.): Springer-Verlag.

Sheth, A., & Larson, J. (1990). Federated database systems for managing distributed, heterogeneous and autonomous databases. *ACM Computing Surveys, 22*(3).

Thalhamer, M., Schrefl, M., & Mohania, M. (2001). Active data warehouses: Complementing OLAP with analysis rules. *Data & Knowledge Engineering, 39(3),* 241-269.

Vassiliadis, C., Quix, Y., Vassiliou, M., & Jarke, M. (2001). Data warehouse process management. Information System, *26.*

Chapter XII
Using Active Rules to Maintain Data Consistency in Data Warehouse Systems

Shi-Ming Huang

National Chung Cheng University, Taiwan

John Tait

Information Retrieval Faculty, Austria

Chun-Hao Su

National Chung Cheng University, Taiwan

Chih-Fong Tsai

National Central University, Taiwan

ABSTRACT

Data warehousing is a popular technology, which aims at improving decision-making ability. As the result of an increasingly competitive environment, many companies are adopting a "bottom-up" approach to construct a data warehouse, since it is more likely to be on time and within budget. However, multiple independent data marts/cubes can easily cause problematic data inconsistency for anomalous update transactions, which leads to biased decision-making. This research focuses on solving the data inconsistency problem and proposing a temporal-based data consistency mechanism (TDCM) to maintain data consistency. From a relative time perspective, we use an active rule (standard ECA rule) to monitor the user query event and use a metadata approach to record related information. This both builds relationships between the different data cubes, and allows a user to define a VIT (valid interval temporal) threshold to identify the validity of interval that is a threshold to maintain data consistency. Moreover, we propose a consistency update method to update inconsistent data cubes, which can ensure all pieces of information are temporally consistent.

INTRODUCTION

Background

Designing and constructing a data warehouse for an enterprise is a very complicated and iterative process since it involves aggregation of data from many different departments and extract, transform, load (ETL) processing (Bellatreche et al., 2001). Currently, there are two basic strategies to implementing a data warehouse, "top-down" and "bottom-up" (Shin, 2002), each with its own strengths, weaknesses, and using the appropriate uses.

Constructing a data warehouse system using the bottom-up approach will be more likely to be on time and within budget. But inconsistent and irreconcilable results may be transmitted from one data mart to the next due to independent data marts or data cubes (e.g. distinct updates time for each data cube) (Inmon, 1998). Thus, inconsistent data in the recognition of events may require a number of further considerations to be taken into account (Shin, 2002; Bruckner et. al, 2001; Song & Liu, 1995):

- **Data availability:** Typical update patterns for a traditional data warehouse on weekly or even monthly basis will delay discovery, so information is unavailable for knowledge workers or decision makers.
- **Data comparability:** In order to analyze from different perspectives, or even go a step further to look for more specific information, data comparability is an important issue .

Real-time updating in a data warehouse might be a solution which can enable data warehouses to react "just-in-time" and also provide the best consistency (Bruckner et al., 2001) (e.g. real-time data warehouse). But, not everyone needs or can benefit from a real-time data warehouse. In fact, it is highly possible that only a relatively small portion of the business community will realize a justifiable ROI (return on investment) from a real time data warehouse (Vandermay J., 2001). Real-time data warehouses are expensive to build, requiring a significantly higher level of support and significantly greater investment in infrastructure than a traditional data warehouse. In additional, real-time update will also require high time cost for response and huge storage space for aggregation.

As a result, it is desirable to find an alternative solution for data consistency in a data warehouse system (DWS) which can achieve near real-time outcome but does not require a high cost.

Motivation and Objective

Integrating active rules and data warehouse systems has been one of the most important treads in data warehousing (DM Review, 2001). Active rules have also been used in databases for several years (Paton & Daz, 1999; Roddick & Schrefl, 2000), and much research has been done in this field. It is possible to construct relations between different data cubes or even the data marts. However, anomalous updates could occur when each of the data marts has its own timestamp for obtaining the same data source. Therefore, problems with controlling data consistency in data marts/data cubes are raised.

There have been numerous studies discussing the maintenance of data cubes dealing with the space problem and retrieval efficiency, either by pre-computing a subset of the "possible group-bys" (Harinarayan et al., 1996; Gupta et al., 1997; Baralis et al., 1997), estimating the values of the group-bys using approximation (Gibbons & Matias, 1998; Acharya et al., 2000) or by using online aggregation techniques (Hellerstein et al., 1997; Gray et al., 1996). However, these solutions still focus on single data cube consistency, not on the overall data warehouse environment's respective. Thus, each department in the enterprise will still face problems of temporal inconsistency over time.

In the paper, we seek to develop temporal-based data consistency by proposing a Temporal-based Data Consistency Mechanism (TDCM) as an alternative solution for data consistency in data warehouse systems (DWS). Through our TDCM, we can ensure that all related information retrieved from a DWS in on a consistent time basis. Thus, this mechanism can enhance data quality an potentially increase real-world competitiveness.

RELATED WORK

Active Rule and Data Warehouse Integration

Active rules have been used in databases for several years (Paton & Dazo, 1999). Most active database rules are defined by production rules and often an event-based rule language, in which a rule is triggered by an event such as the insertion, deletion or modification of data. The event-condition-action (ECA) model for active database is widely used, in which the general form of rules is as follows:

On event
If condition
Then action

The rule is triggered when the event occurs. Once the rule is triggered then, the condition is checked. If the condition is satisfied, the action is executed. Ariel (Hanson, 1996), STRIP (Adelberg et al., 1997), Ode (Arlein et al., 1995), and HiPAC (Paton & Dazo, 1999) are all systems of this type. The aim of an active database is to (1) perform automatic monitoring of conditions defined over the database state (2) take action (possibly subject to timing constraints) when the state of the underlying database changes (transaction-triggered processing).

Active rules have also been integrated into data warehouse architecture recently to provide further analysis, real-time reaction, or materialized views (Thalhammer et al., 2001; Huang et al., 2000; Adelberg, 1997). Also recently data warehouse vendors have concentrated on real-time reaction and response in actual applications, in their active data warehouse systems (Dorinne, 2001).

View Maintenance and Temporal Consistency

Materialized Data Consistency of View Maintenance

Many researchers have studied the view maintenance problem in general (Yang et al., 2000; Ling et al., 1999; Zhuge et al., 1995; Gupta & Mumick, 1995) and a survey of the view maintenance literature can be found in Gupta & Mumick, (1995; Ciferri, 2001), where views are defined as a subset of relational algebraic expressions.

Maintaining the consistency of materialized views in a data warehouse environment is much more complex than maintaining consistency in single database systems (Ciferri, 2001). Following the aforementioned literature, we separate view maintenance approaches into two parts: "Incremental Maintenance" and "Self-Maintenance".

"Incremental Maintenance" is a popular approach to maintaining materialized view consistency (Saeki et al., 2002; Ling et al., 1999), and it is characterized by access through the base data sources. In contrast, the characteristic of "Self-Maintenance" is maintaining materialized view without access to the base data (Ciferri et al., 2001), because base data comes from sources that may be inaccessible. Furthermore, it may be very expensive or time-consuming to query the databases. Thus, to minimize or simply not to perform external access on those information sources during the maintenance process represents an important incremental view maintenance issue (Amo, 2000; Yang et al., 2000). Table 1, illustrates there two materialized view maintenance approaches.

Table 1. Materialized view maintenance approaches

Materialized View Maintenance Approaches	
Approach	**Features**
Incremental Maintenance (Saeki, 2002) (Moro, 2001) (Ling, 1999)	Maintain a materialized view in response to modifications to the base relations. Applicable to nearly all types of database updates. It is more efficient to apply this algorithm to the view than to re-compute the view from the database.
Self-Maintenance (Amo, 2000) (Yang, 2000) (Samtani, 1999)	Maintain the materialized views at the DW without access to the base relations. (e.g. by replicating all or parts of the base data at the DW or utilizing the key constraints information.)

Temporal Consistency

The term "temporal consistency" comes from Real-Time DB systems (Heresar et. al, 1999), where the value of objects must correctly reflect the state of environment. Previous work (Ramamritham, 1993; Xiong et al., 1996; Tomic et al., 2000) has defined temporal consistency in real-time database systems (RTDBS) as follows. An RTDBS must maintain absolute consistency, that is, any changes in the real world should be promptly reflected in the database. If the age of a data object is within some specified threshold, called the absolute threshold "Ta", the data object is absolutely consistent. An RTDBS must also maintain relative consistency, so that the data presents a consistent snapshot of the real world at a given time. Relative consistency requires that the set of data objects is considered to be relatively consistent if the dispersion of ages is smaller than a relative threshold "Tr".

Temporal consistency was also defined using validity intervals in a real-time database to address the consistency issue between the real world state and the reflected value in the database (Ramamritham, 1993). Temporal data can be further classified into base data and derived data. Base data objects import the view of the outside environment. In contrast derived data object can be derived from possibly multiple base/derived data (e.g. data warehouse repository).

In this research, we focus on maintaining data consistency within a temporal-based consistency approach when users send a query from DWS. Mumick (1997) proposes a method of maintaining an aggregate view (called summary-delta table method), and uses it to maintain summary tables in the data warehouse. Like many other incremental view maintenance techniques, we use a "delta" table to record insertion and deletion in the source data. We also combine active rule and temporal consistency concepts and adjusted these methods to construct a Temporal-based Data Consistency Mechanism (TDCM), through which we are able to simultaneously update related data cubes from different data marts.

TEMPORAL-BASED DATA CONSISTENCY

Overview

The proposed TDCM is an alternative solution for data warehouse system (DWS), which uses active rules to maintain data consistency. Because temporal consistency is often ensured either by extended use of time stamps, or by validity status (Bruckner et al., 2001), we let knowledge workers or decision makers define a VIT (Valid Interval Temporal) as a threshold in this mechanism. This ensures that every piece of information captured from a DWS is delivered in a temporally correct manner. We define Temporal-based Data Consistency as following:

Definition: *Temporal-based Data Consistency (TDC)*

The set the dispersion of data object remains within a specified threshold, *VIT.* The threshold VIT reflects the temporal requirements of the application. The dispersion of two data objects x_i and x_j, denoted as $T(x_i, x_j)$ is defined as $T(x_i, x_j) = | t(x_i) - t(x_j)$, where $t(x_i)$ and $t(x_j)$ are the time-stamps of two objects, x_i and x_j. Thus, the set S, of data objects is said to have Temporal-based Data Consistency if:

$$\forall x_i, x_j \in S, T(x_i, x_j) \le VIT(S).$$

Temporal-based Data Consistency Mechanism

Data Warehouse Event and Active Rule Syntax

In a data warehouse environment, multi-dimensional query events can be classified into dimension events and measurement events (Huang et al., 2000; Gray et al., 1996). Figure 1 illustrates the event classification in multi-dimensional query and data consistency.

Figure 2 shows our active rule syntax, which includes two parts: a rule body and a coupling model. The rule body describes the ECA base active rules, while the coupling model describes how the active rules can be integrated into the database query. The rule body is composed of three main components: a query predicate, an optional condition, and an action. The query predicate controls rule triggering; and the condi-

Figure 2: Active rule syntax

```
Rule Body:
Define Rule ::= <rule-name>
On ::= <query-predicate>
[ if <conditions> := true ]
then
[evaluate query-commalist]
execute ::= <action>
query-predicate ::= event [,event [,event]]
event ::= drill down | roll up | push | slice|
pull | dice | select| insert| delete| update
alter | drop
condition ::= query-commalist
query-commalist ::= query [,query]*
query ::= table-expression
Coupling Model:
Query_coupling = Same | Separate
EC_coupling   = Before | After,
CA_coupling   = Immediate | Deferred,
Execute_mode  = Repeat | Once,
[precedes <rule_names> ]
[follows < rule_names> ]
```

Figure 1. Event classification

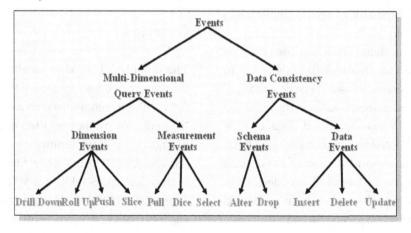

tion specifies an additional predicate that must be true if a triggered rule is to automatically execute its action. Active rules are triggered by database state transitions – that is, by execution of operation blocks. After a given transition, those rules whose transition predicate holds with respect to the effect of the transition are triggered. The coupling models give database designers the flexibility of deciding how the rule query is integrated within the Multi-Dimensional Query (MDQ) (Gingras, & Lakshmanan, 1998).

There are five different execution attributes to determine the semantic of an active rule, as follows:

Query_coupling: treating the execution of a rule as a query in DWS, e.g. a rule query. If the Query_coupling is set to 'same', then the MDQ is committed only when the RQ (Rule Query) and DQ (Data Query) are both committed. If the Query_coupling is set to 'separate', then the MDQ commitment will depend only on the DQ. This suggests that the Query_coupling should be set to 'Separate' when the active rule does not have any effect on the DQ, in order to enhance the system performance by reducing query execution time.

EC_coupling: defining the execution sequence of the event and condition part for a relational active rule. The 'before' EC_coupling means that the rule condition is evaluated immediately before the DQ is executed. The 'after' EC_coupling means that the rule condition is evaluated after the DQ is in the prepare-to-commit state.

CA_coupling: presenting the execution sequence of the condition and action part for an active rule. The 'immediate' CA_coupling means that the rule action is executed immediately after the rule condition is evaluated and satisfied. The rule action executed after DQ is in the prepare-to-commit state, when CA_coupling is specified to 'defer'.

Execute_mode: the triggered rule will automatically be deactivated after it is committed, when its Execute_mode is specified as 'once'.

On the other hand, the rule is always active if its Execute_mode is specified to 'repeat'.

Precedes_Follows: The optional 'precedes' and 'follows' clauses are used to induce a partial ordering on the set of defined rules. If a rule r1 specifies a rule r2 in its 'precedes' list, or if r2 specifies r1 in its 'follows' list, then r1 is higher than r2 in the ordering.

Temporal-Based Data Consistency and Active Rule Integration

Active rules have been integrated into data warehouse architecture to maintain data consistency in the materialized views (Adelberg, 1997). Using temporal perspective, anomalies updated to obtain timely information by end-users' queries will cause data inconsistencies in daily transactions. In this research, we focus on temporal-based data consistency as defined previously. according to which, the TDC Evaluation Protocol is described as in Figure 3.

The following example (Figure 4) is of integrated active rule and temporal-based data consistency evaluation protocol to maintain data consistency. When a user is browsing Data CubeA and using a drill-down OLAP operation (In "Months" level and Measurement<= "20"),

Figure 3. TDC Evaluation protocol

```
Temporal-based Data Consistency Evaluation Protocol
    //Set the timestamp of object xᵢ, t(xᵢ)
    //Set the timestamp of object xⱼ, t(xⱼ)
    For each related object
IF t(xᵢ) = t(xⱼ) THEN
//Temporal-based Data Consistency
ELSE
    IF |t(xᵢ) = t(xⱼ)| <= VIT (Valid Interval Temporal) THEN
    //Temporal-based Data Consistency
    ELSE
IF (xᵢ) = t(xⱼ) THEN
        Consistency Update xⱼ From t(xⱼ) to t(xᵢ)
    ELSE
        Consistency Update xᵢ From t(xᵢ) to t(xⱼ)
//Temporal-based Data Consistency
    END IF
    END IF
END IF
```

the active rule Analysis-Rule1 will be triggered for rule evaluation. If the user needs to retrieve more detail or related information from other data cubes, TDCM will be launched to maintain data consistency. Through the timestamp of each data cube and VIT threshold, we are able to decide which data cube needs to be updated.

Active Rule Activation Model

This section discusses our active rule activation model by extending the model specified in (Paton & Daz, 1999; Huang et al., 2000) which shows how a set of rules is treated at runtime. The execution sequence of data query and triggered rules will influence the result and correctness of active rules. The coupling model provides more semantics for rule triggering and execution. Our temporal-based data consistency mechanism working process is shown in Figure 5.

- The *Signaling* phase includes to the appearance of an event occurrence caused by an event source.
- The *Triggering* phase takes the events produced and triggers the corresponding rules. The association of a rule with its event occurrence forms a rule instantiation.
- The *CE (Condition Evaluation): The true* phase evaluates the condition of the triggered rules which are satisfied.
- The *RE (Relation Evaluation): The true* phase evaluates the relations between different data objects that have existed or not.
- The *IE (Inconsistency): The true* phase detects a data inconsistency with related data object caused by a user anomaly updating a daily transaction. It will be considered inconsistent if the dispersion interval of two data objects is smaller then VIT threshold.
- The *Scheduling* phase indicates how the rule conflict set is processed. In this model,

Figure 4. Active rule for data consistency within TDCM

```
Define Rule Analysis-Rule1
//E (Event)
On dimensional drill down
//C (Condition)
If {Level = "Months" and
Dimensions = ("Product" , "Years"),
and Measurement = "TQuantity", and Measurement<= "20", and
Select Years, Months, Product, TQuantity
From CubeA
Where Product = "ALL" and MONTH>= "7" or MONTH <= "12"}
//A (Action)
then execute {
        // Temporal-based Data Consistency Evaluation Protocol
        // Set t1 and t2 are the timestamp of CubeA and CubeB
        IF | t1-t2 | <= 1 (Month) Then
        Retrieve "CubeB"
        ELSE
          IF t1 > t2 then
            Consistency_Update (CubeB to t1)
        ELSE
            Consistency_Update (CubeA to t2)
          END IF
          END IF}
Coupling Model:
  Query_coupling = Separate
  EC_coupling = After
  CA_coupling = Deferred
  Execute_Mode = Once
```

Figure 5. TDCM working process

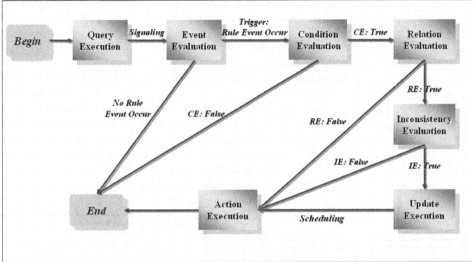

rules are partially ordered. For any two rules, one rule can be specified as having higher priority than an other rule without ordering being required.

The semantics of the data warehouse active rule syntax determines how rule processing will take place at run-time once a set of rules has been defined. It also determines how rules will interact with the arbitrary data warehouse event and queries that are submitted by users and application programs. Even for relatively small rule sets, rule behavior can be complex and unpredictable, so precise execution semantics is essential (Huang et al, 2000). Figure 7 presents the detailed rule activation processing flow of our system. The detail rule activation process flow is as seen in Figure 6.

Figure 6. The detail rule activation process flow.

Step1: Query coupling evaluation:
    If *Query_coupling* is *Separate*, the system will submit the triggered rule to QM (query manager) as a new query. Otherwise, the system will proceed with the following steps.
Step 2: Event-Condition coupling evaluation-- *Before*
    2a. Reasoning rules, which its *EC_coupling* is equal to *Before*.
    2b. If the condition evaluation result is true, then the following two possible situations may happen.
        2b.1. The action part will be executed immediately if its *CA_coupling* is equal to *Immediate*.
        2b.2. The action part will be saved into a queue if its *CA_coupling* is equal to *Deferred*.
    2c. Repeating the steps 2a, 2b until no more rules are reasoned by step 2a.
Step 3: Executing the data query.
Step 4: Executing the queued rules, which are stored by step 2b.2.
Step 5: Event-Condition evaluation--*After:*
    5a. Reasoning rules, which its *EC_coupling* is equal to *After*.
    5b. If the condition evaluation result is true, there are the following two possible situations.
        5b.1. The action part will be executed immediately if its *CA_coupling* is equal to *Immediate*.
        5b.2. The action part will be saved into a queue if its *CA_coupling* is equal to *Deferred*.
    5c. Repeating steps 5a, 5b until no more rules is reasoned by step 5a.
Step 6: Executing queued rules, which are stored by step 5b.2.
Step 7: Committing the query if and only if all sub-queries are committed.

Figure 7. Process flow of rule activation

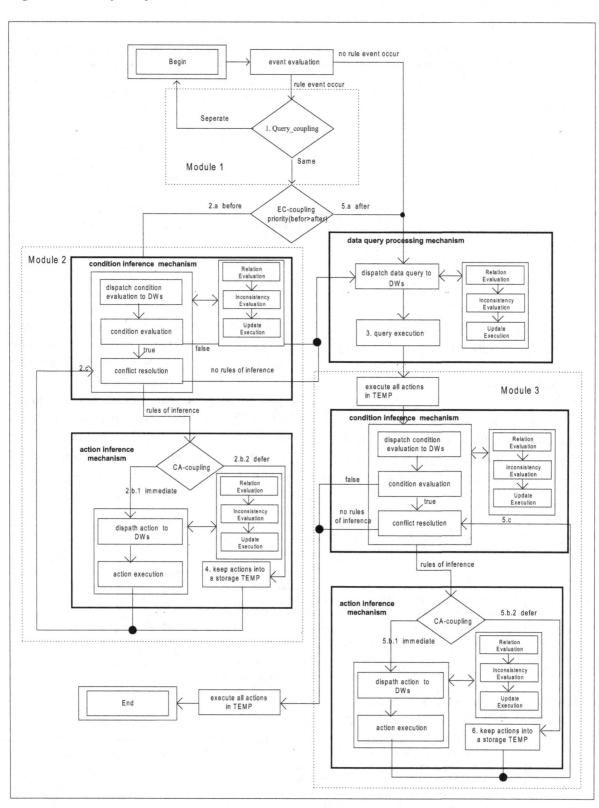

Taxonomy for Situations of Temporally-Based Data Consistency Mechanism

We can identify several possible different situations for the Temporally-based Data Consistency Mechanism. We can have at least four distinct situations: 1. timestamp of all data cubes are the same; 2. timestamp of one data cube is expired; 3. timestamp of one data cube is new; 4. all of the timestamps of the data cubes are different from each other .

Consider that there are three data cubes (Data Cube1, Data Cube2, and Data Cube3) and three different times (t1, t2, and t3). Suppose t1 > t2 > t3 and the browsing sequence is Data Cube1—Data Cube2—Data Cube3. Thus, we can classify these events into several different situations:

In situation1, the timestamp of all three data cubes are the same ("t1"). Thus, we do not have to update any data cube. According to our definition, they are temporally consistent.

In situation2, the timestamp of Data Cube1 (t1) is not equal to Data Cube2 (t2), so Data Cube2 and Data Cube3 have temporal-based data consistency. As a result, when user browsing Data Cube1 and Data Cube2, our mechanism will update Data Cube1 (from t1 to t2). Thus our mechanism will update once for temporal-based data consistency.

In situation3, the timestamp of Data Cube1 is equal to Data Cube2 (TDC), so Data Cube2 and Data Cube3 are inconsistent. As a result, when users are browsing Data Cube1 and Data Cube2, they do not have to update; but when users are browsing Data Cube2 and Data Cube3, our mechanism will update both Data Cube2 (from t2 to t3) and Data Cube1 (from t2 to t3). Thus, our mechanism will update twice for temporal-based data consistency.

Situation 1. (t1, t1, t1)

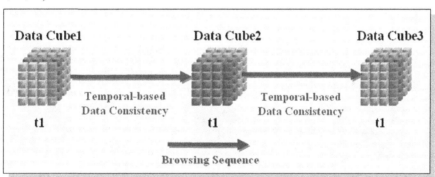

Situation 2. (t1, t2, t2)

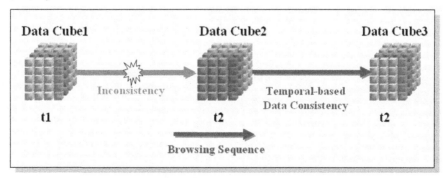

Situation 3. (t2, t2, t3)

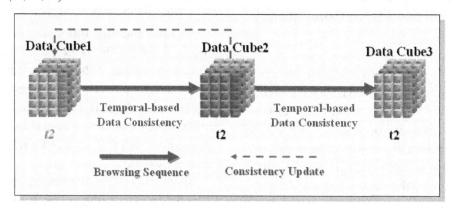

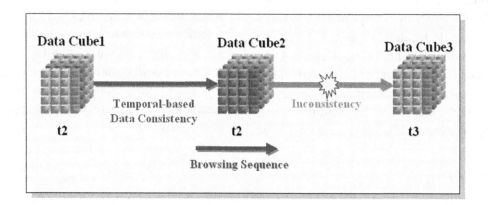

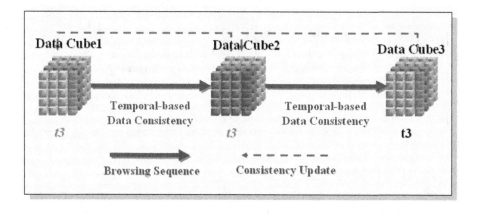

Situation 4. (t1, t2, t3)

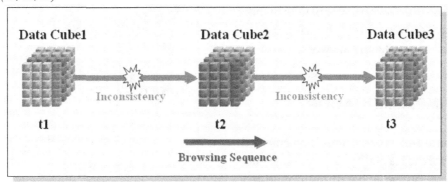

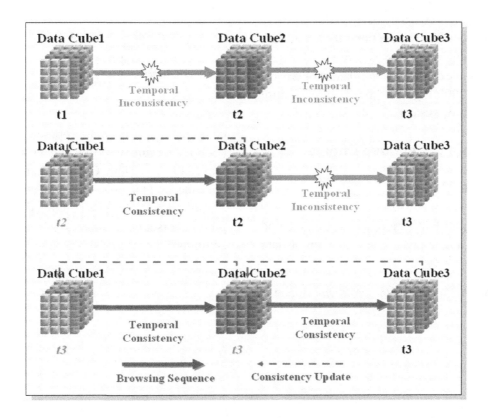

In situation4, the timestamps of all three data cubes are different, so when a user is browsing Data Cube1 and Data Cube2, our mechanism will update Data Cube1 (from t1 to t2); when a user is browsing Data Cube2 and Data Cube3, our mechanism will update both Data Cube1 (from t2 to t3) and Data Cube (from t2 to t3). Thus, our mechanism will update 3 times for temporal-based data consistency.

Summary

In this section, we introduce a methodology to develop the TDCM. Through active rule and metadata repositories, we can provide consistent data to knowledge workers or decision makers when they query a data warehouse system. Using active rules to maintain temporal-based data consistency of stored facts does not guarantee a timely, correct view of the modeled real world. But it does ensure that every piece of information captured by a data warehouse system is provided in a temporally consistent framework.

SYSTEM IMPLEMENTATION

In this section, a prototype system is implemented to demonstrate the feasibility to our mechanism. Our prototype system is based on a multi-tier environment. The client is an active cube browser system, which is coded by using JDK (Java Development Kit). The middle tier is the active data warehouse engine, which is written in Visual Basic. The cube database is designed in Microsoft SQL Server 2000. Figure 8 shows the architecture of the prototype system.

Active Data Warehouse Engine

Data Cube Manager

Our Data Cube Manager provides an easy method to generate a data cube. The algorithm of data

Figure 9. Data cube generation algorithm

```
/* Subprogram */
Procedure AF(M1,M2,.....Mm) {
    For x← 0 to 2^N-1
    do
       S(x) ← S(x) + Aggregation Function (measurements)
    } // end of AF procedure
Procedure Generate_SQL(){
       for i←0 to 2^N-2
       do

          Select{ S(i) }, { AF(M1,M2,.....Mm) }

          From Data_Base

          Group BY S(i)

          Union
          Select{ S(2^N-1) }, { AF(M1,M2,.....Mm) }
                From Data_Base
                Group BY S(2^N-1)
} //end of Generate_SQL Procedure
```

cube creation we use was proposed by Gray et al. (1996). There are two kinds of data, which will be moved to our system. One is dimension data for the cube, and the other is fact data for the cube.

Creating a data cube requires generating the power set (set of all subsets) of the aggregation columns. Since the cube is an aggregation opera-

Figure 8. Architecture of the prototype system

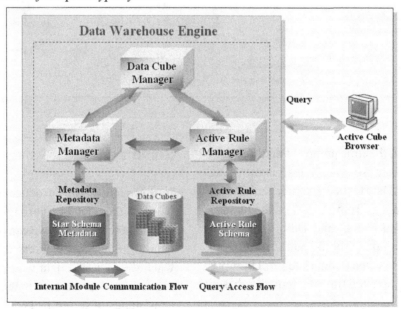

tion, it makes sense to externalize it by overloading the SQL GROUP BY operator. In fact, the cube is a relational operator, with GROUP BY and ROLL UP as degenerate forms of the operator. Overloading the SQL GROUP BY can conveniently specify by overloading the SQL GROUP BY. If there are N dimensions and M measurements in the data cube, there will be 2N – 1 super-aggregate values. If the cardinality of the N attributes are D1, D2..., DN then the cardinality of the result of cube relation is $\Pi(Di + 1)$. Figure 9 shows the fact data algorithm.

Active Rule Manager

The active rule manager is specified the rules of data cube, and the grammar of active rules in our system follows the standard ECA (Event, Condition, and Action) rule. We designed an Active Rule Wizard, which is included with a friendly user interface and takes the designer through four easy steps to construct an active rule. Figure 10 shows the active rule construction process.

Two Metadata Repositories in the Implementation

The Metadata Repository and the Metadata Manager are responsible for storing schema (Meta-Model) and providing metadata management. Thus there are two metadata repositories in our system, as follows:

Figure 10. Active rule construction process

(a)

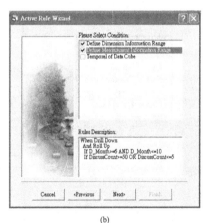

(b)

(c)

(d)

- Star schema metadata

The most popular design technique used to implement a data warehouse is the star schema. The star schema structure takes advantage of typical decision support queries by using one central fact table for the subject area and many dimension tables containing de-normalized descriptions of the facts. After the fact table is created, OLAP tools can be used to pre-aggregate commonly accessed information. Figure 11 displays the OMT model of star schema metadata.

- Active rule schema metadata

Many useful semantics are included in the proposed active rule schema metadata. The active rule schema is in two parts: a rule body table and a coupling model table. The rule body table is used to describe the ECA base active rules schema and the coupling model table is used to describe how the active rules can be integrated into the MDQ. Figure 12 presents an OMT model of an active rule schema.

Active Data Cube Browser

The active cube browser provides an OLAP function for user queries. When users browse cubes,

Figure 11. OMT model of the star schema

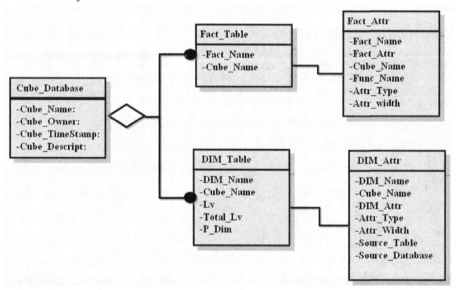

Figure 12. OMT model of an active rule schema

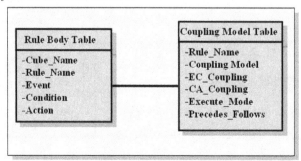

Figure 13. Active cube browser

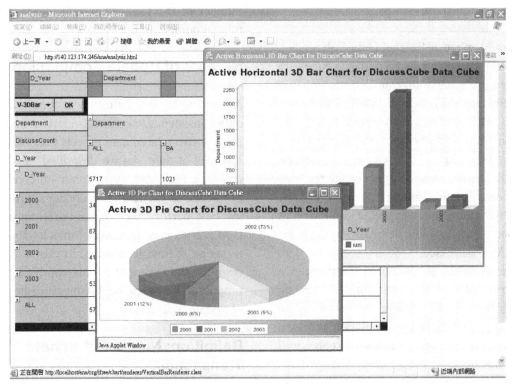

several OLAP events (e.g. Drill-Down, Roll-Up, Slice, Dice...) will be triggered. The data warehouse engine detects the event and employs an active rule mechanism to go one step further to analyze and return a warning to the active cube browser. At the same time, our mechanism will also follow a consistency rule to automatically maintain temporal consistency.

Moreover, in order to represent the query result in an easily understood manner, we use the adopting JFreeChart API from an open-source organization called JFreeChart. Our active cube browser provides several charts (e.g. Pie Chart, 3D Pie Chart, Horizontal Bar Chart, Vertical Bar Chart...) for clearer comparison analysis. Figure 13 shows the Data Warehouse Engine detection when a dimension drill down event occurs, the rule of DiscussCube is triggered to browse another cube and be shown in the Active Frame.

SYSTEM EVALUATION

System Simulation

Previous studies (Song & Liu, 1995) have considered only a general measure of temporal consistency, called %Inconsistency, which indicates the percentage of transactions which are either absolutely or relatively inconsistent. In this simulation, we use the number of inconsistencies to measure temporal consistency in top-down and bottom-up architecture.

Definition: Number of Inconsistencies

The number of all possible data inconsistencies due to user anomalies in updating transactions.

We used the following parameters in this simulation for purposes stated:

- The Number of Related Data Cubes ($|N|$): To decide how many related data cubes are used in a simulation run.
- Valid Interval Temporal ($|VIT|$): The threshold value specifies the temporal-based data consistency of data required by the DWS. The time interval of each two data objects with greater then VIT is considered out-of-date. In our simulation, we give VIT the same value of 1. We expected the number of inconsistency would be smaller as the value of VIT increased.
- The Number of update transactions in a period ($|U|$): The user anomalies update transactions to retrieve the newest data from the DWS. In our simulation, we use a randomizer to decide which data cubes will be updated.
- Simulation Run Periods ($|P|$): Total run period in our simulation.
- Simulation Times ($|T|$): The total execution time of our simulation.

In each series of experiments, we started to simulate the number of inconsistencies with a transitional Bottom-up and Top-Down data warehouse architecture. In the Bottom-up data warehouse architecture, given $|N|$ is 10, $|VIT|$ is 1, $|U|$ 3, and $|P|$ is 10. The objective of our TDCM is to avoid possible inconsistent situations under the Bottom-up architecture.

In the Top-down data warehouse architecture, we gave the same parameters for the simulation program. The only difference between Bottom-up and Top-down is that Top-down architecture has a reload period (set reload period is 3) which can centrally refresh the data warehouse after a specified period.

As time proceeds, the number of inconsistencies will increase with Top-down or Bottom-up architectures, a problem our TDCM seeks to

resolve. With detailed investigation, we show the number of inconsistencies will increase as the related number of data cubes $|N|$ increases.

Number of Update Comparsion

According to our definition of temporal-based data consistency, we use a consistent update for each of two related data objects that are considered out-of-date. As we described in chapter1, real-time updates have no temporal consistency problems, so the real-time update approach has the best performance in temporal consistency. However its enormous cost limits its applicability as an optimum solution. In this section, we compare the real-time update approach and the proposed TDCM approach to measure the number of update transaction.

Definition: Number of Update Transaction

All possible consistency updating transaction of data objects permute with different timestamps.

We used the following parameters in this simulation for the purposes stated:

- The Number of Related Data Cubes ($|N|$): To decided how many related data cubes in a simulation run.
- Valid Interval Temporal ($|VIT|$): The threshold value specifies the temporally-based data consistency of data required by the DWS. The time interval of each two data objects with greater then VIT is considered out-of-date. In this simulation, we give VIT the same value of 0 for the worst case situation.

Considering the worst case, $L = \{X_1, X_2, X_3, ..., X_n\}$ is a set of data objects and T_{now} is the current time. $T = \{t_1, t_2, t_3, ..., t_n\}$ ($t_n > t_{n-1} > t_{n-2} ... > t_1$) is a set of timestamps where the user browsing sequence will be followed by a sequence, such as:

$X_1 \rightarrow X_2 \rightarrow X_3 .... \rightarrow X_n$. Our program simulates all possible situations to calculate the number of update transactions in the real-time and TDCM approaches.

To contrast the real-time update and TDCM approach, we use an easily compared and analyzed metric %Update Number (specific weight) to illustrate the results. The simulation results are shown in Figure 14:

Figure 14 shows that under the worst case situation, if data cube relationship is in a specified range (less than 7), our TDCM approach is better than the real-time update. Considering the other situations, including 1 to m relations or given a VIT threshold greater than 0, we expected the number of update transaction will be decreased. Figure 15 shows the simulation result under VIT=1 situation.

Because we use a system simulation to evaluate our effectiveness, we not only compare the number of inconsistencies in the Top-down and Bottom-up architectures, but also calculate the number of update transactions for real-time update and for our TDCM approach. We also found the point to reach temporal-based data consistency is on VIT threshold setting. A useful and suitable VIT can not only maintain temporal-based data consistency easily but also greatly reduce the update time cost.

CONCLUSION

In this research, we have defined temporal-based data consistency in a data warehouse system and established a TDCM to maintain data consis-

Figure 14(a). Simulation result 7

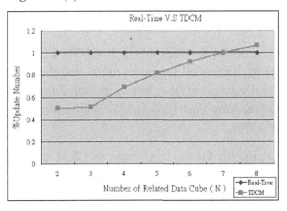

Figure 14(b). Simulation result 8

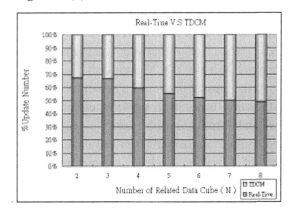

Figure 15(a). Simulation result 9

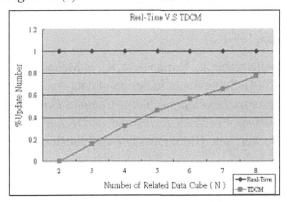

Figure 15(b). Simulation result 10

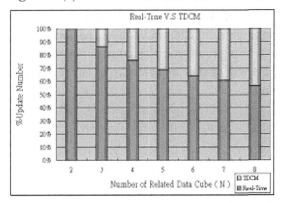

Table 2. Summary compare result

	DWS with TDCM	**Traditional DWS**
Update Cost	Less	More
Data Quality	High	Low
Data Consistency	Temporally-based	Inconsistent
Availability	Available	Partially Available
Comparability	Comparable	Partially Comparable

tency through an active rule. We implemented our mechanism into a data warehouse system to evaluate the correctness of the proposed TDCM, with the results indicating that TDCM can systematically detect and solve data inconsistencies in a data warehouse system. Finally we use simulation method to evaluate the effectiveness of our TDCM approach. The result indicates that, in contrast to real-time update, our approach incurs a high cost when the relation hierarchy of data cubes is within a specified range. In particular, determining a suitable VIT threshold is the most important issue of concern. Table 2 summarizes a comparison result between traditional DWS approach and our TDCM approach.

At the present time our implementation is not sufficiently efficient to perform effectively on real scale problems with rapidly changing data and complex constraints between data. Finding ways of improving efficiency is therefore a major focus of our current work.

Our current results apply only to a single data warehouse situation. Although such situations are common in practice, future practical applications on the internet will involve access to multiple heterogeneous data warehouses and data sources exhibiting more complex consistency problems. This will also be an objective of our research in future.

REFERENCE

Acharya, S., Gibbons, P. B., & Poosala, V. (2000). Congressional samples for approximate answering of group-by queries. *Proceedings of ACM SIG-MOD International Conference on Management of Data*, (pp. 487-498).

Adelberg, B., Garcia-Molina, H., & Widom, J. (1997). The STRIP rule system for efficiently maintaining derived data. *Proceedings of the ACM SIGMOD, International Conference on Management of Data*, (pp. 147-158).

Amo, S. D., & Alves, M. H. F. (2000). Efficient maintenance of temporal data warehouses. *Proceedings of the International Database Engineering and Applications Symposium*, (pp. 188-196).

Arlein, R., Gava, J., Gehani, N., & Lieuwen, D. (1995). Ode 4.2 (Ode <EOS>) user manual. *Technical report*. AT&T Bell Labs.

Baralis, E., Paraboschi, S., & Teniente, E. (1997). Materialized view selection in a multidimensional database. *Proceedings. of VLDB Conference*, (pp. 156-165).

Bellatreche, L., Karlapalem, K., & Mohania, M. (2001). Some issues in design of data warehouse systems. *Developing Quality Complex Database Systems: Practices, Techniques, and Technologies*, Becker, S.A. (Ed.), Ideas Group Publishing.

Bruckner, R.M., List, B., Schiefer, J., & Tjoa, A. M. (2001). Modeling temporal consistency in data warehouses. *Proceedings of the 12th International Workshop on Database and Expert Systems Applications*, (pp. 901-905).

Ciferri, C. D. A., & Souza, F. F. (2001). Materialized views in data warehousing environments. *Proceedings of the XXI International Conference of the Chilean Computer Science Society*, (pp. 3-12).

Gibbons, P. B., & Matias, Y. (1998). New sampling-based summary statistics for improving approximate query answers. *Proceeding of ACM SIGMOD International Conference on Management of Data*, (pp. 331-342).

Gingras, F., & Lakshmanan, L. (1998). nD-SQL: A multi-dimensional language for interoperability and OLAP. *Proceedings of the 24th VLDB Conference*, (pp. 134-145).

Gray, J., Bosworth, A., Layman, A., & Pirahesh, H. (1996). Data cube: A relational aggregation operator generalizing group-by, cross-tab, and sub-totals. *Proceeding of the 12th International Conference on Data Engineering*, (pp. 152-159).

Griffoen, J., Yavatkar, R., & Finkel, R. (1994). Extending the dimensions of consistency: Spatial consistency and sequential segments. *Technical Report*, University of Kentucky.

Gupta, A., & Mumick, I. S. (1995). Maintenance of materialized views: Problems, techniques, and applications. *IEEE Data Engineering Bulletin, Special Issue on Materialized Views and Warehousing, 18*(2), 3-18.

Gupta, H., Harinarayan, V., Rajaraman, A., & Ullman, J. (1997). Index selection for OLAP. *Proceedings of the International Conference on Data Engineering*, (pp. 208-219).

Hanson, E.N. (1996). The design and implementation of the ariel active database rule system. *IEEE Transaction on Knowledge and Data Engineering, 8*(1),157-172.

Harinarayan, V., Rajaraman, A., & Ullman, J. D. (1996). Implementing data cubes efficiently. *Proceeding of ACM SIGMOD Conference*, (pp. 205-216).

Hellerstein, J.M., Haas, P.J., & Wang, H. (1997). Online aggregation. *Proceedings of ACM SIGMOD Conference*, (pp. 171–182).

Haisten, M. (1999, June). Real-time data warehouse. *DM Review.*

Huang, S. M., Hung, Y. C., & Hung, Y. M. (2000). Developing an active data warehouse System. *Proceeding of 17th International Conference on Data and Information for the Coming Knowledge Millennium.*

Inmon, W. H. (1998, December). Information management: Charting the course. *DM Review.*

Ling, T. W., & Sze, E. K. (1999). Materialized View Maintenance Using Version Numbers. *Proceedings of the 6th International Conference on Database Systems for Advanced Applications*, 263-270.

Moro, G., & Sartori, C. (2001). Incremental maintenance of multi-source views. *Proceedings of the 12th Australasian Database Conference*, (pp. 13-20).

Mumick, I. S., Quass, D., & Mumick, B. S. (1997). Maintenance of data cubes and summary tables in a warehouse. *Proceeding of ACM SIGMOD Conference*, (pp. 100-111).

Paton, N.W. & Daz, O. (1999). Active database systems. *ACM Computing Surveys, 31*(1), 63-103.

Ramamritham, K. (1993). Real-time databases. *International Journal of Distributed and Parallel Databases, 1*(2), 199-226.

Roddick, J.F., & Schrefl, M. (2000). Towards an accommodation of delay in temporal active databases. *Proceedings of the 11ᵗʰ International Conference on Australasian Database Conference*, (pp. 115-119).

Samtani, S., Kumar, V., & Mohania, M. (1999). Self maintenance of multiple views in data warehousing. *Proceedings of the International Conference on Information and knowledge management*, (pp. 292-299).

Shin, B. (2002). A case of data warehousing project management. *Information and Management*, *39*(7), 581-592.

Song, X., & Liu, J. (1995). Maintaining temporal consistency: Pessimistic vs. optimistic concurrency control. *IEEE Transactions on Knowledge and Data Engineering*, *7*(5), 786-796.

Thalhammer, T., Schrefl, M., & Mohania, M. (2001). Active data warehouses: Complementing OLAP with analysis rules. *Data and Knowledge Engineering*, *39*(3), 241-269.

Torp, K., Jensen, C. S., & Snodgrass, R. T. (2000). Effective time stamping in databases. *Journal of Very Large Database*, *8*(3), 267-288.

Xiong, M., Stankovic, J., Rammritham, K. Towsley, D., & Sivasankaran, R. (1996). Maintaining temporal consistency: Issues and algorithms. *Proceeding of the 1ˢᵗ International Workshop on Real-Time Databases*, (pp. 1-6).

Zhuge, Y., Garcia-Molina, H., Hammer, J., & Widom, J. (1995). View maintenance in a warehousing environment. *Proceedings of the ACM SIGMOD International Conference on Management of Data*, (pp. 316-327).

Zhug,e Y., Molina, H. G., & Wiener, J. (1998). Consistency algorithms for multi-source warehouse view maintenance. *Journal of Distributed and Parallel Databases*, *6*(1), 7-40.

Chapter XIII
Distributed Approach to Continuous Queries with kNN Join Processing in Spatial Telemetric Data Warehouse

Marcin Gorawski
Silesian Technical University, Poland

Wojciech Gębczyk
Silesian Technical University, Poland

ABSTRACT

This chapter describes realization of distributed approach to continuous queries with kNN join process-ing in the spatial telemetric data warehouse. Due to dispersion of the developed system, new structural members were distinguished: the mobile object simulator, the kNN join processing service, and the query manager. Distributed tasks communicate using JAVA RMI methods. The kNN queries (k Nearest Neighbour) joins every point from one dataset with its k nearest neighbours in the other dataset. In our approach we use the Gorder method, which is a block nested loop join algorithm that exploits sorting, join scheduling, and distance computation filtering to reduce CPU and I/O usage.

INTRODUCTION

With expansion of location-aware technologies such as the GPS (Global Positioning System) and growing popularity and accessibility of the mobile communication, location-aware data management becomes a significant problem in the mobile computing systems. Mobile devices become much more available with concurrent growth of their computational capabilities. It is expected that future mobile applications will require scalable architecture that will be able to process very large and quickly growing number of mobile objects, and to evaluate compound queries over their locations (Yiu, Papdias, Mamoulis, Tao, 2006).

The paper describes realization of distributed approach to the *Spatial Location and Telemetric Data Warehouse* (SDW(l/t)), which bases on the *Spatial Telemetric Data Warehouse* (STDW)), which consist of telemetric data containing information about water, gas, heat and electricity consumption (Gorawski, Wróbel, 2005). DSDW(l/t) (*Distributed Spatial Location and Telemetric Data Warehouse*) is supplied with datasets from *Integrated Meter Reading* (IMR) data system and by mobile objects location.

Integrated Meter Reading data system enables communication between medium meters and telemetric database system. Using GPRS or SMS technology, measurements from meters located on a wide geographical area are transferred to database, where they are processed and put forward for further analysis.

The SDW(l/t) supports making tactical decisions about size of medium productivity on the base of short-termed consumption predictions. Predictions are calculated basing on data stored in a data warehouse by ETL process.

DESIGNED APPROACH

First figure illustrates designed approach architecture. We can observe multiple, concurrently running mobile objects (query points), the *Gorder* (Chenyi, Hongjun, Beng Chin, Jing 2004) service responsible for processing simultaneous continuous queries over *k* nearest neighbors, RMI's *SDWServer* and the central part of the designed data system - SDW(l/t), which is also referenced as a query manager. Communication between

SDW(l/t) and query processing service is maintained with Java's Remote Method Invocation (RMI) solutions.

Principal goal of the described approach is to distribute the previously designed system over many independent nodes. As a result we expect faster and more efficient processing of similarity join method *Gorder*. In the previous approach, all components shown in figure 1 were linked together on a single computer. All active processes were using the same CPU. Because of high CPU usage and long evaluation time we decided to distribute the SDW (l/t) into independent services, linked together with Java RMI technology. The most efficient solution assumes moving the *Gorder* service to separate computer because it causes the highest CPU consumption from all components. Other components may be executed on different computers, or on the same computer; their influence on the CPU usage is insignificant.

The designed system works as follows. First, using SDW(l/t), we have to upload a road map and meters into a database running on Oracle Server, .Then we start the *SDWServer*, the *Gorder* service and as many mobile objects as we want to evaluate. Every new mobile object is registered in the database. In SDW(l/t) we define new queries for active mobile objects. Queries are also registered in the database. The *Gorder* service

Figure 1. A scheme of DSDW(l/t) structure

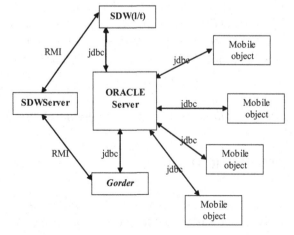

verifies periodically, if there are any new queries defined. Every query is processed during each cycle of the *Gorder* process. Results are sent to SDW(l/t), where they are submitted for further analysis. *SDWServer* secures steady RMI connection between running processes.

MOBILE OBJECTS SIMULATOR

For the designed approach's evaluation we developed a mobile object simulator that corresponds to any moving object like car, man or airplane. Being in constant movement, mobile object is perfect to act as a query point. Continuous changes in its locations forces data system to continuously process queries to maintain up-to-date information about object's *k* nearest neighbours. While designing the mobile object mechanism we made a few assumptions. On the one hand, mobile objects are not allowed to interfere with system's behaviour, but on the other hand, they provide everything that is necessary to conduct experiments which verifies the system system against realistic, natural conditions.

Mobile object simulator is a single process that represents any moving object. It constantly changes its actual location and destination. We assume that a moving object has ability to send updates on its location to the Oracle server, which is the core of DSDW (l/t). It is justifiable assumption because the GPS devices are getting cheaper every day.

In real terms, the location-aware monitoring systems are not aware of mobile object problem of choosing the right direction, because it is not the system that decides where specific object is heading to. System only receives information about current object location and makes proper decisions on the way of processing it. Since our project is not a realistic system, but only a simulation, with a goal to evaluate new solutions, we do not have access to the central system containing information about mobile objects positions.

Therefore, we had to develop an algorithm that will decide on mobile objects movements in order to make SDW(l/t) more realistic.

GORDER QUERY SERVICE

k Nearest Neighbor (*k*NN) join combines each point of one dataset R with its *k* nearest neighbors in the other dataset S. *Gorder* is a block nested loop join algorithm which achieves its efficiency thanks to data sorting, join scheduling and distance computation reduction. Firstly, it sorts input datasets into order called *G-order* (an order based on grid). As a result, datasets are ready to be partitioned into blocks proper for efficient scheduling for join processing. Secondly, scheduled block nested loop join algorithm is applied to find *k* nearest neighbors for each block of R data points within data blocks of S dataset.

Gorder achieves its efficiency due to inheritance of strength of the block nested loop join. Applying this approach it is able to reduce the number of random reads. Moreover the algorithm makes use of a pruning strategy, which prunes away unpromising data blocks using properties of G-ordered data. Furthermore, *Gorder* utilizes two-tier partitioning strategy to optimize CPU and I/O time and reduces distance computation cost by pruning away redundant computations.

G-Ordering

The *Gorder* algorithm authors designed an ordering based on grid called *G-ordering* to group nearby data points together, hence in the scheduled block nested loop join phase they can identify the partition of a block of G-ordered data and schedule it for join.

Firstly, *Gorder* conducts the PCA transformation (*Principal Component Analysis*) on input datasets. Secondly, it applies a grid on a data space and partitions it into l^d square cells, where l is the number of segments per dimension.

275

Figure 2. PCA transformation and grid ordering

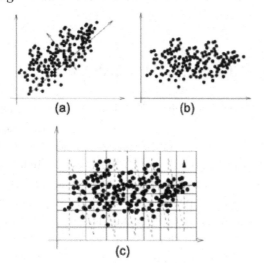

(a)   (b)

(c)

While figure 2a illustrates the original data space, figure 2b sketches the same data space after performing PCA transformation. In figure 2c we can observe grid applied on a two-dimensional data space.

Definition 1. (kNN join) (Chenyi, Hongjun, Beng Chin, Jing, 2004) *Given two data sets R and S, an integer k and the similarity metric dist(), the kNN-join of R and S, denoted as R×kNN S, returns pairs of points (p_i; q_j) such that p_i is from the outer dataset R and q_j from the inner dataset S, and q_j is one of the K-nearest neighbours of p_i.*

$$dist(p,q) = \left(\sum_{i=1}^{d} |p.x_i - q.x_i|^\rho \right)^{\frac{1}{\rho}}, 1 \le \rho \le \infty \quad (1)$$

For further notice we have to define the *identification vector*, as a *d*-dimensional vector $v = <s_1,...,s_d>$, where s_i is the segment number to which the cell belongs to in i^{th} dimension. In our approach we deal with two-dimensional identification vectors.

Bounding box of a data block B is described by the lower left $E = <e_1, ..., e_d>$ and upper right

$T = <t_1, ..., t_d>$ point of data block B (Böhm, Braunmüller, Krebs, Kriegel 2001).

$$e_k = \begin{cases} (v_1.s_k - 1) \cdot \frac{1}{l} & dla \quad 1 \le k \le a \\ 0 & dla \quad k > a \end{cases} \quad (2)$$

$$t_k = \begin{cases} v_m.s_k \cdot \frac{1}{l} & dla \quad 1 \le k \le a \\ 0 & dla \quad k > a \end{cases} \quad (3)$$

where α is an active dimension of data block. In the designed approach points will be represented by only two dimensions: $E = <e_x, e_y>$, $T = <t_x, t_y>$.

Scheduled G-ordered data join

In the second phase of *Gorder*, G-ordered data from R and S datasets is examined for joining. Let's assume that we allocate n_r and n_s buffer pages for data of R and S. Next, we partition R and S into blocks of the allocated buffer sizes. Blocks of R are allocated sequentially and iteratively into memory. Blocks of S are loaded into memory in order based on their similarity to blocks of R, which are already loaded. It optimizes *k*NN processing by scheduling blocks of S so that the blocks which are most likely to contain nearest neighbors can be loaded into memory and processed as first.

Similarity of two G-ordered data blocks is measured by the distance between their bounding boxes. As shown in the previous section, bounding box of a block of G-ordered data may be computed by examining the first and the last point of data block. The minimum distance between two data blocks B_r and B_s is denoted as $MinDist(B_r, B_s)$, and is defined as the minimum distance between their bounding boxes (Chenyi, Hongjun, Beng Chin, Jing, 2004). *MinDist* is a lower bound of the distance of any two points from blocks of R and S.

$$MinDist(B_r, B_s) = \sum_{k=1}^{d} d_k^2 \quad d_k = \max(b_k - u_k, 0)$$

$$b_k = \max(B_r.e_k, B_s.e_k) \quad (4)$$

$$u_k = \min(B_k.t_k, B_s.t_k)$$

$$\forall p_r \in B_r, p_s \in B_s \; MinDist(B_r, B_s) \le dist(p_r, p_s) \quad (5)$$

According to the explanations given above we can deduce two pruning strategies (Chenyi, Hongjun, Beng Chin, Jing, 2004):

1. If $MinDist(B_r, B_s)$ > pruning distance of p, B_s does not contain any points belonging to the k-nearest neighbors of the point p, and therefore the distance computation between p and points in B_s can be filtered. Pruning distance of a point p is the distance between p and its kth nearest neighbor candidate. Initially, it is set to infinity.

2. If $MinDist(B_r, B_s)$ > pruning distance of B_r, B_s does not contain any points belonging to the k-nearest neighbors of any points in B_r, and hence the join of B_r and B_s can be pruned away. The pruning distance of an R block is the maximum pruning distance of the R points inside.

Join algorithm firstly sequentially loads blocks of R into memory. For the block B_r of R loaded into memory, blocks of S are sorted in an order according to their distance to B_r. At the same time blocks with $MinDist(B_r, B_s)$ > pruning distance of B_r are pruned (pruning strategy (2)). That is why only remaining blocks are loaded into memory one by one. For each pair of blocks of R and S the *MemoryJoin* method is processed. After processing all unpruned blocks of S with block of R, list of kNN candidates for each point of B_r, is returned as a result.

Memory Join

To join blocks B_r and B_s each point p_r in B_r is compared with B_s. For each point p_r in B_r we find that if $MinDist(B_r, B_s)$ > pruning distance of p_r, according to first pruning strategy, B_s can not contain any points that could be candidates for k nearest neighbours of p_r, so B_s can be skipped. In the other way function *CountDistance* is called for

p_r and each point p_s in B_s. Function *CountDistance* inserts into a list of kNN candidates of p_r those of p_s, whose $dist(p_r, p_s)$ > pruning distance of p_r. d_α^2 is a distance between the bounding boxes of B_r and B_s on the α-th dimension, where $\alpha = min(B_r.\alpha, B_s.\alpha)$.

SDW(L/T)

SDW(l/t) acts as a coordinator of all running processes and initiates configuration changes. It affects efficiency of the whole DSDW (l/t). The SDW(l/t) is responsible for loading a virtual road map in the database. All objects included in the input dataset for the *Gorder* join processing service are displayed on the map. In this application we can define all query execution parameters that may affect computation time. We correspond to this part of system as a „query manager" because all queries are defined, and maintained in this service.

The SDW(l/t) enables generation of test datasets for experimental issues. It is also an information centre about all defined mobile objects and about their current locations. One of the most important features of the SDW(l/t) is the ability of tracing current results for continuousqueries.

Query manager provides information about newly defined or removed queries to the *SDWServer*. Afterwards, this information is fetched by *Gorder* service, which recalculates the input datasets for kNN join and returns them for further query processing.

EVALUATION OF DISTRIBUTED SDW(L/T)

All experiments were performed on a road map of size 15x15 km. Map was generated for 50 nodes per 100 km^2 and for 50 meters per 100 km^{2} for each type of medium (gas, electricity, water). Only evaluation on effect of number of meters was carried for a few different maps. The number of segments per dimension was set to 10. Block size was 50 data points. Those values were considered as optimal after performing additional tests that are not described in this paper. In the study we performed experiments for a non-distributed SDW(1/t) and distributed versions of SDW(1/t) – DSDW(1/t). Results illustrate the influence of distribution on system's effectiveness and query computation time.

Testing Architecture DSDW(l/t)

Figure 3 illustrates hardware architecture used during evaluation of DSDW(l/t). The first computer run Oracle 10g with the designed database, RMI server, SDWServer and the SDW(1/t) for managing queries. On the separate computer we placed mobile objects because they do not use much of computer computation power and many processes may be run simultaneously. On the last computer we run only the *Gorder* service for better evaluation time.

Single Query Experiments

For single query experiments we define one mobile object. Figure 4a. illustrates that an average evaluation time of query about one type of meters (1) is more or less on constant level for non-distributed version SDW(1/t). We can notice distractions for k equals 6 or 8 but they are very small, measured in milliseconds. For query concerning

Figure 4a. Effect of value k SDW(l/t).

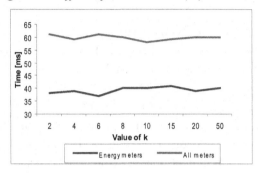

all meters (2) (for higher number of meters) an average query evaluation time increases with the growth of value k starting from value 8, where minimum is achieved. However, this increase is also measured in milliseconds. For DSDW(1/t) we can observe a little higher average measured time, but it is constant and it does not change with the increase of k value.

When testing the influence the number of meters has on query evaluation time we set parameter k on value 20 (Figure 5). Conducted experiments show that, with the growth of number of meters the query evaluation time increases. However, time does not grow up very quickly. After increasing number of meters six times, query evaluation time increased for about 77 % for non-distributed SDW(1/t). For DSDW(1/t) we can notice little higher average evaluation time. That is caused by the need of downloading all data concerning meters to another computer.

Figure 3. DSDW(l/t) testing architecture

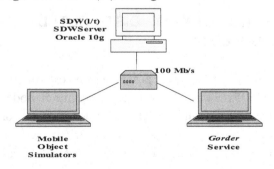

Figure 4b. Effect of value k DSDW(l/t).

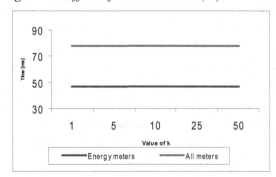

Simultaneous Queries Experiments

The time of full *Gorder* process was measured during experiments for simultaneous queries. It means that we measured the average summary evaluation time for all defined queries that are processed during single round of *Gorder* process.

Figure 6 summarizes the effect of number of simultaneous queries on average *Gorder* process evaluation time. All queries were defined for the same type of meters. That is why the evaluation time of one cycle of the *Gorder* process was evaluated during one single call of the *Gorder* algorithm. Along with previous results, the influence of *k* value on the process evaluation time is insignificant. However, with the growth of number of simultaneous queries, the time of conducted computations increases. For SDW(l/t) experiments were performed for only 5 mobile objects because of to high CPU usage caused by running entire system on one computer. It was

Figure 5. Effect of number of meters per 100 km² – SDW(l/t) (first figure) and DSDW(l/t) (second figure)

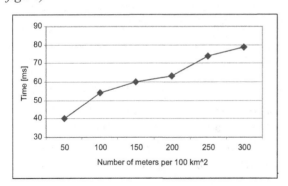

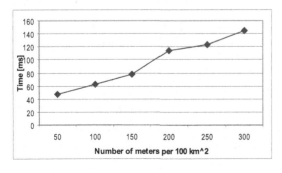

needless to run experiments for greater number of mobile objects. Average evaluation times increase with the growth of the number of queries. Each additional query causes the time to grow for about 10ms. For distributed version of the system we could process 12 objects and more. Average evaluation time is a little higher but it is more constant and increases slowly.

Differentiation of queries (Figure 7) caused that in every single cycle of *Gorder* process, *Gorder* algorithm was called separately for every type of query. Therefore, for four queries about four different types of meters *Gorder* process called *Gorder* algorithm four times. Given results for non-distributed SDW(l/t) proved that with the growth of number of differential queries, process evaluation time significantly increases. We processed only three queries with input datasets with the same size.

In the DSDW(l/t) we performed experiments for 12 queries. 3 queries concerned water meters, 3 concerned gas meters and 3 concerned electricity meters. Each of them with the same input dataset size. We also added 3 queries concerning all meters. Adding queries successively, one by one, from each type of query, we measured average evaluation time of the entire process. Given results show that with the growth of the number of different queries the average evaluation time increases slowly. The growth is much less significant than in non-distributed version and we are able to process much more queries.

SUMMARY

Pilotage system SDW(l/t) is currently improving in terms of searching for new simultaneously continuous queries processing techniques. Distributed approach of the designed system, DSDW(l/t), shows that this development course should be considered for further analysis. Furthermore, using incremental execution paradigm as the way to achieve high scalability during simultaneous execution of continuous spatio-temporal queries is a promising approach. Queries should be grouped in the unique list of continuous, spatio-temporal queries, so that spatial joins could be processed between moving objects and moving queries.

We also consider implementing a solution for balanced, simultaneous and distributed query processing to split execution of queries of the

Figure 7. Effect of differentiation of simultaneous queries – DSDW(l/t).

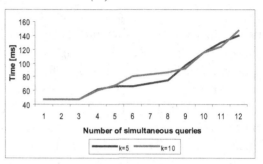

same type on different computers, depending on their CPU usage prediction.

REFERENCES

Böhm Ch., Braunmüller B., Krebs F., & Kriegel, H., (2001). Epsilon Grid oOrder: An aAlgorithm for the sSimilarity jJoin on mMassive hHigh-dDimensional dData, *Proceedings. ACM SIG-MOD INT. Conf. on Management of Data,* Santa Barbara, CA, 2001.

Chenyi, Xia,, Hongjun, Lu, Beng, Chin, Ooi, & Jing, Hu, (2004). *GORDER: An eEfficient mMethod for KNN jJoin pProcessing,* VLDB 2004,(pp. 756-767).

Gorawski M., & Malczok R., (2004). Distributed sSpatial dData wWarehouse iIndexed with vVirtual mMemory aAggregation tTree. The *5th Workshop on Spatial-Temporal DataBase Management (STDBM_VLDB'04),* Toronto, Canada 2004.

Gorawski M., & Wróbel W., (2005). Realization of kNN qQuery tType in sSpatial tTelemetric dData wWarehouse. *Studia Informatica, vol.26, nr 2*(63), pp.1-22.

Gorawski, M., & Gebczyk, W., (2007)., *Distributed approach of continuous queries with knn join processing in spatial data warehouse,* ICEIS, Funchal, Madeira, 2007, (pp. :131-136).

Figure 6a. Effect of number of simultaneous

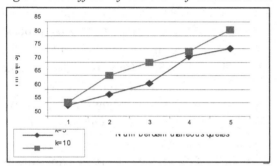

Figure 6b. Effect of number of simultaneous queries –DSDW(l/t) (second figure)

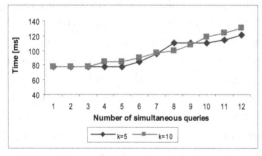

Figure 7a. Effect of differentiation of simultaneous queries – SDW(l/t)

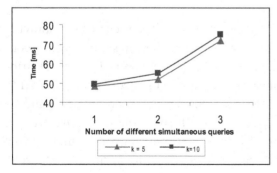

Hammad, M. A., Franklin, M. J., Aref, W. G., & Elmagarmid, A. K., (2003). *Scheduling for shared window joins over data streams.* VLDB.

Mouratidis, K., Yiu, M., Papadias, D., & Mamoulis, N., (2006, September 12-16). Continuous nNearest nNeighbor mMonitoring in rRoad nNetworks. To appear in the *Proceedings of the Very Large Data Bases Conference (VLDB)*, Seoul, Korea, Sept. 12 - Sept. 15, 2006.

Yiu, M., Papadias, D., Mamoulis, N., & Tao, Y. (2006).. Reverse nNearest nNeighbors in lLarge gGraphs. *IEEE Transactions on Knowledge and Data Engineering (TKDE),18*(4), 540-553, 2006.

Chapter XIV
Spatial Data Warehouse Modelling

Maria Luisa Damiani
Università di Milano, Italy & Ecole Polytechnique Fédérale, Switzerland

Stefano Spaccapietra
Ecole Polytechnique Fédérale de Lausanne, Switzerland

ABSTRACT

This chapter is concerned with multidimensional data models for spatial data warehouses. Over the last few years different approaches have been proposed in the literature for modelling multidimensional data with geometric extent. Nevertheless, the definition of a comprehensive and formal data model is still a major research issue. The main contributions of the chapter are twofold: First, it draws a picture of the research area; second it introduces a novel spatial multidimensional data model for spatial objects with geometry (MuSD – multigranular spatial data warehouse). MuSD complies with current standards for spatial data modelling, augmented by data warehousing concepts such as spatial fact, spatial dimension and spatial measure. The novelty of the model is the representation of spatial measures at multiple levels of geometric granularity. Besides the representation concepts, the model includes a set of OLAP operators supporting the navigation across dimension and measure levels.

INTRODUCTION

A topic that over recent years has received growing attention from both academy and industry concerns the integration of spatial data management with multidimensional data analysis techniques. We refer to this technology as spatial data warehousing, and consider a spatial data warehouse to be a multidimensional database of spatial data. Following common practice, we use here the term spatial in the geographical sense, i.e., to denote data that includes the description of how objects and phenomena are located on the Earth. A large variety of data may be considered to be spatial, including: data for land use and socioeconomic analysis; digital imagery and geo-sensor data; location-based data acquired through GPS or other positioning devices; environmental phenomena. Such data are collected and possibly marketed by organizations such as public administrations, utilities and other private companies, environmental research centres and spatial data infrastructures. Spatial data warehousing has been recognized as a key technology in enabling the interactive analysis of spatial data sets for decision-making support (Rivest et al., 2001; Han et al., 2002). Application domains in which the technology can play an important role are, for example, those dealing with complex and worldwide phenomena such as homeland security, environmental monitoring and health safeguard. These applications pose challenging requirements for integration and usage of spatial data of different kinds, coverage and resolution, for which the spatial data warehouse technology may be extremely helpful.

Origins

Spatial data warehousing results from the confuence of two technologies, spatial data handling and multidimensional data analysis, respectively. The former technology is mainly provided by two kinds of systems: spatial database management systems (DBMS) and geographical information systems(GIS). Spatial DBMS extend the functionalities of conventional data management systems to support the storage, efficient retrieval and manipulation of spatial data (Rigaux et al., 2002). Examples of commercial DBMS systems are Oracle Spatial and IBM DB2 Spatial Extender. A GIS, on the other hand, is a composite computer based information system consisting of an integrated set of programs, possibly including or interacting with a spatial DBMS, which enables the capturing, modelling, analysis and visualization of spatial data (Longley et al., 2001). Unlike a spatial DBMS, a GIS is meant to be directly usable by an end-user. Examples of commercial systems are ESRI ArcGIS and Intergraph Geomedia. The technology of spatial data handling has made significant progress in the last decade, fostered by the standardization initiatives promoted by OGC (Open Geospatial Consortium) and ISO/TC211, as well as by the increased availability of off-the-shelf geographical data sets that have broadened the spectrum of spatially-aware applications. Conversely, multidimensional data analysis has become the leading technology for decision making in the business area. Data are stored in a multidimensional array (cube or hypercube) (Kimball, 1996; Chaudhuri & Dayla, 1997; Vassiliadis & Sellis, 1999). The elements of the cube constitute the facts (or cells) and are defined by measures and dimensions. Typically, a measure denotes a quantitative variable in a given domain. For example, in the marketing domain, one kind of measure is sales amount. A dimension is a structural attribute characterizing a measure. For the marketing example, dimensions of sales may be: time, location and product. Under these example assumptions, a cell stores the amount of sales for a given product in a given region and over a given period of time. Moreover, each dimension is organized in a hierarchy of dimension levels, each level corresponding to a different granularity for the dimension. For example, *year* is one level of the *time* dimension, while the sequence *day, month, year* defines a simple hierarchy of increasing granularity for the time dimension. The basic operations for online analysis (OLAP operators) that can be performed over data cubes are: *roll-up*, which moves up along one or more dimensions towards more aggregated data (e.g., moving from monthly sales amounts to yearly sales amounts); *drill-down*, which moves down dimensions towards more detailed, disaggregated data and *slice-and-dice*, which performs a selection and projection operation on a cube.

The integration of these two technologies, spatial data handling and multidimensional analysis, responds to multiple application needs. In business data warehouses, the spatial dimension is increasingly considered of strategic relevance for the analysis of enterprise data. Likewise, in engineering and scientific applications, huge amounts of measures, typically related to environmental phenomena, are collected through sensors, installed on ground or satellites, and continuously generating data which are stored in data warehouses for subsequent analysis.

Spatial Multidimensional Models

A data warehouse (DW) is the result of a complex process entailing the integration of huge amounts of heterogeneous data, their organization into denormalized data structures and eventually their loading into a database for use through online analysis techniques. In a DW, data are organized and manipulated in accordance with the concepts and operators provided by a multidimensional data model. Multidimensional data models have been widely investigated for conventional, non-spatial data. Commercial systems based on these models are marketed. By contrast, research on spatially aware DWs (SDWs) is a step behind. The reasons are diverse: The spatial context is peculiar and complex, requiring specialized techniques for data representation and processing; the technology for spatial data management has reached maturity only in recent times with the development of SQL3-based implementations of OGC standards; finally, SDWs still lack a market comparable in size with the business sector that is pushing the development of the technology. As a result, the definition of spatial multidimensional data models (SMDs) is still a challenging research issue.

A SMD model can be specified at conceptual and logical levels. Unlike the logical model, the specification at the conceptual level is independent of the technology used for the management of spatial data. Therefore, since the representation is not constrained by the implementation platform, the conceptual specification, that is the view we adopt in this work, is more flexible, although not immediately operational.

The conceptual specification of an SMD model entails the definition of two basic components: a set of representation constructs, and an algebra of spatial OLAP (SOLAP) operators, supporting data analysis and navigation across the representation structures of the model. The representation constructs account for the specificity of the spatial nature of data. In this work we focus on one of the peculiarities of spatial data, that is the availability of spatial data at different levels of granularity. Since the granularity concerns not only the semantics but also the geometric aspects of the data, the location of objects can have different geometric representations. For example, representing the location of an accident at different scales may lead to associating different geometries to the same accident.

To allow a more flexible representation of spatial data at different geometric granularity, we propose a SDM model in which not only dimensions are organized in levels of detail but also the spatial measures. For that purpose we introduce the concept of *multi-level spatial measure*.

The proposed model is named MuSD (multigranular spatial data warehouse). It is based on the notions of *spatial fact*, *spatial dimension* and *multi-level spatial measure*. A spatial fact may be defined as a fact describing an event that occurred on the Earth in a position that is relevant to know and analyze. Spatial facts are, for instance, road accidents. Spatial dimensions and measures represent properties of facts that have a geometric meaning; in particular, the spatial measure represents the location in which the fact occurred. A multi-level spatial measure is a measure that is represented by multiple geometries at different levels of detail. A measure of this kind is, for example, the location of an accident:

Depending on the application requirements, an accident may be represented by a point along a road, a road segment or the whole road, possibly at different cartographic scales. Spatial measures and dimensions are uniformly represented in terms of the standard spatial objects defined by the Open Geospatial Consortium. Besides the representation constructs, the model includes a set of SOLAP operators to navigate not only through the dimensional levels but also through the levels of the spatial measures.

The chapter is structured in the following sections: the next section, *Background Knowledge*, introduces a few basic concepts underlying spatial data representation; the subsequent section, *State of the Art on Spatial Multidimensional Models*, surveys the literature on SDM models; the proposed spatial multidimensional data model is presented in the following section; and research opportunities and some concluding remarks are discussed in the two conclusive sections.

BACKGROUND KNOWLEDGE

The real world is populated by different kinds of objects, such as roads, buildings, administrative boundaries, moving cars and air pollution phenomena. Some of these objects are tangible, like buildings, others, like administrative boundaries, are not. Moreover, some of them have identifiable shapes with well-defined boundaries, like land parcels; others do not have a crisp and fixed shape, like air pollution. Furthermore, in some cases the position of objects, e.g., buildings, does not change in time; in other cases it changes more or less frequently, as in the case of moving cars. To account for the multiform nature of spatial data, a variety of data models for the digital representation of spatial data are needed. In this section, we present an overview of a few basic concepts of spatial data representation used throughout the chapter.

The Nature of Spatial Data

Spatial data describe properties of phenomena occurring in the world. The prime property of such phenomena is that they occupy a position. In broad terms, a position is the description of a location on the Earth. The common way of describing such a position is through the coordinates of a coordinate reference system.

The real world is populated by phenomena that fall into two broad conceptual categories: entities and continuous fields (Longley et al., 2001). Entities are distinguishable elements occupying a precise position on the Earth and normally having a well-defined boundary. Examples of entities are rivers, roads and buildings. By contrast, fields are variables having a single value that varies within a bounded space. An example of field is the temperature, or the distribution, of a polluting substance in an area. Field data can be directly obtained from sensors, for example installed on satellites, or obtained by interpolation from sample sets of observations.

The standard name adopted for the digital representation of abstractions of real world phenomena is that of *feature* (OGC, 2001, 2003). The feature is the basic representation construct defined in the reference spatial data model developed by the Open Geospatial Consortium and endorsed by ISO/TC211. As we will see, we will use the concept of feature to uniformly represent all the spatial components in our model. Features are spatial when they are associated with locations on the Earth; otherwise they are non-spatial. Features have a distinguishing name and have a set of attributes. Moreover, features may be defined at instance and type level: *Feature instances* represent single phenomena; *feature types* describe the intensional meaning of features having a common set of attributes. Spatial features are further specialized to represent different kinds of spatial data. In the OGC terminology, *coverages* are the spatial features that represent continuous fields and consist of discrete functions taking values over space partitions. Space partitioning results from either the subdivision of space in a set of regular units or cells (*raster* data model) or the subdivision of space in irregular units such as triangles (*tin* data model). The discrete function assigns each portion of a bounded space a value.

In our model, we specifically consider *simple spatial features*. Simple spatial features ("features" hereinafter) have one or more attributes of geometric type, where the geometric type is one of the types defined by OGC, such as point, line and polygon. One of these attributes denotes the position of the entity. For example, the position of the state Italy may be described by a multipolygon, i.e., a set of disjoint polygons (to account for islands), with holes (to account for the Vatican State and San Marino). A simple feature is very close to the concept of entity or object as used by the database community. It should be noticed, however, that besides a semantic and geometric characterization, a feature type is also assigned a coordinate reference system, which is specific for the feature type and that defines the space in which the instances of the feature type are embedded.

More complex features may be defined specifying the topological relationships relating a set of features. Topology deals with the geometric properties that remain invariant when space is elastically deformed. Within the context of geographical information, topology is commonly used to describe, for example, connectivity and adjacency relationships between spatial elements. For example, a road network, consisting of a set of interconnected roads, may be described through a graph of nodes and edges: Edges are the topological objects representing road segments whereas nodes account for road junctions and road endpoints.

To summarize, spatial data have a complex nature. Depending on the application requirements and the characteristics of the real world phenomena, different spatial data models can be adopted for the representation of geometric

and topological properties of spatial entities and continuous fields.

STATE OF THE ART ON SPATIAL MULTIDIMENSIONAL MODELS

Research on spatial multidimensional data models is relatively recent. Since the pioneering work of Han et al. (1998), several models have been proposed in the literature aiming at extending the classical multidimensional data model with spatial concepts. However, despite the complexity of spatial data, current spatial data warehouses typically contain objects with simple geometric extent.

Moreover, while an SMD model is assumed to consist of a set of representation concepts and an algebra of SOLAP operators for data navigation and aggregation, approaches proposed in the literature often privilege only one of the two aspects, rarely both. Further, whilst early data models are defined at the logical level and are based on the relational data model, in particular on the star model, more recent developments, especially carried out by the database research community, focus on conceptual aspects. We also observe that the modelling of geometric granularities in terms of multi-level spatial measures, which we propose in our model, is a novel theme.

Often, existing approaches do not rely on standard data models for the representation of spatial aspects. The spatiality of facts is commonly represented through a geometric element, while in our approach, as we will see, it is an OGC spatial feature, i.e., an object that has a semantic value in addition to its spatial characterization.

A related research issue that is gaining increased interest in recent years, and that is relevant for the development of comprehensive SDW data models, concerns the specification and efficient implementation of the operators for spatial aggregation.

Literature Review

The first, and perhaps the most significant, model proposed so far has been developed by Han et al. (1998). This model introduced the concepts of spatial dimension and spatial measure. Spatial dimensions describe properties of facts that also have a geometric characterization. Spatial dimensions, as conventional dimensions, are defined at different levels of granularity. Conversely, a spatial measure is defined as "a measure that contains a collection of pointers to spatial objects", where spatial objects are geometric elements, such as polygons. Therefore, a spatial measure does not have a semantic characterization, it is just a set of geometries. To illustrate these concepts, the authors consider a SDW about weather data. The example SDW has three thematic dimensions: {temperature, precipitation, time}; one spatial dimension: {region}; and three measures: {region_map, area, count}. While area and count are numeric measures, region_map is a spatial measure denoting a set of polygons. The proposed model is specified at the logical level, in particular in terms of a star schema, and does not include an algebra of OLAP operators. Instead, the authors develop a technique for the efficient computation of spatial aggregations, like the merge of polygons. Since the spatial aggregation operations are assumed to be distributive, aggregations may be partially computed on disjoint subsets of data. By pre-computing the spatial aggregation of different subsets of data, the processing time can be reduced.

Rivest et al. (2001) extend the definition of spatial measures given in the previous approach to account for spatial measures that are computed by metric or topological operators. Further, the authors emphasize the need for more advanced querying capabilities to provide end users with topological and metric operators. The need to account for topological relationships has been more concretely addressed by Marchant et al. (2004), who define a specific type of dimension implementing spatio-temporal topological operators at different levels of detail. In such a way, facts may be partitioned not only based on dimension values but also on the existing topological relationships.

Shekhar et al. (2001) propose a *map cube operator,* extending the concepts of data cube and aggregation to spatial data. Further, the authors introduce a classification and examples of different types of spatial measures, e.g., spatial distributive, algebraic and holistic functions.

GeoDWFrame (Fidalgo et al., 2004) is a recently proposed model based on the star schema. The conceptual framework, however, does not include the notion of spatial measure, while dimensions are classified in a rather complex way.

Pederson and Tryfona (2001) are the first to introduce a formal definition of an SMD model at the conceptual level. The model only accounts for spatial measures whilst dimensions are only non-spatial. The spatial measure is a collection of geometries, as in Han et al. (1998), and in particular of polygonal elements. The authors develop a pre-aggregation technique to reduce the processing time of the operations of merge and intersection of polygons. The formalization approach is valuable but, because of the limited number of operations and types of spatial objects that are taken into account, the model has limited functionality and expressiveness.

Jensen et al. (2002) address an important requirement of spatial applications. In particular, the authors propose a conceptual model that allows the definition of dimensions whose levels are related by a partial containment relationship. An example of partial containment is the relationship between a roadway and the district it crosses. A degree of containment is attributed to the relationship. For example, a roadway may be defined as partially contained at degree 0.5 into a district. An algebra for the extended data model is also defined. To our knowledge, the model has been the first to deal with uncertainty in data warehouses, which is a relevant issue in real applications.

Malinowski and Zimanyi (2004) present a different approach to conceptual modelling. Their SMD model is based on the Entity Relationship modelling paradigm. The basic representation constructs are those of *fact relationship* and *dimension*. A *dimension* contains one or several related levels consisting of entity types possibly having an attribute of geometric type. The *fact relationship* represents an n-ary relationship existing among the dimension levels. The attributes of the *fact relationship* constitute the measures. In particular, a spatial measure is a measure that is represented by a geometry or a function computing a geometric property, such as the length or surface of an element. The spatial aspects of the model are expressed in terms of the MADS spatio-temporal conceptual model (Parent et al., 1998). An interesting concept of the SMD model is that of *spatial fact relationship*, which models a spatial relationship between two or more spatial dimensions, such as that of spatial containment. However, the model focuses on the representation constructs and does not specify a SOLAP algebra.

A different, though related, issue concerns the operations of *spatial aggregation*. Spatial aggregation operations summarize the geometric properties of objects, and as such constitute the distinguishing aspect of SDW. Nevertheless, despite the relevance of the subject, a standard set of operators (as, for example, the operators Avg, Min, Max in SQL) has not been defined yet. A first comprehensive classification and formalization of spatio-temporal aggregate functions is presented in Lopez and Snodgrass (2005). The operation of aggregation is defined as a function that is applied to a collection of tuples and returns a single value. The authors distinguish three kinds of methods for generating the set of tuples, known as *group composition*, *partition composition* and *sliding window composition*. They provide a formal definition of aggregation for conventional, temporal and spatial data based on this distinction. In addition to the conceptual

aspects of spatial aggregation, another major issue regards the development of methods for the efficient computation of these kinds of operations to manage high volumes of spatial data. In particular, techniques are developed based on the combined use of specialized indexes, materialization of aggregate measures and computational geometry algorithms, especially to support the aggregation of dynamically computed sets of spatial objects (Papadias, et al., 2001; Rao et al., 2003; Zhang & Tsotras, 2005).

A MULTIGRANULAR SPATIAL DATA WAREHOUSE MODEL: MUSD

Despite the numerous proposals of data models for SDW defined at the logical, and more recently, conceptual level presented in the previous section, and despite the increasing number of data warehousing applications (see, e.g., Bedard et al., 2003; Scotch & Parmantoa, 2005), the definition of a comprehensive and formal data model is still a major research issue.

In this work we focus on the definition of a formal model based on the concept of spatial measures at multiple levels of geometric granularity.

One of the distinguishing aspects of multidimensional data models is the capability of dealing with data at different levels of detail or granularity. Typically, in a data warehouse the notion of granularity is conveyed through the notion of dimensional hierarchy. For example, the dimension *administrative units* may be represented at different decreasing levels of detail: at the most detailed level as municipalities, next as regions and then as states. Note, however, that unlike dimensions, measures are assigned a unique granularity. For example, the granularity of sales may be homogeneously expressed in euros.

In SDW, the assumption that spatial measures have a unique level of granularity seems to be too restrictive. In fact, spatial data are very often available at multiple granularities, since data are collected by different organizations for different purposes. Moreover, the granularity not only regards the semantics (semantic granularity) but also the geometric aspects (spatial granularity) (Spaccapietra et al., 2000; Fonseca et al., 2002). For example, the location of an accident may be modelled as a measure, yet represented at different scales and thus have varying geometric representations.

To represent measures at varying spatial granularities, alternative strategies can be prospected: A simple approach is to define a number of spatial measures, one for each level of spatial granularity. However, this solution is not conceptually adequate because it does not represent the hierarchical relation among the various spatial representations.

In the model we propose, named MuSD, we introduce the notion of *multi-level spatial measure*, which is a spatial measure that is defined at multiple levels of granularity, in the same way as dimensions. The introduction of this new concept raises a number of interesting issues. The first one concerns the modelling of the spatial properties. To provide a homogeneous representation of the spatial properties across multiple levels, both spatial measures and dimensions are represented in terms of OGC features. Therefore, the locations of facts are denoted by feature identifiers. For example, a feature, say p1, of type *road accident*, may represent the location of an *accident*. Note that in this way we can refer to spatial objects in a simple way using names, in much the same way Han et al. (1998) do using pointers. The difference is in the level of abstraction and, moreover, in the fact that a feature is not simply a geometry but an entity with a semantic characterization.

Another issue concerns the representation of the features resulting from aggregation operations. To represent such features at different granularities, the model is supposed to include a set of operators that are able to dynamically decrease the spatial granularity of spatial measures. We

call these operators *coarsening operators*. With this term we indicate a variety of operators that, although developed in different contexts, share the common goal of representing less precisely the geometry of an object. Examples include the operators for cartographic generalization proposed in Camossi et al. (2003) as well the operators generating imprecise geometries out of more precise representations (*fuzzyfying* operators).

In summary, the MuSD model has the following characteristics:

- It is based on the usual constructs of (spatial) measures and (spatial) dimensions. Notice that the spatiality of a measure is a necessary condition for the DW to be spatial, while the spatiality of dimensions is optional;
- A spatial measure represents the location of a fact at multiple levels of spatial granularity;
- Spatial dimension and spatial measures are represented in terms of OGC features;
- Spatial measures at different spatial granularity can be dynamically computed by applying a set of coarsening operators; and
- An algebra of SOLAP operators is defined to enable user navigation and data analysis.

Hereinafter, we first introduce the representation concepts of the MuSD model and then the SOLAP operators.

Representation Concepts in MuSD

The basic notion of the model is that of *spatial fact*. A spatial fact is defined as a fact that has occurred in a location. Properties of spatial facts are described in terms of measures and dimensions which, depending on the application, may have a spatial meaning.

A *dimension* is composed of *levels*. The set of levels is partially ordered; more specifically, it constitutes a lattice. Levels are assigned values belonging to *domains*. If the domain of a level consists of features, the level is *spatial*; otherwise it is *non-spatial*. A *spatial measure*, as a dimension, is composed of levels representing different granularities for the measure and forming a lattice. Since in common practice the notion of granularity seems not to be of particular concern for conventional and numeric measures, non-spatial measures are defined at a unique level. Further, as the spatial measure represents the location of the fact, it seems reasonable and not significantly restrictive to assume the spatial measure to be unique in the SDW.

As Jensen et al. (2002), we base the model on the distinction between the intensional and extensional representations, which we respectively call *schema* and *cube*. The schema specifies the structure, thus the set of dimensions and measures that compose the SDW; the cube describes a set of facts along the properties specified in the schema.

To illustrate the concepts of the model, we use as a running example the case of an SDW of road accidents. The *accidents* constitute the spatial facts. The properties of the accidents are modelled as follows: The number of *victims* and the *position* along the road constitute the measures of the SDW. In particular, the position of the accident is a spatial measure. The *date* and the *administrative unit* in which the accident occurred constitute the dimensions.

Before detailing the representation constructs, we need to define the spatial data model which is used for representing the spatial concepts of the model.

The Spatial Data Model

For the representation of the spatial components, we adopt a spatial data model based on the OGC simple features model. We adopt this model because it is widely deployed in commercial spatial DBMS and GIS. Although a more advanced spatial data model has been proposed (OGC, 2003), we do not lose in generality by adopting the simple

feature model. Features (simple) are identified by names. Milan, Lake Michigan and the car number AZ213JW are examples of features. In particular, we consider as spatial features entities that can be mapped onto locations in the given space (for example, Milan and Lake Michigan). The location of a feature is represented through a *geometry*. The geometry of a spatial feature may be of type point, line or polygon, or recursively be a collection of disjoint geometries. Features have an application-dependent semantics that are expressed through the concept of *feature type*. Road, Town, Lake and Car are examples of feature types. The *extension* of a feature type, *ft*, is a set of semantically homogeneous features. As remarked in the previous section, since features are identified by unique names, we represent spatial objects in terms of feature identifiers. Such identifiers are different from the pointers to geometric elements proposed in early SDW models. In fact, a feature identifier does not denote a geometry, rather an entity that has also a semantics. Therefore some spatial operations, such as the spatial merge when applied to features, have a semantic value besides a geometric one. In the examples that will follow, spatial objects are indicated by their names.

Basic Concepts

To introduce the notion of schema and cube, we first need to define the following notions: *domain, level, level hierarchy, dimension* and *measure*. Consider the concept of domain. A domain defines the set of values that may be assigned to a property of facts, that is to a measure or to a dimension level. The domain may be single-valued or multi-valued; it may be spatial or non-spatial. A formal definition is given as follows.

Definition 1 (Domain and spatial domain): Let V be the set of values and F the set f features with $F \subseteq V$. A domain Do is single-valued if Do $\subseteq V$; it is multi-valued if Do $\subseteq 2^V$, in which case the elements of the domain are subsets of values.

Further, the domain Do is a single-valued spatial domain if Do $\subseteq$ F; it is a multi-valued spatial domain if Do $\subseteq 2^F$. We denote with DO the set of domains $\{Do_1 ..., Do_k\}$.

Example 1: In the road accident SDW, the single-valued domain of the property victims is the set of positive integers. A possible spatial domain for the position of the accidents is the set $\{a4, a5, s35\}$ consisting of features which represent roads. We stress that in this example the position is a feature and not a mere geometric element, e.g., the line representing the geometry of the road.

The next concept we introduce is that of *level*. A level denotes the single level of granularity of both dimensions and measures. A level is defined by a name and a domain. We also define the notion of partial ordering among levels, which describes the relationship among different levels of detail.

Definition 2 (Level): A level is a pair $< Ln, Do >$ where Ln is the name of the level and Do its domain. If the domain is a spatial domain, then the level is spatial; otherwise it is non-spatial.

Let Lv1 and Lv2 be two levels, dom(Lv) the function returning the domain of level Lv, and $\leq_{lv}$ a partial order over V. We say that $Lv1 \leq_{lv} Lv2$ iff for each $v1 \in dom(Lv1)$, it exists $v2 \in dom(Lv2)$ such that $v1 \leq_{lv} v2$. We denote with LV the set of levels. The relationship $Lv1 \leq_{lv} Lv2$ is read: Lv1 is less coarse (or more detailed) than Lv2.

Example 2: Consider the following two levels: L_1=<AccidentAtLargeScale, PointAt1:1'000>, L_2=<AccidentAtSmallScale, PointAt1:50'000>. Assume that Do_1 = PointAt1:1'000 and Do2 = PointAt1:50'000 are domains of features representing accidents along roads at different scales. If we assume that $Do_1 \leq_{lv} Do_2$ then it holds that AccidentAtLargeScale$\leq_{lv}$ AccidentAtSmallScale.

The notion of level is used to introduce the concept of *hierarchy of levels*, which is then applied to define dimensions and measures.

Definition 3 (Level hierarchy): Let L be a set of n levels L = $\{Lv_1, ..., Lv_n\}$. A level hierarchy H is a lattice over L: H =<L, $\leq_{lv}$, Lvtop, Lvbot> where $\leq_{lv}$ is a partial order over the set L of levels, and Lvtop, Lvbot, respectively, the top and the bottom levels of the lattice.

Given a level hierarchy H, the function LevelsOf(H) returns the set of levels in H. For the sake of generality, we do not make any assumption on the meaning of the partial ordering. Further, we say that a level hierarchy is of type *spatial* if all the levels in L are spatial; *non-spatial* when the levels are non-spatial; *hybrid* if L consists of both spatial and non-spatial levels. This distinction is analogous to the one defined by Han et al. (1998).

Example 3: Consider again the previous example of hierarchy of administrative entities. If the administrative entities are described by spatial features and thus have a geometry, then they form a spatial hierarchy; if they are described simply by names, then the hierarchy is non-spatial; if some levels are spatial and others are non-spatial, then the hierarchy is hybrid.

At this point we introduce the concepts of *dimensions*, *measures* and *spatial measures*. *Dimensions* and *spatial measures* are defined as hierarchies of levels. Since there is no evidence that the same concept is useful also for numeric measures, we introduce the notion of hierarchy only for the measures that are spatial. Further, as we assume that measures can be assigned subset of values, the domain of a (spatial) measure is multivalued.

Definition 4 (Dimension, measure and spatial measure): We define:

- A dimension D is a level hierarchy. The domains of the dimension levels are single-valued. Further, the hierarchy can be of type: spatial, non-spatial and hybrid;
- A measure M is defined by a unique level < M, Do >, with Do a multi-valued domain; and
- A spatial measure SM is a level hierarchy. The domains of the levels are multi-valued. Moreover the level hierarchy is spatial.

To distinguish the levels, we use the terms *dimension* and *spatial measure levels*. Note that the levels of the spatial measure are all spatial since we assume that the locations of facts can be represented at granularities that have a geometric meaning. Finally, we introduce the concept of *multigranular spatial schema* to denote the whole structure of the SDW.

Definition 5 (Multigranular spatial schema): A multigranular spatial schema S (schema, in short) is the tuple S =<D1, ..Dn, M1, ...Mm, SM> where:

- Di is a dimension, for each i =1, .., n;
- Mj is a non-spatial measure, for each j =1, .., m; and
- SM is a spatial measure.

We assume the spatial measure to be unique in the schema. Although in principle that could be interpreted as a limitation, we believe it is a reasonable choice since it seems adequate in most real cases.

Example 4: Consider the following schema S for the road accidents SDW:

S =<date, administrativeUnit, victims, location> where:

- {*date, administrativeUnit*} are dimensions with the following simple structure:
  - date =<{year, month } , $\leq_{date}$, month, year> with month $\leq_{date}$ year
  - administrativeUnit =<{municipality, region, state}, $\leq_{adm}$, municipality, state> with municipality $\leq_{adm}$ region $\leq_{adm}$ state;
- victims is a non-spatial measure;
- location is the spatial measure. Let us call M1 = AccidentAtLargeScale and M2 = AccidentAtSmallScale, two measure levels representing accidents at two different scales. Then the measure is defined as follows: <{M1, M2} $\leq$pos, M1, M2> such that M1$\leq$pos M2.

Finally, we introduce the concept of *cube* to denote the extension of our SDW. A cube is a set of cells containing the measure values defined with respect a given granularity of dimensions and measures. To indicate the level of granularity of dimensions, the notion of *schema level* is introduced. A schema level is a schema limited to specific levels. A cube is thus defined as an instance of a schema level.

Definition 6 (Schema level): Let $S = <D_1, ..D_n, M_1, ...M_m, SM>$ be a schema. A schema level SL for S is a tuple: $<DLv_1, ..DLv_n, M_1, ...M_m, Slv>$ where:

- $DLv_i \in$ LevelsOf (D_i), is a level of dimension D_i (for each i = 1, ..., n);
- M_i is a non-spatial measure (for each i =1, ..., m); and
- $Slv \in$ LevelsOf (SM) is a level of the spatial measure SM

Since non-spatial measures have a unique level, they are identical in all schema levels. The cube is thus formally defined as follows:

Definition 7 (Cube and state): Let $SL = <DLv_1,$ $..DLv_n, M_1, ...M_m, Slv>$ be a schema level.

A cube for SL, C_{SL} is the set of tuples (cells) of the form: $<d_1, ..., d_n, m_1, ..., m_m, sv>$ where:

- d_i is a value for the dimension level DLv_i;
- m_i is a value for the measure M_i; and
- sv is the value for the spatial measure level Slv.

A state of a SDW is defined by the pair $<SL, C_{SL}>$ where SL is a schema level and C_{SL} a cube.

The *basic cube* and *basic state* respectively denote the cube and the schema level at the maximum level of detail of the dimensions and spatial measure.

Example 5: Consider the schema S introduced in example 4 and the schema level <month, municipality, victims, accidentAtlargeScale>. An example of fact contained in a cube for such a schema level is the tuple <May 2005, Milan, 20, A4> where the former two values are dimension values and the latter two values are measure values. In particular, A4 is the feature representing the location at the measure level accidentAt-LargeScale.

Spatial OLAP

After presenting the representation constructs of the model, we introduce the spatial OLAP operators. In order to motivate our choices, we first discuss three kinds of requirements that the concept of hierarchy of measures poses on these operators and thus the assumptions we have made.

Requirements and Assumptions

Interrelationship Between Dimensions and Spatial Measures

A first problem due to the introduction of the hierarchy of measures may be stated in these

terms: Since a measure level is functionally dependent on dimensions, is this dependency still valid if we change the granularity of the measure? Consider the following example: assume the cube in example 4 and consider an accident that occurred in May 2005 in the municipality of Milan, located in point *P* along a given road, and having caused two victims. Now assume a decrease in the granularity of the position, thus representing the position no longer as a point but as a portion of road. The question is whether the dimension values are affected by such a change. We may observe that both cases are possible: (a) The functional dependency between a measure and a dimension is not affected by the change of spatial granularity of the measure if the dimension value does not depend on the geometry of the measure. This is the case for the dimension *date of accident;* since the date of an accident does not depend on the geometry of the accident, the dimension value does not change with the granularity. In this case we say that the date dimension is *invariant*; (b) The opposite case occurs if a spatial relationships exists between the given dimension and the spatial measure. For example, in the previous example, since it is reasonable to assume that a relationship of spatial containment is implicitly defined between the administrative unit and the accident, if the granularity of position changes, say the position is expressed not by a point but a line, it may happen that the relationship of containment does not hold any longer. In such a case, the value of the dimension level would vary with the measure of granularity. Since this second case entails complex modelling, in order to keep the model relatively simple, we assume that all dimensions are invariant with respect to spatial measure granularity. Therefore, all levels of a spatial measure have the same functional dependency from dimensions.

Aggregation of Spatial Measures

The second issue concerns the operators for the spatial aggregation of spatial measures. Such operators compute, for example, the union and intersection of a set of geometries, the geometry with maximum linear or aerial extent out of a set of one-dimensional and two-dimensional geometries and the MBB (Minimum Bounding Box) of a set of geometries. In general, in the SDW literature these operators are supposed to be applied only to geometries and not to features. Moreover, as previously remarked, a standard set of operators for spatial aggregation has not been defined yet.

For the sake of generality, in our model we do not make any choice about the set of possible operations. We only impose, since we allow representing spatial measures as features, that the operators are applied to sets of features and return a feature. Further, the result is a new or an existing feature, depending on the nature of the operator. For example, the union (or merge) of a set of features, say states, is a newly-created feature whose geometry is obtained from the geometric union of the features' geometries. Notice also that the type of the result may be a newly-created feature type. In fact, the union of a set of states is not itself a state and therefore the definition of a new type is required to hold the resulting features.

Coarsening of Spatial Measures

The next issue is whether the result of a spatial aggregation can be represented at different levels of detail. If so, data analysis would become much more flexible, since the user would be enabled not only to aggregate spatial data but also to dynamically decrease their granularity. To address this requirement, we assume that the model includes not only operators for spatial aggregation but also operators for decreasing the spatial granularity of features. We call these operators *coarsening operators*. As previously stated, coarsening operators include operators for cartographic generalization (Camossi & Bertolotto, 2003) and fuzzyûcation operators. A simple example of fuzzyfication is the operation mapping of a point of coordinates

(x,y) into a close point by reducing the number of decimal digits of the coordinates. These operators are used in our model for building the hierarchy of spatial measures.

When a measure value is expressed according to a lower granularity, the dimension values remain unchanged, since dimensions are assumed to be invariant. As a simple example, consider the position of an accident. Suppose that an aggregation operation, e.g., MBB computation, is performed over positions grouped by date. The result is some new feature, say *yearly accidents*, with its own polygonal geometry. At this point we can apply a coarsening operator and thus a new measure value is dynamically obtained, functionally dependent on the same dimension values. The process of grouping and abstraction can thus iterate.

Spatial Operators

Finally, we introduce the Spatial OLAP operators that are meant to support the navigation in MuSD. Since numerous algebras have been proposed in the literature for non-spatial DW, instead of defining a new set of operators from scratch, we have selected an existing algebra and extended it. Namely, we have chosen the algebra defined in Vassiliadis, 1998. The advantages of this algebra are twofold: It is formally defined, and it is a good representative of the class of algebras for cube-oriented models (Vassiliadis, 1998; Vassiliadis & Sellis, 1999), which are close to our model.

Besides the basic operators defined in the original algebra (LevelClimbing, Packing, FunctionApplication, Projection and Dicing), we introduce the following operators: MeasureClimbing, SpatialFunctionApplication and CubeDisplay. The *MeasureClimbing* operator is introduced to enable the scaling up of spatial measures to different granularities; the *SpatialFunctionApplication* operator performs aggregation of spatial measures; *CubeDisplay* simply visualizes a cube as a map. The application of these operators causes

Table 1. Cb= Basic cube

Month	Location	Victims
Jan 03	P1	4
Jeb 03	P2	3
Jan 03	P3	3
May 03	P4	1
Feb 04	P5	2
Feb 04	P6	3
Mar 04	P7	1
May 04	P8	2
May 04	P9	3
May 04	P10	1

Table 2. Cube 1

Year	Location	Victims
03	P1	4
03	P2	3
03	P3	3
03	P4	1
04	P5	2
04	P6	3
04	P7	1
04	P8	2
04	P9	3
04	P10	1

a transition from the current state to a new state of the SDW. Therefore the navigation results from the successive application of these operators.

Hereinafter we illustrate the operational meaning of these additional operators. For the sake of completeness, we present first the three fundamental operators of the native algebra used to perform data aggregation and rollup.

In what follows, we use the following conventions: S indicates the schema, and ST denotes the set of states for S, of the form <SL, C> where SL is the schema level <DLv_1, ..., DLv_i, ..., DLv_n, M_1, ..., M_m, Slv> and C, a cube for that schema level. Moreover, the dot notation $SL.DLv_i$ is used to denote the DLv_i component of the schema level. The examples refer to the schema presented in Example 4 (limited to one dimension) and to the basic cube reported in Table 1.

Level Climbing

In accordance with the definition of Vassiliadis, the LevelClimbing operation replaces all values of a set of dimensions with dimension values of coarser dimension levels. In other terms, given a state S = <SL, C>, the operation causes a transition to a new state <SL', C'> in which SL' is the schema level including the coarser dimension level, and

C' is the cube containing the coarser values for the given level. In our model, the operation can be formally defined as follows:

Definition 8 (LevelClimbing): The LevelClimbing operator is defined by the mapping: LevelClimbing: ST x D x LV→ ST such that, given a state SL, a dimension D_i and a level lv_i of D_i, LevelClimbing(<SL, Cb>, D_i, lv_i) = <SL', Cb > with lv_i = $SL'.Dlv_i$.

Example 6: Let SL be the following schema levels: SL=<Month, AccidentPoint, Victims>. Cube 1 in Table 2 results from the execution of Level_Climbing (<SL, Basic_cube>, Time, Year).

Packing

The Packing operator, as defined in the original algebra, groups into a single tuple multiple tuples having the same dimension values. Since the domain of measures is multi-valued, after the

Table 3. Cube 2

year	Location	#Victims
03	{P1,P2,P3,P4}	{4,2,3,1,2,1}
04	{P5,P6,P7,P8,P9,P19}	{3,3,1,3}

operation the values of measures are sets. The new state shows the same schema level and a different cube. Formally:

Definition 9 (Packing): The Packing operator is defined by the mapping: Packing: ST→ ST such that Packing(<SL, C>) = <SL, C'>

Example 7: Cube 2 in Table 3 results from the operation: Pack (SL,Cube1)

FunctionApplication

The FunctionApplication operator, which belongs to the original algebra, applies an aggregation function, such as the standard avg and sum, to the non-spatial measures of the current state. The result is a new cube for the same schema level. Let M be the set of non-spatial measures and AOP the set of aggregation operators.

Definition 10 (FunctionApplication): The FunctionApplication operator is defined by the mapping: FunctionApplication: ST×AOP×M→ ST, such that denoting with op(C, M_i) the cube resulting from the application of the aggregation operator op to the measure Mi of cube C, FunctionApplication(<DLv_1, ..., DLv_n, M_1, ...M_i, ..., M_m, op, M_i) = <SL, C'> with cube C' = op(C, M_i).

SpatialFunctionApplication

This operator extends the original algebra to perform spatial aggregation of spatial measures. The operation is similar to the previous Function-Application. The difference is that the operator is meant to aggregate spatial measure values.

Table 4. Cube 3

Year	#Victims	Location
03	13	Area1
04	10	Area2

Definition 11 (SpatialFunctionApplication): Let SOP be the set of spatial aggregation operators. The SpatialFunctionApplication operator is defined by the mapping:

SpatialFunctionApplication: ST×SOP→ ST such that, denoting with op(C, Slv) the cube resulting from the application of the spatial aggregation operator sop to the spatial measure level Slv of cube C, SpatialFunctionApplication(<DLv_1, ..., DLv_n, M_1, ..., M_m, Slv >, sop) = <SL, C'> with C' = sop(C, Slv).

Example 8: Cube 3 in Table 4 results from the application of two aggregation operators, respectively on the measures victims and AccidentPoint. The result of the spatial aggregation is a set of features of a new feature type.

Measure Climbing

The MeasureClimbing operator enables the scaling of spatial measures to a coarser granularity. The effect of the operation is twofold: a) it dynamically applies a coarsening operator to the values of the current spatial measure level to obtain coarser values; and b) it causes a transition to a new state defined by a schema level with a coarser measure level.

Defnition 12 (MeasureClimbing): Let COP be the set of coarsening operators. The Measure-Climbing operator is defined by the mapping: MeasureClimbing : ST×COP→ ST such that denoting with:

- op(Slv): a coarsening operator applied to the values of a spatial measure level Slv
- SL =<DLv1, ..., DLvi, ..., DLvn, M1, ..., Mm, Slv>
- SL' =< DLv1, ..., DLvi, ..., DLvn, M1, ..., Mm, Slv' >

Table 5. Cube 4

Year	#Victims	FuzzyLocation
03	13	Id
04	10	Id2

MeasureClimbing(SL, op)=SL' with Slv' = op(Slv);

Example 9: Cube 4 in Table 5 results from the application of the MeasureClimbing operator to the previous cube. The operation applies a coarsening operator to the spatial measure and thus changes the level of the spatial measure, reducing the level of detail. In Cube 4, "FuzzyLocation" is the name of the new measure level.

DisplayCube

This operator is introduced to allow the display of the spatial features contained in the current cube in the form of a cartographic map. Let MAP be the set of maps.

Defnition 13 (DisplayCube): The operator is defined by the mapping: DisplayCube: ST → MAP so that, denoting with m, a map: DisplayCube(<SL, C>) =m.

As a concluding remark on the proposed algebra, we would like to stress that the model is actually a general framework that needs to be instantiated with a specific set of aggregation and coarsening operators to become operationally meaningful. The definition of such set of operators is, however, a major research issue.

FUTURE TRENDS

Although SMD models for spatial data with geometry address important requirements, such models are not sufficiently rich to deal with more complex requirements posed by innovative applications. In particular, current SDW technology is not able to deal with complex objects. By complex spatial objects, we mean objects that cannot be represented in terms of simple geometries, like points and polygons. Complex spatial objects are, for example, continuous fields, objects with topology, spatio-temporal objects, etc. Specific categories of spatio-temporal objects that can be useful in several applications are diverse trajectories of moving entities. A trajectory is typically modelled as a sequence of consecutive locations in a space (Vlachos, 2002). Such locations are acquired by using tracking devices installed on vehicles and on portable equipment. Trajectories are useful to represent the location of spatial facts describing events that have a temporal and spatial evolution. For example, in logistics, trajectories could model the "location" of freight deliveries. In such a case, the delivery would represent the spatial fact, characterized by a number of properties, such as the freight and destination, and would include as a spatial attribute the trajectory performed by the vehicle to arrive at destination. By analyzing the trajectories, for example, more effective routes could be detected. Trajectories result from the connection of the tracked locations based on some interpolation function. In the simplest case, the tracked locations correspond to points in space whereas the interpolating function determines the segments connecting such points. However, in general, locations and interpolating functions may require a more complex definition (Yu et al., 2004). A major research issue is how to obtain summarized data out of a database of trajectories. The problem is complex because it requires the comparison and classification of trajectories. For that purpose, the notion of trajectory similarity is used. It means that trajectories are classified to be the same when they are sufficiently similar. Different measures of similarity have been proposed in the literature (Vlachos et al., 2002). A spatial data warehouse of trajectories could provide the unifying representation framework to integrate data mining techniques for data classification.

CONCLUSION

Spatial data warehousing is a relatively recent technology responding to the need of providing users with a set of operations for easily exploring large amounts of spatial data, possibly represented at different levels of semantic and geometric detail, as well as for aggregating spatial data into synthetic information most suitable for decision-making. We have discussed a novel research issue regarding the modelling of spatial measures defined at multiple levels of granularity. Since spatial data are naturally available at different granularities, it seems reasonable to extend the notion of spatial measure to take account of this requirement. The MuSD model we have defined consists of a set of representation constructs and a set of operators. The model is defined at the conceptual level in order to provide a more flexible and general representation. Next steps include the specialization of the model to account for some specific coarsening operators and the mapping of the conceptual model onto a logical data model as a basis for the development of a prototype.

REFERENCES

Bedard, Y., Gosselin, P., Rivest, S., Proulx, M., Nadeau, M., Lebel, G., & Gagnon, M. (2003). Integrating GIS components with knowledge discovery technology for environmental health decision support. *International Journal of Medical Informatics, 70*, 79-94.

Camossi, E., Bertolotto, M., Bertino, E., & Guerrini, G. (2003). A multigranular spatiotemporal data model. *Proceedings of the 11th ACM International Symposium on Advances in Geographic Information Systems, ACM GIS 2003,* New Orleans, LA (pp. 94-101).

Chaudhuri, S., & Dayal, U. (1997). An overview of data warehousing and OLAP technology. *ACM SIGMOD Record, 26*(1) , 65-74.

Clementini, E., di Felice, P., & van Oosterom, P. (1993). A small set of formal topological relationships suitable for end-user interaction. In *LNCS 692: Proceedings of the 3rd International Symposyium on Advances in Spatial Databases, SSD '93* (pp. 277-295).

Fidalgo, R. N., Times, V. C., Silva, J., & Souza, F. (2004). GeoDWFrame: A framework for guiding the design of geographical dimensional schemas. In *LNCS 3181: Proceedings of the 6th International Conference on Data Warehousing and Knowledge Discovery, DaWaK 2004* (pp. 26-37).

Fonseca, F., Egenhofer, M., Davies, C., & Camara, G. (2002). Semantic granularity in ontology-driven geographic information systems. *Annals of Mathematics and Artificial Intelligence, Special Issue on Spatial and Temporal Granularity, 36*(1), 121-151.

Han, J., Altman R., Kumar, V., Mannila, H., & Pregibon, D. (2002). Emerging scientific applications in data mining. *Communication of the ACM, 45*(8), 54-58.

Han, J. , Stefanovic, N., & Kopersky, K. (1998). Selective materialization: An efficient method for spatial data cube construction. *Proceedings of Research and Development in Knowledge Discovery and Data Mining, Second Pacific-Asia Conference, PAKDD'98* (pp. 144-158).

Jensen, C., Kligys, A., Pedersen T., & Timko, I. (2002). Multidimensional data modeling for location-based services. In *Proceedings of the 10th ACM International Symposium on Advances in Geographic Information Systems* (pp. 55-61).

Kimbal, R. (1996). *The data warehouse toolkit.* New York: John Wiley & Sons.

Longley, P., Goodchild, M., Maguire, D., & Rhind, D. (2001). *Geographic information systems and science.* New York: John Wiley & Sons.

Lopez, I., & Snodgrass, R. (2005). Spatiotemporal

aggregate computation: A survey. *IEEE Transactions on Knowledge and Data Engineering, 17*(2), 271-286.

Malinowski, E. & Zimanyi, E. (2004). Representing spatiality in a conceptual multidimensional model. *Proceedings of the 12th ACM International Symposium on Advances in Geographic Information Systems, ACM GIS 2004*, Washington, DC (pp. 12-21).

Marchant, P., Briseboi, A., Bedard, Y., & Edwards G. (2004). Implementation and evaluation of a hypercube-based method for spatiotemporal exploration and analysis. *ISPRS Journal of Photogrammetry & Remote Sensing, 59*, 6-20.

Meratnia, N., & de By, R. (2002). Aggregation and Comparison of Trajectories. *Proceedings of the 10th ACM International Symposium on Advances in Geographic Information Systems, ACM GIS 2002*, McLean, VA (pp. 49-54).

OGC--OpenGIS Consortium. (2001). *OpenGIS^{â} abstract specification, topic 1: Feature geometry (ISO 19107 Spatial Schema)*. Retrieved from http://www.opengeospatial.org

OGC—Open Geo Spatial Consortium Inc. (2003). *OpenGIS^{â} reference model*. Retrieved from http://www.opengeospatial.org

Papadias, D., Kalnis, P., Zhang, J., & Tao, Y. (2001). Efficient OLAP operations in spatial data warehouses. *LNCS: 2121, Proceedings of the 7h Int. Symposium on Advances in Spatial and Temporal Databases* (pp. 443-459).

Pedersen, T., & Tryfona, N. (2001). Pre-aggregation in spatial data warehouses. *LNCS: 2121, Proceedings. of the 7h Int. Symposium on Advances in Spatial and Temporal Databases* (pp. 460-480).

Rao, F., Zhang, L., Yu, X., Li, Y., & Chen, Y. (2003). Spatial hierarchy and OLAP-favored search in spatial data warehouse. *Proceedings of the 6th*

ACM International Workshop on Data Warehousing and OLAP, DOLAP '03 (pp. 48-55).

Rigaux,. P., Scholl, M., & Voisard, A. (2002). *Spatial databases with applications to Gis*. New York: Academic Press.

Rivest, S., Bedard, Y., & Marchand, P. (2001). Towards better support for spatial decision making: Defining the characteristics of spatial on-line analytical processing (SOLAP). *Geomatica, 55*(4), 539-555.

Savary, L., Wan, T., & Zeitouni, K. (2004). Spatio-temporal data warehouse design for human activity pattern analysis. *Proceedings of the 15th International Workshop On Database and Expert Systems Applications (DEXA04)* (pp. 81-86).

Scotch, M., & Parmantoa, B. (2005). SOVAT: Spatial OLAP visualization and analysis tools. *Proceedings of the 38th Hawaii International Conference on System Sciences.*

Shekhar, S. , Lu. C. T., Tan, X., Chawla, S., & Vatsavai, R. (2001). Map cube: A visualization tool for spatial data warehouse. In H. J. Miller & J. Han (Eds.), *Geographic data mining and knowledge discovery.* Taylor and Francis.

Shekhar, S., & Chawla, S. (2003). *Spatial databases: A tour*. NJ: Prentice Hall.

Spaccapietra, S., Parent, C., & Vangenot, C. (2000). GIS database: From multiscale to multirepresentation. In B. Y.Choueiry & T. Walsh (Eds.), Abstraction, reformulation, and approximation, LNAI 1864. *Proceedings of the 4th International Symposium, SARA-2000*, Horseshoe Bay, Texas.

Theodoratos, D., & Sellis, T. (1999). Designing data warehouses. *IEEE Transactions on Data and Knowledge Engineering, 31*(3), 279-301.

Vassiliadis, P. (1998). Modeling multidimensional databases, cubes and cube operations. *Proceedings of the 10th Scientific and Statistical Da-*

tabase Management Conference (SSDBM '98) (pp. 53-62).

Vassiliadis, P., & Sellis, T. (1999). A survey of logical models for OLAP databases. *ACM SIG-MOD Record, 28*(4), 64-69.

Vlachos, M., Kollios, G., & Gunopulos, D.(2002). Discovering similar multidimensional trajectories. *Proceedings of 18th ICDE* (pp. 273-282).

Wang, B., Pan, F., Ren, D., Cui, Y., Ding, D. et al. (2003). Efficient olap operations for spatial data using peano trees. *Proceedings of the 8th ACM SIGMOD Workshop on Research Issues in Data Mining and Knowledge Discovery* (pp. 28-34).

Worboys, M. (1998). Imprecision in finite resolution spatial data. *GeoInformatica, 2*(3), 257-279.

Worboys, M., & Duckam, M. (2004). *GIS: A computing perspective* (2nd ed.). Boca Raton, FL: CRC Press.

Yu, B., Kim, S. H., Bailey, T., & Gamboa R. (2004). Curve-based representation of moving object trajectories. *Proceedings of the International Database Engineering and Applications Symposium, IDEAS 2004* (pp. 419-425).

Zhang, D., & Tsotras, V. (2005). Optimizing spatial Min/Max aggregations. *The VLDB Journal, 14*, 170-181.

Section IV
Benchmarking and Evaluation

Chapter XV
Data Warehouse Benchmarking with DWEB

Jérôme Darmont
University of Lyon (ERIC Lyon 2), France

ABSTRACT

Performance evaluation is a key issue for designers and users of Database Management Systems (DBMSs). Performance is generally assessed with software benchmarks that help, for example test architectural choices, compare different technologies, or tune a system. In the particular context of data warehousing and On-Line Analytical Processing (OLAP), although the Transaction Processing Performance Council (TPC) aims at issuing standard decision-support benchmarks, few benchmarks do actually exist. We present in this chapter the Data Warehouse Engineering Benchmark (DWEB), which allows generating various ad-hoc synthetic data warehouses and workloads. DWEB is fully parameterized to fulfill various data warehouse design needs. However, two levels of parameterization keep it relatively easy to tune. We also expand on our previous work on DWEB by presenting its new Extract, Transform, and Load (ETL) feature, as well as its new execution protocol. A Java implementation of DWEB is freely available online, which can be interfaced with most existing relational DMBSs. To the best of our knowledge, DWEB is the only easily available, up-to-date benchmark for data warehouses.

INTRODUCTION

Performance evaluation is a key issue for both designers and users of Database Management Systems (DBMSs). It helps designers select among alternate software architectures, performance optimization strategies, or validate or refute hypotheses regarding the actual behavior of a system. Thus, performance evaluation is an essential component in the development process of efficient and well-designed database systems. Users may also employ performance evaluation, either to compare the efficiency of different technologies before selecting one, or to tune a system. In many fields including databases, performance is generally assessed with the help of software benchmarks. The main components in a benchmark are its database model and workload model (set of operations to execute on the database).

Evaluating data warehousing and decision-support technologies is a particularly intricate task. Though pertinent, general advice is available, notably on-line (Pendse, 2003; Greenfield, 2004a), more quantitative elements regarding sheer performance, including benchmarks, are few. In the late nineties, the OLAP (On-Line Analytical Process) APB-1 benchmark has been very popular. Henceforth, the Transaction Processing Performance Council (TPC) (1), a non-profit organization, defines standard benchmarks (including decision-support benchmarks) and publishes objective and verifiable performance evaluations to the industry.

Our own motivation for data warehouse benchmarking was initially to test the efficiency of performance optimization techniques (such as automatic index and materialized view selection techniques) we have been developing for several years. None of the existing data warehouse benchmarks suited our needs. APB-1's schema is fixed, while we needed to test our performance optimization techniques on various data warehouse configurations. Furthermore, it is no longer supported and somewhat difficult to find. The TPC currently supports the TPC-H decision-support benchmark (TPC, 2006). However, its database schema is inherited from the older and obsolete benchmark TPC-D (TPC, 1998), which is not a dimensional schema such as the typical star schema and its derivatives that are used in data warehouses (Inmon, 2002; Kimball & Ross, 2002). Furthermore, TPC-H's workload,

though decision-oriented, does not include explicit OLAP queries either. This benchmark is implicitly considered obsolete by the TPC that has issued some draft specifications for its successor: TPC-DS (TPC, 2007). However, TPC-DS, which is very complex, especially at the ETL (Extract, Transform, and Load) and workload levels, has been under development since 2002 and is not completed yet.

Furthermore, although the TPC decision-support benchmarks are scalable according to Gray's (1993) definition, their schema is also fixed. For instance, TPC-DS' constellation schema cannot easily be simplified into a simple star schema. It must be used "as is". Different ad-hoc configurations are not possible. Furthermore, there is only one parameter to define the database, the Scale Factor (SF), which sets up its size (from 1 to 100,000 GB). Users cannot control the size of dimensions and fact tables separately, for instance. Finally, users have no control on workload definition. The number of generated queries directly depends on SF.

Eventually, in a context where data warehouse architectures and decision-support workloads depend a lot on application domain, it is very important that designers who wish to evaluate the impact of architectural choices or optimization techniques on global performance can choose and/or compare among several configurations. The TPC benchmarks, which aim at standardized results and propose only one configuration of warehouse schema, are ill-adapted to this purpose. TPC-DS is indeed able to evaluate the performance of optimization techniques, but it cannot test their impact on various choices of data warehouse architectures. Generating particular data warehouse configurations (e.g., large-volume dimensions) or ad-hoc query workloads is not possible either, whereas it could be an interesting feature for a data warehouse benchmark.

For all these reasons, we decided to design a full data warehouse benchmark that would be able to model various configurations of database and workload: DWEB, the Data Warehouse Engineering Benchmark (Darmont *et al.*, 2005; Darmont *et al.*, 2007). In this context (variable architecture, variable size), using a real-life benchmark is not an option. Hence, DWEB helps generate ad-hoc synthetic data warehouses (modeled as star, snowflake, or constellation schemas) and workloads, mainly for engineering needs. DWEB may thus be viewed more as a benchmark generator than an actual, single benchmark.

This chapter presents the full specifications of DWEB's database and workload models, and expands our previous work with a new ETL process and a new execution protocol that have recently been included into DWEB. All models, parameters and pseudo-code algorithms are provided. The remainder of this chapter is organized as follows. We first present the state of the art decision-support benchmarks, with a particular focus on the current and future standards TPC-H and TPC-DS. Then, we detail DWEB's specifications: database model, workload model, ETL process and execution protocol. We present a short tutorial to illustrate DWEB's usage, and finally conclude this chapter and provide future research directions.

STATE OF THE ART DECISION-SUPPORT BENCHMARKS

To the best of our knowledge, relatively few decision-support benchmarks have been designed out of the TPC. Some do exist, but their specification is sometimes not fully published (Demarest, 1995). The most notable is presumably the OLAP APB-1 benchmark, which was issued in 1998 by the OLAP council, a now inactive organization founded by four OLAP vendors. APB-1 has been quite extensively used in the late nineties. Its data warehouse schema is architectured around four dimensions: *Customer*, *Product*, *Channel* and *Time*. Its workload of ten queries is aimed at sale forecasting. APB-1 is quite simple and proved

limited, since it is not "differentiated to reflect the hurdles that are specific to different industries and functions" (Thomsen, 1998). Finally, some OLAP datasets are also available on-line (2), but they do not qualify as benchmarks, being only raw databases (chiefly, no workload is provided).

In the remainder of this section, we focus more particularly on the TPC benchmarks. The TPC-D benchmark (Ballinger, 1993; Bhashyam, 1996; TPC, 1998) appeared in the mid-nineties, and forms the base of TPC-H and TPC-R that have replaced it (Poess & Floyd, 2000). TPC-H and TPC-R are actually identical, only their usage varies. TPC-H (TPC, 2006) is for ad-hoc querying (queries are not known in advance and optimizations are forbidden), while TPC-R (TPC, 2003) is for reporting (queries are known in advance and optimizations are allowed). TPC-H is currently the only decision-support benchmark supported by the TPC. Its designated successor, TPC-DS (Poess *et al.*, 2002; TPC, 2007), is indeed still currently under development and only available as a draft.

TPC-H

TPC-H exploits the same relational database schema as TPC-D: a classical *product-order-supplier* model (represented as a UML class diagram in Figure 1); and the workload from TPC-D supplemented with five new queries. This workload is constituted of twenty-two SQL-92 parameterized, decision-oriented queries labeled Q1 to Q22; and two refresh functions RF1 and RF2 that essentially insert and delete tuples in the ORDER and LINEITEM tables.

The query parameters are substituted with the help of a random function following a uniform distribution. Finally, the protocol for running TPC-H includes a load test and a performance test (executed twice), which is further subdivided into a power test and a throughput test. Three primary metrics describe the results in terms of power, throughput, and a composition of the

Figure 1. TPC-D, TPC-H, and TPC-R database schema

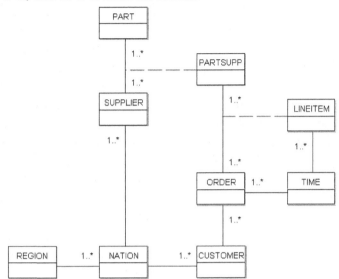

two. Power and throughput are respectively the geometric and arithmetic average of database size divided by execution time.

TPC-DS

TPC-DS more clearly models a data warehouse than TPC-H. TPC-DS' database schema, whose fact tables are represented in Figure 2, models the decision-support functions of a retail product supplier as several snowflake schemas. Catalog and web sales and returns are interrelated, while store management is independent. This model also includes fifteen dimensions that are shared by the fact tables. Thus, the whole model is a constellation schema.

TPC-DS' workload is made of four classes of queries: reporting queries, ad-hoc decision-support queries, interactive OLAP queries, and data extraction queries. A set of about five hundred queries is generated from query templates written in SQL-99 (with OLAP extensions). Substitutions on the templates are operated using non-uniform random distributions. The data warehouse maintenance process includes a full ETL process and a specific treatment of dimensions. For instance, historical dimensions preserve history as new dimension entries are added, while non-historical dimensions do not store aged data any more. Finally, the execution model of TPC-DS consists of four steps: a load test, a query run, a data maintenance run, and another query run. A single

Figure 2. TPC-DS data warehouse schema

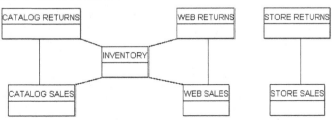

throughput metric is proposed, which takes the query and maintenance runs into account.

DWEB SPECIFICATIONS

We present in this section the fullest specifications of DWEB as of today. The main components in a benchmark are its database and workload models, but we also detail DWEB's new ETL capability and new execution protocol, which were previously assumed to be similar to TPC-DS's.

Database Model

Schema

Our design objective for DWEB is to be able to model the different kinds of data warehouse architectures that are popular within a ROLAP (Relational OLAP) environment: classical star schemas, snowflake schemas with hierarchical dimensions, and constellation schemas with multiple fact tables and shared dimensions. To achieve this goal, we propose a data warehouse metamodel (represented as a UML class diagram in Figure 3) that can be instantiated into these different schemas.

We view this metamodel as a middle ground between the multidimensional metamodel from the Common Warehouse Metamodel (CWM) (OMG, 2003; Poole *et al.*, 2003) and the eventual benchmark model. Our metamodel may actually be viewed as an instance of the CWM metamodel, which could be qualified as a meta-metamodel in our context. The upper part of Figure 3 describes a data warehouse (or a datamart, if a datamart is viewed as a small, dedicated data warehouse) as constituted of one or several fact tables that are each described by several dimensions. Each dimension may also describe several fact tables (shared dimensions). Each dimension may be constituted of one or several hierarchies made of different levels. There can be only one level if the dimension is not a hierarchy. Both fact tables and dimension hierarchy levels are relational tables, which are modeled in the lower part of Figure 3. Classically, a table or relation is defined in intention by its attributes and in extension by its tuples or rows. At the intersection of a given attribute and a given tuple lies the value of this attribute in this tuple.

Our metamodel is quite simple. It is sufficient to model the data warehouse schemas we aim at (star, snowflake, and constellation schemas), but it is limited and cannot model some particulari-

Figure 3. DWEB data warehouse metaschema

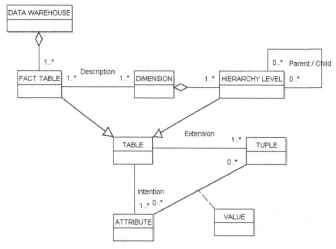

ties that are found in real-life warehouses, such as many-to-many relationships between facts and dimensions, or hierarchy levels shared by several hierarchies. This is currently a deliberate choice, but the metamodel might be extended in the future.

Parameterization

DWEB's database parameters help users select the data warehouse architecture they need in a given context. They are aimed at parameterizing metaschema instantiation to produce an actual data warehouse schema. When designing them, we try to meet the four key criteria that make a "good" benchmark, according to Gray (1993):

- *Relevance,* the benchmark must answer our engineering needs (cf. Introduction);
- *Portability,* the benchmark must be easy to implement on different systems;
- *Scalability,* it must be possible to benchmark small and large databases, and to scale up the benchmark;
- *Simplicity,* the benchmark must be understandable; otherwise it will not be credible nor used.

We further propose to extend Gray's scalability criterion to *adaptability.* A performance evaluation tool must then propose different database or workload configurations that help run tests in various experimental conditions. Such tools might be qualified as benchmark generators, though we term them, possibly abusively, tunable or generic benchmarks. Aiming at adaptability is mechanically detrimental to simplicity. However, this criterion is fundamental and must not be neglected when designing a generic tool. It is thus necessary to find means to ensure good adaptability while not sacrificing simplicity; in short, to find a fair tradeoff between these criteria.

Relevance and adaptability on one hand, and simplicity on the other hand, are clearly two orthogonal goals. Introducing too few parameters

reduces the model's expressiveness, while introducing too many parameters makes it difficult to apprehend by potential users. Furthermore, few of these parameters are likely to be used in practice. In parallel, the generation complexity of the instantiated schema must be mastered. To solve this dilemma, we capitalize on the experience of designing the OCB object-oriented database benchmark (Darmont & Schneider, 2000). OCB is generic and able to model all the other existing object-oriented database benchmarks, but it is controlled by too many parameters, few of which are used in practice. Hence, we propose to divide the parameter set into two subsets.

The first subset of so-called low-level parameters allows an advanced user to control everything about data warehouse generation (Table 1). However, the number of low-level parameters can increase dramatically when the schema gets larger. For instance, if there are several fact tables, all their characteristics, including dimensions and their own characteristics, must be defined for each fact table.

Thus, we designed a layer above with much fewer parameters that may be easily understood and set up (Table 2). More precisely, these high-

Table 1. DWEB warehouse low-level parameters

Parameter name	Meaning
NB_FT	Number of fact tables
NB_DIM(f)	Number of dimensions describing fact table #f
TOT_NB_DIM	Total number of dimensions
NB_MEAS(f)	Number of measures in fact table #f
DENSITY(f)	Density rate in fact table #f
NB_LEVELS(d)	Number of hierarchy levels in dimension #d
NB_ATT(d,h)	Number of attributes in hierarchy level #h of dimension #d
HHLEVEL_SIZE(d)	Cardinality of the highest hierarchy level of dimension #d
DIM_SFACTOR(d)	Size scale factor in the hierarchy levels of dimension #d

level parameters are average values for the low-level parameters. At database generation time, the high-level parameters are exploited by random functions (following a Gaussian distribution) to automatically set up the low-level parameters. Finally, unlike the number of low-level parameters, the number of high-level parameters always remains constant and reasonable (less than ten parameters).

Users may choose to set up either the full set of low-level parameters, or only the high-level parameters, for which we propose default values that correspond to a snowflake schema. Note that these parameters control both schema and data generation.

Remarks:

- Since shared dimensions are possible,

$$TOT\_NB\_DIM \le \sum_{i=1}^{NB\_FT} NB\_DIM(i).$$

- The cardinal of a fact table is usually lower or equal to the product of its dimensions' cardinals. This is why we introduce the no-

tion of density. A density rate of one indicates that all the possible combinations of the dimension primary keys are present in the fact table, which is very rare in real-life data warehouses. When density rate decreases, we progressively eliminate some of these combinations (cf. Workload Generation).

- This parameter helps control the size of the fact table, independently of the size of its dimensions, which are defined by the *HHLEVEL_SIZE* and *DIM_SFACTOR* parameters (see below).

- Within a dimension, a given hierarchy level has normally a greater cardinality than the next level. For example, in a *town-region-country* hierarchy, the number of towns must be greater than the number of regions, which must be in turn greater than the number of countries. Furthermore, there is often a significant scale factor between these cardinalities (e.g., one thousand towns, one hundred regions, ten countries). Hence, we model the cardinality of hierarchy levels by assigning a "starting" cardinality to the highest level in the hierarchy (*HHLEVEL_SIZE*), and

Table 2. DWEB warehouse high-level parameters

Parameter name	Meaning	Default value
AVG_NB_FT	Average number of fact tables	1
AVG_NB_DIM	Average number of dimensions per fact table	5
AVG_TOT_NB_DIM	Average total number of dimensions	5
AVG_NB_MEAS	Average number of measures in fact tables	5
AVG_DENSITY	Average density rate in fact tables	0.6
AVG_NB_LEVELS	Average number of hierarchy levels in dimensions	3
AVG_NB_ATT	Average number of attributes in hierarchy levels	5
AVG_HHLEVEL_SIZE	Average cardinality of the highest hierarchy levels	10
DIM_SFACTOR	Average size scale factor within hierarchy levels	10

then by multiplying it by a predefined scale factor (*DIM_SFACTOR*) for each lower-level hierarchy.

- The global size of the data warehouse is assessed at generation time so that the user retains full control over it.

Generation Algorithm

The instantiation of the DWEB metaschema into an actual benchmark schema is done in two steps:

1. Build the dimensions;
2. Build the fact tables.

The pseudo-code for these two steps is provided in Figures 4 and 5, respectively. Each of these steps is further subdivided, for each dimension or each fact table, into generating its intention and extension. In addition, dimension hierarchies must be managed. Note that they are generated starting from the highest level of hierarchy. For instance, for our *town-region-country* sample hierarchy, we build the country level first, then

Figure 4. DWEB dimensions generation algorithm

```
For i = 1 to TOT_NB_DIM do
  previous_ptr = NIL
  size = HHLEVEL_SIZE(i)
    For j = 1 to NB_LEVELS(i) do
    // Intention
    h1 = New(Hierarchy_level)
    h1.intention = Primary_key()
    For k = 1 to NB_ATT(i,j) do
        h1.intention = h1.intention
            ∪ String_member()
    End for
    // Hierarchy management
    h1.child = previous_ptr
    h1.parent = NIL
    If previous_ptr ≠ NIL then
        previous_ptr.parent = h1
        // Foreign key
        h1.intention = h1.intention
            ∪ previous_ptr.intention.primary_key
    End if
    // Extension
    h1.extension = ∅
    For k = 1 to size do
        new_tuple = Integer_primary_key()
        For l = 1 to NB_ATT(i,j) do
            new_tuple = new_tuple ∪ Random_string()
        End for
        If previous_ptr ≠ NIL then
            new_tuple = new_tuple
                ∪ Random_key(previous_ptr)
            End if
            h1.extension = h1.extension ∪ new_tuple
        End for
        previous_ptr = h1
        size = size * DIM_SFACTOR(i)
  End for
  dim(i) = h1 // First (lowest) level of the hierarchy
End for
```

Figure 5. DWEB fact tables generation algorithm

```
For i = 1 to TOT_NB_FT do
    // Intention
    ft(i).intention = ∅
    For k = 1 to NB_DIM(i) do
        j = Random_dimension(ft(i))
        ft(i).intention = ft(i).intention
            ∪ ft(i).dim(j).primary key
    End for
    For k to NB_MEAS(i) do
        ft(i).intention = ft(i).intention
            ∪ Float_measure()
    End for
    // Extension
    ft(i).extension = ∅
    For j = 1 to NB_DIM(i) do // Cartesian product
        ft(i).extension = ft(i).extension
            × ft(i).dim(j).primary key
    End for
    to_delete = DENSITY(i) * |ft(i).extension|
    For j = 1 to to_delete do
        Random_delete(ft(i).extension)
    End for
    For j = 1 to |ft(i).extension| do
    // With |ft(i).extension| updated
    For k = 1 to NB_MEAS(i) do
        Ft(i).extension.tuple(j).measure(k)
            = Random_float()
        End for
    End for
End for
```

the region level, and eventually the town level. Hence, tuples from a given hierarchy level can refer to tuples from the next level (that are already created) with the help of a foreign key.

We use three main classes of functions and one procedure in these algorithms.

1. `Primary_key()`, `String_member()` and `Float_measure()` return attribute names for primary keys, members in hierarchy levels, and measures in fact tables, respectively. These names are labeled sequentially and prefixed by the table's name (e.g., DIM1_1_DESCR1, DIM1_1_DESCR2...).

2. `Integer_primary_key()`, `Random_key()`, `Random_string()` and `Random_float()` return sequential integers with

respect to a given table (no duplicates are allowed), random instances of the specified table's primary key (random values for a foreign key), random strings of fixed size (20 characters) selected from a precomputed referential of strings and prefixed by the corresponding attribute name, and random single-precision real numbers, respectively.

3. `Random_dimension()` returns a dimension that is chosen among the existing dimensions that are not already describing the fact table in parameter.

4. `Random_delete()` deletes one tuple at random from the extension of a table.

Except in the `Random_delete()` procedure, where the random distribution is uniform, we use Gaussian random distributions to introduce a skew, so that some of the data, whether in the fact tables or the dimensions, are referenced more frequently than others as it is normally the case in real-life data warehouses.

Remark: The way density is managed in Figure 5 is grossly non-optimal. We chose to present the algorithm that way for the sake of clarity, but the actual implementation does not create all the tuples from the cartesian product, and then delete some of them. It directly generates the right number of tuples by using the density rate as a probability for each tuple to be created.

Workload Model

In a data warehouse benchmark, the workload may be subdivided into:

1. A load of decision-support queries (mostly OLAP queries);
2. The ETL (data generation and maintenance) process.

To design DWEB's workload, we inspire both from TPC-DS' workload definition (which is very elaborate) and information regarding data warehouse performance from other sources (BMC, 2000; Greenfield, 2004b). However, TPC-DS' workload is quite complex and somehow confusing. The reporting, ad-hoc decision-support and OLAP query classes are very similar, for instance, but none of them include any specific OLAP operator such as Cube or Rollup. Since we want to meet Gray's simplicity criterion, we propose a simpler workload. In particular, we do not address the issue of nested queries for now. Furthermore, we also have to design a workload that is consistent with the variable nature of the DWEB data warehouses.

We focus in this section on the definition of a query model that excludes update operations.

The ETL and warehouse refreshing processes are addressed in the next section.

Query Model

The DWEB workload models two different classes of queries: purely decision-oriented queries involving common OLAP operations, such as cube, roll-up, drill-down and slice and dice; and extraction queries (simple join queries). We define our generic query model (Figure 6) as a grammar that is a subset of the SQL-99 standard, which introduces much-needed analytical capabilities to relational database querying. This increases the ability to perform dynamic, analytic SQL queries.

Parameterization

DWEB's workload parameters help users tailor the benchmark's load, which is also dependent from the warehouse schema, to their needs. Just like DWEB's database parameter set (cf. previous section), DWEB's workload parameter set (Table 3) has been designed with Gray's simplicity criterion in mind. These parameters determine how the query model from Figure 6 is instantiated. These parameters help define workload size and complexity, by setting up the proportion of complex OLAP queries (i.e., the class of queries) in the workload, the number of aggregation operations, the presence of a Having clause in the query, or the number of subsequent drill-down operations.

Here, we have only a limited number of high-level parameters (eight parameters, since *PROB_ EXTRACT* and *PROB_ROLLUP* are derived from *PROB_OLAP* and *PROB_CUBE*, respectively). Indeed, it cannot be envisaged to dive further into detail if the workload is as large as several hundred queries, which is quite typical.

Remark: *NB_Q* is only an *approximate* number of queries because the number of drill-down op-

Figure 6. DWEB query model

Query ::-	
Select	![<Attribute Clause> | <Aggregate Clause> | [<Attribute Clause>, <Aggregate Clause>]]
From	!<Table Clause> [<Where Clause> || [<Group by Clause> * <Having Clause>]]
Attribute Clause ::-	*Attribute name* [[, <Attribute Clause>] | ⊥]
Aggregate Clause ::-	![*Aggregate function name (Attribute name)*] [As Alias] [[, <Aggregate Clause>] | ⊥]
Table Clause ::-	*Table name* [[, <Table Clause>] | ⊥]
Where Clause ::-	**Where** ![<Condition Clause> | <Join Clause>| [<Condition Clause> **And** <Join Clause>]]
Condition Clause ::-	![*Attribute name* <Comparison operator> <Operand Clause>] [[<Logical operator> <Condition Clause>] | ⊥]
Operand Clause ::-	[*Attribute name* | *Attribute value* | *Attribute value list*]
Join Clause ::-	![*Attribute name i = Attribute name j*] [[**And** <Join Clause>] | ⊥]
Group by Clause ::-	**Group by** [**Cube** | **Rollup**] <Attribute Clause>
Having Clause ::-	[*Alias* | *Aggregate function name (Attribute name)*] <Comparison operator> [*Attribute name* | *Attribute value list*]
Key:	The [and] brackets are delimiters.
	!<A>: A is required.
	*<A>: A is optional.
	<A || B>: A or B.
	<A | B>: A exclusive or B.
	⊥: empty clause.
	SQL language elements are indicated in bold.

Table 3. DWEB workload parameters

Parameter name	Meaning	Default value
NB_Q	Approximate number of queries in the workload	100
AVG_NB_ATT	Average number of selected attributes in a query	5
AVG_NB_RESTR	Average number of restrictions in a query	3
PROB_OLAP	Probability that the query type is OLAP	0.9
PROB_EXTRACT	Probability that the query is an extraction query	1 - *PROB_OLAP*
AVG_NB_AGGREG	Average number of aggregations in an OLAP query	3
PROB_CUBE	Probability of an OLAP query to use the Cube operator	0.3
PROB_ROLLUP	Probability of an OLAP query to use the Rollup operator	1 - *PROB_CUBE*
PROB_HAVING	Probability of an OLAP query to include a Having clause	0.2
AVG_NB_DD	Average number of drill-downs after an OLAP query	3

erations after an OLAP query may vary. Hence we can stop generating queries only when we actually have generated as many or more queries than *NB_Q*.

Generation Algorithm

The pseudo-code of DWEB's workload generation algorithm is presented in Figures 7a and 7b. The algorithm's purpose is to generate a set of SQL-99 queries that can be directly executed on the synthetic data warehouse defined in the previous section. It is subdivided into two steps:

1. Generate an initial query that may be either an OLAP or an extraction (join) query;
2. If the initial query is an OLAP query, execute a certain number of drill-down operations based on the first OLAP query. More precisely, each time a drill-down is performed, a member from a lower level of dimension hierarchy is added to the attribute clause of the previous query.

Step 1 is further subdivided into three substeps:

1. The Select, From, and Where clauses of a query are generated simultaneously by randomly selecting a fact table and dimensions, including a hierarchy level within a given dimension hierarchy;
2. The Where clause is supplemented with additional conditions;
3. Eventually, it is decided whether the query is an OLAP query or an extraction query. In the second case, the query is complete. In the first case, aggregate functions applied to measures of the fact table are added in the query, as well as a Group by clause that may include either the Cube or the Rollup operator. A Having clause may optionally be added in too. The aggregate function we apply on measures is always Sum since it is the most common aggregate in cubes. Furthermore, other aggregate functions bear similar time complexities, so they would not

bring in any more insight in a performance study.

We use three classes of functions and a procedure in this algorithm.

1. Random_string() and Random_float() are the same functions than those already described in the Database Generation section. However, we introduce the possibility for Random_float() to use either a uniform

Figure 7a. DWEB workload generation algorithm

```
n = 0
While n < NB_Q do
    // Step 1: Initial query
    // Step 1.2: Select, From and Where clauses
    i = Random_FT() // Fact table selection
    attribute_list = ∅
    table_list = ft(i)
    condition_list = ∅
    For k = 1 to Random_int(AVG_NB_ATT) do
        // Dimension selection
        j = Random_dimension(ft(i))
        l = Random_int(1, ft(i).dim(j).nb_levels)
        // Positioning on hierarchy level l
        hl = ft(i).dim(j) // Current hierarchy level
        m = 1 // Level counter
        fk = ft(i).intention.primary_key.element(j)
        // This foreign key corresponds to
        // ft(i).dim(j).primary_key
        While m < l and hl.child ≠ NIL do
            // Build join
            table_list = table_list ∪ hl
            condition_list = condition_list
                ∪ (fk = hl.intention.primary_key)
            // Next level
            fk = hl.intention.foreign_key
            m = m + 1
            hl = hl.child
        End while
        attribute_list = attribute_list
            ∪ Random_attribute(hl.intention)
    End for
    // Step 1.2: Supplement Where clause
    For k = 1 to Random_int(AVG_NB_RESTR) do
        condition_list = condition_list
            ∪ (Random_attribute(attribute_list)
                = Random_string())
    End for
    // Step 1.3: OLAP or extraction query selection
    p1 = Random_float(0, 1)
    If p1 ≤ PROB_OLAP then // OLAP query
    // Aggregate clause
    aggregate_list = ∅
    For k = 1 to Random_int(AVG_NB_AGGREG) do
        aggregate_list = aggregate_list
            ∪ (Random_measure(ft(i).intention)
    End for
                                                ../..
```

or a Gaussian random distribution. This depends on the function parameters: either a range of values (uniform) or an average value (Gaussian). Finally, we introduce the `Random _ int()` function that behaves just like `Random _ float()` but returns integer values.

2. `Random _ FT()` and `Random _ dimension()` help select a fact table or a dimension describing a given fact table, respectively. They

Figure 7b. DWEB workload generation algorithm (continued)

```
../..
    // Group by clause
    group_by_list = attribute_list
    p2 = Random_float(0, 1)
    If p2 ≤ PROB_CUBE then
      group_by_operator = CUBE
    Else
      group_by_operator = ROLLUP
    End if
    // Having clause
    P3 = Random_float(0, 1)
    If p3 ≤ PROB_HAVING then
        having_clause
              = (Random_attribute(aggregate_list), ≥,
                  Random_float())
    Else
        having_clause = ∅
    End if
    Else // Extraction query
      group_by_list = ∅
      group_by_operator = ∅
      having_clause = ∅
    End if
    // SQL query generation
    Gen_query(attribute_list, aggregate_list, table_list,
      condition_list, group_by_list, group_by_operator,
      having_clause)
    n = n + 1
    // Step 2: Possible subsequent DRILL-DOWN queries
    If p1 ≤ PROB_OLAP then
      k = 0
      While k < Random_int(AVG_NB_DD)
        and hl.parent ≠ NIL do
        k = k + 1
        hl = hl.parent
        att = Random_attribute(hl.intention)
        attribute_list = attribute_list ∪ att
        group_by_list = group_by_list ∪ att
        Gen_query(attribute_list, aggregate_list,
          table_list, condition_list, group_by_list,
          group_by_operator, having_clause)
      End while
      n = n + k
    End if
End while
```

both use a Gaussian random distribution, which introduces an access skew at the fact table and dimension levels. `Random_dimension()` is also already described in the Database Generation section.

3. `Random_attribute()` and `Random_measure()` are very close in behavior. They return an attribute or a measure, respectively, from a table intention or a list of attributes. They both use a Gaussian random distribution.

4. `Gen_query()` is the procedure that actually generates the SQL-99 code of the workload queries, given all the parameters that are needed to instantiate our query model.

ETL Process

When designing DWEB's ETL process, we have to consider again the relevance *vs.* simplicity tradeoff (cf. Gray's criteria). Though the ETL phase may take up to 80% of the time devoted to a data warehousing project, it would not be reasonable to include its full complexity in a benchmark tool. Hence, we balanced in favor of simplicity. However, we present here a first step toward including a full ETL phase into DWEB; extensions are definitely possible.

Model

Since the DWEB software is a standalone tool that generates data and workloads, we chose not to include an extraction phase in its ETL capability. Data updates are performed directly in the database to keep DWEB's usage simple and minimize external file management. However, data updates could also easily be recorded into flat files before being applied, to simulate an extraction phase.

We did not include any transformation in the process either, despite it is a very important phase in the ETL process. However, in a benchmark, such transformations are simulated to consume

CPU time (this is the tactic adopted in TPC-DS). In DWEB, we consider that the processing time of various tests in the insert and modify procedures related to the loading phase might be considered as equivalent to simulating transformations.

We thus focus on the loading phase. A data warehouse schema is built on two different concepts: facts and dimensions. Updates might be insertions, modifications or deletions. Since data are normally historicized in a data warehouse, we do not consider deletions. Hence, we can identify four warehouse refreshing types for which we adopt specific strategies.

1. *Insertions in fact tables* are simple. They involve few constraints at the schema level, save that we cannot use an existing primary key in the related fact table. To achieve an insertion, we randomly fetch one primary key in each dimension to build an aggregate fact table key, and then add random measure values to complete the fact.

2. *Insertions in dimensions* raise a new issue. They must be dispatched in all hierarchy levels. Hence, for each dimension, we seek to insert elements from the highest hierarchy level (coarsest granularity grain) into the lowest hierarchy level (finest granularity grain). New dimension members only need a new, unique primary key to be inserted in a given hierarchy level.

3. *Modifications in fact tables* only necessitate randomly fetching an existing fact and modifying its measure values.

4. *Modifications in dimensions* must finally take dimension hierarchy levels in into account to avoid introducing inconsistencies in the hierarchy.

Parameterization

DWEB's ETL parameters help users tune how the data warehouse is refreshed. Like the other parameters in DWEB, they have been designed with Gray's simplicity criterion in mind. These parameters direct how the ETL model is applied. They basically define refresh and insertion/modification rates. We voluntarily define only a small number (three, since *FRR* and *MR* are derived from *DRR* and *IR*, respectively) of high-level parameters (Table 4).

GRR represents the total number of records from fact and dimension tables that must be refreshed (insertion and modifications included), with respect to current warehouse size. *DRR* and *FRR* control the proportion of these updates that are performed on dimension and fact tables, respectively. Finally, *IR* and *MR* control the proportion of insertions and modifications, respectively.

Refresh Algorithms

The refresh phase in DWEB is actually achieved with the help of two refresh procedures, one for dimensions and one for fact tables. Their pseudo-code is presented in Figures 8 and 9, respectively. Both procedures follow the same principle:

1. Compute the number of tuples to insert or update with respect to parameters *GRR*,

Table 4. DWEB ETL parameters

Parameter name	Meaning	Default value
GRR	Global refresh rate	0.01
DRR	Dimension refresh rate	0.05
FRR	Fact refresh rate	1 – DRR
IR	Insert rate	0.95
MR	Modification rate	1 – IR

DRR, *FRR*, *IR*, and *MR*, as well as the total number of tuples in the warehouse *GLOBAL_SIZE*;

2. Insert or modify as many tuples in the corresponding table — modifications affect a randomly selected tuple. Furthermore, dimension updates are dispatched on all hierarchy levels.

We use two new classes of procedures in this algorithm.

1. `Insert_into_Dim()` and `Insert_into_FT()` insert new tuples into dimension and fact tables, respectively. The main difference between these two procedures is that dimension insertion manages foreign key selection for pointing to the next hierarchy

Figure 8. DWEB dimension refresh procedure

```
For i = 1 to TOT_NB_DIM do
    ins_nb = ((GLOBAL_SIZE * GRR * DRR * IR)
        / TOT_NB_DIM) / NB_LEVELS(i)
    mod_nb = ((GLOBAL_SIZE * GRR * DRR * MR)
        / TOT_NB_DIM) / NB_LEVELS(i)
    For j = NB_LEVELS(i) to 1 step -1 do
        // Insertions
        For k = 1 to ins_nb do
            Insert_into_Dim(dim(i).level(j))
        End for
        // Modifications
        For k = 1 to mod_nb do
            Modify_Dim(Random_Key(dim(i).level(j))
        End for
    End for
End for
```

Figure 9. DWEB fact table refresh procedure

```
For i = 1 to NB_FT do
    For j = 1 to (GLOBAL_SIZE * GRR * FRR * IR)
        / |ft(i).extension| do
        Insert_into_FT(ft(i))
    End for
    For j = 1 to (GLOBAL_SIZE * GRR * FRR * MR)
        / |ft(i).extension| do
        Modify_FT(Random_Key(ft(i))
    End for
End for
```

level, whereas there is no such constraint in a fact table.

2. `Modify_Dim()` and `Modify_FT()` modify one tuple, identified by its primary key, from a dimension or fact table, respectively. Primary keys are provided by the `Random_key()` function (cf. Database Model section), which returns random instances of the specified table's primary key. `Modify_Dim()` and `Modify_FT()` only differ by the updated attribute's nature: dimension members are strings, while fact measures are numerical. They are generated with the `Random_string()` and `Random_float()` functions, respectively (cf. Database Model section).

Execution Protocol

Protocol

DWEB's test protocol is quite classical for a benchmark, and is actually a variation of TPC-DS'. It is constituted of two distinct parts:

1. A *load test* that consists in filling the data warehouse structure with data;
2. A *performance test* that evaluates system response and that is further subdivided into two steps:
   2.1. A *cold run* in which the workload is applied onto the test warehouse once;

2.2. A *warm run* that is replicated *REPN* times and that includes the warehouse refresh process and another execution of the workload.

The pseudo-code for the performance test is presented in Figure 10. The main difference between DWEB's and TPC-DS' execution protocols is that DWEB's warm run may be executed many times instead of just one.

Remark: The *GRR* parameter may be set to zero if users do not want to include warehouse refresh tests.

Performance Metric

The performance metric we retained in DWEB is *response time*. It is computed separately for work-

Figure 10. Performance test algorithm

```
// Cold run
etime[0] = time()
Execute_Workload()
etime[0] = time() - etime[0]
// Warm run
For i = 1 to REPN do
    rtime[i] = time()
    Execute_Refresh(GLOBAL_SIZE)
    rtime[i] = time() - rtime[i]
    etime[i] = time()
    Execute_Workload()
    etime[i] = time() - etime[i]
End for
```

load execution and data warehouse refreshing, so that any run time (e.g., cold run time, refresh time in warm run replication #*i*...) can be displayed. Global, average, minimum and maximum execution times are also computed, as well standard deviation. Note that this kind of atomic approach for assessing performance allows to derive any more complex, composite metrics, such as TPC-H's and TPC-D's, if necessary.

DWEB TUTORIAL

We present in this section a short tutorial that illustrates DWEB's usage and shows how DWEB's execution protocol is implemented in practice. DWEB is a Java application. Its main GUI (Graphical User Interface) is depicted in Figure 11. It is divided into three sections/panels:

1. *Database connection:* JDBC (Java Database Connectivity) connection to a database server and database;
2. *Action:* the actual benchmark interface that helps set parameters and launch tests;
3. *Information:* this window displays messages when an event or error occurs.

    Actually using DWEB through the "Action" panel is a four-step process.

Data Warehouse Generation

Clicking on the "Generate DW" command button helps set either the full range of low-level parameters or only the high-level parameters (Figure 12), which we recommend for most performance tests. Then, the data warehouse's (empty) structure is automatically created.

Load Test

The second subpanel in the "Action" panel features three command buttons. Since DWEB's param-

Figure 11. DWEB GUI

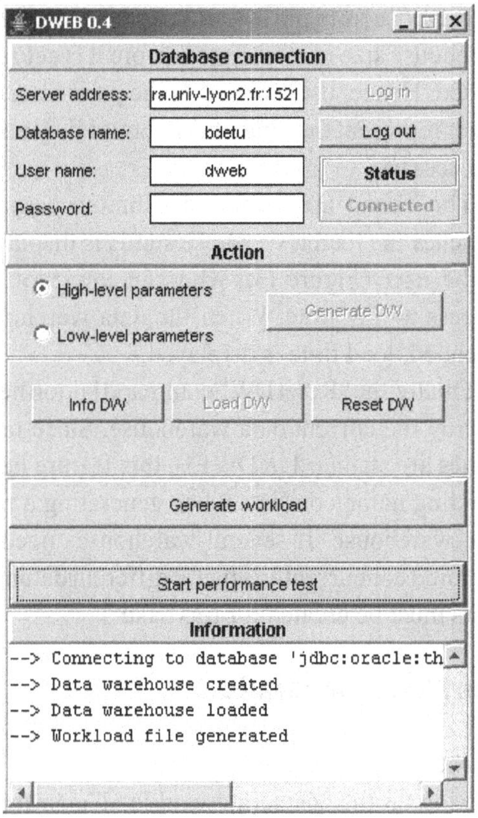

Figure 12. DWEB database parameterization

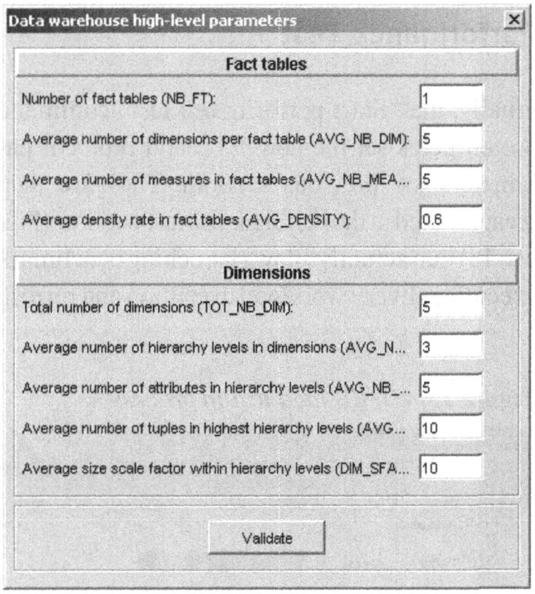

eters might sound abstract, we provide through the "Info DW" command button an estimation of data warehouse size in megabytes before it is actually loaded. Hence, users can reset the parameters to better represent the kind of warehouse they need, if necessary.

The "Load DW" command button actually launches the load test, whose status is displayed to the user (Figure 13), who can interrupt the process at any time. When the data warehouse is loaded, load time is displayed.

Finally, the "Reset DW" command button helps destroy the current data warehouse. Since table names are standard in DWEB, this feature helps avoiding name conflicts when generating a new data warehouse. If several warehouses need to be stored concurrently, several different database users must be created for this sake.

Workload Generation

Workload generation is simply achieved by clicking on the "Generate workload" command button, which triggers workload parameter setup (Figure 14) and save its queries into an external file, so that they can be reused.

Performance Test

Finally, the "Start performance test" command button helps set the new ETL and protocol parameters (cf. previous section). They are then recapitulated in the performance test window (Figure 15) that actually allows launching benchmark execution. Every workload execution and refresh

Figure 13. DWEB load test in process

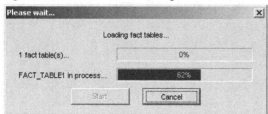

Figure 14. DWEB workload parameterization

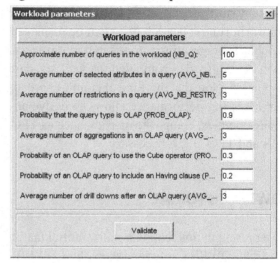

operation time is displayed and also recorded separately in a CSV (Comma-Separated Values) file that can later be processed in a spreadsheet or any other application. Warm run total, average, minimum and maximum times, as well as standard deviation, for refresh operations, workload executions, and both (refresh + workload total), are computed. Performance tests may be reiterated any number of times, with or without generating a new workload each time.

CONCLUSION AND PERSPECTIVES

We have mainly proposed DWEB, which is currently the only operational data warehouse benchmark to the best of our knowledge, to help data warehouse designers select among alternate architectures and/or performance optimization techniques. However, it can also be used, as the TPC benchmarks, for sheer performance comparisons. It is indeed possible to save a given warehouse and its associated workload to run tests on different systems and/or with various optimization techniques.

To satisfy the relevance and adaptability criteria, DWEB can generate various ad-hoc synthetic

Figure 15. DWEB performance test window

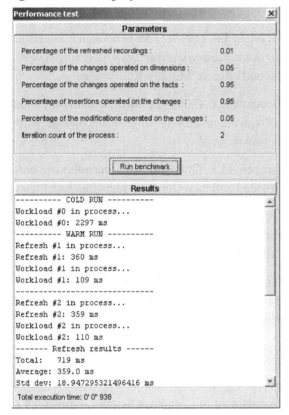

data warehouses and their associated workloads. Popular data warehouse schemas, such as star, snowflake, and constellation schemas, as well as much-used decision-support operators such as cube, roll-up or drill-down, are indeed supported by our tool. These features are piloted by a full set of low-level parameters, but we have also proposed a series of high-level parameters that are limited in number, not to sacrifice too much Gray's simplicity criterion. Finally, we have opted to implement DWEB with the Java language to satisfy the portability criterion. DWEB's code is freely available on-line (3).

We have illustrated sample usages of DWEB by evaluating the efficiency of several indexing techniques on various data warehouse configurations (Darmont *et al.*, 2005; Darmont *et al.*, 2007). Though these experiments were not actually new, they helped us demonstrate DWEB's relevance.

We indeed obtained results that were consistent with previously published results regarding bitmap join indices (O'Neil & Graefe, 1995) and star-join indices (Bellatreche *et al.*, 2002). We could underline again the crucial nature of indexing choices in data warehouses. Furthermore, since such choices depend on the warehouse's architecture, we showed DWEB's usefulness in a context where "mono-schema" benchmarks are not relevant.

Our work opens up many perspectives for further developing and enhancing DWEB. First, the warehouse metamodel and query model are currently deliberately simple. They could definitely be extended to be more representative of real data warehouses, i.e., more relevant. For example, the warehouse metamodel could feature many-to-many relationships between dimensions and fact tables, and hierarchy levels that are shared by several dimensions. Our query model could also be extended with more complex queries such as nested queries that are common in OLAP usages. Similarly, our DWEB's ETL feature focuses on the loading phase, and could be complemented by extraction and transformation capabilities. TPC-DS' specifications and other existing studies (Labrinidis & Roussopoulos, 1998) could help us complementing our own tool.

We have also proposed a set of parameters for DWEB that suit both the models we developed and our expected usage of the benchmark. However, a formal validation would help select the soundest parameters. More experiments should also help us to evaluate the pertinence of our parameters and maybe propose sounder default values. Other parameters could also be considered, such as the domain cardinality of hierarchy attributes or the selectivity factors of restriction predicates in queries. This kind of information may indeed help designers to choose an architecture that supports some optimization techniques adequately.

Finally, we only used response time as a performance metric. Other metrics must be envisaged, such as the metrics designed to measure the quality of data warehouse conceptual models (Serrano *et al.*, 2003; Serrano *et al.*, 2004). Formally validating these metrics would also improve DWEB's usefulness.

ACKNOWLEDGMENT

The author would like to thank Audrey Gutierrez and Benjamin Variot for coding DWEB's latest improvements.

REFERENCES

Ballinger, C. (1993). TPC-D: Benchmarking for decision support. *The benchmark handbook for database and transaction processing systems*, second edition. Morgan Kaufmann.

Bellatreche, L., Karlapalem, K., & Mohania, M. (2002). Some issues in design of data warehousing systems. *Data warehousing and web engineering*.(pp. 22-76). IRM Press.

Bhashyam, R. (1996). TCP-D: The challenges, issues and results. *The 22th International Conference on Very Large Data Bases*, Mumbai (Bombay), India. *SIGMOD Record, 4*, 593.

BMC Software. (2000). Performance management of a data warehouse. *http://www.bmc.com*

Darmont, J., Bentayeb, F., & Boussaïd, O. (2005). DWEB: A data warehouse engineering benchmark. *The 7th International Conference on Data Warehousing and Knowledge Discovery (DaWaK 05), Copenhagen, Denmark. LNCS, 3589*, 85-94.

Darmont, J., Bentayeb, F., & Boussaïd, O. (2007). Benchmarking data warehouses. *International Journal of Business Intelligence and Data Mining, 2*(1), 79-104.

Darmont, J., & Schneider, M. (2000). Benchmarking OODBs with a generic tool. *Journal of Database Management, 11*(3), 16-27.

Demarest, M. (1995). A data warehouse evaluation model. *Oracle Technical Journal. 1*(1), 29.

Gray, J., Ed. (1993). *The benchmark handbook for database and transaction processing systems*, second edition. Morgan Kaufmann.

Greenfield, L. (2004). Performing data warehouse software evaluations. *http://www.dwinfocenter. org/evals.html*

Greenfield, L. (2004). What to learn about in order to speed up data warehouse querying. *http://www. dwinfocenter.org/fstquery.html*

Inmon, W.H. (2002). *Building the data warehouse*, third edition. John Wiley & Sons.

Kimball, R., & Ross, M. (2002). *The data warehouse toolkit: The complete guide to dimensional modeling*, second edition. John Wiley & Sons.

Labrinidis, A., & Roussopoulos, N. (1998). *A performance evaluation of online warehouse update algorithms*. Technical report CS-TR-3954. Department of Computer Science, University of Maryland.

OMG. (2003). *Common warehouse metamodel (CWM) specification version 1.1.* Object Management Group.

O'Neil, P.E., & Graefe, G. (1995). Multi-table joins through bitmapped join indices. *SIGMOD Record, 24*(3), 8-11.

Pendse, N. (2003). The OLAP report: How not to buy an OLAP product. *http://www.olapreport. com/How_not_to_buy.htm*

Poess, M., & Floyd, C. (2000). New TPC benchmarks for decision support and Web commerce. *SIGMOD Record, 29*(4), 64-71.

Poess, M., Smith, B., Kollar, L., & Larson, P.A. (2002). TPC-DS: Taking decision support benchmarking to the next level. *2002 ACM SIGMOD International Conference on Management of Data*, Madison, Wisconsin, USA. (pp. 582-587).

Poole, J., Chang, D., Tolbert, D., & Mellor, D. (2003). *Common warehouse etamodel developer's guide*. John Wiley & Sons.

Serrano, M., Calero, C., & Piattini, M. (2003). Metrics for data warehouse quality. *Effective Databases for Text & Document Management.* (pp. 156-173).

Serrano, M., Calero, C., Trujillo, J., Lujan-Mora, S., & Piattini, M. (2004). Towards a metrics suite for conceptual models of datawarehouses. *1st International Workshop on Software Audit and Metrics (SAM 04)*, Porto, Portugal. (pp. 105-117).

Thomsen, E. (1998). Comparing different approaches to OLAP calculations as revealed in benchmarks. *Intelligence Enterprise's Database Programming & Design.* http://www.dbpd.com/vault/9805desc.htm

TPC. (1998). *TPC Benchmark D Standard Specification Version 2.1.* Transaction Processing Performance Council.

TPC. (2003). *TPC Benchmark R Standard Specification Revision 2.1.0.* Transaction Processing Performance Council.

TPC. (2006). *TPC Benchmark H Standard Specification Revision 2.6.1.* Transaction Processing Performance Council.

TPC. (2007). *TPC Benchmark DS Standard Specification Draft version 52.* Transaction Processing Performance Council.

ENDNOTES

1. http://www.tpc.org
2. http://cgmlab.cs.dal.ca/downloadarea/datasets/
3. http://bdd.univ-lyon2.fr/download/dweb.zip

Chapter XVI
Analyses and Evaluation of Responses to Slowly Changing Dimensions in Data Warehouses*

Lars Frank
Copenhagen Business School, Denmark

Christian Frank,
Copenhagen Business School, Denmark

ABSTRACT

*A **Star Schema Data Warehouse** looks like a star with a central, so-called **fact table**, in the middle, surrounded by so-called **dimension tables** with one-to-many relationships to the central fact table. Dimensions are defined as **dynamic** or **slowly changing** if the attributes or relationships of a dimension can be updated. Aggregations of fact data to the level of the related dynamic dimensions might be misleading if the fact data are aggregated without considering the changes of the dimensions. In this chapter, we will first prove that the problems of SCD (Slowly Changing Dimensions) in a datawarehouse may be viewed as a special case of the read skew anomaly that may occur when different transactions access and update records without concurrency control. That is, we prove that aggregating fact data to the levels of a dynamic dimension should not make sense. On the other hand, we will also illustrate, by examples, that in some situations it does make sense that fact data is aggregated to the levels of a dynamic dimen-*

sion. That is, it is the semantics of the data that determine whether historical dimension data should be preserved or destroyed. Even worse, we also illustrate that for some applications, we need a history preserving response, while for other applications at the same time need a history destroying response. Kimball et al., (2002), have described three classic solutions/responses to handling the aggregation problems caused by slowly changing dimensions. In this chapter, we will describe and evaluate four more responses of which one are new. This is important because all the responses have very different properties, and it is not possible to select a best solution without knowing the semantics of the data.

INTRODUCTION

A *data warehouse* is an *OLAP* (*On Line Analytical Processing*) database (Codd, 1993 and Codd et al. 1993), where the data is loaded/updated periodically. In other words, a data warehouse is not an *OLTP* (*On Line Transaction Processing*) database (e.g., Gray and Reuter, 1993). The data warehouse *drill functions* (e.g., Kimball et al., 1998) have been developed to accommodate the special needs for aggregating the data stored in the fact table of a data warehouse.

The traditional *drill-down* functions use the one-to-many relationships of the data warehouse to find more detailed information. If we take accumulated data as an example, the drill-down function will show the more detailed data elements of the accumulated data. The *roll-up* function can use the one-to-many relationships of the data warehouse to generate an overview of the detailed information. However, the aggregating drill functions may give misleading results as old fact data may be aggregated to dimension levels that have changed since the fact data were created. In this paper, we will evaluate the following 7 different techniques for handling the aggregation problems of slowly changing dimensions (Responses to SCD). The first three responses are the classic techniques described by Kimball et al. (1998).

- **Type 1 response:** Overwrite the dimension record with the new values by which historical information is lost.

- **Type 2 response:** Create a new additional dimension record with the current information.

- **Type 3 response:** Create a "Previous" field in the dimension record to store the immediate previous attribute value.

- **Type 4 response:** Create a new dimension using a dynamic dimension hierarchy

- **Type 5 response:** Store dynamic dimension data as fact data

- **Type 6 response:** Use finer granularity in combination with response 1 or 3

- **Type 7 response:** Store the dynamic dimension data as static facts in another data mart

Table 1 gives an overview of the most important properties of the different responses, and in section 4 the evaluation is described in more details. The most important evaluation criterion for responses to Slowly Changing Dimensions is whether the responses preserve historical information. In the next section, we will illustrate by examples that it is the semantics of the data that determine whether historical information should be preserved. That is, both history preserving and history destroying responses are important. Therefore, it is important to know that only the Type 1 and 3 responses can overwrite historical information in an effective way. The Type 3 and 6 responses do not preserve all the details of historical information but may be a good choice in special situations. Response Types 2, 4, 5, and

7 preserves historical information in an effective way but it is often application dependent to select the best solution as e.g. performance depends on what data is aggregated.

The paper is organized as follows. In this paper, we will first prove that the problems of Slowly Changing Dimensions in a data warehouse may be viewed as a special case of the read skew anomaly that may occur when different transactions access and update records without concurrency control. The next section will describe the most important concepts in dimensional modelling used in this paper. The following section offers more detailed descriptions and an evaluation of the different responses to Slowly Changing Dimensions. Concluding remarks and suggestions for further research are presented at the end of the paper.

Related Research

Many authors working with data warehouse design have also analyzed the problems of aggregating fact data to the levels of slowly changing dimensions (e.g., Kimball et al., 1998; Anahory and Murray, 1997). The Type 4 technique of splitting a dynamic dimension into two independent dimensions to simplify the dynamicity may also be applied to groups of dimension attributes. Kimball et al. (1998) describe this as *Rapidly changing monster dimensions* because a group with all the dynamic attributes of a dimension may change rather frequently. However, as long as several dynamic attributes/ relationships are grouped together, the technique cannot be used as a response that solves the problem of slowly

Table 1.

Response type	Evaluation criteria		
	Is historical information preserved	Aggregation performance	Storage consumption
Response 1 where dimension records are overwritten	No	In the evaluation, we define this solution to have average performance	Only the current dimension record version is stored. No redundant data is stored
Response 2 where new versions are created	Yes	Version records makes performance slower proportional to the number of changes	All old versions of dimension records are stored often with redundant attributes
Response 3 where only one historical version is saved	The current version and a single history destroying version are saved	No performance degradation occurs if either the current or the historical version are used in a query	Normally, only a single extra attribute version is stored
Response 4 that use the top of a dynamic dimen-sion hierarchy as a new static dimen-sion	Yes	Better or worse depen-ding on whether both dimension tables are used in a query	The relatively large fact table must have an extra foreign key attribute
Response 5 with dimension data as fact data	Yes	Better or worse depen-ding on whether the new fact data are used in a query	The relatively large fact table must have an extra attribute for each dynamic dimension attribute
Response 6 that use fine granularity in combination with response 1 or 3	The finer the granularity, the more historical state information is preserved	The finer the granularity, the slower the performance	The finer the granularity, the more storage consumption
Response 7 that stores dynamic dimension data as static facts in another data mart	Yes	Better or worse depen-ding on whether both fact tables are used in a drill across query	This is the most storage consuming solution as at least a new fact and foreign key are stored in the new fact table

changing dimensions. Anyway, if the static attributes/relationships are separated in a dimension by themselves, it may be cheaper to implement a response for the dynamic attributes/relationships. Therefore, the same technique may be used to solve different problems.

Levene and Loizou (2003) have evaluated the snowflake schema and conclude that it has several desirable properties such as new "normalization" possibilities. Therefore, it should be easy to understand as a good model of the real world, and the design should have a minimum of redundancy. We agree that a design, that is a good model of the real world, is useful but "normalization" may conflict with some of the most important responses to slowly changing dimensions, and minimizing redundancy is traditionally not the most important objective in data warehouse design. The relatively new Type 4 response has earlier been described by Frank et al., 2005 and 2006, and some of its properties have been evaluated. Frank, 2008, have described but not evaluated the Type 5 and 6 responses.

SLOWLY CHANGING DIMENSIONS MAY BE VIEWED AS AN ANOMALY

When transactions are executed without isolation, the so called *isolation anomalies* (Berenson et al., 1995) may occur. Isolation anomalies may totally change the real values of the data read by a transaction, and if the transaction stores its view of data, the wrong data values may be made permanent. Isolation anomalies may be dealt with by using countermeasures (Frank and Zahle, 1998) as the so called *long duration transactions* (e.g., Gray and Reuter, 1993) can not be managed by using traditional concurrency control. In the same way, the anomalies caused by dynamic dimensions may be dealt with by using the so called *responses* to SCD. As with countermeasures against isolation anomalies it is the semantics of the data that determine witch

response type is the best choice. Therefore, the evaluation criteria "Aggregation performance" and "Storage consumption" from Table 1 are only relevant after it is decided whether the response should preserve, destroy and/or preserve historical information in minor detail.

An isolation anomaly is defined by its *history* that consists of the reads, writes, commits, and aborts executed by the involved transactions. Histories can be written in shorthand notation in the following way (Berenson et al., 1995):

- "w1(x)" means a write by transaction 1 on record x.
- "r2(y)" means a read of record y by transaction 2.
- Transaction 1's commit and abort are written "c1" and "a1", respectively.
- Transaction 1's reading and writing of a set of records satisfying a predicate P is denoted by "r1 (P)" and "w1 (P)", respectively.

Using histories the classic isolation anomalies may be described as follows (Berenson et al., 1995):

- The lost update anomaly: r1(x)...w2(x)... w1(x)...c1...
- The dirty read anomaly: w1(x)...r2(x)... a1...
- The non-repeatable read anomaly or fuzzy read: r1(x)...w2(x)... c2...r1(x)...
- The phantom anomaly: r1 (P)...w2(y in P)...c2...r1 (P)...
- The read skew anomaly: r1(x)...w2(x)... w2(y)...c2... r1(y)...
- The write skew anomaly: r1(x)... r2(y)... w2(y)...w1(x)...c1...c2...

The *read skew anomaly* is a situation where a first transaction reads a record. Next, a second transaction updates the record and a related record. The updates are committed. Finally, the first transaction reads the related record. In this situation, the first transaction may find that the integration of the semantic meaning of the data stored in x and y do not make sense.

The problem of Slowly Changing Dimensions in a data warehouse is not an isolation anomaly as the updating and reading transactions are executed in different time slots. However, in this section we will illustrate that the problems in data warehouses with Slowly Changing Dimensions may be viewed as a special case of the read skew anomaly.

In the following example, x is Fact data while y is Dimension data in a data warehouse. In this situation, the interpretation of the x data may depend on the y data. In the example, the evaluation of x data may change from "acceptable" to "unacceptable" depending on the value of a "size" attribute in y.

Example 1

Let us suppose x is a set of records with the monthly sale of a department in a store and y is the corresponding department record. And let us suppose that the department record has an attribute with the number of salesmen in the department.

As Fact data normally is not updated, the Read skew history in a data warehouse is reduced to

$$r1(x)\dots w2(y)\dots c2\dots r1(y)\dots$$

From an information point of view, this Read skew history is equivalent to following history as the Fact data x is not changed.

$$\dots w2(y)\dots c2\dots r1(x)\dots r1(y)\dots$$

However, this is the history of an OLAP transaction that reads fact data x created before a dimension update in a Slowly Changing Dimension y. Therefore, the Read skew anomaly may be seen as a special case of the problem of Slowly Changing Dimensions.

In the example above, it is important to preserve the relationship between record x and the historical version of record y as the monthly sale normally is very dependent on the number of salesmen in the department. However, it is semantics of the data that determine whether it is right to preserve relationships to historical dimension versions or not. This is illustrated in the following example.

Example 2

Let us suppose x is the sale of products in a department store and y is the department records without the attribute with the number of salesmen. In order to se how the departments are performing, it should be possible to aggregate the sale to each department periodically. However, suppose that at a point in time the departments are reorganized in such a way that some products are sold in other departments and vice versa. If the managers now want to see how the departments have performed over time the question can be answered with or without using historical dimension data. If the historical relationship between a sale x and the department y where x was sold is preserved, it may not make any sense to compare the sale of a department over time as the products sold are not the same over time. On the other hand, if historical dimension data is not used all the sales of a product are related to the department from where it is currently sold and the aggregated sales do not correspond to the sales of the real departments. Anyway, in this situation it makes sense to compare the sales of the departments over time, as the aggregated sales correspond to the real sales over time of a static group of products.

In the following example, we will illustrate that the historical versions of a dynamic dimension may only be used by some applications. That is, it is semantics of the data that determine whether historical dimension data should be preserved, destroyed, preserved without always using the historical information, or preserved in only one historical version.

Example 3

Let us suppose x is the sale of products in a department store and y is the department records including an attribute with the monthly costs of the departments. In order to see the monthly revenue of the departments over time, it should be possible to aggregate the sales to the departments periodically. As the monthly costs per department vary with the number of employees, the department dimension is dynamic, and the historical dimension data should be preserved in order to subtract the monthly costs of a department from the corresponding aggregated monthly sale.

Again, we suppose that at a point in time the departments are reorganized in such a way that some products are sold in other departments and vice versa. In this situation, it may also be of interest to compare the performance of the departments with the performance that would have occurred if the reorganization had not taken place. However, in this situation we only need the product-department relationships before and after the reorganization and not all the history of the departments. As seen in Table 1, response 3 is tailored to deal with such a situation.

TYPES OF DYNAMICITY IN SLOWLY CHANGING DIMENSIONS

Dynamicity in slowly changing dimensions can be group after whether it is a dimension attribute or a dimension relationship that is dynamic. *Dynamic dimension attributes* are normal dimension attributes that may be updated. Aggregations to a dimension with a dynamic dimension attribute may be misleading as fact data created before the change are aggregated to a dimension level with changed properties. *Dynamic dimension relationships* are dimension relationships that

may be updated. Aggregations to a level with a dynamic relationship towards the fact table may be problematic as fact data created before the changes may be aggregated to levels with which they had no relationship when they were created. The reason why we distinguish between dynamic dimension attributes and dynamic dimension relationships is that the aggregation problems with dynamic dimension relationships normally are more serious than the aggregation problems with dynamic dimension attributes. For example, a change in a dimension attribute value may have no or minor correlation with the aggregated fact data, while a change in a dimension relationship always will change the aggregations made through the relationship. A more technical reason for the distinction is that the dynamic attributes are stored in the dimension itself while the dynamic relationships are stored as foreign keys in the related table. Therefore, overwriting a dynamic dimension relationship must be implemented by updating the related table and not by updating the dynamic dimension itself. If the related table is the fact table, then the fact table must be updated even though fact data by definition is static.

Dynamicity in slowly changing dimensions can also be grouped after whether a history preserving response or a more or less history destroying response should be used from a semantic point of view. Normally, it is important to select responses to slowly changing dimensions that preserve historical information as data warehouses are used to analyze changes over time. However, as described in the previous section, it may be important to more or less destroy historical information. In these situations, it is important to use a proper response type that makes the aggregations over time meaningful. It is the semantics of the aggregated data that should be used to decide whether a history preserving or a more or less history destroying response should be used. Therefore, this question must be answered for all dynamic attributes/keys before the responses are chosen. As described in the previous section it may even be necessary to implement both history preserving and history destroying responses for the same dimension because different applications may have different needs.

A *dimension hierarchy* (e.g., Kimball et al., 1998) is a hierarchy of tables connected through one-to-many relationships towards the fact table. If the tables in a dimension hierarchy are joined together to a single dimension table, we say that the joined dimension has an *internal dimension hierarchy*. In practice, internal dimension hierarchies are often used as they normally improve the speed of executing aggregation at the costs of extra space for storing redundant information. Normally, the fact table of a data warehouse has a *Time dimension hierarchy* that enables the users to aggregate fact data to the level of day, month or year. The time hierarchy may be internal or stored in separate tables as a dimension hierarchy. In the following example, the Time dimension has been designed with an internal dimension hierarchy for performance reasons. This will not produce aggregation problems as the Time dimension including its hierarchies is static. However, the example also illustrates that both internal and external dimension hierarchies with dynamic

dimension relationships automatically will have serious aggregation problems.

Example

In Figure 1, the central fact table of the snowflake schema has three dimensions and a dimension hierarchy. Therefore, the fact table has attributes for the four corresponding dimension foreign keys. In the figure, the primary key of each table is underlined.

The Product dimension is dynamic as the Product-group of a Product may change. The Salary-group of the dimension hierarchy is dynamic as its relationship to a Salesman may change. The Salary-group dimension is stored in a hierarchy as this may save a lot of storage space if many salesmen are related to a few salary-groups with many attributes to describe the salary contracts. It may be interesting to aggregate the turnover (Qty*Price) to both the Salesman and Salary-group levels to evaluate each individual salesman as well as groups of salesmen. However, the aggregation to the Salary-group level is without meaning as some salesmen may have changed salary group. For these salesmen, the turnover that should have

Figure 1.

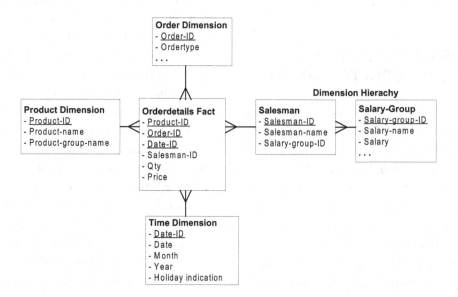

been aggregated to the previous salary group is wrongly aggregated to the new salary group. Therefore, a response type that preserves historical information should be used.

In Figure 1, the Product dimension has an internal dimension hierarchy as each Product has a relationship to one Product-group and each Product-group may have relationships to many Products. This relationship is dynamic, and, therefore, aggregation to the Product-group level in the internal Product hierarchy may be wrong. However, the Product-group is a dynamic classification criterion as one or more products may change their Product to Product-group relationship by a management decision. However, the same static Product-group definition should be used over time in aggregations even though the groups may have changed over time. Otherwise, it does not make sense from a semantic point of view to compare aggregations to the Product-group level over time. Therefore, a response type that destroys historical information should be used when data is aggregated from the Product level to the Product-group level.

The Time dimension is implemented with an internal hierarchy, too. This will give no aggregation problems as both the attributes of the dimension and the internal relationships between day, month, and year are static. However, in the real world, the Time dimension may be dynamic as some event may change a weekday to a holiday. Anyway, this may be handled as an error in the initial load of the Time dimension, and therefore the history destroying Type 1 response to slowly changing dimensions can be recommended.

RESPONSES TO SLOWLY CHANGING DIMENSIONS

In this section, we will describe and evaluate the different responses to slowly changing dimensions in more details. First, we will describe the fourth response. We describe the Type 4 response first to

illustrate that it is important to examine whether it is possible to change dynamic information to static information by changing the design of the datawarehouse. The Type 7 response will also create new entities in the datawarehouse. Next, we will describe and evaluate the classic responses originally described by Kimball. Finally, we will describe and evaluate three new responses.

The Type 4 Response: Create a New Dimension Using a Dynamic Dimension Hierarchy

The aggregation problems in internal and external dynamic dimension hierarchies may disappear if the data corresponding to a dynamic entity in the hierarchy is removed and stored in a separate independent dimension directly related to the fact table. By doing so the dynamic data is either changed to static dimensions or changed to dynamic dimensions with reduced aggregation problems. Response 4 may be used recursively as different layers of dynamic entities may occur in both internal and external dimension hierarchies. The Type 4 response should only be used to transform dimensions with dynamic relationships to the fact table where it is important to preserve historical information.

Example 5

In Figure 2, the dynamic Salesmen dimension hierarchy from example 1 has been divided into two independent dimensions corresponding to the entities Salesman and Salary-group. These dimensions still have dynamic attributes, but they do not have dynamic hierarchies and therefore response 4 cannot be used any more. However, the transformation has solved all the aggregation problems as the turnover can be aggregated to the Salary-group level in a meaningful way. Anyway, the dimensions are still dynamic as historical information may be lost when the dimension attributes are updated. Therefore, it may still be

Figure 2.

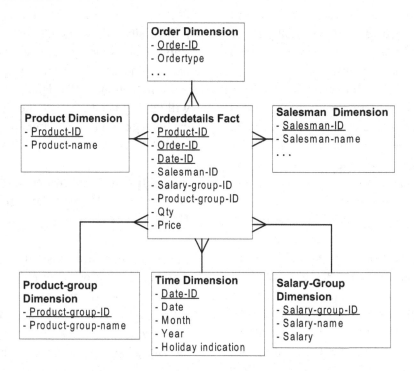

useful to use one of the other responses to slowly changing dimensions.

The implementation of a new salary-group dimension uses more storage space than the solution with a dimension hierarchy as the foreign key now is stored in the fact table and not in the Salesman dimension.

The Type 4 solution also gives a worse performance than the solution with a dimension hierarchy if data from both Salesman table and the Salary-group table are to be used in query. However, the Type 4 solution is best when only the Salary-group information is needed in a query.

The dynamic internal dimension hierarchy of the Products dimension from example 1 has also been divided into two independent dimensions corresponding to the entities Product and Product-group. However, in this case the Type 4 response is used in a wrong way from a semantic point of view, as it normally does not make sense to aggregate the turnover to Product-groups where the Products per Product-group may change over time. In order to make it possible to compare the

turnover per Product-group over time, a static set of Products per Product-group should be used even though the Products per Product-group are dynamic. For example, if it turns out that some Garden products are not waterproof, management may decide to group them under Furniture products in the future. However, to make it possible to compare the turnover per Product group over time, the non-water proof furniture should also be grouped as Furniture products in past fact records. This is not possible with the type 4 response as it preserves historical information. A correct solution to the problem is described under the Type 1 and 3 responses where historical information is not preserved, and, therefore, the turnover per Product group per time period will be corrected automatically.

The Type 1 Response: Overwrite with the New Values

Inc case of a dynamic dimension attribute, this is the simplest response to use, and the response functions correctly if a response type that destroys historical information is needed or if the historical information of the attribute is not important from a semantic point of view. Normally, data is not important from "a semantic point of view" if the value of the attribute is not correlated to the result of the aggregations. The problem is that the fact data created before the change of the dynamic attribute are aggregated to a level where the attribute may have changed in a misleading way with respect to the correlated aggregated data. However, the Type 1 response is also the most inflexible solution, and the decision to use this response is normally irreversible as the response destroys the historical information. The following example illustrates situations where the Type 1 response may be useful.

Example 6

In Figure 2, the name attributes like Product-name, Salesman-name, and Salary-name may be changed, but normally these changes are not important from a semantic point of view. In such situations, the information can be overwritten without problems. In Figure 1, the Type 1 response may also be useful when the turnover is aggregated to the Product-group level as historical information must not be used when the turnover is aggregated to the current definition of the Product-groups.

The following examples will illustrate that the Type 1 response may give misleading aggregations if either the value of a dynamic attribute is correlated to the result of the aggregations or if a response type that preserves historical information is needed.

Example 7

In Figure 2 the Salary attribute in the Salary-Group dimension is dynamic. One may expect that Salesmen with a high salary will sell more than Salesmen with a low salary, i.e. the Salary

attribute is probably correlated to the result of the aggregations. Therefore, the Type 1 response that destroys historical information, may give misleading aggregations if the user wants to analyze the aggregated turnover as a function of the Salary attribute. In Figure 1, the Type 1 response may also give misleading results when the turnover is aggregated to the Salary-group level as historical information must be used if the turnover has to be aggregated to the correct Salary-groups.

Example 8

The following star schema illustrates a data warehouse in a bank where the fact data is calculated and loaded periodically each month. For a customer that changes the relationship of an account to a branch office, half of the aggregated interest and costs for the month in question will in average be aggregated to a wrong branch office, i.e. aggregations to the branch office level may be misleading. However, if the granularity of the fact table is reduced to a day there will be no aggregation errors as banks normally calculate interest/costs on a daily basis.

The Type 2 Response: Create a New Additional Record

This response creates a new dimension record version with the changed data each time the dimension record is changed. By using the historical dimension versions, it is always possible to aggregate fact data correctly through a dynamic dimension hierarchy. However, this will increase the complexity of the datawarehouse, and the

Figure 3.

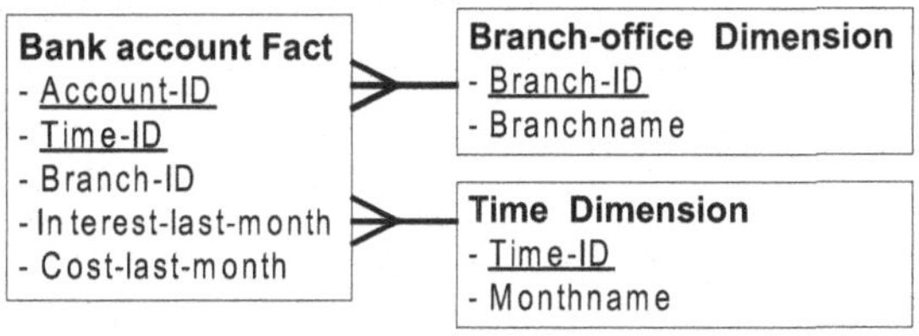

333

knowledge workers making data warehouse applications must know that different versions of dimension records are stored. For example, count statistics must always control that only "living" versions are counted. The following examples illustrate that the Type 2 response is useful both as a response to dynamic dimension attributes and to dynamic dimension relationships.

Example 9

In Figure 2, the Salary attribute in the Salary-group dimension may change. As we believe the Salary attribute is correlated to the result of the aggregations, the Type 2 response can give a better description of the relationship between the aggregated sale and the salary of the salesmen for each time period than the Type 1 response.

Example 10

In Figure 3, it is possible to use the Type 2 response to changes in the accounts relationships to the branch offices. However, as the changed relationship is stored in the fact table, a new version of the fact record must be created to keep track of the changed relationship. In this situation, it is possible to divide the fact data according to the time the accounts have been related to each branch office. With this solution, special care must be taken with statistics where the number of accounts per branch office is aggregated.

The Type 3 Response: Create a "Previous" Field for the Updated Attribute

With this solution, it is not possible to keep track of all changes as only the current values and a single historical version are stored. Therefore, the Type 3 response is grouped together with the Type 1 response as a response that destroys historical information. However, as described earlier the limited historical information stored by this solution makes it an ideal choice in an analysis of a reorganization or structural change where the situation before the structural change is compared with the situation after the structural change.

Example 11

Dimension tables are often used to group the fact data in business-defined groups like Product-groups, Departments and Regions, where management may decide to change the groupings overnight. In contrast to the previous responses, we are now interested in solutions that will allow us to aggregate all the fact data to either the previous or the new groupings. In this situation, we will recommend using the Type 3 response to store both the new and the previous foreign keys as illustrated in the Figure 4.

In the snowflake schema above, it is possible to aggregate the fact data to both the new and the

Figure 4.

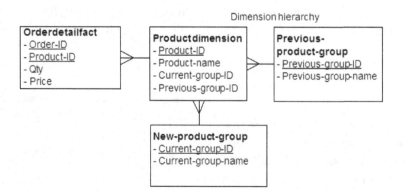

previous product groups. Normally, it should be enough to store two groupings of foreign keys, because the only reason for storing previous groupings is to evaluate whether it was wise to make the latest change in the grouping. The two dimension hierarchies illustrated in the Figure may be joined together with the Product dimension to form a product dimension with two dynamic internal hierarchies. As we have seen in Figure 2, these may be removed by using the Type 4 response. However, the aggregations to the product group level in different time periods cannot be compared if a product is aggregated to different product groups depending on when the product group relationship was changed. Therefore, the Type 1 and 3 responses are the only correct solutions in this situation.

The Type 5 Response: Store Dynamic Dimension Data as Fact Data

Any dynamic dimension attribute may be stored as a static fact attribute. We will call this solution *the Type 5 response* to slowly changing dimensions. The Type 5 response is very costly in storage space compared with the Type 2 response as the data of the attribute is redundant except for the first time a new version is stored. However, if the attribute is used in aggregations to other dimensions than its own, it may improve performance considerably as illustrated in the following example.

Example 12

In Figure 1 the Price of a product should be stored as a dynamic dimension attribute in the Product dimension to ensure that there always is an up-to-date version of the Price. However, the price is stored as a static redundant fact attribute in Figure 1. This may be done for two different reasons. The first reason relates to performance as it is possible to aggregate the turnover to any aggregation level without reading a Type 2 version

of the Product dimension, where the correct version of the Price can be stored. The other reason for storing the Price as a fact attribute is that the salesman who uses this solution is able to select a special price for a customer.

The Type 6 Response: Use Fine Granularity in Response 1 or 3

The idea of this response is to use a fine granularity in the fact table in combination with the Type 1 or 3 responses. This can diminish or totally eliminate aggregation errors caused by the Type 1 or 3 responses in situations where state fact data only can be aggregated to aggregation levels, which they were related to at the end of the state periods. By diminishing the granularity (i.e. the state period and the accumulated state fact data), the number of the fact data aggregated to wrong dimensions is diminished correspondingly. The example of Figure 3 illustrates how it is possible to eliminate errors in an account data warehouse by changing the granularity from monthly state data to daily state data.

The Type 7 Response: Store the Dynamic Dimension Data as Static Facts in another Mart

In response type 5 the dynamic dimension attribute was stored as a static measure in the fact table. This is always possible but it may be a short-term solution if the dynamic attribute from a business and normalization point of view origins from another business entity.

Example 13

Let us suppose a fact table stores the sale of products in a department store as described in the examples of the second section. In this example the department records are without the attribute with the number of salesmen as well as the attribute with the monthly costs of the departments. That is, the department dimension may be static. The missing dynamic attribute values of the original department dimension of the previous examples may in this situation be calculated from new fact tables. As examples, the number of employees per department may be aggregated from an employee data mart, and the monthly cost per department may be calculated by drilling across from the employee data mart with salary information to a new procurement data mart and further to a new promotion data mart etc. This solution will be the most flexible solution as historical data may be stored in most details. However, it is normally costly and time consuming and therefore unrealistic to develop this solution for all dynamic dimension attributes.

CONCLUSION

In this paper, we have illustrated that the problems of SCD (Slowly Changing Dimensions) in a datawarehouse may be viewed as a special case of the read skew anomaly that may occur when different transactions access and update records without concurrency control. That is, we have proved that the aggregating fact data to the levels of a dynamic dimension may not make any sense. In this situation, historical information about the changes in dimension data should be preserved. On the other hand, we also illustrate that in some situations, it is necessary to overwrite historical information in order to make aggregations meaningful. The reason for this is that data aggregated periodically across time periods with a structural chance, may not give any meaning, if the structural reorganization change the groupings to which data are aggregated.

However, historical information may also be overwritten if there is no correlation between the values of a dynamic attribute and the result of the aggregations. That is, it is the semantics of the data that determine whether historical information should be preserved, destroyed, preserved

without always using the historical information, or preserved in minor details. Therefore, it is important to know that only the Type 1 and 3 responses can overwrite historical information in an effective way. The Type 3 response is only the best choice in situations where exactly two versions should be saved. This is illustrated with a reorganisation example where only the latest versions before and after the reorganization are saved. Response Types 2, 4, 5, and 7 all preserve historical information in an effective way but it is often application dependent to select the best solution as e.g. performance depends on what data is aggregated.

Both the classic and four new responses to Slowly Changing Dimensions have been described and evaluated in this paper. Table 1 of the paper gives an overview of the most important properties of the different solutions.

REFERENCES

Anahory, S., & Murray, D. (1997). *Data warehousing in the real world*. Addison Wesley.

Bischoff, J., & Alexander, T. (1997). *Data warehouse: Practical advice from experts*. Prentice Hall.

Codd, E. F. (1993). *Providing OLAP (On-line Analytical Processing) to user-analysts: An IT mandate*. Technical Report, E.F. Codd and Associates.

Codd, E. F., Codd, S. B., & Salley, C. T. (1993, July). Beyond decision support. *Computerworld*, *27*(30), 87-89.

Frank, L., (2008). *Databases and applications with relaxed ACID properties*. Doctoral Dissertation, Copenhagen Business School, Samfundslitteratur.

Frank, L., & Christian, Frank (2006). Evaluation and selection of responses to slowly changing dimensions in data warehouses. *Proceedings of the Fourth International Conference on Computer Applications, ICCA2006*, (pp. 33-42).

Frank, L., Christian, F., Christian, S., Jensen, & Torben Bach P. (2005). Dimensional modelling by using a new response to slowly changing dimensions. *Proceedings of the 2nd International Conference on Information Technology*, Amman

Frank, L., & Zahle, T, (1998). Semantic ACID properties in multidatabases Uuing remote procedure calls and update propagations. *Software - Practice & Experience, 28*, 77-98.

Gray, J., & Reuter, A. (1993). *Transaction processing*. Morgan Kaufman.

Gray, J., Bosworth, A., Layman, A., & Pirahesh, H. (1996). Data cube: A relational aggregation operator generalizing group-by, cross-tab, and sub-totals. *Proceedings of the Twelfth International Conference on Data Engineering*, New Orleans, LA, February, (pp. 152-159).

Kimball, R., Reeves, L., Ross, M., & Thornthwaite, W. (1998). *The data warehouse lifecycle toolkit: Expert methods for designing, developing, and deploying data warehouses*. John Wiley & Sons.

Kimball, R., & Ross, M. (2002). *The data warehouse toolkit: The complete guide to dimensional modelling*. 2nd Edition, John Wiley & Sons.

Levene, M., & Loizou, G. (2003). Why is the snowflake schema a good data warehouse design? *Information Systems, 28*, 225-240.

Pedersen, T. B., Christian, S., Jensen, & Curtis E., Dyreson (2001). *A foundation for capturing and querying complex multidimensional data', Information Systems, 26*, 283-423.

ENDNOTE

*   This research is partly funded by the 'Danish Foundation of Advanced Technology Research' as part of the 'Third Generation Enterprise Resource Planning Systems' (3gERP) project, a collaborative project between Department of Informatics at Copenhagen Business School, Department of Computer Science at Copenhagen University, and Microsoft Business Systems.

Compilation of References

Abello et al., (2006). Abelló, A., Samos J., & Saltor, F. (2006). YAM²: A multidimensional conceptual model extending UML. *Journal of Information Systems (IS)*, *31*(6), 541-567.

Abello, A., Samos, J., & Saltor, F. (2006). *A data warehouse multidimensional models classification*. Technical Report LSI-2000-6. Universidad de Granada.

Abello, A., Samos, J., & Saltor, F. (2001). A framework for the classification and description of multidimensional data models. In *Proceedings of 12ᵗʰ Int. conf. on Database and Expert Systems Applications (DEXA)*, LNCS 2113, (pp. 668-677). Springer.

Abello, A., Samos, J., & Saltor F. (2003). Implementing operations to navigate semantic star schemas. *Proceedings of the Sixth International Workshop on Data Warehousing and OLAP (DOLAP 2003)* (pp. 56–62). New York: ACM Press.

Abelló, A., Samos, J., & Saltor, F. (2002, July 17-19). YAM2 (Yet another multidimensional model): An extension of UML. In *Proceedings of the International Database Engineering & Applications Symposium* (pp. 172-181). Edmonton, Canada.

Abelló, A., Samos, J., & Saltor, F. (2006). *YAM2, A multidimensional conceptual model extending UML. Information Systems, 31*(6),541-567.

Abelló, A., Samos, J., & Saltor, F. (2002). *YAM2 (Yet Another Multidimensional Model): An extension of UML*. In *Proceedings of the Int. DB Engineering and Application Symposium*, (pp. 172-181).

Acharya, S., Gibbons, P. B., & Poosala, V. (2000). Congressional samples for approximate answering of group-by queries. *Proceedings of ACM SIGMOD International Conference on Management of Data*, (pp. 487-498).

Adelberg, B., Garcia-Molina, H., & Widom, J. (1997). The STRIP rule system for efficiently maintaining derived data. *Proceedings of the ACM SIGMOD, International Conference on Management of Data*, (pp. 147-158).

Agrawal, R., Gupta, A., & Sarawagi, S. (1995). *Modeling multidimensional databases* (IBM Research Report). IBM Almaden Research Center, San Jose, CA.

Albrecht, J., Bauer, A., Deyerling, O., Gunzel, H., Hummer, W., Lehner, W., & Schlesinger, L. (1999). Management of multidimensional aggregates for efficient online analytical processing. *Proceedings: International Database Engineering and Applications Symposium*, Montreal, Canada, (pp. 156-164).

Al-Kazemi, B. & Mohan, C.K. (2002). Multi-phase discrete particle swarm optimization. *Proceedings from the International Workshop on Frontiers in Evolutionary Algorithms*, (pp. 622-625).

Amo, S. D., & Alves, M. H. F. (2000). Efficient maintenance of temporal data warehouses. *Proceedings of the International Database Engineering and Applications Symposium*, (pp. 188-196).

Anahory, S., & Murray, D. (1997). *Data warehousing in the real world*. Addison Wesley.

Ananthakrishna, R., Chaudhuri, S., & Ganti, V. (2002). Eliminating fuzzy duplicates in data warehouses. In

Proceedings of 28th International Conference on Very Large Databases (VLDB '02).

Angeline, P. (1998, May 4-9). Using selection to improve particle swarm optimization. Proceedings from *The IEEE International Conference on Evolutionary Computation (ICEC'98),* Anchorage, Alaska, USA.

Annoni, E. (2007, November). Eléments méthodologique pour le développement de systèmes décisionnels dans un contexte de réutilisation. Thesis in computer sciences, University Paul Sabatier, Toulouse, France.

Araque, F. (2002). Data warehousing with regard to temporal characteristics of the data source. *IADIS WWW/Internet Conference.* Lisbon, Portugal.

Araque, F. (2003). Integrating heterogeneous data sources with temporal constraints using wrappers. *The 15th Conference On Advanced Information Systems Engineering. Caise Forum.* Klagenfurt, Austria.

Araque, F. (2003). Real-time data warehousing with temporal requirements. *Decision Systems Engineering, DSE'03 (in conjunction with the CAISE'03 conference).* Austria: Klagen-furt/Velden.

Araque, F., Carrasco, R., Salguero, A., Delgado, C., & Vila, M. (2007). Fuzzy integration of a Web data sources for data warehousing. *Lecture Notes in Computer Science,4739. ISSN: 0302-9743. Springer-Verlag.*

Araque, F., Salguero, A., & Abad, M. (2006). Application of data warehouse and decision support system in soaring site recommendation. *Information and Communication Technologies in Tourism, ENTER 2006.* Lausanne, Switzerland: Springer Verlag.

Araque, F., Salguero, A., & Delgado, C. Information system architecture for data warehousing. *Lecture Notes in Computer Science.* ISSN: 0302-9743. Springer-Verlag.

Araque, F., Salguero, A., & Delgado, C. (2007). Monitoring Web data sources using temporal properties as an external resources of a data warehouse. *The 9th International Conference on Enterprise Information Systems,* (pp.. 28-35). Funchal, Madeira.

Araque, F., Salguero, A., Delgado, C., & Samos, J. (2006). Algorithms for integrating temporal properties of data in data warehousing. *The 8th Int. Conf. on Enterprise Information Systems (ICEIS).* Paphos, Cyprus.

Araque, F., & Samos, J. (2003). Data warehouse refreshment maintaining temporal consistency. *The 5th Intern. Conference on Enterprise Information Systems, ICEIS.* Angers, France.

Arlein, R., Gava, J., Gehani, N., & Lieuwen, D. (1995). Ode 4.2 (Ode <EOS>) user manual. *Technical report.* AT&T Bell Labs.

Artz, J. (2005). Data driven vs. metric driven data warehouse design. In *Encyclopedia of Data Warehousing and Mining,* (pp. 223 – 227). Idea Group.

Baeza-Yates & Ribeiro-Neto, 1999Baeza-Yates, R.A., & Ribeiro-Neto, B.A. (1999). *Modern information retrieval.* ACM Press/Addison-Wesley.

Ballinger, C. (1993). TPC-D: Benchmarking for decision support. *The benchmark handbook for database and transaction processing systems,* second edition. Morgan Kaufmann.

Ballou, D.P., & Pazer, H.L. (1985). Modeling data and process quality in multi-input, multi-output information systems. *Management Science, 31*(2), 150–162.

Ballou, D.P, Wang, R.Y., Pazer H.L., & Tayi, G.K. (1998). Modelling information manufacturing systems to determine information product quality.,*Management Science, 44*(4), 462–484.

Baralis, E., Paraboschi, S., & Teniente, E. (1997). Materialized view selection in a multidimensional database. *Proceedings. of VLDB Conference,* (pp. 156-165).

Bauer, A., & Lehner, W. (2003). On solving the view selection problem in distributed data warehouse architectures. *Proceedings: 15th International Conference on Scientific and Statistical Database Management (SSDBM'03), IEEE,* (pp. 43-51).

Bedard, Y. (1999). *Visual modeling of spatial databases: towards spatial PVL and UML. Geomantic 53*(2), 169-186.

Bedard, Y., & Bernier, E. (2002). *Supporting multiple representations with spatial databases views management and the concept of VUEL. Proceedings of the Joint Workshop on Multi-Scale Representations of Spatial Data, ISPRS.*

Bedard, Y., Gosselin, P., Rivest, S., Proulx, M., Nadeau, M., Lebel, G., & Gagnon, M. (2003). Integrating GIS components with knowledge discovery technology for environmental health decision support. *International Journal of Medical Informatics, 70,* 79-94.

Bellatreche, L., Karlapalem, K., & Mohania, M. (2002). Some issues in design of data warehousing systems. *Data warehousing and Web engineering.*(pp. 22-76). IRM Press.

Belo, O. (2000, November). Putting intelligent personal assistants working on dynamic hypercube views updating. *Proceedings of 2nd International Symposium on Robotics and Automation (ISRA'2000)*, Monterrey, México.

Ben-Abdallah, M., Ben, Saïd N., Feki, J., & Ben-Abdallah, H. (2007, November). MP-Builder : A tool for multidimensional pattern construction , *Arab International Conference on Information Technology (ACIT 2007)*, Lattakia, Syria.

Ben-Abdallah, M., Feki, J., & Ben-Abdallah, H. (2006, 9-11 Mai). Designing Multidimensional patterns from standardized real world entities. *International Conference on Computer and Communication Engineering ICCCE'06,* Kuala Lumpur, Malysia.

Ben-Abdallah, M., Feki, J., & Ben-Abdallah, H. (2006, 7-9 December). MPI-EDITOR : Un outil de spécification de besoins OLAP par réutilisation logique de patrons multidimensionnels. *Maghrebian Conference on Software Engineering and Artificial Intelligence MCSEAI'06,* Agadir, Morocco.

Benefelds, J., & Niedrite, L. (2004). Comparison of approaches in data warehouse development in financial services and higher education. In *Proceedings of the 6th Int. Conf. of Enterprise Information Systems (ICEIS 2004), 1,* 552-557. Porto.

Berloto, M. (1998). *Geometric modeling of spatial entities at multiple levels of resolution.* PhD Thesis, Uni. degli Studi di Genova.

Bernier, E., Badard, T., Bédard, Y., Gosselin, P., & Pouliot, J. (2007). Complex spatio-temporal data warehousing and OLAP technologies to better understand climate-related health vulnerabilities. *Special number of International Journal of Biomedical Engineering and Technology on "Warehousing and Mining Complex Data: Applications to Biology, Medicine, Behavior, Health and Environment".*

Bettini, C., Jajodia, S., & Wang, S. (2000). *Time granularities in databases, data mining and temporal reasoning,* Secaucus, NJ, USA. Ed. New York: Springer-Verlag Inc. Secaucus, NJ, USA.

Beyer, K.S., Chamberlin, D.D., Colby, L.S., Ozcan, F., Pirahesh, H., & Xu Y. (2005). Extending XQuery for analytics, *ACM SIGMOD Int. Conf. on Management of Data (SIGMOD)* (pp. 503–514). ACM Press.

Bezdek, J. C. (1981). *Pattern recognition with fuzzy objective function algorithms.* New York: Plenum Press.

Bhashyam, R. (1996). TCP-D: The challenges, issues and results. *The 22th International Conference on Very Large Data Bases,* Mumbai (Bombay), India. *SIGMOD Record, 4,* 593.

Bilenko, M., & Mooney, R. J. (2003, August). Adaptive duplicate detection using learnable string similarity measures. *Proceedings of the Ninth ACM SIGKDD International Conference on Knowledge Discovery and Data Mining (KDD'03)*, Washington, DC (pp. 39-48).

Bischoff, J., & Alexander, T. (1997). *Data warehouse: Practical advice from experts.* Prentice Hall.

Blaschka, M., Sapia, C., Hofling, G., & Dinter, B. (1998). Finding your way through multidimensional data models. In *Proceedings of 9th Int. Conf. on Database and Expert Systems Applications (DEXA), LNCS 1460,* 198-203. Springer,

Blickle, T., & Thiele, L. (1996). A comparison of selection schemes used in evolutionary algorithms. *Evolutionary Computation 4*(4), 361-394.

BMC Software. (2000). Performance management of a data warehouse. *http://www.bmc.com*

Boehnlein, M. & Ulbrich-vom-Ende, A. (2000). Business process-oriented development of data warehouse structures. In *Proceedings of Int. Conf. Data Warehousing 2000* (pp. 3-16). Physica Verlag.

Böhm Ch., Braunmüller B., Krebs F., & Kriegel, H., (2001). Epsilon Grid oOrder: An aAlgorithm for the sSimilarity jJoin on mMassive hHigh-dDimensional dData, *Proceedings. ACM SIGMOD INT. Conf. on Management of Data,* Santa Barbara, CA, 2001.

Böhnlein, M., & Ulbrich-vom, Ende, A. (1999). Deriving initial data warehouse structures from the conceptual data models of the underlying operational information systems.

Bonifati, A., Cattaneo, F., Ceri, S., Fuggetta, A., & Paraboschi, S. (2001). Designing data marts for data warehouses. In *ACM Transactions on Software Engineering and Methodology, 10*(4), 452-483.

Bordawerkar et al., (2005). Bordawekar, R., & Lang, C. A. (2005). Analytical processing of XML documents: Opportunities and challenges. *SIGMOD Record, 34*(2), 27-32.

Borges, K. A. V., Davis Jr., C.A.., & Laender, A. H. F. (2001). *OMT-G: An object-oriented data model for geographic applications Geo Informatics 5*(3), 221-260.

Boussaid et al., 2006Boussaid, O., Messaoud, R.B., Choquet, R., & Anthoard, S. (2006). X-Warehousing: An XML-based approach for warehousing complex data. In *10ᵗʰ East European Conf. on Advances in Databases and Information Systems (ADBIS 2006)* (pp. 39–54). Springer.

Bouzeghoub, M., Fabret, F., & Matulovic, M. (1999). Modeling data warehouse refreshment process as a workflow application. In *Proceedings of the International Workshop on Design and Management of Data Warehouses*, Heidelberg, Germany.

Brinkkemper, S. (1996). Method engineering: Engineering of information systems development methods and tools. In *Information and Software Technology, 38*(4), 275- 280.

Browne, J., Harhen, J., & Shivnan, J. (1996). *Production management systems.* Addison-Wesley.

Bruckner, R., & Tjoa, A. (2002). Capturing delays and valid times in data warehouses: Towards timely consistent analyses. *Journal of Intelligent Information Systems (JIIS), 19*(2,)169-190. *Kluwer Academic Publishers.*

Bruckner, R.M., List, B., Schiefer, J., & Tjoa, A. M. (2001). Modeling temporal consistency in data warehouses. *Proceedings of the 12th International Workshop on Database and Expert Systems Applications,* (pp. 901-905).

Burigat, S., Chittaro, L., & De Marco, L. (2005) Bringing dynamic queries to mobile devices: A visual preference-based search tool for tourist decision support. *Proceedings of INTERACT 2005: 10th IFIP International Conference on Human-Computer Interaction* (pp. 213-226. Berlin: Springer Verlag.

Cabibbo, L., & Torlone, R. (2000). The design and development of a logical OLAP system. *2nd International Conference of Data Warehousing and Knowledge Discovery (DaWaK'00),* London, UK: Springer, LNCS 1874, (pp. 1-10).

Cabibbo, L., & Torlone, R. (1998, March 23-27). A logical approach to multidimensional databases. In *Proceedings of the International Conference on Extending Database Technology* (pp. 183-197). Valencia, Spain.

Calero, C., Piattini, M., Pascual, C., & Serrano, M.A. (2001). Towards data warehouse quality metrics. *Proceedings of International Workshop on Design and Management of Data Warehouses*, (pp. 2/1-10).

Calvanese, D., De Giacomo, G., Lenzerini, M., Nardi, D., & Rosati, R. (1998, August 20-22). Information integration: Conceptual modeling and reasoning support. In *Proceedings of the International Conference on Cooperative Information Systems* (pp. 280-291). New York.

Camossi, E., Bertolotto, M., Bertino, E., & Guerrini, G. (2003b). *A multigranular spactiotemporal data model. Proceedings of the 11th ACM international symposium.* Advances in GIS, (pp. 94-101). New Orleans, USA.

Camossi, E., Bertolotto, M., Bertino, E., & Guerrini, G. (2003). A multigranular spatiotemporal data model. *Proceedings of the 11th ACM International Symposium on Advances in Geographic Information Systems, ACM GIS 2003,* New Orleans, LA (pp. 94-101).

Campbell, B., Collins, P., Hadaway, H., Hedley, N., & Stoermer, M. (2002). Web3D in ocean science learning environments: Virtual big beef creek. *Proceedings of the 7th International Conference on 3D Web Technology,* (pp. 85-91).

Carpani, F., & Ruggia, R. (2001). An integrity constraints language for a conceptual multidimensional data model. *13th International Conference on Software Engineering & Knowledge Engineering (SEKE'01),* Argentina.

Carrasco, R., Araque, F., Salguero, A., & Vila, A. (2008). Applying fuzzy data mining to tourism area. En J. Galindo, *Handbook of Research on Fuzzy Information Processing in Databases.* Hershey, PA, USA: Information Science Reference.

Castellanos, M. (1993). *Semiautomatic semantic enrichment for the integrated access in interoperable databases. PhD thesis,* . Barcelona, Spain: Dept. Lenguajes y Sistemas Informáticos, Universidad Politécnica de Cataluña, Barcelona.

Chang, J. (2004). The current state of BPM technology. *Journal of Business Integration.*

Chaudhuri, S., & Dayal, U. (1997). An overview of data warehousing and OLAP technology. *ACM SIGMOD Record, 26*(1) , 65-74.

Chaudhuri, S., Ganti, V., & Motwani, R. (2005). Robust identification of fuzzy duplicates. In *Proceedings of the 21st international Conference on Data Engineering (ICDE'05),* Washington, DC (pp. 865-876).

Cheesman, J., & Daniels, J. (2000). UML Components: A simple process for specifying component-based software. Addison Wesley.

Chen, Y., Dehne, F., Eavis, T., & Rau-Chaplin, A. (2006). Improved data partitioning for building large ROLAP data cubes in parallel. *Journal of Data Warehousing and Mining, 2(*1), 1-26.

Chengalur-Smith, I.N., Ballou, D.P., & Pazer, H.L. (1999). The impact of data quality information on decision making: An exploratory analysis. *IEEE Transactions on Knowledge and Data Engineering, 11*(6), 853-864.

Chenyi, Xia,, Hongjun, Lu, Beng, Chin, Ooi, & Jing, Hu, (2004). *GORDER: An eEfficient mMethod for KNN jJoin pProcessing,* VLDB 2004,(pp. 756-767).

Chittaro, L., & Ranon, R. (2007). Web3D technologies in learning, education and training: Motivations, issues, opportunities. *Computers & Education Journal, 49*(1), 3-18..

Chittaro, L., & Scagnetto, I. (2001). Is semitransparency useful for navigating virtual environments? *Proceedings of VRST-2001: 8th ACM Symposium on Virtual Reality Software & Technology,* pp. 159-166. New York: ACM Press.

Chittaro, L., Combi, C., & Trapasso, G. (2003, December). Data mining on temporal data: A visual approach and its clinical application to hemodialysis. *Journal of Visual Languages and Computing, 14*(6), 591-620.

Chiu, S. (1994). Fuzzy model identification based on cluster estimation. *Journal of Intelligent & Fuzzy Systems, 2*(3).

Chrisment, C., Pujolle, G., Ravat, F., Teste, O., & Zurfluh, G. (2006). *Bases de données décisionnelles.* Encyclopédie de l'informatique et des systèmes d'information. Jacky Akoka, Isabelle Comyn-Wattiau (Edition.), Vuibert, I/5, pp. 533-546.

Ciferri, C. D. A., & Souza, F. F. (2001). Materialized views in data warehousing environments. *Proceedings of the XXI International Conference of the Chilean Computer Science Society,* (pp. 3-12).

Clementini, E., di Felice, P., & van Oosterom, P. (1993). A small set of formal topological relationships suitable for end-user interaction. In *LNCS 692: Proceedings of the 3rd International Symposyium on Advances in Spatial Databases, SSD '93* (pp. 277-295).

Codd, E.F., Codd, S.B., & Salley, C.T. (1993). *Providing OLAP (On Line Analytical Processing) to user analyst: An*

IT mandate, technical report, E.F. Codd and associates, (white paper de Hyperion Solutions Corporation).

Codd, E. F. (1993). *Providing OLAP (On-line Analytical Processing) to user-analysts: An IT mandate*. Technical Report, E.F. Codd and Associates.

Codd, E. F., Codd, S. B., & Salley, C. T. (1993, July). Beyond decision support. *Computerworld, 27*(30), 87-89.

Codd, E.F. (1970, June). A relational model of data for large shared data banks. *Communication of the ACM, 13*(6), 3776-387.

Codd, E.F., Codd, S.B., & Salley, C.T. (1993). Providing OLAP (On-Line Analytical Processing) to user analysts: An IT mandate. *White Paper*, E.F. Codd & Associates.

Cohen, W., Ravikumar, P., & Fienberg, S. (2003). A comparison of string distance metrics for name-matching tasks. In *Proceedings of the Eighth International Joint Conference on Artificial Intelligence: Workshop on Information Integration on the Web (IIWeb-03)*.

Colliat, 1996Colliat, G. (1996). OLAP, relational, and multidimensional database systems. *SIGMOD Record, 25*(3), 64-69.

Coors, V., & Jung, V. (1998). Using VRML as an interface to the 3D data warehouse. *Proceedings of the third Symposium on Virtual Reality Modeling Language*. ACM Press.

Creese, G. (2005). Volume analytics: Get ready for the process warehouse. *DMReview.* http://www.dmreview. com.

Cutting-Decelle, A.F., & Michel, J.J. (2003). ISO 15531 MANDATE: A standardized data model for manufacturing management. *International Journal of Computer Applications in Technology, 18*(1-4).

Darmont, J., & Schneider, M. (2000). Benchmarking OODBs with a generic tool. *Journal of Database Management, 11*(3), 16-27.

Darmont, J., Bentayeb, F., & Boussaïd, O. (2005). DWEB: A data warehouse engineering benchmark.

The 7th International Conference on Data Warehousing and Knowledge Discovery (DaWaK 05), Copenhagen, Denmark. LNCS, 3589, 85-94.

Darmont, J., Bentayeb, F., & Boussaïd, O. (2007). Benchmarking data warehouses. *International Journal of Business Intelligence and Data Mining, 2*(1), 79-104.

Datta, A., & Thomas, H. (1997). A conceptual model and algebra for on-line analytical processing in data warehouses. In *Proceedings of the Workshop for Information Technology and Systems* (pp. 91-100).

De Amicis, F., & Batini, C. (2004). A methodology for data quality assessment on financial data. *Studies in Communication Sciences, 4,*(2), 115-136.

Delaney, B. (1999). The NYSE's 3D trading floor. *IEEE Computer Graphics and Applications 19*(6), 12-15.

Demarest, M. (1995). A data warehouse evaluation model. *Oracle Technical Journal. 1*(1), 29.

Deshpande, P. M., Naughton, J. K., Ramasamy, K., Shukla, A., Tufte, K., & Zhao, Y. (1997). Cubing algorithms, storage estimation, and Storage and processing alternatives for OLAP. *Data Engineering Bulletin, 20*(1), 3-11.

Dresner, H. (2002). Business activity monitoring: New age BI?. *Gartner Research LE-15-8377.*

Eberhart, R. C., & Shi, Y. (2001). Particle swarm optimization: Developments, applications and resources. *Proceedings from the 2001 Congress on Evolutionary Computation,.1,* 81-86.

Eberhart, R.C., & Kennedy, J. (1995). A new optimizer using particle swarm theory. *Proceedings from the Sixth International Symposium on Micro Machine and Human Science*, Nagoya, Japan, IEEE Service Center, Piscataway, NJ, (pp. 39-43).

Elmagarmid, A. K., Ipeirotis, P. G., & Verykios, V. S. (2007). Duplicate record detection: A survey. *IEEE Transactions on Knowledge and Data Engineering, 19*(1), 1-16.

Elmasri, R, & Navathe, S.(2007). *Fundamental of database systems*, Pearson International/Addison Wesley Editorial, 5ª edition.

English, L.P. (1999). Improving data warehouse & business information quality: Methods for reducing costs and increasing profits. Wiley and Sons.

Fahrner, C., & Vossen, G. (1995). A survey of database transformations based on the entity-relationship model. *Data & Knowledge Engineering, 15*(3), 213-250.

Fankhauser, P., & Klement, T. (2003). XML for data warehousing chances and challenges (Extended Abstract). In *5th Int. Conf. on Data Warehousing and Knowledge Discovery* (*DaWaK 2003*) (pp. 1-3). Springer.

Feki, J., & Ben-Abdallah, H. (2007, March). Multidimensional pattern construction and logical reuse for the design of data marts. *International Review on Computers and Software (IRECOS), 2*(2), 124-134, ISSN 1882-6003.

Feki, J., Ben-Abadallah, H., & Ben Abdallah, M. (2006). Réutilisation des patrons en étoile. *XXIVème Congrès INFORSID'06*, (pp. 687-701), Hammamet, Tunisie.

Feki, J., & Ben-Abdallah, H. (2006, 22-24 Mai). Star patterns for data mart design: Definition and logical reuse operators. *International Conference on Control, Modeling and Diagnosis ICCMD'06*, Annaba Algeria.

Feki, J., Majdoubi, J., & Gargouri, F. (2005, July). A two-phase approach for multidimensional schemes integration. *17th International Conference on Software Engineering and Knowledge Engineering (SEKE'05)*, (pp. 498-503), Taipei, Taiwan, Republic of China. ISBN I-891706-16-0.

Feki, J., Nabli, A., Ben-Abdallah, H., & Gargouri, F. (2008, August). An automatic data warehouse conceptual design approach. encyclopedia of data warehousing and mining, John Wang Edition (To appear August).

Fidalgo, R. N., Times, V. C., Silva, J., & Souza, F. (2004). GeoDWFrame: A framework for guiding the design of geographical dimensional schemas. In *LNCS 3181: Proceedings of the 6th International Conference on Data Warehousing and Knowledge Discovery, DaWaK 2004* (pp. 26-37).

Fitzgerald, B. & Fitzgerald, G. (1999). Categories and contexts of information systems developing: Making sense of the mess. In *Proceedings of European Conf. on Information Systems*, (pp.194-211).

Fonseca, F., Egenhofer, M., Davies, C., & Camara, G. (2002). Semantic granularity in ontology-driven geographic information systems. *Annals of Mathematics and Artificial Intelligence, Special Issue on Spatial and Temporal Granularity, 36*(1), 121-151.

Franconi, E., & Kamble, A. (2004a, June 7-11). The GMD data model and algebra for multidimensional information. In *Proceedings of the Conference on Advanced Information Systems Engineering* (pp. 446-462). Riga, Latvia.

Franconi, E., & Kamble, A. (2004b). A data warehouse conceptual data model. In *Proceedings of the International Conference on Statistical and Scientific Database Management* (pp. 435-436).

Frank, L., (2008). *Databases and applications with relaxed ACID properties*. Doctoral Dissertation, Copenhagen Business School, Samfundslitteratur.

Frank, L., & Christian, Frank (2006). Evaluation and selection of responses to slowly changing dimensions in data warehouses. *Proceedings of the Fourth International Conference on Computer Applications, ICCA2006*, (pp. 33-42).

Frank, L., Christian, F., Christian, S., Jensen, & Torben Bach P. (2005). Dimensional modelling by using a new response to slowly changing dimensions. *Proceedings of the 2nd International Conference on Information Technology*, Amman

Frank, L., & Zahle, T, (1998). Semantic ACID properties in multidatabases Uuing remote procedure calls and update propagations. *Software - Practice & Experience, 28*, 77-98.

Fuhr & Großjohann, (2001). Fuhr, N., & Großjohann, K. (2001). XIRQL: A query language for information retrieval in XML documents. In *Proceedings of the 24th Intl. Conf. on Research and Development in Information Retrieval (SIGIR 2001)* (pp. 172–180). ACM Press.

Galhardas, H., Florescu, D., et al. (2001). Declarative data cleaning: Language, model and algorithms. In *Proceedings of the 27ᵗʰ International Conference on Very Large Databases (VLDB'01)*, Rome (pp. 371-380).

Galindo, J., Urrutia, A., & Piattini, M. (2006). *Fuzzy databases: Modeling, design and implementation.* Hershey, PA: Idea Group Publishing.

Gamma, E., Helm, R., Johnson, J. & Vlissides, J. (1999). *Design patterns: Elements of reusable object-oriented software.* Addisson-Wesley.

Gascueña, C. (2008). *Propousal of a conceptual model for the Representation of spatio temporal multigranularity in multidimensional databases.* PhD Thesis. University Politecnica of Madrid, Spain.

Gascueña, C. M., & Guadalupe, R. (2008). *A study of the spatial representation in multidimensional models. Proceedings of the 10th International Conference on Enterprise Information Systems*, Spain, ICEIS 2008.

Gascueña, C. M., & Guadalupe, R.. (2008). *Some types of spatio-temporal granularities in a conceptual multidimensional model. Aplimat-Journal of Applied Mathematics, 1*(2), 215-216.

Gascueña, C. M., Cuadra, D., & Martínez, P. (2006). *A multidimensional approach to the representation of the spatiotemporal multigranularity. Proceedings of the 8th International Conference on Enterprise Information Systems*, Cyprus. ICEIS 2006.

Gascueña, C. M., Moreno, L., & Cuadra, D. (2006). *Dos Perspectivas para la Representación de la Multi-Granularidad en Bases de Datos Espacio-Temporales.* IADIS 2005 conferences.

Ghozzi, F. (2004). Conception et manipulation de bases de données dimensionnelles à contraintes. *Thesis in computer sciences,* University Paul Sabatier, Toulouse, France.

Gibbons, P. B., & Matias, Y. (1998). New sampling-based summary statistics for improving approximate query answers. *Proceeding of ACM SIGMOD International Conference on Management of Data*, (pp. 331-342).

Gingras, F., & Lakshmanan, L. (1998). nD-SQL: A multi-dimensional language for interoperability and OLAP. *Proceedings of the 24th VLDB Conference*, (pp. 134-145).

Giorgini, P., Rizzi, S., & Garzetti, M. (2005). Goal-oriented requirement analysis for data warehouse design. In *Proceedings of 8ᵗʰ ACM Int. Workshop DOLAP*, (pp. 47-56).

Giorgini, P., Rizzi, S., & Garzetti, M. (2005, November 4-5). Goal-oriented requirement analysis for data warehouse design. In *Proceedings of the ACM International Workshop on Data Warehousing and OLAP* (pp. 47-56). Bremen, Germany.

Goeken, M. (2005). Anforderungsmanagement bei der Entwicklung von data-warehouse-systemen. Ein sichtenspezifischer Ansatz. In *Proceedings der DW 2004 - Data Warehousing und EAI,* (pp. 167 – 186).

Goldberg, D.E. (1989). *Genetic algorithms in search, optimization, and machine learning.* Reading, MA: Addison-Wesley.

Golfarelli et al., (1998). Golfarelli, M., Maio, D., & Rizzi, S. (1998). The dimensional fact model: A conceptual model for data warehouses, invited paper. *Intl. Journal of Cooperative Information Systems (IJCIS), 7*(2-3), 215-247.

Golfarelli et al., (2001). Golfarelli, M., Rizzi, S., & Vrdoljak, B. (2001). Data warehouse design from XML sources. In *4ᵗʰ ACM Int. Workshop on Data Warehousing and OLAP (DOLAP 2001)* (pp. 40-47). ACM Press.

Golfarelli, M., & Rizzi, S. (2001, April 2-6). WᴀɴD: A CASE tool for data warehouse design. In *Demo Proceedings of the International Conference on Data Engineering* (pp. 7-9). Heidelberg, Germany.

Golfarelli, M., Maio, D., & Rizzi, S. (1998). Conceptual design of data warehouses from E/R schemes. In *Proceedings of Hawaii Int. Conf. on System Sciences, 7*, 334-343.

Golfarelli, M., Maio, D., & Rizzi, S. (1998). Conceptual design of data warehouses from E/R schemes. *31st Hawaii International Conference on System Sciences.*

Golfarelli, M., Maio, D., & Rizzi, S. (1998). The dimensional fact model: A conceptual model for data warehouses. *International Journal of Cooperative Information Systems, 7*(2-3), 215-247.

Golfarelli, M., Mario, D., & Rizzi, S. (1998). *The dimensional fact model: A conceptual model for data warehouses.* (IJCIS) 7(2–3), 215-247.

Golfarelli, M., Rizzi, S., & Saltarelli, E. (2002). WAND: A case tool for workload-based design of a data mart. SEBD, (pp. 422-426).

Gorawski M., & Malczok R., (2004). Distributed sSpatial dData wWarehouse iIndexed with vVirtual mMemory aAggregation tTree. The *5th Workshop on Spatial-Temporal DataBase Management (STDBM_VLDB'04)*, Toronto, Canada 2004.

Gorawski M., & Wróbel W., (2005). Realization of kNN qQuery tType in sSpatial tTelemetric dData wWarehouse. *Studia Informatica, vol.26, nr 2*(63), pp.1-22.

Gorawski, M., & Gebczyk, W., (2007)., *Distributed approach of continuous queries with knn join processing in spatial data warehouse,* ICEIS, Funchal, Madeira, 2007, (pp. :131-136).

Gray, J., Bosworth, A., Layman, A., & Pirahesh, H. (1996). Data cube: A relational aggregation operator generalizing group-by, cross-tab, and sub-totals. *Proceeding of the 12th International Conference on Data Engineering,* (pp. 152-159).

Gray, J., & Reuter, A. (1993). *Transaction processing.* Morgan Kaufman.

Gray, J., Bosworth, A., Layman, A., & Pirahesh, H. (1996). Data cube: A relational aggregation operator generalizing group-by, cross-tab, and sub-totals. *Proceedings of the Twelfth International Conference on Data Engineering,* New Orleans, LA, February, (pp. 152-159).

Gray, J., Ed. (1993). *The benchmark handbook for database and transaction processing systems,* second edition. Morgan Kaufmann.

Greenfield, L. (2004). Performing data warehouse software evaluations. *http://www.dwinfocenter.org/evals.html*

Greenfield, L. (2004). What to learn about in order to speed up data warehouse querying. *http://www.dwinfocenter.org/fstquery.html*

Grefenstette, J..J., & Baker, J.E. (1989). How genetic algorithms work: A critical look at implicit parallelism. In J. David Schaffer, (ed.) *Proceedings: the Third International Conference on Genetic Algorithms*, San Mateo, CA, (pp. 20-27). Morgan Kaufmann Publishers

Griffoen, J., Yavatkar, R., & Finkel, R. (1994). Extending the dimensions of consistency: Spatial consistency and sequential segments. *Technical Report*, University of Kentucky.

Gupta, A., & Mumick, I. S. (1995). Maintenance of materialized views: Problems, techniques, and applications. *IEEE Data Engineering Bulletin, Special Issue on Materialized Views and Warehousing, 18*(2), 3-18.

Gupta, H., & Mumick, I.S. (1999). Selection of views to materialize under a maintenance-time constraint. *Proceedings of the International Conference on Database* Theory.

Gupta, H., Harinarayan, V., Rajaraman, A., & Ullman, J. (1997). Index selection for OLAP. *Proceedings of the International Conference on Data Engineering,* (pp. 208-219).

Gyssens, M., & Lakshmanan, L.V.S. (1997). A foundation for multi-dimensional databases, *23rd Int. Conf. on Very Large Data Bases (VLDB)* (pp. 106-115), Morgan Kaufmann.

Gyssens, M., & Lakshmanan, L. V. S. (1997). A foundation for multi-dimensional databases. In *Proceedings of the International Conference on Very Large Data Bases* (pp. 106-115), Athens, Greece.

Haidarian Shahri, H., & Barforush, A. A. (2004). A flexible fuzzy expert system for fuzzy duplicate elimination in data cleaning. *Proceedings of the 15th International Conference on Database and Expert Systems Applications (DEXA'04)* (LNCS 3180, pp. 161-170). Springer Verlag.

Haidarian Shahri, H., & Shahri, S. H. (2006). Eliminating duplicates in information integration: An adaptive, extensible framework. *IEEE Intelligent Systems, 21*(5), 63-71.

Haisten, M. (1999, June). Real-time data warehouse. *DM Review.*

Haller, M., Proll, B., Retschitzgger, W., Tjoa, A., & Wagner, R. (2000). Integrating heterogeneous tourism information in TIScover - The MIRO-Web approach. *Proceedings Information and Communication Technologies in Tourism, ENTER.* Barcelona , Spain

Hammad, M. A., Franklin, M. J., Aref, W. G., & El-magarmid, A. K., (2003). *Scheduling for shared window joins over data streams.* VLDB.

Han, J. , Stefanovic, N., & Kopersky, K. (1998). Selective materialization: An efficient method for spatial data cube construction. *Proceedings of Research and Development in Knowledge Discovery and Data Mining, Second Pacific-Asia Conference, PAKDD'98* (pp. 144-158).

Han, J., Altman R., Kumar, V., Mannila, H., & Pregibon, D. (2002). Emerging scientific applications in data mining. *Communication of the ACM, 45*(8), 54-58.

Hanson, E.N. (1996). The design and implementation of the ariel active database rule system. *IEEE Transaction on Knowledge and Data Engineering, 8*(1),157-172.

Harinarayan, V., Rajaraman, A., & Ullman, J. (1996). Implementing data cubes efficiently. *Proceedings of ACM SIGMOD Conference.* Montreal: ACM.

Harmsen, F. (1997). *Situational method engineering.* Dissertation Thesis, University of Twente, Moret Ernst & Young Management Consultants.

Hayes, R., & Wheelright, S. (1984). *Restoring our competitive edge*: *Competing through manufacturing.* John Wiley & Sons.

Hellerstein, J.M., Haas, P.J., & Wang, H. (1997). Online aggregation. *Proceedings of ACM SIGMOD Conference,* (pp. 171–182).

Hellinger, M., & Fingerhut, S. (2002). Business activity monitoring: EAI meets data warehousing. *Journal of Enterprise Application Integration (EAI).*

Hernandez, M. A., & Stolfo, S. J. (1998). Real-world data is dirty: Data cleansing and the merge/purge problem. *Data Mining and Knowledge Discovery, 2*(1), 9-37.

Holland, J.H. (1992). *Adaptation in natural and artificial systems.* Cambridge, MA, (2nd edition): MIT Press.

Hollingworth, D. (1995). *The workflow reference model.* Technical Report TC00-1003, Workflow Management Coalition, Lighthouse Point, Florida, USA.

Horner, J., Song, I-Y., & Chen, P.P. (2004). An analysis of additivity in OLAP systems. In *7th ACM Int. Workshop on Data Warehousing and OLAP (DOLAP 2004)* (pp. 83-91). ACM Press.

Horng, J.T., Chang, Y.J., Liu, B.J., & Kao, C.Y. (1999, July). Materialized view selection using genetic algorithms in a data warehouse. *Proceedings from the World Congress on Evolutionary Computation,* Washington D.C.

Huang, S. M., Hung, Y. C., & Hung, Y. M. (2000). Developing an active data warehouse System. *Proceeding of 17th International Conference on Data and Information for the Coming Knowledge Millennium.*

Huang, Y.-F., & Chen, J.-H. (2001). Fragment allocation in distributed database design. In *Journal of Information Science and Engineering 17*(2001), 491-506.

Hurtado, C.A., & Mendelzon, A.O. (2002, June). OLAP dimension constraints. *21st ACM SIGACT-SIGMOD-SIGART Symposium on Principles of Database Systems (PODS'02),* Madison, USA, (pp. 169-179).

Hüsemann, B., Lechtenbörger, J., & Vossen, G. (2000). Conceptual data warehouse design. *Proc. of the Int'l Workshop on Design and Management of Data Warehouses,* Stockholm, Sweden, (pp. 6.1-6.11).

Hüsemann, B., Lechtenbörger, J., & Vossen, G. (2000). Conceptual data warehouse design. In *Proceedings of the International Workshop on Design and Management of Data Warehouses,* Stockholm, Sweden.

Hutter, M. (2002, May). Fitness uniform selection to preserve genetic diversity. *Proceedings in the 2002 Congress on Evolutionary Computation (CEC-2002),* Washington D.C, USA, *IEEE* (pp. 783-788).

Inmon, W. (2002). *Building the data warehouse.* John Wiley & Sons.

Inmon, W. H. (1998, December). Information management: Charting the course. *DM Review.*

ISO (2004). ISO Technical Committee TC 184/SC 4. ISO 10303-1:1994. *Industrial automation systems and integration - Product data representation and exchange - Part 1: Overview and fundamental principles.* International Organization for Standardization.

ISO (2005). ISO Technical Committee 184/SC 4. ISO 15531-32 (2005). *Industrial automation systems and integration - Industrial manufacturing management data: Resources usage management - Part 32: Conceptual model for resources usage management data.* International Organization for Standardization.

Jang, J. S. R. (1993). ANFIS: Adaptive network-based fuzzy inference systems. *IEEE Transactions on Systems, Man, and Cybernetics, 23*(3), 665-685.

Jang, J. S. R., & Sun, C. T. (1995). Neuro-fuzzy modeling and control. *Proceedings of the IEEE*, 378-406.

Jarke, M., Jeusfeld, M.A., Quix, C., & Vassiliadis, P. (1999). Architecture and quality in data warehouses: An extended repository approach. *Information Systems, 24*(3), 229-253.

Jensen, M.R., Møller, T.H., & Pedersen, T.B. (2001). Specifying OLAP cubes on XML data, *13th Int. Conf. on Scientific and Statistical Database Management (SSDBM)* (pp. 101-112). IEEE Computer Society.

Jensen, C., Kligys, A., Pedersen T., & Timko, I. (2002). Multidimensional data modeling for location-based services. In *Proceedings of the 10th ACM International Symposium on Advances in Geographic Information Systems* (pp. 55-61).

Jeusfeld, M.A., Quix, C., & Jarke, M. (1998). Design and analysis of quality information for data warehouses. *Proceedings of the International Conference on Conceptual Modeling*, (pp. 349-362).

Jones, C.B., Kidner, D.B., Luo, L.Q., Bundy, G.L., & Ware, J.M. (1996). Databases design for a multi-scale spatial information system. *Int. J., GIS 10*(8), 901-920.

Jones, M. E., & Song, I. Y. (2005). Dimensional modeling: Identifying, classifying & applying patterns. In *Proceedings of the ACM International Workshop on Data Warehousing and OLAP* (pp. 29-38). Bremen, Germany.

Kaldeich, C., & Oliveira, J. (2004). Data warehouse methodology: A process driven approach. In *Proceedings of CAISE*, LNCS, *3084*, 536-549.

Kalnis, P., Mamoulis, N., & D., Papadias (2002). *View selection using randomized search. Data Knowledge Engineering, 42*(1), 89-111.

Kalnis, P., Mamoulis, N., & Papadias, D. (2002). View selection using randomized search. In *Data Knowledge Engineering, 42*(1), 89-111.

Karr, A.F., Sanil, A.P., & Banks, D.L. (2006). Data quality: A statistical perspective. *Statistical Methodology, 3*(2), 137-173.

Keith et al., 2005 Keith, S., Kaser, O., & Lemire, D. (2005). Analyzing large collections of electronic text using OLAP. In *APICS 29th Conf. in Mathematics, Statistics and Computer Science* (pp. 17-26). Acadia University.

Kennedy, J., & Eberhart, R. C. (1995). Particle swarm optimization. In *Proceedings of the International Conference on Neural Networks*, IV. Piscataway, NJ: IEEE Service Center, (pp. 1942-1948).

Kennedy, J., & Eberhart, R.C. (1997). A discrete binary version of the particle swarm optimization algorithm. *Proceedings from the 1997 Conference on Systems, Man and Cybernetics (SMC'97)*, (pp. 4104-4109).

Khatri, V., Ram, S., & Snodgrass, R. T. (2006). *On augmenting database design-support environments to capture the geo-spatio-temporal data semantic*, 2004, Publisher Elsevier Science Ltd, *31*(2), 98-133.

Khrouf, K., & Soulé-Dupuy, C. (2004). A textual warehouse approach: A Web data repository. In Masoud Mohammadian (Eds.), *Intelligent Agents for Data Mining and Information Retrieval* (pp. 101-124), Idea Publishing Group (IGP).

Kimbal, R. (1996). *The data warehouse toolkit.* New York: John Wiley & Sons.

Kimball, R., & Ross, M. (2002). *The data warehouse toolkit: The complete guide to dimensional modeling, second edition.* John Wiley & Sons.

Kimball, R., Reeves, L., Ross, M., & Thornthwaite, W. (1998). *The data warehouse lifecycle toolkit: Expert methods for designing, developing, and deploying data warehouses.* John Wiley & Sons.

Kimball, R., Ross, M., & Merz, R. (2002). *The data warehouse toolkit: The complete guide to dimensional modeling.* John Wiley & Sons.

Kotidis, Y., & Roussopoulos, N. (1999, June). Dynamat. A dynamic view management system for data warehouses. In *Proceedings of the ACM SIGMOD International Conference on Management of Data*, Philadelphia, Pennsylvania, (pp. 371-382).

Koza, J.R. (1992). Genetic programming: On the programming of computers by means of natural selection. Cambridge, Massachusetts: MIT Press.

Kriebel, C.H. (1978). Evaluating the quality of information systems. *Proceedings of the BIFOA Symposium*, (pp. 18-20).

Krink, T., & Løvbjerg, M. (2002, September 7-11). The life cycle model: Combining particle swarm optimization, genetic algorithms and hillclimbers. In *Proceedings of the 7th International Conference on Parallel Problem Solving from Nature (PPSN VII)*, Granada, Spain. *Lecture Notes in Computer Science, 2439*, 621-630. Springer.

Kueng, P., Wettstein, T., & List, B. (2001). A holistic process performance analysis through a process data warehouse. In *Proceedings of the American Conf. on Information Systems*, (pp. 349-356).

Labrinidis, A., & Roussopoulos, N. (1998). *A performance evaluation of online warehouse update algorithms.* Technical report CS-TR-3954. Department of Computer Science, University of Maryland.

Lechtenbörger, J. (2004). Computing unique canonical covers for simple FDs via transitive reduction. *Technical report, Angewandte Mathematik und Informatik*, University of Muenster, Germany: Information Processing Letters.

Lechtenbörger, J. (2001). *Data warehouse schema design* (Tech. Rep. No. 79). DISDBIS Akademische Verlagsgesellschaft Aka GmbH, Germany.

Lechtenbörger, J., Hüsemann, B. J., & Vossen. (2000). Conceptual data warehouse design. *International Workshop on Design and Management of Data Warehouses*, Stockholm, Sweden, (pp. 6.1-6.11).

Lechtenbörger, J., & Vossen, G. (2003, July). Multidimensional normal forms for data warehouse design. *Information Systems Review, 28*(5), 415-434.

Lee, Y.W., Strong, D.M., Kahn, B.K., & Wang, R.Y. (2001). AIMQ: A methodology for information quality assessment. *Information and Management, 40*(2), 133-146.

Lenz, H. J., & Shoshani, A. (1997). Summarizability in OLAP and statistical databases. In *Proceedings of the 9th International Conference on Statistical and Scientific Database Management* (pp. 132-143). Washington, DC.

Leppanen, M., Valtonen, K., & Pulkkinen, M. (2007). Towards a contingency framework for engineering an EAP method. In *Proceedings of the 30th Information Systems Research Seminar in Scandinavia IRIS2007*.

Levene, M., & Loizou, G. (2003). Why is the snowflake schema a good data warehouse design? *Information Systems, 28*, 225-240.

Li, C., & Wang, X. S. (1996). A data model for supporting on-line analytical processing. In *Proceedings of the International Conference on Information and Knowledge Management* (pp. 81-88). Rockville, Maryland.

Li, Y., Brodlie, K., & Philips, N. (2001). Web-based VR training simulator for percutaneous rhizotomy. *Proceedings of Medicine Meets Virtual Reality*, (pp. 175-181).

Liang, W., Wang, H., & Orlowska, M.E. (2001). Materialized view selection under the maintenance cost constraint. In *Data and Knowledge Engineering, 37*(2), 203-216.

Lin, W.-Y., & Kuo, I-C. (2004). A genetic selection algorithm for OLAP data cubes. *Knowledge and Information Systems, 6*(1), 83-102. Springer-Verlag London Ltd.

Ling, T. W., & Sze, E. K. (1999). Materialized View Maintenance Using Version Numbers. *Proceedings of the 6th International Conference on Database Systems for Advanced Applications*, 263-270.

List, B., Bruckner, R. M., Machaczek, K., & Schiefer, J. (2002). A comparison of data warehouse development methodologies. Case study of the process warehouse. In *Proceedings of DEXA 2002, LNCS 2453*, (pp. 203-215). Springer.

Longley, P., Goodchild, M., Maguire, D., & Rhind, D. (2001). *Geographic information systems and science.* New York: John Wiley & Sons.

Lopez, I., & Snodgrass, R. (2005). Spatiotemporal aggregate computation: A survey. *IEEE Transactions on Knowledge and Data Engineering, 17*(2), 271-286.

Loureiro, J., & Belo, O. (2006c, May 23-27). A discrete particle swarm algorithm for OLAP data cube selection. In *Proceedings of 8th International Conference on Enterprise Information Systems (ICEIS 2006)*, Paphos, Cyprus, (pp. 46-53).

Loureiro, J., & Belo, O. (2006b, October 2-6). Evaluating maintenance cost computing algorithms for multi-node OLAP systems. In *Proceedings of the XI Conference on Software Engineering and Databases (JISBD2006)*, Sitges, Barcelona, (pp. 241-250).

Loureiro, J. &Belo, O. (2006b, December 11-14). An evolutionary approach to the selection and allocation of distributed cubes. *Proceedings from 2006 International Database Engineering & Applications Symposium (IDEAS2006)*, Delhi, India, (pp. 243-248).

Loureiro, J., & Belo, O. (2006ª, January). Life inspired algorithms for the selection of OLAP data cubes. In *WSEAS Transactions on Computers, 1*(5), 8-14.

Loureiro, J., & Belo, O. (2006ª, June 5-9). A non-linear cost model for multi-node OLAP cubes. *Proceedings from the CAiSE'06 Forum*, Luxembourg, (pp. 68-71).

Løvbjerg, M., Rasmussen, T., & Krink, T. (2001). Hybrid particle swarm optimization with breeding and subpopulations. *Proceedings from the 3rd Genetic and Evolutionary Computation Conference (GECCO-2001).*

Low, W. L., Lee, M. L., & Ling, T. W. (2001). A knowledge-based approach for duplicate elimination in data cleaning. *Information Systems, 26*, 585-606.

Lujan-Mora, S., Trujillo, J., & Song, I. (2002). Extending the UML for multidimensional modeling. In *Proceedings of UML*, LNCS 2460, (pp. 290-304). Springer.

Luján-Mora, S., Trujillo, J., & Song, I. Y. (2002). Extending the UML for multidimensional modeling. In *Proceedings of the International Conference on the Unified Modeling Language* (pp. 290-304). Dresden, Germany.

Luján-Mora, S., Trujillo, J., & Song, Il- Yeol. (2006). A UML profile for multidimensional modeling in data warehouses. *DKE, 59*(3), 725-769.

Maier, D. (1983). The theory of relational databases. *Computer Science Press.*

Malinowski, E., & Zimanyi, E. (2006). *A conceptual solution for representing time in data warehouse dimensions.* Proceedings of the 3rd Asia-Pacific (APCCM2006), Hobart, Australia.

Malinowski, E., & Zimányi, E. (2006). Hierarchies in a multidimensional model: From conceptual modeling to logical representation. *Journal of Data & Knowledge Engineering (DKE), 59*(2), 348-377.

Malinowski, E., & Zimanyi, E. (2006). *Inclusion of time-varying measures in temporal data warehouses dimensions.* Proceedings of the 8th International Conference on Enterprise Information Systems, Paphos, Cyprus.

Malinowski, E., & Zimanyi, E. (2004). OLAP hierarchies: A conceptual perspective. In *Proceedings of the 16th Int. Conf. on Advanced Information Systems Engineering*, (pp. 477-491).

Malinowski, E. & Zimanyi, E. (2004). Representing spatiality in a conceptual multidimensional model. *Proceedings of the 12th ACM International Symposium on Advances in Geographic Information Systems, ACM GIS 2004*, Washington, DC (pp. 12-21).

Malinowski, E., & Zimanyi, E. (2005). Spatial hierarchies and topological relationships in the spatial multiDimER model. *Lecture Notes in Computer Science, 3567*, p. 17.

Mamdani, E. H. (1976). Advances in linguistic synthesis of fuzzy controllers. *International Journal on Man Machine Studies, 8*, 669-678.

Mangisengi, O., Pichler, M., Auer, D., Draheim, D., & Rumetshofer, H. (2007). Activity warehouse: Data management for business activity monitoring. *Proceeding from the Ninth International Conference of Enterprise Information Systems (ICEIS),* Madeira, Portugal.

March, S., & Hevner, A. (2005). Integrated decision support systems: A data warehousing perspective. *Decision Support Systems* .

Marchant, P., Briseboi, A., Bedard, Y., & Edwards G. (2004). Implementation and evaluation of a hypercube-based method for spatiotemporal exploration and analysis. *ISPRS Journal of Photogrammetry & Remote Sensing, 59*, 6-20.

Maza, M., & Tidor, B. (1993). An analysis of selection procedures with particular attention paid to proportional and Bolzmann selection. In Stefanic Forrest (ed.) *Proceedings of the Fifth International Conference on Genetic Algorithms*, San Mateo, CA. (pp. 124-131) Morgan Kaufmann Publishers.

McCabe et al., 2000McCabe, C., Lee, J., Chowdhury, A., Grossman, D. A., & Frieder, O. (2000). On the design and evaluation of a multi-dimensional approach to information retrieval. In *23rd Int. ACM Conf. on Research and Development in Information Retrieval (SIGIR)* (pp. 363-365). ACM Press.

McCoy, D. (2001). *Business activity monitoring: The promise and the reality.* Gartner Group.

McDaniel, T. (2001). Ten pillars of business process management. *Journal of Enterprise Application Integration (EAI).*

Meratnia, N., & de By, R. (2002). Aggregation and Comparison of Trajectories. *Proceedings of the 10th ACM International Symposium on Advances in Geographic Information Systems, ACM GIS 2002,* McLean, VA (pp. 49-54).

Miers, D., Harmon, P., & Hall, C. (2006). The 2006 BPM suites report. *Business Process Trends.*

Mirbel, I., & Ralyte, J. (2005). Situational method engineering: Combining assembly-based and roadmap-driven approaches. In *Requirements Engineering, 11*(1), 58-78.

Missier, P., & Batini, C. (2003). An information quality management framework for cooperative information Systems. *Proceedings of Information Systems and Engineering*, Boston, MA, USA, (pp.25–40).

Mitchell, M. (1996). *An introduction to genetic algorithms*. Cambridge, MA: MIT Press.

Monge, A. E., & Elkan, P. C. (1997, May). An efficient domain-independent algorithm for detecting approximately duplicate database records. *Proceedings of the SIGMOD 1997 Workshop on Data Mining and Knowledge Discovery* (pp. 23-29).

Moody, L. D., & Kortink, M. A. R. (2000). From enterprise models to dimensional models: A methodology for data warehouses and data mart design. *International Workshop on Design and Management of Data Warehouses,* Stockholm, Sweden, (pp. 5.1-5.12).

Moro, G., & Sartori, C. (2001). Incremental maintenance of multi-source views. *Proceedings of the 12th Australasian Database Conference*, (pp. 13-20).

Mothe et al., 2003Mothe, J., Chrisment, C., Dousset, B., & Alau, J. (2003). DocCube: Multi-dimensional visualisation and exploration of large document sets. *Journal of the American Society for Information Science and Technology (JASIST), 54*(7), 650-659.

Moura, J., Pantoquillo, M., & Viana, N. (2004). Real-time decision support system for space missions control. *International Conference on Information and Knowledge Engineering.* Las Vegas.

Mouratidis, K., Yiu, M., Papadias, D., & Mamoulis, N., (2006, September 12-16). Continuous nNearest nNeighbor mMonitoring in rRoad nNetworks. To appear in the *Proceedings of the Very Large Data Bases Conference (VLDB),* Seoul, Korea, Sept. 12 - Sept. 15, 2006.

Mumick, I. S., Quass, D., & Mumick, B. S. (1997). Maintenance of data cubes and summary tables in a warehouse. *Proceeding of ACM SIGMOD Conference*, (pp. 100-111).

Nassis, V., Rajugan R., Dillon T.S., & Rahayu, J.W. (2004). Conceptual Design of XML Document Warehouses, *6th Int. Conf. on Data Warehousing and Knowledge Discovery* (*DaWaK 2004*) (pp. 1-14). Springer.

Nesamoney, D. (2004). BAM: Event-driven business intelligence for the real-time enterprise. *DM Review, 14*(3).

Nguyen, T. B., Tjoa, A. M., & Wagner, R. (2000). An object-oriented multidimensional data model for OLAP. In *Proceedings of the International Conference on Web-Age Information Management* (pp. 69-82). Shanghai, China.

Niedrite, L., Solodovnikova, D., Treimanis, M., & Niedritis, A. (2007). The development method for process-oriented data warehouse. In *WSEAS Transactions on Computer Research,,2*(2), 183 – 190.

Niedrite, L., Solodovnikova, D., Treimanis, M., & Niedritis, A. (2007). Goal-driven design of a data warehouse-based business process analysis system. In *Proceedings of WSEAS Int. Conf. on Artificial Intelligence, Knowledge Engineering And Data Bases AIKED '07.*

Niemi et al., 2002Niemi, T., Niinimäki, M., Nummenmaa, J., & Thanisch, P. (2002). Constructing an OLAP cube from distributed XML data. In *5th ACM Int. Workshop on Data Warehousing and OLAP* (*DOLAP*) (pp.22-27). ACM Press.

Niemi, T., Nummenmaa, J., & Thanisch, P. (2001, June 4). Logical multidimensional database design for ragged and unbalanced aggregation. *Proceedings of the 3rd International Workshop on Design and Management of Data Warehouses,* Interlaken, Switzerland (p. 7).

Nishiyama, T. (1999). Using a process warehouse concept a practical method for successful technology transfer. *Proceeding from the Second International Symposium on Object-Oriented Real Time Distributed Computing, IEEE Computer Society*, Saint Malo.

Noser, H., & Stucki, P. (2003). Dynamic 3D visualization of database-defined tree structures on the World Wide Web by using rewriting systems. *Proceedings of the International Workshop on Advance Issues of E-Commerce and Web-Based Information Systems, IEEE Computer Society press*, (pp. 247-254).

O'Neil, P.E., & Graefe, G. (1995). Multi-table joins through bitmapped join indices. *SIGMOD Record, 24*(3), 8-11.

Object Management Group (2006). *Object constraint language (OCL) specification, v2.0.*

Object Management Group, (2005). *Software process engineering metamodel specification, v1.1.*

OGC—Open Geo Spatial Consortium Inc. (2003). *OpenGIS$^{\hat{a}}$ reference model.* Retrieved from http://www.opengeospatial.org

OGC--OpenGIS Consortium. (2001). *OpenGIS$^{\hat{a}}$ abstract specification, topic 1: Feature geometry (ISO 19107 Spatial Schema).* Retrieved from http://www.opengeospatial.org

Oliva, M., & Saltor, F. (1996). A negotiation process approach for building federated databases. *The 10th ERCIM Database Research Group Workshop on Heterogeneous Information Management*, (pp. 43-49). Prague.

Oliva, M., & Saltor, F. (2001). Integrating multilevel security policies in multilevel federated database systems. In B. Thuraisingham, R. van de Riet, K.R. Dittrich, and Z. Tari, editors. Boston: Kluwer Academic Publishers.

OMG (2006). Object Management Group (OMG), Business Process Modeling Notation Specification.http://www.bpmn.org/Documents/OMG%20Final%20Adopted%20BPMN%201-0%20Spec%2006-02-01.pdf.

OMG. (2003). *Common warehouse metamodel (CWM) specification version 1.1.* Object Management Group.

Pankratius, V., & Stucky, W. (2005). A formal foundation for workflow composition, workflow view definition, and workflow normalization based on Petri Nets. *Proceeding from the Second Asia-Pacific Conference on Conceptual Modeling (APCCM 2005).*

Papadias, D., Kalnis, P., Zhang, J., & Tao, Y. (2001). Efficient OLAP operations in spatial data warehouses. *LNCS: 2121, Proceedings of the 7h Int. Symposium on Advances in Spatial and Temporal Databases* (pp. 443-459).

Parent, C., Spaccapietra, S., & Zimanyi, E. (1999). *Spatio-temporal conceptual models: Data structures+space+time. Proceedings of the 7th ACM Symposium on Advances in Geographic Information Systems*, Kansas City, USA.

Parent, C., Spaccapietra, S., & Zimanyi, E. (2006). *The MurMur project: Modeling and querying multi-representation spatio-temporal databases. Information Systems, 31*(8), 733-769.

Park et al., 2005Park, B-K., Han, H., & Song, I-Y. (2005). XML-OLAP: A multidimensional analysis framework for XML warehouses. In *6th Int. Conf. on Data Warehousing and Knowledge Discovery (DaWaK)* (pp.32-42). Springer.

Park, C.S., Kim, M.H., & Lee, Y.J. (2003, November). Usability-based caching of query results in OLAP systems. *Journal of Systems and Software, 68*(2), 103-119.

Park, R.E., Goethert, W.G., & Florac, W.A. (1996). Goal-driven software measurement – A guidebook. In *Technical Report, CMU/SEI-96-HB-002*, Software Engineering Institute, Carnegie Mellon University.

Paton, N.W. & Daz, O. (1999). Active database systems. *ACM Computing Surveys, 31*(1), 63-103.

Payne, T.H. (2000). Computer decision support systems. *Chest: Official Journal of the American College of Chest Physicians, 118*, 47-52.

Pedersen, D., Riis, K., & Pedersen, T.B. (2002). XML-extended OLAP querying. *14th Int. Conf. on Scientific and Statistical Database Management (SSDBM)* (pp.195-206), IEEE Computer Society.

Pedersen, T. B. (2000). *Aspects of data modeling and query processing for complex multidimensional data*, PhD Thesis, Faculty of Engineering and Science, Aalborg University.

Pedersen, T. B., & Jensen, C. (1999). Multidimensional data modeling for complex data. In *Proceedings of the International Conference on Data Engineering* (pp. 336-345). Sydney, Austrialia.

Pedersen, T. B., Christian, S., Jensen, & Curtis E., Dyreson (2001). *A foundation for capturing and querying complex multidimensional data', Information Systems, 26*, 283-423.

Pedersen,T., & Tryfona, N. (2001). Pre-aggregation in spatial data warehouses. *LNCS: 2121, Proceedings. of the 7h Int. Symposium on Advances in Spatial and Temporal Databases* (pp. 460-480).

Pendse, N. (2003). The OLAP report: How not to buy an OLAP product. *http://www.olapreport.com/How_not_to_buy.htm*

Pérez, J.M., Berlanga, Llavori, R., Aramburu, M.J., & Pedersen, T.B. (2005). A relevance-extended multi-dimensional model for a data warehouse contextualized with documents. In *8th Intl. Workshop on Data Warehousing and OLAP (DOLAP)* (pp.19-28), ACM Press.

Pérez-Martinez, J.M., Berlanga-Llavori, R.B., Aramburu-Cabo, M.J., & Pedersen, T.B. (2007). Contextualizing data warehouses with documents. *Decision Support Systems (DSS)*, available online doi:10.1016/j.dss.2006.12.005.

Phipps, C., & Davis, K. (2002). Automating data warehouse conceptual schema design and evaluation. *DMDW'02*, Canada.

Piattini, Mario G., Esperanza, Marcos, Coral, Calero, & Belén, Vela. (2006). *Tecnología y diseño de bases de datos*, Editorial: Ra-Ma.

Pighin, M., & Ieronutti, L. (2007). From database to datawarehouse: A design quality evaluation. *Proceedings of the International Conference on Enterprise Information Systems, INSTICC Eds.*, Lisbon, POR, (pp. 178-185).

Pipino, L., Lee, Y., & Wang, R. (2002. Data quality assessment. *Communications of the ACM, 45*(4), 211-218.

Poess, M., & Floyd, C. (2000). New TPC benchmarks for decision support and Web commerce. *SIGMOD Record, 29*(4), 64-71.

Poess, M., Smith, B., Kollar, L., & Larson, P.A. (2002). TPC-DS: Taking decision support benchmarking to the next level. *2002 ACM SIGMOD International Conference on Management of Data*, Madison, Wisconsin, USA. (pp. 582-587).

Pokorný, 2001Pokorný, J. (2001). Modelling stars using XML. In *4ᵗʰ ACM Int. Workshop on Data Warehousing and OLAP (DOLAP)* (pp.24-31). ACM Press.

Poole, J., Chang, D., Tolbert, D., & Mellor, D. (2003). Common warehouse metamodel developers guide, (p. 704). Wiley Publishing.

Poole, J., Chang, D., Tolbert, D., & Mellor, D. (2003). *Common warehouse etamodel developer's guide*. John Wiley & Sons.

Potter, M.A., & Jong, K.A. (1994). A cooperative co-evolutionary approach to function optimization. *The Third Parallel Problem Solving From Nature*. Berlin, Germany: Springer-Verlag, (pp. 249-257).

Prakash, N., & Gosain, A. (2003). Requirements driven data warehouse development. In *Proceedings of the Conference on Advanced Information Systems Engineering—Short Papers*, Klagenfurt/Velden, Austria.

Priebe, T., & Pernul, G. (2000). Towards OLAP security design: Survey and research issues. In *Proceedings of the ACM International Workshop on Data Warehousing and OLAP* (pp. 33-40). Washington, DC.

Rahm, E., & Do, H. H. (2000). Data cleaning: Problems and current approaches. *Bulletin of the IEEE Computer Society Technical Committee on Data Engineering, 23*(4), 3-13.

Ralyte, J., Deneckere, R., & Rolland, C. (2003). Towards a generic model for situational method engineering. In *Proceedings. of CAiSE'03*, LNCS *2681*, 95-110. Springer-Verlag.

Ramamritham, K. (1993). Real-time databases. *International Journal of Distributed and Parallel Databases, 1*(2), 199-226.

Raman, V., & Hellerstein, J. M. (2001). Potter's Wheel: An interactive data cleaning system. In *Proceedings of the*

27ᵗʰ *International Conference on Very Large Databases (VLDB'01)*, Rome (pp. 381-390).

Rao, F., Zhang, L., Yu,X., Li,Y.,& Chen, Y. (2003). Spatial hierarchy and OLAP-favored search in spatial data warehouse. *Proceedings of the 6th ACM International Workshop on Data Warehousing and OLAP, DOLAP '03* (pp. 48-55).

Ravat, F., Teste, O., Tournier, R., & Zurfluh, G. (2008). Algebraic and graphic languages for OLAP manipulations. *Int. j. of Data Warehousing and Mining (DWM), 4*(1), 17-46.

Ravat, F., Teste, O., & Tournier, R. (2007). OLAP aggregation function for textual data warehouse. In *9ᵗʰ International Conference on Enterprise Information Systems (ICEIS 2007)*, vol. DISI (pp. 151-156). INST-ICC Press.

Ravat, F., Teste, O., Zurfluh, G. (2006, June). Algèbre OLAP et langage graphique. *XIVème congrès INFormatique des ORganisations et Systèmes d'Information et de Décision (INFORSID'06)*, Tunisia, (pp. 1039-1054)

Redman, T.C. (1996). *Data quality for the information age*. Artech House.

Redman, T.C. (1998). The impact of poor data quality on the typical enterprise. *Communications of the ACM, 41*(2), 79-82.

Rigaux,. P., Scholl, M., & Voisard, A. (2002). *Spatial databases with applications to Gis*. New York: Academic Press.

Rivest, S., Bedard, Y., & Marchand, P. (2001). Towards better support for spatial decision making: Defining the characteristics of spatial on-line analytical processing (SOLAP). *Geomatica, 55*(4), 539-555.

Rizzi, S., Abelló, A., Lechtenbörger, J., & Trujillo, J. (2006). Research in data warehouse modeling and design: Dead or alive? In *Proceedings of the 9th ACM Int. Workshop on Data Warehousing and OLAP (DOLAP '06)*, (pp. 3-10) ACM Press.

Robertson, G.G., Card, S.K., & Mackinlay, J.D. (1993). Information visualization using 3D interactive animation. *Communications of the ACM 36*(4), 57-71.

Roddick, J.F., & Schrefl, M. (2000). Towards an accommodation of delay in temporal active databases. *Proceedings of the 11ᵗʰ International Conference on Australasian Database Conference*, (pp. 115-119).

Rolland, C. (1997). A primer for method engineering. In *Proceedings of the INFormatique des ORganisations et Syst`emes d'Information et de D'ecision (INFORSID'97).*

Saidane, M., & Giraudin, J.P. (2002). Ingénierie de la coopération des systèmes d'information. *Revue Ingénierie des Systèmes d'Information (ISI), 7*(4), Hermès.

Salguero, A., & Araque, F. (2008). Ontology based data warehousing for improving touristic Web Sites. *International Conference. International Conference e-Commerce 2008.* Amsterdam, The Netherlands.

Salguero, A., Araque, A., Carrasco, R., Vila, M., & Martínez, L. (2007). Applying fuzzy data mining for soaring area selection. *Computational and ambient intelligence - Lecture Notes in Computer Science, 450,* 597-604, *ISSN: 0302-9743.*

Salguero, A., Araque, F., & Delgado, C. (2008). Data integration algorithm for data warehousing based on ontologies metadata. *The 8th International FLINS Conference on Computational Intelligence in Decision and Control (FLINS).* Madrid, Spain.

Salguero, A., Araque, F., & Delgado, C. (2008). Using ontology metadata for data warehousing. *The 10th Int. Conf. on Enterprise Information Systems (ICEIS).* Barcelona, Spain.

Samos, J., Saltor, F., Sistac, J., & Bardés, A. (1998). Database architecture for data ware-housing: An evolutionary approach. *Proceedings Int'l Conf. on Database and Expert Systems Applications* (pp.. 746-756). Vienna: In G. Quirchmayr et al. (Eds.): Springer-Verlag.

Samtani, S., Kumar, V., & Mohania, M. (1999). Self maintenance of multiple views in data warehousing. *Proceedings of the International Conference on Information and knowledge management,* (pp. 292-299).

SAP. (1998). *Data modeling with BW.* SAP America Inc. and SAP AG, Rockville, MD.

Sapia, C. (2000, September). PROMISE – Modeling and predicting user query behavior in online analytical processing environments. In *Proceedings of the 2nd International Conference on Data Warehousing and Knowledge Discovery (DAWAK'00),* London, UK, Springer.

Sapia, C., Blaschka, M, Höfling, & Dinter, B. (1998). Extending the E/R model for the multidimensional paradigm. In Advances in Database Technologies (ER'98 Workshop Proceedings), Springer-Verlag, 105-116.

Sapia, C., Blaschka, M., Höfling, G., & Dinter, B. (1998). Extending the E/R model for the multidimensional paradigm. In *Proceedings of Advances in Database Technologies, ER '98 Workshops on Data Warehousing and Data Mining, Mobile Data Access, and Collaborative Work Support and Spatio-Temporal Data Management,* LNCS 1552, 105-116). Springer.

Sarawagi, S., & Bhamidipaty, A. (2002). Interactive deduplication using active learning. *Proceedings of Eighth ACM SIGKDD International Conference on Knowledge Discovery and Data Mining (KDD '02)* (pp. 269-278).

Savary ,L., Wan, T., & Zeitouni, K. (2004). Spatio-temporal data warehouse design for human activity pattern analysis. *Proceedings of the 15ᵗʰ International Workshop On Database and Expert Systems Applications (DEXA04)* (pp. 81-86).

Scannapieco, M., Virgillito, A., Marchetti, C., Mecella, M., & Baldoni, R. (2004). The DaQuinCIS architecture: A platform for exchanging and improving data quality in cooperative information systems. *Information Systems, 29*(7), 551-582.

Scheuermann, P., Shim, J., & Vingralek, R. (1996, September 3-6). WATCHMAN: A data warehouse intelligent cache manager. In *Proceedings of the 22th International Conference on Very Large Data Bases VLDB'96*, Bombay, (pp. 51-62).

Schiefer, J., List, B., & Bruckner, R. (2002). A holistic approach for managing requirements of data warehouse systems. In *Proceedings of the Americas Conference on Information Systems.*

Schiefer, J., List, B., & Bruckner, R.M. (2003). Process data store: A real-time data store for monitoring business processes. *Lecture Notes in Computer Science, Database and Expert Systems Applications (DEXA)*, Springer-Verlag.

Schulze-Wollgast, P., Tominski, C., & Schumann, H. (2005). Enhancing visual exploration by appropriate color coding. *Proceedings of International Conference in Central Europe on Computer Graphics, Visualization and Computer Vision*, (pp. 203-210).

Scotch, M., & Parmantoa, B. (2005). SOVAT: Spatial OLAP visualization and analysis tools. *Proceedings of the 38th Hawaii International Conference on System Sciences.*

Sen, A., & Sinha, A. P. (2005). A comparison of data warehousing methodologies. *Communications of the ACM, 48*(3), 79-84.

Serrano, M., Calero, C., & Piattini, M. (2003). Metrics for data warehouse quality. *Effective Databases for Text & Document Management.* (pp. 156-173).

Serrano, M., Calero, C., Trujillo, J., Lujan-Mora, S., & Piattini, M. (2004). Towards a metrics suite for conceptual models of datawarehouses. *1st International Workshop on Software Audit and Metrics (SAM 04)*, Porto, Portugal. (pp. 105-117).

Shekhar, S. , Lu. C. T., Tan, X., Chawla, S., & Vatsavai, R. (2001). Map cube: A visualization tool for spatial data warehouse. In H. J. Miller & J. Han (Eds.), *Geographic data mining and knowledge discovery.* Taylor and Francis.

Shekhar, S., & Chawla, S. (2003). *Spatial databases: A tour.* NJ: Prentice Hall.

Shekhar, S., Lu, C., Tan, X., Chawla, S., & Vatsavai, R. (2001). Map cube: A visualization tool for spatial data warehouses. As *Chapter of Geographic Data Mining and Knowledge Discovery*, Harvey J. Miller and Jiawei Han (eds.), Taylor and Francis.

Sheth, A., & Larson, J. (1990). Federated database systems for managing distributed, heterogeneous and autonomous databases. *ACM Computing Surveys, 22*(3).

Shi, Y., & Eberhart, R.C. (1999). Empirical study of particle swarm optimization. *Proceedings from the 1999 Congress of Evolutionary Cmputation, 3*, 1945-1950. IEEE Press.

Shim, J., Scheuermann, P., & Vingralek, R. (1999, July). Dynamic caching of query results for decision support systems. In *Proceedings of the 11th International Conference on Scientific and Statistical Database Management*, Cleveland, Ohio.

Shin, B. (2002). A case of data warehousing project management. *Information and Management, 39*(7), 581-592.

Shneiderman, B. (1994). Dynamic queries for visual information seeking. *IEEE Software, 11*, 70-77.

Shukla, A., Deshpande, P.M., & Naughton, J.F. (1998). Materialized view selection for multidimensional datasets. *Proceedings of VLDB.*

Simitsis, A. (2005). Mapping conceptual to logical models for ETL processes. In *Proceedings of the ACM International Workshop on Data Warehousing and OLAP* (pp. 67-76). Bremen, Germany.

Solodovnikova, D., & Niedrite, L. (2005). Using data warehouse resources for assessment of E-Learning influence on university processes. In *Proceedings of the 9th East-European Conf. on Advances in Databases and Information Systems (ADBIS)*, (pp. 233-248).

Song, X., & Liu, J. (1995). Maintaining temporal consistency: Pessimistic vs. optimistic concurrency control. *IEEE Transactions on Knowledge and Data Engineering, 7*(5), 786-796.

Spaccapietra, S., Parent, C., & Vangenot, C. (2000). GIS database: From multiscale to multirepresentation. In B. Y. Choueiry & T. Walsh (Eds.), Abstraction, reformulation, and approximation, LNAI 1864. *Proceedings of the 4th International Symposium, SARA-2000*, Horseshoe Bay, Texas.

Stefanovic, N., Han, J., & Koperski, K. (2000). Object-based selective materialization for efficient implementation of spatial data cubes. *IEEE Trans. on Knowledge and Data Engineering, 12*(6), 938-958.

Stell, J., & Worboys, M. (1998). Stratified map spaces: A formal basic for multi-resolution spatial databases. *Proceedings of the 8th International Symposium on Spatial Data Handling, SDH'98* (pp. 180-189).

Sullivan, D. (2001). *Document warehousing and text mining*, Wiley John & Sons Inc.

Takagi, T., & Sugeno, M. (1985). Fuzzy identification of systems and its applications to modeling and control. *IEEE Transactions on Systems, Man, and Cybernetics, 15*, 116-132.

Thalhamer, M., Schrefl, M., & Mohania, M. (2001). Active data warehouses: Complementing OLAP with analysis rules. *Data & Knowledge Engineering, 39(3)*, 241-269.

Theodoratos, D., & Sellis, T. (1999). Designing data warehouses. *IEEE Transactions on Data and Knowledge Engineering, 31*(3), 279-301.

Thomsen, E. (1998). Comparing different approaches to OLAP calculations as revealed in benchmarks. *Intelligence Enterprise's Database Programming & Design.* http://www.dbpd.com/vault/9805desc.htm

Timpf, S. (1999). Abstraction, level of detail, and hierarchies in map series. *International Conference on Spatial Information Theory, COSIT'99*, LNCS 1661, (pp. 125-140).

Tjoa, A.M., List, B., Schiefer, J., & Quirchmayr, G. (2003). The process warehouse – A data warehouse approach for business process management. *Intelligent Management in the Knowledge Economy*, (p. 112-126). Edward Elgar Publishing.

Torlone R. (2003). *Conceptual Multidimensional Models. In Multidimensional databases: problems and solutions*, pages 69-90, Idea Group Publishing, Hershey, PA, USA.

Torlone, 2003Torlone, R. (2003). Conceptual multidimensional models. In M. Rafanelli (ed.), *Multidimensional Databases: Problems and Solutions* (pp. 69-90). Idea Publishing Group.

Torp, K., Jensen, C. S., & Snodgrass, R. T. (2000). Effective time stamping in databases. *Journal of Very Large Database, 8*(3), 267-288.

TPC. (1998). *TPC Benchmark D Standard Specification Version 2.1.* Transaction Processing Performance Council.

TPC. (2003). *TPC Benchmark R Standard Specification Revision 2.1.0.* Transaction Processing Performance Council.

TPC. (2006). *TPC Benchmark H Standard Specification Revision 2.6.1.* Transaction Processing Performance Council.

TPC. (2007). *TPC Benchmark DS Standard Specification Draft version 52.* Transaction Processing Performance Council.

Transaction Processing Performance Council (TPC): TPC Benchmark R (decision support) Standard Specification Revision 2.1.0. tpcr_2.1.0.pdf, available at http://www.tpc.org

Tryfona, N., Busborg, F., & Borch Christiansen, J. G. (1999). starER: A conceptual model for data warehouse design. In *Proceedings of the ACM International Workshop on Data Warehousing and OLAP,* Kansas City, Kansas (pp. 3-8).

Tryfona, N., Busborg, F., & Borch, J. (1999). *StarER a conceptual model for data warehouse design. In Proceedings of the 2nd ACM Int. Workshop on DW and OLAP*, (pp. 3-8).

Tryfona, N., Price, R., & Jensen, C. S.(2003). *Conceptual Models for Spatio-temporal Applications.* In M. Koubarakis et al. (Eds.), Spatio-Temporal DB: The CHOROCHRONOS Approach (pp. 79-116). Berlin, Heidelberg: Verlag.

Tseng, F.S.C., & Chou, A.Y.H (2006). The concept of document warehousing for multi-dimensional modeling of textual-based business intelligence. *Decision Support Systems (DSS), 42*(2), 727-744.

Tsois, A., Karayannidis, N., & Sellis, T. (2001). MAC: Conceptual data modeling for OLAP. *International Workshop on Design and Management of Data Warehouses (DMDW'2001)*, Interlaken, Switzerland.

UNECE (2002). UN/CEFACT - ebXML Core Components Technical Specification, Part 1 V1.8. http//www.unece.org/cefact/ebxml/ebXML_CCTS_Part1_V1-8.

Van den Bergh, F., & Engelbrecht, A.P. (2004, June). A cooperative approach to particle swarm optimization. *IEEE Transactions on Evolutionary Computation, 8*(3), 225-239.

Vargas, da Rocha, L., Edelweiss, L. V., & Iochpe, C. (2001). GeoFrame-T: A temporal conceptual framework for data modelin. *Proceedings of the ninth ACM international symposium on Advances in GIS*, Atlanta, GA, USA.

Vassiliadis, C., Quix, Y., Vassiliou, M., & Jarke, M. (2001). Data warehouse process management. Information System, *26*.

Vassiliadis, P. (1998). Modeling multidimensional databases, cubes and cube operations. In *Proceedings of the 10th International Conference on Statistical and Scientific Database Management*, Capri, Italy.

Vassiliadis, P. (1998). Modeling multidimensional databases, cubes and cube operations. *Proceedings of the 10th Scientific and Statistical Database Management Conference (SSDBM '98)* (pp. 53-62).

Vassiliadis, P., & Sellis, T. (1999). A survey of logical models for OLAP databases. *ACM SIGMOD Record, 28*(4), 64-69.

Vassiliadis, P., Simitsis, A., & Skiadopoulos, S. (2002, November 8). Conceptual modeling for ETL processes. In *Proceedings of the ACM International Workshop on Data Warehousing and OLAP* (pp. 14-21). McLean, VA.

Vlachos, M., Kollios, G., & Gunopulos, D.(2002). Discovering similar multidimensional trajectories. *Proceedings of 18th ICDE* (pp. 273-282).

Vrdoljak, B., Banek, M., & Rizzi S. (2003). Designing Web warehouses from XML schemas. In *5th Int. Conf. on Data Warehousing and Knowledge Discovery (DaWaK)* (pp. 89-98). Springer.

Vrdoljak, B., Banek, M., & Skocir, Z. (2006). Integrating XML sources into a data warehouse. In *2nd Int. Workshop on Data Engineering Issues in E-Commerce and Services (DEECS 2006)* (pp. 133-142). Springer.

Walrand, J., & Varaiya, P. (2000). *High-performance communication networks.* The Morgan Kaufmann Series in Networking.

Wang, B., Pan, F., Ren, D., Cui, Y., Ding, D. et al. (2003). Efficient olap operations for spatial data using peano trees. *Proceedings of the 8th ACM SIGMOD Workshop on Research Issues in Data Mining and Knowledge Discovery* (pp. 28-34).

Wang, H., Li, J., He, Z., & Gao, H. (2005). OLAP for XML data. In *5th Int. Conf. on Computer and Information Technology (CIT)* (pp. 233-237), IEEE Computer Society.

Wang, R.Y., & Strong, D.M. (1996). *Data quality systems evaluation and implementation.* London: Cambridge Market Intelligence Ltd.

Wang, R.Y., Storey, V.C., & Firth, C.P. (1995). A framework for analysis of data quality research. *IEEE Transactions on Knowledge and Data Engineering, 7*(4), 623-640.

Wang, R.Y., Strong, D.M. (1996). Beyond accuracy: What data quality means to data consumers. *Journal of Management Information Systems, 12*(4), 5-33.

Westerman, P. (2001). *Dataw Warehousing using the Wal-Mart model.* (p. 297). Morgan Kaufmann.

White, C. (2003). Building the real-time enterprise. *The Data Warehousing Institute, TDWI Report Series*, A101 Communications Publication.

Widom, J. (1995, November). Research problems in data warehousing. In *Proceedings of the Fourth International Conference on Information and Knowledge Management (CIKM '95)*, Baltimore, Maryland, (pp. 25-30), Invited paper.

Williamson, C., Shneiderman, B. (1992). The dynamic HomeFinder: Evaluating dynamic queries in a real-estate information exploration System. *Proceedings of the Conference on Research and Development in Information Retrieval (SIGIR 92)*, (pp. 338–346). New-York: ACM Press.

Winkler, W. E. (1999). *The state of record linkage and current research problems* (Publication No. R99/04). Internal Revenue Service, Statistics of Income Division.

Winter, R., & Strauch, B. (2003). A method for demand-driven information requirements analysis in data warehousing projects. In *Proceedings of the 36th Hawaii Int. Conf. on System Sciences.*

Wiwatwattana, N., Jagadish, H.V., Lakshmanan, L.V.S., & Srivastava, D. (2007). X³: A cube operator for XML OLAP. In *23rd Int. Conf. on Data Engineering (ICDE)* (pp. 916-925). IEEE Computer Society.

Worboys, M. (1998). Imprecision in finite resolution spatial data. *GeoInformatica, 2*(3), 257-279.

Worboys, M., & Duckam, M. (2004). *GIS: A computing perspective* (2nd ed.). Boca Raton, FL: CRC Press.

Xie, X.-F., Zhang, W.-J., & Yang, Z.-L. (2002). Hybrid particle swarm optimizer with mass extinction. *Proceedings from the Int. Conf. on Communication, Circuits and Systems (ACCCAS)*, Chengdhu, China.

Xiong, M., Stankovic, J., Rammritham, K. Towsley, D., & Sivasankaran, R. (1996). Maintaining temporal consistency: Issues and algorithms. *Proceeding of the 1st International Workshop on Real-Time Databases*, (pp. 1-6).

Yin, X., & Pedersen, T.B. (2004). Evaluating XML-extended OLAP queries based on a physical algebra. In *7th ACM Int. Workshop on Data Warehousing and OLAP (DOLAP)* (pp.73-82). ACM Press.

Yiu, M., Papadias, D., Mamoulis, N., & Tao, Y. (2006).. Reverse nNearest nNeighbors in lLarge gGraphs. *IEEE Transactions on Knowledge and Data Engineering (TKDE),18*(4), 540-553, 2006.

Yu, B., Kim, S. H., Bailey, T., & Gamboa R. (2004). Curve-based representation of moving object trajectories. *Proceedings of the International Database Engineering and Applications Symposium, IDEAS 2004* (pp. 419-425).

Yu, J.X., Choi, C-H, Gou, G., & Lu, H. (2004, May). Selecting views with maintenance cost constraints: Issues, heuristics and performance. *Journal of Research and Practice in Information Technology, 36*(2.

Zadeh, L. A. (2002). From computing with numbers to computing with words: From manipulation of measurements to manipulation of perceptions. *International Journal on Applied Mathematics and Computer Science, 12*(3), 307-324.

Zadeh, L. A. (1975). The concept of linguistic variable and its application to approximate reasoning: Part I. *Information Sciences, 8*, 199-251.

Zadeh, L. A. (1975). The concept of linguistic variable and its application to approximate reasoning: Part II. *Information Sciences, 8*, 301-357.

Zadeh, L. A. (1975). The concept of linguistic variable and its application to approximate reasoning: Part III. *Information Sciences, 9*, 43-80.

Zhang, J., Ling, T.W., Bruckner, R.M., & Tjoa, A.M. (2003). Building XML data warehouse based on frequent patterns in user queries. In *5th Int. Conf. on Data Warehousing and Knowledge Discovery (DaWaK)* (pp. 99-108). Springer.

Zhang, C., Yao, X., & Yang, J. (2001, September). An evolutionary approach to materialized views selection in a data warehouse environment. *IEEE Trans. on Systems, Man and Cybernetics, Part C, 31*(3).

Zhang, D., & Tsotras, V. (2005). Optimizing spatial Min/Max aggregations. *The VLDB Journal, 14*, 170-181.

Zheng, K. (2006, September 2006). Design, implementation, user acceptance, and evaluation of a clinical decision support system for evidence-based medicine practice. *Thesis in information systems and health informatics*, Carnegie Mellon University, H. John Heinz III School of Public Policy and Management, Pittsburgh, Pennsylvania.

Zhuge, Y., Garcia-Molina, H., Hammer, J., & Widom, J. (1995). View maintenance in a warehousing environment. *Proceedings of the ACM SIGMOD International Conference on Management of Data*, (pp. 316-327).

Zhuge Y., Molina, H. G., & Wiener, J. (1998). Consistency algorithms for multi-source warehouse view mainte-nance. *Journal of Distributed and Parallel Databases, 6*(1), 7-40.

About the Contributors

David Taniar received bachelor's, master's, and PhD degrees – all in computer science, specializing in databases. Since completing his PhD in 1997 from Victoria University, Australia, he has been at Monash University, Australia. He also held a lecturing position at RMIT University in 1999-2000 and was a visiting professor at the National University of Singapore for 6 months in 2006. His research primarily focuses on query processing, covering object-relational query processing, XML query processing, mobile query processing, and parallel query processing. He has published more than 50 journal papers in these areas. He has published a book on Object-Oriented Oracle (IGI, 2006) and another book on High Performance Parallel Query Processing and Grid Databases (John Wiley & Sons, 2008). He is a founder editor-in-chief of the International Journal of Data Warehousing and Mining (IGI, USA).

* * *

Hanene Ben-Abdallah received a BS in computer science and a BS in mathematics from the University of Minnesota, MPLS, MN, USA in 1989, a MSE (in 1991) and a PhD in computer and information science from the University of Pennsylvania, Philadelphia, PA, USA in 1996. She joined the Electrical and Computer Engineering Department of the University of Waterloo, CA for a postdoctoral fellowship in 1996. Since 1997, she has been in the Computer Science Department in the Faculty of Economics and Management at the University of Sfax, Tunisia, where she is now an associate professor.

Hanene's research interests include the application of formal methods and reuse techniques in software engineering, and graphical specification languages.

Mounira Ben Abdallah received a BS in computer science (2000) and a master's degree in information systems and new technologies (2003) from the University of Sfax. She is now preparing a doctorate degree at the same university working on applying reuse techniques for the design of data warehouses.

Francisco Araque is an associate professor of computer science at the Software Engineering Department of The University of Granada. He holds a doctorate from the University of Granada. His research specialization is in the areas of decision support systems, data warehousing, e-business and knowledge management. he is a member of the Languages and Computer Systems Research Group at the University of Granada.

Orlando Belo (obelo@di.uminho.pt) is an associate professor in the Department of Informatics at Minho University, Portugal. He is also a member of the Computer Science and Technology Center in the same university, working in areas like data warehousing systems, OLAP, and data mining. His main research topics are related with data warehouse design, implementation and tuning, ETL services, and distributed multidimensional structures processing.

Jérôme Darmont received his PhD degree in computer science from the University of Clermont-Ferrand II, France in 1999. He has been an associate professor at the University of Lyon 2, France since then. His current research interests mainly relate to performance optimization and evaluation in database management systems and data warehouses (benchmarking, auto-administration, optimization techniques...), XML and complex data warehousing and mining, and medical or health-related applications.

Cecilia Delgado is an associate professor of computer science at the Software Engineering Department of The University of Granada. He holds a doctorate from the University of Granada. His research specialization is in the areas of decision support systems, data warehousing, e-business and knowledge management. He is a member of the Languages and Computer Systems Research Group at the University of Granada.

Dirk Draheim holds a diploma in computer science from the Technische Universität Berlin since 1994 and a PhD in computer science from the Freie Universität Berlin since 2002. In spring 2006 he was lecturer in HCI at the University of Auckland and since summer 2006 he is Senior Researcher at the Software Competence Center Hagenberg, Linz, currently in the position of the area manager of database technology. His research interests are business process modeling, requirements engineering and software architecture of enterprise applications, model-driven architecture, and generative programming. Dirk Draheim is member of the ACM.

Jamel Feki received a BS in computer and information systems from the University of Sfax, Tunisia 1981, a master's degree (in 1982) and a thèse troisième cycle in computer science (data base field) from the University Paul SABATIER, Toulouse, France in 1984. He worked as a project manager at the Tunisian Petroleum company ETAP. Since 1986, he has been an assistant professor in the Computer Science Department in the Faculty of Economics and Management at the University of Sfax, Tunisia. He was a visiting professor at the University of Qatar from 1993 until 1999.
Jamel's research interests cover decisional support systems domain: OLAP requirements specification and data warehouse design methods.

Christian Frank has several years of experience as a consultant in the areas of Information Management and Business Intelligence. Located in Copenhagen, Denmark, the primary target customers are Danish organizations. Christian Frank's research interests are among other things enterprise architecture, master data management, governance, strategic planning, and knowledge management. Christian Frank has a Master's degree in Business Economics and Computer Science from Copenhagen Business School. His master thesis explored the coherence between enterprise architecture and information management.

Lars Frank started as associate professor at Copenhagen Business School in 1992, where his research areas have been databases, transaction models, system integration, distributed systems, mobile systems, and data warehousing. In May 2008, he is going to defend his doctoral dissertation with the title *Databases and Applications with Relaxed ACID Properties*. Lars Frank is very interested in research corporation with companies that are interested in practical methods for system integration, and in late 2008 he hope to start a project in analyzing and evaluating methods to integrate the health systems of the Danish hospitals.

Rafael Guadalupe Garcia is PhD in mathematical sciences for Cantabria University, and bachelor's of mathematics sciences for La Laguna University, from Spain. He is currently professor at topography, geodesy and cartography E.T.S.I., in polytechnic of Madrid University. He also has taught at other universities as Laguna, U.N.E.D., and Complutense, from Spain. And East University and I.U.P.F.A.N., from Venezuela Republic. In addition he has directed several Doctoral Theses.

As researcher accumulates more than thirty-four international publications on applied mathematics in computer science, and some on spatial data and its treatment on multidimensional databases, as well as a large number of papers at conferences, seminars and symposiums.

Concepción M. Gascueña is PhD in geographic engineering for Polytechnic of Madrid University, bachelor's in mathematical sciences for complutense of Madrid University, diploma of advanced studies in computer sciences for Carlos III of Madrid University, master's in computer security for Polytechnic of Madrid University, and Master in Computer Audit for Polytechnic of Madrid University, from Spain.

She is currently associate professor at Computer Science department, in Polytechnic of Madrid University. She also has taught at Carlos III of Madrid University, for six years.

In this moment, her research is directed to study on spatial data and its treatment on multidimensional databases, having some international publications and papers at conferences, seminars and symposiums.

Wojciech Gębczyk was born in Gliwice (Poland) in 1981. After graduating from Information Technology Faculty of the Silesian Technical University in 2005 he started a PhD at the same university. Simultaneously he stared work in AIUT company in Gliwice in the telemetric department as a senior database software engineer, where he is responsible for database designing and optimization. His research in data warehousing is focused on developing new solutions to continuous mobile queries in distributed spatio-temporal environments. Designed approaches extends functionality of Spatial Telemetric Data Warehouse developed in Institute of Computer Science of the Silesian Technical University.

Marcin Gorawski is a computer scientist. He graduated the Institute of Computer Science of Silesian University of Technology in Gliwice. He is a doctor of technical sciences in a field of computer technology. He was an assistant professor and director of the Laboratory of Algorithms, Programming and Autonomous Systems in Institute of Computer Science of Silesian University of Technology.

His scientific achievements include about 220 publications and monographs in the national and foreign professional journals, dealing with the problems of industrial processes controlling, fault tolerant technology, data bases security, data bases and warehouses and intelligent managing systems.

Liga Grundmane received a master's degree in Computer Science in 2006 from the University of Latvia in the field of data warehousing. From 2003 until 2006 she was involved in data warehouse development for the University of Latvia within the e-University Project. After 2006 Liga Grundmane took part in several commercial data warehouse development projects. She has published several papers in international conferences. Her current research interests include methods for defining and managing user access rights on database level for dimensional models, data warehouse design problems, particularly managing historical data and importance of data history in data warehouses, specific fact table design issues.

Shi-Ming Huang received his PhD degree at the school of computing and information systems, University of Sunderland, U.K. He is currently a head of Accounting and Information Technology Department and a director for the Research Center of e-Manufacturing and e-Commerce at National Chung Cheng University, Taiwan. He is also a professor in the Department of Information Management. He is 2006 President for International Chinese Information Systems Association (ICISA). He has published five books, three business software and over 40 articles in refereed information system journals, such as *Decision Support Systems, Information and Management, Journal of Computer Information Systems, European Journal of Operational Research, Journal of Database Management, ACM SIGMOD*, etc. He has received over 10 achievement awards in information system area and serves as editorial board member in several international journals. He also serves as an associate editor in *International Journal of Management* and *Enterprise Development*.

Jorge Alexandre de Albuquerque Loureiro has been an associated professor in Superior School of Technology of Viseu, Portugal, in the Computer Science Department, since 1990. Currently he is teaching in areas of intelligent data analysis, data warehousing, OLAP technologies and programming languages. For 11 years (from 1985-1996) he worked as software analyst and developer. He has a PhD in computer science, knowledge area of artificial intelligence, by the University of Minho, being the PhD thesis *Multidimensional Data Structures Dynamic Restructuring in Useful Time*. He also has a master's in systems and information technologies, by the University of Coimbra, Portugal. The title of the master's thesis is *Data Warehousing: Technology and Strategy for DSS*, specializing in the area of computer systems architectures. For many years he has been researching in OLAP and data mining areas, particularly applying life inspired algorithms to the optimization of OLAP structures.

Oscar Mangisengi holds a PhD in computer science from Vienna University of Technology, Vienna, Austria. From September, 2000 to April, 2001 he worked at Software Competence Centre Hagenberg (SCCH) Austria as a scientific research staff. From April 2001 to March, 2002 he worked as a postdoctoral research fellow at the School of Computing, Department of Computer Science, National University of Singapore, Singapore. From April, 2002, he continues working at Software Competence Centre Hagenberg, Austria. His research interests are data warehousing, data and information integration, conceptual modelling, workflow, business process monitoring, and knowledge management.

Laila Niedrite is a lecturer at the University of Latvia since 1996. She received a PhD degree in computer science from University of Latvia in 2008. She is currently teaching courses on data warehousing and system design at the University of Latvia.

She combines the academic work with participation in IT projects at the University of Latvia – information system of University of Latvia as system analyst, Latvian Education Informatization System Project as group manager, and E-university Project at the University of Latvia as data warehouse development group manager since 2003. Her research interests focus on database systems, data warehousing and integration.

Maurizio Pighin is a professor in the Department of Mathematics and Computer Science of the University of Udine, and currently teaches advanced courses of software engineering and information systems. His major research interests are in the area of software engineering and ERP and data warehouse systems. He is the author of more than 60 scientific publications in international journals, books and refereed conference proceedings. He worked at several national and international research and development projects. He is a referee of various international journals. He has been involved in the organization of some important events in the fields of software engineering and information systems.

Lucio Ieronutti received the PhD degree in computer science from the University of Udine, Italy, in 2006. Since 2003, he actively works at IS&SE-Lab (Information Systems and Software Engineering) and the HCI Lab (Human Computer Interaction) and of the University of Udine. His research interests are in information systems, data warehouses, 3D virtual environments and information visualization. He is author of 20 publications on these topics.

Franck Ravat (ravat@irit.fr) was born in 1968 in St Michel de Fronsac (France). He obtained his PhD in computer science from the University of Toulouse 3, France, with a thesis on distributed databases in 1996. Since 1997, Dr. Franck Ravat is associate professor at the University of Toulouse 1 and researcher in the generalised information systems/data warehouse research group (SIG/ED) of the IRIT institute.

His current research interests include all aspects of data warehouse design and languages. His publications appear in major national and international conferences, for which he also serves as reviewer.

Alberto Salguero is a doctoral fellow at the Software Engineering Department of The University of Granada. At the moment he is working on his doctoral dissertation about spatio-temporal data warehouse based on ontology models. He is a member of the Languages and Computer Systems Research Group at the University of Granada.

Darja Solodovnikova received a master's degree in Computer Science in 2006 from the University of Latvia and now she is studying towards PhD in the field of data warehousing. Darja Solodovnikova participates as the system analyst at the e-University Project of the University of Latvia since 2004. She is also teaching the practical classes in databases for undergraduate and graduate students of the University of Latvia since 2007. She has published 7 papers in refereed journals and international conferences in the field of data warehousing and e-learning. Her research interests include data warehouse evolution and schema versioning.

Chun-Hao Su received his master's degree in the Management Information System Department of National Chung Cheng University, Taiwan. He is the member for the Center of e-Manufacturing and e-Commerce (CMCA). His research focuses on database, data Warehousing, ERP solution and E-Commerce. Now, He is a R&D engineer and MIS Manager at Hurco Automation Ltd, focus on embedded system design including OS porting, HMI (Human Machine Interface) software, database, and Web-Enabled Solution.

John Tait obtained a PhD from the University of Cambridge in 1983. After a career in industry he joined the University of Sunderland in 1991, where he eventually became professor of intelligent information systems and associate dean of computing and technology. In September 2007 he became chief scientific officer of the Information Retrieval Facility, a not-for-profit foundation which promotes research in large scale information retrieval. He is a past programme committee chair of the ACM SIGIR conference (2005, an Associate Editor of ACM Transaction on Information Systems and has published over 90 refereed conference and journal papers. His current research focuses on problems of retrieving still and moving images and on patent retrieval.

Ronan Tournier (tournier@irit.fr) was born in 1976 in Lannion (France). Previously a computer technician and sales engineer for computer systems during four years, he obtained his PhD in computer science from the University of Toulouse 3 on the OLAP analysis of document data. He is currently a researcher in the Generalised Information Systems/Data Warehouse research group (SIG/ED) of the IRIT institute.

His research interests include multidimensional modelling, algebras as well as the integration of text-rich documents within data warehouses and OLAP systems.

Maris Treimanis earned his doctorate from the Institute of Cybernetics at Academy of Science in Estonia (1988). Since year 1976 he is lecturing courses on data structures, operating system concepts, contemprorary management and IT Project Management at the University of Latvia. In parallel with academic life, he actively participates in practical IT initiatives aimed to significantly change and improve different educational and business processes. To name some of them - project leader, E-university Project at the University of Latvia (2002-2008); Vice-president IT and member of board at the JSC "SEB Latvijas Unibanka" (1999-2002); project leader, Latvian Education Informatization System Project (1997-1999); project leader and designer, CASE tool IStechnology and treasury, MM, FX management information systems.

Chih-Fong Tsai obtained a PhD at School of Computing and Technology from the University of Sunderland, UK in 2005 for the thesis entitled *Automatically Annotating Images with Keywords*. He is now an assistant professor at the Department of Accounting and Information Technology, National Chung Cheng University, Taiwan. He has published a number of refereed journal papers including *ACM Transactions on Information Systems, Information Processing & Management, Expert Systems with Applications, Expert Systems, Online Information Review, and Neurocomputing*. His current research focuses on researching and developing data mining and artificial intelligence techniques for business and engineering problems.

Index